Lecture Notes in Computer Science   10513

Commenced Publication in 1973
Founding and Former Series Editors:
Gerhard Goos, Juris Hartmanis, and Jan van Leeuwen

More information about this series at http://www.springer.com/series/7409

Regina Bernhaupt · Girish Dalvi
Anirudha Joshi · Devanuj K. Balkrishan
Jacki O'Neill · Marco Winckler (Eds.)

Human-Computer Interaction – INTERACT 2017

16th IFIP TC 13 International Conference
Mumbai, India, September 25–29, 2017
Proceedings, Part I

 Springer

Editors

Regina Bernhaupt
Ruwido Austria GmbH
Neumarkt am Wallersee
Austria

Girish Dalvi
Indian Institute of Technology Bombay
Mumbai
India

Anirudha Joshi
Indian Institute of Technology Bombay
Mumbai
India

Devanuj K. Balkrishan
Indian Institute of Technology Bombay
Mumbai
India

Jacki O'Neill
Microsoft Research Centre India
Bangalore
India

Marco Winckler 🆔
Université Paul Sabatier
Toulouse
France

ISSN 0302-9743   ISSN 1611-3349   (electronic)
Lecture Notes in Computer Science
ISBN 978-3-319-67743-9   ISBN 978-3-319-67744-6   (eBook)
DOI 10.1007/978-3-319-67744-6

Library of Congress Control Number: 2017953425

LNCS Sublibrary: SL3 – Information Systems and Applications, incl. Internet/Web, and HCI

Printed on acid-free paper

This Springer imprint is published by Springer Nature
The registered company is Springer International Publishing AG
The registered company address is: Gewerbestrasse 11, 6330 Cham, Switzerland

Foreword

The 16th IFIP TC13 International Conference on Human–Computer Interaction, INTERACT 2017, took place during September 25–29, 2017, in Mumbai, India. This conference was held on the beautiful campus of the Indian Institute of Technology, Bombay (IIT Bombay) and the Industrial Design Centre (IDC) was the principal host. The conference was co-sponsored by the HCI Professionals Association of India and the Computer Society of India, in cooperation with ACM and ACM SIGCHI. The financial responsibility of INTERACT 2017 was taken up by the HCI Professionals Association of India.

The International Federation for Information Processing (IFIP) was created in 1960 under the auspices of UNESCO. The Technical Committee 13 (TC13) of the IFIP aims at developing the science and technology of human–computer interaction (HCI). TC13 has representatives from 36 countries, apart from 16 expert members and observers. TC13 started the series of INTERACT conferences in 1984. These conferences have been an important showcase for researchers and practitioners in the field of HCI. Situated under the open, inclusive umbrella of the IFIP, INTERACT has been truly international in its spirit and has attracted researchers from several countries and cultures. The venues of the INTERACT conferences over the years bear a testimony to this inclusiveness.

In 2017, the venue was Mumbai. Located in western India, the city of Mumbai is the capital of the state of Maharashtra. It is the financial, entertainment, and commercial capital of the country and is the most populous city in India. *Mumbaikars* might add that it is also the most hardworking.

The theme of INTERACT 2017 was "Global Thoughts, Local Designs." The theme was designed to let HCI researchers respond to challenges emerging in the new age of global connectivity where they often design products for users who are beyond their borders belonging to distinctly different cultures. As organizers of the conference, we focused our attention on four areas: *India, developing countries, students,* and *research*.

As the first INTERACT in the subcontinent, the conference offered a distinctly Indian experience to its participants. The span of known history of India covers more than 5,000 years. Today, India is the world's largest democracy and a land of diversity. Modern technology co-exists with ancient traditions within the same city, often within the same family. Indians speak 22 official languages and hundreds of dialects. India is also a hub of the information technology industry and a living laboratory of experiments with technology for developing countries.

INTERACT 2017 made a conscious effort to lower barriers that prevent people from developing countries from participating in conferences. Thinkers and optimists believe that all regions of the world can achieve human development goals. Information and communication technologies (ICTs) can support this process and empower people to achieve their full potential. Today ICT products have many new users and many new uses, but also present new challenges and provide new opportunities. It is no surprise that HCI researchers are showing great interest in these emergent users. INTERACT 2017 provided a platform to explore these challenges and opportunities but also made it easier for people from developing countries to participate. We also introduced a new track called Field Trips, which allowed participants to directly engage with stakeholders within the context of a developing country.

Students represent the future of our community. They bring in new energy, enthusiasm, and fresh ideas. But it is often hard for students to participate in international conferences. INTERACT 2017 made special efforts to bring students to the conference. The conference had low registration costs and several volunteering opportunities. Thanks to our sponsors, we could provide several travel grants. Most importantly, INTERACT 2017 had special tracks such as Installations, a Student Design Consortium, and a Student Research Consortium that gave students the opportunity to showcase their work.

Finally, great research is the heart of a good conference. Like its predecessors, INTERACT 2017 aimed to bring together high-quality research. As a multidisciplinary field, HCI requires interaction and discussion among diverse people with different interest and background. The beginners and the experienced, theoreticians and practitioners, and people from diverse disciplines and different countries gathered together in Mumbai to learn from each other and to contribute to each other's growth. We thank all the authors who chose INTERACT 2017 as the venue to publish their research.

We received a total of 571 submissions distributed in two peer-reviewed tracks, five curated tracks, and seven juried tracks. Of these, the following contributions were accepted:

- 68 Full Papers (peer reviewed)
- 51 Short Papers (peer reviewed)
- 13 Case Studies (curated)
- 20 Industry Presentations (curated)
- 7 Courses (curated)
- 5 Demonstrations (curated)
- 3 Panels (curated)
- 9 Workshops (juried)
- 7 Field Trips (juried)
- 11 Interactive Posters (juried)
- 9 Installations (juried)
- 6 Doctoral Consortium (juried)
- 15 Student Research Consortium (juried)
- 6 Student Design Consortium (juried)

The acceptance rate for contributions received in the peer-reviewed tracks was 30.7% for full papers and 29.1% for short papers. In addition to full papers and short papers, the present proceedings feature contributions accepted in the form of case studies, courses, demonstrations, interactive posters, field trips, and workshops.

The final decision on acceptance or rejection of full papers was taken in a Program Committee meeting held in Paris, France, in March 2017. The full-paper chairs, the associate chairs, and the TC13 members participated in this meeting. The meeting discussed a consistent set of criteria to deal with inevitable differences among the large number of reviewers. The final decisions on other tracks were made by the corresponding track chairs and reviewers, often after additional electronic meetings and discussions.

INTERACT 2017 was made possible by the persistent efforts over several months by 49 chairs, 39 associate chairs, 55 student volunteers, and 499 reviewers. We thank them all. Finally, we wish to express a special thank you to the proceedings publication co-chairs, Marco Winckler and Devanuj Balkrishan, who did extraordinary work to put together four volumes of the main proceedings and one volume of adjunct proceedings.

September 2017

Anirudha Joshi
Girish Dalvi
Marco Winckler

IFIP TC13 (http://ifip-tc13.org/)

Established in 1989, the International Federation for Information Processing Technical Committee on Human–Computer Interaction (IFIP TC 13) is an international committee of 37 member national societies and 10 Working Groups, representing specialists of the various disciplines contributing to the field of human–computer interaction (HCI). This includes (among others) human factors, ergonomics, cognitive science, computer science, and design. INTERACT is its flagship conference of IFIP TC 13, staged biennially in different countries in the world. The first INTERACT conference was held in 1984 running triennially and became a biennial event in 1993.

IFIP TC 13 aims to develop the science, technology, and societal aspects of HCI by: encouraging empirical research; promoting the use of knowledge and methods from the human sciences in design and evaluation of computer systems; promoting better understanding of the relation between formal design methods and system usability and acceptability; developing guidelines, models, and methods by which designers may provide better human-oriented computer systems; and, cooperating with other groups, inside and outside IFIP, to promote user-orientation and humanization in system design. Thus, TC 13 seeks to improve interactions between people and computers, to encourage the growth of HCI research and its practice in industry and to disseminate these benefits worldwide.

The main focus is to place the users at the center of the development process. Areas of study include: the problems people face when interacting with computers; the impact of technology deployment on people in individual and organizational contexts; the determinants of utility, usability, acceptability, and user experience; the appropriate allocation of tasks between computers and users especially in the case of automation; modeling the user, their tasks, and the interactive system to aid better system design; and harmonizing the computer to user characteristics and needs.

While the scope is thus set wide, with a tendency toward general principles rather than particular systems, it is recognized that progress will only be achieved through both general studies to advance theoretical understanding and specific studies on practical issues (e.g., interface design standards, software system resilience, documentation, training material, appropriateness of alternative interaction technologies, guidelines, the problems of integrating multimedia systems to match system needs, and organizational practices, etc.).

In 2015, TC 13 approved the creation of a Steering Committee (SC) for the INTERACT conference. The SC is now in place, chaired by Jan Gulliksen and is responsible for:

- Promoting and maintaining the INTERACT conference as the premiere venue for researchers and practitioners interested in the topics of the conference (this requires a refinement of the aforementioned topics)
- Ensuring the highest quality for the contents of the event

- Setting up the bidding process to handle the future INTERACT conferences; decision is made up at TC 13 level
- Providing advice to the current and future chairs and organizers of the INTERACT conference
- Providing data, tools and documents about previous conferences to the future conference organizers
- Selecting the reviewing system to be used throughout the conference (as this impacts the entire set of reviewers)
- Resolving general issues involved with the INTERACT conference
- Capitalizing history (good and bad practices)

In 1999, TC 13 initiated a special IFIP Award, the Brian Shackel Award, for the most outstanding contribution in the form of a refereed paper submitted to and delivered at each INTERACT. The award draws attention to the need for a comprehensive human-centered approach in the design and use of information technology in which the human and social implications have been taken into account. In 2007, IFIP TC 13 also launched an Accessibility Award to recognize an outstanding contribution in HCI with international impact dedicated to the field of accessibility for disabled users. In 2013 IFIP TC 13 launched the Interaction Design for International Development (IDID) Award that recognizes the most outstanding contribution to the application of inter-active systems for social and economic development of people in developing countries. Since the process to decide the award takes place after papers are sent to the publisher for publication, the awards are not identified in the proceedings.

IFIP TC 13 also recognizes pioneers in the area of HCI. An IFIP TC 13 pioneer is one who, through active participation in IFIP Technical Committees or related IFIP groups, has made outstanding contributions to the educational, theoretical, technical, commercial, or professional aspects of analysis, design, construction, evaluation, and use of interactive systems. IFIP TC 13 pioneers are appointed annually and awards are handed over at the INTERACT conference.

IFIP TC 13 stimulates working events and activities through its Working Groups (WGs). Working Groups consist of HCI experts from many countries, who seek to expand knowledge and find solutions to HCI issues and concerns within their domains. The list of Working Groups and their area of interest is given here.

WG13.1 (Education in HCI and HCI Curricula) aims to improve HCI education at all levels of higher education, coordinate and unite efforts to develop HCI curricula and promote HCI teaching.

WG13.2 (Methodology for User-Centered System Design) aims to foster research, dissemination of information and good practice in the methodical application of HCI to software engineering.

WG13.3 (HCI and Disability) aims to make HCI designers aware of the needs of people with disabilities and encourage the development of information systems and tools permitting adaptation of interfaces to specific users.

WG13.4 (also WG2.7) (User Interface Engineering) investigates the nature, con-cepts, and construction of user interfaces for software systems, using a framework for reasoning about interactive systems and an engineering model for developing user interfaces.

WG 13.5 (Resilience, Reliability, Safety and Human Error in System Development) seeks a frame-work for studying human factors relating to systems failure, develops leading-edge techniques in hazard analysis and safety engineering of computer-based systems, and guides international accreditation activities for safety-critical systems.

WG13.6 (Human-Work Interaction Design) aims at establishing relationships between extensive empirical work-domain studies and HCI design. It promotes the use of knowledge, concepts, methods, and techniques that enable user studies to procure a better apprehension of the complex interplay between individual, social, and organizational contexts and thereby a better understanding of how and why people work in the ways that they do.

WG13.7 (Human–Computer Interaction and Visualization) aims to establish a study and research program that will combine both scientific work and practical applications in the fields of HCI and visualization. It integrates several additional aspects of further research areas, such as scientific visualization, data mining, information design, computer graphics, cognition sciences, perception theory, or psychology, into this approach.

WG13.8 (Interaction Design and International Development) is currently working to reformulate its aims and scope.

WG13.9 (Interaction Design and Children) aims to support practitioners, regulators, and researchers to develop the study of interaction design and children across international contexts.

WG13.10 (Human-Centered Technology for Sustainability) aims to promote research, design, development, evaluation, and deployment of human-centered technology to encourage sustainable use of resources in various domains.

New Working Groups are formed as areas of significance in HCI arise. Further information is available on the IFIP TC13 website at: http://ifip-tc13.org/

IFIP TC13 Members

Officers

Chair

Philippe Palanque, France

Vice-chair for Growth and Reach Out INTERACT Steering Committee Chair

Jan Gulliksen, Sweden

Vice-chair for Working Groups

Simone D.J. Barbosa, Brazil

Vice-chair for Awards

Paula Kotze, South Africa

Treasurer

Virpi Roto, Finland

Secretary

Marco Winckler, France

Webmaster

Helen Petrie, UK

Country Representatives

Australia
Henry B.L. Duh
Australian Computer Society

Austria
Geraldine Fitzpatrick
Austrian Computer Society

Brazil
Raquel Oliveira Prates
Brazilian Computer Society (SBC)

Bulgaria
Kamelia Stefanova
Bulgarian Academy of Sciences

Canada
Lu Xiao
Canadian Information Processing Society

Chile
Jaime Sánchez
Chilean Society of Computer Science

Croatia
Andrina Granic
Croatian Information Technology
  Association (CITA)

Cyprus
Panayiotis Zaphiris
Cyprus Computer Society

Czech Republic
Zdeněk Míkovec
Czech Society for Cybernetics
  and Informatics

Denmark
Torkil Clemmensen
Danish Federation for Information
  Processing

Finland
Virpi Roto
Finnish Information Processing
  Association

France
Philippe Palanque
Société informatique de France (SIF)

Germany
Tom Gross
Gesellschaft für Informatik e.V.

Hungary
Cecilia Sik Lanyi
John V. Neumann Computer Society

India
Anirudha Joshi
Computer Society of India (CSI)

Ireland
Liam J. Bannon
Irish Computer Society

Italy
Fabio Paternò
Italian Computer Society

Japan
Yoshifumi Kitamura
Information Processing Society of Japan

Korea
Gerry Kim
KIISE

The Netherlands
Vanessa Evers
Nederlands Genootschap voor
  Informatica

New Zealand
Mark Apperley
New Zealand Computer Society

Nigeria
Chris C. Nwannenna
Nigeria Computer Society

Norway
Dag Svanes
Norwegian Computer Society

Poland
Marcin Sikorski
Poland Academy of Sciences

Portugal
Pedro Campos
Associacão Portuguesa para o Desen-
volvimento da Sociedade da Informação
  (APDSI)

Singapore
Shengdong Zhao
Singapore Computer Society

Slovakia
Wanda Benešová
The Slovak Society for Computer
  Science

Slovenia
Matjaž Debevc
The Slovenian Computer Society
  INFORMATIKA

South Africa
Janet L. Wesson
The Computer Society of South Africa

Spain
Julio Abascal
Asociación de Técnicos de Informática
  (ATI)

Sweden

Jan Gulliksen

Swedish Interdisciplinary Society
  for Human–Computer Interaction

Swedish Computer Society

Switzerland

Denis Lalanne

Swiss Federation for Information
  Processing

Tunisia

Mona Laroussi

Ecole Supérieure des Communications
  De Tunis (SUP'COM)

UK

José Abdelnour Nocera

British Computer Society (BCS)

United Arab Emirates

Ghassan Al-Qaimari

UAE Computer Society

USA

Gerrit van der Veer

Association for Computing Machinery
  (ACM)

Expert Members

Dan Orwa	University of Nairobi, Kenya
David Lamas	Tallinn University, Estonia
Dorian Gorgan	Technical University of Cluj-Napoca, Romania
Eunice Sari	University of Western Australia, Australia and UX Indonesia, Indonesia
Fernando Loizides	Cardiff University, UK and Cyprus University of Technology, Cyprus
Frank Vetere	University of Melbourne, Australia
Ivan Burmistrov	Moscow State University, Russia
Joaquim Jorge	INESC-ID, Portugal
Marta Kristin Larusdottir	Reykjavik University, Iceland
Nikolaos Avouris	University of Patras, Greece
Paula Kotze	CSIR Meraka Institute, South Africa
Peter Forbrig	University of Rostock, Germany
Simone D.J. Barbosa	PUC-Rio, Brazil
Vu Nguyen	Vietnam
Zhengjie Liu	Dalian Maritime University, China

Observer

Masaaki Kurosu, Japan

Working Group Chairs

**WG 13.1 (Education in HCI
and HCI Curricula)**

Konrad Baumann, Austria

**WG 13.2 (Methodologies
for User-Centered System Design)**

Marco Winckler, France

WG 13.3 (HCI and Disability)

Helen Petrie, UK

WG 13.4/2.7 (User Interface Engineering)

José Creissac Campos, Portugal

WG 13.5 (Resilience, Reliability, Safety, and Human Error in System Development)

Chris Johnson, UK

WG 13.6 (Human-Work Interaction Design)

Pedro Campos, Portugal

WG 13.7 (HCI and Visualization)

Peter Dannenmann, Germany

WG 13.8 (Interaction Design and International Development)

José Adbelnour Nocera, UK

WG 13.9 (Interaction Design and Children)

Janet Read, UK

WG 13.10 (Human-Centered Technology for Sustainability)

Masood Masoodian, Finland

Conference Organizing Committee

General Conference Chairs

Anirudha Joshi, India
Girish Dalvi, India

Technical Program Chair

Marco Winckler, France

Full-Paper Chairs

Regina Bernhaupt, France
Jacki O'Neill, India

Short-Paper Chairs

Peter Forbrig, Germany
Sriganesh Madhvanath, USA

Case Studies Chairs

Ravi Poovaiah, India
Elizabeth Churchill, USA

Courses Chairs

Gerrit van der Veer, The Netherlands
Dhaval Vyas, Australia

Demonstrations Chairs

Takahiro Miura, Japan
Shengdong Zhao, Singapore
Manjiri Joshi, India

Doctoral Consortium Chairs

Paula Kotze, South Africa
Pedro Campos, Portugal

Field Trips Chairs

Nimmi Rangaswamy, India
José Abdelnour Nocera, UK
Debjani Roy, India

Industry Presentations Chairs

Suresh Chande, Finland
Fernando Loizides, UK

Installations Chairs

Ishneet Grover, India
Jayesh Pillai, India
Nagraj Emmadi, India

Keynotes and Invited Talks Chair

Philippe Palanque, France

Panels Chairs

Antonella De Angeli, Italy
Rosa Arriaga, USA

Posters Chairs

Girish Prabhu, India
Zhengjie Liu, China

Student Research Consortium Chairs

Indrani Medhi, India
Naveen Bagalkot, India
Janet Wesson, South Africa

Student Design Consortium Chairs

Abhishek Shrivastava, India
Prashant Sachan, India
Arnab Chakravarty, India

Workshops Chairs

Torkil Clemmensen, Denmark
Venkatesh Rajamanickam, India

Accessibility Chairs

Prachi Sakhardande, India
Sonali Joshi, India

Childcare Club Chairs

Atish Patel, India
Susmita Sharma, India

Food and Social Events Chair

Rucha Tulaskar, India

Local Organizing Chairs

Manjiri Joshi, India
Nagraj Emmadi, India

Proceedings Chairs

Marco Winckler, France
Devanuj Balkrishan, India

Sponsorship Chair

Atul Manohar, India

Student Volunteers Chairs

Rasagy Sharma, India
Jayati Bandyopadhyay, India

Venue Arrangements Chair

Sugandh Malhotra, India

Web and Social Media Chair

Naveed Ahmed, India

Program Committee

Associated Chairs

Simone Barbosa, Brazil
Nicola Bidwell, Namibia
Pernille Bjorn, Denmark
Birgit Bomsdorf, Germany
Torkil Clemmensen, Denmark
José Creissac Campos, Portugal
Peter Forbrig, Germany
Tom Gross, Germany
Jan Gulliksen, Sweden
Nathalie Henry Riche, USA
Abhijit Karnik, UK
Dave Kirk, UK
Denis Lalanne, Switzerland
Airi Lampinen, Sweden
Effie Law, UK
Eric Lecolinet, France
Zhengjie Liu, China
Fernando Loizides, UK
Célia Martinie, France
Laurence Nigay, France

Monique Noirhomme, Belgium
Philippe Palanque, France
Fabio Paterno, Italy
Helen Petrie, UK
Antonio Piccinno, Italy
Kari-Jouko Raiha, Finland
Dave Randall, Germany
Nimmi Rangaswamy, India
John Rooksby, UK
Virpi Roto, Finland
Jan Stage, Denmark
Frank Steinicke, Germany
Simone Stumpf, UK
Gerrit van der Veer, The Netherlands
Dhaval Vyas, India
Gerhard Weber, Germany
Janet Wesson, South Africa
Marco Winckler, France
Panayiotis Zaphiris, Cyprus

Reviewers

Julio Abascal, Spain
José Abdelnour Nocera, UK
Silvia Abrahão, Spain
Abiodun Afolayan Ogunyemi, Estonia
Ana Paula Afonso, Portugal
David Ahlström, Austria
Muneeb Ahmad, Australia
Deepak Akkil, Finland
Sarah Alaoui, France
Komathi Ale, Singapore
Jan Alexandersson, Germany
Dzmitry Aliakseyeu, The Netherlands
Hend S. Al-Khalifa, Saudi Arabia
Fereshteh Amini, Canada
Junia Anacleto, Brazil
Mads Schaarup Andersen, Denmark
Leonardo Angelini, Switzerland
Huckauf Anke, Germany
Craig Anslow, New Zealand
Nathalie Aquino, Paraguay
Oscar Javier Ariza Núñez, Germany
Parvin Asadzadeh, UK
Uday Athavankar, India
David Auber, France
Nikolaos Avouris, Greece
Sohaib Ayub, Pakistan
Chris Baber, UK
Cedric Bach, France
Naveen Bagalkot, India
Jan Balata, Czech Republic
Emilia Barakova, The Netherlands
Pippin Barr, Denmark
Oswald Barral, Finland
Barbara Rita Barricelli, Italy
Michel Beaudouin-Lafon, France
Astrid Beck, Germany
Jordan Beck, USA
Roman Bednarik, Finland
Ben Bedwell, UK
Marios Belk, Germany
Yacine Bellik, France
David Benyon, UK
François Bérard, France

Arne Berger, Germany
Nigel Bevan, UK
Anastasia Bezerianos, France
Sudhir Bhatia, India
Dorrit Billman, USA
Pradipta Biswas, India
Edwin Blake, South Africa
Renaud Blanch, France
Mads Bødker, Denmark
Cristian Bogdan, Sweden
Rodrigo Bonacin, Brazil
Claus Bossen, Denmark
Paolo Bottoni, Italy
Nadia Boukhelifa, France
Nina Boulus-Rødje, Denmark
Judy Bowen, New Zealand
Margot Brereton, Australia
Roberto Bresin, Sweden
Barry Brown, Sweden
Emeline Brulé, France
Nick Bryan-Kinns, UK
Sabin-Corneliu Buraga, Romania
Ineke Buskens, South Africa
Adrian Bussone, UK
Maria Claudia Buzzi, Italy
Marina Buzzi, Italy
Federico Cabitza, Italy
Diogo Cabral, Portugal
Åsa Cajander, Sweden
Eduardo Calvillo Gamez, Mexico
Erik Cambria, Singapore
Pedro Campos, Portugal
Tara Capel, Australia
Cinzia Cappiello, Italy
Stefan Carmien, Spain
Maria Beatriz Carmo, Portugal
Luis Carriço, Portugal
Stefano Carrino, Switzerland
Géry Casiez, France
Fabio Cassano, Italy
Thais Castro, Brazil
Vanessa Cesário, Portugal
Arnab Chakravarty, India

Rosella Gennari, Italy
Werner Geyer, USA
Giuseppe Ghiani, Italy
Anirban Ghosh, Canada
Sanjay Ghosh, India
Martin Gibbs, Australia
Patrick Girard, France
Victor Gonzalez, Mexico
Rohini Gosain, Ireland
Nicholas Graham, Canada
Tiago Guerreiro, Portugal
Yves Guiard, France
Nuno Guimaraes, Portugal
Tauseef Gulrez, Australia
Thilina Halloluwa, Sri Lanka
Martin Halvey, UK
Dave Harley, UK
Richard Harper, UK
Michael Harrison, UK
Heidi Hartikainen, Finland
Thomas Hartley, UK
Mariam Hassib, Germany
Ari Hautasaari, Japan
Elaine Hayashi, Brazil
Jonas Hedman, Denmark
Ruediger Heimgaertner, Germany
Tomi Heimonen, USA
Mattias Heinrich, Germany
Ingi Helgason, UK
Wilko Heuten, Germany
Uta Hinrichs, UK
Daniel Holliday, UK
Jonathan Hook, UK
Jettie Hoonhout, The Netherlands
Heiko Hornung, Brazil
Axel Hösl, Germany
Lara Houston, UK
Roberto Hoyle, USA
William Hudson, UK
Stéphane Huot, France
Christophe Hurter, France
Husniza Husni, Malaysia
Ebba Thora Hvannberg, Iceland
Aulikki Hyrskykari, Finland
Yavuz Inal, Turkey
Petra Isenberg, France

Poika Isokoski, Finland
Minna Isomursu, Denmark
Howell Istance, Finland
Kai-Mikael Jää-Aro, Sweden
Karim Jabbar, Denmark
Isa Jahnke, USA
Abhishek Jain, India
Mlynar Jakub, Switzerland
Yvonne Jansen, France
Camille Jeunet, France
Nan Jiang, UK
Radu Jianu, UK
Deepak John Mathew, India
Matt Jones, UK
Rui José, Portugal
Anirudha Joshi, India
Dhaval Joshi, China
Manjiri Joshi, India
Mike Just, UK
Eija Kaasinen, Finland
Hernisa Kacorri, USA
Sanjay Kairam, USA
Bridget Kane, Ireland
Shaun K. Kane, USA
Jari Kangas, Finland
Ann Marie Kanstrup, Denmark
Evangelos Karapanos, Cyprus
Turkka Keinonen, Finland
Pramod Khambete, India
Munwar Khan, India
NamWook Kim, USA
Yea-Seul Kim, USA
Jennifer King, USA
Reuben Kirkham, UK
Kathi Kitner, South Africa
Søren Knudsen, Denmark
Janin Koch, Finland
Lisa Koeman, The Netherlands
Uttam Kokil, USA
Christophe Kolski, France
Paula Kotze, South Africa
Dennis Krupke, Germany
Sari Kujala, Finland
David Lamas, Estonia
Eike Langbehn, Germany
Rosa Lanzilotti, Italy

Marta Larusdottir, Iceland
Yann Laurillau, France
Elise Lavoué, France
Bongshin Lee, USA
Matthew Lee, USA
Barbara Leporini, Italy
Agnes Lisowska Masson, Switzerland
Netta Livari, Finland
Kiel Long, UK
Víctor López-Jaquero, Spain
Yichen Lu, Finland
Stephanie Ludi, USA
Bernd Ludwig, Germany
Christopher Lueg, Australia
Ewa Luger, UK
Stephan Lukosch, The Netherlands
Jo Lumsden, UK
Christof Lutteroth, UK
Kris Luyten, Belgium
Miroslav Macik, Czech Republic
Scott Mackenzie, Canada
Allan MacLean, UK
Christian Maertin, Germany
Charlotte Magnusson, Sweden
Jyotirmaya Mahapatra, India
Ranjan Maity, India
Päivi Majaranta, Finland
Sylvain Malacria, France
Marco Manca, Italy
Kathia Marçal de Oliveira, France
Panos Markopolous, The Netherlands
Paolo Masci, Portugal
Dimitri Masson, France
Stina Matthiesen, Denmark
Claire McCallum, UK
Roisin McNaney, UK
Indrani Medhi-Thies, India
Gerrit Meixner, Germany
Johanna Meurer, Germany
Luana Micallef, Finland
Takahiro Miura, Japan
Judith Molka-Danielsen, Norway
Naja Holten Moller, Denmark
Giulio Mori, Italy
Alistair Morrison, UK
Aske Mottelson, Denmark

Omar Mubin, Australia
Michael Muller, USA
Lennart Nacke, Canada
Amit Nanavati, India
David Navarre, France
Carla Nave, Portugal
Luciana Nedel, Brazil
Matti Nelimarkka, Finland
Julien Nembrini, Switzerland
David Nemer, USA
Vania Neris, Brazil
Maish Nichani, Singapore
James Nicholson, UK
Diederick C. Niehorster, Sweden
Shuo Niu, USA
Manuel Noguera, Spain
Nicole Novielli, Italy
Diana Nowacka, UK
Marcus Nyström, Sweden
Marianna Obrist, UK
Lars Oestreicher, Sweden
Thomas Olsson, Finland
Juliet Ongwae, UK
Dympna O'Sullivan, UK
Antti Oulasvirta, Finland
Saila Ovaska, Finland
Xinru Page, USA
Ana Paiva, Portugal
Sabrina Panëels, France
Smitha Papolu, USA
Hugo Paredes, Portugal
Susan Park, Canada
Oscar Pastor, Spain
Jennifer Pearson, UK
Simon Perrault, Singapore
Mark Perry, UK
Anicia Peters, Namibia
Kevin Pfeil, USA
Jayesh Pillai, India
Marcelo Pimenta, Brazil
Aparecido Fabiano Pinatti de Carvalho,
   Germany
Claudio Pinhanez, Brazil
Stefania Pizza, Italy
Bernd Ploderer, Australia
Andreas Poller, Germany

Sponsors and Partners

Silver Sponsors

LEAD PARTNERS

facebook

Gala Dinner Sponsor

Design Competition Sponsor

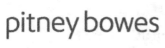

Pitney Bowes

Education Partners

Interaction Design Foundation (IDF)

Friends of INTERACT

Ruwido GmBH, Austria   Oxford University Press

Converge by CauseCode Technologies

Exhibitors

balsamiq®

Partners

International Federation for Information Processing

In-cooperation with ACM   In-cooperation with SIGCHI

**IDC
IIT Bombay**

**HCI Professionals'
Association of India**

Industrial Design Centre, IIT Bombay   HCI Professionals' Association of India

Computer Society of India   IIT Bombay

Contents

Co-design Studies

Cultural Differences and Communication Technology

Design Rationale and Camera-Control

Adaptive Design and Mobile Applications

A Minimalist Approach for Identifying Affective States for Mobile Interaction Design

Subrata Tikadar[✉], Sharath Kazipeta, Chandrakanth Ganji, and Samit Bhattacharya

Indian Institute of Technology Guwahati, Guwahati, India
subratatikadar@gmail.com, sharathkazipeta@gmail.com,
chandu8594@gmail.com, samit3k@gmail.com

Abstract. Human Computer Interaction (HCI) can be made more efficient if the interactive systems are able to respond to the users' emotional state. The foremost task for designing such systems is to recognize the users' emotional state during interaction. Most of the interactive systems, now a days, are being made touch enabled. In this work, we propose a model to recognize the emotional state of the users of touchscreen devices. We propose to compute the affective state of the users from 2D screen gesture using the number of touch events and pressure generated for each event as the only two features. No extra hardware setup is required for the computation. Machine learning technique was used for the classification. Four discriminative models, namely the Naïve Bayes, K-Nearest Neighbor (KNN), Decision Tree and Support Vector Machine (SVM) were explored, with SVM giving the highest accuracy of 96.75%.

Keywords: Affective state · Arousal and valence · Emotion · Touch gesture

1 Introduction

With the ubiquitous explosion of mobile touch input devices, mobile HCI has become very important to improve usability of such devices. Affective touch interaction, which takes into account the affect and emotion of mobile touchscreen users, has the potential to significantly improve usability of these devices. The first and most important step for designing an affective interactive system is to recognize the affective state of the user. This may be followed by the design and implementation of appropriate interface and interaction that complement and/or change the users' emotional state. We can also make changes in the way tasks are performed depending on the current state of the user emotion. For instance, changing the look/contents of a webpage based on the emotional state of the user.

Mobile devices have limited capabilities in terms of their processor, storage and power back up. Moreover, the mobility aspect demands simplicity; these devices should not require too many extra attachments and wires. Literature contain many works on emotion recognition. In most of those cases, methods were proposed to recognize emotion from facial expression, gesture, posture and physiological signals. These mostly involved computer vision and image processing techniques, which are computationally

R. Bernhaupt et al. (Eds.): INTERACT 2017, Part I, LNCS 10513, pp. 3–12, 2017.
DOI: 10.1007/978-3-319-67744-6_1

expensive. In addition, such methods often require additional set ups such as cameras or probes and wires to record physiological signals. Consequently, most of the existing approaches are not suitable or feasible to detect emotional state of mobile users. The added hardware may affect the mobility and affordability of the devices. Therefore, an alternative approach is to predict affective state from the touch interaction behavior represented by the touch gestures (finger strokes). The finger strokes are *indirect cues* to the affective state of a touch screen user.

The indirect cue based approach has a major advantage: we do not require additional expensive sensors or wires to record the finger strokes. Further, the computations are much less compared to other approaches. We propose one such indirect cue based approach in this work.

A controlled experiment was conducted to establish the model with the empirical data of 29 users. For training and testing set of data, the random permutation cross validation technique[1] was used. Only two touch interaction characteristics: the *number of touch events* and *average pressure of the events* are used to determine the emotional state of a mobile touchscreen user in our proposed approach. We have not found any work that can detect emotion with such high accuracy from only two input features. Hence, our approach provides a unique and novel method. The proposed approach along with the data collection and analysis are described in this article.

2 Related Works

A wide class of emotion detection techniques use facial expressions (e.g., [12, 14, 18, 19, 25]), inspired by the theory proposed by Ekman et al. [5]. Body movement and postures are also commonly used as cues to detect emotional states [3, 9]. Physiological signal such as electrooculogram (EOG), galvanic skin response (GSR), heart rate (HR), electrocardiogram (ECG), frontal brain electrical activity: electroencephalography (EEG) and eye blinking rate (EBR) were also used for emotion recognition (e.g., [1, 10, 16–18]). Some of the works are, in fact, based on the 'multi-modal' approach. For instance, both EEG and peripheral physiological signal were used by Koelstra et al. [17] for recognition of arousal-valence dimensional emotions induced by music videos.

All these works involve significant computations. Moreover, extra hardware, equipment and expensive sensors were used in most of those cases. We, on the other hand, are looking to detect the affective state of touch screen users, assuming small handled devices such as smartphones and tablets.

It has been reported that emotion can be recognized by keystroke patterns and dynamics [6, 15, 23, 35]. Our approach does not depend only upon keyboard dependent data. However, the works demonstrate that features such as pressure on a key or typing speed can be used to detect emotion.

Sano and Picard [30], Bauer and Lukowicz [2] and Ciman et al. [4] used user-smartphone interaction data to detect the users' sate. The aim of these works was to identify the stress level of the users, so that it can be applied for taking care about the health condition of the users. We want to recognize more number of emotional states

---

[1] http://scikit-learn.org/stable/modules/cross_validation.html.

instead of restricting just two states like stress and no-stress. Moreover, some of these works [2, 30] used privacy sensitive data of the users like SMS, phone call, location etc. In our approach, we do not require such kind of personal or private data.

A system developed by Gao et al. [8] was able to recognize the players' emotional states into four discrete states (Bored, Excited, Frustrated and Relaxed) as well as 2 levels of valence and 2 levels of arousal while playing game. They also used the finger stroke information for state prediction. However, emotion detection was done using the extracted touch information from a high-end device (iPod^{TM}). Moreover, relatively large number of features (17 features) were used in their emotion recognition system. Shah et al. [32] tried to overcome this limitation with a smaller set of features (10 features). However, some of these features, for instance, deviation in the number of strikes and deviation in the number of taps, may be difficult to know beforehand for use in automatic prediction. By considering just two features from the 2D screen (touch) gestures, number of touch events, and average pressure, our proposed approach addresses the issues discussed above. Consequently, the approach is expected to be less computational, easy to understand, and hence, easy to implement. The approach is described next.

3   Proposed Approach

In order to detect emotion, we propose to use discrete emotional states based on the *circumplex model of affect* [27, 28, 31]. An alternative set of circumplex emotional states, where the dimensional states are discretised, has been reported based on the arousal and valence level.

We based our idea of the four states on the Geneva Emotional Wheel (GEW[2]) [29] and the circumplex model of affect proposed by Posner et al. [27]. The GEW is a theoretically derived and empirically tested instrument, to measure emotional reactions to objects, events, and situations. The GEW contains 20 different emotion families with their intensities diverging out as shown in Fig. 1. The emotion families are arranged in a wheel shape with the axes being defined by two major dimensions of emotional experience: valence (x-direction) and arousal (y-direction).

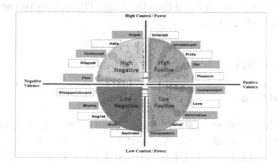

Fig. 1. The Geneva Emotional Wheel (GEW) and our proposed partitions of the wheel into four abstract discrete emotional states based on circumplex model of affect.

---

[2] http://www.affective-sciences.org/en/gew/.

We propose to represent each of the four quadrants of the GEW as a distinct emotional state based on the circumplex model of emotion. Thus, the top-right quadrant is the *high positive* state, the top-left quadrant is the *high negative* state, the bottom-left quadrant is the *low negative* state and the bottom-right quadrant is the *low positive* state. High and low indicate arousal level whereas positive and negative indicate valence level. The arousal-valence level emotional states are also equally important and are being identified and applied in many areas (e.g., [8, 21, 22, 33]). In fact, this type of states are more suitable in some particular research; e.g.; for identifying students' engagement level in classroom [34].

It has been reported that the user is likely to exert more pressure on the touch screen in high arousal state [8]. Number of touch events is also higher in the high arousal state [8, 35]. Typing speed also increases in high positive state [15]. The arousal dimension has been suggested to reflect the intensity of either appetitive or aversive systems [13, 20]. Aversive responses are high in high BIS (*behaviour inhibition system*) or BAS (*behavioural activation system*, formerly known as *approach system*). This clearly indicates that behavioural responses increase in high arousal state. Hence, the behavioural touch features such as frequency of touch, pressure applied while touching is expected to increase while a user is in high arousal state.

Depending on the value of number of events and pressure generated, it is possible to decide if the arousal level is high or low. The valence level is decided by assuming the basic human psychology that when a user is in positive mood s/he want to stay in that mood, but in case of negative mood s/he does not want to stay on that mood. When a player wins at the time of game playing, s/he doesn't want to lose. On the other hand, when s/he loses, s/he does not want to lose, s/he wants to win, i.e., s/he wants to change her/his state from negative to positive. This implies winning mode means positive valence, losing mood means negative valence. Previous works [7, 21, 24, 25] support this assumption. Once arousal levels are computed for every time interval, valence level can be measured by observing the rate of change of arousal.

We have used machine learning technique for the classification. Using the number of touch events and pressure generated on each event as feature attributes, our predictive model classifies the users into one of the four emotional states. We have conducted an empirical study with 29 users to build the classifier. The details of the empirical study are described in the next section.

4   Details of Empirical Study

4.1   Experimental Setup

In order to collect the emotional data of touchscreen users, we designed a small game application: 'Emotion Estimator' for Android OS. On the game screen, there are 4 buckets namely, 'BUCKET 1', 'BUCKET 2', 'BUCKET 3' and 'BUCKET 4'. At each instant, a ball is placed in one of the four buckets. The position of the ball changes once a player interacts with the touchscreen depending upon the modes described below. A player tries to guess in which bucket the ball is. Each wrong guess attracts a penalty of 2 and each correct guess gains an increment in score by 4. Time is displayed at the top left corner of the screen and total score is displayed at the top right corner of the screen. The duration of the game is 2 minutes (120 seconds). Figure 2 shows the game interfaces for two particular instants.

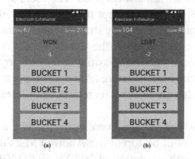

Fig. 2. The Emotion Estimator game interface with two possible situations. (a) is an example screenshot when a player guess right bucket, and hence, wins; (b) is an example screenshot when a player guess wrong bucket, and hence, loses.

The game consists of the following three modes. However, the players were not informed about these modes.

- Winning Mode: In this mode, the player always wins, irrespective of in which bucket the player tries to guess the ball is in.
- Losing Mode: In this mode, the player always loses, irrespective of in which bucket the player tries to guess the ball is in.
- Regular Mode: In this mode, the position of the ball changes after each touch interaction and if the player guesses correctly s/he wins, else s/he loses.

The game design strategy and timeline division is summarized in Fig. 3.

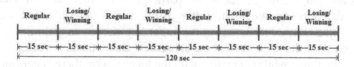

Fig. 3. Timeline division-strategy of the game for a particular instance.

We required 2 types of data: when a player wins & when s/he loses. However, we placed a regular mode interval between a winning & a losing mode interval so that within that interval the user's arousal level might be neutralized. It also helped not to overlap the 2 modes of the game. Random placing of winning and losing mode, each time the game started, has been followed to overcome the effect of biasness.

We chose 15 s interval for each mode because we assumed that 5 consecutive intervals (each of 3 s) are sufficient to capture the emotional data of a user. We collected data of each mode for a particular user twice to analyze whether the nature of touch interaction data were same, for a particular user for a particular mode. At the same time, we couldn't choose longer interval for each mode because if a user won continuously for a long time, s/he might feel bored. Similarly, continuous losing might lead to user frustration.

In conventional way of data collection (asking the users about their emotional states), the quality of emotional data are not always good. The users themselves may not be sure about their emotional state. It may interrupt the interaction and may irritate the users also. So, we collected the data by the gaming strategy. Furthermore, the gaming approach is able to change the emotional state of the user naturally while playing the game. Generally, when a player wins, s/he feels positive (pleasure, joy, pride, admiration etc.). Similarly if a player lose, s/he feels negative (anger, disappointed, sadness, shame etc.). Hence, this helps us to gather the touchscreen data of different emotional state of the user.

The smartphone with which the data were collected was a 'OnePlus One' running on Cyanogen based OS 11 built on top of the Android Marshmallow. The screen size of the phone was 5.5 inch with resolution of 1080×1920 (401 pixels per inch density i.e. ppi). Number of touch events and pressure generated by each event were captured using the Android APIs onTouchEvent() and getPressure(), respectively.

4.2 Participants

We collected data from 29 users who voluntarily took part in the study. All of them were male UG/PG students of IIT Guwahati. The users were within the age group of 19–24 years, with the average age of 21 years. All of them were regular users of touchscreen devices, including both tablets and smartphones.

5 Data Analysis

From the empirical data of 29 users, we computed the sum of the number of *touch events* across the game playing modes for all the participants for each interval. Generally, a 'tap' is considered as 'Action Down' followed by 'Action Up' only, and occurs in an ideal case. 'Action Down' means putting the finger on touchscreen of the device. 'Action Up' means releasing the finger from the touchscreen. But in the real world, due to some movement of the finger while contacting with the touchscreen, there occurs an auxiliary action called 'Action Move' in between Action Down and Action Up, even in case of a tap. In this work all these three actions: 'Action Down', 'Action Move' and 'Action Up' are considered as events.

We assumed a 3 s time interval for data analysis. Choice of an appropriate time interval is not easy and we should keep in mind the way individuals react to stimuli. For example, emotional reaction to a text message may be dependent on a series of events and activities: getting a notification about the message, followed by reading the sender's name and figuring out the sender's identity (e.g., whether from boss or friend), followed by reading of the text. The affective state at the end of all these activities may depend on all of them. Thus, the particular state is arrived at after some seconds that was spent for all these activities. While trying to determine the affective state, we should consider this entire duration. We assume 3 s to be an appropriate duration to capture all the actions/events in any touch interaction in general and the game play scenario in particular that affects the emotional state of a user.

Along with the number of touch events, the average pressure of the touch events per time interval was also calculated. Equations (1) and (2) were used to calculate the number of events and the pressure of the touch events, respectively.

Let us consider that there are n number of taps that have taken place during the 3-sec interval. For each of these taps, we determine the number of events N_i. Number of events for a time interval is determined by calculating the sum of the number of events (N_i) for n taps.

$$\text{Number of events (in a particular interval)} = \sum_{i=1}^{n} N_i \tag{1}$$

For determining pressure value, let us consider there are N events in a time interval. Let P_i be the pressure at each event. The average pressure is calculated as follows:

$$\text{Average pressure (in a particular interval)} = (\sum_{i=1}^{N} P_i)/N \tag{2}$$

5.1 Classification of Data

Four classifiers, namely the K-Nearest Neighbour (KNN), Support Vector Machine (SVM), Decision Tree and the Naïve Bayes have been explored. The observed accuracies were 94.57%, 96.75%, 96.4% and 88.4%, respectively. Although the highest accuracy was found in case of SVM, the other classifiers also gave good enough results. Hence, we can claim that any of the four classifiers are equally applicable for our proposed model.

6 Discussion

We have found only one work (Gao et al. [8]) which is similar to this work. They achieved 89% of accuracy while discriminating between 2 levels of arousal and 2 levels of valence. Whereas we have achieved highest accuracy of 96.75%.

'Duration' along with pressure and frequency of touch could be considered while detecting the emotional state, but we avoided it because some of the previous works sometimes contradicted one another when duration was considered as a feature [8]. For instance, Matsuda et al. [23] had shown that duration in the joy state is shorter and it is longer in the sad state. On the other hand, Hertenstein et al. [11] observed that the touch duration in joy is longer than anger. Moreover, Use of only two features to detect the emotional state makes the model simpler and less expensive in terms of computing.

We considered, as mentioned earlier, a 3 s interval for observing the rate of change of arousal. We considered this 3 s interval both in non-overlapping way (0–3, 3–6 …) as well as in overlapping way (0–3, 1–4, 2–5, 3–6 …). Considering the 3 s interval in overlapping way, number of data points increased to 1740 (29 users × 4 winning/losing mode × 15 interval for each mode) while that was 580 (29 users × 4 winning/losing mode × 5 interval for each mode) in case of non-overlapping way.

Although the data points varied, we could not find any variation in results. In both the cases, the prediction accuracy of four arousal-valence dimensional emotional state were same. This also indicate that the 3 s is a perfect choice of interval for measuring valence level in this context.

Other ways of expressing emotion, e.g., facial expression may be fake or disguised [15, 26]. Emotion detection by sensing physiological/psychophysiological signal, or even from multimodal approach may give better result [18, 19, 25], but these types of methods involve expensive hardware and equipment to be attached with the device. We have, therefore, chosen to consider the behavioral features to detect the emotional states. This fit best for the approach to detect emotional states of the users of the ubiquitously affordable touchscreen devices, with high accuracy.

We could not go for the questionnaire/SAM (Self-Assessment Manikin) approach as we intended to follow the non-intrusive (i.e., without intruding the user) method to observe the change of the emotional state in real time. Therefore, an alternative approach to validate the model is to compare the emotional states calculated from physiological signal (like EEG recorded at the time of data collection) with the emotional states identified by our approach. We are currently working on this.

Naturally, someone may have doubt that something can be lost with this minimalist approach. Yes, as we're using only 2 features, it may not finely classify all the states, if the number of emotional states is large, e.g., 20. But for arousal-valence level emotion identification, our approach is good enough. In future, we plan to design more suitable game and to collect more data to refine and validate the model so that the identified emotional states can be used in real time affective systems, specifically in affective classroom.

7 Conclusion

A minimalist approach for identifying emotional state of a touchscreen user has been proposed in this work. We claim that only two features: number of touch events and pressure generated for each event are sufficient to identify the users' emotional state into any of the four states: high-positive, high-negative, low-positive and low-negative. High and low indicate the arousal level whereas positive and negative indicate the valence level. We intend to work on the use of affective state information for the interface and interaction design in future.

Acknowledgements. We are thankful to all the 29 users who voluntarily took part in the empirical studies.

References

1. AlZoubi, O., D'Mello, S.K., Calvo, R.A.: Detecting naturalistic expressions of nonbasic affect using physiological signals. IEEE Trans. Affect. Comput. **3**(3), 298–310 (2012)
2. Bauer, G., Lukowicz, P.: Can smartphones detect stress-related changes in the behaviour of individuals? In: 2012 IEEE International Conference on Pervasive Computing and Communications Workshops (PERCOM Workshops). IEEE (2012)
3. Camurri, A., Lagerlöf, I., Volpe, G.: Recognizing emotion from dance movement: comparison of spectator recognition and automated techniques. Int. J. Hum Comput Stud. **59**(1), 213–225 (2003)
4. Ciman, M., Wac, K., Gaggi, O.: iSenseStress: assessing stress through human-smartphone interaction analysis. In: 2015 9th International Conference on Pervasive Computing Technologies for Healthcare (PervasiveHealth). IEEE (2015)
5. Ekman, P., Sorenson, E.R., Friesen, W.V.: Pan-cultural elements in facial displays of emotion. Science **164**(3875), 86–88 (1969)
6. Epp, C., Lippold, M., Mandryk, R.L.: Identifying emotional states using keystroke dynamics. In: Proceedings of the SIGCHI Conference on Human Factors in Computing Systems. ACM (2011)
7. Frederickx, S., et al.: The relationship between arousal and the remembered duration of positive events. Appl. Cogn. Psychol. **27**(4), 493–496 (2013)
8. Gao, Y., Bianchi-Berthouze, N., Meng, H.: What does touch tell us about emotions in touchscreen-based gameplay? ACM Trans. Comput.-Hum. Interact. (TOCHI) **19**(4), 31 (2012)
9. Glowinski, D., et al.: Toward a minimal representation of affective gestures. IEEE Trans. Affect. Comput. **2**(2), 106–118 (2011)
10. Hazlett, R.L.: Measuring emotional valence during interactive experiences: boys at video game play. In: Proceedings of the SIGCHI Conference on Human Factors in Computing Systems. ACM (2006)
11. Hertenstein, M.J., et al.: The communication of emotion via touch. Emotion **9**(4), 566 (2009)
12. Isbister, K., et al.: The sensual evaluation instrument: developing an affective evaluation tool. In: Proceedings of the SIGCHI Conference on Human Factors in Computing Systems. ACM (2006)
13. Kambouropoulos, N., Staiger, P.K.: Personality and responses to appetitive and aversive stimuli: the joint influence of behavioural approach and behavioural inhibition systems. Personality Individ. Differ. **37**(6), 1153–1165 (2004)
14. Kätsyri, J., Sams, M.: The effect of dynamics on identifying basic emotions from synthetic and natural faces. Int. J. Hum Comput Stud. **66**(4), 233–242 (2008)
15. Khanna, P., Sasikumar, M.: Recognising emotions from keyboard stroke pattern. Int. J. Comput. Appl. **11**(9), 1–5 (2010)
16. Koelstra, S., et al.: Deap: a database for emotion analysis; using physiological signals. IEEE Trans. Affect. Comput. **3**(1), 18–31 (2012)
17. Koelstra, S., et al.: Single trial classification of EEG and peripheral physiological signals for recognition of emotions induced by music videos. In: Yao, Y., Sun, R., Poggio, T., Liu, J., Zhong, N., Huang, J. (eds.) BI 2010. LNCS, vol. 6334, pp. 89–100. Springer, Heidelberg (2010). doi:10.1007/978-3-642-15314-3_9
18. Kolodyazhniy, V., et al.: An affective computing approach to physiological emotion specificity: toward subject-independent and stimulus-independent classification of film-induced emotions. Psychophysiology **48**(7), 908–922 (2011)

19. Lang, P.J., et al.: Looking at pictures: affective, facial, visceral, and behavioral reactions. Psychophysiology **30**(3), 261–273 (1993)
20. Lee, S., Lang, A.: Discrete emotion and motivation: Relative activation in the appetitive and aversive motivational systems as a function of anger, sadness, fear, and joy during televised information campaigns. Media Psychol. **12**(2), 148–170 (2009)
21. Lerner, J.S., Keltner, D.: Beyond valence: toward a model of emotion-specific influences on judgement and choice. Cogn. Emot. **14**(4), 473–493 (2000)
22. Lottridge, D., Chignell, M., Jovicic, A.: Affective interaction understanding, evaluating, and designing for human emotion. Rev. Hum. Factors Ergon. **7**(1), 197–217 (2011)
23. Matsuda, Y., et al.: Emotional communication in finger braille. Adv. Hum.-Comput. Interact. **2010**, 4 (2010)
24. Murphy, S.T., Zajonc, R.B.: Affect, cognition, and awareness: affective priming with optimal and suboptimal stimulus exposures. J. Pers. Soc. Psychol. **64**(5), 723 (1993)
25. Partala, T., Surakka, V.: The effects of affective interventions in human–computer interaction. Interact. Comput. **16**(2), 295–309 (2004)
26. Picard, R.W.: Affective computing: challenges. Int. J. Hum Comput Stud. **59**(1), 55–64 (2003)
27. Posner, J., Russell, J.A., Peterson, B.S.: The circumplex model of affect: an integrative approach to affective neuroscience, cognitive development, and psychopathology. Dev. Psychopathol. **17**(03), 715–734 (2005)
28. Russell, J.A.: A circumplex model of affect. J. Pers. Soc. Psychol. **39**(6), 1161–1178 (1980)
29. Sacharin, V., Schlegel, K., Scherer, K.R.: Geneva emotion wheel rating study. Center for Person, Kommunikation, Aalborg University, NCCR Affective Sciences. Aalborg University, Aalborg (2012)
30. Sano, A., Picard, R.W.: Stress recognition using wearable sensors and mobile phones. In: 2013 Humaine Association Conference on Affective Computing and Intelligent Interaction (ACII). IEEE (2013)
31. Schlosberg, H.: Three dimensions of emotion. Psychol. Rev. **61**(2), 81 (1954)
32. Shah, S., Teja, J.N., Bhattacharya, S.: Towards affective touch interaction: predicting mobile user emotion from finger strokes. J. Interact. Sci. **3**(1), 1–15 (2015)
33. Stickel, C., Ebner, M., Steinbach-Nordmann, S., Searle, G., Holzinger, A.: Emotion detection: application of the valence arousal space for rapid biological usability testing to enhance universal access. In: Stephanidis, C. (ed.) UAHCI 2009. LNCS, vol. 5614, pp. 615–624. Springer, Heidelberg (2009). doi:10.1007/978-3-642-02707-9_70
34. Woolf, B., Burleson, W., Arroyo, I., Dragon, T., Cooper, D., Picard, R.: Affect aware tutors: recognising and responding to student affect. Int. J. Learn. Technol. **4**(3/4), 129–164 (2009)
35. Zimmermann, P., et al.: Affective computing—a rationale for measuring mood with mouse and keyboard. Int. J. Occup. Saf. Ergon. **9**(4), 539–551 (2003)

Automatic Generation of User Interface Layouts for Alternative Screen Orientations

Clemens Zeidler[1]([envelope]), Gerald Weber[1], Wolfgang Stuerzlinger[2], and Christof Lutteroth[3]

[1] University of Auckland, Auckland, New Zealand
{clemens.zeidler,g.weber}@auckland.ac.nz
[2] School of Interactive Arts and Technology (SIAT),
Simon Fraser University, Vancouver, Canada
w.s@sfu.ca
[3] University of Bath, Bath, UK
c.lutteroth@bath.ac.uk

Abstract. Creating multiple layout alternatives for graphical user interfaces to accommodate different screen orientations for mobile devices is labor intensive. Here, we investigate how such layout alternatives can be generated automatically from an initial layout. Providing good layout alternatives can inspire developers in their design work and support them to create adaptive layouts. We performed an analysis of layout alternatives in existing apps and identified common real-world layout transformation patterns. Based on these patterns we developed a prototype that generates landscape and portrait layout alternatives for an initial layout. In general, there is a very large number of possibilities of how widgets can be rearranged. For this reason we developed a classification method to identify and evaluate "good" layout alternatives automatically. From this set of "good" layout alternatives, designers can choose suitable layouts for their applications. In a questionnaire study we verified that our method generates layout alternatives that appear well structured and are easy to use.

Keywords: Automatic layout · Layout design · Screen rotation · Device independence

1   Introduction

Today, mobile apps need to support different screen orientations, i.e., landscape and portrait, and need to have reasonable layouts for both orientations. To support this need, mobile platform user interface (UI) development frameworks enable developers to specify flexible UIs, which can adapt to different conditions through two means: UI designers can use *layout managers* to resize a UI automatically to the available screen space, and UI designers can specify *layout alternatives* for different screen orientations.

© IFIP International Federation for Information Processing 2017
Published by Springer International Publishing AG 2017. All Rights Reserved
R. Bernhaupt et al. (Eds.): INTERACT 2017, Part I, LNCS 10513, pp. 13–35, 2017.
DOI: 10.1007/978-3-319-67744-6_2

 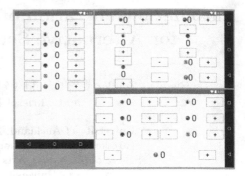

Fig. 1. Left: portrait layout. Top right: original layout in landscape mode; space is not optimally used. Bottom right: layout adapted to landscape mode.

Fig. 2. There are many possible layout alternatives for a given portrait layout. Top right: an example of a reasonable good alternative. Bottom right: an example for a bad alternative.

Layout managers adapt the size of each UI widget to the available space, but in general preserve the overall arrangement of the widgets. An example of this is shown in Fig. 1: the left parts shows a UI designed for portrait orientation, and at the top-right, the same UI is shown in landscape. As this UI's layout manager keeps relative positioning intact, the landscape UI still has the same overall layout as the original design on the left. Yet, due to the different aspect ratio between portrait and landscape orientation, the UI at the top-right does not make optimal use of the available space: the interface is stretched horizontally while the list view displays only a few items.

Some layout managers, such as a flow layout, can make a layout more adaptive to different screen sizes. However, such adaptive layout managers may not always be powerful enough or can lead to undesirable results. For example, a flow layout may break a row of widgets at an undesired position. Also, multiple flow layouts in the same layout may result in undefined behavior since multiple solutions are possible. To avoid this, many UI designers today manually specify separate layout alternatives for certain screen conditions, e.g., for landscape. In Fig. 1, such a layout is shown at the bottom-right: widgets are rearranged to make better use of the available space. Yet, manually creating alternative layouts is laborious and error prone. Regardless of the used layout manager, the developer has to consider the layout carefully for each screen condition. Automatic generation of layout alternatives would not only make it easier for developers to adapt their layouts to alternative screen orientations, but also support their creativity by providing new layout ideas they may not have envisioned as an alternative.

The number of possible layout alternatives grows exponentially with the number of widgets in the layout, i.e., in a complex layout there is a huge number of ways widgets can be rearranged. This makes it difficult to analyze all possible options and, more importantly, it is not clear how to identify "good" layout alternatives from the huge set of possible alternatives. For example, Fig. 2 shows two possible landscape alternatives for a relatively simple portrait layout; while intuitively the bottom alternative is better than the top one, it is not directly clear how to automatically detect this. Here, we develop a novel classification method to identify "good" alternatives.

To address the question of how layout alternatives should be generated, we analyzed 815 existing mobile apps to identify common layout transformation patterns. Based on the findings we define transformation rules between layouts and apply these transformation rules systematically to a given layout to create appropriate alternatives. The generated alternatives are then ranked using a novel objective function, which is then used to provide a shortlist of suggestions to a GUI designer. In our survey of existing apps, we identified that landscape alternatives for portrait layouts contain the most changes, which motivated us to tackle this transformation first. In many cases, this transformation is the more appropriate option for the design process, as the default orientation of a mobile UI is portrait and the landscape alternative is typically added after [1,2]. However, our prototype also supports the generation of portrait alternatives for a landscape layout. In a questionnaire study, we found that our method is able to generate and identify landscape layout alternatives that appear to be well structured, easy to use, and that the automatic generation of layout alternatives can support GUI design.

Our contributions are:

1. An empirical study summarizing the use of layout alternatives in existing apps.
2. An automatic method to generate landscape and portrait layout alternatives.
3. An objective function to identify a set of "good" layout alternative candidates.
4. An evaluation of the approach.

2   Related Work

A variety of design guidelines and UI design patterns exist for mobile devices [3–5]. Nilsson [6] summarized design patterns for mobile UIs; some of these patterns focus on utilizing screen space, including the switch between portrait and landscape mode. Scarr et al. [7] compared the performance of three adaptation techniques for displaying a set of icons – scaling, scrolling and reflow – and illustrated the usability benefits of preserving spatial layout consistency. However, the mentioned work does not provide guidelines or patterns to adapt layouts to different screen orientations or conditions.

Adaptive layout classes can adapt a GUI to different screen sizes [8]. This technique is also used for web-based document layouts [9,10]. However, as discussed earlier, such adaptive layout classes are not always sufficient for more drastic aspect ratio changes where widgets need to be rearranged.

UI generators generate UIs automatically [11–14], and are typically based on UI models which are specified by designers, such as task models, abstract UI models and concrete UIs [15]. In this approach layout templates are filled with widgets from a specification to form a concrete layout. This has also been used to generate multiple user interfaces from a single specification [16–18]. Similarly, documents with dynamic content can be rendered using multiple templates, selected based on constraints [19], or web pages can be transformed into layout templates [20]. Lee et al. [21] provide predefined layout examples and generate the final web document from a selected example. With this approach, the output layout is predefined by a designer while in our approach the layout is generated dynamically.

In our work we use an objective function to find an optimal layout alternative for the given screen conditions. This technique has also been used to improve the usability and aesthetics of UIs created in a sketching tool [22] as well as for automatic document formatting [23]. Sears [24] proposed an objective function for UI layouts which accumulates the expected time required to perform common tasks. Similarly, SUPPLE [25,26] adapts layouts to user's motor and vision capabilities by choosing optimal widgets. Our objective function is based on design patterns and designed to find "good" layouts using layout information *only* available at design time. The designer is then able to select an alternative layout from a list of possibly "good" layouts. SUPPLE also optimizes layout containers, e.g., the orientation of a linear layout, to make a layout fit to different screen sizes. Compared to SUPPLE, we perform more complex changes to the layout topology by re-grouping widgets and recursively applying a set of layout transformations.

Layout graph grammars, a.k.a. spatial graph grammars, have been proposed as a formal method for layout transformation. Brandenburg [27] described how context-free graph grammars can be extended with layout specifications to visualize a graph. Others extended this work and showed how context-sensitive graph grammars with layout specifications and actions can be used to describe certain adaptations of web pages [28,29]. However, transformations still have to be defined manually.

Web pages often need to be adapted for viewing on mobile devices. Roudaki et al. [30] summarized various approaches for this purpose. Qiu et al. [31] compared methods for adapting and rendering web pages on small display devices by breaking them down into a structural overview and detail views for content. Florins and Vanderdonckt [32] proposed rules for graceful degradation of UIs when they are used on more constrained devices. Yu and Kong [33] compared small-screen UI design patterns for news websites. In our work we target layout transformations for screen orientation changes where the screen area stays the same.

Personalized UIs have been proposed as a way to adapt UIs dynamically to different users and situations. Hinz et al. [34] proposed to mine personalized content adaptation rules from user interactions for the optimization of web content presentation on mobile devices. The Framework for Agile Media Experiences (FAME) [35] permits developers to define logical page models that are dynamically filled with content deemed appropriate for a certain user while satisfying given constraints. However, these approaches use predefined layout specifications to render the UI.

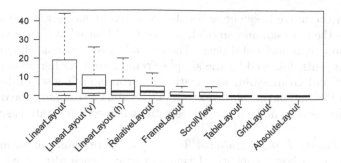

Fig. 3. Boxplot of number of layouts per application.

UI builders are development tools for specifying resizable UI layouts. Constraint-based layouts, such as Auto Layout[1], are often used to make a layout resizable [8,36–38]. Hottelier et al. [39] proposed a technique which allows designers to generalize and specialize constraint-based layout specifications using direct manipulation. Xu et al. proposed methods that make it easier for designers to beautify UIs by inferring layout constraints [40] and to arrange graphic elements with commands [41] based on the way they are visually grouped. The Auckland Layout Editor [42] maps simple drag&drop operations to linear layout constraints. However, little help is available when existing layouts need to be adapted to new requirements.

3   Analysis of Existing Layout Alternatives

To get an overview of current practices in layout adaptation, we surveyed existing layouts in real software projects, and analyzed how such layouts are adapted to different screen conditions. Also, we were interested in identifying commonly used adaptation patterns. To answer these questions we automatically analyzed the source code of all 815 (in 2014) available open source Android apps from the F-Droid project[2]. Android uses a standardized way to specify layout alternatives for different screen conditions in XML files, which provided the data for our study. Layouts can also be specified directly in Java code, but in our data set only 2% of the layouts were instantiated that way.

Usage of Layout Models. Our survey identifies layout models that are frequently used in Android layout specifications. This enables us to get a better grasp on the types of layout arrangements that need to be transformed in practice. Android offers many of the common layout models, such as: LinearLayout for arranging widgets vertically in a column or horizontally in a row; RelativeLayout, which is a form of constraint-based layout; FrameLayout, which usually contains only a single widget; and GridLayout, which arranges widgets in a grid. Figure 3 shows

---

[1] developer.apple.com/design/adaptivity.
[2] f-droid.org.

a boxplot of the usage frequencies for different layout models in the apps. LinearLayout is the most common model, and vertical LinearLayouts are somewhat more common than horizontal ones. The second most frequent class of layouts is RelativeLayouts, followed by the simple FrameLayout. Other models, such as TableLayout and GridLayout, are relatively uncommon. These results are consistent with the findings of Shirazi et al. [43]. ScrollView is not a layout model, but is usually used to make a layout resizable when screen estate is scarce.

Analysis of Layout Transformations. To analyze the relevance of layout alternatives, we surveyed how frequently developers specify such alternatives for their apps. Furthermore, we analyzed how much each layout alternative differs from the corresponding default layout. To measure this, we looked at the widgets that we were able to uniquely identify (by their ID) in a layout alternative as well as in the corresponding default layout. We counted how many of these widgets are at a different structural position ($\Delta_{position}$) in a layout alternative compared to the default. Widgets were considered to be at different positions if their paths to the root of the layout hierarchy, as given in the XML file, differed.

Among the 815 apps with 11,110 layouts we found 365 (3.2%) alternatives for landscape layouts and 397 (3.5%) alternatives for different layout sizes (247 (2.2%) alone for large[3] layout sizes). The low percentage of layout alternatives alone already supports the need for automatic layout alternative generation. We found that the layout alternatives for landscape contain on average more widgets at different positions than the alternatives for different sizes ($\Delta_{position} = 6.5$ vs. $\Delta_{position} = 3.6$).

To understand how a layout specification is typically adapted to different screen sizes and orientation, we manually analyzed 99 of the layout alternatives in detail (63 landscape and 36 other resizing alternatives). In particular, we selected those layout alternatives in which the widget positions changed significantly, i.e., with $\Delta_{position} \geq 10$, plus 15 randomly selected layouts with a smaller difference. Since we did not know what layout adaption techniques we would encounter, we first identified layout adaptation categories by manually analyzing the layouts. In a second step another researcher classified the layouts into these categories. We identified the following categories of transformations in the layouts:

1. **Appearance**: changes in fonts, text labels, image content, spacing or insets, widget size (but not arrangement), etc.
2. **Widgets**: widgets were added or removed.
3. **Horizontal Flow**: a row of widgets was broken into several adjacent rows, or adjacent rows were joined.
4. **Vertical Flow**: a column of widgets was broken into several adjacent columns, or adjacent columns were joined.
5. **Pivot**: a horizontal linear layout was transformed into a vertical one, or vice versa.
6. **Scrolling**: a scrollable container was inserted to deal with overflowing content.

---

[3] developer.android.com/guide/practices/screens_support.html.

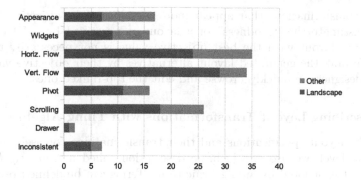

Fig. 4. Histogram of the identified transformation categories found in landscape layout alternatives and in alternatives for different screen sizes.

7. **Drawer**: widgets were moved to a hidden "drawer" container to make room.
8. **Inconsistent**: clear misalignment of widgets or unnecessary changes in widget order.

Figure 4 shows the distribution of categories for layout alternatives. Note that each alternative can be in multiple categories, e.g., a linear layout may have been pivoted as well as split into multiple columns. As the vertical space is reduced in landscape, the most common adaptation is unsurprisingly vertical flow. Scrolling is very frequent; it offers a simple – if not always user friendly – solution to content overflow. Overall, the results indicate that transformations of linear layouts, such as flow across columns and rows, as well as pivoting are frequently used for creating a landscape alternative.

4   Automatic Generation of Layouts

Building on the findings and identified transformation patterns from the previous section, we developed a tool that generates layout alternatives for a given layout. This is a challenging problem since the solution space grows exponentially with the number of changes applied to the initial layout. Moreover, defining an objective function that can identify "good" layout alternatives is demanding: the "goodness" of a layout is a complex construct that incorporates aesthetic and semantic criteria, which are hard to define (or even recognize) in a way that can be easily automated. As identified in the previous section, landscape layout alternatives contain the most layout changes. For this reason we first target layout transformations between portrait and landscape orientation. To address the complexity of the solution space, we focus on the most common transformations for landscape alternatives, i.e., flow and pivot (Fig. 4).

We treat the generation of good landscape alternatives as a constrained discrete optimization problem. We define a set of layout transformations and, starting with the initial layout, search the solution space by applying transformations repeatedly. To limit the search, we define and apply an objective function to prioritize transformations that appear more promising. The objective function can only estimate the "goodness" of a layout as perceived by a UI designer, therefore the layout with the best objective value is not necessarily the best choice. We rank the generated layout alternatives by their objective value and allow UI designers to quickly browse and edit the top-ranked ones.

4.1 Describing Layout Transformations with Tiling Algebra

To describe layout specifications and their transformations concisely at a high abstraction level, we use an algebraic description called a *tiling algebra* [44]. Every layout is denoted by an algebraic term. Terms can be defined recursively as follows, based on two associative tiling operators | and /:

1. **Atoms**: The smallest terms of the algebra are individual widgets (i.e., layouts containing only a single widget). They are given capitalized names, e.g., *Button* or *B*.
2. **Horizontal Tiling** |: If a and b are terms representing layouts, then the term $a|b$ represents a horizontal layout in which layout a is arranged to the left of layout b.
3. **Vertical Tiling** /: If a and b are terms representing layouts, then the term a/b represents a vertical layout in which layout a is arranged on top of layout b.

Then, a horizontal linear layout with three widgets A, B and C is written as $A|B|C$.

Fragments: Terms in the tiling algebra can nest analogously to layouts, and we call the nested sub-layouts in a term *fragments*. This is similar to binary space partitioning layouts [45]. For example, $l_1 = (A|B)/(C|D)$ describes that a layout $l_2 = A|B$ is above a layout $l_3 = C|D$. l_2 and l_3 are fragments of l_1.

Named Tabstops: To describe more complex layouts, such as table and grid layouts, we introduce named tabstops, i.e., named grid lines between fragments. A named tabstop can occur multiple times in a fragment which allows us to describe alignments within a fragment. For example, the fragment of a simple 2×2 grid can be described using a named tabstop i: $(A|B)/(C|D)$. This means the tabstop i occurs in the first and the second row of the grid.

Levels: Terms can be described by abstract syntax trees (ASTs), where each inner node is a tiling operator and the leaf nodes are widgets. We call the fragments that are formed at a depth n of an AST, i.e., the fragments combined at the same nesting depth n, the nth *level* of the term. For example, consider the layout $l_1 = (A|B)/(C|D|(E/F))$: the first level contains only l_1 itself; the second one contains $A|B$ and $C|D|(E/F)$; the third level contains C, D and $E|F$; and the fourth one contains E and F.

The tiling algebra is well suited to describe LinearLayouts, FrameLayouts, TableLayouts and many GridLayouts. Transforming RelativeLayouts automatically to a tiling algebra is not always possible and non-trivial. Some complex,

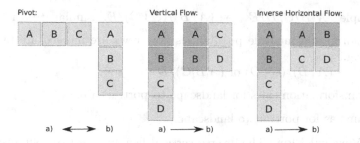

Fig. 5. Examples for the transformation rules.

interleaved grid layouts cannot be described using a single fragment and named tabstops. However, for the layouts analyzed in our survey, we were able to describe all GridLayouts and manually replace RelativeLayouts by layout classes that can be described using tiling algebra.

4.2 Transformation Rules

Based on the most common transformations identified in our survey of existing landscape alternatives, we define three basic transformation rules on fragments for the transformation from portrait to landscape: pivot, vertical flow and inverse horizontal flow. We define the inverse transformation rules for the transformation from landscape to portrait layouts analogously. Figure 5 visualizes the transformation rules.

We use the right-arrow symbol $\rightarrow$ to denote transformations from one layout to another. Note that the variables in the rules (e.g., a) represent fragments, i.e., they are not necessarily widgets but can possibly be broken down further.

Transformation rules for portrait to landscape:

Pivot: The pivot transformation changes the orientation of a fragment, i.e., the $|$ operator becomes $/$, and vice versa. For example, $I/C/L \rightarrow I|C|L$. The pivot transformation generalizes to table layouts, e.g., $(A|B)/(C|D) \rightarrow_i$
$(A/B)|(C/D)$, i.e., the grid is transposed.

Vertical Flow: The vertical flow transformation breaks a column, i.e., vertical LinearLayout, into two adjacent ones:

$$a_1/\ldots/a_n \rightarrow (a_1/\ldots/a_k)|(a_{k+1}/\ldots/a_n).$$

The vertical flow transformation takes multiple break positions into account. For example, $I/C/L$ can be transformed to $(I|C)/L$ or alternatively to $I|(C/L)$.

Inverse Horizontal Flow: This transformation splits a column into multiple rows:

$$a_1/\ldots/a_n \rightarrow (a_1|\ldots|a_i)/\ldots/(a_k|\ldots|a_n).$$

For example, $A/B/C/D/E \rightarrow (A \mid B)/(C \mid D)/E$. Similar to the vertical
$\qquad\qquad\qquad\quad m \qquad m$
flow transformation multiple possibilities how rows are merged are taken into
account, e.g.,
$A/B/C/D \rightarrow (A \mid B)/(C \mid D)$ or $(A|B|C)/D$.
$\qquad\quad m \qquad m$

The transformation rules for landscape to portrait are:

Pivot: Same as for portrait to landscape.

Inverse Vertical Flow: The inverse vertical flow merges two columns:

$$(a_1/\ldots/a_k) \mid (a_{k+1}/\ldots/a_n) \rightarrow a_1/\ldots/a_n.$$

Horizontal Flow: The horizontal flow merges multiple rows into a column:

$$(a_1 \mid \ldots \mid a_i)/\ldots/(a_k \mid \ldots \mid a_n) \rightarrow a_1/\ldots/a_n.$$

4.3   Grouping of Fragments

In order to transform a layout meaningfully, it is useful to group logically related
widgets together. Logically related widgets are sometimes already grouped in a
layout specification, but this is not always the case. For example, consider a UI
layout in which three labels L are logically paired with editable text fields E:
the correct grouping may already be encoded in the layout specification with a
separate nested layout for each of the pairs, i.e., $l_1 = (L/E)/(L/E)/(L/E)$, but
the layout may also simply be defined in a single layout as $l_2 = L/E/L/E/L/E$.
l_1 is easier to transform meaningfully, as related widgets stay together when
applying the previously defined transformations. For example, a vertical flow
transformation may split a pair of label and text field: $l_2 \rightarrow (L/E/L) \mid (E/L/E)$.
However, a similar transformation on the groups of l_2 would leave the pairs
intact: $l_1 \rightarrow ((L/E)/(L/E)) \mid (L/E)$.

Our grouping approach is inspired by Gestalt principles [46]: it forms groups
according to repeated patterns of fragments (principle of similarity) to make
sure that the fragments in each group are transformed together (principle of
common fate). To group the fragments in a linear layout, we (1) identify
the longest repeated consecutive pattern of fragments in the layout, and (2)
group all occurrences of the pattern into new fragments, i.e., linear sub-layouts.
Step (1) is equivalent to the well-known longest repeated substring problem,
which can be solved in linear time. For example, to group a layout $l_3 = a/L/L/E/L/E/L/L/E/L/E/b$ the algorithm (1) identifies $l_4 = (L/L/E/L/E)$
as the longest repeating consecutive pattern, and (2) groups the occurrences of
the pattern so that $l_3 \rightarrow a/l_4/l_4/b$. The grouping process can be recursively
repeated, i.e., we can look for groups in the fragments a, l_4 and b, which results
in $l_4 \rightarrow L/l_5/l_5$ with $l_5 = (L/E)$. Sometimes there are multiple ways how items
can be grouped in which case the grouping algorithm returns multiple solutions,
e.g., $L|E|L|E|L$ can be grouped as $(L|E)|(L|E)|L$ or $L|(E|L)|(E|L)$.

It is possible that the grouping produced by this approach is wrong, i.e., does not match the logical relations in the UI. Therefore, this grouping is only considered as a possible fragment when applying transformations. By itself, the grouping does not change a layout. However, after grouping a fragment, transformations on that fragment are more likely to respect the aforementioned Gestalt principles.

4.4 Objective Function

We define an objective function $f(l)$ to estimate the quality of a layout specification l. Smaller values of l indicate better layouts. The function is a weighted sum:

$$f(l) = w_{min} \cdot t_{min}(l) + w_{pref} \cdot t_{pref}(l) + w_{ratio} \cdot t_{ratio}(l)$$
$$+ w_{nTra} \cdot t_{nTra}(l) + w_{sym} \cdot t_{sym}(l) + w_{level} \cdot t_{level}(l)$$

with t being quality terms that are calculated for a layout, and w being constant weights which are chosen empirically. This sum can be extended to incorporate additional criteria. In the following we briefly summarize the definitions of the quality terms and the heuristics behind them. The first three quality terms correspond directly to commonly-used penalty functions, e.g., in constraint-based UI layouts [8,47]. These terms take the minimum and preferred widget and layout sizes into account. Here, the preferred size is the natural size of a widget or a layout, i.e., the size a widget or a layout would obtain if their are no other constraints, such as the window size, forcing it to a different size. The other quality terms are motivated by research into UI aesthetics and usability [7,48,49]. We focused on terms that are well-motivated by previous work, but acknowledge that more terms, e.g., to account for alignment, could be added to the objective function.

Minimum Size: "A layout that can be shrunk to a compact size is likely to have a good structure [8,47]."

$$t_{min} = \frac{min_w^2 + min_h^2}{screen_w^2 + screen_h^2}$$

min_w, min_h, $screen_w$ and $screen_h$ are the width and height of the minimum and the screen size. The divisor normalizes the value to the screen size. If the layout in its minimum size does not fit on the screen, we assign t_{min} a very large value.

Preferred Size: "If the widgets of a layout have a size close to their preferred size, the space is well used [8,47]."

$$t_{pref} = \frac{\sum_i ((pref_{w,i} - size_{w,i})^2 + (pref_{h,i} - size_{h,i})^2)}{screen_w^2 + screen_h^2}$$

$pref_i$ and $size_i$ are the preferred and the actual size of each widget.

Aspect Ratio: "A good layout in its preferred size has an aspect ratio close to that of the target screen [8,47,50]."

$$t_{ratio} = |ratio_{pref} - ratio_{screen}|/ratio_{screen}$$

We constrain $t_{ratio} \leq 1$ to limit the impact of this term.

Number of Transformations: "A smaller number of transformations is preferable as this preserves the spatial consistency of the UI [7]." t_{nTra} is the number of transformations which was applied to derive the layout from the initial one. We constrain $t_{nTra} \leq 5$ to limit the impact of this term.

Symmetry: "Layouts with a high symmetry are preferable [48,49]." We chose a simple, screen-independent definition of symmetry based on the AST of a layout fragment: a fragment is symmetric if it consists of topologically equivalent parts. That is, layouts are symmetric if all the sub-layouts they contain are structurally equivalent and simple widgets are symmetric by definition. This can be understood intuitively through examples: $(A/B)|(C/D)|(E/F)$ is symmetric because A/B, C/D and E/F are structurally equivalent (vertical tilings of two widgets). The fragment $(A|B)/(C|D)/E$ is not symmetric because E is a single widget and not a horizontal tiling of two widgets as the other sub-fragments. Based on this notion,

$$t_{sym}(l) = 1 - \frac{s(l)}{widgetCount(l)^2 \cdot nLevels(l)}$$

with s defined recursively on a fragment $l = a_1/\ldots/a_n$ or $l = a_1|\ldots|a_n$ as

$$s(l) = \begin{cases} nWidgets(l)^2 \cdot nLevels(l) & \text{, if } l \text{ symmetric} \\ \sum_{i=1..n} s(a_i) & \text{, otherwise} \end{cases}$$

$s(l)$ measures the degree of symmetry in l: if l is symmetric, the value returned is higher with the size of l, i.e., with its number of widgets $nWidgets$ and levels $nLevels$. If l itself is not symmetric, the same logic is applied to its sub-layouts, summing up the value of each symmetric sub-layout found. The divisor ensures that $0 \leq t_{sym}(l) \leq 1$.

Transformation Level: "A transformation close to the root of the fragment hierarchy is better as this preserves the spatial consistency of larger sub-layouts [7]." t_{level} is the deepest level that has been changed by the transformations that derived the layout from the initial one. For example, consider an initial layout $l_1 = (A/(B/C))/(D/E)$ with three levels. If we transform $l_1 \rightarrow l_2 = (A/(B/C))|(D/E)$ (pivot of the first/on level 1) and then $l_2 \rightarrow l_3 = (A|(B/C))|(D/E)$ (pivot of/at level 2), then $t_{level}(l_3) = \max(1,2) = 2$. We constrain $t_{level} \leq 5$ to limit the impact of this term.

4.5 Empirical Optimization of Parameters

The weights of the objective function are parameters of the layout generation approach. They should be chosen so that the objective function correlates with the "goodness" of a layout. Initially, we had no data about the "goodness" of landscape layout alternatives, i.e., no ground truth. Thus, we had to optimize the weights based on our own subjective ratings of "goodness", facing the following two challenges:

1. **Precision**: It is hard for an individual to tell precisely how "good" a layout alternative should be rated.
2. **Local Optimization**: Adjusting the weights to create a more appropriate objective value for a specific layout can reduce the objective value for other layouts.

We addressed the precision challenge as follows: while it is hard to get precise ratings, it is usually possible for an experienced individual to recognize layout alternatives that are clearly unsuitable ("bad" layouts) and layout alternatives that could be suitable ("good" layouts). Using our automatic layout transformation approach, we generated a variety of landscape alternatives for a number of portrait layouts and then selected a set of "good" and "bad" layouts from them, based on subjective judgment. The weights were chosen in a way that maximizes the discriminatory power of the objective function, i.e., so that the "good" layouts had low and the "bad" layouts high objective values.

To address the challenge of local optimization, we used a form of linear regression based on quadratic programming. For each possible pair of a "good" landscape layout alternative l_{good} and a "bad" alternative l_{bad} for a given portrait layout, a soft constraint is added to a linear constraint system: $f(l_{bad}) - f(l_{good}) \geq 1$. This difference should be at least 1 for every such pair, so the layouts can be discriminated. Note that we do not add constraints for every possible pair of good and bad layout alternatives. We only add constraints for every possible pair derived from the same layout, as the layout generation approach compares only such alternatives with each other.

Overall, this yields a set of weights for the objective function. In the following table, the *man* row gives the values for the initial manual process and the *opt* row gives the results for the subsequent constraint optimization.

	w_{min}	w_{pref}	w_{ratio}	w_{nTra}	w_{sym}	w_{level}
man	0.2	10	0.4	0.04	1	0.2
opt	2.8	10	0.2	0.4	2.5	0.8

The values are scaled to $w_{pref} = 10$. Note that the weights of different objective function terms are not directly comparable as the terms are not normalized to each other.

4.6 Search Strategy

In order to find suitable landscape layouts, starting with the given layout, we search the space of possible layouts by repeatedly applying the transformation rules. The solution space grows exponentially with the number of transformation steps: at each step, the number of transformations that can be applied is roughly linear to the layout size. The pivot rule can be applied to any fragment in a layout; the vertical flow and inverse horizontal flow rules can be applied to any vertical fragment, usually in more than one way; and grouping can be applied recursively on fragments containing repetitions.

As a result, a brute force search is not practical in many cases. To search the solution space more efficiently, we perform transformations on intermediate layouts with a good objective value. That is, we generally try to optimize a layout already estimated to be comparatively good before looking at worse layouts. Furthermore, in order to preserve symmetry in a layout (one of the quality terms of the objective function), we use a heuristic that favors a transformation to be consistently applied to a whole level of the layout. That is, we first apply the same transformation to all fragments of a chosen level: if the fragments on that level are similarly structured, i.e., if there is symmetry between them, then applying the same transformation to each of them is likely to preserve that symmetry. For example, applying the pivot transformation to the entire (symmetric) second level of $(A/B)|(A/B)$ yields a symmetric layout $(A|B)|(A|B)$.

However, using this search strategy, we found that calculating a sufficient number of good layout alternatives still takes up to several minutes. This is not acceptable for a tool that supports the interactive design process of a developer. A performance analysis revealed that most time was spent in the relatively complex calculation of the minimum and actual layout size needed for the objective function evaluation. To solve this problem we split the objective function into a part that is quick to calculate and a second that is slower: $f = f_{fast} + f_{slow}$ with $f_{fast} = w_{nTra} \cdot t_{nTra} + w_{sym} \cdot t_{sym} + w_{level} \cdot t_{level}$ and $f_{slow} = w_{min} \cdot t_{min} + w_{pref} \cdot t_{pref} + w_{ratio} \cdot t_{ratio}$. We found that there is a good correlation between f and f_{fast}, i.e., for the analyzed layouts we found that the six best layouts chosen by f were among the 23 best layouts chosen by f_{fast}. This allows us to perform a coarse search using f_{fast} followed by a detailed search on the found layouts using the full objective function f. With this approach we can perform the search for good layout alternatives in under a second on a i5-4300U CPU at 1.90 GHz.

5   Implementation

We implemented the layout alternative generation approach as a plugin for the Android Studio development environment, the official development environment for Android, which has an integrated design editor for XML layout files[4]. With our plugin the user can generate landscape and portrait layout alternatives from a layout XML file. As shown in Fig. 6, the user can quickly browse the top-ranked layout alternatives and edit a chosen alternative if desired. Internally, the plugin transforms the input into a constraint-based layout [8,47] in order to calculate the size properties required for the objective function.

---

[4] The source code is available on: gitlab.com/czeidler/layoutalternatives.

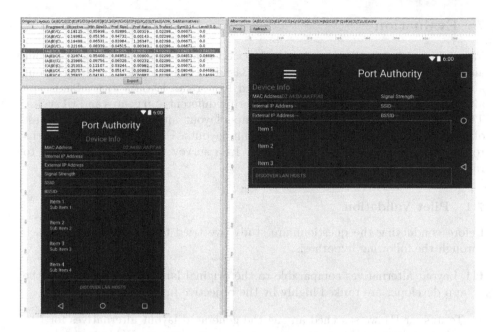

Fig. 6. Screenshot of the implementation: a list of the layout alternatives with the best objective values (top-left), the original portrait layout (bottom-left), and the selected landscape layout alternative (right).

6   Limitations

In the following we discuss limitations of our approach. In our analysis of existing layouts (Sect. 3) we focused on Android and it is not clear if our results can be generalized to other platforms, e.g., iOS. However, the main Android layout classes are similar to those on other mobile platforms, and mobile design patterns are comparable across platforms [5]. With a fairly large number of analyzed layouts we believe we captured a representative picture of existing transformation patterns and that our results are transferable to different platforms.

Currently, our prototype does not handle dynamic layouts, e.g., layouts that change on user interaction. While it is possible that our prototype could handle multiple intermediate steps of a dynamic layout, such a feature is currently difficult to implement since dynamic behavior is not specified in the layout XML files.

To limit the solution space we focused on a small set of transformations (Sect. 4). This makes it sometimes difficult or even impossible to generate some rarer layout alternatives, e.g., multiple transformations may have to be applied to achieve a certain result. To solve this problem more specialized transformations need to be introduced.

7 Evaluation

We evaluated how well our objective function is able to identify "good" layout alternatives using a questionnaire study. Based on our analysis of existing layout alternatives in real-world apps, we selected 15 portrait layouts with a landscape alternative that changed significantly, covering different app genres and UI styles. Then we generated a ranking of landscape layout alternatives with the best objective values for each of the 15 portrait layouts. Finally, the quality of the resulting landscape layouts was assessed. In a survey we asked participants to rate the layout alternatives.

7.1 Pilot Validation

Before conducting the questionnaire study, we tried to validate our approach through the following hypothesis:

H1 Layout alternatives comparable to the original landscape layouts from the app developer are ranked highly by the objective function.

To answer H1 we searched among the generated layout alternatives for layouts that are comparable to the original landscape layouts. We judged a layout alternative as comparable if it follows the general layout topology of the original, i.e., if the correct layout transformations had been applied. Here, minor details that our transformations cannot achieve, e.g., font size changes or widget alignment, were ignored. For all 15 layouts we were able to identify layout alternatives that were comparable to the original landscape layout. Figure 7 shows that most of these layout alternatives were ranked among the top three candidates. That is, they were among the top three generated layouts according to their objective values, and therefore near the top of the list of alternatives in our prototype. This supports H1, i.e., that the prototype generates the expected layout and that the layout is ranked highly by the objective function.

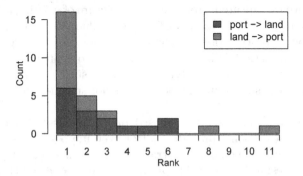

Fig. 7. Automatic ranking of the layout alternatives which are comparable to the original landscape and portrait layouts created by the app developer. Our objective function ranks the original layout alternatives highly.

For further validation we performed the inverse test, i.e., generated portrait layout alternatives from the generated landscape alternatives. We were able to transform all landscape layouts back to their original portrait ones. Furthermore, the layout alternative matching the original portrait layout was also ranked highly (Fig. 7). Interestingly, the portrait alternative matching the original portrait layout were generally ranked higher than the landscape alternative matching the original landscape layout. An explanation for this is that the transformation rules for landscape to portrait are simpler than the inverse rules. For example, while there are generally multiple ways to break a column into two columns using the vertical flow transformation, there is only one way to merge two columns.

7.2   Methodology

In our questionnaire study we aimed to verify the following hypotheses:

H2 The layout alternatives that are ranked highly contain acceptable layouts.
H3 Such layouts are useful as a starting point for designing landscape alternatives.

We used a web questionnaire to evaluate the six best layout alternatives, i.e., those with the smallest objective values, generated for each of the 15 portrait layouts. Note that the six best layout alternatives always contained the *original landscape alternative* (see Fig. 7). After questions about demographics and previous experience with UI design, the 15 portrait layouts and their generated landscape alternatives were shown in randomized order. For each portrait layout, a participant was first asked to rate the portrait layout itself and then each of the landscape layout alternatives in randomized order. To facilitate comparisons, we showed each layout alternative next to the original portrait layout. For each portrait layout and each layout alternative we asked the following 5-point Likert-scale questions (which are loosely based on [51]), ranging from strongly disagree to strongly agree:

Q1 The portrait/landscape layout appears well structured.
Q2 The portrait/landscape layout appears easy to use.
Q3 There are problems with this portrait/landscape layout.

After each of the 15 layouts, i.e., the portrait layout and its six landscape alternatives, we asked the following questions, again using the 5-point Likert scale:

Q4 Some of the proposed layout alternatives were as I expected them to be.
Q5 The proposed layout alternatives were missing one or more layouts that I would have expected.
Q6 The proposed layout alternatives contained good layouts that were unexpected.
Q7 The proposed layout alternatives gave me a good overview of how the layout can be transformed to landscape.

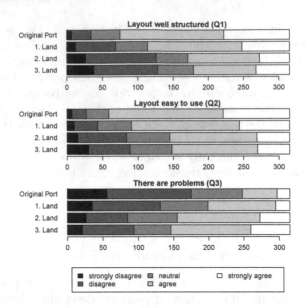

Fig. 8. Answers to Q1, Q2, Q3 for the original portrait and the three best automatically ranked alternatives. For 15 layouts, 21 participants gave $21 \cdot 15 = 315$ answers for the original layout and its alternatives.

Q8 The proposed layout alternatives contained a good starting point for the design of a landscape layout alternative.

At the end of the questionnaire the participants were asked to answer the following 5-point Likert-scale questions:

Q9 As a layout designer I would like to use a tool that proposes layout alternatives for different screen conditions, e.g., landscape alternative for a given portrait layout.
Q10 I do not think a tool that proposes layout alternatives would be useful for layout designers.

Finally, we gave participants the option to leave free-text comments.

7.3   Results and Discussion

21 participants (9 female, 12 male, average age 31) responded to our ad and filled the questionnaire. According to the responses, 13 had UI design experience, seven were familiar with UI layout design tools, and eight had designed layout alternatives for different screen conditions. The participants were a mix of professionals working in IT, designers, and computer science students. In total, $15 \times 7 \times 21 = 2205$ quality ratings for $15 \times 7 = 105$ layouts were submitted (15 apps with $(6 + 1)$ layouts each).

To validate H2 we consider the ratings of the best generated layout alternatives in comparison to that of the original portrait layout. In Fig. 8 we can see that layout alternatives ranked higher by the objective function generally also got better ratings. The first and second best alternatives received a positive rating by more than half of the participants. The third alternative received a borderline result. The fact that two layouts received a positive rating by the majority can be interpreted as a form of resilience of the tool output; we can expect more than one proposed layout to be acceptable by many. Overall, these results are a good support for hypothesis H2.

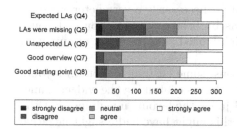

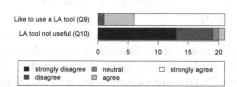

Fig. 9. Combined answers to Q7-Q11 for all layouts.

Fig. 10. Questions Q9-Q10 at the end of the questionnaire.

To validate H3 we looked in particular at the answers to the summary questions about the layout alternatives for each of the portrait layouts (Fig. 9). Q8 addresses H3 most directly and was answered strongly in the affirmative, supporting acceptance of H3. Q7 addresses more the added value of the whole set of layout alternatives and the positive result strengthens H3 further. For Q5, agreement signals potential shortcomings of the tool, but less than half the responses agree, so this does not seem to be a limiting factor. For Q6, a majority of positive answers is not necessarily expected, and the positive responses indicate benefits for at least some of the users. If a sizable fraction of users finds unexpected layouts of reasonable quality, this would mean that the tool can provide a useful service designing new layouts through stimulating creativity. In that sense, Q6 adds an important additional dimension to the evaluation of H3. Q4 complements Q6 to some degree and addresses whether the tool is able to obtain reasonable layouts automatically. The answers show that the tool appears predictable to the users in that it delivers at least some expected layouts. We can therefore accept H3 in two ways: first, the tool eases the UI design work as seen in the answers to Q4 and Q8, and second, the tool might also provide new ideas, as indicated in the answers to Q6. Figure 10 shows that there was a strong agreement among the participants that a tool that proposes layout alternatives would generally be useful. This was also backed by comments from the participants. For example: "A tool that automatically displays alternatives for layout designs is extremely useful." or "Some of the layouts were really good, especially ones that are aligned symmetrically."

Study Limitations. One threat to validity of the questionnaire results is acquiescence bias, which could lead to alternatives being rated overly positive.

We addressed this threat by asking for three quality measures (Q1-Q3), which allowed participants to express a differentiated judgment. Furthermore, agreement to Q3 signals a negative judgment. The fact that higher ranked alternatives got better ratings even though the order in the survey was randomized (Fig. 8) speaks against a strong acquiescence bias. Similarly, a variety of questions (Q4-Q8) was used to investigate H3 and to obtain a differentiated understanding of possible benefits.

Another threat to validity is a possible selection bias in the layouts chosen for the user study. The population of layouts is necessarily a very heterogeneous space, and we tried to mitigate such a bias by basing our selection of layouts on the layout survey described earlier, which looked at a larger set of apps and layouts.

A minor issue is that for technical reasons, some custom widgets in layouts were not rendered correctly, i.e., only as gray boxes containing the widget name. We told the participants to expect this and judge the layouts imagining that the gray boxes were appropriate widgets. Still, this might have had a slight negative effect on ratings.

8   Conclusion

In this paper we investigated how layout alternatives for alternative screen orientations can be generated automatically. To identify suitable layout transformation patterns we analyzed layouts from 815 existing Android apps. Based on this analysis, we designed a set of rules to transform layouts and presented a new way to computationally estimate the quality of a transformed layout. Using this quality measure as objective function, we automatically generated landscape and portrait layout alternatives for a given layout. Finally, we validated the utility of our implementation and whether the objective function is able to identify "good" layouts in a questionnaire study. We found that layout alternatives ranked highly by the objective function were rated well by the participants. Generated layout alternatives appeared to be well structured and easy to use. Moreover, our method generated good layouts that were not anticipated by the participants, which means our prototype can actively help developers to design new GUIs.

In future work, we plan to identify other transformation rules, e.g., rules which apply visual appearance changes or change the layout more drastically. Yet, to improve the accuracy of the corresponding objective function, we need to simultaneously investigate new quality terms, such as a term that encapsulates additional Gestalt principles. Also, we plan to improve the quality of the layout alternatives by learning from the alternative choices designers made for their layouts while using our system. Finally, transformations between different screen sizes, e.g., tablet to phone, should be supported.

References

1. Morris, J.: Android User Interface Development: Beginner's Guide. Packt Publishing, Birmingham (2011)
2. Sahami Shirazi, A., Henze, N., Dingler, T., Kunze, K., Schmidt, A.: Upright or sideways?: analysis of smartphone postures in the wild. In: Proceedings of 15th International Conference on HCI with Mobile Devices and Services, pp. 362–371 (2013)
3. Adipat, B., Zhang, D.: Interface design for mobile applications. In: AMCIS 2005 Proceedings, p. 494 (2005)
4. Tidwell, J.: Designing Interfaces: Patterns for Effective Interaction Design. O'Reilly Media Inc., Sebastopol (2010)
5. Neil, T.: Mobile Design Pattern Gallery: UI Patterns for Smartphone Apps. O'Reilly Media Inc., Sebastopol (2014)
6. Nilsson, E.G.: Design patterns for user interface for mobile applications. Adv. Eng. Softw. **40**(12), 1318–1328 (2009). Designing, modelling and implementing interactive systems
7. Scarr, J., Cockburn, A., Gutwin, C., Malacria, S.: Testing the robustness and performance of spatially consistent interfaces. In: Proceedings of the SIGCHI Conference on Human Factors in Computing Systems, pp. 3139–3148 (2013)
8. Zeidler, C., Lutteroth, C., Weber, G.: Constraint solving for beautiful user interfaces: how solving strategies support layout aesthetics. In: Proceedings of the 13th International Conference of the NZ Chapter of the ACM's Special Interest Group on HCI, CHINZ 2012, pp. 72–79 (2012)
9. Frain, B.: Responsive web design with HTML5 and CSS3 (2012)
10. Nebeling, M., Matulic, F., Streit, L., Norrie, M.C.: Adaptive layout template for effective web content presentation in large-screen contexts. In: Proceedings of the 11th ACM Symposium on Document Engineering, DocEng 2011, pp. 219–228 (2011)
11. Raneburger, D., Popp, R., Vanderdonckt, J.: An automated layout approach for model-driven wimp-ui generation. In: Proceedings of the 4th ACM SIGCHI Symposium on Engineering Interactive Computing Systems, EICS 2012, pp. 91–100 (2012)
12. Yanagida, T., Nonaka, H., Kurihara, M.: Personalizing graphical user interfaces on flexible widget layout. In: Proceedings of the 1st ACM SIGCHI Symposium on Engineering Interactive Computing Systems, EICS 2009, pp. 255–264 (2009)
13. Kim, W.C., Foley, J.D.: Providing high-level control and expert assistance in the user interface presentation design. In: Proceedings of the INTERACT 1993 and CHI 1993 Conference on Human Factors in Computing Systems, pp. 430–437 (1993)
14. Talton, J., Yang, L., Kumar, R., Lim, M., Goodman, N., Měch, R.: Learning design patterns with bayesian grammar induction. In: Proceedings of the 25th ACM Symposium on User Interface Software and Technology, pp. 63–74 (2012)
15. Paterno, F., Santoro, C.: One model, many interfaces. In: Kolski, C., Vanderdonckt, J. (eds.) Computer-Aided Design of User interfaces III, pp. 143–154. Springer, Dordrecht (2002). doi:10.1007/978-94-010-0421-3_13
16. Nichols, J., Myers, B.A., Higgins, M., Hughes, J., Harris, T.K., Rosenfeld, R., Pignol, M.: Generating remote control interfaces for complex appliances. In: Proceedings of the 15th Annual ACM Symposium on User Interface Software and Technology, UIST 2002, pp. 161–170 (2002)

17. Nichols, J., Rothrock, B., Chau, D.H., Myers, B.A.: Huddle: automatically generating interfaces for systems of multiple connected appliances. In: Proceedings of the 19th Annual ACM Symposium on User Interface Software and Technology, UIST 2006, pp. 279–288 (2006)
18. Nichols, J., Chau, D.H., Myers, B.A.: Demonstrating the viability of automatically generated user interfaces. In: Proceedings of the SIGCHI Conference on Human Factors in Computing Systems, CHI 2007, pp. 1283–1292 (2007)
19. Schrier, E., Dontcheva, M., Jacobs, C., Wade, G., Salesin, D.: Adaptive layout for dynamically aggregated documents. In: Proceedings of the 13th International Conference on Intelligent User Interfaces, IUI 2008, pp. 99–108 (2008)
20. Kumar, R., Talton, J.O., Ahmad, S., Klemmer, S.R.: Bricolage: example-based retargeting for web design. In: Proceedings of the SIGCHI Conference on Human Factors in Computing Systems, CHI 2011, pp. 2197–2206 (2011)
21. Lee, B., Srivastava, S., Kumar, R., Brafman, R., Klemmer, S.R.: Designing with interactive example galleries. In: Proceedings of the SIGCHI Conference on Human Factors in Computing Systems, CHI 2010, pp. 2257–2266 (2010)
22. Todi, K., Weir, D., Oulasvirta, A.: Sketchplore: sketch and explore with a layout optimiser. In: Proceedings of the 2016 ACM Conference on Designing Interactive Systems, pp. 543–555 (2016)
23. Hurst, N., Li, W., Marriott, K.: Review of automatic document formatting. In: Proceedings of the 9th ACM Symposium on Document Engineering, pp. 99–108 (2009)
24. Sears, A.: Layout appropriateness: a metric for evaluating user interface widget layout. IEEE Trans. Softw. Eng. 19(7), 707–719 (1993)
25. Gajos, K., Weld, D.S.: SUPPLE: automatically generating user interfaces. In: Proceedings of the 9th International Conference on Intelligent User Interfaces, IUI 2004, pp. 93–100 (2004)
26. Gajos, K.Z., Wobbrock, J.O., Weld, D.S.: Automatically generating user interfaces adapted to users' motor and vision capabilities. In: Proceedings of the 20th Annual ACM Symposium on User Interface Software and Technology, pp. 231–240 (2007)
27. Brandenburg, F.J.: Designing graph drawings by layout graph grammars. In: Tamassia, R., Tollis, I.G. (eds.) GD 1994. LNCS, vol. 894, pp. 416–427. Springer, Heidelberg (1995). doi:10.1007/3-540-58950-3_395
28. Zhang, K., Kong, J., Qiu, M., Song, G.L.: Multimedia layout adaptation through grammatical specifications. Multimedia Syst. 10(3), 245–260 (2005)
29. Kong, J., Zhang, K., Zeng, X.: Spatial graph grammars for graphical user interfaces. ACM Trans. Comput.-Hum. Interact. 13(2), 268–307 (2006)
30. Roudaki, A., Kong, J., Yu, N.: A classification of web browsing on mobile devices. J. Vis. Lang. Comput. 26, 82–98 (2015)
31. Qiu, M.K., Zhang, K., Huang, M.: An empirical study of web interface design on small display devices. In: Proceedings of the 2004 IEEE/WIC/ACM International Conference on Web Intelligence, WI 2004, pp. 29–35 (2004)
32. Florins, M., Vanderdonckt, J.: Graceful degradation of user interfaces as a design method for multiplatform systems. In: IUI 2004, vol. 4, pp. 140–147 (2004)
33. Yu, N., Kong, J.: User experience with web browsing on small screens: experimental investigations of mobile-page interface design and homepage design for news websites. Inf. Sci. 330, 427–443 (2016). sI: Visual Info Communication
34. Hinz, M., Fiala, Z., Wehner, F.: Personalization-based optimization of web interfaces for mobile devices. In: Brewster, S., Dunlop, M. (eds.) Mobile HCI 2004. LNCS, vol. 3160, pp. 204–215. Springer, Heidelberg (2004). doi:10.1007/978-3-540-28637-0_18

35. Lempel, R., Barenboim, R., Bortnikov, E., Golbandi, N., Kagian, A., Katzir, L., Makabee, H., Roy, S., Somekh, O.: Hierarchical composable optimization of web pages. In: Proceedings of the 21st International Conference on World Wide Web, pp. 53–62 (2012)
36. Zeidler, C., Müller, J., Lutteroth, C., Weber, G.: Comparing the usability of grid-bag and constraint-based layouts. In: Proceedings of the 24th Australian Computer-Human Interaction Conference, OzCHI 2012, pp. 674–682 (2012)
37. Lok, S., Feiner, S.: A survey of automated layout techniques for information presentations. Proc. SmartGraphics 2001, 61–68 (2001)
38. Borning, A., Marriott, K., Stuckey, P., Xiao, Y.: Solving linear arithmetic constraints for user interface applications. In: Proceedings of the 10th Annual ACM Symposium on User Interface Software and Technology, UIST 1997, pp. 87–96 (1997)
39. Hottelier, T., Bodik, R., Ryokai, K.: Programming by manipulation for layout. In: Proceedings of the 27th Annual ACM Symposium on User Interface Software and Technology, UIST 2014, pp. 231–241 (2014)
40. Xu, P., Fu, H., Igarashi, T., Tai, C.L.: Global beautification of layouts with interactive ambiguity resolution. In: Proceedings of the 27th Annual ACM Symposium on User Interface Software and Technology, UIST 2014, pp. 243–252 (2014)
41. Xu, P., Fu, H., Tai, C.L., Igarashi, T.: Gaca: group-aware command-based arrangement of graphic elements. In: Proceedings of the 33rd Annual ACM Conference on Human Factors in Computing Systems, CHI 2015, pp. 2787–2795 (2015)
42. Zeidler, C., Lutteroth, C., Sturzlinger, W., Weber, G.: The Auckland Layout Editor: an improved GUI layout specification process. In: Proceedings of the 26th Annual ACM Symposium on User Interface Software and Technology, pp. 343–352 (2013)
43. Sahami Shirazi, A., Henze, N., Schmidt, A., Goldberg, R., Schmidt, B., Schmauder, H.: Insights into layout patterns of mobile user interfaces by an automatic analysis of Android apps. In: Proceedings of the 5th ACM SIGCHI Symposium on Engineering Interactive Computing Systems, pp. 275–284 (2013)
44. Zeidler, C., Weber, G., Gavryushkin, A., Lutteroth, C.: Tiling algebra for constraint-based layout editing. J. Log. Algebr. Methods Program. 89, 67–94 (2017)
45. Hertzog, P.: Binary space partitioning layouts to help build better information dashboards. In: Proceedings of the 20th International Conference on Intelligent User Interfaces, IUI 2015, pp. 138–147 (2015)
46. Köhler, W.: Gestalt Psychology: An Introduction to New Concepts in Modern Psychology. Liveright Publishing Corporation, New York (1947)
47. Lutteroth, C., Strandh, R., Weber, G.: Domain specific high-level constraints for user interface layout. Constraints 13(3), 307–342 (2008)
48. Lavie, T., Tractinsky, N.: Assessing dimensions of perceived visual aesthetics of web sites. Int. J. Hum. Comput. Stud. 60(3), 269–298 (2004)
49. Ngo, D.C.L., Teo, L.S., Byrne, J.G.: Modelling interface aesthetics. Inf. Sci. 152, 25–46 (2003)
50. Nebeling, M., Matulic, F., Norrie, M.C.: Metrics for the evaluation of news site content layout in large-screen contexts. In: Proceedings of the SIGCHI Conference on Human Factors in Computing Systems, CHI 2011, pp. 1511–1520 (2011)
51. Moshagen, M., Thielsch, M.T.: Facets of visual aesthetics. Int. J. Hum. Comput. Stud. 68(10), 689–709 (2010)

Defining Gestural Interactions for Large Vertical Touch Displays

Robin Andersson[1]([⊠]), Jonas Berglund[1], Aykut Coşkun[2], Morten Fjeld[1], and Mohammad Obaid[3]

[1] Computer Science and Engineering, Chalmers University of Technology, Gothenburg, Sweden
k.robin.andersson@gmail.com
[2] KUAR, Media and Visual Arts Department, Koç University, Istanbul, Turkey
[3] Department of Information Technology, Uppsala University, Uppsala, Sweden

Abstract. As new technologies emerge, so do new ways of interacting with the digital domain. In this paper, the touch interaction paradigm is challenged for use on large touch displays of 65 in. in size. We present a gesture elicitation study with 26 participants carried out on twelve actions commonly used on touch displays. The results and analysis of 312 touch gestures revealed agreement rates for each action. We report several findings including the results of a set of ten unique (and a few secondary) gestures, a taxonomy classifying the defined gestures, a pilot study on the defined gestures, and explicit design implications. We discuss the results and include several important factors for future considerations. We aim at helping future designers and engineers to design interactions for large touch displays.

Keywords: Large touch display · User-defined · Gestural interaction

1 Introduction

Gestural interactions have attracted researchers to enable the next generations of intuitive input. In the context of large touch display technologies, most research looks at platform specific gestural input, for example a study on multi-touch walls [3], and studies focusing on how to improve drag-and-drop operations on large displays [4,5,11]. However, little focuses on using a user-centred approach to investigate and define the gestural interactions for common actions such as moving an item, copying or accessing a menu item as in Fig. 1.

Saffer [27] writes that the following years will likely see designers and engineers define the next generation of inputs to be used for decades. He states that designing gestural interfaces is no different to designing any interface, where the needs of the user and preferences are to be defined first. Wobbrock et al. [32] have followed a user-centered approach when defining gestural inputs for surface top interactions, inspiring other researchers in other domains to define gestures

© IFIP International Federation for Information Processing 2017
Published by Springer International Publishing AG 2017. All Rights Reserved
R. Bernhaupt et al. (Eds.): INTERACT 2017, Part I, LNCS 10513, pp. 36–55, 2017.
DOI: 10.1007/978-3-319-67744-6_3

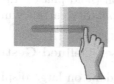

Fig. 1. Examples drawn from the user-defined gesture set: the three gestures *Move*, *Copy*, and *Menu Access* received high, intermediate, and low agreement scores.

in a similar process [13, 19, 23, 25, 32]. Related studies looking into improving the methodology [29], cultural differences [15], and legacy bias [12, 20], also exist.

With the emergence of large vertical touch displays, defining user preferences for gestural interactions has yet to be conducted. This paper attempts to remedy this gap by investigating user-defined gestures for large touch display. The word gesture is used as short for multi touch gesture in this paper if not stated otherwise. We contribute the following to the community: (1) a set of user-defined touch gestures for common actions on large touch displays, (2) a classification of the touch gestures through an existing taxonomy, (3) user agreement rates for each action, along with (4) design implications for future designers and engineers to use when designing for the platform. We confirm the contributions via a pilot evaluation with a high-fidelity prototype.

2 Background

Designing gestural interaction depends largely on the user and the technology at hand. Borrowing gestures from one technology to another (e.g. tabletops to mobiles devices) might not be appropriate [21]. Thus, in this section we present the bases of the related literature to our research which includes work on human gestures, user-defined gestures, and studies on large display interactions.

2.1 Human Gestures

There has been much research aimed at explaining and comprehending human gestures, and attempts at describing and categorizing them. Two commonly used taxonomies are employed in the examples below. Efron [6] groups gestures into five categories, namely *physiographics*, *kinetographics*, *ideographics*, *deictics*, and *batons*. Four different categories were later defined by Ekman and Friesen [7], namely *emblems*, *illustrators*, *regulators* and *adaptors*.

McNeill [16] groups gestures into five categories: *cohesive*, *beat*, *deictic*, *iconic*, and *metaphoric*. In later work, McNeill [17] defines four phases that gestures consist of; namely *preparation*, *stroke*, *hold*, and *retraction*. These phases describe the steps from first positioning the body so that it is ready to carry out the gesture (preparation phase), to performing the gesture (stroke phase), and lastly returning to the original position (hold phase). In our work, we adopt the definition by McNeill due to its popularity currency in elicitation studies [23,24].

.2.2 Large Displays and User-Defined Gestures

There has been much research done on large displays in general. For example, Chen et al. [3] introduced an approach to design interactions for Multi-Touch Interactive Wall displays, and Mateescu et al. [14] introduced a *Wall*, which is an agile team collaboration tool for large multi-touch wallsystems. Nolte et al. [22], on the other hand, present a system that aims to improve collaboration when using a large interactive wall-mounted touch display. These examples present approaches and applications; however for interactions with large vertical touch displays there is a need to establish and understand users' preferences for gestural touch interactions with large displays.

Elicitation studies to define interaction is an approach that puts the user at the center of gestural design. Wobbrock et al. [31] introduced a guessability methodology to allow users, through elicitation, to suggest gestures for an interface that for them feels natural. The work was followed by another elicitation study by Wobbrock et al. [32] which lets users come up with appropriate gestures to execute a set of tasks on a tabletop platform. Many other studies have adopted the same approach of user-defined gestures into different areas of interest, such as single-handed microgestures [2], non-touch display gestures for smartwatches [1], free-hand TV control [28], navigating a humanoid robot [23], navigating a drone [24], and mid-air gestures on large wall-mounted displays [30]. Kou et al. [13] studied freehand gestures for vertical displays.

Of interest to this paper is the study by Mauney et al. [15] which investigates the effect culture has on gestures by using the same gesture-elicitation methodology. In their study, participants from China, India, the US, the UK, Germany, Finland, France, and Spain were examined to determine cultural differences in user-defined gestures on small hand-held touch displays. In our work, we also consider the cultural impact on the user-defined gestures.

In considering the literature to date, there seems to be no specific research into or design of user-defined gestural interaction for large vertical touch displays, opening a promising gap in the current state of research for large touch displays. Thus, we adopt a similar approach to [32] who studied interactions with a horizontal display (tabletops). In this context, the prospective usage of the interfaces (horizontal versus a vertical touch display) and possible applications inherently differ in several ways; for instance, while users are often seated at horizontal screens, users of vertical screens typically stand [26]. Users seated at horizontal displays often experience undesired effects of both parallaxis [18] and leaning [9]. Even though [32] did not study those effects, their existence serves as a "capstone argument" that gestures which have been found to work for horizontal displays cannot directly be transferred to vertical displays, motivating us to revisit the actions and gestures studied in [32]. Our contributions have the possibility of providing guidelines for interacting with the intended platform as well as a valuable foundation for future research to expand or investigate further.

3   User Study

While the overarching methodology is specified in the study by Wobbrock et al. [32], the details still need to be adapted to the context of a large touch display. The study included 12 actions. These were in part based on the previous work in [32] describing common actions performed on a touch screen and in part based on a brief observation session. The session consisted of video-recording user interactions with a large screen planning application during four stand-up meetings with approximately 10 participants each, followed by an analysis examining the most frequently used actions. From the observation session, four actions were found to be commonly used; specifically *Mark as complete, Enter Edit mode, Change Color* and *Create an Object*. In addition, we included eight actions featured in [32], namely *Delete, Long Copy, Short Copy, Fire up a context menu, Expand, Move, Undo single delete,* and *Undo multiple delete*. To enable the actions for the study we developed a tool that has a set of predetermined animations for the 12 actions. Figure 2 illustrates the initial state of the Move action that was shown on the display using the tool.

Two instructors followed a script to run the study; one guided the user through the session, and the other acted as a Wizard of Oz who remotely used the tool to activate the animated actions.

Fig. 2. Screenshot of how the move action was shown to participants (left) and illustration of its animation (right). The green object was animated in a continuous movement from the top left corner to the lower right corner. (Color figure online)

Each action contained a simple green square object displayed on a dark background, leaving out any unnecessary distraction during the pre-defined animation. The animations were designed to provide the user with the lead of what is required in the requested action, providing the user with before and after states for the green square. For the actions *Create* and *Delete an object* the object appeared and disappeared. The Long and Short *Copy* actions, and the *Move* action had a continuous animation showing the object moving along the display for a set duration to its position, see Fig. 2. For the action *Fire up a context menu*, a radial menu (also known as a pie menu) appeared around the object. The *Change Color* simply switched between green and red color abruptly.

On *Expand*, the green object contained an example text that was partially hidden until the object was expanded to twice its size. *Mark as complete* presented a check mark on the object. The *Enter Edit mode* action showed an already expanded object with an example text, and switched from a flat green background into the same background but also with darker green diagonal stripes, while showing a cursor-like line blinking for a few seconds. Both *Undo* actions (i.e. undo single delete and undo multiple delete) started by showing one or six objects respectively disappearing from the display (simulating the objects being deleted) and later re-appearing at their previous locations.

3.1 Participants

In total, 26 participants volunteered in the study (14 female). The average age was 24.3 years ($SD = 4.0$) and the average body height was 169.2 cm ($SD = 7.9$). Three participants were left handed. Most were students within the fields of Engineering, Design, Business or Psychology. Eighteen were of Turkish nationality and the remainder were comprised of one each from Singapore, England, Lebanon, Mexico, USA, and Sweden, and two from Germany. Twenty three of the participants self rated themselves as having either high or very high experience using touch displays (of any kind). It is important to note is that our participants were not chosen with their touch screen experience in mind; rather, the norm in our society is to own and fluently use smartphones with touch capabilities. Finally, participants were each offered a coffee voucher for their participation.

3.2 Apparatus

The study was set up in a studio room measuring 9×5 m, as can be seen in Fig. 3. The introduction area in the figure was used for introducing users to the study and having them read and sign the consent form before moving over to the main area. A 65 in. (165 cm) TV display was used to display the actions to the users - the exact size of the TV was selected for its suitability for use in an open office space. Two cameras - one Canon 700D DSLR camera and one Apple iPhone 6 camera - were set up on tripods at the sides of the display to record the participants' interactions throughout the study process.

3.3 Study Procedure

Each participant was first given a description of the study and asked to fill in the questionnaire. The participants were then asked to stand at a marker on the floor approximately three meters in front of the display. They watched simple animations, one at a time, of the 12 actions executed on the display, and after each one they were asked to perform a touch gesture on the display that they believed would repeat the demonstrated action. At the same time as the participant performed the gesture, the animation was triggered on the display.

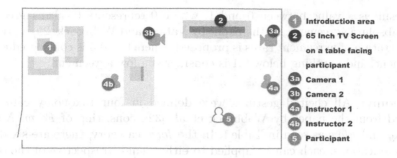

Fig. 3. Sketch of the user study setup.

After completing a gesture, the participants were asked to rate how easy it was to think of a gesture intended for the action executed on a 5-point Likert scale. The participants were also given the opportunity to add any extra comments about the completed gesture. This procedure was repeated for all 12 actions, but the order of the actions was randomized using an online random list generator[1] for each participant. This was done to avoid any order effect. One gesture was given for each action and with all 26 participants in the study, a total of $26 \times 12 = 312$ gestures were recorded for analysis. Each session took about 30–45 min to complete.

3.4 Measurements

Several aspects were measured during the study. An initial questionnaire asked for demographic data, such as nationality, age, gender, body height and dominant hand, along with technical background and profession or course of study. The video recordings were annotated using the ELAN Annotation Tool [8], marking each gesture with "start" and "end". Two researchers cross checked the annotated files. One researcher did $\approx$27% of the data independent of the other researcher. The two researchers discussed and resolved any inconsistencies. In addition, all video files were independently examined by the authors multiple times and given descriptive classifications. Based on this data, the agreement rate, taxonomy and a gesture set were defined.

Agreement Rate: The agreement rate has been calculated based the formula presented in [29] and seen in Eq. 1:

$$AR(r) = \frac{|P|}{|P|-1} \sum_{P_i \subseteq P} \left(\frac{|P_i|}{|P|} \right)^2 - \frac{|1|}{|P|-1} \tag{1}$$

where P is a set of gestures for action r, $|P|$ is the size of the proposed set of gestures, and P_i represents the size of a subset of identical gestures within P.

---

[1] https://www.random.org/lists/.

The result is a value between 0 and 1, where 0 represents total disagreement and 1 absolute agreement. In the paper by Vatavu and Wobbrock [29] a possible interpretation of agreement rates is proposed, where 0.3–0.5 is considered a high agreement, and anything below 0.1 is considered a low agreement.

Taxonomy: All elicited gestures were defined in four taxonomy categories adopted from the paper by Wobbrock et al. [32], consisting of *Form*, *Nature*, *Binding* and *Flow* as seen in Table 1. In the *form* category, there are six different classifications; each can be applied to either hand irrespective of the other. Gestures defined as *static pose* imply that the hand is kept in the same spot and does not change its posture throughout the gesture. Gestures defined as *dynamic pose* have the used hand's pose change while it's still being held in the same position. The gestures classified as *static pose and path* gestures has the hand posture being the same through all of the gesture while the hand moves along some path. *Dynamic pose and path* gestures have the hand change its posture in the gesture while the hand moves. The *one-point touch* and *one-point path* gestures concern themselves only with a single touch point. These groups include gestures where the user might have touched the display with several fingers but with the intention of still being a single touch point. The *one-point touch* gestures contains *static pose* gestures but using only one finger. *One-point path* however is the same as the *static pose and path* form, but using only one finger.

Table 1. Taxonomy of touch display gestures adopted from the work by [32].

Taxonomy		
Form	Static pose	Hand pose is held in one location
	Dynamic pose	Hand pose changes in one location
	Static pose and path	Hand pose is held as hand moves
	Dynamic pose and path	Hand pose changes as hand moves
	One-point touch	Static pose with one finger
	One-point path	Static pose & path with one finger
Nature	symbolic	Gesture visually depicts a symbol
	Physical	Gesture acts physically on objects
	Metaphorical	Gesture indicates a metaphor
	Abstract	Gesture-referent mapping is arbitrary
Binding	object-centric	Location defined w.r.t. object features
	World-dependent	Location defined w.r.t. world features
	World-independent	Location can ignore world features
	Mixed dependencies	World-independent plus another
Flow	Discrete	Gesture occurs once
	Continuous	Gesture takes place over a period of time

Gesture Set: In a gesture set, a gesture can at most be nominated to one action; however one action can have more than one gesture assigned to it. This approach is based on previous research by Wobbrock et al. [31].

To finalize a gesture set based on the users' behaviour, the actions with higher agreement rates were prioritized to get their most frequently occurring gestures assigned to them. An action sharing the same top pick gesture with other actions - but where the action itself had a lower agreement rate - would be assigned the gesture with its second most (or third most, and so on) occurrence for that particular action.

4 Results

In this section we present the results on the agreement rates for all actions, a taxonomy for the collected data, and a user-defined set of gestures for the 12 actions included in this study. There were also other noticeable results, such as that the participants graded their previous experience with touch displays to be 4.38 ($SD = 0.68$) on a 5-point Likert scale, indicating that they were very well versed in the use of touch displays. Statements from the participants however show that gestures were inspired from both touch interfaces and the desktop (or laptop) paradigm. For instance, one participant said *"I was inspired from my MacBook. I use all the fingers and the menu appears" [par 24]*, while another said *"Easy since I have used it on my smartphone" [par 15]*.

4.1 Agreement Rates

The agreement rates for each action were calculated, following the procedure by Vatavu and Wobbrock [29]. The results show noticeable leaps in agreement rates which divide the actions into groups, such as the leaps between the actions *Move* and *Mark complete*, *Mark complete* and *Copy short*, and also between *Delete* and *Color change* (see Fig. 4).

4.2 Taxonomy

As previously explained, all elicited gestures were defined according to four taxonomy categories (see Table 1). The results of these definitions can be seen in Fig. 5. Out of all the 312 gestures provided during the study, 251 were performed using only the right hand, 20 with only the left hand, and 41 with both hands. Only two of the left handed gestures were performed by a right-handed user. In total; 23 right-handed participants provided two left-handed gestures, while the three left-handed participants provided seven right-handed gestures.

Looking at the collected data and the results represented in Figs. 4 and 5, it seems that actions within the Nature and Binding categories that are classified as physical and object-centric (also continuous from the Flow category) generally score higher. In fact, the four actions that were ranked the lowest in terms of agreement rates were also the only four that had predominantly gestures classified in the Abstract category.

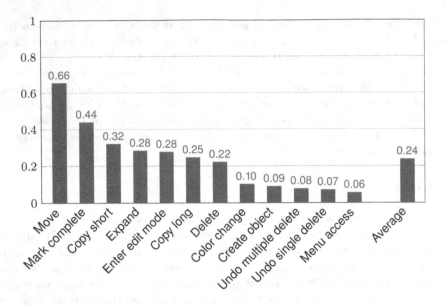

Fig. 4. Agreement rates for the 12 actions in descending order.

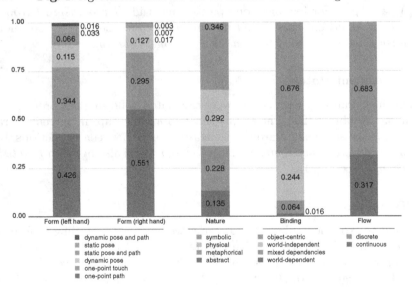

Fig. 5. Taxonomy distribution, color coded by category: *Form, Nature, Binding, Flow.*

4.3   Gesture Set

A gesture set was produced as shown in Table 2 and illustrated in Fig. 6. Each single gesture corresponds to an action; a gesture is defined by its form, nature, binding, and flow (all defined in Table 2). Since the results did not show any major differences between the actions *Copy long* and *Copy short* they were

Table 2. The gesture set for the user study's actions with occurrence data. The gestures elicited for Copy long and Copy short barely differed and were thus joined into Copy. Undo single delete and Undo multiple delete were similarly joined into Undo. oc = object centric, md = mixed dependencies, wi = world independent. cont = continuous, disc = discrete. opp = one-point path, opt = one-point touch, dp = dynamic pose

Action	Gesture	Form	Nature	Binding	Flow	Occurrence
Move	Drag	opp	physical	oc	cont	81 %
Expand	Spread	dp	metaphorical	oc	cont	77 %
Mark complete	Draw Check	opp	symbolic	oc	disc	73 %
Copy	Pre-Action + Drag	opp	physical	oc	cont	62 %
	Tap S + Tap D	opt	abstract	md	disc	23 %
Delete	Flick	opp	physical	oc	disc	46 %
	Draw "X"	opp	symbolic	oc	disc	12 %
Edit mode	Double Tap	opt	metaphorical	oc	disc	42 %
Color change	Slide	opp	metaphorical	oc	disc	31 %
Create	Draw Square D	opp	symbolic	wi	disc	23 %
	Tap D	opt	abstract	wi	disc	12 %
Menu access	Tap and Hold	opt	abstract	oc	disc	19 %
Undo	Slide W	opp	abstract	wi	disc	21 %
	Rotate (CCW)	dp	metaphorical	wi	cont	10 %

combined into *Copy*. Similarly, *Undo single delete* and *Undo multiple delete* were treated the same way and were thus combined into *Undo*. This resulted in a set of 10 actions in total.

4.4   Cultural Differences

Breaking down the combined results as presented in Figs. 4 and 5 exposes the differences in agreement rate and taxonomy distribution on the cultural level. The international group (non-Turkish participants) scored overall higher agreement rates, measuring in at 0.38 compared to 0.22 for the Turkish group. Looking at individual actions, the agreement rates follow largely the same trends. There are however noticeable differences for both copy actions that show higher agreement rates for the international users (0.58 versus 0.17 for Copy Long, and 0.61 versus 0.24 for Copy Short). As for the taxonomy, both groups had almost identical numbers, with the exception of the international group not having performed any gestures defined in the forms *Dynamic pose and path, static pose & Static pose and path*, and instead having a larger share of one-point-path gestures.

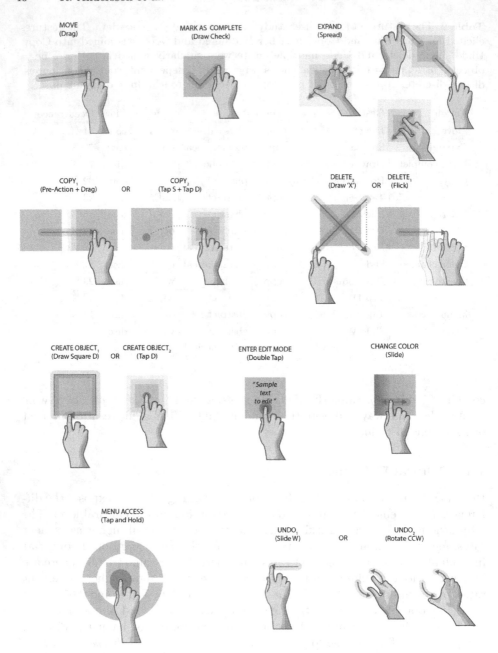

Fig. 6. Illustrations of the user-defined gesture set. Gestures illustrated with 1 finger can also be performed with 2 or 3 fingers. "S" is short for source and "D" for destination.

5   Pilot Study

The pilot study featured a fully functional system deployed on a 55 in. touch display placed in an open space at an office. The system consisted of pre-defined gestural actions deployed on a planning application (Visual Planning, by Yolean[2]) - a web based visual management tool used in organisations to visualise and organize employees' tasks on various platforms. We chose a 55 in. display as it allowed us to test the gestures on a large display of different size, suggesting how the results might be generalisable. This is considered to be a contribution to the base of several iterative cycles to validate the results, and further studies into generalisability are required and beyond the scope of the study presented in this paper.

To get an indication on whether the proposed gesture set had merit and would be well received, a prototype of four user-defined gestures was implemented. Four gestures considered to be of varying difficulty, from easy to hard, were selected based on their agreement scores (*Create an Object, Mark as complete, Enter Edit mode*, and *Delete*) that allowed for comparison with corresponding pre-defined gestures in the existing planning application. The pre-defined counterparts were all except one executed through a tap and hold to bring up a menu and then tapping the corresponding button. The one difference was *Create and Object* which were accomplished through dragging an object from the top right of the application.

Thus, the study had two conditions A and B, where condition A was the new version containing the implemented gestures (user-defined), and condition B had the pre-defined gestures from the planning application. We counter-balanced the conditions between each session to avoid any order-effect.

The hypothesis of the pilot study was that the majority of participants would favor their experience when interacting with the user-defined gestures (condition A) over the system's pre-defined gestures (B) both overall as well as for each individual metric. To test for our hypothesis, subjective ratings were collected of the users' performances via the commonly used NASA-TLX questionnaires [10] which evaluate the experience of the condition according to a set of workload performance qualities (mental demand, physical demand, temporal demand, performance, effort, and frustration). The procedure of the study had three steps:

In step one, the study instructors provided a demonstration and got the participant accustomed to the application and gestures used for the condition. Participants then got the chance to use the application, first by a guided scenario and then on their own for as long as they needed. The instructor also explained the details of the questionnaire forms that were to be completed after the session.

In step two, the participant carried out the main study task, which had the following set of instructions (kept consistent throughout the study conditions):

– "Create FOUR notes on week 43 for John Doe. Name them Task a, b, c, and d."

---

[2] Yolean is a company located in Gothenburg (Sweden) that develop web applications to support lean methodologies.

- "Mark Tasks a, b and c, d, as well as TASKS 1, 2, 3 and 4 as complete."
- "Remove Tasks 1, 2 and 3, and a, b and c."

The third step consisted of collecting subjective evaluations using the NASA-TLX questionnaire. In addition, participants were asked which of the two conditions they preferred in general when interacting with the application.

5.1 Pilot Evaluation

In total 20 participants took part in the pilot study, of which 17 were male, two were female and one identified as *other*. The average age was 25.9 ($SD =$ 2.7), and 19 were right-handed. Out of all participants, one was Chinese and the rest were Swedish. The participants all self-rated themselves as of high technical experience. Only two participants had any experience of the planning software.

The overall results from the collected NASA-TLX subjective data can be seen in Fig. 7. A Paired t-test was conducted to compare the NASA-TLX ratings for Condition A and Condition B. The results revealed an overall significant difference between Condition A ($M = 22.61$, $SD = 13.02$) and Condition B ($M = 28.9, SD = 15.76$); $t(19) = 2.91$, $p = 0.004$. This suggests that Condition A had lower overall NASA-TLX scores. Looking at the individual metric elements, the paired t-test shows a significant difference for the elements Physical Demand (A ($M = 26$, $SD = 20.49$) and B ($M = 33.25, SD = 22.08$); $t(19) = 1.91$, $p = 0.036$) and Frustration (A ($M = 21$, $SD = 16.19$) and B ($M = 33, SD = 20.42$); $t(19) = 3.29$, $p = 0.002$), while the other elements were not significant. When participants were asked about their preferences between condition A and B, the majority chose condition A, as shown in Table 3.

Table 3. The numbers of participants that preferred one condition over the other. Note that even though there were 20 participants some columns do not add up to 20; the reason being that some participants did not pick a preferred condition.

	Create	Edit	Complete	Delete	Overall
A	19	17	14	13	18
B	0	2	3	5	2

These results give us positive indications on the usability of the user-defined gestures, and allow us to further explore how they can be tested. In the following section we discuss the overall results and future directions for our investigation.

6   Discussion

Agreement Rates: The similarities between higher agreement rates and the Nature and Binding taxonomy categories seems to indicate that users more easily

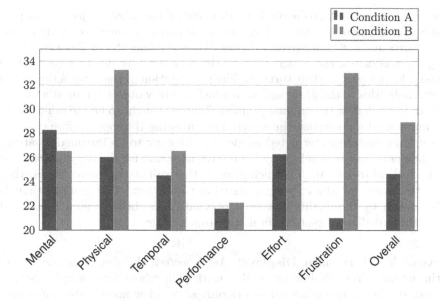

Fig. 7. The computed results from the NASA-TLX form used in the pilot study. Values range from 5 to 100. Lower is better in all metrics, and Condition A (blue) corresponds to the new gestures while Condition B (red) corresponds to the old gestures. (Color figure online)

think of gestures that relate to something they know, such as moving an object by dragging, rather than pairing their gesture with something abstract such as a tap and hold for opening up a menu. Looking at the group with lower rates (scoring <0.1), from the authors' own recollection these actions all seem to lack unique gestures on touch display devices. The actions are believed to generally be initiated through other means, such as through a dedicated button or accessed through a menu, this could be investigated in future work. If this is indeed true then the study's participants would not have been exposed to such gestures, thus resulting in the diverse set of elicited gestures as seen in the results.

Actions with low agreement rates for some actions seem to coincide to the seemingly low commonality of them having dedicated gestures. It also seems that actions with high agreement rates coincide with high commonality of dedicated gestures. For instance, *Move*, *Expand*, and *Delete* are all perceived by the authors to commonly have specific gestures devoted to them - as with the move action on iPhone which uses drag for positioning objects.

However, *Mark Complete*, *Copy Short*, *Copy Long* are not thought to commonly have dedicated gestures assigned to them. Furthermore, *Delete* is also recognized to often be situated in a menu or executed through a button. In these cases it is thought to be more fine-grained reasons for the agreement rates turning out the way they did. In the case of *Mark Complete*, the presentation of the action during the user study is perceived to be quite symbolic with the showing of an explicit green check mark covering the whole object on display. This is thought to have been guiding the participants' gestures, hence more similar gestures and the high agreement rate. When it comes to the *Copy Short* and *Copy Long* gestures, the presentation in the user study is also believed to have played a higher part in their turnout. The presentation of the copy actions show many similarities to the *Move* action in which the new object is moved while the "old" object is left at the original position. This is thought to be the main reason why many used a pre-action (interpreted as initiating the copy) before conducting the drag gesture (interpreted as moving the copy to its intended location). As a side note, having a relatively high agreement rate for the copy actions is in line with Wobbrock et al. [32] which gives further validity to the result. Furthermore, the reason for *Delete* being situated at the bottom of its group is thought to be caused by the duality discussed previously, i.e. being present both with and without dedicated gestures in mobile touch devices.

Vertical Vs Horizontal Displays: As expected, the results confirm many of the findings from Wobbrock et al.'s work [32], where for example the patterns shown in the taxonomy categories only show a few noteworthy differences. Furthermore, agreement rates for similar actions between the studies are also quite similar. The actions might however be misleading to compare directly since explanations of them are often missing from [32], for example the animation and presentation of *Menu access* in both studies risk being too different even though the intention is most likely the same. Furthermore, the *Nature* category in this study showed a greater share of symbolic gestures.

There were some differences in the *Binding* category, which showed a very low value for *world-dependent*. The reason for these differences is believed to be related to differing legacy bias between the two studies; specifically from usage of mobile phones and touch interfaces, which in general have become more common in recent years [15,27]. A few comments from the participants confirm this, for example *"I had to remember how to do it on my phone; had to relate to something I know" [par 11]*. It makes sense that the users relied less on gestures that made use of *world-dependent* widgets (e.g. buttons and toolbars) or other paradigms closely tied to the desktop design space. Looking at the given gestures in general, few of them are more complex or require more advanced body gestures compared to that of mobile touch displays. It seems as if the participants did not fully utilize the possibilities offered by the increased display size.

Something that is not present in the results compared to the study by Wobbrock et al. [32] is that there were no gestures elicited that moved objects to or from beyond the edges of the display. This most probably has to do with the differences in display formats between the two studies. Where the display in [32] had a wide flat edge outside of the active display suitable for such gestures, this study's display had a protruding bezel a couple of centimetres wide.

Interfering Gestures: One aspect in the proposed gesture set considered how some gestures might interfere with others so that one gesture would be identified

instead of another during an interaction. For instance, the *Mark as complete*
action has the user draw a check symbol, which is essentially the same as tracing
a check mark with the drag gesture. As such, the *Mark as complete* action
interferes with the *Move* action. This problem can however be designed and
developed around, which is why seemingly interfering gestures are still present
in the gesture set (see Sect. 6.1). Looking at the study by Wobbrock et al. [32],
there is no emphasis on interfering gestures, possibly because their gestures do
not naturally overlap each other.

One-Handed Versus Two-Handed: Finally, the study allows users to choose
if they want to perform the gesture with one or two hands. This was decided
since whatever felt natural to the participants was the desired outcome. The
fact that most people did provide one-handed gestures should then be seen as
an indication for the preferred way to interact on large touch displays.

Successful Pilot Study Results: The pilot study results indicate that participants generally preferred the user-defined gestures over the pre-defined ones.
   The pilot study was run with Swedish participants, which is a different culture
from the majority of the data that constructed the user-defined set. Nevertheless,
participants still leaned towards the user-defined gesture set over the pre-defined
one; furthermore, as the display used in the pilot study was 55 in., which is
smaller than the one used in the elicitation study, this shows promise for more
general applicability. In addition, we suspect that using a planning application
on a vertical display is not a common thing, and this might have affected some
results for both A and B in regard to the NASA-TLX scores. However, the
results indicate that user-defined gestures are less physically demanding and less
frustrating, with an overall acceptance of the gestures. These are indications
only, and further studies need to be conducted to validate the user-defined set
on different large touch displays and the cultural impact on the user-defined set.

Cultural Impact: The higher agreement rates for the international users can in
some regard be attributed to the lower participant count as stated by Vatavu and
Wobbrock [29], i.e. high agreement rates correlate with low participant counts.
The difference in user-defined gestures between cultures should be quite low, as
stated by Mauney et al. [15]. Low differences between cultures could also be a
direct result of culturally similar legacy bias. However, the nationalities present
in both studies covered only four participants (two Germans, one British and
one American), and as such these ratiocinations need to be investigated further.

6.1   Design Implications

Looking at the agreement rate it seems like the higher agreement rates coincide
with the Nature and Binding categories. The higher agreement rates for *Physical* and *Object-centric* gestures gives a good indication that such actions are
easier to think of for users, moreso compared to gestures classified towards the

Abstract spectrum. As such, designers should design interactions geared towards something more relatable; perhaps even similar to how real-world objects would behave. As there were low agreement rates for world-independent actions (and nonexistent gestures in the world-dependent *Binding*), designers should also preferably design gestures with respect to objects' positions on the display.

Participants often reached for previous knowledge when coming up with gestures and their feedback indicated this (especially referencing mobile devices), e.g. *"Seemed pretty easy, like on an iPhone" [par 12]*, *"[...] like on Android" [par 14]*, *"In every software (when editing text) you click on it" [par 16]*, *"Like Photoshop, crop and drag" [par 08]*, *"[...] like in Word or Powerpoint" [par 05]*. Designing gestures similar to those of applications in the same domain, or those on more common touch devices, should make the gestures easier to remember.

When designing interactions for even larger touch displays, tests and considerations have to be made regarding the move and copy gesture. Most user study participants did not think they would have chosen other gestures if the display was bigger, for example one participant indicated *"No I don't think so, even if it were super big" [par 21]*. A few however mentioned that drag gestures would not be suitable. For instance, one participant indicated that *"The only one that would be different is the one where I dragged. The rest would be the same." [par 12]*, another answered *"As long as the arms are able to cover the display. Might be changed otherwise. Might be abstract gestures if not reachable" [par 07]*.

Important to consider is the possibility of interfering gestures. While it is possible to develop software around interfering gestures, it should be done with care and with an understanding of its difficulties. A possible way for some of the user-defined actions could be to recognize several gestures at the same time, and then execute or discontinue one gesture on its completion or failure.

To compensate for situations similar to the pilot study's result showing higher mental demand for the suggested gesture set, both a unique gesture and a common menu-like alternative could be assigned. This could serve as a fallback if the user forgot the dedicated gesture.

6.2 Limitations

It was inevitable for the design of the gesture's animation presentation to have affected the results in some way, as showing some animation for an action could be expected to guide the user into performing a certain type of gesture. This aspect could have been improved by allowing participants to give not only one elicited gesture but multiple gestures.

For some gestures, the part of the gesture that involved "selecting" an object was removed from the interpretation of that gesture during the result computation. This was most commonly shown in the *copy*, *undo*, and *move* actions. The gesture set given by Wobbrock et al. [32] shows selection as a unique action that was incorporated into their research; thus the inclusion of selection in our study should have been considered as an action.

Our study had mostly participants from Turkish background (approx 70%), which makes our data and results dominated by the gestures performed in the Turkish culture. However, approx (30%) of our participants came from several other countries, which to some extent had an influence on the gestural set. We elaborate on the cultural impact in our paper; however, to fully understand how to generalise the results in a more diverse cultural setup, it requires further investigations and study designs.

Furthermore, our study did not include any measures for reducing legacy bias; many gestures in the proposed set contains interactions that relate to those elicited on other platforms. While not reducing legacy bias can be advantageous as to not reinvent what does not need to be reinvented [12], there are techniques that can be used for doing so e.g. *priming* (preparing the participants for the new platform), *production* (letting participants propose multiple interactions) *partners* (letting participants participate in groups), which can yield more novel interaction techniques specific for the platform [20].

7   Conclusion and Future Work

This paper has presented a user study investigating user-defined touch gestures for large displays. In total, we analysed 312 elicited gestures from 26 participants for 12 actions commonly used on touch displays. The results and analysis reported agreement rate of user-gestures, a taxonomy of user-gestures, and a user-defined gesture set. We gave results of a pilot study evaluation of a gesture set used on a high fidelity prototype, which showed great promise in the user-defined gesture set. In addition, this paper discusses the results in detail and gives design implications to aid designers and engineers when developing interfaces for large touch displays.

This paper provides a basis for several future directions. The study by Kou et al. [13] shows that there are interesting findings to be made by allowing participants to provide multiple gestures for each action, and one can consider investigating the presented study by asking participants to provide multiple gestures for each action. Another angle for future work is considering several touch display sizes, which might reveal interesting gestural interactions depending on how large the touch display is. In addition, future studies could consider legacy bias in investigating differences in outcome by using techniques as presented by Morris et al. [20] or simply by actively selecting participants with low experience with touch screens. This could provide valuable insights into how legacy bias affects user-defined gestures on a touch display and perhaps provide more novel interactions. Finally, cultural impact on the user-defined gestures was only briefly touched upon in this paper, and future research could consider carrying out a full investigation on this important aspect that impacts upon how we interact with the interface.

Acknowledgements. The authors would like to thank Oğuzhan Özcan, Asım Evren Yantaç, Ayça Adviye Ünlüer and Doğa Çorlu for assisting in the user study. We thank Arçelik's support in providing us with equipment to run the study. In addition, we thank Yolean for supplying the pilot study equipment and development expertise. Finally, we thank our participants both in Turkey and Sweden for their time and input.

References

1. Arefin Shimon, S.S., Lutton, C., Xu, Z., Morrison-Smith, S., Boucher, C., Ruiz, J.: Exploring non-touchscreen gestures for smartwatches. In: the 2016 Conference on Human Factors in Computing Systems, pp. 3822–3833. ACM (2016)
2. Chan, E., Seyed, T., Stuerzlinger, W., Yang, X.D., Maurer, F.: User elicitation on single-hand microgestures. In: Proceedings of the 2016 CHI Conference on Human Factors in Computing Systems, pp. 3403–3414. ACM (2016)
3. Chen, W., Lao, S.Y., Lee, H., Smeaton, A.F.: Interaction design for multi-touch interactive walls. In: 2012 Second International Conference on Intelligent System Design and Engineering Application, pp. 310–313, January 2012
4. Collomb, M., Hascoët, M., Baudisch, P., Lee, B.: Improving drag-and-drop on wall-size displays. In: Proceedings of Graphics Interface 2005, GI 2005, pp. 25–32. Canadian Human-Computer Communications Society, School of Computer Science, University of Waterloo, Waterloo (2005)
5. Doeweling, S., Glaubitt, U.: Drop-and-drag: Easier drag & drop on large touchscreen displays. In: Proceedings of the 6th Nordic Conference on Human-Computer Interaction: Extending Boundaries, NordiCHI 2010, pp. 158–167. ACM, New York (2010). http://doi.acm.org/10.1145/1868914.1868936
6. Efron, D.: Gesture and Environment. King's Crown Press, New York (1941)
7. Ekman, P., Friesen, W.V.: The repertoire of nonverbal behavior: Categories, origins, usage, and coding. Semiotica 1(1), 49–98 (1969)
8. ELAN the language archive. https://tla.mpi.nl/tools/tla-tools/elan/. Accessed 21 Jan 2017
9. Gerken, J., Jetter, H.C., Schmidt, T., Reiterer, H.: Can "touch" get annoying?. In: Proceeding of the ACM International Conference on Interactive Tabletops and Surfaces, ITS 2010, pp. 257–258. ACM, New York (2010)
10. Hart, S.G.: NASA-Task Load Index (NASA-TLX); 20 years later. In: Proceedings of the Human Factors and Ergonomics Society Annual Meeting, vol. 50, pp. 904–908. Sage Publications (2006)
11. Kobayashi, M., Igarashi, T.: Boomerang: Suspendable drag-and-drop interactions based on a throw-and-catch metaphor. In: Proceedings of the 20th Annual ACM Symposium on User Interface Software and Technology, UIST 2007, pp. 187–190. ACM, New York (2007)
12. Köpsel, A., Bubalo, N.: Benefiting from legacy bias. Interactions 22(5), 44–47 (2015)
13. Kou, Y., Kow, Y.M., Cheng, K.: Developing intuitive gestures for spatial interaction with large public displays. In: Streitz, N., Markopoulos, P. (eds.) DAPI 2015. LNCS, vol. 9189, pp. 174–181. Springer, Cham (2015). doi:10.1007/978-3-319-20804-6_16
14. Mateescu, M., Kropp, M., Burkhard, R., Zahn, C., Vischi, D.: aWall: A sociocognitive tool for agile team collaboration using large multi-touch wall systems. In: Proceedings of the 2015 International Conference on Interactive Tabletops & Surfaces, ITS 2015, pp. 405–408. ACM, New York (2015)
15. Mauney, D., Howarth, J., Wirtanen, A., Capra, M.: Cultural similarities and differences in user-defined gestures for touchscreen user interfaces. In: CHI 2010 Extended Abstracts on Human Factors in Computing Systems, CHI EA 2010, pp. 4015–4020. ACM, New York (2010)
16. McNeill, D.: So you think gestures are nonverbal? Psychol. Rev. 92(3), 350 (1985)

17. McNeill, D.: Hand and Mind: What Gestures Reveal about Thought. University of Chicago press, Chicago (1992)
18. Migge, B., Kunz, A.: Interaction error based viewpoint estimation for continuous parallax error correction on interactive screens. In: Proceedings of the IADIS International Conference: ICT, Society and Human Beings (2011)
19. Morris, M.R.: Web on the wall: Insights from a multimodal interaction elicitation study. In: Proceedings of the 2012 ACM International Conference on Interactive Tabletops and Surfaces, ITS 2012, pp. 95–104. ACM, New York (2012)
20. Morris, M.R., Danielescu, A., Drucker, S., Fisher, D., Lee, B., Schraefel, M.C., Wobbrock, J.O.: Reducing legacy bias in gesture elicitation studies. Interactions **21**(3), 40–45 (2014)
21. Nielsen, M., Störring, M., Moeslund, T.B., Granum, E.: A procedure for developing intuitive and ergonomic gesture interfaces for HCI. In: Camurri, A., Volpe, G. (eds.) GW 2003. LNCS, vol. 2915, pp. 409–420. Springer, Heidelberg (2004). doi:10.1007/978-3-540-24598-8_38
22. Nolte, A., Brown, R., Poppe, E., Anslow, C.: Towards collaborative modelling of business processes on large interactive touch display walls. In: Proceedings of the 2015 International Conference on Interactive Tabletops & Surfaces, ITS 2015, pp. 379–384. ACM, New York (2015)
23. Obaid, M., Kistler, F., Häring, M., Bühling, R., André, E.: A framework for user-defined body gestures to control a humanoid robot. Int. J. Soc. Robot. **6**(3), 383–396 (2014)
24. Obaid, M., Kistler, F., Kasparavičiūtė, G., Yantaç, A.E., Fjeld, M.: How would you gesture navigate a drone?: a user-centered approach to control a drone. In: Proceedings of the 20th International Academic Mindtrek Conference, pp. 113–121. ACM (2016)
25. Ruiz, J., Li, Y., Lank, E.: User-defined motion gestures for mobile interaction. In: Proceedings of the SIGCHI Conference on Human Factors in Computing Systems, CHI 2011. ACM, New York (2011)
26. Ryall, K., Forlines, C., Shen, C., Morris, M.R., Everitt, K.: Experiences with and observations of direct-touch tabletops. In: Proceedings of the First IEEE International Workshop on Horizontal Interactive Human-Computer Systems, TABLETOP 2006, pp. 89–96. IEEE Computer Society, Washington, DC (2006)
27. Saffer, D.: Designing Gestural Interfaces: Touchscreens and Interactive Devices. O'Reilly Media, Inc., Sebastopol (2008)
28. Vatavu, R.D.: User-defined gestures for free-hand TV control. In: Proceedings of the 10th European Conference on Interactive TV and Video, EuroITV 2012, pp. 45–48. ACM, New York (2012)
29. Vatavu, R.D., Wobbrock, J.O.: Formalizing agreement analysis for elicitation studies: New measures, significance test, and toolkit. In: Proceedings of the 33rd Annual ACM Conference on Human Factors in Computing Systems, CHI 2015, pp. 1325–1334. ACM, New York (2015)
30. Wittorf, M.L., Jakobsen, M.R.: Eliciting mid-air gestures for wall-display interaction. In: Proceedings of the 9th Nordic Conference on Human-Computer Interaction, NordiCHI 2016, pp. 3:1–3:4. ACM, New York (2016)
31. Wobbrock, J.O., Aung, H.H., Rothrock, B., Myers, B.A.: Maximizing the guessability of symbolic input. In: CHI 2005 Extended Abstracts on Human Factors in Computing Systems, pp. 1869–1872. ACM, New York (2005)
32. Wobbrock, J.O., Morris, M.R., Wilson, A.D.: User-defined gestures for surface computing. In: Proceedings of the SIGCHI Conference on Human Factors in Computing Systems, CHI 2009, pp. 1083–1092. ACM, New York (2009)

MyCarMobile: A Travel Assistance Emergency Mobile App for Deaf People

Tânia Rocha[1,2(✉)], Hugo Paredes[1,2], Diogo Soares[1],
Benjamim Fonseca[1,2], and João Barroso[1,2]

[1] University of Trás-os-Montes and Alto Douro,
Quinta de Prados, 5000-801 Vila Real, Portugal
{trocha,hparedes,benjaf,jbarroso}@utad.pt
[2] INESC TEC, C Campus da FEUP, Rua Dr. Roberto Frias,
4200-465 Porto, Portugal

Abstract. Deaf people face serious communication problems. The use of smartphones has been explored as a solution for breaking communication barriers and enhancing their communication, by providing access to basic services. This paper explores the usage of iconographic interfaces in smartphones as a means for contributing to further autonomy for deaf people. We applied the model for asynchronous and non-verbal communication through iconographic and interactive flows to develop the MyCarMobile application, a travel assistance android mobile application for deaf people. Our research explores a solution which enables travel assistance services without involving audio, using an iconographic interface to report road accidents. A user centered design approach was applied in the development of the prototype and usability tests were performed with eleven deaf users, in order to validate the mobile application. The results revealed a good performance and user satisfaction when interacting with the application.

Keywords: Accessibility · Usability · Mobile · Android · Deaf community

1 Introduction

Driving is a daily activity for many people and, since no one is immune to road problems, there are services that provide on-the-spot assistance for drivers. Unfortunately, deaf people are unable to make use of travel assistance services which rely on the traditional voice-based services. In addition, there are problems common to other users, such as people with sudden problems of word articulation, vocal diseases, or situations of shock and panic caused by violent occurrences.

Consequently, there is an increased drive to overcome barriers to human communication and interaction, as well as to make improvements in the quality of life of the deaf community, promising to meet the needs of deaf drivers. Hence, the research question is: can a mobile application based on visual interface be a usable solution for emergency situations for the deaf community?

Thus, we present the MyCarMobile application for mobile devices, which allows the user to contact assistance on the road through a smartphone without need of audio.

R. Bernhaupt et al. (Eds.): INTERACT 2017, Part I, LNCS 10513, pp. 56–65, 2017.
DOI: 10.1007/978-3-319-67744-6_4

The solution presented is a native mobile application that is always available through rapid prototyping for multiplatform, by simply defining the application flow, with the integration of services permanently available through a mediation server and dynamic communication channels. In previous works [1] we focused on literature and technical issues. Specifically, in this paper we focused on assessment.

The paper is structured as follows: in the second section, we list and analyze related studies; in the third, MyCarMobile we identify travel assistance problems to be overcome, then we reveal the development process (methodology, architecture design and implementation) and the usability assessment results; in the fourth, we present the conclusions and future work.

2 Related Studies

The popularity and the massification of smartphone usage has boosted the development of mobile applications, which provide huge benefits to their users [2, 3]. However, they started to be developed and designed without any consideration of accessibility and usability, challenging the interaction of users with disabilities. Indeed, developers of mobile applications ignore the fact that almost one in five people in the world live with recognized disability [4] and they are all potential users of these technologies [5]. Despite this fact, there are already some mobile applications developed to minimize their limitations of their use, helping people with special needs in their daily lives [6, 7], particularly for deaf people, with visual or speech impairment [8].

Although they are similar, each development platform has its own accessibility guidelines regarding the mobile application development, such as the guidelines for Android [9], mobile applications for the Windows Phone [10], and for the iOS mobile [11]. Furthermore, there are also guidelines for accessibility (such as: the Word Wide Web Consortium (W3C) accessibility guidelines (WAI - WCAG 2.0) [12] and the European standard EN 301 549 [13]) and usability [14, 15] (such as: ISO 9241-11 [16], ISO 13407 [17] and ISO 9241-210 an improved update of ISO 13407 [18]).

Moreover, when developing communication systems easy-to-use tools can facilitate a clear and efficient conversation. The CommunicateHealth design team presented three tools specifically for health communication systems, which focused on the increment communication during health emergencies. They were the following: the Show Me booklet ("a spiral-bound, laminated, dry erase booklet for use in emergency shelters"), the Show Me mobile app (a mobile application for volunteers and staff who work in a particular location or going door-to-door); and, the Show Me FAC mobile app (for staff and volunteers at family assistance centers). The booklet and the two mobile apps used icon-based forms of communication [19].

In the work of Buttussi et al. (2010), a mobile system is also presented for use in the health context. The solution proposed was based on a "collection of emergency-related sentences, showing videos of the corresponding translations in sign language to the deaf patients" [20].

The eCall system, presented in the work of Cabo et al. (2014), automatically calls for help in case of a car accident. This system works by sending the geographic location and the vehicle identification data containing information, while at the same time executing a 112-voice connection. The interface of the eCall System Proposal relies on text –based communication [21].

Another solution presented is the PeacePHONE, a simulated mobile phone, designed to compensate for existing functions on mobile phones that were not practical for deaf individuals, by providing an evaluation of these functions and a conceptual design based on the daily life requirements of the Deaf community. These functions are related to the global interaction in a multifunction mobile phone [22].

The system proposed by Constantinou et al. (2010) consists of a mobile application that provides feedback of an emergency situation to the emergency services. The solutions allowed for three emergency contact options: to the police, to an ambulance, and to the fire department. It is a text and icon-based communication [23].

Also, Weppner and Lukowicz (2014) presented an application that lets people with hearing and speech impairments make emergency calls to standard emergency call centers, but the interaction with the interface is mostly done by text input and output [24].

As it can be seen, the icon-based communication is considered a powerful tool in the development of interfaces for deaf users, as it allows communication feedback between the user in need and the emergency services. This design solution can be considered for other users, not only for deaf people, as it can be useful for people with low literacy and/or communication challenges [19].

Regarding commercial solutions, there are also current solutions (mobile applications) that come as a workaround solution for replacing the phone call for getting in touch with the travel assistance, describing their claim and asking for proper assistance. In this context, we analyzed several apps for travel assistance; however, their service was provided throughout a telephone call, unsuitable for the deaf or people with speech impairments, and/or need to have an internet connection to report occurrences. For example, the Portuguese company AXA offers the My AXA mobile application for Android and iPhone devices. In terms of accessibility, the solution does not meet the requirements for deaf users because during the car claim process the user is requested to make an emergency call in case of injuries. In addition, it also requests a call to the assistance if the vehicle is immobile. These call options are inaccessible to deaf users as it requires audio in order to be used [25]. Another solution is iBrisa. It is an application for iOS (iPhone and iPad), Android and Windows 8, which is a fundamental tool for drivers on the Brisa Group's motorways. Specifically, in terms of accessibility for deaf users, the iBrisa application travel assistance system is not feasible because it requires audio stimulus for proper assistance to be obtained [26]. Another example is the Seguros Directo company, which offers Direct mobile application for Android and iOS devices. The application provides a travel assistance service via telephone call to the company number, but in terms of accessibility for deaf users this service is not feasible due to the need for audio [27].

3   MyCarMobile

After analyzing the apps described above, we felt it was necessary to develop an automatic system for mediation of non-verbal and asynchronous communication which would overcome the necessity of using the audio stimulus to make the emergency call and/or must be connected to report occurrences. As an alternative, we present a solution that is a rapid development method of native mobile applications. These are always available through rapid prototyping for multiplatform, by simply defining the application flow, with the integration of services permanently available through a mediation server and dynamic communication channels. This solution focuses on the provision of a generic service that guarantees interactive solutions based on iconographic flows for non-verbal communication, such as an integrated system of mediation and communication between different entities [28]. The idea arose as a means for facilitating the daily activities of the deaf through mobile applications.

Therefore, the first application based on this system was the SOSPhone mobile application, which aimed at assisting deaf users although it is not specifically geared towards travel assistance. The concept of SOSPhone is to get in touch with emergency services without using a voice call. The application has an iconographic interface that facilitates the process of interaction with the deaf users, allowing to select images that describe the problem that is intended to be reported. This selection of images results in an SMS message containing all the codes corresponding to the selected information, which is immediately sent to the emergency services. The solution was developed to ensure access to emergency services for the Deaf community, but could be used by the general population given its universal design [29].

Furthermore, the same concept was applied in two other scenarios: setting up medical appointments (M3App) and travel assistance (MyCarMobile).

The MyCarMobile application is presented in more detail in the next section.

3.1 MyCarMobile: Identifying the Problem

Travel assistance services aim to provide support to all drivers; however, when a deaf driver gets stuck on the road due to a road problem or accident, he/she cannot call assistance using a telephone call) because this action involves audio stimulus.

To understand how deaf people overcome this situation, we carried out a survey with the Portuguese Deaf community, aiming to collect statistical data on the major impediments that deaf people felt when communicating with travel assistance services [30].

On the basis of the statistical data from the survey it was found that 80% of the respondents had a driving license, and 56% of them have had to resort to travel assistance at least once. The means they used to contact the travel assistance differs: 55% said that they had to send an SMS to a friend/family member to call the travel assistance; 30% asked another driver to make the call; 5% contacted a Sign Language interpreter by 3G; 5% contacted FPAS by GNR; and 5% used another form of contact, not specified.

Furthermore, 40% of participants in the study said they were no longer being assisted due to communication problems and 64% agreed that travel assistance companies do not have support services for communication with low-hearing or deaf people.

3.2 MyCarMobile: Presenting the Mobile Application

Through the survey results and the analysis of some of the most relevant mobile travel assistance applications currently available, we have found that current solutions for

Deaf people with travel assistance services are not efficient and there is a need to develop a solution that can be used, autonomously, by deaf people.

Accordingly, the solution MyCarMobile is presented as a mobile application which allows calls without requiring the usual telephone emergency call in order to guarantee use by the Deaf or people who are incapacitated to speak. The application provides an iconographic interface allowing the user to report occurrences through simple touches on the smartphone's touch screen. This way, the user can easily and intuitively contact travel assistance and report a specific occurrence. The design developed takes into consideration the accessibility and usability guidelines referenced in Sect. 2.

Regarding the application development process, it followed the ISO 9241-210 standard, which addresses a user-centered design methodology [31].

The solution requires two functional prototypes in particular. The first prototype operates as a client application and the second prototype operates as a server application.

The **client application prototype** was implemented under the Android operating system. It used the Integrated Development Environment (IDE) Eclipse, as well as the support components for Java programming language, the Java Development Kit (JDK) and Java Runtime Environment (JRE).

The prototype developed has two main phases of operation. The first collects the data for a given occurrence. The second consists in sending the data through an SMS message to the server application of the travel assistance services.

In the first phase, a simple and intuitive interface was implemented, which was capable of collecting all the necessary information to characterize a given occurrence. Thus, the user can quickly provide data by simply tapping the smartphone's touch screen. This method is intended to simplify the process of using the travel assistance service because the user can use the service describing its occurrence without having to enter text or involve an audio call. The content that will be displayed in the interface focuses on the description of the occurrences, which can be defined in three different types of main categories (malfunction, accident, or other situations) with three different degrees (light, serious or very serious). In case of another situation, a list of other situations that may have occurred (broken glasses, loss or locked keys, lack of fuel or battery, robbery or theft, fire or explosion) is available.

During the data collection phase, the user always has an option available that allows to change data that has already been selected using a slide menu. Note that during the process of data collecting, the values are subsequently stored in strings defined as global variables, so that the contents can be accessed in any part of the application interface. At the end of all options, a global string containing all the required information of the occurrence is obtained. The same coordinates are automatically added to the GPS coordinates of the location of the occurrence. To do this, the user must activate the appropriate GPS permissions. Once data has been collected, the content stored is sent via an SMS message to the server application with all the necessary information of a particular occurrence. Before sending the message, the application checks the network coverage to avoid failure messages or lost information. If it is not possible to send the message, a failure message is shown to the user during sending, so that he/she is aware that the request for assistance has not been sent and that he/she needs to send it again. At the end of the information collection and in case the SMS message with its occurrence information is sent successfully, the user has the possibility to use a live

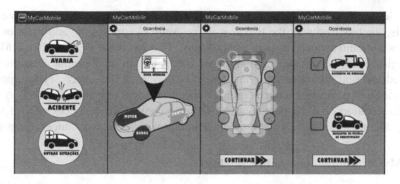

Fig. 1. Screenshots of the client application prototype implemented in Android.

chat implemented in the application to add additional information. This live chat also works by exchanging SMS messages, which are displayed by the interface in a synchronized way, in real time, as they are transferred between the client application and the server application. In Fig. 1, we can see the MyCarMobile client application interface running on the Android operating system.

The server application prototype was developed with Microsoft Visual Studio Ultimate 2012. To transmit information from one application to another through the SMS messaging service, the communication solution uses a GSM modem to access the GSM network and ensure communication [32]. To implement GSM technology, a GSM modem with a SIM card connected to the computer's serial port is required. Since the exchange of information between the computer and the GSM modem uses a protocol designated by the AT command (command language used to control the modem), it is essential to define the AT commands that will perform the intended operation.

When the application is executed, the communication window is shown to the user. For user interaction, it is first necessary to open the serial port that connects the application with the modem, and only then use the application that has access to the GSM network so that it is able to send and receive information. This method of communication ensures a solid solution to its integration.

Once the application integration is ensured through a viable communication source to avoid data loss, then the mechanism that allows it to manage and analyze occurrences was implemented. This management is based on messages received from the prototype of the Android application.

The server application is constantly listening to new messages, but only hosts the messages that are sent by the Android application, because these messages contain a code that validates them. Messages that do not contain this code will be ignored. Whenever there are new messages, the server application shows the number of new occurrences as a notification on the upper left corner of the window. You can click on these notifications to list all occurrences that have not yet been viewed on the screen.

Each message received is stored by the application so that it can be consulted at any time. To list all occurrences registered, users simply click on the query button of the server application, which immediately checks the text files and displays the occurrences on the screen.

In addition to these features, the server application includes the option of a live chat, which is synchronized with the live chat in the Android application, and the messages are shown simultaneously in both applications. This live chat system also works by exchanging SMS messages, which are listed on the screen, in a similar chat interface. Received and sent messages are immediately displayed on the screen. The purpose of this service is to complement the recording of occurrences in case there is a need to detail a certain situation or if the user wants to ask questions to the helpdesk or vice versa, offering the possibility of a greater user interaction with travel assistance services.

3.3   MyCarMobile: Assessing Usability

An assessment phase was performed to evaluate the usability of the MyCarMobile mobile application, also with the intention of validation the interface by deaf users.

Regarding participants, the tests were carried out with the collaboration of the Deaf Association of Porto. This phase included eleven deaf participants who were invited to participate in the pilot study (five women and six men). Of the total participants, 26% of the ages ranged from 20 to 29 years old; 37% were between 30 and 39 years old; and 37% were between 40 and 49 years old. The educational level of participants was the 12th grade or lower. In the group 10% had a Master's degree; 18% had a Bachelor's degree; 36%, 12th grade; and less than 36% had left school before the 12th degree.

In relation to procedures, a script was elaborated in order to perform the user tests. This script was translated by a Sign Language interpreter and was used to make a short introduction of the MyCarMobile app. After this introduction, the tests started, with all participants performing the tests individually, under the same conditions. After having completed the tests, a Computer System Usability Questionnaire (CSUQ) was filled out by the participants to gather usability results.

To perform the tests, an Android smartphone was used, with the MyCarMobile application installed. The smartphone had the following features: HTC One X (Android 4.2.2) with a 4.7″ (720 × 1280) pixels monitor.

Concerning the experimental design, each user followed the script provided to them, with scenario information and specific tasks.

After performing the tasks, users answered a CSUQ questionnaire to assess the prototype [33]. This questionnaire is an instrument that measures user satisfaction regarding the computer system usability. The questionnaire consists of 19 questions, with a likert scale of seven points for each answer, where point 1 corresponds to "I totally disagree" and point 7 corresponds to "I totally agree". The 19 questions are grouped into 4 subscales: overall, overall system satisfaction measurement (all 19 questions); sysuse, measures the system utility (questions 1 to 8); infoqual, measures the quality of information (questions 9 to 15); and, interqual, measures the quality of the interface (questions 16 to 18).

Summarizing, users had to follow the instructions of the script (translated by a Sign Language interpreter), perform the scenario described in the script, and then respond to the questionnaire to provide data.

For the results, we used the likert scale (1 to 7) and the average obtained in each response was calculated to ascertain the level of user agreement for each question. Also, the standard deviation of the responses was calculated, as well as the total number of responses (Total N) entered in the average calculation. Furthermore, when users gave a not applicable response (N/A), the number was also considered.

The results showed users evaluated MyCarMobile regarding simplicity of system usage, with an average of 6.60 and a standard deviation of 0.52. Also, in terms of general satisfaction, the application obtained an average of 6.55 with a standard deviation of 0.69. Despite the positive results in the simplicity usage and satisfaction, users expected to encounter more functions and capacities (5.91 with a standard deviation of 1.22). Overall, concerning the average and standard deviation of the usability metrics under analysis, the system satisfaction rate was 6.31 (up to 7) with a standard deviation of 0.18. Also in the other metrics, Sysuse (average: 6.35 and standard deviation: 0.19), Inforqual (average: 6.30 and standard deviation: 0.12) and interqual (average: 6.16 and standard deviation: 0.22), showed a good user assessment. It is important to note that users found the MyCarMobile mobile application easy to use and were satisfied with it, even when they wished it had more features.

4 Conclusions and Future Work

To create the MyCarMobile mobile application, we took into consideration accessibility and usability standards to develop a client application, which allowed the use of travel assistance services without audio recourse, but also a server application that could receive and manage the occurrences sent by the client application. After the prototypes were implemented successfully, the client prototype was validated with the Deaf users, through user tests. The results showed that the MyCarMobile can be a useful solution for travel assistance for deaf people, as it proved to be easy to use and users where satisfied after usage. However, as future studies, we propose adding new functionalities to the application, since the tests revealed that despite the satisfaction of the users regarding their ability to easily use this application to call the travel assistance services, they would have liked to have more functionalities in the application.

Acknowledgements. This work was supported by the Project "Accessible metaphor for non-text Web browsing" financed the Prize for Digital Inclusion and Literacy by Fundação para a Ciência e a Tecnologia (FCT).

References

1. Paredes, H., Fonseca, B., Barroso, J.: Developing iconographic driven applications for nonverbal communication: a roadside assistance app for the deaf. In: Stephanidis, C., Antona, M. (eds.) Universal Access in Human-Computer Interaction. Aging and Assistive Environments, UAHCI 2014. LNCS, vol. 8515, pp. 762–771. Springer, Cham (2014). doi:10.1007/978-3-319-07446-7_72
2. Riviere, E.: Edge-centric computing: vision and challenges. ACM SIGCOMM Comput. Commun. Rev. **45**(5), 37–42 (2015)
3. Lopez, P.: Internet Society. Global Internet Report 2015, Mobile evolution and development of the Internet. Internet Society, Reston (2015). http://www.internetsociety.org/globalinternetreport/assets/download/IS_web.pdf

4. Global Accessibility Reporting Initiative (GARI). http://www.gari.info/index.cfm
5. Rocha, T.: Metáfora de Interação para o Acesso à Informação Digital de uma Forma Autónoma por Pessoas com Deficiência Intelectual (2014)
6. Lagoá, P., Nicolau, H., Guerreiro, T., Gonçalves, D., Jorge, J.: Acessibilidade Móvel: Soluções para Deficientes Visuais. In: Proceedings of the 3th National Conference on Human-Computer Interaction (2008)
7. Blind, T.: Accessible Apps. How to be Blind: A Community for the Blind and Visually Impaired (2012). http://htb2.com/apps/
8. Global Accessibility Reporting Initiative (GARI): Find Mobile Apps (2012). http://www.gari.info/findapps-results.cfm
9. Google: Making Applications Accessible. Developer Android (2012). https://developer.android.com/guide/topics/ui/accessibility/apps.html
10. Microsoft: Guidelines for designing accessible apps. MSDN Microsoft (2014). http://msdn.microsoft.com/en-us/library/windows/apps/hh700407.aspx
11. Apple: Making Your iOS App Accessible. Developer Apple (2014). https://developer.apple.com/library/ios/documentation/UserExperience/Conceptual/iPhoneAccessibity/Making_Application_Accessible/Making_Application_Accessible.html#//apple_ref/doc/uid/TP40008785-CH102-SW5
12. World Wide Web Consortium (W3C): Web Content Accessibility Guidelines (WCAG) 2.0. http://www.w3.org/TR/2008/REC-WCAG20-20081211/
13. Martínez, L., Pluke, M.: Mandate M 376: new software accessibility requirements. Procedia Comput. Sci. **27**, 271–280 (2014). doi:10.1016/j.procs.2014.02.030
14. Ribeiro, A., Silva, R.: Survey on cross-platforms and languages for mobile apps. In: IEEE (ed.) Quality of Information and Communications Technology (QUATIC), pp. 255–260 (2012). doi:10.1109/QUATIC.2012.56
15. Macedo, K., Pereira, A.T.: Desenvolvimento de Recomendações de Acessibilidade e Usabilidade para Ambientes Virtuais de Aprendizagem Voltados para o Utilizador Idoso. Centro Interdisciplinar de Novas Tecnologias na Educação – CINTED. Universidade Federal do Rio Grande do Sul - UFRGS (2009)
16. International Organization for Standardization – (ISO): ISO 9241-11 Ergonomic requirements for office work with visual display terminals (VDTs) - Part 11: Guidance on usability (1998). http://www.it.uu.se/edu/course/homepage/acsd/vt09/ISO9241part11.pdf
17. International Organization for Standardization – (ISO): ISO 13407: Human Centred Design Process for Interactive Systems (1998). http://www.iso.org/iso/catalogue_detail.htm?csnumber=21197
18. International Organization for Standardization – (ISO): ISO 9241-210:2010 Ergonomics of human-system interaction - Part 210: Human-centred design for interactive systems (2010). http://www.iso.org/iso/catalogue_detail.htm?csnumber=52075
19. Patton, A., Griffin, M., Tellez, A., Petti, M.A., Scrimgeour, X.: Using icons to overcome communication barriers during emergencies: a case study of the show me interactive tools. Visible Lang. **49**(1/2), 81 (2015). http://visiblelanguagejournal.com/issue/161/article/931
20. Buttussi, F., Chittaro, L., Carchietti, E., Coppo, M.: Using mobile devices to support communication between emergency medical responders and deaf people. In: Proceedings of the 12th International Conference on Human Computer Interaction with Mobile Devices and Services. ACM (2010)
21. Cabo, M., Fernandes, F., Pereira, T., Fonseca, B., Paredes, H.: Universal access to eCall system. Procedia Comput. Sci. **27**, 104–112 (2014)
22. Liu, C., Chiu, H., Hsieh, C., Li, R.: Optimizing the usability of mobile phones for individuals who are deaf. Assist. Technol. **22**(2), 115–127 (2010)

23. Vaso, C., Ioannou, A., Diaz, P.: Inclusive access to emergency services: an action research project focused on hearing-impaired citizens. Univ. Access Inf. Soc., 1–9 (2016)
24. Weppner, J., Lukowicz, P.: Emergency app for people with hearing and speech disabilities: design, implementation and evaluation according to legal requirements in Germany. In: Proceedings of the 8th International Conference on Pervasive Computing Technologies for Healthcare. ICST (Institute for Computer Sciences, Social-Informatics and Telecommunications Engineering) (2014)
25. AXA: AXA Apps: aplicações móveis para o seu smartphone. AXA. http://www.axa.pt/axa-mobile.aspx
26. Brisa: Aplicação iBrisa. Brisa. http://www.brisa.pt/PresentationLayer/conteudo.aspx?menuid=437
27. Seguro Directo: A Direct no seu telefone. Seguro Directo (2017). http://www.segurodirecto.pt/servicos/app.html
28. Fonseca, B., Azevedo, D., Fernandes, F., Paredes, H., Cabo, M., Pereira, T.: Automatic asynchronous mediation of nonverbal communication for interactive streams iconographic (2013)
29. Paredes, H., Fonseca, B., Cabo, M., Pereira, T., Fernandes, F.: SOSPhone: a mobile application for emergency calls. Univ. Access Inf. Soc. 13, 277–290 (2013). doi:10.1007/s10209-013-0318-z
30. Baptista, B.: Interface de intermediação de comunicação entre surdos e serviços de assistência em viagem (2012)
31. Usability Partners: ISO standards. Usability Partners (2010). http://www.usabilitypartners.se/about-usability/iso-standards
32. Mouly, M., Pautet, M.-B.: The GSM System for Mobile Communications. Telecom Publishing (1992). ISBN: 0945592159
33. Lewis, J.R.: IBM computer usability satisfaction questionnaires: psychometric evaluation and instructions for use. Int. J. Hum. Comput. Interact. Arch. 7(1), 57–78 (1995)

Touch Shadow Interaction and Continuous Directional User Interface for Smartphone

Sanjay Ghosh[1(✉)], Joy Bose[1], Rajkumar Darbar[2],
and Punyashlok Dash[2]

[1] Samsung R&D Institute, Bangalore, Karnataka, India
{sanjay.ghosh,joy.bose}@samsung.com
[2] Indian Institute of Technology, Kharagpur, Kharagpur, India
rajdarbar.r@gmail.com, punyashlok.com@gmail.com

Abstract. We propose a new touch screen interaction named as Touch Shadow, which is based on the contact area and the resultant shape of the fingertip when it touches the touch surface. The results of our feasibility evaluation established three degrees of freedom for the Touch Shadow interaction based on three fundamental parameters, the touch surface area, displacement of the touch centroid and direction of the press. For this interaction, we designed several user interface options that can support continuous interaction. Based on the review feedback from 6 UI designers, we finally selected three of them, the Bubble Shadow, Rectangular Shadow and Beam Shadow for user evaluation. A proof of concept prototype was developed for Android smartphones and was tested with 10 users for maps application scenario. The participants rated the experience of using Touch Shadow with continuous direction UI on the map to be high.

Keywords: Touch interaction · Capacitive touch interface · Finger touch degrees of freedom · Continuous touch interaction · Directional touch

1 Introduction

Existing touch gestures are primarily two dimensional in nature, as they are limited by the position and movement of fingers or stylus across locations on the touch screen. Moreover, most of the existing touch interactions are committable or discrete by nature, and not exploratory or continuous. This means that, when a user performs any existing touch action, say, tap or long press on a button, the mapped event is bound to happen. Thus, existing touch interactions assume that the user is certain about which action to perform for which task. However, several applications with real life situations require the user to explore various possible options and then take a decision. Examples are: searching for a hotel using a map or choosing a particular family picture from the phone gallery. For such instances, the interaction as well as the user interface needs to be designed to support the cognitive mental model of ambiguity.

To support such a requirement, the interaction must be inherently continuous in nature, which would enable the user to give continuous input to the device using simple interactions, similar to that which is possible using a joystick. Designing such

R. Bernhaupt et al. (Eds.): INTERACT 2017, Part I, LNCS 10513, pp. 66–74, 2017.
DOI: 10.1007/978-3-319-67744-6_5

interactions would need the touch hardware to respond to more degrees of freedom (DOF) which a user can control using touch actions. The existing touch gestures only allow limited degrees of freedom, limited by the touch coordinates on a touch screen. Although pinch, pan, and scroll among the current touch gestures are of continuous nature, these are also tightly coupled with the distance traveled by the user's fingers on the touch surface. The user is still required to move his finger on the 2D touch surface in order to perform these gestures. Position 3D touch or Pressure Touch [1], which is patented by Apple, is beyond just 2D touch and allows one additional degree of freedom along the Z-axis with three intermediate interaction levels, but it may still be considered as discrete interaction rather than a continuous one. Moreover, techniques such as Apple's 3D touch require specialized embedded hardware to detect the finger pressure during the touch. Our research objective was to develop a new touch interaction with above mentioned capabilities without employing additional hardware.

In this paper, we propose and evaluate a new touch interaction method for smartphones which we call as Touch Shadow, wherein the user can perform continuous input without lifting and moving his finger. Shadow here is a metaphor used to represent the variable surface area of the finger tip that touches the touch surface. When different levels of pressure are applied to the finger on a touch surface, the resultant surface area and shape of the finger contact slightly changes. Also, the bulge of the fingertip depends on the direction of the applied pressure. The advantage of the touch shadow interactions over the existing touch interaction includes the ability to continuously interact with UI elements in the display. In this study, our objective was to evaluate how clearly these slight changes could be detected and could be mapped to interactions. To that end, we developed a proof of concept prototype on an Android smartphone with a capacitive touch screen to demonstrate the concept. The detection of this interaction is based on the measurement of the total capacitance value from the surface area of the finger touch and hence no additional hardware was employed. We evaluate the feasibility of detection along three possible degrees of freedom, i.e. change in the touch area, change in direction and change in the touch centroid, on our prototype with 10 users. We also identified and implemented 3 UI elements using the interaction on a map application in Android, and evaluated with 10 users for ease of use. Thus, this study established the feasibility of the proposed interaction for smartphone applications.

2 Related Work

There are several research prototypes which detect the finger pressure [2] or shear force [3, 4] to perform continuous interactions. Most of these employ relevant sensors below the touch screen to augment a device such as a smartphone. There are a few approaches which detect an equivalent of finger pressure in some form without actually using any pressure sensors. WatchMI [5] is one such prototype which detects different levels of continuous touch pressure through finger movements data recorded in the built-in IMU sensor in the Smartwatch. Contrastingly, there are also few prototypes which use various actions of the finger on 2D touch surface as a close proxy to the pressure, an approach used in our Touch Shadow interaction method. Wang et al. [6] performed an empirical evaluation of the three key properties of the finger touch, i.e. contact area, contact shape and contact orientation and proposed to use these for defining additional degrees of freedom for touch gestures on a 2D touch surface. This forms one of the inspirations for our research. Xiao et al. [7] proposed to use the finger movement along the pitch and yaw relative to a touch surface to trigger actions on a smartphone and a smartwatch. Roudaut et al. [8] proposed MicroRolls gestures using the thumb, wherein the stationary thumb acquires six small magnitude rolling positions which can be detected on the touch surface. TapSense [9] prototype detects the portion of the user's finger including the tip, pad, nail, and knuckle that is used to make the touch interaction. Angle pose [10] estimated a finger's 3D pose and angle based on the model using cumulative capacitive values and used them for improved accuracy of touch. Work by Wang et al. [11] could detect finger orientation based on the directionality and the shape of the touch surface. Closely relevant to our work is that of Boring et al. [12] which uses the change in thumb's contact size along various threshold levels for mapping different user interaction. Here the elliptical size of thumb contact portion was considered virtually equivalent to the finger pressure.

Notably, most of the above mentioned works focused only on one of the additional aspects of finger touch other than just the location and movement along the x-y coordinate of the 2D touch surface. This additional aspect may either be the touch angle or pose of the finger or size of the touch surface or the slight movement of the finger. However, our Touch Shadow gesture is based on 3 aspects: change in touch area, change in direction and change in the touch centroid. Also unlike ours, most of the prior works do not primarily define the continuous aspect of the interaction.

3   Detection Parameters for Touch Shadow Interaction

We here explain the fundamental detection parameters for detecting Touch Shadow.

3.1   Change in Area/Shape

When the user rolls or presses the finger, the fingertip bulges, resulting in a change in the area of the finger in contact with the screen. This change can be in the positive or negative direction, which represents one of the degrees of freedom. By measuring the change in this area or shape we mapped it to different interaction categories.

3.2   Displacement of the Centroid

The centroid of the ellipse formed by the touch surface of the finger with the touch-screen gets displaced towards the direction of the tangential force, resulting in an additional degree of freedom. If (x_1, y_1) are the initial touch coordinates and (x_2, y_2) the final touch coordinates, the displacement is given by $\sqrt{((x_2 - x_1)^2 + (y_2 - y_1)^2)}$.

3.3   Directionality

The direction of movement of the finger can also be identified and serves as an additional degree of freedom. The x and y touch coordinates of the touch point, along with the touch major and touch minor of the ellipse created by the finger can be used to calculate the Displacement Angle of centroid Θ, given by $\tan^{-1}(y_2 - y_1)/(x_2 - x_1)$.

4   Touch Shadow Detection Feasibility

We performed a detection feasibility experiment to study the degrees of freedom that are possible for our Touch Shadow interaction. We used three Android devices with different levels of screen resolutions: Samsung S6, Samsung J7, and Motorola G3. The prototype, as shown in Fig. 1(a), had a circular touch sensitive area for users to move their finger with seven different tasks as mentioned in Table 1.

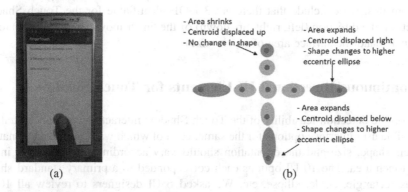

(a)   (b)

Fig. 1. (a) Prototype used for the feasibility evaluation. (b) Pattern of finger touch shapes, area and centroid displacements during evaluation.

Table 1. The captured values for the touch ellipse for the feasibility experiment, averaged over 10 users, using a Samsung Galaxy S6.

Test action	Touch major	Touch minor	X co-ordinate	Y co-ordinate	Area
Normal touch (Default light press)	2.93	2.93	737.23	1993.13	0.02
Radial shadow (Medium press)	4.83	3.42	738.28	2021.88	0.03
Radial shadow (Strong press)	5.86	5.86	717.19	2031.88	0.05
Left shadow (Light press)	2.93	2.93	657.07	1991.88	0.02
Max left shadow (Light press)	4.88	3.42	605.04	2008.75	0.03
Right shadow (Light press)	3.42	3.42	766.05	2005	0.03
Max right shadow (Light press)	3.42	1.95	919.34	2043.21	0.02
Up shadow (Light press)	1.95	1.95	717.19	1938.75	0.02
Max up shadow (Light press)	1.95	1.95	720	1853.75	0.02
Bottom shadow (Light press)	3.42	3.42	730.20	2051	0.03
Max bottom shadow (Light press)	5.37	3.91	734.06	2113.13	0.04

We tested it with 10 users, all heavy users of smartphone applications in the age group of 24–35 years (Mean Age = 28.3 years; SD = 2.8; 4 Female; 6 Male), and then took the average of the values to normalize for the size of the fingers and other parameters readings. We actually did not observe high within-subject variations. In fact, the readings for touch major, touch minor, and area for all the 10 users differed not more than 10%. This also assured sufficient accuracy in terms of detecting the correct interaction. The results for Samsung S6 are tabulated in Table 1. We obtained similar results using the other devices as well. We recorded the values of the x and y coordinates of the touch point and the minor and major axes of the ellipse around the touch point. The key aspect of the results is as follows: the touch surface area expanded in a pattern similar to as shown in Fig. 1(b) when the finger was rolled from the initial position to the left, right, or down position. It shrunk slightly when the finger was rolled up. From this, we conclude that there are 3 DOF identifiable for the Touch Shadow interaction: the direction (left, right, up, down) of the finger movement, the (x, y) touch coordinates and the surface area of touch (size).

5   Continuous Directional UI Elements for Touch Shadow

Based on the detection feasibility of the Touch Shadow interaction, we conceptualized 10 possible user interface options for the same, each of which was continuous in nature, i.e. their shape, size and the orientation should vary according to the change in the finger touch area. The 10 UI options each corresponded to a primary standard shape, such as rectangle, circle, ellipse, etc. We asked 6 UI designers to review all 10 UI options with respect to a set of 10 different hypothetical application use cases which required continuous interaction, the use cases being provided as stimulus in form of mobile wireframe illustrations. Few of these use cases were: exploring and selecting a music track, searching for a particular photo in a gallery, selecting a video, etc. We performed a subjective analysis of the feedback and reasoning received and selected the three most preferred continuous directional UI options, i.e. Bubble, Rectangular and Beam Shadow for further evaluation. Most of the participants found these three UI options to be appropriate for the majority of the application use cases.

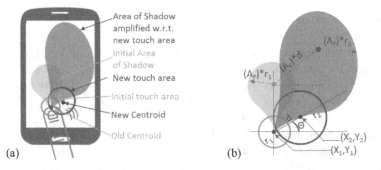

Fig. 2. Illustration of (a) a bubble shaped UI element created by the user in the direction of change of touch area, and (b) the area and direction of the UI element.

5.1 Bubble Shadow

A bubble shaped UI element is created in the direction of change of the touch area. Figure 2 shows the calculation of the touch area and direction of expansion for the gesture. The touch region is assumed to be a circle for the sake of easier understanding, whose centre is at a distance d and angle Θ from the initial coordinates of the touch point. Here (x_1, y_1) and (x_2, y_2) are the initial and final coordinates of the centroid.

5.2 Rectangular Shadow

Here the UI element is in the shape of a rectangle. Here Θ assumes one of the following four values: 0, 90, 180, or 270°, depending on the predominant cardinal direction of the finger displacement (up, bottom, left, right). As in the bubble UI, the rectangle amplified the displacement of the touch point by an amplification factor A_{F1}. So the movement of the center of the rectangle = $A_{F1} * \Delta d$.

5.3 Beam Shadow

In this case, the UI element is in the shape of a beam (similar to the light of a torch), where the angle Θ made by the beam is a value between 0 and 90° in the predominant cardinal direction of the finger displacement, as before. The length of the arc r is proportional to the displacement of the centroid Δd, amplified by an amplification factor A_F. The arc angle is proportional to ΔA, the change of touch area.

Table 2 describes the 3 UI elements w.r.t. the 3 DOF parameters.

Table 2. Illustration of the modes of using the Touch Shadow gesture

Touch Gesture	Touch expansion by pressing the Center of the finger	Touch expansion by pressing on upper right tip of the finger	Touch expansion by pressing on lower portion of the finger
Interaction	Radial Shadow	Right Shadow	Left Shadow
Detection Conditions	a1. ΔA=Small;Δd=0;Θ=0 a2. ΔA=Large;Δd=0;Θ=0	b1. ΔA=0;Δd=Small;Θ=-45°to+45° b2. ΔA=0;Δd=Large;Θ=-45°to+45°	c1. ΔA=Small;Δd=Small;Θ=+135°to-135° c2. ΔA=Large;Δd=Large;Θ=+135°to-135°
Shadow UI - I (Bubble)			
Shadow UI - II (Rectangle)			
Shadow UI - III (Beam)			

In our prototype, we were able to detect at least 64 (43 for 3 DOF parameter with 4 levels for each DOF parameter) different instances of detection conditions, Only 6 of those 64 detection conditions are described in the three columns of Table 2. At least one of the 3 DOF parameters, i.e. ΔA, Δd and Θ should vary beyond the threshold limit for a valid instance of a detection condition. The three UI options, Bubble, Rectangular, and Beam are illustrated for these 6 different instances of detection conditions. For detection condition a1 and a2, the only ΔA varied continuously; while Δd and Θ were constant, a condition achieved by pressing the center of finger touch area. Similarly, other corresponding detection instances can be inferred from Table 2.

6 Prototype Implementation Details

We implemented a prototype of the Touch Shadow UI, using a Samsung Galaxy S6 smartphone running Android version 7. For simplicity, we assumed the movement of only one of the following: up, bottom, left, right, or radial. For the simplicity of

---

IDENTIFY-DIRECTION-FINGER-MOVEMENT () // Identify direction

1   T_x, T_y = Threshold for min. movement of touch point centroid in the X axis; //Input
2   T_A = Threshold for min. change in area of the touch ellipse; // Input
3   x_1, y_1, A_1 = Initial touch coordinates, touch area; //using getX, getY, getArea functions
4    $touchMajor_1$, $touchMinor_1$ = Initial major and minor axes of touch ellipse;
5   x_2, y_2 = New touch coordinates; A_2 = New touch area;
6    $d_x = x_2 - x_1$, $d_y = y_2 - y_1$; //movement of the centroid of touch point
7    $d_A = A_2 - A_1$; //change in area of the touch ellipse
8   **if** (abs(d_x) < T_x and abs(d_y) > T_y) //movement in up-down direction
9   if (d_y > 0) then $direction$ = DIR_UP; else $direction$ = DIR_BOTTOM;
10   **if** (abs(d_x) > T_x and abs(d_y) < T_y) //movement in left-right direction
11   if (d_x > 0) then $direction$ = DIR_RIGHT; else $direction$ = DIR_LEFT;
12   **if** (abs(d_x) < T_x and abs(d_y) < T_y) //no movement, press down at same point
13   if (d_A > T_A) then $direction$ = DIR_RADIAL;
14   **return** $direction$;

PLOT-UI-ELEMENT () // Plot the UI element based on identified direction

1   T_1 = Polling interval in millseconds; // Input
2   A_1, A_2 = Amplification factors for UI, based on the model of device used; //input
3    $direction$ = Identified direction of finger movement; //input
4   **for**(;;)
5   CLEAR_CANVAS();
6       $touchMajor_1$, $touchMinor_1$, x_1, y_1, A_1 = GET-TOUCH-PARAMETERS();
7       $r_1 = touchMajor_1 * A_1$; $r_2 = touchMinor_1 * A_1$;
8   **if**($direction$ ==DIR_LEFT)
9   c = abs(x_2-x_1)*A_2; PLOT-UI-ELLIPSE($x1$-c, $y1$, r_1, r_2);
10   **if**($direction$ ==DIR_RIGHT)
11   c = abs(x_2-x_1)*A_2; PLOT-UI-ELLIPSE($x1$+c, $y1$, r_1, r_2);
12   **if**($direction$ ==DIR_UP)
13   c = abs(y_2-y_1)*A_2; PLOT-UI-ELLIPSE($x1$, $y1$+c, r_1, r_2);
14   **if**($direction$ ==DIR_BOTTOM)
15   c = abs(y_2-y_1)*A_2; PLOT-UI-ELLIPSE($x1$, $y1$-c, r_1, r_2);
16   **if**($direction$ ==DIR_RADIAL) PLOT-UI-ELLIPSE($x1$, $y1$, r_1, r_2);
17   sleep(T_1); // Poll every T1 millisec
18   **return**;

explaining the interaction detection logic and UI rendering logic, we provide the pseudo code only for the Bubble UI, with the bubble shape approximated by an ellipse.

7 User Interface Evaluation

We conducted an evaluation with 10 users, the same set of people involved earlier in initial feasibility evaluation. They used the prototype with the 3 UI elements, bubble, rectangular and beam, overlaid on a map for a task to explore hotels around a fixed location (convention center). The users were asked to place their index finger on the location and explore the hotels in the region under one of the 3 UI elements using the continuous directional Touch Shadow interaction. Based on the changing UI shape, the interface displayed information such as hotel distance, cost, rating and discounts as in Fig. 3. For the prototype, we simulated only dummy values in the map interface. Post user trials, we collected their subjective feedback in terms of usefulness of the Touch Shadow interaction and ease of use of the 3 UI elements.

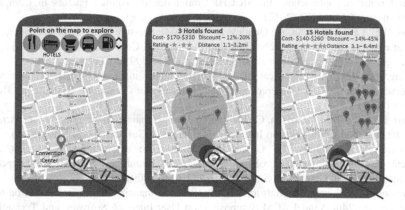

Fig. 3. Wireframe illustration of the Bubble Shadow UI on a maps application.

Majority of the users found the rectangular UI to be the easiest to control with Touch Shadow interaction, since the rectangular UI overlay covered appropriate portions of the rectangular smartphone display. A user suggested adapting default aspect ratios of the rectangular UI based on the smartphone used. Many users found the Beam UI to be most relevant for scenarios where a pivot point of interest is important, as in the test use case of finding hotels around a location. Users found the Rectangular UI relevant when a portion of display interface or an area was important. For some users, finger occlusion was the primary concern while using the Beam UI element, so they preferred the bubble UI considering it to be a superior variant of the Beam UI. Overall, almost all the users rated their experience of the Touch Shadow interaction to be high and found this to be highly useful for application use cases.

8 Conclusion

We proposed and evaluated a new interaction method called Touch Shadow, with the ability to continuously interact with UI elements enabling the user to continuously explore options and then choose. In future, we plan to implement the Touch Shadow interaction and corresponding UI elements for other key smartphone applications.

References

1. Apple, Inc. Multi-touch gesture dictionary, US Patent 20070177803 (2008)
2. Clarkson, E.C., Patel, S.N., Pierce, J.S., Abowd, G.D.: Exploring continuous pressure input for mobile phones. Georgia Institute of Technology (2006)
3. Heo, S., Lee, G.: Force gestures: augmenting touch screen gestures with normal and tangential forces. In: 24th Annual ACM Symposium on User Interface Software and Technology, pp. 621–626 (2011)
4. Harrison, C., Hudson, S.: Using shear as a supplemental two-dimensional input channel for rich touchscreen interaction. In: SIGCHI Conference on Human Factors in Computing Systems, pp. 3149–3152 (2012)
5. Yeo, H.S., Lee, J., Bianchi, A., Quigley, A.: WatchMI: pressure touch, twist and pan gesture input on unmodified smartwatches. In: 18th International Conference on Human-Computer Interaction with Mobile Devices and Services, pp. 394–399 (2016)
6. Wang, F., Ren, X.: Empirical evaluation for finger input properties in multi-touch interaction. In: SIGCHI Conference on Human Factors in Computing Systems, pp. 1063–1072 (2009)
7. Xiao, R., Schwarz, J., Harrison, C.: Estimating 3D finger angle on commodity touchscreens. In: International Conference on Interactive Tabletops & Surfaces, pp. 47–50 (2015)
8. Roudaut, A., Lecolinet, E., Guiard, Y.: MicroRolls: expanding touch-screen input vocabulary by distinguishing rolls vs. slides of the thumb. In: SIGCHI Conference on Human Factors in Computing Systems, pp. 927–936 (2009)
9. Harrison, C., Schwarz, J., Hudson, S.E.: TapSense: enhancing finger interaction on touch surfaces. In: 24th Annual ACM Symposium on User Interface Software and Technology, pp. 627–636 (2011)
10. Rogers, S., Williamson, J., Stewart, C., Murray-Smith, R.: AnglePose: robust, precise capacitive touch tracking via 3D orientation estimation. In: SIGCHI Conference on Human Factors in Computing Systems, pp. 2575–2584 (2011)
11. Wang, F., Cao, X., Ren, X., Irani, P.: Detecting and leveraging finger orientation for interaction with direct-touch surfaces. In: 22nd Annual ACM Symposium on User Interface Software and Technology, pp. 23–32 (2009)
12. Boring, S., Ledo, D., Chen, X.A., Marquardt, N., Tang, A., Greenberg, S.: The fat thumb: using the thumb's contact size for single-handed mobile interaction. In: 14th International Conference on Human-Computer Interaction with Mobile Devices and Services, pp. 39–48 (2012)

Aging and Disabilities

Age-Related Effects of Task Difficulty on the Semantic Relevance of Query Reformulations

Saraschandra Karanam and Herre van Oostendorp[⊠]

Utrecht University, Utrecht, The Netherlands
{s.karanam, h.vanoostendorp}@uu.nl

Abstract. This study examined the semantics of query reformulations in relation to age and task difficulty. Task difficulty was manipulated using a metric called task preciseness defined as the semantic similarity of the task description with the content of the target page(s) containing the answer. A behavioral experiment was conducted in which 24 younger adults and 21 older adults solved six low precise and six high precise information search tasks. The behavioral outcomes were found to be in line with preceding work indicating that the metric was successful in differentiating different levels of task difficulty. Analysis of the semantic relevance of queries showed that for low precise tasks, the queries generated by younger adults had significantly higher mean semantic relevance than that of older adults whereas for high precise tasks, it was the other way round. When analyzed across reformulations, it was found that the mean semantic relevance of queries generated by older adults, decreased for both low and high precise tasks. For younger adults, it remained constant for high precise tasks and even increased for low precise tasks. Implications of these findings for the design of information search systems are discussed.

Keywords: Information search · Aging · Task preciseness · Query reformulations

1 Introduction

Searching for information on the Internet is a complex cognitive activity involving a number of cognitive processes such as attention, comprehension, decision making and problem solving. Naturally, these cognitive processes are in turn affected by a number of cognitive factors such as age [8], domain knowledge [35], experience with the Internet [51] etc., leading to wide variations in the adoption of the Internet and its efficient use. The focus of this paper is particularly on the effect of aging on information search performance. Older adults are now one of the fastest growing users of the Internet [2, 10]. The Internet is known to decrease isolation by enabling alternate means of communication with near and dear, foster independence, enhance attention and memory [41], and keep the mind active, thereby increasing overall health and well-being of the elderly [33].

However, a number of barriers still exist preventing large scale adoption and usage of the Internet by the elderly. Older adults are known to be slow and less efficient when

© IFIP International Federation for Information Processing 2017
Published by Springer International Publishing AG 2017. All Rights Reserved
R. Bernhaupt et al. (Eds.): INTERACT 2017, Part I, LNCS 10513, pp. 77–96, 2017.
DOI: 10.1007/978-3-319-67744-6_6

using the Internet because of their natural decline in motor skills and fluid intelligence involving processing speed, cognitive flexibility or ability to switch processing strategies, attentional control and visuospatial span [16, 17, 48]. Crystallized intelligence, on the other hand, increases and/or becomes more stable with aging. Crystallized intelligence involves prior knowledge, experience and vocabulary skills. Therefore it is often higher for older adults compared to younger adults [16, 17, 48]. These cognitive abilities directly influence the cognitive processes underlying information search resulting in lower efficiency of older adults on information search tasks. For example, lower processing speed could lead to longer time in evaluating search results or hyperlinks on a website, difficulty in switching strategies could lead to difficulty in reformulating unsuccessful queries or difficulty in getting out of an unsuccessful path, lack of attentional control could lead to inefficient handling of relevant and irrelevant search results or hyperlinks and finally lower visuospatial span could mean less efficient exploration of the search result page or a website.

This is reflected in the outcomes of research from human factors and information science communities: older adults were found to generate less queries, use less keywords per query, reformulate less, spend longer time evaluating the search engine result pages (SERPs, henceforth), spend more time evaluating the content of websites opened from SERPs, switch fewer number of times between SERPs and websites and find it difficult to reformulate unsuccessful queries [8, 11, 24, 26, 37]. Studies that investigated the differences in search strategies employed by younger and older adults show that older adults follow a more structured and methodical approach such as careful selection of query terms and spending longer time evaluating the search results and younger adults are more impulsive which involves frequent switches and clicks on irrelevant search results [52]. Younger adults are able to adapt their strategy more often than older adults [8] and younger adults explore more (number of search results opened for any given query) and exploit less (number of websites and hyperlinks within those websites visited for any given query) whereas older adults exploit more and explore less [9].

The research on search strategies has, however, paid less attention to the impact of aging on query reformulation strategies and the actual content of the queries during reformulations. By actual content, we mean here the semantic aspects of the query terms. These, precisely, form the main focus of this paper. Researchers from the information retrieval community have studied query reformulations extensively [19, 21, 39, 44] and modeled query reformulation behavior based on certain structural patterns such as addition and deletion of terms, observed in them [20, 22, 42]. Researchers from the human factors and information science communities have examined a number of factors that influence query reformulations such as task type [31], cognitive style [28], query type [1], prior domain knowledge and familiarity with the topic of the search [14, 18]. For example, the study of [14] showed that participants with low familiarity tend to alter the spelling and use stemming for query reformulation whereas participants with medium or higher topic familiarity are inclined to add new terms and phrases to reformulate queries. Participants with a higher topic familiarity were also found to make less spelling errors and preferred to use specific terms or search from different aspects [18]. The focus of the above studies is largely on the structural aspects of query reformulations such as addition, retention and deletion of terms and not on the semantic aspects. They also do not involve any age-related differences. However, it has been known since long that knowledge-based query reformulation strategies are more efficient, as shown by Shute and Smith in [40]. A recent study by [24] investigated both the structural aspects (that is, the type of reformulation: generalization vs. specialization) and the semantic relevance (that is, the semantic relatedness of queries with target information) of query reformulations. Their study found that younger adults used a specialization strategy to reformulate queries significantly more often than older adults. A generalization strategy was also used significantly more often by younger adults, especially for difficult tasks. The semantic relevance of queries with target information was found to be significantly higher for difficult tasks compared to simple tasks. When measured across reformulations, it showed a decreasing trend for older adults and remained constant for younger adults, indicating that as older adults reformulated, they produced queries that were further away from the target information.

It is useful to note from the above studies that the age-related differences in information search performance (in terms of time spent on search results vs. websites, number of clicks on search results, number of queries generated, number of reformulations), search strategies employed (exploration vs. exploitation, structured vs. impulsive) and structural aspects of query reformulations (generalization vs. specialization) were more prominent for difficult tasks. In the next section, we give a brief overview of how task difficulty was characterized in literature.

2   Task Difficulty

The effect of task difficulty on information search performance has been a focus of research for several decades [3, 6, 7, 15, 27, 30, 46, 49]. It is the most frequently incorporated attribute, to assess the performance of a user interacting with an information source (or a system). In spite of this, there is no consensus on how to operationalize task difficulty objectively and how to distinguish between different levels of task difficulty, as is evident from the number of different approaches that exist in literature: availability (simple tasks) or non-availability (difficult tasks) of keywords in the task description that could be used as queries [8, 11], size (small for simple tasks vs. large for difficult tasks) and complexity (low for simple tasks vs. high for difficult tasks) of the search space [37], availability (simple tasks) or non-availability (difficult tasks) of the answer in the search snippets [24, 26]. Gwidzka and Spence [15] proposed to assess task difficulty objectively using three factors: path length (the length of the navigation path leading to the target information), page complexity (the complexity of navigation choices on each web-page) and page information assessment (the difficulty of relevance judgement on pages that contain the desired information). [36, 47] extended the work of Gwidzka and Spence by introducing a metric called path relevance which measures the degree to which the task description overlaps in meaning with the hyperlink text on the optimal path to the target page.

In this paper, we define an objective measure of task difficulty called *task preciseness*. Task preciseness measures the degree to which the task description overlaps in meaning with the content of the target page(s) containing the answer to the task. Let us say, the user is searching for an answer to the following task: "What name is given to the valve that protects food from entering your lungs when you swallow?" and let us assume that the target page contains the following text "The epiglottis is a flap of soft cartilage, covered by a mucous membrane. It is attached to the back of the tongue and acts as a valve during swallowing to prevent food and liquid from entering the lungs." It is clear from the above example that the degree of overlap between the task description and the actual text on the target page is very high (swallow-swallowing, prevent-protect, food-food, lungs-lungs, valve-valve), almost directly giving the answer the user is searching for. If instead, the target page contains the following text: "Lips and tongue keep food in the mouth and in place prior to swallowing. The soft tissue created by the cricopharyngeus muscle, also called as epiglottis, at the top of the esophagus keeps air out of the digestive system during breathing", the degree of overlap between the task description and the actual text on the target page is very low (swallow-swallowing). The answer is not directly available and has to be indirectly inferred by the user. In order to validate the efficacy of task preciseness, we conduct an experiment with low and high precise information search tasks created using the new metric and check if the information search performance of real subjects on these tasks is indeed in line with known prior outcomes on task difficulty or not. We use Latent Semantic Analysis (LSA, henceforth) [29] to compute the degree of overlap in meaning or semantic similarity values. While we are aware of other methodologies to compute semantic similarity values such as LDA [4], HAL [32], PMI-IR [45] etc., we use LSA in our study because LSA scores have been shown to significantly overlap with those of human scores on synonym, antonym and subject matter tests. LSA has been successful in mimicking human sorting and category judgments, accurately estimating passage coherence, learnability of passages and the quality and the quantity of knowledge in an essay [12, 34, 50]. LSA is a machine-learning technique that builds a semantic space representing a given user population's understanding of words, short or whole texts by applying statistical computations, singular value decomposition and represents them as a vector in a multidimensional space of about 300 dimensions. The cosine value (+1 if identical and 0 if unrelated) between two vectors in this representation gives the measure of the semantic relatedness. It has been shown that higher semantic relatedness between two texts relates to higher overlap in the meanings associated with those two texts. Therefore, a high LSA value indicates a high overlap in the description of the task and the content pages containing the answer to the task.

As an example of a high precise task, for the task (presented in Dutch) *"Bij patient Jansen is waarschijnlijk sprake van een hersenbloeding omdat er een bloeding in en rondom de hersenen lijkt te zijn geweest. Op een CT-scan is een misvormd bloedvat te zien. Welke opties voor een operatieve behandeling heeft de neurochirurg? (Patient Jansen has probably a cerebral haemorrhage because of bleeding in and around the brain. A CT scan shows a malformed blood vessel. What options for a surgical procedure does a neurosurgeon have?)"*, the target page containing the answer also contains words such as *"hersenbloeding (cerebral haemorrhage)"*, *"misvormd bloedvat (malformed blood vessel)"*, *"CT-scan"*, *"neurochirurg (neurosurgeon)"* etc. leading to a high degree of overlap between the task description and the content of the target page (LSA value = 0.75).

Similarly, a low LSA value indicates a low overlap in the description of the task and the content pages containing the answer to the task. As an example of a low precise task, for the task (presented in Dutch), "*Fieke, pas 6 jaar, heeft behoefte aan veel water drinken en moet ook vaak plassen. Ook is ze vaak erg uitgeput. De arts stelt vast dat de waarde van haar glucose veel te hoog is. Wat zou er aan de hand kunnen zijn, wees specifiek. Welke behandeling zal de arts dan inzetten? (Fieke, 6 years old, needs to drink plenty of water and must urinate frequently. She is often very exhausted. The doctor notes that the value of its glucose is too high. What could be the problem, be specific. What treatment will deploy the doctor?)*", the words such as "*veel water drinken (drink plenty of water)*", "*vaak plassen (urinate frequently)*", "*uitgeput (exhausted)*", "*glucose veel te hoog (glucose level is too high)*" are not part of the target page containing the answer, leading to a low degree of overlap between the task description and the content of the target page (LSA value = 0.38).

Therefore, tasks with a high LSA value of task preciseness provide better, more precise contextual information pointing to the target information. Tasks with a low LSA value of task preciseness would, on the other hand, require the user to engage in higher level cognitive activities such as using his/her own knowledge to understand the task, generate relevant queries, examine search results and determine their usefulness etc. The advantage of using LSA is that it provides us an automatic and objective way of calculating overlap in meaning.

Overall, we make the following contributions in this paper:

1. We investigate the age-related differences in information seeking performance on varying levels of task difficulty.
2. We examine the age-related variations in the semantic aspects of query reformulations under varying levels of task difficulty.
3. We examine the age-related variations in the semantic aspects of queries measured across reformulations.

The remainder of this paper is organized as follows. Section 3 lists the research questions of this paper. Sections 4 and 5 give details of the experiment conducted and results obtained. Section 6 concludes the paper with a discussion on future directions.

3 Research Questions

There were three main research questions that motivated this study:

1. What impact does task difficulty, operationalized as task preciseness, have on information search performance, measured in terms of task-completion time, number of clicks, task accuracy and number of reformulations? **(RQ1)**.
2. How would the information seeking performance vary between younger and older adults on different levels of task difficulty? **(RQ2)**.
3. How does the semantic relevance of a query with the target information sought vary in relation to age and task difficulty? **(RQ3a)**. How does the semantic relevance of a query with target information sought vary in relation to age and task difficulty when analyzed at a more granular level: across reformulations? **(RQ3b)**.

4 Experiment

4.1 Method

Participants. 24 younger adults (17 males and 7 females) ranging from 18 to 27 years ($M = 21.08$, $SD = 1.9$), and 21 older adults (11 males and 10 females) ranging from 66 to 88 years ($M = 75.52$, $SD = 6.85$) participated in the study.

Design. We followed a 2 (Age: Young vs. Old) X 2 (Task Preciseness: Low vs. High) mixed design with age as between-subjects variable and task preciseness as within-subjects variable.

Material. *Websites.* Five mockup websites based on material from popular Dutch medical and health websites were built. The URLs of the real websites from which the content of our mockup websites was sourced and adapted, the number of topics, the number of pages and the maximum depth of each website are presented in Table 1.

Table 1. Details of mockup websites used.

Website	Number of topics	Number of pages	Maximum depth
Website 1[a]	6	37	6
Website 2[b]	11	194	6
Website 3[c]	10	124	5
Website 4[d]	11	38	4
Website 5[e]	10	65	5

[a]https://www.hartstichting.nl/.
[b]https://www.dokterdokter.nl/.
[c]https://www.gezondheidsplein.nl/.
[d]http://www.gezondheid.nl/.
[e]https://gezondnu.nl.

It was ensured that the websites look realistic both in terms of content (text and pictures) and the visual layout and information architecture. These five websites were indexed using Google's custom search engine[1]. We ran our experiment on mockup material that was designed by us because of the following reason: we need to know the target pages in advance in order to be able to compute task preciseness.

Material. *Information Search Tasks.* The experiment was conducted with twelve simulated information search tasks [5], all from the domain of health (because it is interesting for older adults), divided into six low precise and six high precise tasks based on the semantic similarity between the task description and the content of the target page(s). We used LSA [29] to compute the similarity value between a task description and the content of its corresponding target page(s). An independent samples t-test between the semantic similarity values obtained for low and high precise tasks showed a significant difference $t(10) = -2.2$, $p < .05$. The mean semantic similarity

---

[1] https://cse.google.com.

between the task description and the content of the target page(s) was significantly higher for high precise tasks ($M = 0.7$, $SD = 0.058$) compared to low precise tasks ($M = 0.54$, $SD = 0.15$), indicating that the amount of overlap between the task description and the corresponding target page(s) is significantly higher in high precise tasks compared to low precise tasks. The tasks were all presented in Dutch.

4.2   Procedure

Participants first filled out a demographic questionnaire in which they were asked details about their age, gender, number of hours spent on the Internet per week and number of years of experience with computers. Based on the self-reported answers, older adults ($M = 20.73$, $SD = 14.6$) were found to be spending significantly less number of hours on the Internet compared to younger adults ($M = 37.8$, $SD = 13.14$) $t(20) = 3.78$, $p < .001$. Older adults were significantly longer experienced with computers ($M = 24.7$ years, $SD = 10.92$) than younger adults ($M = 13.0$ years, $SD = 2.16$) $t(20) = -4.78$, $p < .001$.

They were next presented with two tests: a computerized version of a Dutch vocabulary test, adapted from Hill Mill Vocabulary (HMV) test [38], and a fluid intelligence test: a computerized version of the Trail Making Test (TMT Part B) [43]. The score on the vocabulary test gives us an indication of the amount of crystallized intelligence and the score on the trail making test gives us an indication of the amount of fluid intelligence. For the vocabulary test, participants were presented with 24 Dutch keywords (one followed by the other) along with six other keywords presented as multiple choice options. For each test keyword, the participants had to choose an option from the six alternatives that is closest in meaning to it. There was only one possible correct answer for each test keyword. Correct choices were scored 1 and wrong choices were scored 0. Thus the maximum possible score on this test is 24 and the minimum possible score is 0. In line with the traditional cognitive aging literature, it was found that the scores of older adults ($M = 18.52$, $SD = 2.7$) on the vocabulary test were significantly higher than that of the scores of younger adults ($M = 15.3$, $SD = 2.45$)

Fig. 1. Interface showing the (a) Google custom search interface and the (b) main screen in which the information search tasks are solved by participants

$t(20) = -3.7$, $p < .001$ indicating that they had significantly higher crystallized knowledge compared to younger adults.

For the trail making test, participants were shown 25 circles containing both numbers (1 to 13) and alphabets (A to L) on the computer screen. The participants had to click on the circles in ascending pattern alternating between numbers and alphabets (1-A-2-B-3-C and so on) starting from the number 1. If the circle clicked by a participant is right, it turned green, otherwise it turned red. We measured the time taken to finish the test correctly. In line with the traditional cognitive aging literature, significant differences were found in fluid abilities of younger and older adults. Older adults ($M = 80.75$, $SD = 38.94$) took significantly longer to finish this test ($t(20) = -4.04$, $p < .001$) than younger adults ($M = 49.37$, $SD = 31.98$) indicating that they had significantly lower fluid abilities compared to younger adults.

After the TMT test, participants were allowed a break of five minutes. They were then presented with the twelve information search tasks (six high precise and six low precise). The order of the presentation of tasks was counter balanced. Participants were first shown the task and then directed to the home page of Google's custom search engine. Participants were not allowed to use any other search engine. We show in Fig. 1a the interface of Google custom search engine and in Fig. 1b the main screen of our interface that participants used while solving the information search tasks. It was ensured the size and placement of Google logo and the search bar below it were exactly similar to the standard interface of Google search. Participants could enter queries as they normally would on any browser and the corresponding search results appeared on the next screen. Users had to always go back to the first screen (Fig. 1a) in order to reformulate a query. The task description was made available to the participant at all times in the top left corner. An empty text box was provided in the top right corner for the participant to enter his/her answer. A time limit of 8 min was set for each task beyond which the interface automatically took the participant to the next task. All the queries generated by the users, the corresponding search engine result pages and the URLs opened by them were logged in the backend using Visual Basic. We first report the results of information seeking performance in terms of task-completion time, number of clicks, task accuracy and number of reformulations. Next, we report the results of analyzing the semantic relevance of queries across reformulations with target information.

5   Analysis

5.1   Analysis of Search Performance

In this section we will examine the impact of task difficulty on search performance measured in task-completion time, number of clicks, task accuracy and number of reformulations (RQ1), as well as the impact of age (RQ2).

Measures. We used the following metrics to analyze search performance: task-completion time, number of clicks, accuracy and number of reformulations.

Task-completion time. Task-completion time is computed from the moment of opening a browser and typing in the first query to the moment of answering the question.

This includes the time it takes in typing queries, evaluating search results, clicking on one of the search results, evaluating the content of the websites opened from the search results and finally typing the answers.

Number of clicks. Number of clicks is the total number of clicks made by a participant for each task. This includes the clicks made on the search results as well as the clicks made on websites opened from the search results.

Accuracy. Accuracy is measured as 0, 0.25, 0.5, 0,75 or 1 depending on whether the participant's answer was correct (in which case the score is 1) or partially correct (in which case the score is 0.25, 0.5 or 0.75) or wrong (in which case the score is 0). Two researchers scored the participant's answers for their accuracy using the above definition and the inter-scorer reliability (Cronbach's alpha) was found to be very high (>0.8).

Number of reformulations. Number of reformulations is the total number of unique queries that a user could come up with for each task in the process of answering it (e.g., if participant added, deleted keywords or created new ones, we counted them as reformulations of query).

Results. Data of only those tasks was included in the analysis for which the participants successfully completed the tasks. 14 data points out of a total number of (12 tasks X 45 participants) = 540 data points (2.6%) were therefore dropped. For all the four dependent variables, a 2 (Age: Young vs. Old) X 2 (Task Preciseness: Low vs. High) mixed ANOVA was conducted with age as between-subjects variable and task preciseness as within-subjects variable.

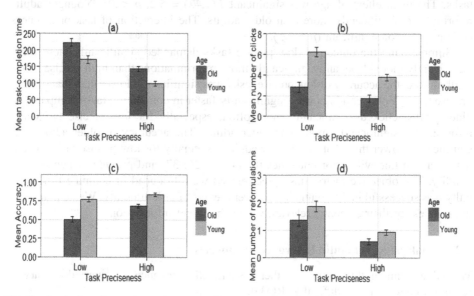

Fig. 2. Analysis of search performance in terms of (a) task-completion time, (b) clicks, (c) accuracy and (d) number of reformulations in relation to age and task preciseness

Task-completion time. The main effect of task preciseness was significant $F(1,43) =$ 84.76, $p < .001$. Low precise tasks demanded significantly more time than high precise tasks. See Fig. 2a. The main effect of age was significant $F(1,43) = 18.46$, $p < .001$. Older adults took significantly longer to complete tasks compared to younger adults. The interaction of task preciseness and age was not significant ($p > .05$).

Number of clicks. The main effect of task preciseness was significant $F(1,43) = 29.62$, $p < .001$. See Fig. 2b. Participants clicked significantly more often for low precise tasks compared to high precise tasks. The main effect of age was significant $F(1,43) =$ 31.67, $p < .001$. Younger adults clicked significantly more often than older adults. The interaction of task preciseness and age was significant $F(1,43) = 4.33$, $p < .05$. Younger adults clicked significantly more often than older adults, especially for low precise tasks.

Accuracy. The main effect of task preciseness was significant $F(1, 43) = 19.85$, $p < .001$. See Fig. 2c. Accuracy on high precise tasks was significantly higher than accuracy on low precise tasks. The main effect of age was significant $F(1,43) = 37.41$, $p < .001$. Younger adults found significantly more accurate answers than older adults. The interaction of age and task preciseness was also significant $F(1,43) = 4.45$, $p < .05$. Post-hoc tests showed that there was no effect of task preciseness on the accuracy of answers found by younger adults. The accuracy of answers found by older adults, however, dropped significantly for low precise tasks compared to high precise tasks.

Number of reformulations. The main effect of task preciseness was significant $F(1,43)$ = 40.0, $p < .001$. See Fig. 2d. Queries corresponding to low precise tasks were reformulated significantly more often than the queries corresponding to high precise tasks. The main effect of age was significant $F(1,43) = 5.2$, $p < .05$. Younger adults reformulated significantly more than older adults. The interaction of task preciseness and age was not significant ($p > .05$).

Summarizing the outcomes, low precise tasks demanded significantly more time, significantly more clicks and significantly more reformulations than high precise tasks. Furthermore, the accuracy of low precise tasks was significantly lower than that of high precise tasks. Younger adults were significantly faster in completing tasks compared to older adults, clicked significantly more often, especially for low precise tasks and reformulated significantly more than older adults. The accuracy of older adults was significantly lower than that of younger adults, especially for low precise tasks. These results are in-line with prior outcomes [8, 11, 24, 26, 37] and provide evidence to its validity. The objective metric (task preciseness) we introduced to compute task difficulty was successful in differentiating different levels of task difficulty. We next analyse the queries for their semantic relevance with the target information.

5.2   Analysis of Semantic Relevance of Queries

We will examine in this section whether the semantic relevance of a query does vary in relation to age and task difficulty (RQ3a).

Measures. Semantic relevance was used in the past as a metric to evaluate the content of hyperlink texts (to predict navigation behavior on websites) [13, 23, 25] or the snippets of the search results on the SERPs (to predict interaction behavior with search engines) [26]. However, the semantic aspects of queries are not well studied. In this section, we analyse the semantic aspects of queries using a metric called semantic relevance of query.

Semantic Relevance of Query (SRQ). For each task and each query corresponding to that task, semantic relevance was computed between the query and the target information sought using LSA [29]. We compute SRQ in the following way: we used 65,000 Dutch documents (consisting of 60% newspaper articles and 40% medical and health related articles) as a corpus to create first a semantic space in Dutch. The LSA values were then computed between a query and the target information for each task. This is repeated for all queries of the task and a mean LSA value is computed. This is repeated again for all the tasks of a participant and finally for all the participants. This metric gives us an estimate of how close in semantic similarity the queries generated by the participants are to the target information. So in general, the higher the SRQ value is, the more relevant the query is.

Results. Data of two older participant had to be dropped for this analysis due to some technical registration problems.

Semantic Relevance of Query (SRQ): A 2 (Age: Young vs. Old) X 2 (Task Preciseness: Low vs. High) mixed ANOVA was conducted with age as between-subjects variable and task preciseness as within-subjects variable. The main effects of task preciseness and age were not significant ($p > .05$). However, interestingly, the interaction of age and task preciseness was highly significant $F(1,41) = 15.26, p < .001$. Post-hoc tests showed that for low precise tasks, the mean SRQ was significantly higher for younger adults compared to older adults. For high precise tasks, it was the other way round (Fig. 3). Based on the literature, there can be two possible reasons that can explain this interaction effect: differences in fluid abilities and differences in crystallized knowledge between younger and older adults. We examined each possibility further.

(1) *Fluid ability*: We saw earlier in Sect. 4.2 that younger adults reformulated significantly more often than older adults. We could not observe this main effect when the scores on the fluid intelligence test were included as a covariate in the analysis, which indicates that, after controlling for fluid abilities, there was no significant age-related difference in the number of reformulations. This increases the possibility that fluid intelligence is also the reason behind the interaction effect observed between age and task preciseness for mean SRQ. To examine this, we included once more, the scores on the fluid intelligence test as a covariate and repeated the ANOVA analysis with mean SRQ as dependent variable. The interaction of age and task preciseness was still significant $F(1,40) = 13.53$, $p < .001$. Together with the outcome on the number of reformulations, it indicates that after controlling for the differences in fluid abilities between younger and older adults, there is no significant difference in the number of reformulations performed by younger and older adults, however, there is still a strong interaction between age and task preciseness on the mean SRQ. Therefore, fluid ability cannot explain the interaction effect.

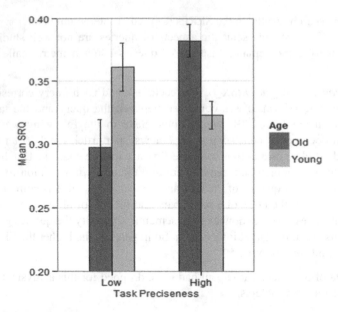

Fig. 3. Mean SRQ of queries with target information in relation to age and task preciseness

(2) *Crystallized intelligence:* We divided both younger and older adults into two groups of high and low crystallized intelligence based on the median scores on the HMV test. In the high HMV group, we had 14 younger adults and 10 older adults. In the low HMV group, we had 10 younger adults and 9 older adults. For each group, separately, we conducted a 2 (Age: Young vs. Old) X 2 (Task Preciseness: Low vs. High) mixed ANOVA with age as between-subjects variable and task preciseness as within-subjects variable. For the high HMV group, only the interaction of age and task preciseness was significant $F(1,22) = 6.72$, $p < .05$ and no other effects were significant ($p > .05$). See Fig. 4b. Post-hoc tests showed that for low precise tasks, there was no significant difference in the mean SRQ between younger and older adults ($p > .05$). Whereas, for high precise tasks, the mean SRQ was significantly higher ($p < .05$) for older adults compared to younger adults.

For the low HMV group, also, only the interaction of age and task preciseness was significant $F(1,17) = 8.32$, $p < .01$ and no other effects were significant ($p > .05$). See Fig. 4a. However, post-hoc tests revealed an interesting difference with the high HMV group. For high precise tasks, there was no significant difference in the mean SRQ between younger and older adults ($p > .05$). Whereas, for low precise tasks, the mean SRQ was significantly ($p < .05$) lower for older adults compared to younger adults.

Summarizing the outcomes relevant to RQ3a, for high precise tasks, the mean SRQ was significantly higher for older adults compared to younger adults only in the high HMV group and not in the low HMV group. Whereas for low precise tasks, the mean SRQ was significantly lower for older adults compared to younger adults only in the low HMV group and not in the high HMV group. These outcomes indicate that,

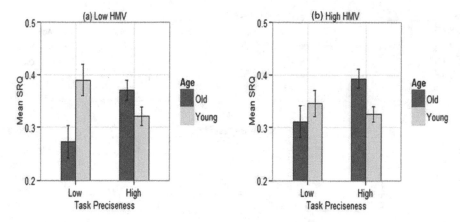

Fig. 4. Mean semantic relevance of queries with target information for participants with (a) low crystallized knowledge and (b) high crystallized knowledge (HMV) in relation to age and task preciseness

older adults, due to their higher crystallized intelligence, are able to utilize the higher contextual information present in the high precise tasks much better than younger adults. But, when it comes to low precise tasks, which demand generating own queries using one's own knowledge and understanding of the task, older adults perform poorly compared to younger adults.

5.3   Analysis of SRQ Across Reformulations

In this section we will examine the impact of age and task difficulty on the semantic relevance of a query across reformulations (RQ3b). For this we analyzed the mean semantic relevance of the queries with the target information at a more granular level by looking at each reformulation cycle separately. The first cycle corresponds to the first query, the second cycle corresponds to the second subsequent query, and the third cycle corresponds to the third query and so on. The mean semantic relevance was computed for all the queries of all the tasks of a particular type (high precise and low precise separately), generated by young and old participants *in each reformulation cycle*. To achieve higher reliability, only those cycles were considered for which there were at least 4 queries (per reformulation cycle). By doing so, only 3.2% of data was excluded from the analysis. The resulting graphs are shown in Fig. 5. It is clear from Fig. 5 that younger adults reformulated much longer, that is, more successive queries than older adults.

We tried to answer the following questions in relation to Fig. 5:

(a) How does the mean SRQ vary across reformulations for younger and older adults? And what effect does task preciseness have on it? For high precise tasks, there was no significant difference in the mean SRQ across reformulations for younger adults whereas for older adults, it decreased as they reformulated (the mean semantic relevance of the ending queries was lower than that of the starting

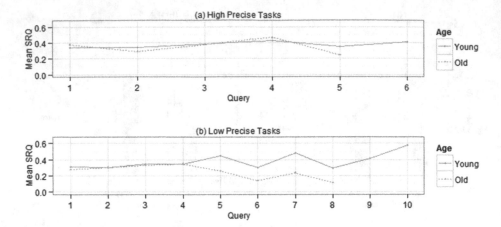

Fig. 5. Mean semantic relevance of queries with target at each reformulation cycle for (a) high precise and (b) low precise tasks

queries, $t(23) = 1.88$, $p = .07$). For low precise tasks, the mean SRQ increased across reformulations for younger adults (the mean semantic relevance of ending queries was significantly higher than that of the starting queries, $t(26) = -3.5$, $p < .005$), whereas it decreased for older adults (the mean semantic relevance of the ending queries was significantly lower than that of the starting queries, $t(20) = 2.15$, $p < .05$).

(b) Do younger and older adults start a search task with a similar SRQ? What happens to this difference as they reformulate? And what is the effect of task preciseness in this context? For high precise tasks, there was no significant age difference in the semantic relevance of either the starting or the ending queries. For low precise tasks as well, there was no significant age difference in the semantic relevance of the starting queries. However, the ending queries of younger adults had a higher mean semantic relevance than the ending queries of older adults and this difference was close to conventional significance, $t(5) = 2.2$, $p = .07$. Because of the small number of observations for low precise tasks, we examined the difference between the first four and the last four queries of a session and found no significant age difference between the first four queries. However, for the last four queries, the mean SRQ was significantly higher for younger adults compared to older adults, $t(18) = -3.22$, $p < .001$.

6   Conclusions and Discussion

This study focused on the semantics of query reformulations in relation to age and task difficulty. Task difficulty was manipulated using a metric called task preciseness defined as the degree to which the task description overlaps with the content of the target page(s) containing the answer. It is computed as the semantic similarity between the task description and the content of the target pages using LSA. We conducted an experiment in which 24 younger adults and 21 older adults solved twelve information retrieval tasks divided into two levels of task difficulty based on our task preciseness metric making use of LSA. For low precise tasks, the semantic similarity value was low and for high precise tasks, it was high. Analysis of search performance on these two groups of tasks shows significant differences: low precise tasks demanded significantly more time, significantly more clicks and significantly more reformulations than high precise tasks. Furthermore, the accuracy of low precise tasks was significantly lower than that of high precise tasks. These outcomes are in-line with outcomes reported in prior work [24] (RQ1). It indicates that our objective measure was valid and sensitive enough in differentiating two levels of task difficulty.

We next examined the effects of age (RQ2), younger adults were, as expected, significantly faster in completing tasks compared to older adults, clicked significantly more often, especially for low precise tasks and reformulated significantly more than older adults. The accuracy of older adults in task performance was significantly lower than that of younger adults, especially for low precise tasks. These outcomes are also in-line with aging-related literature [8, 11, 24, 26, 37] (RQ2). It indicates that our task preciseness metric is able to successfully simulate the effects of task difficulty on aging.

We next analysed the age-related differences in the semantic relevance of queries with target information. For low precise tasks, the mean SRQ was significantly higher for younger adults compared to older adults. For high precise tasks, it was the other way round (RQ3a). We ruled out the possibility that fluid abilities could be the underlying cause for the interaction effect by including the score on our fluid intelligence test as a covariate. The interaction effect was still found to be significant. We then checked if differences in crystallized intelligence could explain the interaction effect. We divided both younger and older adults into two groups of high and low crystallized intelligence based on the median scores on our HMV test and repeated the analysis on each group separately. For high precise tasks, the mean SRQ was significantly higher for older adults compared to younger adults only in the high HMV group and not in the low HMV group. Whereas for low precise tasks, the mean SRQ was significantly lower for older adults compared to younger adults only in the low HMV group and not in the high HMV group. These outcomes indicate that, older adults, due to their higher crystallized intelligence, are able to utilize the better specified contextual information present in the high precise tasks more efficiently than younger adults. But, when it comes to low precise tasks, which demand generating own queries using one's own knowledge and understanding of the task, older adults perform poorly compared to younger adults.

Lastly, we examined the age-related differences in the mean SRQ *across reformulations*. Younger adults were found to reformulate much longer than older adults. For older adults, the mean SRQ decreased for both low and high precise tasks. For younger adults, the mean SRQ remained constant for high precise tasks and even increased for low precise tasks. Furthermore, both younger and older adults start a session with queries of similar SRQ value. They also end a session with queries of similar SRQ value for high precise tasks. For low precise tasks at the end of a session, the mean SRQ was found to be significantly higher for younger adults compared to older adults (RQ3b). It is important to note that these outcomes are largely in line with [24].

One of the main limitations of our work is that the task preciseness metric we defined can be used only for those types of tasks for which there is a known target answer page (s). Therefore, it is necessary to know the target page(s) in advance to compute the task preciseness. Though this limits the applicability of the metric in real environments where neither the user intent nor the target answer are known before hand, it can be very useful in providing training and support to users with low information search skills. We describe how this training and support can be provided in the next section.

7   Design Implications

Based on the behavioral outcomes and the analysis of the content of search queries during reformulations, we come up with the design and methodology of constructing two types of automatic tools that can support interaction with a search engine.

7.1   Support Tool 1

We saw in the analysis of search outcomes that older adults take much longer time to finish tasks than younger adults (See Fig. 2). One of the possible reasons could be that they are unable to differentiate between a relevant and a non-relevant search result as efficiently as the younger adults do. We propose a support tool that visually highlights the most relevant search results for a given query, as shown in Fig. 6. This methodology was successfully used in the past to provide navigation support within websites [23]. We propose to extend the same methodology to generate support for interaction with a search engine.

Given a query, semantic relevance is computed between the query and each of the search results on the basis of LSA. The search result with the maximum semantic relevance is highlighted with a green arrow as shown in Fig. 6. This form of support would enable older adults to spend less mental resources in differentiating between a relevant and a non-relevant search result which in turn would lead to better accuracy.

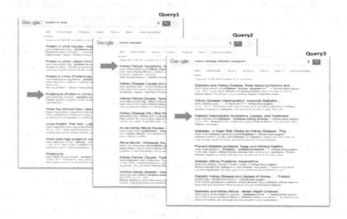

Fig. 6. Design of a support tool for interacting with a search engine that highlights the most relevant search result for a given query. (Color figure online)

7.2   Support Tool 2

We saw in the analysis of semantic relevance of queries across reformulations that the SRQ of younger adults remained constant and that of the older adults decreased as they reformulated further. In other words, older adults were going further away in semantic distance from the target information as they reformulate, which probably could be one of the reasons for their lower accuracy (See Fig. 2). This support tool is intended to ensure that a user does not digress too far away from the goal information in the form of irrelevant queries. To address this problem, we propose a second support tool that monitors - based on the LSA value - the average semantic relevance of the SERPs with the goal information derived from the query and warns the user when it falls below a threshold as shown in Fig. 7. This form of support would indicate to the users that their search results on a page are not relevant enough and they can use this information to take corrective actions such as generating a more relevant query.

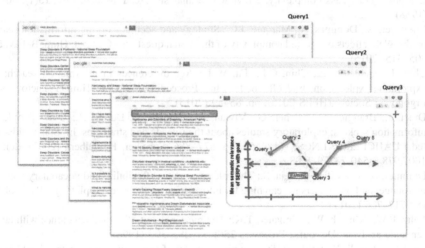

Fig. 7. Design of a support tool for interacting with a search engine that monitors the average semantic relevance of the user's queries to the goal information

The study of [24] and the results of our study indicate that such a support system would be of immense help to older adults in improving their overall search performance. We envision both tools to be used for training purposes with a large collection of tasks and their corresponding expected answers. The efficacy of such a training and support mechanism in improving the semantic relevance of search queries of older adults in real contexts needs to be empirically verified.

Acknowledgements. This research was supported by Netherlands Organization for Scientific Research (NWO), ORA Plus project MISSION (464-13-043).

References

1. Aloteibi, S., Sanderson, M.: Analyzing geographic query reformulation: an exploratory study. J. Assoc. Inf. Sci. Technol. **65**(1), 13–24 (2014)
2. Aula, A.: User study on older adults' use of the Web and search engines. Univ. Access Inf. Soc. **4**(1), 67–81 (2005)
3. Bell, D.J., Ruthven, I.: Searcher's assessments of task complexity for web searching. In: McDonald, S., Tait, J. (eds.) ECIR 2004. LNCS, vol. 2997, pp. 57–71. Springer, Heidelberg (2004). doi:10.1007/978-3-540-24752-4_5
4. Blei, D.M., Ng, A.Y., Jordan, M.I.: Latent dirichlet allocation. J. Mach. Learn. Res. **3**, 993–1022 (2003)
5. Borlund, P., Ingwersen, P.: The development of a method for the evaluation of interactive information retrieval systems. J. Doc. **53**(3), 225–250 (1997)
6. BystrÖm, K.: Information and information sources in tasks of varying complexity. J. Am. Soc. Inform. Sci. Technol. **53**(7), 581–591 (2002)
7. Campbell, D.J.: Task complexity: a review and analysis. Acad. Manag. Rev. **13**(1), 40–52 (1988)
8. Chevalier, A., Dommes, A., Marquié, J.C.: Strategy and accuracy during information search on the Web: effects of age and complexity of the search questions. Comput. Hum. Behav. **53**, 305–315 (2015)
9. Chin, J., Anderson, E., Chin, C.L., Fu, W.T.: Age differences in information search: an exploration-exploitation tradeoff model. In: Proceedings of the Human Factors and Ergonomic Society (HFES 2015), pp. 85–89 (2015)
10. Dinet, J., Brangier, E., Michel, G., Vivian, R., Battisti, S., Doller, R.: Older people as information seekers: exploratory studies about their needs and strategies. In: Stephanidis, C. (ed.) UAHCI 2007. LNCS, vol. 4554, pp. 877–886. Springer, Heidelberg (2007). doi:10. 1007/978-3-540-73279-2_98
11. Dommes, A., Chevalier, A., Lia, S.: The role of cognitive flexibility and vocabulary abilities of younger and older users in searching for information on the web. Appl. Cogn. Psychol. **25**(5), 717–726 (2011)
12. Foltz, P.W., Kintsch, W., Landauer, T.K.: The measurement of textual coherence with latent semantic analysis. Discourse Processes **25**(2–3), 285–307 (1998)
13. Fu, W.T., Pirolli, P.: SNIF-ACT: a cognitive model of user navigation on the World Wide Web. Hum.-Comput. Interact. **22**(4), 355–412 (2007)
14. Ghosh, D.: Effects of topic familiarity on query reformulation strategies. In: Proceedings of the 2016 ACM on Conference on Human Information Interaction and Retrieval, pp. 261–264. ACM (2016)
15. Gwizdka, J., Spence, I.: What can searching behavior tell us about the difficulty of information tasks? A study of Web navigation. Proc. Am. Soc. Inf. Sci. Technol. **43**(1), 1–22 (2006)
16. Horn, J.L.: The theory of fluid and crystallized intelligence in relation to concepts of cognitive psychology and aging in adulthood. In: Craik, F.I.M., Trehub, S. (eds.) Aging and Cognitive Processes. Advances in the Study of Communication and Affect, vol. 8, pp. 237–278. Springer, Boston (1982). doi:10.1007/978-1-4684-4178-9_14
17. Horn, J.L., Cattell, R.B.: Age differences in fluid and crystallized intelligence. Acta Physiol. **26**, 107–129 (1967)
18. Hu, R., Lu, K., Joo, S.: Effects of topic familiarity and search skills on query reformulation behavior. Proc. Am. Soc. Inf. Sci. Technol. **50**(1), 1–9 (2013)

19. Huang, J., Efthimiadis, E.N.: Analyzing and evaluating query reformulation strategies in web search logs. In: Proceedings of the 18th ACM Conference on Information and Knowledge Management, pp. 77–86. ACM (2009)
20. Jansen, B.J., Booth, D.L., Spink, A.: Patterns of query reformulation during Web searching. J. Assoc. Inf. Sci. Technol. **60**(7), 1358–1371 (2009)
21. Jansen, B.J., Spink, A., Narayan, B.: Query modifications patterns during web searching. In: Fourth International Conference on Information Technology, 2007. ITNG 2007, pp. 439–444. IEEE (2007)
22. Jiang, J., Ni, C.: What affects word changes in query reformulation during a task-based search session? In: Proceedings of the 2016 ACM on Conference on Human Information Interaction and Retrieval, pp. 111–120. ACM (2016)
23. Juvina, I., van Oostendorp, H.: Modeling semantic and structural knowledge in Web navigation. Discourse Processes **45**(4–5), 346–364 (2008)
24. Karanam, S., van Oostendorp, H.: Age-related differences in the content of search queries when reformulating. In: Proceedings of the 2016 CHI Conference on Human Factors in Computing Systems, pp. 5720–5730. ACM (2016)
25. Karanam, S., van Oostendorp, H., Fu, W.T.: Performance of computational cognitive models of web-navigation on real websites. J. Inf. Sci. **42**(1), 94–113 (2016)
26. Karanam, S., van Oostendorp, H., Sanchiz, M., Chevalier, A., Chin, J., Fu, W.T.: Modeling and predicting information search behavior. In: Proceedings of the 5th International Conference on Web Intelligence, Mining and Semantics, article no. 7. ACM (2015)
27. Kim, J.: Task as a predictable indicator for information seeking behavior on the Web. ProQuest (2006)
28. Kinley, K., Tjondronegoro, D., Partridge, H., Edwards, S.: Human-computer interaction: the impact of users' cognitive styles on query reformulation behaviour during web searching. In: Proceedings of the 24th Australian Computer-Human Interaction Conference, pp. 299–307. ACM (2012)
29. Landauer, T.K., McNamara, D.S., Dennis, S., Kintsch, W.: Handbook of Latent Semantic Analysis. Erlbaum, Mahwah (2007)
30. Li, Y.: Exploring the relationships between work task and search task in information search. J. Am. Soc. Inform. Sci. Technol. **60**(2), 275–291 (2009)
31. Liu, C., Gwizdka, J., Liu, J., Xu, T., Belkin, N.J.: Analysis and evaluation of query reformulations in different task types. Proc. Am. Soc. Inf. Sci. Technol. **47**(1), 1–9 (2010)
32. Lund, K., Burgess, C.: Producing high-dimensional semantic spaces from lexical co-occurrence. Behav. Res. Methods Instr. Comput. **28**(2), 203–208 (1996)
33. Mellor, D., Firth, L., Moore, K.: Can the Internet improve the well-being of the elderly? Ageing Int. **32**(1), 25–42 (2008)
34. Millis, K., Magliano, J., Wiemer-Hastings, K., Todaro, S., McNamara, D.S.: Assessing and improving comprehension with latent semantic analysis. In: Handbook of Latent Semantic Analysis, pp. 207–225 (2007)
35. Monchaux, S., Amadieu, F., Chevalier, A., Mariné, C.: Query strategies during information searching: effects of prior domain knowledge and complexity of the information problems to be solved. Inf. Process. Manage. **51**(5), 557–569 (2015)
36. Puerta Melguizo, M.C., Vidya, U., Can Oostendorp, H.: Seeking information online: the influence of menu type, navigation path complexity and spatial ability on information gathering tasks. Behav. Inf. Technol. **31**(1), 59–70 (2012)
37. Queen, T.L., Hess, T.M., Ennis, G.E., Dowd, K., Grühn, D.: Information search and decision making: effects of age and complexity on strategy use. Psychol. Aging **27**(4), 817 (2012)
38. Raven, J.C., Court, J.H.: Raven's Progressive Matrices and Vocabulary Scales. Oxford Psychologists Press, Oxford (1998)

39. Rieh, S.Y.: Analysis of multiple query reformulations on the web: the interactive information retrieval context. Inf. Process. Manage. **42**(3), 751–768 (2006)
40. Shute, S.J., Smith, P.J.: Knowledge-based search tactics. Inf. Process. Manage. **29**(1), 29–45 (1993)
41. Slegers, K., Van Boxtel, M.P., Jolles, J.: Computer use in older adults: determinants and the relationship with cognitive change over a 6 year episode. Comput. Hum. Behav. **28**(1), 1–10 (2012)
42. Sloan, M., Yang, H., Wang, J.: A term-based methodology for query reformulation understanding. Inf. Retr. J. **18**(2), 145–165 (2015)
43. Strauss, E., Sherman, E.M., Spreen, O.: A compendium of neuropsychological tests: administration, norms, and commentary. American Chemical Society (2006)
44. Teevan, J., Adar, E., Jones, R., Potts, M.A.: Information re-retrieval: repeat queries in Yahoo's logs. In: Proceedings of the 30th Annual International ACM SIGIR Conference on Research and Development in Information Retrieval, pp. 151–158. ACM (2007)
45. Turney, P.D.: Mining the Web for synonyms: PMI-IR versus LSA on TOEFL. In: De Raedt, L., Flach, P. (eds.) ECML 2001. LNCS, vol. 2167, pp. 491–502. Springer, Heidelberg (2001). doi:10.1007/3-540-44795-4_42
46. Vakkari, P.: Task-based information searching. Ann. Rev. Inf. Sci. Technol. **37**(1), 413–464 (2003)
47. van Oostendorp, H., Madrid, R., Melguizo, M.C.P.: The effect of menu type and task complexity on information retrieval performance. Ergon. Open J. **2**, 64–71 (2009)
48. Wang, J.J., Kaufman, A.S.: Changes in fluid and crystallized intelligence across the 20-to 90-year age range on the K-BIT. J. Psychoeduc. Assess. **11**(1), 29–37 (1993)
49. Wildemuth, B., Freund, L., Toms, E.G.: Untangling search task complexity and difficulty in the context of interactive information retrieval studies. J. Doc. **70**(6), 1118–1140 (2014)
50. Wolfe, M.B., Schreiner, M.E., Rehder, B., Laham, D., Foltz, P.W., Kintsch, W., Landauer, T.K.: Learning from text: matching readers and texts by latent semantic analysis. Discourse Processes **25**(2–3), 309–336 (1998)
51. Wood, E., De Pasquale, D., Mueller, J.L., Archer, K., Zivcakova, L., Walkey, K., Willoughby, T.: Exploration of the relative contributions of domain knowledge and search expertise for conducting Internet searches. Ref. Libr. **57**(3), 182–204 (2016)
52. Youmans, R.J., Bellows, B., Gonzalez, C.A., Sarbone, B., Figueroa, I.J.: Designing for the wisdom of elders: age related differences in online search strategies. In: Stephanidis, C., Antona, M. (eds.) UAHCI 2013. LNCS, vol. 8010, pp. 240–249. Springer, Heidelberg (2013). doi:10.1007/978-3-642-39191-0_27

Could People with Stereo-Deficiencies Have a Rich 3D Experience Using HMDs?

Sonia Cárdenas-Delgado[1], M.-Carmen Juan[1(✉)],
Magdalena Méndez-López[2], and Elena Pérez-Hernández[3]

[1] Instituto Universitario de Automática e Informática Industrial,
Universitat Politècnica de València, Camino de Vera, s/n, 46022 València, Spain
{scardenas,mcarmen}@dsic.upv.es
[2] Departamento de Psicología y Sociología,
Universidad de Zaragoza, Saragossa, Spain
mmendez@unizar.es
[3] Departamento de Psicología Evolutiva y de la Educación,
Universidad Autónoma de Madrid, Madrid, Spain
elena.perezh@uam.es

Abstract. People with stereo-deficiencies usually have problems for the perception of depth using stereo devices. This paper presents a study that involves participants who did not have stereopsis and participants who had stereopsis. The two groups of participants were exposed to a maze navigation task in a 3D environment in two conditions, using a HMD and a large stereo screen. Fifty-nine adults participated in our study. From the results, there were no statistically significant differences for the performance on the task between the participants with stereopsis and those without stereopsis. We found statistically significant differences between the two conditions in favor of the HMD for the two groups of participants. The participants who did not have stereopsis and could not perceive 3D when looking at the Lang 1 Stereotest did have the illusion of depth perception using the HMD. The study suggests that for the people who did not have stereopsis, the head tracking largely influences the 3D experience.

Keywords: HMD · Large stereo screen · Virtual reality · Stereopsis · 3D experience · Stereoblindness · Stereo-deficiency · Head tracking

1 Introduction

Stereopsis refers to the perception of depth through visual information that is obtained from the two eyes of an individual with normally developed binocular vision [1]. The perception of depth is also possible with information visible from only one eye. In this case, the person uses differences in object size and motion parallax in order to have such perception [2]. However, according to Barry [3], the impression of depth cannot be as vivid as that obtained from binocular disparities.

Virtual Reality (VR) has received numerous definitions. According to LaViola [4], "VR is a user interface technology that provides an immersive and realistic, three dimensional computer simulated world". Dionisio et al. [5] defined VR as a

© IFIP International Federation for Information Processing 2017
Published by Springer International Publishing AG 2017. All Rights Reserved
R. Bernhaupt et al. (Eds.): INTERACT 2017, Part I, LNCS 10513, pp. 97–116, 2017.
DOI: 10.1007/978-3-319-67744-6_7

computer-generated simulation of three-dimensional objects or environments with seemingly real, direct, or physical user interaction. Different devices or systems can be used to display a virtual environment. Different taxonomies have been established according to the level of immersion. For example, Muhanna [6] classified the VR systems as:

- Basic: hand-based and monitor-based.
- Partially immersive: wall projectors, immersive-desk, and monocular head-based.
- Fully immersive: room-based (vehicle simulation and CAVE) and binocular head-based.

In a subject of Virtual and Augmented Reality of a Master's program in Computer Science, we observed that students who did not have stereopsis (checked using the Lang 1 Stereotest) did not have perception of depth when using VR devices such as a CAVE, a large stereo screen and even with autostereoscopic displays. However, the same students had the sensation of depth using the Oculus Rift. This motivated us to design a study to compare the Oculus Rift with another stereo device that we have already used in order to test our hypothesis. The visualization system chosen for the comparison was a large stereo screen. However, other Head-Mounted Displays (HMD) or different visualization systems (CAVE, autostereoscopic displays, or other HMDs) could also be used. Since the appearance of the first HMD developed by Sutherland [7], many different commercial devices and non-commercial prototypes have been developed (e.g., Oculus Rift, HTC VIVE, Google Cardboard, Samsung Gear VR, or Microsoft HoloLens). Therefore, other comparisons could be considered in the future work.

In this paper, we present a study in which users were exposed to a maze navigation task in a 3D environment in two conditions: using a HMD (Oculus Rift) and using polarization glasses with a large stereo screen. Two groups of users participated in our study: a group who did not have stereopsis (no stereopsis), and a group who had stereopsis (stereopsis). Our main hypothesis was that the users that did not have stereopsis would have a statistically richer 3D experience with the HMD than with a large stereo screen.

2 Background

2.1 Stereopsis Recovery

Several previous works have focused on the idea of restoring stereopsis in adults. Two cases in which this recovering was described were experienced by Barry [3] and Bridgeman [8]. Barry [3] recovered from strabismus after visual therapy in adulthood. Bridgeman [8], with stereo-deficiency, acquired stereopsis when watching a 3D movie. Besides these two personal experiences, other works have also been interested in stereopsis recovery. For example, Ding & Levi [9] carried out a case study involving 5 adults who were stereoblind or stereoanomalous. After perceptual learning, the participants showed substantial recovery of stereopsis. Ding & Levi [9] concluded that "some human adults deprived of normal binocular vision can recover stereopsis at least partially". In the same year, Astle et al. [10] carried out another case study involving two humans with anisometropic amblyopia whose stereopsis also improved after following a training course. In 2014, Xi et al. [11] carried out a case study involving 11 participants with anisometropic or ametropic amblyopia. Those participants were trained with anaglyphic textures with different disparities. They also experienced stereopsis improvement. Vedamurthy et al. [12] trained adults who were stereo blind or stereodeficient using a natural visuomotor task (a Virtual Reality environment). They conclude that "some adults deprived of normal binocular vision and insensitive to the disparity information can, with appropriate experience, recover access to more reliable stereoscopic information". Therefore, all these previous works indicate that human adults can recover or acquire stereopsis in adulthood.

2.2 Users' Perceptions

In this section, we focus on users' perceptions in which two different visualization devices have been compared. To our knowledge, no previous work has studied users' perceptions considering people with stereo vision versus stereo blindness. However, several studies of users' perceptions have been carried out with groups in which specific problems had not been defined.

With regard to the comparison between different HMDs, Young et al. [13] compared the Oculus Rift and a high-cost Nvis SX60 HMD, which differ in resolution, field of view, and inertial properties, among other factors. In this comparison, both HMDs were fully immersive. Young et al. [13] assessed simulator sickness and presence. They found that the Oculus Rift consistently outperformed the Nvis SX60 HMD, but some people were more subject to simulator sickness with the Oculus Rift. Buń et al. [14] used the nVisor MH60 V HMD, the Oculus Rift DK1, and Samsung Gear VR with students of medical disciplines to learn anatomy. In this study, the three HMDs were fully immersive. Twenty students from the Poznan University of Technology participated in a study concerning perception. The participants were asked to select the preferred HMD and interaction method. Most of them chose the Gear VR in combination with Kinect and gamepad as the preferred solution.

Other works have compared HMDs with different visualization systems. For example, Tan et al. [15] presented a study involving 10 participants who played a first-person shooter game using the Oculus Rift and a traditional desktop computer-monitor. In that study, the authors compared a fully immersive VR system with a basic or low immersive VR system. They concluded that the participants had heightened experiences, a richer engagement with passive game elements, a higher degree of flow, and a deeper immersion with the Oculus Rift than on a traditional desktop computer-monitor. However, they also mentioned the problems of cybersickness and lack of control. Gutiérrez-Maldonado et al. [16] developed a VR system to train diagnostic skills for eating disorders and compared two visualization systems (Oculus Rift DK1 vs. a laptop with a stereoscopic 15.6-inch screen). In that study, the authors also compared a fully immersive VR system with a basic or low immersive VR system. Fifty-two undergraduate students participated in their study. No differences were found in either effectiveness or usability with regard to skills training in a psychopathological exploration of eating disorders through virtual simulations.

Juan & Pérez [17] carried out a comparison study of the levels of presence and anxiety in an acrophobic environment that was viewed using a Computer Automatic Virtual Environment (CAVE) and a 5DT HMD. In this environment, the floor fell away, and the walls rose up. To determine whether either of the two visualization systems induced a greater sense of presence/anxiety in non-phobic users, an experiment comparing the two visualization systems was carried out. Twenty-five non-phobic participants took part in their study. The CAVE induced a significantly higher level of presence in users. Their results indicated that both visualization systems provoked anxiety, but that the CAVE provoked more anxiety than the HMD.

Other works have compared different versions of the same environment using HMDs. For example, Davis et al. [18] used the Oculus Rift and compared two different virtual roller coasters, each with different levels of fidelity. They found that the more realistic roller coaster with higher levels of visual flow had a significantly greater chance of inducing cybersickness.

Therefore, previous works have compared HMDs with low and fully immersive VR systems. In contrast, we compare a HMD with a partially immersive VR system.

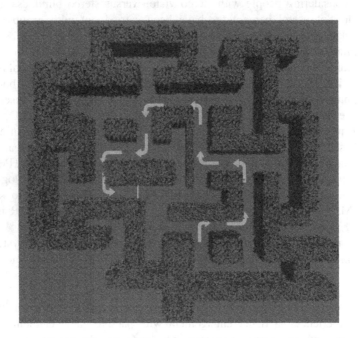

Fig. 1. Virtual environment. Maze viewed from above.

3   Virtual Environment

The virtual environment is based on the Cincinnati Water Maze [19]. The virtual environment is a maze with nine intersections (see Fig. 1). The maze has a wall of hedges that are two meters high and pathways of grass that are two meters wide. A first-person avatar represents the participant's point of view (the participant sees the maze through the eyes of the avatar). Therefore, this avatar personifies the movements of the user in the maze. The participant controls the avatar with a gamepad. At each intersection, there is an arrow on the ground; the color of the arrow and the direction it points depend on the scene. The system has three stages: habituation, retention, and testing. The habituation stage has an environment with a short route. The path has four intersections and a straight road at the end. This is a trial stage to train participants to handle the system properly. The retention stage consists of an environment in which the participant follows another route with nine intersections and is guided by green arrows. The participant must learn the route. The testing stage has yellow arrows that show options at each intersection. The participant must remember and follow the same path that was followed in the retention stage. When the participant makes a mistake, the system shows a warning message and they are automatically relocated back to the starting position. Each participant has five attempts to reach the end of the maze. The time increases with the number of attempts. The experience lasts around six minutes. However, the time could increase based on the number of attempts. A more detailed description of the virtual environment can be found in [20].

3.1 Hardware and Software

The virtual environment ran on an Intel Core i7 computer, 3.5 GHz processor with 16 GB RAM, an NVIDIA GeForce GTX-970 with a video card of 4 GB, and Windows 8 Operating System. For the development of the system, we used Unity Edition Professional (http://unity3d.com), version 4.6.0f3 as the game engine, and C# and Java-Script as the programming languages. Blender was used to create and modify the 3D models that were included in the environment. Adobe Photoshop was used to modify textures and images.

Two loudspeakers were used to provide messages and instructions to the participants. AB-Move Gamepad BG Revenge was used as the input device. Thanks to the gamepad, the user controlled the avatar, indicating the direction to follow (i.e., go forward, turn to the right, or turn to the left). The gamepad was integrated into the system thanks to the controller Input Manager of Unity, which enabled functions and personalized the use of the device in the two visualization systems. The collision of objects in the environment was controlled to keep the participants from colliding with the walls.

3.2 Oculus Rift

We used an Oculus Rift DK2. It has a resolution of 960×1080 per eye, a field-of-view of 100 nominal, a weight of 0.32 kg, and an optical frame rate of 75 Hz. It has head tracking and positional tracking. Figure 2 shows a view of the Maze with the Oculus Rift. Figure 3 shows a user handling the Oculus Rift.

The head tracking of the Oculus Rift was used to let the user to look around in the position where he/she was. To integrate the Oculus Rift with the system, we used the plugins provided by the manufacturer (Oculus SDK 0.4.2, Oculus Runtime, and Oculus Unity Integration Package).

Fig. 2. View of the Maze with the Oculus Rift.

Fig. 3. A participant carrying out the task with the gamepad.

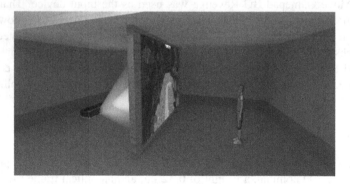

Fig. 4. Testing room for the large stereo screen condition.

3.3   Large Stereo Screen

A large stereo screen was placed in a room with some special characteristics. First, the room was divided into two areas (the projection area and the user area); these areas were separated by a wall and a translucent 120-inch screen. Figure 4 shows a representation of this room. Two projectors placed in the projection area project two images onto the screen. Specifically, we used two InFocus IN1503 short throw projectors. These projectors could generate an image of 177 × 111 cm. at a throw distance of 140 cm. They produced a brightness of 3000 ANSI lumens and had a resolution of 1280 × 800 pixels. These two images are polarized and a 3D image is created. The user must wear linear polarized 3D glasses in order to see the image correctly. Figure 5 shows a user in the large stereo screen condition. A library was developed to create the 3D sensation. This library allows the user to have the right point of view by placing the two virtual cameras to simulate the two eyes of the user. The cameras are located at a standard intraocular distance (63 mm) [21] and at a field of view of 60°. This value for the field of view was calculated from the real dimensions of the screen and the distance between the participant and the screen. This condition did not include head tracking.

Fig. 5. A participant in front of the large stereo screen handling the gamepad.

4 Study

All of the participants were duly informed about the purpose of the study before each session. They signed the Informed Consent for participation, and the study was conducted according to the principles stated in the Declaration of Helsinki. The Ethics Committee of the Universitat Politècnica de València (UPV) approved this study.

Before each session, all of the participants filled out the Personal Data Questionnaire (PDQ). Afterwards, they were checked for stereopsis using the Lang 1 Stereotest cards [22, 23]. The participants were divided into two groups. Each group participated in only one session and was exposed to only one of the two different conditions. One group used the HMD and the other group used the large stereo screen (intersubject analysis). Finally, when they had finished, they completed the questionnaire about previous experiences (PEQ), and another questionnaire (PQ) to know their perceptions about interaction, the 3D sensations, and satisfaction. Most of the questions of the PQ were adapted from the Presence Questionnaire proposed by Witmer & Singer [24].

4.1 Participants

Students of the UPV participated in this study (N = 59; mean age 25.83 ± 3.97; 35 men and 24 women). A recruitment campaign was conducted to find the participants by advertising within the campus facilities. The participants were randomly assigned to each condition. Since the task was the same, each participant used only one of the two conditions. The participants were assigned randomly to two groups (30 participants for the HMD condition, and 29 for the large stereo screen condition).

4.2 Control Variables

To carry out the current study, two control variables were defined. The main goal was to establish homogeneous groups in terms of previous experiences with 3D and to determine which participants had stereopsis and which ones did not.

First, the PEQ was used to determine whether the participants of both groups had previous experience with 3D and video games. The PrevExperience variable combines the answers to questions related to previous experience (Table 1). The questionnaire used a Likert scale [from 1 to 5 (1 being 'none' or ('extremely low'), and 5 being 'very high')]. For the group of participants who did not have stereopsis, the mean for the HMD condition was 3.09 ± 0.61, and the mean for the large stereo screen condition was 2.78 ± 0.58. These means indicate that those participants had moderate experience with 3D. For the group of participants who had stereopsis, the mean for the HMD condition was 3.10 ± 0.59, and the mean for the large stereo screen condition was 2.96 ± 0.61. These means indicate that those participants had moderate experience with 3D. There were no statistically significant differences in previous 3D experiences between the HMD condition and the large stereo screen condition ($U = 34$, $Z = 0.714$, $p = 0.483$, $r = 0.184$). This result demonstrates the homogeneity of the sample regarding this aspect.

Table 1. Questionnaire on previous experience with 3D.

#Q	Questions
QX1	I perform activities in 3D
QX2	I play 3D games
QX3	I see movies in 3D

Second, the Lang 1 Stereotest was applied to determine which participants had stereopsis and which ones did not. Brown et al. [23] administered the Lang 1 Stereotest to 292 participants and concluded that this test correctly identified people with vision defects associated with reduced stereopsis and that it was appropriate for vision screening of both adults and children. The Lang 1 Stereotest has three objects. We followed the protocol suggested by Brown et al. [23]. A participant passed the test when he/she had 3/3 positive responses, 3/3 partial positive responses, or 2/3 positive and/or partial positive responses where the negative response was at the 550" level. A participant failed the test when he/she had 3/3 negative responses and 2/3 negative responses where the single positive or partial positive response was at the 1200" level.

In our sample, 22 participants were successful in the Lang 1 Stereotest for the HMD condition (73.33%), and 22 participants were successful for the large stereo screen condition (75.86%). Therefore, 8 participants failed the Lang 1 Stereotest in the HMD condition (26.67%), and 7 participants failed in the large stereo screen condition (24.14%). These results ensure an equivalent number of participants in the two conditions. In Brown et al.'s study [23], 6.5% of the participants failed the test. Other studies have indicated that this percentage can be between 5% and 10% [25], or as high as 34% in older subjects [26]. In our case, this percentage is considerably higher than in normal population. This is because we especially invited people who we knew did not have stereopsis to participate in our study. The objective was to have the sample of participants without stereopsis as large as possible to compare them with the population with stereopsis.

4.3   Procedure

The study compared the participant's perceptions using a 3D environment in two conditions (HMD and a large stereo screen). The same VR environment was used with each condition. In order to move around the virtual environment, the participants held a gamepad in their hands. In the HMD condition, the participants were seated in a chair and wore an Oculus Rift DK2 with head tracking enabled. The lenses of the HMD were positioned properly for each user's eyes. This adjustment was achieved by turning the lateral adjuster to fix the separation between the participant's eyes (inter-pupillary distance). The HMD was kept firmly in place by strapping it tightly to the participant's face.

In the large stereo screen condition, the participants were standing in front of the large, high-resolution display. Displacement and rotation depend on the decision points shown in the virtual environment. Each participant was instructed about how to use the gamepad, the HMD, and the polarized glasses. The participant was also urged to pay attention at each stage of the exposure. Each participant was instructed to remember the route in order to find a way out of the maze.

After ending the session, the participants answered a questionnaire on the interaction with the system, 3D sensations, and satisfaction (PQ). The questions of the questionnaire are shown in Table 2.

5   Results

This section presents the analysis of the data collected from this study. Data normality was checked and the pertinent statistical tests were carried out based on those results. The Shapiro-Wilk and Anderson-Darling are inferential tests that were used to check data normality. Since the tests reported that our data did not fit the normal distribution, non-parametric statistical tests (the Mann-Whitney U test) were applied for the Likert questions to determine whether or not there were statistically significant differences for our questionnaire (Table 2). There were two groups: one group used the HMD and the other group used the large stereo screen. These two groups were also divided into two different populations, those participants who had stereopsis and those participants who

Table 2. Questionnaire on the interaction, 3D-sensations, and satisfaction. The questionnaire used a Likert scale [from 1 to 5 (1 being 'none' or ('extremely low') and 5 being 'very high')].

# QI	Interaction
QI1	How natural was the mechanism that controlled movement through the environment?
QI2	How natural did your interactions with the 3D environment seem?
QI3	How well could you concentrate on the required tasks rather than on the mechanisms used to perform those tasks?
QI4	The environment was easy to use
# QE	Virtual Environment and 3D-sensations
QE1	How involved were you in the 3D virtual environment experience?
QE2	How much did your experiences in the virtual environment seem consistent with your real-world experiences?
QE3	How closely were you able to examine objects?
QE4	How quickly did you adjust to the 3D virtual environment experience?
QE5	At times it seems to me that objects have depth?
QE6	My 3D experience compared to others previous 3D experiences has been ...
# QS	Satisfaction
QS1	To what degree did you feel general discomfort during or at the end of the task?
QS2	In general, rate the experience of movement and interaction with the virtual environment
QS3	Rate your visualization experience from 1–5 (1-least satisfying)

did not have stereopsis. The data from the study were analyzed using the statistical open source toolkit R (http://www.r-project.org) with the R-Studio IDE (http://www.rstudio.com).

The results of our questionnaire were grouped by Interaction, 3D Sensations, and Satisfaction. The results are shown in Tables 3, 4, 5, 6, 7 and 8.

5.1   Interaction Outcomes

As Tables 3 and 4 show, no statistically significant differences were found in the QI2–QI4 questions between the HMD condition and the large stereo screen condition. The participants thought that the interaction with the 3D environment seemed natural (QI2). The users were concentrated on the assigned task rather than on the mechanisms used to perform it (QI3). The participants did not perceive significant differences for ease of use (QI4). However, there was a statistically significant difference in QI1 in favor of the HMD. In Q1, the participants perceived the mechanism, which controlled movement through the environment, to be more natural. These results were obtained for the two groups of participants (stereopsis vs. no stereopsis).

For the HMD condition and the two population groups (stereopsis vs. no stereopsis), no statistically significant differences were found in the QI1–QI4 questions. The same result was obtained for the large stereo screen condition and the two population groups.

Table 3. Means and Standard deviations, Mann-Whitney U test analysis, and r effect size between the HMD condition and the large stereo screen condition of those who did not have stereopsis for the questions about interaction. The ** indicates statistically significant differences.

# Q	HMD	Large stereo screen	U	Z	p	r
QI1	4.38 ± 0.52	1.14 ± 0.38	56.0	3.426	<0.001**	0.885
QI2	4.88 ± 0.35	4.43 ± 1.13	33.0	0.829	0.446	0.214
QI3	4.00 ± 0.93	3.86 ± 0.69	30.5	0.308	0.962	0.079
QI4	4.13 ± 0.64	3.14 ± 1.22	41.5	1.662	0.101	0.429

Table 4. Means and Standard deviations, Mann-Whitney U test analysis, and r effect size between the HMD condition and the large stereo screen condition of those who had stereopsis for the questions about interaction. The ** indicates statistically significant differences.

# Q	HMD	Large stereo screen	U	Z	p	r
QI1	4.00 ± 0.93	1.14 ± 0.35	481.0	5.906	<0.001**	0.890
QI2	4.64 ± 0.73	4.36 ± 0.66	307.0	1.757	0.101	0.265
QI3	4.09 ± 0.68	3.59 ± 0.91	319.0	1.952	0.055	0.294
QI4	4.00 ± 0.93	3.77 ± 1.31	255.5	0.332	0.747	0.050

5.2   3D-Sensation Outcomes

To determine the outcomes for 3D sensations, the participants answered questions QE1–QE6 after their exposure to the virtual environment in two conditions (HMD vs. large stereo screen). Statistically significant differences were found in all six questions in favor of the HMD. These statistically significant differences can be observed for the group of participants who did not have stereopsis (Table 5 and Fig. 6) and those who had (Table 6 and Fig. 6). Overall, the HMD allowed the participants to feel a more enhanced experience than the large stereo screen for the two groups (stereopsis vs. no stereopsis).

For the HMD condition and the two groups of population (stereopsis vs. no stereopsis), no statistically significant differences were found in the QE1–QE6 questions. For the large stereo screen condition, no statistically significant differences were found for any of the questions, except for QE3 in favor of the participants who had stereopsis ($U = 32$, $Z = -2.687$, $p = 0.011$, $r = 0.499$). Although the means of the two groups for QE3 are low, the participants who had stereopsis were able to closely examine objects to a significantly greater extent than the participants who did not have stereopsis. Moreover, the participants who had stereopsis in the large stereo condition scored higher in all the questions (except QE1) than those who did not have stereopsis.

In QS1, there were no statistically significant differences between the two conditions for the participants who did not have stereopsis regarding general discomfort during or at the end of the session (see Table 7). However, in QS1, there was a statistically significant difference between the two conditions and for the participants who had stereopsis (see Table 8). The values of the means for the two groups show that the participants who had stereopsis felt greater general discomfort with the HMD.

Table 5. Means and Standard deviations, Mann-Whitney U test analysis, and r effect size between the HMD condition and the large stereo screen condition of those who did not have stereopsis for the questions about 3D sensations. The ** indicates statistically significant differences.

# Q	HMD	Large stereo screen	U	Z	p	r
QE1	4.63 ± 0.52	3.57 ± 0.54	50.0	2.750	0.009**	0.710
QE2	3.62 ± 0.74	1.14 ± 0.38	56.0	3.392	<0.001**	0.876
QE3	3.88 ± 0.84	1.14 ± 0.38	56.0	3.376	<0.001**	0.872
QE4	4.38 ± 0.74	3.43 ± 0.54	46.5	2.277	0.034**	0.588
QE5	4.00 ± 0.54	2.29 ± 0.76	54.5	3.210	<0.001**	0.829
QE6	3.75 ± 0.89	1.71 ± 1.11	50.5	2.726	0.008**	0.704

Table 6. Means and Standard deviations, Mann-Whitney U test analysis, and r effect size between the HMD condition and the large stereo screen condition of those who had stereopsis for the questions about 3D sensations. The ** indicates statistically significant differences.

# Q	HMD	Large stereo screen	U	Z	p	r
QE1	4.18 ± 0.96	3.50 ± 1.01	338.0	2.365	0.018**	0.357
QE2	3.68 ± 1.13	1.18 ± 0.40	465.0	5.510	<0.001**	0.831
QE3	3.96 ± 0.84	1.73 ± 0.46	476.0	5.712	<0.001**	0.861
QE4	4.46 ± 0.51	3.50 ± 0.91	385.0	3.590	<0.001**	0.541
QE5	4.14 ± 0.77	2.64 ± 1.18	405.0	3.964	<0.001**	0.598
QE6	3.96 ± 1.09	1.86 ± 1.21	423.5	4.398	<0.001**	0.663

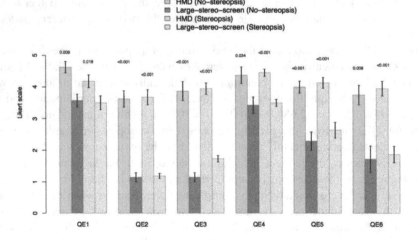

Fig. 6. Participants who had stereopsis and participants who did not have stereopsis (HMD vs. large stereo screen). Barplot and error bars for QE1–QE6 questions. Confidence interval of 95%. Statistically significant differences are found in all questions. Satisfaction outcomes

Table 7. Means and Standard deviations, Mann-Whitney U test analysis, and r effect size between the HMD condition and the large stereo screen condition of those who did not have stereopsis for the questions about satisfaction. The ** indicates statistically significant differences.

# Q	HMD	Large stereo screen	U	Z	p	r
QS1	1.50 ± 0.53	1.14 ± 0.37	38.0	1.414	0.282	0.365
QS2	3.75 ± 0.46	1.43 ± 0.53	56.0	3.395	<0.001**	0.877
QS3	4.38 ± 0.52	3.57 ± 0.53	46.0	2.372	0.039**	0.612

Table 8. Means and Standard deviations, Mann-Whitney U test analysis, and r effect size between the HMD condition and the large stereo screen condition of those who had stereopsis for the questions about satisfaction. The ** indicates statistically significant differences.

# Q	HMD	Large stereo screen	U	Z	p	r
QS1	1.55 ± 0.80	1.14 ± 0.35	311.0	2.084	0.055**	0.314
QS2	4.09 ± 0.81	3.32 ± 0.48	369.0	3.241	<0.001**	0.489
QS3	4.45 ± 0.74	3.59 ± 0.85	371.5	3.209	<0.001**	0.484

In QS2 and QS3, the results show that there were statistically significant differences between the two conditions in favor of the HMD (see Tables 7 and 8). This means that, in general, the participants had a more satisfying experience using the HMD.

For the HMD condition and the two population groups (stereopsis vs. no stereopsis), no statistically significant differences were found in the QS1–QS3 questions. For the large stereo screen condition, no statistically significant differences were found for any of the questions, except for QS2 in favor of the participants who had stereopsis. This result for QS2 implies that the participants who had stereopsis rated the experience of movement and interaction with the virtual environment significantly higher than the participants who did not have stereopsis. When comparing the HMD column of Tables 7 and 8 (HMD condition, no stereopsis vs. stereopsis), the participants who had stereopsis scored higher on all the questions than the participants who did not have stereopsis. The results for the comparison of the large stereo screen column were similar.

5.3 Task Outcomes

To determine the performance on the task, we calculated the following: the time for completion of the task in seconds (Time), the number of head turns by the participant performed at intersections (Headings), the number of attempts made to successfully complete the path (Attempts), and the score (Score). The Score was obtained by adding the number of correct directions chosen in each of the five attempts established to complete the path. We defined ten points per attempt and a maximum Score of fifty points. Specifically, the Score variable was obtained as follows. Each participant had five attempts to reach the end of the maze. If the participant reached the end of the maze on the first attempt, the task ended. If a participant chose the wrong direction at an intersection, the participant automatically returned to the starting point and made another attempt. If the participant went through all five attempts, the task ended.

The participants received a point for each correct choice of an intersection at each attempt. There were 10 intersections in total. The participants received 10 points for each attempt that they did not have to complete. Therefore, if the participants reached the end of the maze on the first attempt, they received 50 points (10 for the first attempt, and 40 for the 4 attempts that they did not have to complete).

The results for the participants with stereopsis and those without stereopsis using the HMD condition are shown in Table 9. Table 10 shows the results considering gender. The results for the participants with stereopsis and those without stereopsis using the large stereo condition are shown in Table 11. Table 12 shows the results taking gender into account. For the two conditions considered independently, the results show that there were no statistically significant differences for the performance on the task between the participants with stereopsis and the participants without stereopsis. The performance on the task was also independent for gender.

Table 9. Means and Standard deviations, Mann-Whitney U test analysis, and r effect size for the HMD condition and between the participants without stereopsis and those with stereopsis.

	No-stereopsis	Stereopsis	U	Z	p	r
Score	48.0 ± 2.88	47.68 ± 3.23	97.0	0.459	0.667	0.084
Attempts	1.62 ± 0.74	2.05 ± 1.09	70.0	−0.898	0.395	0.164
Time	350.5 ± 191.50	295.89 ± 109.63	106.0	0.844	0.414	0.154

Table 10. Means and Standard deviations, Kruskal-Wallis test analysis for the HMD condition and for gender. Atte. = Attempts.

	No-stereopsis		Stereopsis		χ^2	df	p
	Men	Women	Men	Women			
Score	48.00 ± 3.16	48.00 ± 2.83	48.83 ± 2.37	46.30 ± 3.68	0.21	1	0.646
Atte.	1.67 ± 0.82	1.50 ± 0.71	2.00 ± 1.34	2.10 ± 0.74	0.77	1	0.379
Time	364.1 ± 218.40	309.70 ± 116.6	296.30 ± 129.40	295.4 ± 87.0	0.71	1	0.399

Table 11. Means and Standard deviations, Mann-Whitney U test analysis, and r effect size for the large stereo condition for the participants without stereopsis and those with stereopsis.

	No-stereopsis	Stereopsis	U	Z	p	r
Score	41.43 ± 9.41	38.09 ± 11.36	91.0	0.729	0.484	0.135
Attempts	2.14 ± 1.46	2.95 ± 1.76	58.5	−0.983	0.373	0.183
Time	114.5 ± 31.56	137.53 ± 59.34	67.0	−0.510	0.636	0.095

Table 12. Means and Standard deviations, Kruskal-Wallis test analysis for the large stereo condition and for gender. Atte. = Attempts

	No-stereopsis		Stereopsis		χ^2	df	p
	Men	Women	Men	Women			
Score	41.00 ±10.82	41.75 ± 9.95	40.14 ± 9.94	43.50 ± 13.44	0.37	1	0.541
Atte.	1.67 ± 0.58	2.50 ± 1.91	2.79 ± 1.72	3.25 ± 1.91	0.31	1	0.579
Time	99.69 ± 15.69	125.59 ± 38.01	130.71 ± 59.73	149.47± 60.66	1.23	1	0.268

Table 13. Multifactorial ANOVA test for the Headings variable, N = 30.

Factor	F	p	Effect size (η^2)
Gender	0.009	0.924	<0.01
Group (no stereopsis/stereopsis)	0.003	0.961	<0.01
Gender:Group	0.046	0.832	<0.01

For the HMD condition, Table 13 shows the results for the Headings variable (head turnings) taking into account gender and group (no stereopsis vs. stereopsis). The results show that there were no statistically significant differences for gender and group.

When the Score variable for the group who did not have stereopsis is analyzed and the HMD (48.00 ± 2.88) and large stereo screen (41.43 ± 9.41) conditions are compared, there were no statistically significant differences (U = 38.5, Z = 1.318, p = 0.210, r = 0.340). When the Score variable for the group who had stereopsis is analyzed and the HMD (47.68 ± 3.23) and large stereo screen (38.09 ± 11.36) conditions are compared, there were statistically significant differences (U = 354, Z = 2.725, p = 0.006**, r = 0.411) in favor of the HMD condition.

6 Discussion

As mentioned in the background section, HMDs have already been compared with different visualization systems. In this paper, we have compared a HMD (Oculus Rift DK2) with a partially immersive VR system. Previous works have compared the Oculus Rift with a fully immersive VR system [13] and with a non-immersive VR system [15]. Our results are in line with these works. Although other works have suggested that a large projection screen may be an effective substitute for a HMD [27], our results indicate that participants had a better 3D experience using a HMD than using a large stereo screen. Juan & Pérez [17] compared a HMD and a CAVE and observed that the CAVE induced a significantly higher level of presence. The features of their HMD were: 800 × 600 and 40° FOV. The features of the current HMDs are significantly better. We used a HMD with 960 × 1080 and 100° FOV. Another aspect to consider is the inclusion in the system of head tracking. The motion parallax cue plays an important role in stereoscopy. In a fair comparison, the projected stereoscopic display should have head tracking. From our results (QI1 and QS2), non-inclusion of head tracking has negatively affected the results for our large stereo screen condition.

In any case, considering our work and previous works, it is possible to conclude that current HMDs offer advantages over basic, partially, or fully immersive VR systems.

Also mentioned in the introduction section, the study was motivated by the observation of students who did not have stereopsis and did not have depth perception with other VR devices (e.g., CAVE, a large stereo screen, or autostereoscopic displays). However, those same students did have the sensation of depth using the Oculus Rift. Our study corroborated our main hypothesis that current HMDs allow users with stereopsis problems to have the illusion of depth perception. Our explanation for this is that the field of view of current HMDs is much more similar to the human eye than other VR devices or systems. The inclusion of head tracking and a low latency are also very important. Nearly all of the current HMDs include head tracking. As Carmack [28] indicated that "The latency between the physical movement of a user's head and updated photons from a HMD reaching their eyes is one of the most critical factors in providing a high quality experience". Thus, all the new features of current HMDs allow the users to perceive the virtual environment similarly to the way they perceive reality, and, therefore, they feel similar sensations. Stereo blind individuals rely more heavily on motion based cues for depth. Therefore, the 3D experience could largely be influenced by the head tracking. Our argument that the head tracking largely influences the 3D experience was shared by one of the participants without stereopsis. This participant was a computer graphics PhD student, and he explained his experience in an interview after 3 months of his participation in our study. The participant was not able to identify any of the figures that appear in the Lang 1 Stereotest. He did not perceive 3D with an autostereoscopic screen, or with the large stereo screen used in our study, or in the 3D cinemas. However, for the first time in his life, he did experience the feeling of depth with a VR environment using the Oculus Rift. With our virtual maze, he could perceive that the virtual elements were at his side and he could notice the distance they were from. His personal opinion was that the changes in perspective while moving his head enabled him to have that 3D feeling. After this first 3D experience, he tested other stereoscopic devices and he has only been able to appreciate 3D with HMDs that include head tracking. This participant added that when using HMDs that do not include head tracking, instead of perceiving 3D, he suffered from cybersickness. He also experienced cybersickness with the Oculus Rift and with environments that do not allow navigation using head turns. These 3D experiences have not changed the way he perceives objects in the real world. Other statements expressed by other participants without stereopsis during the experience were as follows: 'Oh my God, I can perceive 3D for the first time in my life with this VR device'. This reaction was in line with that reported by the participants in the study carried out by Ding & Levi [9], "depth 'popped out' in daily life, and I enjoyed 3D movies for the first time".

Previous works have used VR for training adults who were stereo blind or stereodeficient [12]. After the training, some of those participants recovered or acquired stereopsis. Our work tested the same virtual environment with two different visualization systems (HMD vs. a large stereo screen) and with people with stereopsis and without stereopsis. From the results, the HMD allowed the participants to feel a richer 3D experience than the large stereo screen for both groups (stereopsis vs. no stereopsis). This also indicates that full stereopsis may not be necessary for rich 3D experiences. The performance on the task for the HMD was independent from the participants' condition (stereopsis vs. no stereopsis) and gender. Therefore, our work and previous works are complementary and their union opens up new possibilities for people with stereoblindness or stereodeficiency. We believe that the use of HMDs in training people for recovering or acquiring stereopsis could have implications for the recovery of visual function in real life. Several studies have indicated that between 5% and 10% of the population do not have stereoscopic vision [23, 25]. This percentage can be as high as 34% in older subjects [26]. Therefore, current HMDs could help this population to experience depth perception using VR. As mentioned in the background section, Bridgeman [8], with stereo-deficiency, acquired stereopsis when watching a 3D movie. A current HMD has been used for watching 3D movies as an observer or as an actor [29]. Oculus Story Studios (https://storystudio.oculus.com/en-us) made their first two movies, *Lost* (2015) and *Henry (2016)*. The possibility of watching movies in 3D as an observer or as an actor is interesting for people with stereopsis, but it also opens up a new possibility for people with stereopsis problems that could be explored.

In this study, we have used a gamepad for the interaction. However, other devices or types of interaction can also be used, e.g., using touch motion controllers, which can be combined with the Oculus Rift CV1. Another possibility is to use VR Manus gloves, or to use Leap Motion for gesture interaction. Leap Motion can be attached to the HMD, allowing interaction with the user's hands.

Even though current HMDs have several benefits, they also have some drawbacks. One of them is the cybersickness that they may induce. As Davis et al. [18] indicated, the more realistic the environment with higher levels of visual flow, the greater the chance of inducing cybersickness. Other works have also studied cybersickness. For example, Sharples et al. [30] studied VR induced symptoms and effects comparing a HMD, a desktop, a projection screen (smaller than ours), and a reality theatre. The participants using the HMD and the projection screen experienced a significant increase in symptoms pre–post exposure for oculomotor, disorientation, and total scored. Moreover, the participants using the HMD also reported a significant increase in nausea. We have not carried out a formal study about cybersickness, but the data for the SQ1 question (*To what degree did you feel general discomfort during or at the end of the task?*) indicates that the participants who had stereopsis scored significantly higher on SQ1 using the HMD than using the large stereo screen condition. Taking into account the differences, our observations are in line with the conclusions obtained by Sharples et al. [30]. Recent studies indicate that the Oculus Rift induces motion sickness [31]. However, further studies are needed to determine whether this or other current HMDs induce more cybersickness than other VR systems, and comparisons between them should also be made. Another drawback is that cables must be connected to the computer. Therefore, wireless HMDs (e.g., Samsung Gear VR, Google Cardboard or HoloLens) that offer freedom of movement could also be considered.

7   Conclusion

We have compared two different visualization systems: a partially immersive large stereo screen, and a fully immersive HMD. The study involved participants who had stereopsis and participants who did not have stereopsis. To our knowledge, this is the first comparison involving those two different visualization systems and those two population groups. The HMD has provided a significantly better VR experience than the large stereo screen. Users that have stereopsis problems and cannot perceive 3D when looking at the Lang 1 Stereo test or using other VR systems (CAVE, large stereo screens, or autostereoscopic displays) do have the sensation of depth when using the HMD. Therefore, our findings indicate that people without stereopsis may benefit from a 3D experience with current HMDs.

As future work regarding the perceptions of people that do not have stereopsis when using current HMDs, a study could be carried out to determine the weight of the different aspects that influence stereoscopy (especially, motion parallax). The Oculus Rift, other HMDs, or other 3D-display technologies could be used to design VR environments for training and to facilitate recovery of stereo vision by people with stereo-deficiencies. We hope to help people who are afflicted with stereo-deficiencies to have rich 3D experiences in VR with the work and ideas presented here.

Acknowledgments.
- This work was mainly funded by the Spanish Ministry of Economy and Competitiveness (MINECO) through the CHILDMNEMOS project (TIN2012-37381-C02-01) and cofinanced by the European Regional Development Fund (FEDER).
- Other financial support was received from the Government of the Republic of Ecuador through the Scholarship Program of the Secretary of Higher Education, Science, Technology and Innovation (SENESCYT), the *Conselleria d'Educació, Investigació, Cultura i Esport* through the grant for consolidable research groups (2017–2018), the Government of Aragon (Department of Industry and Innovation), and the European Social Fund for Aragon.
- We would like to thank the following for their contributions:
  - David Rodríguez Andrés, Mauricio Loachamín Valencia, and Juan Fernando Martín for their help.
  - DSIC and ASIC for allowing us to use its facilities during the testing phase, especially to Vicente Blasco and Manuel Jiménez.
  - The users who participated in the study.
  - The reviewers for their valuable comments.

References

1. Howard, I.P., Rogers, B.J.: Binocular Vision and Stereopsis. Oxford University Press, New York (1995)
2. Howard, I.P., Rogers, B.J.: Perceiving in depth, vol. 3. Oxford University Press, New York (2012)
3. Barry, S.R.: Fixing My Gaze: A Scientist's Journey Into Seeing in Three Dimensions. Basic Books, New York (2009)
4. LaViola, J.L.: A discussion of cybersickness in virtual environments. ACM SIGCHI Bull. **32** (January), 47–56 (2000)
5. Dionisio, J.D.N., Burns III, W.G., Gilbert, R.: 3D virtual worlds and the metaverse: current status and future possibilities. ACM Comput. Surv. **45**(3), 34 (2013)
6. Muhanna, M.A.: Virtual reality and the CAVE: taxonomy, interaction challenges and research directions. J. King Saud Univ. Comput. Inf. Sci. **27**, 344–361 (2015)

7. Sutherland, I.E.: A head-mounted, three-dimensional display. In: The Fall Joint Computer Conference, pp. 757–764 (1968)
8. Bridgeman, B.: Restoring adult stereopsis: a vision researcher's personal experience. Optom. Vis. Sci. **91**, e135–e139 (2014)
9. Ding, J., Levi, D.M.: Recovery of stereopsis through perceptual learning in human adults with abnormal binocular vision. Proc. Natl. Acad. Sci. **108**(37), E733–E741 (2011). USA
10. Astle, A.T., McGraw, P.V., Webb, B.S.: Recovery of stereo acuity in adults with amblyopia. BMJ Case Rep. 2011: bcr0720103143 (2011)
11. Xi, J., Jia, W.-L., Feng, L.-X., Lu, Z.-L., Huang, C.-B.: Perceptual learning improves stereoacuity in amblyopia. Invest. Ophthalmol. Vis. Sci. **55**, 2384–2391 (2014)
12. Vedamurthy, I., Knill, D.C., Huang, S.J., Yung, A., Ding, J., Kwon, O.-S., Bavelier, D., Levi, D.M.: Recovering stereo vision by squashing virtual bugs in a virtual reality environment. Philos. Trans. R. Soc. Lond. B Biol. Sci. **371**(1697), 20150264 (2016)
13. Young, M.K., Gaylor, G., B., Andrus, S.M., Bodenheimer, B.: A comparison of two cost-differentiated virtual reality systems for perception and action tasks. In: The ACM Symposium on Applied Perception, pp. 83–90 (2014)
14. Buń, P., Górski, F., Wichniarek, R., Kuczko, W., Hamrol, A., Zawadzki, P.: Application of professional and low-cost head mounted devices in immersive educational application. Procedia Comput. Sci. **75**, 173–181 (2015)
15. Tan, C.T., Leong, T.W., Shen, S., Dubravs, C., Si, C.: Exploring gameplay experiences on the oculus rift. In: CHI PLAY 2015, pp. 253–263 (2015)
16. Gutiérrez-Maldonado, J., Ferrer-García, M., Plasanjuanelo, J., Andrés-Pueyo, A., Talarn-Caparrós, A.: Virtual reality to train diagnostic skills in eating disorders. comparison of two low cost systems. Stud. Health Tech. Inf. **219**, 75–81 (2015)
17. Juan, M.C., Pérez, D.: Comparison of the Levels of presence and anxiety in an acrophobic environment viewed via HMD or CAVE. Presence Teleoper. Virtual Environ. **18**(3), 232–248 (2009)
18. Davis, S., Nesbitt, K., Nalivaiko, E.: Comparing the onset of cybersickness using the Oculus Rift and two virtual roller coasters. In: the 11th Australasian Conference on Interactive Entertainment, vol. 167, pp. 3–14 (2015)
19. Arias, N., Méndez, M., Arias, J.L.: Brain networks underlying navigation in the Cincinnati water maze with external and internal cues. Neurosci. Lett. **576**, 68–72 (2014)
20. Cárdenas-Delgado, S., Méndez-López, M., Juan, M.C., Pérez-Hernández, E., Lluch, J., Vivó, R.: Using a Virtual Maze Task to assess spatial short-term memory in adults. In: International Conference on Computer Graphics Theory and Applications, pp. 46–57 (2017)
21. Dodgson, N. A.: Variation and extrema of human interpupillary distance. In: SPIE 5291, Stereoscopic Displays and Virtual Reality Systems XI, pp. 36–46 (2004)
22. Lang, J.: A new stereotest. J. Pediatr. Ophthalmol. Strabismus **20**(2), 72–74 (1983)
23. Brown, S., Weih, L., Mukesh, N., McCarty, C., Taylor, H.: Assessment of adult stereopsis using the Lang 1 Stereotest: a pilot study. Binocular Vis. Strabismus Q. **16**(2), 91–98 (2001)
24. Witmer, B.G., Singer, M.J.: Measuring presence in virtual environments: a presence questionnaire. Presence Teleoper. Virtual **7**(3), 225–240 (1998)
25. Castanes, M.S.: Major review: The underutilization of vision screening (for amblyopia, optical anomalies and strabismus) among preschool age children. Binocular Vis. Strabismus Q. **18**(4), 217–232 (2003)
26. Zaroff, C.M., Knutelska, M., Frumkes, T.E.: Variation in stereoacuity: normative description, fixation disparity, and the roles of aging and gender. Invest. Ophthalmol. Vis. Sci. **44**, 891–900 (2003)

27. Patrick, E., Cosgrove, D., Slavkovic, A., Rode, J.A., Verratti, T., Chiselko, G.: Using a large projection screen as an alternative to head-mounted displays for virtual environments. In: SIGCHI Conference on Human Factors in Computing Systems, pp. 478–485 (2000)
28. Carmack, J.: John Carmack's Latency mitigation strategies (2013). http://www.pcgamesn.com/virtual–reality–john–carma. Accessed 20 Jan 2017
29. van den Boom, A.A.L.F.M., Stupar-Rutenfrans, S., Bastiaens, O., van Gisbergen, M.S.: Observe or participate: the effect of point-of-view on presence and enjoyment in 360 degree movies for head mounted displays. In: the European Conference on Ambient Intelligence (2015). http://ceur-ws.org/Vol-1528/paper13.pdf. Accessed 20 Jan 2017
30. Sharples, S., Cobb, S., Moody, A., Wilson, J.R.: Virtual reality induced symptoms and effects (VRISE): comparison of head mounted display (HMD), desktop and projection display systems. Displays **29**(2), 58–69 (2008)
31. Munafo, J., Diedrick, M., Stoffregen, T.A.: The virtual reality head-mounted display Oculus Rift induces motion sickness and is sexist in its effects. Exp. Brain Res. **235**, 889–901 (2016)

How Older People Who Have Never Used Touchscreen Technology Interact with a Tablet

Roberto Menghi[1(✉)], Silvia Ceccacci[1], Francesca Gullà[1],
Lorenzo Cavalieri[1], Michele Germani[1], and Roberta Bevilacqua[2]

[1] Department of Industrial Engineering and Mathematical Sciences,
Università Politecnica delle Marche,
Via Brecce Bianche, 12, 60131 Ancona, Italy
{r.menghi, s.ceccacci, f.gulla, lorenzo.cavalieri,
m.germani}@univpm.it
[2] Istituto Nazionale di Ricerca e Cura per Anziani,
via della Montagnola, 81, 60131 Ancona, Italy
r.bevilacqua@inrca.it

Abstract. Touchscreen technologies have become increasingly common in personal devices, so it seems necessary to improve their accessibility and usability for the older people. In the past years, a lot of studies have been conducted to improve touch interfaces, however, most them do not consider older people with very low attitude with ICTs. Moreover, the majority of studies date back 2014, so they lack to consider the most innovative technologies available today. The present study involves a sample of older people without previous experience with ICTs with the aim of analyzing how basic features of a touchscreen interface affect their performances with typical touch-gestures. A total of 22 participants have been involved. Results partially confirm the existent literature and partially reveal new interesting findings that can be useful to improve the touch screen accessibility for older people.

Keywords: Touchscreen interface · Older people · Usability · Accessibility · Touch gestures · Human computer interaction

1 Introduction

Nowadays, several attempts have been made to analyze the impact of the new technologies for the older users, in terms of accessibility, usability and acceptability: studies of technology use, attitudes and skills have shown that they are less incline to use technology compared with younger ones [1]. However, depicting the older adults as technophobes represents an erroneous preconception as many evidences suggests that older users desire interaction with new technologies to remain active in the society and independent [2]. In fact, older adults can strongly benefit of new information and communication technologies (ICTs) [3], although there are practical issues that explain why older users do not use technologies: lack of motivation or reason to use ICT devices, lack of experience with current technology, cognitive differences and age-related decline, lack of knowledge on how to use ICTs, no access to the technological artifacts, no understanding of what to do with a device, and usability problems [4, 5].

© IFIP International Federation for Information Processing 2017
Published by Springer International Publishing AG 2017. All Rights Reserved
R. Bernhaupt et al. (Eds.): INTERACT 2017, Part I, LNCS 10513, pp. 117–131, 2017.
DOI: 10.1007/978-3-319-67744-6_8

The most effective way to overcome the scarce use of technologies in the older population is to design technologies taking into account their abilities and preferences since the beginning [6–9], in order to support them in using the available services that are becoming more technology based, in particular embedded with touchscreen technologies.

In recent years, touch technology has flourished, so that it has become essential in everyday life: practically all personal devices (e.g., smartphones, tablets, PCs) implement it [10]. The reasons for the success of touchscreen interfaces is mostly due to the fact they allow direct input, and consequently support human-computer interaction in a more intuitive and accessible way. In fact, this imply a screen size larger than no-touch interfaces and virtual button items bigger than those of a keyboard based interface (i.e., large enough to be pressed with a finger).

In the case of touchscreen technologies, some studies have shown that also younger adults may encounter some frustrations during the use, suggesting that improving the design of touchscreen interface for older adults will improve the rate of usability also for the other user groups [1]. On this matter, several studies have been carried out to try to define a set of informal guidelines for interface design for seniors [11]. The dimension of the screen and the characteristics of the screen items (e.g., size, color, grouping, etc.) have been studied to guarantee that touchscreen interactions result accessible and usable for older people [12]. These studies demonstrated that larger items, figure and links should be used to improve interaction. Regarding button size, at least 20 mm square is recommended to ensure an optimal finger selection [13, 14], while the minimum recommended width is 13 mm [15]. Regarding button spacing, a space at least equal to 3.17 mm seems to lower performance error rate for older people [16] although other studies found that gap size does not affect user performance [14].

Some studies [17, 18] found that the interface should support older people to interact without difficulty and should avoid the focus loss, especially for user with visual and cognitive impairment. As a result, they suggest designing the visual objects (e.g., text, icons) with appropriate featured using high contrast colors, and a layout based on clearness and simplicity. In particular, the dark color of background should not be used because it stands out fingerprints and intensifies glare, although the major tablet operating systems provide it as an accessibility setting [19]. To keep attention on the interface, the information should be provided in a simple way, avoiding the unnecessary objects like decorative animations, useless pictures, wallpaper patterns, moving text or flashing text [18] and replace data entry with other simpler choice (e.g., tapping on predefined values, providing sliders or button for incrementing and decrementing values, etc. [19]). Finally, several studies have analyzed the user's gestures (i.e., tap, slide, drag, pinch, swipe, etc.) while they interact with a tablet. These sought to evaluate which of these gestures best support user performance for older people [11]. Their results show that, older users with high manual dexterity prefer dragging and pinching rather than tapping [20].

The literature study showed that there is a strong interest to understand the interaction on touch interface related to age. Nevertheless, most of the existing studies on the usability of the touchscreen devices get primarily involved older people with previous experience using computers and/or other touchscreen technologies (i.e. smartphones, tablet, e-book reader etc.) [11]. Indeed, only few studies in literature have involved subjects without experience with ICTs. Moreover, although in the recent years, touchscreen technology is considerably improved [21, 22], studies on interaction of older people with these recent technologies are still lacking.

In this context, the present study involves a sample of older people without previous experience with ICTs (except for traditional mobile phone) with the aim of analyzing how basic features of a touchscreen interface affect their interactions. For this purpose, the paper inspects the older people performances, during their first experience with the latest generation touchscreen. In detail, this exploratory study aims to: (a) verify whether the guidelines relating to the GUI design for older people based on studies conducted on older technologies are still valid today with latest technologies; (b) assess the level of accessibility of current technologies for older people without prior experience in the use of touchscreen and scarce experience in the use of ICTs.

2 Touchscreen Application

To support the evaluation of the interaction, a touch screen application has been developed, to assess the performance of the participants with tapping, dragging and pinching gestures. The application is composed by three game sessions:

- Tap: tapping a button on the screen;
- Drag and drop: dragging an object on the screen;
- Pinch-to-zoom: expanding or shrinking an object on the screen using two fingers.

The architecture of application (Fig. 1) is composed by three main functional modules. The Application Manager allows to read pattern configuration and startup application parameters and manage all the interaction flow during the three different sessions. Every session manages the items' appearance and behavior according with the configuration data loaded by the manager: these sub-models provide to configure the user interface.

In addition, a background routine is in running during the user interaction in order to collect performance data that are stored in a dedicated report as shown in Fig. 1.

Each session provides a set of mini-tasks in which the target object changes its attributes (e.g. position, shape, color, size, etc.), which are described in detail in the sections below. Each session uses predetermined patterns to change the appearance attributes of the target object, which were randomly assigned. Furthermore, each session can collect key performance parameters useful for the data analysis, which are described in detail in the following paragraphs. Each parameter allows to detect an aspect of user performance: the *Task completion time* (in milliseconds) is the time within the user completes the mini-task, while the *Success value* give the success/failure condition. In order to determine the failure condition, a *Limit time session* is defined for each game. A session is considered failed if the participant does not correctly complete the gesture within the prescribed time.

The interface application was realized to comply the standards and the design guidelines related to web accessibility [23–25].

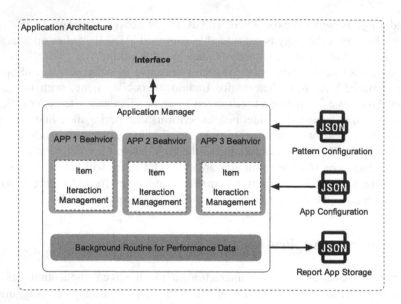

Fig. 1. Architecture of pilot application.

2.1 Tapping

The first application tries to investigate the tapping interaction (Fig. 3a). The user's task consists in tapping a graphical target item (i.e. colored circle): it can be modified about size, contrast, shape and screen position.

The variability range of the first session can be summarized in Fig. 2 and has the same structure in the other experimental sessions. The four attributes used in App1 are:

- **Position**: the screen surface is divided into 6 regions and the target object to be manipulated appears in the center of the assigned region;
- **Shape**: three different shapes are selected (square, square with rounded edges and circle);
- **Color**: three different variants are chosen for the color variability: more precisely, contrast combinations between object and background are defined to test the influence of the choice of color in the interface design. The three variants shown in Fig. 2 are low-contrast, high-contrast and reverse high contrast;
- **Size**: according to the accessibility guidelines three variants of size attribute are defined (small with 38×38px, medium with 76×76px and large with 113×113px).

According with the appearance variables, random combinations of the target item aspect is generated: the total number of the combinations is 162. The item appears on the screen and when the user taps it disappears and the next one is shown. If the user does not achieve the task within the limit time session (4.000 ms), the next step is triggered to guarantee the session conclusion.

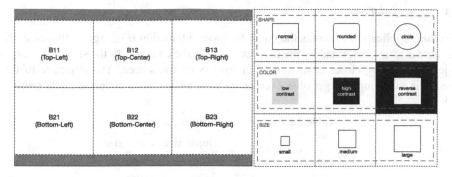

Fig. 2. Variability ranges of object attributes

2.2   Drag and Drop

The second app is focused on the drag and drop interaction (Fig. 3b). Two circles (colored target item and white endpoint) with same size are displayed on the screen. The user must hook the target item (colored) and move it into the white one. When it is left, and does not match with the endpoint circle, its position is reset. In this case, the attributes of the target object are two:

1. **Type of gesture**: a classification of possible dragging trajectories has been defined (see Table 1), which is based on the possible combinations of positions the two displayed objects may assume in the six areas of the screen defined above.
2. **Size**: the three sizes mentioned above are proposed again for both displayed items.

The second session provides 90 combinations. A limit time session equal to 5000 ms determines timeout for the step duration.

Table 1. The considered dragging gestures

Typologies of gestures	Dragging trajectories
Vertical up	B21 → B11, B22 → B12, B23 → B13
Vertical down	B11 → B21, B12 → B22, B13 → B23
Long horizontal right	B11 → B13, B21 → B23
Long horizontal left	B11 → B13, B23 → B21
Short horizontal right	B11 → B12, B12 → B13, B21 → B22, B22 → B23
Short horizontal left	B12 → B11, B13 → B12, B22 → B21, B23 → B22
Long diagonal upper right	B21 → B13
Long diagonal upper left	B23 → B11
Long diagonal bottom right	B11 → B23
Long diagonal bottom left	B13 → B21
Short diagonal upper right	B21 → B12, B22 → B13
Short diagonal upper left	B22 → B11, B23 → B12
Short diagonal bottom right	B11 → B22, B12 → B23
Short diagonal bottom left	B12 → B21, B13 → B22

2.3   Pinch-to-Zoom

The third application concerns the pinch-to-zoom interaction (Fig. 3c). In this case, the possible actions performed by the user are two: he/she can modify the size of the target object by moving closer or away his/her fingers on the screen. The objective of this session is matching a target object (colored) with a concentric endpoint circle (white).

Table 2. The considered zoom percentage

			Object size	Circle size
% Zoom	Zoom out	44%	340px	150px
		62%	240px	150px
		70%	340px	240px
	Zoom in	141%	240px	340px
		160%	150px	240px
		226%	150px	340px

The considered attributes in this session are position (the same six defined above) and the zoom percentage. The zoom percentage is compute as the ratio between the size of the target object and the endpoint circle (see Table 2). The total combination for Pinch-to-zoom interaction are 36. A limit time session equal to 7000 ms determines timeout for the step duration.

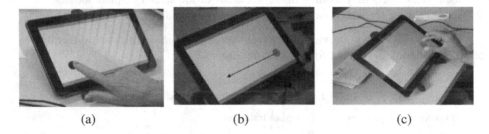

(a)   (b)   (c)

Fig. 3. (a) Tap interaction; (b) Drag & Drop interaction; (c) Pinch-to-zoom interaction

3   Material and Method

3.1   Participants

For the purpose of the study, volunteer subjects were recruited in facilities of the local municipality. To be enrolled, the following inclusion criteria were fixed:

- Age 60 and older;
- Native speakers of the trial language;
- Mini Mental State Examination (MMSE) score ≥ 24;
- Geriatric Depression Scale (GDS) score ≤ 10;

- Subjects should not have any significant mobility impairment (upper or lower extremity);
- Fulfill hearing and vision criteria set by self-reported questionnaires (hearing and vision criteria anticipate that both could be augmented, i.e., via eyeglasses or hearing aids);
- Ability to make time commitment;
- No previous experience in the use of computers, Internet or other ICTs (except for old-fashioned mobile phone).

The total sample was composed of 22 participants, 5 males and 17 females, with a mean age of 76 years old (SD $\pm$ 6.69). The totality of the sample was retired and the most income source is constituted by pension. Almost all the subjects (13 out of 22) were married and live with the partner, while 8 subjects live alone and 1 with the sons. Eight participants (8 out of 22) use mobile phone, while 14 never owned it. On the cognitive side, the mean value of the MMSE is 29.31 (SD $\pm$ 0.77), while the mean score obtained at the GDS is 3.72 (SD $\pm$ 2.54).

3.2 Experimental Equipment

The touch application was presented on a Samsung Galaxy Tab A (10.1″). The whole interaction with the pilot application was recorded by means of dedicated cameras. Specifically, two cameras (Nikon d5300 + AF-P DX 18-55 VR) were placed in the environment and recorded participant's actions to allow offline computer-supported structured video-analysis. Finally, the BORIS software (Behavioral Observation Research Interactive Software) [26] is used to support a video-analysis.

3.3 Procedure

The experiment took place in appropriate equipped room. On a large table, the participants had access to the tablet placed on a fixed special support.

Each participant was asked to sit in front of the tablet. In order to set the correct distance between the user and the tablet, the user has been asked to hold the tablet and position the chair in the way to make a 120° angle between his arm and forearm. Furthermore, the experimenter has assured that the user was taking the correct position and posture. Participants are required to maintain head and neck aligned with the screen focused area, to keep their hips and knees lined up and parallel to the floor, to maintain their back in contact with the chair, avoiding to tilt on the back and to take care that the arms were parallel to the work surface. In the experiment, subjects were also asked to operate with just one hand. The hand choice was not restricted to the left hand or the right hand but was primarily based on the subject's handedness. Anyway, all the users that participated in the tests were right-handed. This test configuration was set to ensure the user comfort during the test and the same interaction conditions for all the users.

The participants were welcomed in the laboratory room and researches have presented the trial objectives and collected the informed consents.

Before starting, the experimenter explained to the participants the three MiniApps operation through the aid of a video demonstration and they were informed about the

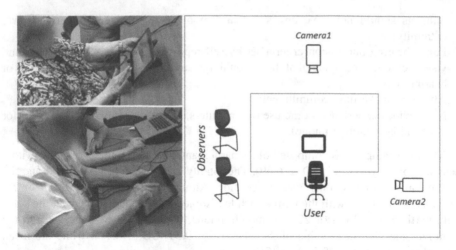

Fig. 4. The experimental setting.

total duration of the test. Then the participants received a full explanation of how the touch application was structured and how to operate it (Fig. 4).

The experimenter started the video-recording and the experimental phase began with the experimenter asked the users starting the first Mini App. Later, the users were asked to interact with others developed MiniApps, according to the functional sequence described in the previous paragraph. In additions, during the entire interaction, users were encouraged to express their thoughts, feelings, possible boredom signs and opinions aloud while the experimenter was taken annotation of the performance, errors and user attitudes. The experimental session was completed when the user has completed the three MiniApps. The total experimentation time about 22.5 min has been established and all involved users have concluded the experiment without any breaks between sessions.

4   Results

Tests show interesting results which partially confirm the existent literature and partially reveal new findings that can be useful to improve the touch screen accessibility for older people.

In general, for tapping we obtained a success rate equal to 78.09%, while success rate decreases to 44.83% for dragging and falls down to 24.49% for pinching. According to the literature [11, 20] this confirms that tapping is the easier gesture for older people.

To assess if gender may affect user performance in term of task completion time, a t-test has been carried out. As show in Table 3, the results illustrate that did not evidenced significant differences between gender.

Table 3. Task completion user performance related to participant's gender

		Mean time (ms)	SD	t	p
Tapping	*Male*	1886,14	627,08	t(2782) = 0,78	0,435
	Female	1864,08	593,39		
Dragging	*Male*	3569,09	1004,94	t(865) = 1,88	0,061
	Female	3427,79	926,28		
Pinching	*Male*	4702,18	1309,02	t(192) = 1,02	0,31
	Female	4468,52	1557,8		

In order to analyze how the considered features of the interface affect user inter-action, different ANOVA analysis were individually performed. To assess equality of variance, Levine's test was used.

4.1   Tapping

Four One-way ANOVA analysis were performed on the experimental results for the tapping task. The first one used size (38px, 76px and 113px) as an independent variable to investigate the effect of size on performance value (i.e., Task Completion Time). The second one used the position of target on the screen area (B11, B12, B13, B21, B22, B23) to analyze the effect of the target position on older people performance. The third one used target contrast (low, high and reverse contrast) as independent variable to investigate the effect of target visibility on performance. The last one used the icon shape (square, square with rounded edge and circle) as independent variable to understand the effect of the shape of the targets on the users' performances.

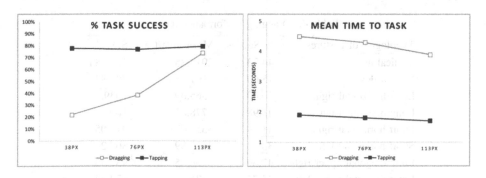

Fig. 5. Tapping and dragging success rate and mean time to task for each target size

Results show that size had a strongly significant effect on the older people per-formance (F(2,2781) = 33.29, p < 0.000). Older people perform more quickly the greater are the targets (Fig. 5): the average of Task Completion Time (T) is equal to 1.77 s with 113px target and increase to 1.84 s and 1.99 s with targets respectively of 76px and 38px width. This confirm results of several previous studies [19, 20]. However, an increase in the size of the targets does not seem to improve success rate: participant performed well also with small targets.

The position of the targets on the screen significant affect older people performance ($F(5,2778) = 3.49$, $p < 0.004$). Older people performed more quickly if targets are located in the middle of the screen ($T_{B12} = 1796.96$ and $T_{B22} = 1845.05$) or on the right side ($T_{B13} = 1841.25$ and $T_{B23} = 1875.75$), while target positioned on the left side slow the performances ($T_{B11} = 1943.02$ and $T_{B21} = 1908.78$). Those results, for right-handed subjects basically confirm the Fitts' law [27]. However, position does not influence the success rate.

Furthermore, there were not significant main effects of the contrast ($F (2,2781) = 1.57$, $p > 0.05$) and of the shape of targets ($F(2,2781) = 0.04$, $p > 0.05$).

4.2 Dragging

Two ANOVA analysis were individually performed on the experimental results for the dragging task. The first one used size (38px, 76px and 113px) as an independent variable to investigate the effect of size on performance value (i.e., Task Completion Time).

The second one was performed to understand how the features of the dragging gesture affects older people performance. To this end, the type of gesture has been used as independent variable to compute the ANOVA analysis.

Results show that size had a strongly significant effect on the older people performance ($F(2,864) = 18.99$, $p < 0.000$). According to the results (Fig. 5), only the targets of 113px width seem to be suitable to be dragged by older people. Regarding the effect of dragging gestures, results show that the type of gesture strongly affects older people performance ($F(13,853) = 6.83$, $p < 0.000$). In particular, older people perform more quickly with vertical gestures and diagonal gestures at the right top (Table 4).

Table 4. Dragging performance data

Typologies of gestures	% Success	Mean time (ms)	SD
Vertical up	44,33	2918,85	1334,84
Verical down	45,60	3101,45	785,84
Long horizontal right	50,00	3565,09	1039,28
Long horizontal left	41,98	3778,87	860,6
Short horizontal right	41,09	3359,09	912,05
Short horizontal left	38,13	3575,89	867,2
Long diagonal upper right	47,69	3306,05	932,53
Long diagonal upper left	43,75	3876,54	624,34
Long diagonal bottom right	47,62	3676,92	758,5
Long diagonal bottom left	57,58	3633,72	826,4
Short diagonal upper right	49,61	3198,97	893,45
Short diagonal upper left	43,85	3873,59	700,77
Short diagonal bottom right	48,06	3606,37	833,99
Short diagonal bottom left	47,29	3461,69	947,08

Moreover, by analysis performance data, it is possible to observe that diagonal gesture resulted in higher success rate than horizontal or vertical gestures (Figs. 6 and 7).

In particular, diagonal trajectories in the lower left resulted in best performance (57.8%), while short horizontal and long horizontal trajectories to the left resulted in lowest success rate.

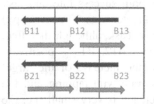

Fig. 6. Short horizontal gestures resulted in worse performances

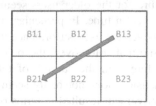

Fig. 7. Diagonal gestures in the lower left resulted in best performance

4.3 Pinching

Two ANOVA analysis were individually performed on the experimental results for the pinching task. The first one used the zoom percentage (see Table 2) as an independent variable to investigate the effect of direction and extension of pinching gesture on performance value (i.e., Task Completion Time). The second one used the position of target on the screen area (B11, B12, B13, B21, B22, B23) to analyze the effect of target position on older people performance.

Results show that the zoom percentage had a strongly significant effect on the older people performance $(F(5,188) = 7.46, p < 0.000)$. According to performance data (Table 5), spreading gesture resulted more ease than pinching. However, it should be observed that zoom ratios that require very broad gestures to be performed (zoom = 226%) result in a dramatic reduction of the success rate. Regarding the effect of object position, results did not reveal significant effect $(F(5,188) = 0.86, p < 0.511)$.

Table 5. Pinching performance results

	% Zoom	% Success	Mean time (ms)	SD
Zoom out	44	18,18	5440,38	1432,18
	62	18,94	4584,32	1929,83
	70	17,42	4169,57	1519,84
Zoom in	141	**43,18**	3710,47	1351,88
	160	**37,12**	4684,43	1344,25
	226	12,12	5511,56	957,57

5 Discussion

From the analysis of the results, it is possible to synthesize some guidelines for the designers of touchscreen interface, to be taken into account in addition to the already available documentation [20, 28].

As already evidenced by the literature [11, 20], it is emerged that the most ease gesture for the older users seems to be tapping, in terms both success rate and task completion time. In particular, a dimension of the object greater than 13 mm (76px) improves the user performance in terms of Time Completion Task, although the effect is minimal. Moreover, the object positions in the screen – B12, B13 – positively interfere with the success of the tapping task. However, the increase of the target dimension does not really seem to influence task success rate with tapping and the improvement resulted in terms of users' performance efficiency is very small (i.e. the task completion task with targets of 113px (i.e. 19 mm) decreases with the target of 38px (i.e. 6 mm) for only 220 ms). This result seems to refute a well-known guideline: that the icon size is very important for older people in performing tapping [13, 14] and at least 13 mm square is recommended to ensure finger selection 13 mm [15].

This result may be due to the improvement of touchscreen technology: in particular, the introduction of the high-resolution screen seems to support users' performance accuracy.

Contrariwise, only targets large at least 113px (19 mm) seem to be suitable to be dragged by older people. This is because the finger occludes the smaller targets during the performance of gesture. Furthermore, the trajectory of dragging gesture influences the performance. In particular, diagonal gestures in the lower left resulted in best performances, while short horizontal gestures resulted in worse performances. Probably this is because such gesture, more than others, avoid the object to be dragged is occluded by the finger or the hand.

Finally, it is emerged that the most difficult gesture for the older users seems to be the pinching/spreading, in terms both success rate and task completion time. Also, this result is consistent with the literature [11, 20]. However, for zoom ratios that do not require very broad gestures to be performed (≤ 160%), spreading gesture resulted more ease than pinching. This result partially confirms the findings of Kobayashi et al. [20]. In fact, in case of pinching/spreading gesture with panning, they found that spreading is generally easier that pinching.

6 Conclusion

Despite the interesting results collected, the sample size of the study is relatively small and this does not allow a proper generalization of the data. For this reason, it is important to take into account the present study as a pilot, with the aim of involving a higher number of users during the next research activities. Within the limits of the study, the most felt one is the neutrality of the application: the tasks were presented by means of stimuli, that do not contain any emotional salience for the users.

From the literature, it is well known that the emotional salience of the events can constitute an important contributor of memory-enhancing effect, for example, using stimuli ranging from pictures to words to narrated slide shows, as well as data from autobiographical memory [29]. For this reason, the personalization of the interfaces may support the successful performance with the tasks, if the screen elements, for example, can be anchored to significant meanings for the users. Despite this, our pilot was focused on achieving information on how to easier the use of any touch screen interfaces in general, by giving a sort of guidelines to be followed during the design, and that can be applied to any kind of contents.

Future studies on touch screen technologies and older users should take into account how the results will vary in consideration of the different attitude level and past experiences with the technological solution [7, 30], considering that improving the design in favor of the older users means also to reduce the frustration with the use for a wider plethora of users [1].

As it is well-known that the older people is represented by a highly heterogeneous group, it is important to find a personalized way - tailored on the individual preferences - to provide a training on technology literacy, in order to empower the users and mitigate the erroneous representations of the technology, often derived by scarce accessibility to the technological solutions.

The improvement of the technological literacy, defined as "the ability to use, manage, assess, and understand technology, involving knowledge, abilities, and the application of both knowledge and abilities to real-world situations, to be obtained through formal or informal educational environments" [31], should be a valuable complement intervention to support the use of the touch screen technologies, and thus collecting new insights for the design of the interfaces.

References

1. Czaja, S., Charness, N., Fisk, A., Hertzog, C., Nair, S., Rogers, W., Sharit, J.: Factors predicting the use of technology: findings from the center for research and education on aging and technology enhancement (CREATE). Psychol. Aging **21**(2), 333–352 (2006)
2. Kurniawan, S.: Older people and mobile phones: a multi-method investigation. Int. J. Hum Comput Stud. **66**(12), 889–901 (2008)
3. Gullà, F., Ceccacci, S., Menghi, R., Germani, M.: An adaptive smart system to foster disabled and elderly people in kitchen-related task. In: Proceedings of the 9th ACM International Conference on PErvasive Technologies Related to Assistive Environments, article no. 27. ACM (2016)
4. van Dijk, J.: The Network Society, Social Aspects of the New Media. Sage Publications, London, Thousand Oaks, New Delhi (n.d.)
5. Czaja, S., Sharit, J.: Age differences in attitudes toward computers. J. Gerontol. **53B**, 329–340 (1998)
6. Goddard, N., Nicolle, C.: What is good design in the eyes of older users? In: Proceedings of the 6th Cambridge Workshop on Universal Access (UA) and Assistive Technology (AT), [CWUAAT], Fitzwilliam College, University of Cambridge, pp. 1–9 (2012)
7. Agarwal, R.: Individual acceptance of information technologies. In: Zmud, R.W. (ed.) Framing the Domains of it Management Research: Glimpsing the Future Through the Past, pp. 85–104. Pinnaflex, Cincinnati (2000)

8. Mackie, R., Wylie, C.: Factors influencing acceptance of computer-based innovations. In: Helander, M. (ed.) Handbook of Human-Computer Interaction, pp. 1081–1106. Elsevier Publishing Co., New York (1998)
9. Mengoni, M., Raponi, D., Ceccacci, S.: A method to identify VR-based set-up to foster elderly in design evaluation. Int. J. Intell. Eng. Inform. 4(1), 46–70 (2016)
10. Lattanzio, F., Abbatecola, A., Bevilacqua, R., Chiatti, C., Corsonello, A., Rossi, L., Bernabei, R.: Advanced technology care innovation for older people in Italy: necessity and opportunity to promote health and wellbeing. J. Am. Med. Dir. Assoc. 15(7), 457–466 (2014)
11. Motti, L.G., Vigouroux, N., Gorce, P.: Interaction techniques for older adults using touchscreen devices: a literature review. In: Proceedings of the 25th Conference on l'Interaction Homme-Machine, p. 125. ACM, November 2013
12. Murata, A., Iwase, H.: Usability of touch-panel interfaces for older adults. Hum. Factors 46, 767–776 (2005)
13. Chung, M., Kim, D., Na, S., Lee, D.: Usability evaluation of numeric entry tasks on keypad type and age. Int. J. Ind. Ergon. 40(1), 97–105 (2010). ISSN 0169-8141
14. Chen, K., Savage, A., Chourasia, A., Wiegmann, D., Sesto, M.: Touch screen performance by individuals with and without motor control disabilities. Appl. Ergon. 44(2), 297–302 (2013)
15. Hwangbo, H., Yoon, S., Jin, B., Han, Y., Ji, Y.: A study of pointing performance of elderly users on smartphones. Int. J. Hum.-Comput. Interact. 29(9), 604–618 (2013)
16. Jin, Z.X., Plocher, T., Kiff, L.: Touch screen user interfaces for older adults: button size and spacing. In: Stephanidis, C. (ed.) UAHCI 2007. LNCS, vol. 4554, pp. 933–941. Springer, Heidelberg (2007). doi:10.1007/978-3-540-73279-2_104
17. Fisk, A.D., Rogers, W.A., Charness, N., Czaja, S.J., Sharit, J.: Designing for Older Adults: Principles and Creative Human Factors Approaches. CRC Press, Boca Raton (2009)
18. Hawthorn, D.: Possible implications of aging for interface designers. Interact. Comput. 12(5), 507–528 (2000)
19. Caprani, N., O'Connor, N.E., Gurrin, C.: Touch screens for the older user. In: Assistive Technologies, pp. 95–118. InTech (2012). ISBN 978-953-51-0348-6
20. Kobayashi, M., Hiyama, A., Miura, T., Asakawa, C., Hirose, M., Ifukube, T.: Elderly user evaluation of mobile touchscreen interactions. In: Campos, P., Graham, N., Jorge, J., Nunes, N., Palanque, P., Winckler, M. (eds.) INTERACT 2011. LNCS, vol. 6946, pp. 83–99. Springer, Heidelberg (2011). doi:10.1007/978-3-642-23774-4_9
21. Ibharim, L.F., Borhan, N., Yatim, M.H.: A field study of understanding child's knowledge, skills and interaction towards capacitive touch technology (iPad). In: Information Technology in Asia (CITA) - 8th International Conference on IEEE (2013)
22. Lee, D.: The state of the touch-screen panel market in 2011. Inf. Disp. 3(11) (2011)
23. ANSI/HFES 100-2007. Human Factors Engineering of Computer Workstations
24. ISO 9241-11: Ergonomics of human-system interaction – Part 11: Usability: Definitions and concepts (1998)
25. World Wide Web Consortium: Web content accessibility guidelines (WCAG) 2.0 (2008)
26. Friard, O., Gamba, M.: BORIS: a free, versatile open-source event-logging software for video/audio coding and live observations. Methods in Ecol. Evol. 7(11), 1325–1330 (2016)
27. Fitts, P.M.: The information capacity of the human motor system in controlling the amplitude of movement. J. Exp. Psychol. 47(6), 381–391 (1954)
28. Díaz-Bossini, J.-M., Lourdes, M.: Accessibility to mobile interfaces for older people. Procedia Comput. Sci. 27, 57–66 (2014)

29. Kensinger, E.: Remembering emotional experiences: the contribution of valence and arousal. Rev. Neurosci. **15**(4), 241–252 (2004)
30. Bevilacqua, R., Di Rosa, M., Felici, E., Stara, V., Barbabella, F., Rossi, L.: Towards an impact assessment framework for ICT-based systems supporting older people: Making evaluation comprehensive through appropriate concepts and metrics. In: Longhi, S., Siciliano, P., Germani, M., Monteriù, A. (eds.) Ambient Assisted Living, 215–222. Springer, Cham (2014). doi:10.1007/978-3-319-01119-6_22
31. ITEA: Standards for technological literacy: content for the study of technology (Reston VA) (2007). http://www.iteaconnect.org/TAA/PDFs/xstnd.pdf. Accessed Jan 2017

MeViTa: Interactive Visualizations to Help Older Adults with Their Medication Intake Using a Camera-Projector System

Robin De Croon[✉], Bruno Cardoso, Joris Klerkx,
Vero Vanden Abeele, and Katrien Verbert

Department of Computer Science, KU Leuven,
Celestijnenlaan 200A, 3001 Leuven, Belgium
{robin.decroon, bruno.cardoso, joris.klerkx,
vero.vandenabeele, katrien.verbert}@kuleuven.be

Abstract. In this paper, we investigate whether augmented reality visualization techniques can empower older adults to explore and understand medication information in an effective and timely manner. Through a user-centered design process involving older adults and health professionals we developed an interactive camera-projector system called MeViTa (Medication Visualization Table) that projects medication information surrounding medication boxes laid on a table. Six designs were iteratively developed. In total 26 older adults, with a mean age of 71 ($\pm$7), participated in the user studies. Although no time benefits were observed, participants perceived MeViTa as an effective means to explore and understand medication information, and as more engaging than the traditional patient information leaflet. Furthermore, by visualizing medication information, our approach provides qualitative findings of the relative ease and difficulty for older adults to learn more about medication information.

Keywords: Medication · Camera-projector · Older adults · User-centered

1 Introduction

Research shows that health literacy - the degree to which people have the capacity to obtain, process, and understand health information - decreases with age [25]. This is problematic as a large part of the older population is dependent on medication. For example, in the United States, more than half of the older population of 65 + needs to take more than five medications per week [41]. Furthermore, accidental medication misuse is also more common with older adults [32]. This misuse is generally related to the fact that medication information can be cumbersome to understand [5]. The work that is presented in this paper attempts to use innovative technology to make it easier for older adults to process medication information. This is an exploratory study focused on the user experience of older adults interacting with our proposed solution.

Several approaches have been proposed to help older adults with technology. Besides typical app-based solutions, the HCI community has shown the potential of using more tangible, interactive technologies to assist people with various deficits and disorders

R. Bernhaupt et al. (Eds.): INTERACT 2017, Part I, LNCS 10513, pp. 132–152, 2017.
DOI: 10.1007/978-3-319-67744-6_9

[3, 24, 44]. In this paper, we extend this body of research with a proof-of-concept that augments older adults in their capability to understand personal medication schemes. Through a user-centered design process involving older adults and health domain professionals (two medical software experts, two legal experts, and two medical researchers) we developed an interactive camera-projector system called MeViTa (Medication Visualization Table). MeViTa makes users' data visible through an augmented reality data visualization and visualizes (1) possible interactions between medication, (2) the user's personalized dosage regimen, and (3) the probability of side-effects. Users can explore, interpret and engage with diverse kinds of information by putting medication boxes on the table, as presented in Fig. 1. Note that our design tries to complement existing systems, such as medication reminders [10], not to replace them. This raises the key question whether allowing older adults to interact with augmented reality visualization techniques empowers them to explore, understand, and recall medication information.

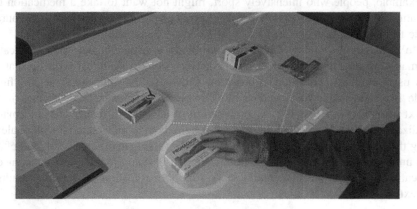

Fig. 1. *Interaction View* of the Final Design. The medication boxes on the table are recognized and medication information is projected surrounding the boxes.

We make the following contributions: first, we present the design and implementation of an open-source camera-projector system that visualizes medication information around medication boxes on a table. Second, we present evaluation results of the perceived usefulness with in total 26 older participants and we describe both weaknesses and benefits for the HCI community working with augmented tools for older persons. Finally, we discuss issues older persons can experience during evaluations with a camera-projector system.

2 Background and Related-Work

To give insight into the challenges posed by medication intake, we provide a short background and briefly discuss the challenges people can experience with medication intake and the effects of medication misuse. We then position our work within related work on camera-projector systems and assistive technologies.

2.1   Medication Use

Correctly taking medication involves of a multitude of tasks: getting the right pre-scription, buying the medication, reading the leaflet[1] and searching for possible interactions between medications, allergies, and even food. One of the problems with medication use is that people can find it difficult to understand the traditional leaflets [23, 30]. According to Liu et al. [30] leaflets *"are inappropriate for use by older adults to manage their medications effectively, which could adversely affect patient safety and adherence to drug therapy."* Furthermore, Ng et al. [33] found users often struggled to make sense of the provided data in its default form and suggest the use of pictograms.

Another problem is medication adherence. People often forget, or refuse, to take their medication for distinct reasons [19]. For example, they have a false idea about the inner workings of medication and feel they are unhealthy and unnecessary [38]. Fur-thermore, people are often interested [11] in, or overestimate [7], potential side-effects. For example, people who intensively sport, might not want to take a medication that has fatigue as a side-effect. However, a general practitioner (GP) might discourage people to lookup side-effects in fear of the nocebo phenomenon [4].

MeViTa aims to empower users by providing transparent and open medication information. Interactive visualizations encourage people to interact with the data. It helps users explore medication information and make the data more meaningful as people may understand and become more interested in medication schemes in the context of their own lives [11]. A combination of augmented reality and information visualization information techniques may also help them to understand the rationale for taking their medication correctly by visualizing the (often small) chance of side-effects in an unambiguous matter. As such, it may support decision-making and adherence to medication. We elaborate on technologies to support medication use for older adults in the next section.

2.2   Health Technologies that Support Older Adults

Several HCI researchers have explored opportunities to use technology to support the older adults. Medication reminders/helpers are well known assistive technologies in the medical domain. While medication adherence is a problem for all age groups, research suggests it is more common among older adults [31]. It is shown that dosage simpli-fication, counseling, reminders, follow-up, supervised self-monitoring, and feedback have the largest positive effect [27, 34]. Medication apps represent a possible strategy to assist non-adherent people [10]. However, older adults are sometimes digital immigrants [48] who might miss prior experience with mobile and other touch enabled devices or prefer not to use them. Another approach are sensor-augmented pillboxes which were developed for older adults [29] or Personal Health Applications [40].

In this paper, we target self-supporting older persons who want to take ownership of their medication. A pill box is sub-optimal as it does not show the rationale and is limited to the medication regime. The overall goal is to empower older adults to explore

---

[1] Also known as: patient information leaflet (PIL) or patient insert.

and understand medication information to address the risks and challenges, such as accidental medication misuse [32], medication interactions [16] and compliance [21].

In our prior work [11], we initially proposed the use of camera-projector technologies as a collaborative tool for improving communication between a GP and a patient. In this paper, we focus on how such technologies might assist older persons with their medication intake. We designed, implemented and evaluated views that represent the interplay between medications, dosage regimen and side-effects.

2.3 Camera-Projector Systems

In this work, we use a stationary camera-projector system. We based our approach on the work of Gugenheimer et al. [15] who "*envision a future where such devices [camera-projector systems] will be sold in hardware stores. They could be available in different form factors, either as a replacement for light bulbs or a simple small box which can be placed in several ways inside the users' environments to be able to blend into the household.*" Evidence of this vision can already be seen in industrial projects. For example, IKEA's kitchen concept 2025 [20] shows an example of an augmented kitchen table. ActiveCues developed a similar system for people with dementia. Results from their initial studies are promising: "*we saw an increase of positive emotions and social activity and a significant increase in their physical activity.*" [1] Such systems can also be used to augment medication information.

The research community has also been exploring the topic. LightSpace [49] for instance explores a variety of interactions between camera-projector surfaces and metaDESK [46] is an important example of interaction techniques using a tangible user interface. Other applications can be devised for this technology. As Jones et al. [22] mentioned, "*[m]any new and exciting possibilities remain to be explored.*" By enabling the projection of interactive visualizations around medication boxes these systems can also be used to augment medication information, and this is in line with our requirement of empowering older persons with actionable knowledge about their medication.

3 Design of MeViTa

A main consideration for the design of MeViTa was the selection of the displayed information. In this section, we give an overview of the final design of MeViTa, shown in Fig. 1, and its technical details. The rationale and major design decisions are presented in Sect. 4.

3.1 Visualizations

The Final Design evolved through five intermediate designs as described in Sect. 4. Finally, as a result from this design process three different views remained to display relevant information to users: first, the *Interaction View* (Fig. 1) represents medication interactions, medication-induced allergies and warnings like alcohol and pregnancy. Second, the *Dosage Regimen View* (Fig. 2) depicts dosage schemes. Finally, the *Side-Effects View* (Fig. 3) shows potential side-effects. To switch between these views, users should move all the boxes on the table to specific areas of the projected interface. No touch interface elements were added to prevent older users from unintentionally activating a function [17]. Thus, only by using tangible objects on the table, users can switch between views.

To start using MeViTa, users are required to put all their medication boxes on the table. The system then recognizes these boxes and displays the *Interaction View*. Red to green colored circles surrounding the boxes indicate whether users can take the medication, or how long they should wait until it is safe to take the medication again. The rationale for taking each medication is described at the bottom of the table (headache/insomnia/etc.). Allergies are listed at the table's top right corner. Warnings are represented as icons around the boxes' surrounding circles. Grey dotted lines are drawn between the medication boxes and their respective rationales. Red lines connecting two boxes represent potential medication interactions. Finally, orange dotted lines connecting boxes with allergies or warning icons represent risk associations to alcohol, pregnancy, breast-feeding, driving, and food (e.g. grapefruit). For example, in Fig. 1 the upper left box shows a warning for alcohol consumption.

To access the *Dosage Regimen View*, users should put the boxes in a designated area on the left side of the table. This view uses a table layout and is a personalized medication scheme based on the system used in the national health platform [47]. It displays the number of pills and the times of each dose.

Finally, to see the *Side-Effects View*, users should put the boxes in the lower designated region of the table. This view also uses a table layout, projecting the list of all known side-effects on the table's first column and the association (probability) that each medication has with each side-effect on the remaining columns. These probabilities are projected above each medication using icon displays: blue-colored icons represent the likelihood of each side-effect.

3.2   Technical Design

The visualizations are implemented using the D3.js (4.2.1) [8] JavaScript library, in combination with Underscore (1.8.3) for data calculations, and SAT.js (0.6.0) for collision detection. Both the patient record and medication information is stored in JSON files. The recognition of medication boxes is done using a slightly modified version of Labbé's find-object (0.6.0) tool [28], which uses OpenCV (3.1). The Speeded Up Robust Features (SURF) [6] algorithm is used for keypoint detection and description. It took the system approximately 0.2 s per medication box to determine the location in the scene. The visualization itself updated every 0.5 s to adapt for changed locations within trial-and-error determined thresholds.

MeViTa consists of a standard webcam, i.e. Logitech c930e camera, with a 1920×1080 resolution and a 90 degrees' field, a short throw Acer H6517ST projector with a 1920×1080 resolution and 3000 lm, and a MacBookPro12.1, which is a standard setup for a camera-projector system [51]. Since the essential part of the information is projected around the medication boxes, the system is mounted on the ceiling with both the projector and the camera pointing down towards the table. Calibration is done manually for each new location by registering the outer areas of the

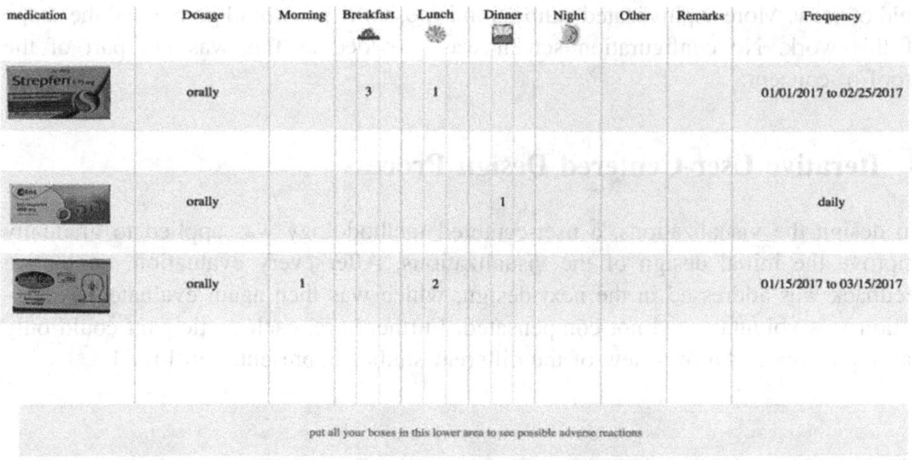

medication	Dosage	Morning	Breakfast	Lunch	Dinner	Night	Other	Remarks	Frequency
Strepfen	orally		3	1					01/01/2017 to 02/25/2017
	orally				1				daily
	orally	1		2					01/15/2017 to 03/15/2017

put all your boxes in this lower area to see possible adverse reactions

Fig. 2. Dosage *Regimen View*, this view is shown when all boxes are put on the left side of the table. For example, the user should orally take 3 pills during breakfast, and 1 during lunch of Strepfen.

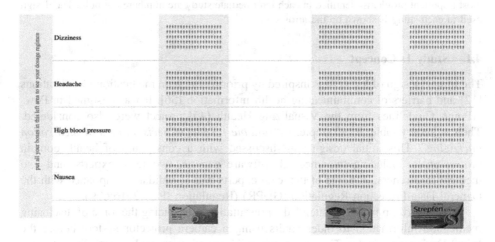

Fig. 3. *Side-Effects View*, this view is shown when all boxes are put on the bottom. For example, in this fictive scenario Strepfen has a very high chance (60%) of headache and a 30% chance of causing high blood pressure. Percentages are not displayed in number but by coloring human figures proportionally.

field of view. More sophisticated calibration is possible, but would go beyond the scope of this work. No configuration screen was provided as this was not part of the proof-of-concept.

4   Iterative User-Centered Design Process

To design the visualizations, a user-centered methodology was applied to gradually improve the initial design of the visualizations. After every evaluation, qualitative feedback was addressed in the next design, which was then again evaluated. Participation was voluntary and not compensated. Furthermore, each participant could only participate once. An overview of the different studies is presented in Fig. 4.

Fig. 4. Timeline that shows the studies and the participants in each iteration. Keywords from the most important problems identified in each intermediate study are numbered in bold. The design used in each study is shown on the arrows.

4.1   Study 1: Concept

The Initial Design of MeViTa is inspired by prior research on medication visualizations [12] and barriers of communicating health information [36]. It was designed in PowerPoint. Guidelines from the Visualizing Health [45] project were also considered. Their summary table, for example, is *"suitable for use in decision aids or medication packaging."* This initial design was discussed with a consortium of health domain professionals, including two medical software experts, two legal experts, and two medical researchers. The role of the legal experts was to validate compliance with the General Data Protection Regulation (GDPR) (Regulation (EU) 2016/679).

All consortium members attended a presentation introducing the topic of disclosing medication information to older adults using a camera projector system before the Initial Design was shown. The design primarily served as an exploration of the domain and formed the basis for Low-Fidelity Design 1. Two major attention points were raised: **Problem (1)** the overview was too crowded: too much information was displayed at once which can be confusing to older adults since the ability to suppress irrelevant representations or response tendencies is known to degrade with age [18]; and **Problem (2)** absolute percentages to visualize changes of side-effects are hard to grasp [13].

4.2   Study 2: Usability

The Initial Design helped to design the Low-Fidelity Design 1 as shown in Fig. 5. The information was divided into four different projections to address Problem 1:

1. interactions and reasons (Figure 5A) → *Interaction View*,
2. dosage regimen (Figure 5B) → *Dosage Regimen View*,
3. side-effects (Figure 5C) → *Side-Effects View*,
4. schedule (Figure 5D) → *Schedule View*.

The circles were not used for the dosage regimen anymore and were now used to visualize the half-life, which is the time the medication remains in the blood. Furthermore, the side-effects were now visualized based on [43] instead of percentages (Problem 2). Users could switch between modes by putting their medication boxes in a respective region. To make this design more realistic, it was developed in PowerPoint so that it could be projected on a table during the expert user evaluation. Five HCI experts were asked to perform a list of typical user tasks to expose usability issues. Two key issues were exposed: **Problem (3)** all information in the schedule was redundantly visualized in the *Dosage Regimen View* (3/5), and **Problem (4)** it is cognitively hard to remember the four regions to put medication (4/5).

4.3 Study 3: Medical Validity

An attempt was made to solve these issues in Low-Fidelity Design 2. The *Schedule View* was removed (Problem 3), thus there are only three main regions to put the medication boxes (Problem 4). This updated design was evaluated with an expert GP from the academic center for general practice to test medical relevance. Two problems were identified: **Problem (5)** the thickness of an interaction line showed the severity, and an orange-to-red hue indicated the probability of a possible interaction. However,

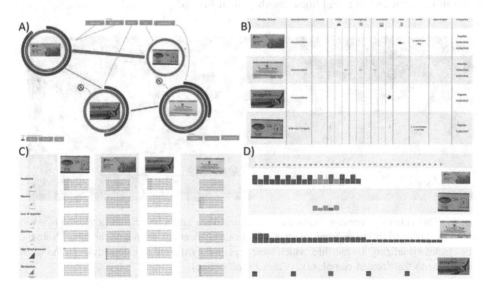

Fig. 5. Overview of the Low-Fidelity Design 1. The view projected depends on the location of the boxes. When they are divided over the table the user sees the (A) *Interaction View*; when they are on the left side the (B) *Dosage Regimen View*, at the top the (C) *Side-Effects View*, and on the right side the (D) *Schedule View*.

this information is often not available in real patient records; and **Problem (6)** the severity of a side-effect is a very personal experience and an impersonal, independently determined severity level is thus best not shown.

4.4   Study 4: Explorative Evaluation with Older Adults

Based on previous feedback a fully working High Fidelity Design was built as presented in Fig. 6. To cope with earlier remarks, we only showed one type of connection between medications from the start (Problem 5): once there was the chance of an interaction a line was drawn between the two medications, hence the severity, and probability were not shown. Furthermore, the severity of side-effects was not shown (Problem 6), only the occurrence.

This intermediate study consisted of four parts: (1) an initial questionnaire exploring demographics and existing attitudes towards medication intake; (2) a task-based scenario; (3) a perceived usefulness questionnaire based on [35] complemented with additional questions; and finally (4) the System Usability Scale (SUS) [9]. Participants were recruited through a paper invitation distributed amongst people at a local older adults' community. Eleven older persons (74 ± 8.3, 5 females) participated in this study. One participant did not take any medication, four participants needed to take only one pill a day and the six others took 3 to 10 pills per day. Three received help from their partner and two received a letter from their GP to prepare a pill box. MeViTa was installed in the home of one participant as the community was a far distance from the research center and it was impossible for some participants to travel the distance. The other participants were invited to this participant's home. Thus, the evaluation happened in a real home as shown in Fig. 6.

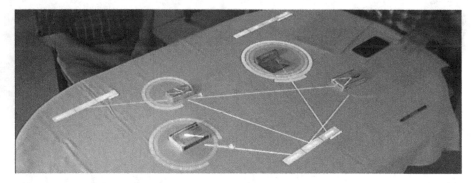

Fig. 6. This video's screenshot shows the *Interaction View* and a participant (left) who is asked by the facilitator (right) to perform a certain task. Four medications are put on the table. Note the blue circles visualizing the half-life, which were replaced by the red to green circles in the latest design due to the deemed complexity. (Color figure online)

Comparison with the Leaflet. To enable a comparison between MeViTa and the leaflet, participants were initially asked to answer five questions using the leaflet. However, we did not complete this part of the study as five participants did not want to read the leaflet (**Problem 7**) because their doctor, who might consider the nocebo phenomenon [4], advised them to not read leaflets. Moreover, two participants mentioned their partner read it. Three other participants could either not find (2/11) or read (1/11) the information. Hence, only 1 out of 11 participants could successfully read the traditional leaflet.

Task-Based Scenario. During the task-based scenario participants were asked to answer seven questions. All participants had to answer the same questions on the medication scheme which was based on a real medication scheme. This scheme contained of four medications and served as a simple use case of medication intake. However, it was discussed at the Academic Center for General Practice in Leuven to represent a realistic use case. To avoid that participants could answer questions from memory and not look at the table to complete their task, fictional medication boxes were used with altered medication names. Unfortunately, most participants were confused by the medication they did not recognize (**Problem 8**). For example, when asked to answer why Cymbolto was used two participants said without looking at the table: "*I don't know, I don't take this medication.*" In total five out of 11 participants did not look at the table and immediately indicated they did not know the answer. Similar observations were made during the other tasks.

The question about the medication's half-life did not interest our participants (**Problem 9**). A participant summarized it perfectly: "*I don't care; my doctor should know this.*" It is interesting to note that although participants were told that they could touch and move medication boxes on the table, none of the participants touched the boxes, unless explicitly asked to do so. However, when they needed to move the boxes to switch views we observed some difficulties reaching the upper part of the table (**Problem 10**).

Perceived Usefulness and System Usability. The fact that participants were confused between the real medication and the imaginary medication that had some letters changed (Problem 8) was also clear in the average SUS score of 64, which is below the average score of 68 [2]. Participants responded neutral when asked whether they felt confident using the system. Answers on the perceived usefulness questionnaire are shown in Fig. 7. Notwithstanding the difficulties with the name confusion, the whiskers show both the mean and median range above neutral.

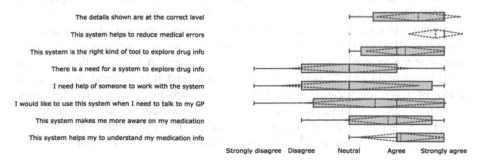

Fig. 7. Answers from the 11 participants ranging from strongly disagree to strongly agree. The boxes visualize the answers on the perceived usefulness questions. Dotted lines indicate the mean and standard deviations.

4.5 Study 5: Evaluation Setup Validation

Before conducting the final user study, the updated design setup was evaluated in a short intermediate study. To address Problem 9, the circles visualizing the medication's half-life were replaced by simpler circles that show whether it is OK to take the medication. Furthermore, to enhance reachability (Problem 10) the area for side-effects was moved to the bottom of the table. This time, participants received a 1-minute demonstration of MeViTa using a box of iron staples to show that the meaning of the boxes was not important. We deliberately chose not to show a legend to evaluate whether the visualizations were clear without it. In contrast to Study 4: Elderly Community (Sect. 4.4), it was strongly emphasized they were not looking at their own medication but at the medication scheme of Julie Janssens, a fictive woman of 73 years old weighing 76 kg. Furthermore, only the colors of the boxes were mentioned by the main researcher to address Problem 8.

We tested this High-Fidelity Design 2 with three participants that were initially recruited for the final evaluation (Sect. 5). Only one minor usability issue was discovered and optimized in the Final Design: a grey area was added to the bottom to indicate more clearly the area for side-effects. Another grey area was added on the left of the table to indicate the area for the medicine schedule.

5 Final Evaluation

This section describes the final user evaluation of the Final Design resulting from the five prior studies as described in Sect. 4. This evaluation explores whether allowing older adults to interact with augmented reality visualization techniques empowers them to explore, understand, and recall medication information in an effective and timely manner.

5.1 Participants

Participants were found using a call for participation published in a major health insurance members' magazine. We did not impose an age limit and all self-identified seniors could participate. These self-supporting older adults are the actual target group of MeViTa. In total, 45 people responded to the call and were contacted by the main researcher explaining the research and planned evaluation in more detail. Each participant was asked to attend an evaluation session of maximum one hour at the nursing home or at the university's computer science department. A mileage allowance was offered in return. In total 22 participants were willing and able to attend an evaluation session, of which seven canceled last minute due to personal reasons. The first three participants were used to validate the updated evaluation setup (Sect. 4.5). Hence, in total 12 older adults (3 females) participated in the final evaluation. They were on average 67.5 ($\pm$5.5) years old and took on average 9 ($\pm$5.5) pills every day.

5.2 Experimental Setup and Measurements

At the start, each participant received an information sheet and was asked to sign an informed consent. Like Studies 4 and 5 the evaluation started with an initial demographic questionnaire. After a tutorial, similar to Study 5: Evaluation Setup Validation (Sect. 4.5), participants were asked (1) to find two side-effects, and (2) the dosage regimen of Motilium using a leaflet. Next, using MeViTa, the same two tasks and five additional tasks were asked in random order. The same approach as in Study 5: Evaluation Setup Validation was applied. It was emphasized they were not looking at their own medication but at the medication scheme of a fictive woman. Participants were asked to think aloud. The following parameters were measured:

- *Time.* How much time does a participant need to complete a given task from the scenario? These timings are extracted from the recorded video files and compared to the time needed to find information in a traditional leaflet.
- *Interaction strategies.* Based on the recordings each interaction performed was logged and analyzed to detect potential strategies participants applied.
- *Memorability.* We wanted to learn if participants recalled more information when they visually saw the information instead of reading the information from leaflets. Participants were asked to recall information from two tasks they performed using both the leaflet and MeViTa.

After this task-based scenario seven perceived usefulness questions based on O'Leary et al. [35] and ten SUS [9] questions were asked.

5.3 Traditional Leaflet and Task-Based Scenario

Table 1 provides an overview of each task and the average completion time. To avoid the pitfalls of Study 4: Elderly Community (Problem 7), participants were asked to perform only two tasks using the leaflet. To account for GPs' nocebo phenomenon concerns [4] the leaflet of an off-the-market medication Motilium was provided.

Task (1) *"Can you tell me the side-effects of Motilium"* or for MeViTa *"Can you tell me the side-effects of the white/red box?"* was successfully completed by nine out of 12 participants using the leaflet (69 s ± 37 s). However, three participants were not able to list the side-effects. To solve this task using MeViTa, participants had to move all boxes on the table to the bottom to switch to the *Side-Effects View*. Compared to the leaflet, it took participants longer to answer the question (107 s ± 55 s) because they initially moved just one box. On the other hand, all participants could successfully find all side-effects.

Task (2) *"On which times during the day can Julie use Motilium"* and *"On which times during the day can Julie use the red box"* was answered correctly by all 12 participants both by using the leaflet (29 s ± 19 s) and by using MeViTa (45 s ± 33 s). With MeViTa, participants first had to move all boxes to the left side of the table to switch to the *Dosage Regimen View*. Then a table with the dosage regimen is projected on the table. Each row is the regimen for the corresponding medication. In contrast to the prior task, only four participants initially moved only one box.

This indicated they remembered how to switch modes using the boxes: "*Then I have to get to that other screen for sure?*"

To alleviate potential resistance to reading the leaflet, participants were asked only two questions using the leaflet. Therefore, the following tasks were only performed using MeViTa. Task (3) "*Why do you think Julie should take this blue box?*" could easily be solved using the *Interaction View*. A grey dotted line connected the blue box with '*fibromyalgia*'. This task was completed swiftly (5 s ± 2 s) and correctly by all 12 participants.

Task (4) "*How do you rate the chance Julie will get a dry throat?*" could be solved by moving all boxes to the bottom of the table and thus switch to the *Side-Effects View*. There, a medication's side-effects are shown in a column above the medication box (see Fig. 3). As the tasks were given in random order, some participants already started from the *Side-Effects View* while others first needed to move all boxes. However, all 12 participants completed the task correctly 10 s ± 10 s. Interestingly, participants rated the likelihood of side-effects lower than prescribed in the leaflet. When there were ten or less out of hundred person icons colored, participants rated the likelihood as uncommon, while the leaflet would list them as common.

Task (5) "*Do you think Julie can drink alcohol while taking these medications?*" could be solved using the *Interaction View*. As shown in Fig. 1 orange dotted lines are drawn from the medication box to an alcohol symbol when an interaction is possible. However, this task created confusion with our participants as they were always taught not to drink any alcohol when on medication: "*Of course, I assume that you do not drink alcohol, that is obvious.*" Five participants therefore first moved all boxes to the bottom of the table to spot the side-effects, which also weights on the average time (20 s ± 21 s).

Task (6) "*Can Julie combine these two blue boxes*" could be solved using the *Interaction View*. One of the primary features of the *Interaction View* is the opportunity to check for medication-medication interactions. When two medications harmfully interact with each other a red line is drawn between the two boxes. However, three out of 12 participants switched to the *Side-Effects View* thinking that two similar side-effects might strengthen each other. Eventually, all 12 participants spotted the red line between two boxes and could finish this task successfully (53 s ± 66 s). Moreover, participants remembered to divide the boxes over the table for a better overview: "*but you [I] should not put the boxes too close to each other.*"

Task (7) "*How much longer before Julie can take a pain killer for her headache?*" could be solved using two different approaches. The *Interaction View* shows a green circle surrounding a medication box when the user can take that medication now. Users can also use the *Dosage Regimen View* to see if enough time has passed since the last dose. Ten out of 12 participants completed the task (30 s ± 27 s): four participants used the *Dosage Regimen View* to complete this task, while six other participants used the *Interaction View*. Two participants were unable to complete this task: "*How should I know this?*" and "*I don't know, it depends on what the doctor says.*"

Table 1. Average time needed to perform each task and the view needed.

Task	Leaflet	MeViTa	Δ	View
1. Can you tell me the side-effects of that white/red box?	69 s ± 37 s	107 s ± 55 s	+70 s	*Side-effects*
2. On which times during the day can Julie use the red box?	29 s ± 19 s	45 s ± 33 s	+16 s	*Dosage regimen*
3. Why do you think Julie should take this blue box?	/	5 s ± 2 s	/	*Interaction*
4. How do you rate the chance Julie will get a dry throat?	/	10 s ± 10 s	/	*Side-effects*
5. Do you think Julie can drink alcohol while taking these medications?	/	20 s ± 21 s	/	*Interaction*
6. Can Julie combine these two blue boxes?	/	53 s ± 66 s	/	*Interaction*
7. How much longer before Julie can take a pain killer for her headache?	/	30 s ± 27 s	/	*Interaction* or *dosage regimen*

5.4 Results on the Perceived Usefulness and Usability Questionnaire

As illustrated in Fig. 8, answers to Likert scale questions scored consistently high. When participants were asked whether MeViTa increased their comprehension of medication schemes 10 out of 12 participants agreed. The two participants that were less positive argued they first needed to get acquainted with the system. All participants agreed that the design can create medication awareness. Ten participants answered they would like to use the system when they would need to talk to their GP. One participant who responded neutral indicated her doctor "*is 82 years old, and doesn't like computers.*" The strongest benefit mentioned is that both the user and the GP would have the same overview which makes it is easier to signal a certain problem to their caregiver. Participants also liked the fact that a general overview of all their medication is generated. This could be particularly useful when they need to go a different specialist. Participants agreed that there is a need for a system to interact with medication as "*young caregivers need to search too much information, anciens [older, more experienced caregivers] already know all of that.*" Participants agreed MeViTa is 'a' right kind of tool, yet seven participants responded neutral as it is not necessarily 'the' right kind of tool. Eight out of 12 participants strongly agreed and 4 agreed that the system can prevent medical mistakes, such as for example medication-medication interactions. Finally, the details are at the right level for 11 out of 12 participants. The scores on the SUS questionnaire was on average 81.5, ranking MeViTa with an A grade [37]. The question on whether they would like to use the system frequently scored lowest. Two out of 12 participants who answered negatively mentioned they would only like to use it when they were prescribed new medication, or when they have a question. In contrast to prior evaluation, both questions: "*I felt very confident using the system*" and "*I think*

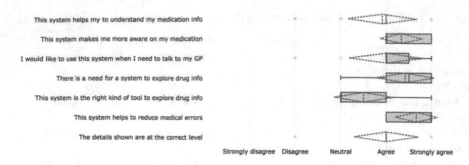

Fig. 8. Answers from the 12 participants ranging from strongly disagree to strongly agree. The box plots visualize the answers on the perceived usefulness questions. Dotted lines indicate the mean and standard deviations.

that I would need the support of a technical person to be able to use this system." scored positive suggesting an improvement over the previous setup.

5.5   Interaction Strategies

In Study 4: Elderly Community (Sect. 4.4) participants only touched the medication boxes when they explicitly needed to move them to alternate between views. In this evaluation, however, other interaction strategies were observed. We observed two kind of actions. The first kind of actions we call *'better overview'*: some participants moved the boxes in such a way to eliminate line intersections or moved boxes further apart to create more distance between the visualization elements for a better overview. The second type of interactions we classify as *'remove'*: some participants took non-relevant boxes from the table to simplify the visualization. Initially, we also logged when participants touched the boxes to confirm they were answering the questions of the right box and when they, unintentionally, held something above the boxes so the camera lost track of the box. All actions were logged using the video recordings and manually extracted. Table 2 shows a summary of all actions logged.

No relation, nor trend was found between the amount of times a participant performed an interaction and how he or she performed on a task. Nor was there any trend observed between the amount of interactions and the answers on the questionnaires. However, as explained above, two strategies were observed for obtaining a better

Table 2. Overview of the number of times participants interacted with the medication boxes ranked per task.

	Task 1	Task 2	Task 3	Task 4	Task 5	Task 6	Task 7	Total
Better overview	2	6	0	2	1	1	0	12
Remove	0	6	2	0	0	6	0	14
switch between views	0	14	2	1	9	9	1	36
Touch to confirm box	2	6	0	5	1	2	2	18
Block From camera	0	3	0	2	1	1	0	7
Total	4	35	4	10	12	19	3	

overview: moving boxes or removing them. The latter strategy was mostly used when participants needed to move boxes to switch between views. They moved the box they were interested in to the right location and took the other boxes away. Finally, the view from the camera was blocked seven times of which three occurrences are related to one participant. This was not an issue as this primarily occurred while participants were moving other boxes around so they did not even notice this occurrence.

5.6 Memorability

After each evaluation participants were asked (1) if they could still name the side-effects of Motilium and the side-effects of the white/red box, and (2) if they could say the dosage regimen of both Motilium and the red box. Question 1 and 2 were answered correctly by respectively five and eight participants who used the leaflet.

Using MeViTa, correct responses were lower: question 1 and 2 were answered correctly by two and five participants respectively. From these results, we cannot show MeViTa helps participants recall medication information more effectively.

6 Discussion

6.1 MeViTa as a Tool to Explore Medication Information

In this paper, we proposed MeViTa to empower older adults to explore medication information. MeViTa is designed using a user-centered methodology. Thus, changes made to each intermediate design improved general usability and functionality. Suggestions raised during the five iterative studies were incorporated in each updated version as described in Sect. 4.

It is important to optimize and minimize the information shown to the user. On the other hand, Shneiderman's mantra [39] advocates to first show an overview and afterwards let the user find the details on demand. However, our initial design was deemed too complex by our expert consortium members (Problem 1). Furthermore, it showed redundant (Problem 3) or non-interesting information (Problem 9), such as the medication's half-life, which could make it harder to remember how to switch between views (Problem 4). In Study 3: Medical Validity we learned which medication information is locally available (Problem 5) and that health-related issues are a personal experience (Problem 6). Finally, especially when working with an older audience, reachability should be considered (Problem 10), as they can experience issues reaching the far end of a table.

Although none of our participants had interacted with a camera-projector system before, most remarks concerned the visualization's learning curve and not the use of a camera-projector system. We thus argue that the technical choice was appropriate to test our visualizations. Alternative solutions include a tabletop that can recognize tangibles or a tablet. All participants mentioned they liked this approach as they did not need to learn any new interaction paradigms. The positive perception is also reflected in the average SUS score of 81.5.

Finally, we observed that by showing the little colored people icons to show uncertainty [43] people were generally less concerned with the likelihood of a side-effect. When they visually saw 1 in 100 people, they realized the likelihood is smaller than they initially thought when just reading 1% or 'uncommon'. As our sample size is small, we cannot draw strong conclusions from this observation, but the observation is interesting for further research.

6.2   Lessons Learned with Older Participants

Important lessons were learned by analyzing the qualitative evaluation data and by observing our participants performing each task. Foremost, like Kobayashi et al. [26] our participants in Study 4: Elderly Community were easily confused. In the succeeding studies participants were therefore better informed about the medication on the table not being their own medication for evaluation purposes. Furthermore, the name of Julie was always mentioned as a reminder and colors were used to refer to medication.

Like Wrede-Sach et al. [50], we also learned older adults place a lot of trust in their GP. Some participants were not willing to read an unknown leaflet as their doctor told them not to read their leaflets. Moreover, in Study 4: Elderly Community only one participant could successfully read the leaflet. Therefore, in the final evaluation, we only asked participants to do two tasks using the leaflet and used an off-the-market medication to consider their doctors' concern. Even then, we could sometimes notice some frustration when they were asked a second question using the leaflet. Although we observed faster timings when participants were asked to perform a similar task, this chosen methodology limited us to ask the participant to perform similar tasks to eliminate learning effects.

6.3   Evaluation Results

Answers on the perceived usefulness questions improved compared to Study 4: Elderly Community. Reasons can be twofold. First, both the issues with the non-interesting half-life and the reachability were addressed and consequently participants received a better experience. Second, the participants in the first iteration were on average seven years older and were recruited through a community, whereas participants in the final evaluation were recruited using a public call in a health magazine and were asked to register online.

Only basic interaction strategies were discovered. Participants moved boxes for a better overview, took boxes from the table to simplify the visualization and sometimes touched the box to ask for confirmation. Given our limited number of participants, no statistically relevant results could be discovered. However, in contrast to Harada et al. [17], we did not discover any unintentional interactions by using objects as an input mechanism to control the views [14].

6.4   Limitations

The number of participants (in total 26) and the absence of a control condition can be seen as a limitation of our current work. However, like Sonne et al. [42] *"we argue [...]*

that it is more important to first uncover potential problems and understand the use of the technology, than to conduct longer and larger efficacy studies." Furthermore, to allow for a comparison between participants we used a non-personal realistic medication regimen instead of asking each participant to bring their own medication. Moreover, we should first discover potential issues and get medical clearance before showing real, personal medication information.

7 Conclusion

In this study, we made the following contributions: first, we presented the design and implementation of an open-source camera-projector system that visualizes medication information around medication boxes on a table. Second, we presented the results of the evaluation of the perceived usefulness of our design with in total 26 older adults participants, and we described both weaknesses and benefits for the HCI community working with technology for older adults. Finally, we also discussed the issues older adults can experience during evaluations with a camera-projector system. To further validate MeViTa, we already made a tentative agreement with the country's largest medication database provider to use their medically validated data in MeViTa.

We believe that with five intermediate studies as described in Sect. 4, and the final evaluation we could to show the perceived usefulness of MeViTa. Qualitative feedback gathered in the different studies shows that MeViTa can empower older adults by visualizing medication information. Although not everybody agreed MeViTa is the only kind of tool that could help them, they do strongly agree there is a need for an application that helps them explore medication info. Unfortunately, we were not able to proof that MeViTa can augment people's ability to recall medication information better or has a time benefit. However, participants indicated that MeViTa helps to understand medication information and increases awareness, that it helps to reduce medical errors and that they would like to use MeViTa in sessions with their GP.

Acknowledgments. MyHealthData is a project co-funded by imec, a digital research institute founded by the Flemish Government. Project partners are EBMPracticeNet, CEBAM, HealthConnect, CM, and MindBytes with project support from Agentschap Innoveren & Ondernemen. The authors would also like to thank all participants and the anonymous reviewers for their extensive feedback to improve the quality of the paper.

References

1. ActiveCues: Tovertafel original. https://dutchgamesassociation.nl/thoughts/517. Accessed 5 May 2017
2. Bangor, A., Kortum, P., Miller, J.: Determining what individual SUS scores mean: adding an adjective rating scale. J. Usability Stud. **4**(3), 114–123 (2009)
3. Bardram, J.E., Frost, M., Szántó, K., Faurholt-Jepsen, M., Vinberg, M., Kessing, L.V.: Designing mobile health technology for bipolar disorder: a field trial of the monarca system. In: Proceedings of the SIGCHI Conference on Human Factors in Computing Systems, pp. 2627–2636. ACM, New York, April 2013

4. Barsky, A.J., Saintfort, R., Rogers, M.P., Borus, J.F.: Nonspecific medication side effects and the nocebo phenomenon. JAMA **287**(5), 622–627 (2002)
5. Basen, M.M.: The elderly and drugs–problem overview and program strategy. Public Health Rep. **92**(1), 43–48 (1997)
6. Bay, H., Ess, A., Tuytelaars, T., Van Gool, L.: Speeded-Up robust features (SURF). Comput. Vis. Image Underst. **110**(3), 346–359 (2008)
7. Berry, D.C., Knapp, P., Raynor, D.K.: Provision of information about drug sideeffects to patients. Lancet **359**(9309), 853–854 (2002)
8. Bostock, M., Ogievetsky, V., Heer, J.: D^3: data-driven documents. IEEE Trans. Vis. Comput. Graph. **17**(12), 2301–2309 (2011)
9. Brooke, J.: SUS-a quick and dirty usability scale. Usability Eval. Ind. **189**(194), 4–7 (1996)
10. Dayer, L., Heldenbrand, S., Anderson, P., Gubbins, P.O., Martin, B.C.: Smartphone medication adherence apps: potential benefits to patients and providers. J. Am. Pharm. Assoc. **53**(2), 172–181 (2013)
11. De Croon, R., Klerkx, J., Duval, E.: A Proof-of-Concept visualization to increase comprehension of personal medication schemes. In: Proceedings of the 10th EAI International Conference on Pervasive Computing Technologies for Healthcare, pp. 25–32. ICST, Cancun, June 2016
12. Duke, J., Faiola, A., Kharrazi, H.: A novel visualization tool for evaluating medication side-effects in multi-drug regimens. In: Jacko, J.A. (ed.) HCI 2009. LNCS, vol. 5613, pp. 478–487. Springer, Heidelberg (2009). doi:10.1007/978-3-642-02583-9_52
13. Fischoff, B., Brewer, N., Downs, J.: Communicating risks and benefits: an evidencebased user's guide. Technical report, Food and Drug Administration, New Hampshire Ave, Silver Spring (2011)
14. Fitzmaurice, G.W.: Graspable user interfaces. Ph.D. thesis, University of Toronto (1996)
15. Gugenheimer, J., Knierim, P., Winkler, C., Seifert, J., Rukzio, E.: UbiBeam: exploring the interaction space for home deployed projector-camera systems. In: Abascal, J., Barbosa, S., Fetter, M., Gross, T., Palanque, P., Winckler, M. (eds.) INTERACT 2015. LNCS, vol. 9298, pp. 350–366. Springer, Cham (2015). doi:10.1007/978-3-319-22698-9_23
16. Haider, S.I., Johnell, K., Weitoft, G.R., Thorslund, M., Fastbom, J.: The influence of educational level on polypharmacy and inappropriate drug use: a register-based study of more than 600,000 older people. J. Am. Geriatr. Soc. **57**(1), 62–69 (2009)
17. Harada, S., Sato, D., Takagi, H., Asakawa, C.: Characteristics of elderly user behavior on mobile multi-touch devices. In: Kotzé, P., Marsden, G., Lindgaard, G., Wesson, J., Winckler, M. (eds.) INTERACT 2013. LNCS, vol. 8120, pp. 323–341. Springer, Heidelberg (2013). doi:10.1007/978-3-642-40498-6_25
18. Hasher, L.: Zacks, R.T., May, C.P.: Inhibitory control, circadian arousal, and age. In: Attention and Performance XVII, Cognitive Regulation of Performance: Interaction of Theory and Application, pp. 653–675 (1999)
19. Hugtenburg, J.G., Timmers, L., Elders, P.J., Vervloet, M., van Dijk, L.: Definitions, variants, and causes of nonadherence with medication: a challenge for tailored interventions. Patient Prefer. Adherence **7**, 675–682 (2013)
20. Ikea: Concept kitchen 2025. http://conceptkitchen2025.ideo.london/. Accessed 5 May 2017
21. Jimmy, B., Jose, J.: Patient medication adherence: measures in daily practice. Oman Med. J. **26**(3), 155–159 (2011)
22. Jones, B., Sodhi, R., Murdock, M., Mehra, R., Benko, H., Wilson, A., Ofek, E., MacIntyre, B., Raghuvanshi, N., Shapira, L.: RoomAlive: magical experiences enabled by scalable, adaptive projector-camera units. In: Proceedings of the 27th Annual ACM Symposium on User Interface Software and Technology, pp. 637–644. ACM, Honolulu, October 2014

23. Katz, M.G., Kripalani, S., Weiss, B.D.: Use of pictorial aids in medication instructions: a review of the literature. Am. J. Health Syst. Pharm. **63**(23), 2391–2397 (2006)
24. Kientz, J.A., Goodwin, M.S., Hayes, G.R., Abowd, G.D.: Interactive technologies for autism. Synth. Lect. Assistive Rehabilitative Health-Preserving Technol. **2**(2), 1–177 (2013)
25. Kobayashi, L.C., Wardle, J., Wolf, M.S., Wagner, C.: Aging and functional health literacy: a systematic review and meta-analysis. J. Gerontol. B Psychol. Sci. Soc. Sci. **71**(3), 10–1093 (2014)
26. Kobayashi, M., Hiyama, A., Miura, T., Asakawa, C., Hirose, M., Ifukube, T.: Elderly user evaluation of mobile touchscreen interactions. In: Campos, P., Graham, N., Jorge, J., Nunes, N., Palanque, P., Winckler, M. (eds.) INTERACT 2011. LNCS, vol. 6946, pp. 83–99. Springer, Heidelberg (2011). doi:10.1007/978-3-642-23774-4_9
27. Kripalani, S., Yao, X., Haynes, R.B.: Interventions to enhance medication adherence in chronic medical conditions: a systematic review. Arch. Intern. Med. **167**(6), 540–550 (2007)
28. Labbé, M.: Find-object (2011). http://introlab.github.io/find-object
29. Lee, M.L., Dey, A.K.: Real-time feedback for improving medication taking. In: Proceedings of the 32nd Annual ACM Conference on Human Factors in Computing Systems, pp. 2259–2268. CHI 2014. ACM, New York (2014)
30. Liu, F., Abdul-Hussain, S., Mahboob, S., Rai, V., Kostrzewski, A.: How useful are medication patient information leaflets to older adults? a content, readability and layout analysis. Int. J. Clin. Pharm. **36**(4), 827–834 (2014)
31. MacLaughlin, E.J., Raehl, C.L., Treadway, A.K., Sterling, T.L., Zoller, D.P., Bond, C.A.: Assessing medication adherence in the elderly: which tools to use in clinical practice? Drugs Aging **22**(3), 231–255 (2005)
32. Montamat, S.C., Cusack, B.: Overcoming problems with polypharmacy and drug misuse in the elderly. Clin. Geriatr. Med. **8**(1), 143–158 (1992)
33. Ng, A.W.Y., Chan, A.H.S., Ho, V.W.S.: Comprehension by older people of medication information with or without supplementary pharmaceutical pictograms. Appl. Ergon. **58**, 167–175 (2017)
34. Nieuwlaat, R., Wilczynski, N., Navarro, T., Hobson, N., Jeffery, R., Keepanasseril, A., Agoritsas, T., Mistry, N., Iorio, A., Jack, S., Sivaramalingam, B., Iserman, E., Mustafa, R.A., Jedraszewski, D., Cotoi, C., Haynes, R.B.: Interventions for enhancing medication adherence. Cochrane Database Syst. Rev. (11), CD000011 (2014)
35. O'Leary, P., Carroll, N., Richardson, I.: The practitioner's perspective on clinical pathway support systems. In: 2014 IEEE International Conference on Healthcare Informatics, pp. 194–201. IEEE, Verona (2014)
36. Rothman, A.J., Kiviniemi, M.T.: Treating people with information: an analysis and review of approaches to communicating health risk information. J. Natl. Cancer Inst. Monogr. Monogr. **25**, 44–51 (1999)
37. Sauro, J.: A Practical Guide to the System Usability Scale: Background, Benchmarks & Best Practices. CreateSpace Independent Publishing Platform, North Charleston (2011)
38. Schüz, B., Marx, C., Wurm, S., Warner, L.M., Ziegelmann, J.P., Schwarzer, R., Tesch-Römer, C.: Medication beliefs predict medication adherence in older adults with multiple illnesses. J. Psychosom. Res. **70**(2), 179–187 (2011)
39. Shneiderman, B.: The eyes have it: a task by data type taxonomy for information visualizations. In: Proceedings 1996 IEEE Symposium on Visual Languages, pp. 336–343. IEEE Computer Society Press, Boulder, September 1996
40. Siek, K.A., Khan, D.U., Ross, S.E., Haverhals, L.M., Meyers, J., Cali, S.R.: Designing a personal health application for older adults to manage medications: a comprehensive case study. J. Med. Syst. **35**(5), 1099–1121 (2011)

41. Slone Epidemiology Center: Patterns of medication use in the united states 2006. Technical report, Epidemiology Center at Boston University, Boston (2006)
42. Sonne, T., Müller, J., Marshall, P., Obel, C., Grønbæk, K.: Changing family practices with assistive technology: MOBERO improves morning and bedtime routines for children with ADHD. In: Proceedings of the 2016 CHI Conference on Human Factors in Computing Systems, pp. 152–164. ACM, New York, May 2016
43. Spiegelhalter, D., Pearson, M., Short, I.: Visualizing uncertainty about the future. Science 333(6048), 1393–1400 (2011)
44. Tanuwidjaja, E., Huynh, D., Koa, K., Nguyen, C., Shao, C., Torbett, P., Emmenegger, C., Weibel, N.: Chroma: a wearable augmented-reality solution for color blindness. In: Proceedings of the 2014 ACM International Joint Conference on Pervasive and Ubiquitous Computing, UbiComp 2014, pp. 799–810. ACM, New York (2014)
45. The Regents of the University of Michigan and the Robert Wood Johnson Foundation: Visualizing health. http://www.vizhealth.org/. Accessed 5 May 2017
46. Ullmer, B., Ishii, H.: The metaDESK: models and prototypes for tangible user interfaces. In: Proceedings of the 10th Annual ACM Symposium on User Interface Software and Technology, UIST 1997, pp. 223–232. ACM, New York (1997)
47. vitalink: Medicatiegegevens delen. http://www.vitalink.be/medicatiegegevens-delen. Accessed 5 MAy 2017
48. Waycott, J., Vetere, F., Pedell, S., Morgans, A., Ozanne, E., Kulik, L.: Not for me: older adults choosing not to participate in a social isolation intervention. In: Proceedings of the 2016 CHI Conference on Human Factors in Computing Systems, CHI 2016, pp. 745–757. ACM, New York (2016)
49. Wilson, A.D., Benko, H.: Combining multiple depth cameras and projectors for interactions on, above and between surfaces. In: Proceedings of the 23nd annual ACM Symposium on User Interface Software and Technology, pp. 273–282. ACM, New York, October 2010
50. Wrede-Sach, J., Voigt, I., Diederichs-Egidi, H., Hummers-Pradier, E., Dierks, M.L., Junius-Walker, U.: Decision-making of older patients in context of the doctorpatient relationship: a typology ranging from "self-determined" to "doctor-trusting" patients. Int. J. Family Med. 2013, 478498 (2013)
51. Yamamoto, G., Hyry, J., Krichenbauer, M., Taketomi, T., Sandor, C., Kato, H., Pulli, P.: A user interface design for the elderly using a projection tabletop system. In: 2015 3rd IEEE VR International Workshop on Virtual and Augmented Assistive Technology (VAAT), vol. 51, pp. 29–32. IEEE, March 2015

Assistive Technology for Blind Users

Blind FLM: An Enhanced Keystroke-Level Model for Visually Impaired Smartphone Interaction

Shiroq Al-Megren[✉], Wejdan Altamimi, and Hend S. Al-Khalifa

Department of Information Technology, King Saud University,
Riyadh, Saudi Arabia
{salmegren,hendk}@ksu.edu.sa,
wejdanaltamimi@gmail.com

Abstract. The Keystroke-Level Model (KLM) is a predictive model used to numerically predict how long it takes an expert user to accomplish a task. KLM has been successfully used to model conventional interactions, however, it does not thoroughly render smartphone touch interactions or accessible interfaces (e.g. screen readers). On the other hand, the Fingerstroke-level Model (FLM) extends KLM to describe and assess mobile-based game applications, which marks it as a candidate model for predicting smartphone touch interactions.

This paper aims to further extend FLM for visually impaired smartphone users. An initial user study identified basic elements of blind users' interactions that were used to extend FLM; the new model is called "Blind FLM". Then an additional user study was conducted to determine the applicability of the new model for describing blind users' touch interactions with a smartphone, and to compute the accuracy of the new model. Blind FLM evaluation showed that it can predict blind users' performance with an average error of 2.36%.

Keywords: Keystroke-Level Mode (KLM) · Fingerstroke-Level Model (FLM) · Mobile phone · Smartphone · Mobile KLM · Touch interaction · Visually impaired users · Blind users

1 Introduction

In Human Computer Interaction (HCI), predictive models allow for human performance to be measured analytically to evaluate the usability of computer systems' design scenarios using low fidelity prototypes and no user participation [19]. The Model Human Processor (MHP) provides a simplified view of the human information processing system that can be used to predict user behaviour. MHP is one of the key components of Card et al. [5] framework for human performance modelling, and is a central part of the framework's other key component; a set of techniques collectively referred to as Goals, Operators, Methods, and Selection rules (GOMS). This family of techniques is used to compare and evaluate motor behaviour by describing four components of skilled error-free user performance: goals, operators, methods, and selection rules.

The GOMS family is used to model goal hierarchies of defined unit tasks. The tasks are rendered as a composition of actions and cognitive operations. The analysis of the

© IFIP International Federation for Information Processing 2017
Published by Springer International Publishing AG 2017. All Rights Reserved
R. Bernhaupt et al. (Eds.): INTERACT 2017, Part I, LNCS 10513, pp. 155–172, 2017.
DOI: 10.1007/978-3-319-67744-6_10

composition yields quantitative and/or qualitative measures of performance [5]. Members of the GOMS family differ in their analysis complexity and the accuracy of predicted completion times [11, 12]. The Keystroke-Level Model (KLM) is a simplified implementation of GOMS that is used to numerically predict execution times for specific tasks in a desktop environment using mouse and keyboard input [4]. The simple model has been widely applied to predict expert performance of various desktop interfaces and its analysis has proven accurate [23]. This fact demonstrates the aptitude and usefulness of KLM.

Originally intended for desktop systems, KLM has been continually extended to model new paradigms of user interaction. With the advancement of smartphone technologies, the original model has been modified for smartphone interaction to ease and accelerate usability testing in the early phases of development. Smartphone extensions to KLM review the model's decomposition by modifying the original operators, introducing new actions, and revising execution times. These new interactions and extended models include predictive text entry [17], voice recognition [6], Near Field Communication (NFC) technology [10], touch input [20], and touch-less interaction [8].

GOMS techniques and smartphone extensions to KLM model visual desktop and smartphone systems to overcome the drawbacks of usability testing by reducing cost and identifying problems early in the development process. However, these models assume non-disabled users that are able to visually perceive the interface. Visually impaired users [27] utilise assistive tools to decrease or eliminate visual dependency. Screen readers provide auditory descriptions of visual elements on a traditional screen. Similarly, smartphones provide accessible interfaces to compensate for visual impairment. Models formulated exclusively from and for visual computer systems are ill-equipped to represent interfaces accessible to visually impaired users and their interactions.

This paper proposes an extended KLM model that is applicable to visually impaired smartphone interaction, and it makes two main contributions. First, a selected mobile KLM extension is examined and modified to model visually impaired smartphone interactions. Second, the new model is evaluated in two user studies where the model was able to thoroughly render and accurately predict blind users' interactions with a smartphone.

In the following sections, we first describe KLM and recall its benefits and limitations as a predictive model. Next, we review the literature on cognitive models for accessible designs and extensions to KLM. We then present the first study for the purpose of extending KLM. This resulted in an enhancement to FLM that considers accessible designs for blind smartphone users. Furthermore, we validate the extended model in a main experiment. We then present and discuss the results of the validation experiment. Finally, we draw conclusions and future plans.

2   Background and Related Work

The extended KLM for visually impaired smartphone interaction builds upon prior work in predictive models and a stream of KLM expansions in accessible interfaces and smartphones. While this section does not represent a complete review of the state of the art for model based usability evaluation, it, nevertheless, highlights the most relevant work and how they may differ.

2.1 Keystroke-Level Model (KLM)

KLM is one of GOM's simpler techniques that computes the time it takes an expert user to perform an error-free task on a desktop application. KLM inherits several limitations from GOMS that limit analysis to linear, closed tasks that are executed error-free by expert users. Task execution time is predicted in KLM by decomposing a set of tasks into a list of perceptual, cognitive, or motor operators and computing its summation. The model consists of six operators [4]:

- **Keystroke** K key or button press
- **Point** P point at a target with the mouse
- **Home** H move hands to the home position (keyboard or mouse)
- **Draw** D draw a line on a grid
- **Mental act** M mental processing prior to taking an action
- **Response** R system response time

Moreover, the mental operator is governed by a set of heuristic rules that consider cognitive preparation:

- Rule 0: insert M operators in front of all K operators. Also, place M operators in front of all P operators used to select commands.
- Rule 1: remove M operators that appear between two operators anticipated to appear next to each other.
- Rule 2: remove M operators belonging to one cognitive unit except the first; a cognitive unit is a premeditated chunk of cognitive activities.
- Rule 3: remove M operators that precede consecutive terminators.
- Rule 4: remove M operators that preceded terminators of commands.

The unit execution time for each operator (excluding R) have been set from previous HCI research. KLM predicts a task's execution time by adding the operators' unit times for each of the task's activities, where $T_{operator}$ is an operator's total time:

$$T_{execute} = T_K + T_P + T_H + T_D + T_M + T_R$$

KLM was empirically validated against keyboard and mouse based systems and various tasks [4]. The model's predictions were found to be accurate with an error of approximately 21%.

2.2 Cognitive Models in Accessibility

The design of accessible web pages are governed by sets of regulations and guidelines to maximise its use among users of varying capabilities [26]. Automated tools are utilised by designers to assess compliance, however these tools only evaluate checkpoints and do not thoroughly assess other usability issues (e.g. effectiveness and efficiency). Visually impaired computer users use screen readers to navigate applications;

visual content is represented as a coded linear sequence that is synthesised into auditory presentation. The GOMS family of techniques are suited for modelling screen readers' sequential output as the model's application is limited to linear tasks. A handful of research have explored extending predictive models to reproduce screen readers' auditory representation.

Time-oriented aspects of usability were the focus of a new visualisation approach, Blind Usability Visualisation [22]. This approach was later implemented as a disability simulation tool, Accessibility Designer (aDesigner), to evaluate and visualise the usability of web pages for blind users. The tool's most novel feature is the concept of 'reaching time'; the time it takes a blind user using a screen reader to reach a desired destination on a web page from the top of that page. The tool is not a predictive model and while average reaching time can be used to measure the navigability of a web page by blind users, it excludes cognitive decision times or other operations. An extension to one of GOMS techniques addresses this rough estimation of reaching time [24].

User observations and two field studies were performed to provide a broad overview of blind interaction on accessible web pages [24]. The studies identified key findings of blind interactions, this include: reliance on different navigational strategies, frequent speech rate configuration, verification of screen reader output, and activation of interactive elements. Some of these findings were used to introduce new structures to the Natural GOMS Language (NGOMSL) that extended the model for accessible web pages. Configurable speech rates and Braille readings times and their impact were not considered. This modified model aimed to automate the assessment of accessible web page efficiency by calculating the time it takes to execute a task on a web page. Nevertheless, the model remains qualitative in nature and unverifiable which makes its application difficult.

Working with non-disabled users, new models were introduced to assess mouse and keyboard navigation in a web site [21]. The keyboard model focused on users who could not use a pointing devices and quantified keyboard navigation's disadvantage against mouse navigation. The TAB key is used to navigate a chain of links in a web page by first locating the target link then pressing the key n times until the link is reached and finally activated by pressing ENTER. This is clearly problematic for link-intensive web sites. The models extend KLM, each of which introduced new operators. Time estimates for the new keyboard operators were measured in a laboratory experiment with non-disabled expert users. Theoretically the model can be used to render blind interaction, but requires adaptation to consider the time it takes a blind user to hit the TAB key.

Blind users' interaction with web pages via a screen reader were remotely observed and analysed to supplement KLM [25]. CogTool [13], a cognitive modelling tool that supports rapid evaluation analysis of GOMS formulations, was used to validate KLM's efficacy at modelling blind users' interaction. KLM did not accurately model the user's behaviour as it did not consider the screen reader's high speech rate. Additionally, CogTool's rules for placing KLM's mental operators, which were procured from sighted user's interaction with visual content, did not ideally reflect the observed skilled interaction of the blind user. Discarding the mental operators from calculation did not improve accuracy, which suggests the parallel recognition of situations and decisions, as well as auditory reception of the screen reader's speech. A future tool was envisioned for evaluating blind users' interaction on a web page, but was not implemented.

2.3 KLM Extensions

Usability testing is an expensive process that is exacerbated with disabled users as testing will have to be carried out late in production with high fidelity prototypes. The recent direction of model extension address the usability needs of non-disabled smartphone users. These models lend themselves to further modification to address blind smartphone interaction. KLM is typically extended by evaluating original operators and introducing new operators and equations. This section focuses on smartphone extensions to KLM and reviews direct touch models.

In the context of smartphone interaction, studies for extension began with text entry methods and predictive text. An early model extended KLM for three text entry methods using a smartphone's keyboard and compared predictions of typing speeds for each of these methods [7]. Another model identified and validated new operators that represent typical and advanced smartphone interaction (e.g. identification tags and gestures) [9]. The model was later revised to include NFC interactions [10]. An extended model utilised KLM, Fitts' law, and a language model to predict user performance with two types of Chinese input methods on smartphones [17]. For the purpose of presenting a new keyboard, 1Line, KLM was extended to measure multi-finger touchscreen keystrokes [15]. Replacing the keyboard with speech input, a new model investigated the feasibility of a speech-based smartphone interface for text messaging, which adapted original operators and introduced predictive equations to the model [6].

Beyond keyboard or speech input, KLM had been extended to predict user interaction time and system energy consumption on smartphones [18]. KLM was also adapted for next-generation smartphone designs, particularly phones that utilise styli [16]. The new model introduced new operators that uniquely represent stylus interactions, and presented the concept of operator block (a sequence of operators that can be used with high repeatability). For direct touch interaction, KLM was modified to model middle-sized touch screens in Integrated Control Systems (ICSs) [1], where the prediction error was less than 5%.

Touch-based smartphones later replaced traditional phones where new extensions were required to assess this new paradigm of human interaction. The Touch Level Model (TLM) was proposed to support interaction with touch devices via direct interaction [20]. Several operators were retained from KLM as they remain applicable to touch input (keystroking K, homing H, mental act M, and system response time R), but discarded the drawing D operator. Several new operators were freshly introduced or inherited from other extensions to KLM that were not developed for touch input: distraction X [9], gesture G, pinch P, zoom Z, initial act I [9], tap T, swipe S, tilt L (degrees), rotate $O(degrees)$, and drag D. TLM has the potential for benchmarking users' touch interactions, but the new operators are without baseline values and the model has yet to be validated. Retained operators' unit times will likely need to be reexamined as well.

Fitts' law is a descriptive model that considers the physical aspects of a Graphical User Interface (GUI) and predicts the time it takes to point to a target. In previous research, Fitts' law has been integrated with KLM to produce enhanced smartphone versions of the model and to compute average execution time based on physical interface features (e.g. [17]). One enhancement extended KLM with three common touch interactions: swipe, tap, and zoom [3]; interactions similarly modelled in TLM [20]. Unlike TLM [20], unit operators' times were formulated using Fitts' law. Nevertheless, the model's potential has not been verified against their intended interaction and application.

Mobile games have increased in popularity as smartphones are becoming more durable and supportive of direct touch interaction. The Fingerstroke-Level Model (FLM) is a modified version of KLM developed for the evaluation of mobile gaming efficacy [14]. FLM adapted original operators and introduced new ones to cope with the new interactions. The model is comprised of six operators: tap T, point P, drag D, flick F, mental thinking M, and response time R. FLM shares P, M, and R with the original KLM, and tapping and dragging (i.e. swiping) with TLM [20] and El Batran et al. extension [3]. Unlike the original KLM and its extensions [3, 20] that results in a single deterministic value, FLM is a regression model. FLM was applied to a mobile game where it was able to predict its execution time more accurately than KLM.

3   KLM Extension for Blind Interaction

The main objective of the first user study was to explore blind users' interaction with touch-based smartphones. Prior to the study, an online screening questionnaire was distributed to better understand blind users' smartphone interaction. The questionnaire's main objectives were to identify commonly used smartphones, popular applications, and blind users' experience with smartphones. The questionnaire was conducted in Arabic and garnered twenty-one respondents, the majority of which were female with an average age of 26.57 years (standard deviation, SD = ±9.66). Excluding one participant, the entire sample used iPhones with the majority (81%) having at least three years of experience with the device. The respondents ranked Twitter, WhatsApp, and YouTube as their most often used applications.

3.1   Methodology

Two instruments were used in this study: structured interviews and observation. The interview was designed to discover popular actions utilised by blind users when using applications on a smartphone. The vocalised actions were then confirmed via observation.

Participants. Three female blind participants with a mean age of 20 years took part. The participants were university students in the College of Education at King Saud University. All participants had good experience with using an iPhone (average experience of 5.6 years) and gave vocal informed consent.

Apparatus. The iPhone was screened as the most commonly used smartphone and its use was observed in this study. VoiceOver is a built-in speech synthesiser that assists visually impaired users when interacting with iOS devices (e.g. iPhone) and applications. Along with specific gestures, users are able to navigate and activate interface element. For instance, a user taps to select an element and listen to its auditory description which informs upcoming actions. Keyboard input is also facilitated with audio. Speech rate of the synthesiser is adjustable in VoiceOver via a rotor that is manipulated by rotating two fingers on the screen. However, this action is often infrequent during a task and is therefore excluded from consideration.

Materials. Interview questions were predetermined starting with an introductory question regarding the smartphone used and its version. The following question prompted the participant for any set of actions that are typically adopted with iPhone applications. The participant was asked to list these actions if she was able to identify a particular set of actions repeatedly used among various application. Otherwise, the participant is asked to describe her interaction with iPhone applications. For the study's instrument, two tasks for Twitter and WhatsApp were prepared for observation. In the Twitter task, the participant was asked write and send a tweet on her personal account. For WhatsApp's task, the participant was asked to write and send a message to someone from her contact list.

Procedure. Sessions were held in a quiet room and lasted approximately 40 min. First, the participant was welcomed and the general research idea was introduced. Two instruments were used in this study, interviews and observations, which were conducted in the same session in sequence. First, the questions were put forth to the participant in Arabic. Second, the participant was asked to carry out the Twitter or WhatsApp scenario under observation. The choice of task and application was dependent on the participant's familiarity with said applications.

3.2 Results

From the interviews, all three participants agreed that they did not follow a series set of actions when interacting with their iPhones. Nevertheless, when asked to describe the sequence of actions typically taken when interacting with an application, the participants identified the following sequence: listen, navigate to a certain button or content (via flick operation), then activate the element (via double tap). These reported actions were then verified with observation.

Two of the participants performed the WhatsApp task, while the third participant carried out the Twitter task. In the Twitter task, the participant opened the application with a double tap and then navigated within the application by flicking the screen with her finger. At times, the participant listened to the complete audio description of the visual element before deciding on an action. Other times, the participant was satisfied with a partial description. For text input, the participant tapped on the screen until the textfield was located (this was vocalised with VoiceOver) and used double tap to activate the keyboard. The writing process started with a tap on the approximate position of the intended character to hear the description. These actions were similarly observed with the WhatsApp task.

Blind users' smartphone interaction via the device's screen reader can be summarised into four actions: tap, double tap, flick, and drag. Tap actions are used to select an element. The selected element is activated via a double tap action. Flicking a finger on the screen is used to navigate the application's elements. Vertical and horizontal scrolling is achieved by sliding or dragging three finger across the screen.

3.3 Revised FLM for Blind Users

The user study identified a series of operations that were frequently carried out by blind users interacting with a smartphone application: tap, double tap, flicking a finger on the screen, or scrolling vertically or horizontally by dragging three fingers across the display. These actions were mapped against the previously reviewed touch-based smartphone extensions to KLM (see Sect. 2.3 and Table 1).

Table 1. The observed blind actions mapped against the same/similar actions (i.e. operators) in TLM [20], El Batran et al.'s model [3], and FLM [14].

Action/Model	TLM [20]	El Batran et al. [3]	FLM [14]
Tap	Tap T	Tap	Tap T
Flick	Swipe S	Short swipe	Flick F
Double tap			
Drag	Drag D	Long swipe	Drag D

The four observed actions related to three operators from TLM [20], El Batran et al. [3], and FLM [14]. Tap actions are a common direct touch behaviour that corresponds well to the Keystroke K operator in KLM and was identified in the previous literature [3, 14, 20]. The observed flick action was a single finger swipe that is short and quick and directly mapped against FLM's Flick F [14]. TLM [20] defined Swipe S as placing one or more fingers on the screen and moving that finger in a single direction for a period of time, while El Batran et al. [3] described swipe as a short or long action to achieve tasks such as scrolling. These two actions can roughly represent the observed flick action, while TLM's [20] Drag D and El Batran et al. [3] long swipe can model the observed drag action.

Of the three touch-based smartphone extension to KLM, FLM's [14] operators closely resemble the observed actions. Unlike TLM [20], units times were computed for the various operators in FLM [14] and El Batran et al. [3]. However, El Batran et al. [3] model only provides unit time for a short swipe (resembling a flick) and not for a long swipe. Moreover, the operators in FLM were validated in an experiment where the root mean square error (RMSE) of the observed and predicted execution times was 16.05%. For that purpose, FLM was selected as the prime candidate for extension. The extended FLM model is called Blind FLM, and its operators and unit times are summarised in Table 2 in relation to KLM [4] and FLM [14].

Retained Operators. Five of the original FLM operators are still appropriate to model blind users' interactions on an iPhone mobile device with VoiceOver.

- **Tap T.** A blind user taps anywhere on the smartphone's screen to listen to the audio description of the underlying visual element. This could be a button, text, link, image, or video. Tap is also used to choose the start position for navigation.

Table 2. Retained, excluded, and new operators of the extended FLM (Blind FLM) and their time estimates as compared to the original KLM [4] and FLM [14].

KLM [4]	Time (s)	FLM [14]	Time (s)	Blind FLM	Time (s)
Keystroke K	0.2	Tap T	0.31	•	0.31
Point P	1.1	•	0.43		
Draw D	$0.9n + 0.16l^a$	Drag D	0.17	•	0.17
Home H	0.4				
Mental act M	1.35	•	1.35	•	1.35
Response R	variable	•	variable	•	variable
Extensions					
		Flick F	$0.12_{\text{right-to-left}}$ $0.11_{\text{left-to-right}}$	•	0.12^b
				Double tap DT	0.62

[a] Drawing D assumes n straight line segments having a total length of l.
[b] Flick F value is set at 0.12 s considering error-free navigation that were observed to be typically from right to the left.

- **Drag D.** Vertical and horizontal scrolling is performed by sliding/dragging three fingers across the screen.
- **Flick F.** Unlike dragging D, this action is typically quick and achieved with a single finger to navigate application elements.
- **Mental preparation M.** With the absence of sight, blind users rely on other senses to conceptualise the real world. Blind smartphone users utilise audio description to map their next interaction, i.e. the mental preparation needed to perform the following action. KLM [4] was previously refined to model screen readers and the authors suggested that recognition of the present situation, screen reader's speech, and action decisions occur in parallel. This was also argued for typing actions [25].
- **Response time R.** This operator is system dependent, arguably irrelevant due to the technological advancement and negligible response times. Nevertheless, the variable is still retained to account for different devices and software.

New Operators. New operators are introduced to the extended FLM to account for novel interactions that are afforded by the analysed interface. Tap interactions are frequently utilised by blind users to select an element and is retained from FLM [14]. Double tap actions activate the selected element (via tap). This is unique to blind users' interaction, where the former voices the element and the latter launches the element.

Excluded Operators. The pointing operator P is excluded in Blind FLM as it is not applicable to blind users' interaction since pointing at an element requires visual perception. Instead of pointing, a blind user taps close to a target element or navigates the elements sequentially. Both of which are represented by the original FLM operators: tap and flick, respectively [14]. Thus, the act of pointing works in tandem or is encapsulated with/within the subsequent action and is not used in its singularity.

Operators' Unit Times. The baseline value for the FLM [14] operators were computed with a practical study. The original values are employed for Blind FLM. In the case of the double tap *DT* action, the value of tap *T* is multiplied by two. The mental thinking *M* operator was not changed from the original KLM and is maintained for this extension as well. See Table 2 for execution times for all operators.

4   Blind FLM Validation

The efficacy of a model and the accuracy of its baseline values are typically evaluated through controlled research studies with human subjects. Within-participants experiments were conducted to investigate Blind FLM. The purpose of these two studies were twofold: (1) to determine the applicability of the Blind FLM operators for describing blind users' touch interactions with a smartphone (first user study); (2) to compute the accuracy of the new model by comparing observed execution times with predicted times (second user study).

4.1   First User Study

A preliminary study was carried out to satisfy the first purpose of the experiment; determine if the new model and its operators are fit to fully model blind touch interactions with a smartphone. This study was also used to evaluate the experimental tasks in order to refine the tasks for the next study.

Methodology

Participants. Five female participants with a mean age of 20.2 years (SD = ±0.84) were recruited for the experiment. All participants were familiar with using an iPhone and VoiceOver with an average of 5.8 years of experience (SD = ±1.1). The participants were students recruited from King Saud University. The device's VoiceOver speech rate values ranged from 80% to 100% with an average of 90%.

Apparatus. Apple's iPhone 6 with VoiceOver was used by all participants. Access to the three applications were made via the participants' private accounts. A camera was used to video record participants' interactions.

Task. Based on the previously discussed questionnaire results: Twitter, WhatsApp, and YouTube were the top three used applications in the blind community. For the preliminary study, three sessions were dedicated for each of these applications. Each session consisted of three tasks; one open task and two structured tasks (a total of nine tasks).

- Twitter
  - Structured tasks

    1. View the profile of the first account on the 'Following' page
    2. Write a tweet consisting of a single word in Arabic or English (e.g. 'Hello') and to tweet the message

  - Open task: retweet any tweet from the timeline

- WhatsApp
  - Structured tasks

    1. Make a voice call with the first contact from the chat list
    2. Reply to the first chat from the chat list with a single word in Arabic or English (e.g. 'Hello')

  - Open task: create a new chat group with two contacts
- YouTube
  - Structured tasks

    1. Play the first video in the home page
    2. Subscribe to the channel of the first video in the home page

  - Open task: delete YouTube's browsing history

The open scenario was used to determine if Blind FLM was able to thoroughly represent blind users' interaction with a touch-based smartphone. KLM and extensions of KLM are only equipped to represent error-free interactions and tasks, thus the two structured tasks were used to reduce the space of probability and error. The two structured tasks were presented as a set of steps that begin from a uniform starting point that continued sequentially.

Procedure. Sessions were held in a quiet room with a WiFi connection, and each session lasted approximately 45 min. First, the participant was given verbal instructions about the experiment and its purpose. After which, the participant was given a chance to voice any questions about the study. Consent was then collected and recorded verbally. Each of the nine tasks was presented to the participant with its required steps. Prior to starting a task, the participant practiced the task until it was mastered and completed without error. For the structured task, whenever a mistake occurred the participant was asked to redo the scenario. All sessions were video recorded.

Participants were asked to use their own iPhones for the experiment. To ensure uniform VoiceOver settings for all participants a set of instructions were provided. The speech rate of VoiceOver was set on 80% speed. The volume of the speech synthesiser was set to its highest rate. Typing mode was set to standard typing.

Results. The video recording for all sessions were coded using the Behavioural Observation Research Interactive Software (BORIS) [28]. BORIS, an event logging tool, allowed the experimenter to observe the video recordings and log observations, i.e. Blind FLM's operators.

Structured Tasks. The structured tasks were modelled using Blind FLM to predict execution times. All tasks were first modelled with the proposed Blind FLM physical/motor operators. The response time R operator was not used due to the iPhone's almost instantaneous reaction. Mental act M operators were later added based on the new model's modified heuristic rules. Rules 1, 3, and 4 from the original KLM are not applicable in this context. Rule 1 is related to fully anticipated operators, while Rules 3 and 4 handle syntactic terminators. Rule 0 and 2 were modified from the original KLM to reflect visually impaired smartphone interaction:

- Rule 0 (R0 base rule): insert M operators in front of all K operators that are used to type a text. Also, place M operators in front all P operators that are used to select a method. In Blind FLM, flick F, tap T, double tap DT, and drag D operators substitute keystroke K and point P operations.
- Rule 2 (R2): remove all M operators that are related to one cognitive unit except the first M.

For Twitter's first task, one participant was excluded from the analysis due to multiple mistakes. The observed execution time for that scenario with the four participants was 13.8 s compared to a predicted value of 11.33 s. For the first WhatsApp structured task, the average predicted execution time was 7.72 s compared to an observed value of 8.34 s. The first YouTube task's predicted execution time was 4.04 s compared to the observed value of 5.68 s. The second tasks from all three applications were excluded due to varying typing speed in Twitter and WhatsApp, and for repeated mistakes in YouTube's task. The root mean square error (RMSE) is commonly used to evaluate KLM's predictions [4]. The average computed RMSE for the three structured tasks was 1.73%.

Open Tasks. The average number of actions undertaken for the open task was 14.6 for Twitter, and 19 for YouTube, and 60.8 for WhatsApp. Negligible mistakes were detected, with no more than two errors per task. The Twitter task consisted of 73% flick F actions, 19% double taps DT, and 8% tap T actions. For the WhatsApp scenario, approximately 40% of the interactions were categorised as flick F and 30% were tap T actions. Double tap DT made up 26% of the actions, while drag actions D were only performed 4% of the time. The majority of the interactions in the YouTube task were flick F actions (78%), followed by double tap DT (21%) then tap T (1%). No drag D actions were observed for the Twitter or YouTube tasks. The open tasks were not analysed with Blind FLM as participants were not restricted to a set of predefined task sequences.

Discussion. Blind FLM was well-equipped to model blind user's touch interactions with an iPhone and VoiceOver. This section discusses the findings of the preliminary study for the open and structured tasks.

Structured Tasks. In the original KLM, the observed model error was 21% of the average predicted execution time [4]. This level of accuracy was achieved in the preliminary study. Nevertheless, the sample size was too small to be representative. Additionally, it was observed with the structured tasks that typing speed varied between the participants which may affect the consistency of the computed results. The second structured task for each of the examined applications involved a typing subtask. These tasks will be excluded in the upcoming user study. Unlike the other actions, modelling text entry is complex. Previous findings for text entry identified various factors that impact text entry, this includes: repetition effect (first tap, second, or more), key type (number, alphabet, or character), entry method (e.g. predictive or word completion), typing speed, and language corpus. Due to this distinctiveness, text entry is excluded with a plan for a future extension.

Open Tasks. The open task for each of the three applications were observed to determine Blind FLM's coverage of blind users' interactions. The operators' occurrence rates were computed and indicated the operators' priorities and their weights in the total execution time. The majority of operators were regularly used to model interactions. Of those operators, flick *F* was the most frequently used when interacting with the smartphone. The drag *D* action was the least used operator and was only observed in WhatsApp's open task.

4.2   Second User Study

A second user study was carried out to validate Blind FLM. The purpose of this study was to compute the accuracy of the new model by comparing observed execution times with predicted times. The experiment expanded on parts of the previous study and improved the tasks to overcome inaccuracy concerns.

Methodology

Participants. Twenty right-handed individuals (7 males, 13 females) with a mean age of 21.5 years (SD = ±7.24) took part in the experiment. Participants were recruited from Kafeef organisation (an organisation that is concerned with training and qualifying blind citizens), Alnoor institute (a female school for the blind), and King Saud University. On average the participants had 5.4 years of experience (SD = ±1.5) with using an iPhone and VoiceOver. The average speed rate utilised with VoiceOver was 89%.

Apparatus. Similar to the previous study, an iPhone 6 was used by all participants with VoiceOver. Each participant used their own device, as well as accessed their private Twitter, WhatsApp, and YouTube accounts. The sessions were video recorded with a camera.

Task. The task used with this study were previously examined in the previous experiment. For each of the three applications, a single structured task was used. The steps used in the preliminary study were re-evaluated as new versions of WhatsApp and YouTube were released. The starting position for each of the three tasks was the default position of VoiceOver. In Twitter, the participant was expected to follow the steps necessary to display the profile of the first account on the 'Following' page. The task's steps for Twitter were as follows:

- Flick to the settings button
- Flick to the switch account button
- Flick to edit profile button
- Flick to profile name button
- Flick to user account button
- Flick to location button
- Flick to following button
- Double tap on the following button
- Tap on the screen
- Scroll down once

- Tap on the screen
- Double tap on the first account

For the WhatsApp task, the participant was asked to initiate a video call with the first contact on their chat list (see Table 3 for steps). For the YouTube session, the participant was asked to play the first video on their personal home page by following these steps:

- Flick to 'Upload and Record'
- Flick to the search button
- Flick to personal account
- Flick to first video on the home page
- Double tap on video to play

Table 3. WhatsApp's task modelled with Blind FLM.

Task steps	Operator	Predicted unit time (s)
	M	1.35
Flick to chats	F	0.12
Flick to the compose button	F	0.12
Flick to archived chats	F	0.12
Flick to search field button	F	0.12
Flick to broadcast list	F	0.12
Flick to new group button	F	0.12
Flick to first chat	F	0.12
	M	1.35
Double tap on chat to open	DT	0.62
	M	1.35
Flick to the video call button	F	0.12
	M	1.35
Double tap on button to call	DT	0.62
Predicted execution time		7.6

Procedure. Sessions were held in a quiet room with a WiFi connections, the location varied depending on the participants and their affiliation. Each session lasted approximately 20 min. The participant was welcomed and the purpose of the study was explained. The participant was then given a chance to voice any questions. Next, a consent form was vocalised and the participant's response recorded. Each task was presented to the participant and its steps were explained. The participant was asked to train each task until mistakes are no longer made. The participant was also asked to use his/her own iPhone for the study with a VoiceOver speech rate set on 80%. The speech synthesiser volume was set to the highest rate. All sessions were video recorded.

Results. The three tasks were modelled with Blind FLM to predict execution times (see sample model for WhatsApp's task in Table 3). The tasks were first modelled without any mental thinking M operators. The mental thinking M operator was then incorporated in the model following the modified heuristic rules for M insertion. Observed execution times were logged using BORIS, where video recordings were played frame by frame. Twitter's task was predicted to take 10.97 s and its execution time was observed at 13.28 s. The predicted execution time for the WhatsApp task was 7.6 s (see Table 3) compared to the observed value of 8.7 s. For YouTube's task, execution time was predicted at 3.8 s, while the observed value was 4.8 s. The accuracy of Blind FLM was evaluated using RMSE, which showed an average prediction error of 2.36%. Table 4 shows the predicted and observed execution times for the three tasks, as well as the RMSE for each of these tasks and the average RMSE.

Table 4. Average observed time, predicted execution time, and computed RMSE for each of the three experimental tasks, as well as average RMSE.

Task	Observed time (s)	Predicted time (s)	RMSE
Twitter	13.28	10.97	3.81%
WhatsApp	8.7	7.6	2.01%
YouTube	4.8	3.8	1.27%
Average RMSE			2.36%

Discussion. The results show that all three tasks completion times were under KLM's suggested 21% RMSE [4]. For all tasks combined, the RMSE average was 2.36%. Twitter's task was predicted and observed to be the longest, while YouTube's task took the least time. This was also reflected with the RMSE value where a larger error percentage was incurred for Twitter's task. This indicates the effect of task complexity on the model's prediction error percentage. See Table 4.

The mental thinking M operator's unit value used in Blind FLM is the original value assigned to it with KLM [4]. Many studies similarly retained the original unit measure for M for conventional phones [7] and smartphones [14, 20]. However, these models render visual applications. A previous study observed blind users' web page interactions via a screen reader to extend KLM [25]. The results of the study suggested the parallel recognition, decision, and auditory reception of the screen readers speech, directly affecting the unit time of the model's operators. While this was also observed in the study (e.g. a participant not listening to the complete description of a visual element), completely discarding the mental act M operator did not result in better accuracy. This added complexity to the mental act M operator for accessible interfaces merits a revisit in future research.

For all tasks, Blind FLM underestimated the predicted time (see Table 4). Given that KLM can only model error-free tasks (a limitation passed on to its extensions, including Blind FLM), participants were asked to repeat a task until no errors were recorded. This repetition had lead the participants to caution and it indicates that the observed times are likely upper limits. Thus, the observed extra time highlight the time it took the participants to process the instructions and carry out the task, i.e. contrary to natural interaction.

5 Conclusion and Future Work

KLM and mobile extensions to KLM have popularly been adopted in HCI to predict the time it takes a skilled user to complete an error-free task. Skilled users were inherently assumed to be sighted and the applications relied on visual output. These models cannot thoroughly express visually impaired interaction, where the visual interface is replaced with an audible alternative. This paper makes two contributions. First, FLM [14] was modified further to render visually impaired mobile phone interaction. Some of FLM's operators were retained, while other were excluded. A new operator, double tap DT, significant to blind user's interaction was introduced to the model. These changes were applied after a series of interviews and observations with blind users and their touch-based smartphones. Second, a user study was conducted to validate the new model (Blind FLM), and evaluate its predictions on a number of tasks. The results showed that Blind FLM was able to accurately predict execution time well below the suggested 21% error [4].

The user studies carried out to modify KLM and validate the new model were performed with an iPhone and limited to a set of applications (WhatsApp, YouTube, and Twitter). We intend to evaluate Blind FLM's accuracy with other mobile phones and applications. The model's operators' unit times were not measured and instead original values from KLM [4] and FLM [14] were adopted. In future work, we plan to reexamine these values in controlled human-subject trails. This is particularly important to overcome any inaccuracies due to FLM and Blind FLM's varying application domains. It will also be interesting to reevaluate the mental thinking M operators' unit time and the effects of an audible interface and blind users listening abilities on its value [2]. Due to varying typing speeds, typing tasks in the validation studies were excluded from computation. This exclusion lends itself to future research that considers visually impaired text input and its effect on tap T and double tap DT operators. A final future direction will apply Blind FLM on real-life design cases, where the model is used to compare the designs efficacy to make informed design choices.

References

1. Abdulin, E.: Using the keystroke-level model for designing user interface on middle-sized touch screens. In: Proceedings of the 2011 Annual Conference Extended Abstracts on Human Factors in Computing Systems, pp. 673–686 (2011). doi:10.1145/1979742.1979667
2. Asakawa, C., Takagi, H., Ino, S., Ifukube, T.: Maximum listening speeds for the blind. In: Proceedings of the International Community for Auditory Display, pp. 276–279 (2003)
3. Batran, K.E., Dunlop, M.D.: Enhancing KLM (Keystroke-level Model) to fit touch screen mobile devices. In: Proceedings of the 16th International Conference on Human-computer Interaction with Mobile Devices & Services (MobileHCI 2014), pp. 283–286 (2014). doi:10.1145/2628363.2628385
4. Card, S.K., Moran, T.P., Newell, A.: The keystroke-level model for user performance time with interactive systems. Commun. ACM 23(7), 396–410 (1980). doi:10.1145/358886.358895
5. Card, S.K., Newell, A., Moran, T.P.: The psychology of human-computer interaction. L. Erlbaum Associates Inc., Hillsdale (1983)

6. Cox, A.L., Cairns, P.A., Walton, A., Lee, S.: Tlk or txt? Using voice input for SMS composition. Pers. Ubiquit. Comput. **12**(8), 567–588 (2008). doi:10.1007/s00779-007-0178-8
7. Dunlop, M.D., Crossan, A.: Predictive text entry methods for mobile phones. Pers. Technol. **4**(2), 134–143 (2000). doi:10.1007/BF01324120
8. Erazo, O., Pino, J.A.: Predicting task execution time on natural user interfaces based on touchless hand gestures. In: Proceedings of the 20th International Conference on Intelligent User Interfaces (IUI 2015), pp. 97–109 (2015). doi:10.1145/2678025.2701394
9. Holleis, P., Otto, F., Hussmann, H., Schmidt, A.: Keystroke-level model for advanced mobile phone interaction. In: Proceedings of the SIGCHI Conference on Human Factors in Computing Systems (CHI 2007), pp. 1505–1514 (2007). doi:10.1145/1240624.1240851
10. Holleis, P., Scherr, M., Broll, G.: A revised mobile KLM for interaction with multiple NFC-tags. In: Proceedings of the 13th IFIP TC 13 International Conference on Human-Computer Interaction - Volume Part IV (INTERACT 2011), pp. 204–221 (2011). http://dl.acm.org/citation.cfm?id=2042283.2042306
11. John, B.E., Kieras, D.E.: The GOMS family of user interface analysis techniques comparison and contrast. ACM Trans. Comput.-Hum. Interact. **3**(4), 320–351 (1996). doi:10.1145/235833.236054
12. John, B.E., Kieras, D.E.: Using GOMS for user interface design and evaluation: which technique? ACM Trans. Comput.-Hum. Interact. **3**(4), 287–319 (1996). doi:10.1145/235833. 236050
13. John, B.E., Prevas, K., Salvucci, D.D., Koedinger, K.: Predictive human performance modeling made easy. In: Proceedings of the SIGCHI Conference on Human Factors in Computing Systems (CHI 2004), pp. 455–462 (2004). doi:10.1145/985692.985750
14. Lee, A., Song, K., Ryu, H.B., Kim, J., Kwon, G.: Fingerstroke time estimates for touchscreen-based mobile gaming interaction. Hum. Mov. Sci. **44**, 211–224 (2015). doi:10. 1016/j.humov.2015.09.003
15. Li, F.C.Y., Guy, R.T., Yatani, K., Truong, K.N.: The 1Line keyboard: a QWERTY layout in a single line. In: Proceedings of the 24th Annual ACM Symposium on User Interface Software and Technology (UIST 2011), pp. 461–470 (2011). doi:10.1145/2047196.2047257
16. Li, H., Liu, Y., Liu, J., Wang, X., Li, Y., Rau, P.-L.P.: Extended KLM for mobile phone interaction: a user study result. In: CHI 2010 Extended Abstracts on Human Factors in Computing Systems (CHI EA 2010), pp. 3517–3522 (2010). doi:10.1145/1753846.1754011
17. Liu, Y., Räihä, K.J.: Predicting chinese text entry speeds on mobile phones. In: Proceedings of the SIGCHI Conference on Human Factors in Computing Systems (CHI 2010), pp. 2183–2192 (2010). doi:10.1145/1753326.1753657
18. Luo, L., Siewiorek, D.P.: KLEM: a method for predicting user interaction time and system energy consumption during application design. In: Proceedings of the 2007 11th IEEE International Symposium on Wearable Computers (ISWC 2007), pp. 1–8 (2007). doi:10. 1109/ISWC.2007.4373782
19. MacKenzie, I.S.: Motor behaviour models for human-computer interaction. HCI models, theories, and frameworks: Toward a multidisciplinary science, 27–54 (2003)
20. Rice, A.D., Lartigue, J.W.: Touch-level model (TLM): evolving KLM-GOMS for touchscreen and mobile devices. In: Proceedings of the 2014 ACM Southeast Regional Conference (ACM SE 2014), pp. 53:1–53:6 (2014). doi:10.1145/2638404.2638532
21. Schrepp, M., Fischer, P.: A GOMS model for keyboard navigation in web pages and web applications. In: Miesenberger, K., Klaus, J., Zagler, Wolfgang L., Karshmer, Arthur I. (eds.) ICCHP 2006. LNCS, vol. 4061, pp. 287–294. Springer, Heidelberg (2006). doi:10.1007/ 11788713_43

22. Takagi, H., Asakawa, C., Fukuda, K., Maeda, J.: Accessibility designer: visualizing usability for the blind. In: Proceedings of the 6th International ACM SIGACCESS Conference on Computers and Accessibility (Assets 2004), pp. 177–184 (2004). doi:10.1145/1028630. 1028662
23. Teo, L., John, B.E.: Comparisons of keystroke-level model predictions to observed data. In: CHI 2006 Extended Abstracts on Human Factors in Computing Systems (CHI EA 2006), pp. 1421–1426 (2006). doi:10.1145/1125451.1125713
24. Tonn-Eichstädt, H.: Measuring website usability for visually impaired people-a modified GOMS analysis. In: Proceedings of the 8th International ACM SIGACCESS Conference on Computers and Accessibility (Assets 2006), pp. 55–62 (2006). doi:10.1145/1168987. 1168998
25. Trewin, S., John, B.E. Richards, J., Swart, C., Brezin, J., Bellamy, R., Thomas, J.: Towards a tool for keystroke level modeling of skilled screen reading. In: Proceedings of the 12th International ACM SIGACCESS Conference on Computers and Accessibility (ASSETS 2010), pp. 27–34 (2010). doi:10.1145/1878803.1878811
26. Web Accessibility Initiative (WAI). Introduction to Web Accessibility. https://www.w3.org/WAI/intro/accessibility.php. Accessed 21 Jan 2017
27. World Health Organization (WHO). Visual impairement and blindness
28. Behavioral Observation Research Interactive Software (BORIS). http://www.boris.unito.it/. Accessed 8 Jan 2017

Comparing Two Approaches of Tactile Zooming on a Large Pin-Matrix Device

Denise Prescher(✉) and Gerhard Weber

Institut für Angewandte Informatik,
Technische Universität Dresden, Dresden, Germany
{denise.prescher,gerhard.weber}@tu-dresden.de

Abstract. Zooming on large tactile displays can result in orientation loss, especially if the user's reference point disappears from the visible area afterwards. To avoid such displacement we developed a focus zoom approach which keeps the currently focused element as central point for zooming. In this paper, we compare this approach with a conventional midpoint zoom (the center of the output area is maintained after zooming) on the touch-sensitive BrailleDis 7200 device. In a study with four blind and eight blindfolded sighted participants we could show that the focus zoom significantly reduces displacement of the focused element on the tactile output area. Locating the focus after doing a focus zoom needs significantly less time, reduces the overall workload and is also preferred by the users.

Keywords: Pin-matrix device · Tactile zooming · Focus zoom · Midpoint zoom · Blind user

1 Introduction

To allow visually impaired users an adequate access to graphical information, large tactile displays have been developed for several years (see [18]). Especially for graphics exploration tasks the display should be as large as possible to allow users for bi-manual reading on the tactile output area [17] applying the concept of active touch (see [3]). Novel two-dimensional pin-matrix devices consist of up to 120×60 pins (e. g. BrailleDis 7200 [11]) and, therefore, can present much more information at once compared to conventional single-line Braille displays. For instance, the presentation of interactive tactile graphics is possible besides simple Braille output.

Compared to conventional visual screens the resolution of even such a large tactile display is very low (10 dpi). Furthermore, the intake capacity of the tactual sense is considerable lower than that of the visual sense [2] which results in a more time-consuming perception. For these reasons interaction and presentation techniques have to be adapted. In particular, appropriate zooming and panning techniques are important for interacting with small screens and, therefore, are

© IFIP International Federation for Information Processing 2017
Published by Springer International Publishing AG 2017. All Rights Reserved
R. Bernhaupt et al. (Eds.): INTERACT 2017, Part I, LNCS 10513, pp. 173–186, 2017.
DOI: 10.1007/978-3-319-67744-6_11

often targeted in current research of visual interaction (e. g. comparison of conventional techniques [5], alternative strategies for map navigation [14], zoomable soft keyboards [8,9] etc.).

When dealing with graphical applications on large tactile displays zooming is also necessary. Blind and visually impaired users not only prefer the usage of zooming functionalities for exploring detailed diagrams but they also can improve their accuracy compared to having no zooming possibilities [13].

In the following, we give a brief overview over existing zooming techniques on two-dimensional tactile displays. Afterwards we present a novel zooming approach for the BrailleDis 7200 and compare it with the conventional zooming on this device within a user study.

2   Related Work

Some approaches for large tactile displays are based on a semantical zooming, i. e. the amount of information is adapted to the current zoom level. In this way, enlargement results in showing more and more details while downsizing removes details allowing to simplify the image. For instance, Rotard uses some kind of semantic zooming methods for showing Scalable Vector Graphics (SVG) [15].

Furthermore, there are also approaches in which the algorithm automatically decides which zoom levels are uninformative and, therefore, should not be shown to the user [12,13]. This means, only zoom levels that are significantly different to the previous level are shown, while the cognitive grouping of information is preserved. In a user study with blind subjects, a significant improvement of correct answers was shown compared to a conventional zoom [13]. There was no difference in response time, but fewer clicks were used. However, a large tactile display was not used for exploring the virtual diagram, but a single Braille cell was mounted on a mouse which was moved across a graphics tablet.

If zooming should be realized independently of some knowledge of the presented content, a semantic zoom is not applicable. Instead, geometric zooming is necessary. In graphical applications it normally leads to a continuous change in the scaling. The applicability of such a continuous zooming for tactile displays is unclear. Alternatively, providing 25 discrete zoom levels seem to be enough for handling a haptic zoomable interface [20]. Generally, perception of zooming greatly differs among blind and sighted people as no overview is available when fingers explore the tactile display sequentially. Because of continuous changes in the scaling, visual zooming seems to be rather a sort of morphing of the presented content for sighted people. This allows much more easily to maintain the context compared to some kind of "page flipping feeling" in tactual perception as some blind people have described it to us.

There already exist several approaches to realize a geometric haptic zooming. The most simple one is a kind of *midpoint zoom* as it is used, for example, in the Tangram workstation [1]. In this 1:1 adoption of the visual zooming metaphor used in common graphical user interfaces, the zoom is performed at the center of the current view port. However, in previous user studies it became clear that blind participants often were confused about clipped objects after zooming [1]. This especially occurs if an object is near to the borders and the user does a zoom-in operation leading to an enlargement which is big enough to move the object outside the visible range (see also Fig. 1 right row). As maintaining the context after zooming is pretty complex in tactual exploration anyway, a large displacement of the content should be avoided.

To allow the user to define a position to be zoomed, another approach can be to rely on the *finger position as center* for zooming. One example is the Touch Zoom used in the system of Shimada et al. [16]. The original zooming functionality of this system is also based on the conventional midpoint approach. In their paper, Shimada et al. reported no comparison for conventional zoom and Touch Zoom. Users only rated subjectively how useful and easy to use the new Touch Zoom was [16]. The usage of zoom gestures within the HyperReader system [10] is another example of the finger position approach. Thereby, the starting point of the circular or semi-circular gestures is used as center for zooming. However,

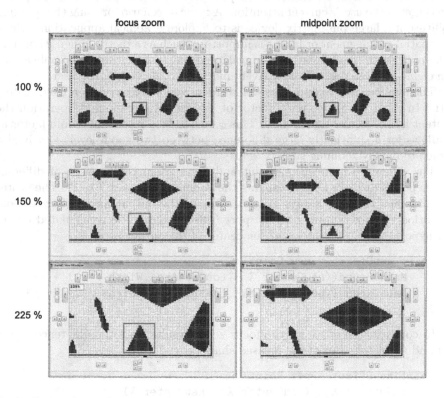

Fig. 1. Screenshots of an example image's tactile output on the pin-matrix device in three different zoom levels based on the focus and midpoint zoom approaches. The triangle shape marked with the surrounding frame is focused (on the pin-matrix device this border is highlighted by blinking pins). The initial view port at the zoom level of 100% is the same, but it changes after zoom-in dependent on the used approach.

to allow for an intuitive and usable gesture interaction, recognition of touch has to be reliable. This can be affected by external influences, such as technical problems, or by ambiguous values which can result from a multitouch input.

3 A Novel Zooming Approach on the BrailleDis Device

Both zooming approaches currently used on the BrailleDis 7200 device, namely 'Midpoint Zoom' [1] and 'HyperReader Zoom Gestures' [10], are not optimal due to the above mentioned problems (clipping of objects after zooming and unreliable touch recognition respectively). Therefore, another approach combining the advantages of both zooming functionalities was implemented. First it uses hardware buttons instead of gesture input, and second it is not performed at the center of the current view, but at the center point of the currently focused element[1]. Unlike the zooming gesture, the finger is not taken as reference point, but the system focus. In the following we call this zooming approach 'Focus Zoom'.

The focused element seems to be appropriate for that purpose as it is often the target of the user's current attention. A typical scenario for using the zooming abilities of a large pin-matrix device is to explore graphical applications where the spatial arrangement or layout is important, such as a tactile image [1] or map [19] application. In information retrieval or editing tasks within such applications the element of interest will be actively marked or selected by the user.

The implemented midpoint as well as focus zoom are based on a fixed scaling ratio. In other words, we use a factor of 1.5, i.e. after a zoom-in operation the content is 50% bigger than before. This seems to be a reasonable zoom factor as it allows for a sufficiently large difference between two zoom levels and it also avoids too many zooming steps.

The difference between midpoint and focus zoom is the usage of different center points displayed after realizing the zooming (compare Fig. 1). The center for midpoint zooming always is the center of the output area. After a zoom operation the position of the view port (offset[2]) has to be recalculated out of the hypothetical new center and the center of the output area:

```
Point newOffset = new Point(
    Math.Round((newCenter.X - (outputArea.Width / 2)) * -1),
    Math.Round((newCenter.Y - (outputArea.Height / 2)) * -1)
);
```

In contrast, the offset for the focus zoom results from the difference of the old and the new center of the focused shape:

```
Point newOffset = new Point(
    oldOffset.X + (oldCenter.X - newCenter.X),
    oldOffset.Y + (oldCenter.Y - newCenter.Y)
);
```

---

[1] The center point of an element is represented by the center of its bounding box.
[2] Note that in our case, the offset is ≤ 0 as it defines how the content is placed in relation to the currently used view port.

In both cases the hypothetical new center is the product of the old center and the scale factor: `newCenter = oldCenter * (newZoom / oldZoom)`. Thereby, the old center is either the center of the output area (midpoint zoom) or the center of the focused shape (focus zoom).

Our hypothesis is that the focus zoom is more efficient than the midpoint zoom. We think, it can reduce loss of orientation by the user as the context is changed less when the focused element does not move after zooming.

4   Experimental Setup

To investigate the above mentioned hypothesis, we conducted a user study to compare the midpoint and focus zoom approach on the BrailleDis 7200 device. The following research questions should be answered:

1. Which zooming approach is more efficient?
2. Which zooming approach reduces the workload?
3. Which zooming approach is preferred by the users?

4.1   Participants

12 participants with a mean age of 33 years took part in the study. Four of them were blind, the others were blindfolded sighted people. The demographic data of the subjects are shown in Table 1.

Table 1. Demographic data of the participants.

Subject ID	Gender	Age	Visual impairment	Experience with BrailleDis
B1	m	42	Late blind	High
B2	f	53	Congenitally blind	Very high
B3	f	32	Congenitally blind	High
B4	f	27	Congenitally blind	No
S1	m	32	Sighted	Very high
S2	m	32	Sighted	High
S3	m	34	Sighted	High
S4	f	31	Sighted	No
S5	f	22	Sighted	Low
S6	f	33	Sighted	Medium
S7	m	33	Sighted	Low
S8	m	24	Sighted	Very low

As no Braille knowledge or experiences in tactual shape recognition were necessary for the study, we also took blindfolded sighted people to increase the number of data sets. Their tactual acuity may be inferior compared to that of blind people [4], but individual differences can be isolated by using a within-group design of the study [7]. This means, every participant performed all test conditions as described below.

4.2   Materials, Task and Procedure

To allow for a comparison of the zooming approaches, a set of focus locating tasks was given to the participants. The focused element should be quickly regained on the tactile display after executing a zoom operation. This kind of task is common for scenarios in which a tactile graphic is explored on a two-dimensional pin-matrix device.

We prepared three test images each consisting of 18 shapes different in size and form that were randomly spread over the document (see also Fig. 2). In each single task, one of these shapes was selected randomly (each shape has been chosen only once). Furthermore, the current view port of the pin-matrix device also was placed randomly, but it was ensured that the focused shape was visible in the initial output.

In a short training phase the two zooming approaches as well as the following task was explained to the participant. Furthermore, an example was shown where the focused shape moved outside the visible view after zooming and, therefore, panning was necessary. To allow the user to locate the shape in this situation, panning operations were explained and trained briefly. After the training, three test runs were conducted.

The three test images were randomly assigned to the three test runs. Each single task (one trial) within these test runs consisted of the following phases:

1. searching for the focused element
2. zoom operation (triggered by the test supervisor)
3. retrieving the focused element as fast as possible

Each test run consisted of ten different zooming conditions (single tasks, see Table 2) which were presented in random order. In the first test run, each zooming approach was assigned five times and in a random order to the zooming conditions. In the second test run, one of the zooming approaches (either focus or midpoint zoom) was used in all the ten different zooming conditions. In the third test run, the remaining zooming approach was used. Each participant had to complete all three test runs (within-group design). In total, there were 30 trials per participant. Before each trial, the user was told by which scale factor the current output will be changed after zooming (see 'zoom mode' in Table 2). Based on this information, the user can make his/her own expectations (mental model) what will happen to the focused element.

4.3   Apparatus and Measurements

The Tangram workstation (see [1]) was used for presenting the graphical shapes on the BrailleDis 7200 device (see Fig. 2). The graphic files were shown in Libre Office Draw[3], captured and converted into a 10 dpi binary tactile image. This image was sent to the BrailleDis 7200 device which has a touch-sensitive tactile

---

[3] https://www.libreoffice.org/discover/draw/.

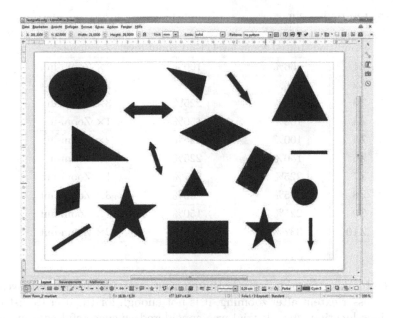

Fig. 2. One of the sample images (Libre Office Draw graphic document with 18 differently sized and formed shapes) presented on the BrailleDis 7200. The tactile output shows all of the image (zoom level = 66%).

output area consisting of 120×60 pins. The size of the tactile area is 30×15 cm which allows users to use both hands for exploring the content.

The focused shape was tactually marked by a blinking frame (its bounding box) at a frequency of about 1.7 Hz. Note that for locating the target element before and after zooming it was not necessary to recognize its shape but only to

Table 2. Ten different zooming conditions used in the experiment.

Condition	Initial zoom level	End zoom level	Zoom mode
Z1	66%	100%	1× Zoom-in
Z2	66%	150%	2× Zoom-in
Z3	66%	225%	3× Zoom-in
Z4	100%	150%	1× Zoom-in
Z5	100%	225%	2× Zoom-in
Z6	150%	225%	1× Zoom-in
Z7	225%	337%	1× Zoom-in
Z8	225%	66%	3× Zoom-out
Z9	225%	150%	1× Zoom-out
Z10	337%	150%	2× Zoom-out

detect the blinking frame[4]. As in both zooming methods the frame moves to a greater or lesser extent after zooming, it is not enough for the user to just touch the previous location. A task/trial was considered as successful as soon as one edge of the bounding box was felt and reported by the participant. Therefore, the user gave oral feedback ("stop").

During the tasks, the following data were recorded in logfiles:

- focused shape: name and center position (before and after the zooming operation)
- zoom level: before and after the zooming operation
- offset of the view port: before and after the zooming operation
- time: when zooming operation was executed and when subject has successfully found the shape again

Out of this, task completion time as well as the distance between the target shape's center position before and after zooming was calculated. Moreover, the user's workload for each of the two zooming approaches was measured by using the NASA-TLX (Task Load Index, see [6]) after the second and third test run. Therefore, the participant verbally had to give a rating between 0 and 100% for each of the TLX factors. At the end of the test, the user should state which zoom approach he prefers. Beside the demographic data these values were recorded in a questionnaire.

---

[4] Locating the blinking pins is the major challenge in a finding focus task on the BrailleDis device. The recognition of a shape is quite a different task, which is not part of our test. The participants could trust in that the focused shape is inside the bounding box. In a real-life scenario on the pin-matrix device, the user must find the blinking pins at first, and then he/she can continue the image exploration. By concentrating only on finding the focus, we can reduce the complexity of the task.

5   Results and Discussion

For exploring the tactile output area nearly all participants used both hands. Merely participant S4 used only her right hand (all fingers and palm). B2 and S2 used their palms in addition to their fingers the whole time. B3 and S3 used only their fingertips. The other subjects added their palms in some cases, for instance if using the fingers was not enough to quickly detect the blinking focus. Although the blinking pins made some mechanical sound, according to the participants of the study it seemed not to be a clue to locate the focus.

A comparison of completion time in midpoint and focus zoom conditions for each participant is presented in Fig. 3. The mean displacements of the focused element are compared in Fig. 4.

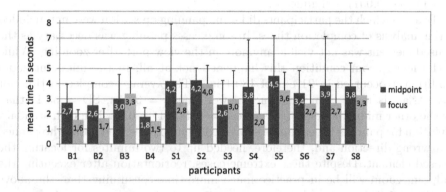

Fig. 3. Time needed for locating the focused object after midpoint and focus zoom (means and standard deviations; $10 \leq n \leq 15$).

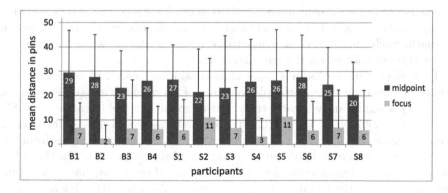

Fig. 4. Distance between the positions of the focused element's center before and after executing midpoint or focus zoom (means and standard deviations; $n = 15$).

Regarding the time needed for locating the focused element after doing a zoom operation, the focus zoom (mean completion time = 2.7 s, SD = 0.8) is more efficient than the midpoint zoom (mean completion time = 3.4 s, SD = 0.8). Comparing the average times of blind (midpoint zoom: mean = 2.5 s, SD = 0.5; focus zoom: 2.1 s, SD = 0.9) and sighted (midpoint zoom: mean = 3.8 s, SD = 0.6; focus zoom: 3.0 s, SD = 0.6) participants separately, it can be found that both user groups needed nearly a quarter more time to locate the focused element after using the midpoint zoom. We suspect this is mainly due to the higher displacement of the focused element after zooming with the midpoint approach (mean distance = 25.2 pins, SD = 2.7) compared to that caused by the focus zoom (mean distance = 6.6 pins, SD = 2.6). Paired t-tests show that the difference in completion time ($t = 3.581$, $df = 11$, $p < 0.01$) as well as in the displacement of the focused element's center point after zooming ($t = 15.093$, $df = 11$, $p < 0.001$) is significant.

Trials in which the participants did some panning operation were not included in the analysis of completion times. In some cases panning was necessary as the focused element was not visible anymore in the view port after zooming. While in the focus zoom condition this happened not at all, in the midpoint zoom condition it occurred in 21 out of 180 trials. The average completion time for these trials is more than ten times slower (mean = 35.5 s, SD = 35.1) than for the other midpoint zoom trials (mean = 3.4 s, SD = 0.8). The high standard deviation for panning times can be explained by unexperienced users who panned in a wrong direction and, therefore, needed up to two minutes for locating the focused element. Despite these extreme cases, reorientation after executing the midpoint zoom will be in practice much more time-consuming than the above mentioned 125% compared to focus zoom.

Considering the distance values in the focus zoom condition, further explanation is required. Normally, the focus zoom results in no or only very little displacements of the focused element[5]. However, in some cases there can be considerable displacements after a zoom-out operation due to keeping the content within the visible range of the pin-matrix device (see Fig. 5). For instance, the positioning of the document in the smallest zoom level (the whole image is visible) is always the same (Fig. 5 right) and does not depend on the used zooming approach. Such an adaptation seems to be necessary to allow for a consistent presentation of content on the pin-matrix device.

This effect also results in a more time-consuming search in zoom-out conditions (see also Fig. 6), i.e. completion time of zoom-out trials (mean = 3.4 s, SD = 1.1) is significantly greater than that of zoom-in trials (mean = 2.8 s, SD = 0.7; $t = -2.902$, $df = 11$, $p < 0.05$). Especially the zoom-out by three steps at once (factor = 4.5, see Fig. 5) doubles the search time on average from 2.6 (average time in one or two step zoom-out conditions) to 5.3 s. On the other side, the tested zoom-in conditions (one, two and three steps) have no significant difference on the completion time ($F_{2,220} = 0.578$, $p > 0.5$). By and large, the effectiveness of the focus zoom approach against the midpoint zoom is more

---

[5] Little displacements of one or two pins may occur due to rounding errors.

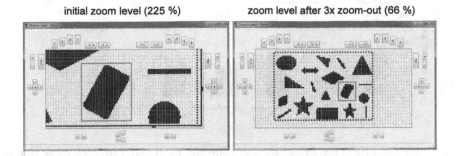

initial zoom level (225 %)   zoom level after 3x zoom-out (66 %)

Fig. 5. Screenshots of tactile output before and after a three-step zoom-out operation – presentation in smallest zoom level (66 %) is equal in focus and midpoint zoom.

significant based on completion time in zoom-in conditions ($t = 3.139$, $df = 11$, $p < 0.01$) than in zoom-out conditions ($t = 1.307$, $df = 11$, $p = 0.22$, no significance). As shown in Fig. 6, these results can be found in both user groups.

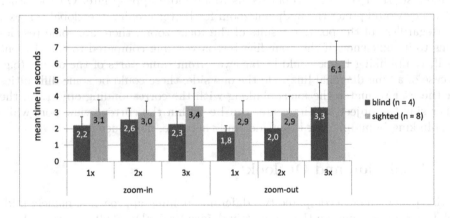

Fig. 6. Mean times needed for locating the focused object based on the zoom condition.

The participants assessed the workload related factors of the TLX significantly lower for focus zoom than for midpoint zoom (see Fig. 7; $t = 4.950$, $df = 5$, $p < 0.01$). Note that low TLX values are better than high values[6]. Although the individual ratings partially deviate greatly from each other, the focus zoom was perceived by every participant as less or, at least, equally demanding as the midpoint zoom in all factors. Thus, with respect to the overall workload, the focus zoom has clear benefits over the midpoint zoom.

---

[6] For instance, a low TLX performance factor means that a user was very successfully in performing a task ("How successful were you in accomplishing what you were asked to do?"; 0 = perfect, 100 = failure).

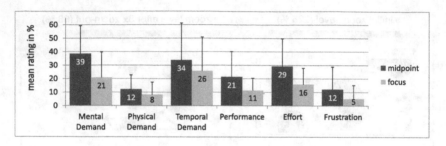

Fig. 7. Rating of the TLX factors for midpoint and focus zoom (0 = very low, 100 = very high; means and standard deviations; $n = 12$).

All participants liked the focus zoom approach very much. 9 of the 12 participants would prefer it over the midpoint zoom, while the other three (one sighted and two blind users) had no preference. Instead, they would like to have both zooming possibilities because they think the suitability of the zoom method highly depends on the current task. For instance, if only the focused element is of interest, then the focus zoom seems to be more appropriate. On the other side, they would prefer the midpoint zoom for better keeping the global context.

Regardless of the positive results of the focus zoom, there are some restrictions to its efficiency. If the bounding box is very big compared to the element itself, the blinking frame could be far away from some parts of the object (e.g. in case of a long diagonal line). On the one side, there could be some difficulties for the user to match the focus blinking with the corresponding object, on the other side the object and its center can be within the current view port while the blinking bounding box is outside, and therefore, not touchable.

6   Conclusion and Outlook

In this paper we have compared two different zooming approaches, namely midpoint and focus zoom, on the pin-matrix device BrailleDis 7200. The task of our study with four blind and eight blindfolded sighted participants was to retrieve the focused element in a tactile graphic after performing a zooming operation. While the midpoint zoom condition maintains the middle of the output area, the focus zoom takes the currently focused element as central point for zooming.

Our results showed that, at least in focus locating tasks, the focus zoom is not only more efficient but also preferred by the users. It allows to better keep orientation in dealing with single tactile graphic elements as it minimizes the displacement of the focused object on the tactile output area after zooming. This again reduces the need for time-consuming panning operations. Besides, the overall workload for focus zoom is significantly lower than that for midpoint zoom.

These results could be shown for both user groups – blind as well as blindfolded sighted people. In fact, the average values for the two tested zooming conditions show that the blind users as well as the sighted users were both about 25% faster in using the focus zoom, regardless of their tactile or visual abilities. Of course, the blind users were faster in all conditions than the sighted users, but for our analysis, the absolute time was not important. Independent of accessibility issues and even for users who are unfamiliar with large tactile displays, a focused-centered zooming approach can support focus finding tasks on two-dimensional tactile displays.

In the end, multiple zooming approaches can be provided redundantly to allow for an efficient interaction on tactile pin-matrix devices in various tasks. On the BrailleDis 7200 the user can choose from the above mentioned zooming methods, namely gesture input, midpoint and focus zoom. For instance, the midpoint zoom is applied if no element is selected and zoom gestures can enable the user to define a fixation point which is independent of the system focus.

Acknowledgments. We thank all participants as well as Jens Bornschein for his work on the extension mechanism of the Tangram workstation. The Tangram project was sponsored by the Federal Ministry of Labour and Social Affairs (BMAS) under the grant number R/FO125423. The paper is part of the Mosaik project which is also sponsored by the BMAS under the grant number 01KM151112. Only the authors of this paper are responsible for its content.

References

1. Bornschein, J., Prescher, D., Weber, G.: Collaborative creation of digital tactile graphics. In: Proceedings of the 17th International ACM SIGACCESS Conference on Computers and Accessibility, pp. 117–126 (2015)
2. Franke, H.W.: Sehen und Erkennen (See and recognize). Bild der Wissenschaft 5/75 (1975). (in German)
3. Gibson, J.: Observations on active touch. Psychol. Rev. **69**(6), 477–491 (1962)
4. Goldreich, D., Kanics, I.M.: Tactile acuity is enhanced in blindness. J. Neurosci. **23**(8), 3439–3445 (2003)
5. Gutwin, C., Fedak, C.: Interacting with big interfaces on small screens: a comparison of fisheye, zoom, and panning techniques. In: Proceedings of Graphics Interface 2004, pp. 145–152. Canadian Human-Computer Communications Society (2004)
6. Hart, S.G., Staveland, L.E.: Development of NASA-TLX (Task Load Index): results of empirical and theoretical research. Adv. Psychol. **52**, 139–183 (1988)
7. Lazar, J., Feng, J.H., Hochheiser, H.: Research Methods in Human-Computer Interaction. Wiley, London (2010)
8. Oney, S., Harrison, C., Ogan, A., Wiese, J.: ZoomBoard: a diminutive QWERTY soft keyboard using iterative zooming for ultra-small devices. In: Proceedings of the SIGCHI Conference on Human Factors in Computing Systems, CHI 2013, pp. 2799–2802. ACM, New York (2013)
9. Pollmann, F., Wenig, D., Malaka, R.: HoverZoom: making on-screen keyboards more accessible. In CHI 2014 Extended Abstracts on Human Factors in Computing Systems, pp. 1261–1266. ACM, New York (2014)
10. Prescher, D., Weber, G., Spindler, M.: A tactile windowing system for blind users. In: Proceedings of the 12th International ACM SIGACCESS Conference on Computers and Accessibility, pp. 91–98 (2010)

11. Prescher, D.: Redesigning input controls of a touch-sensitive pin-matrix device. In: Proceedings of the International Workshop on Tactile/Haptic User Interfaces for Tabletops and Tablets, pp. 19–24 (2014)

12. Rastogi, R., Pawluk, D.T.: Automatic, intuitive zooming for people who are blind or visually impaired. In: Proceedings of the 12th International ACM SIGACCESS Conference on Computers and Accessibility, pp. 239–240 (2010)

13. Rastogi, R., Pawluk, T.V., Ketchum, J.: Intuitive tactile zooming for graphics accessed by individuals who are blind and visually impaired. IEEE Trans. Neural Syst. Rehabil. Eng. 21(4), 655–663 (2013)

14. Robbins, D.C., Cutrell, E., Sarin, R., Horvitz, E.: ZoneZoom: map navigation for smartphones with recursive view segmentation. In: Proceedings of the Working Conference on Advanced Visual Interfaces, AVI 2004, pp. 231–234. ACM, New York (2004)

15. Rotard, M., Otte, K., Ertl, T.: Exploring Scalable Vector Graphics for Visually Impaired Users. In: Miesenberger, K., Klaus, J., Zagler, W.L., Burger, D. (eds.) ICCHP 2004. LNCS, vol. 3118, pp. 725–730. Springer, Heidelberg (2004). doi:10. 1007/978-3-540-27817-7_108

16. Shimada, S., Yamamoto, S., Uchida, Y., Shinohara, M., Shimizu, Y., Shimojo, M.: New design for a dynamic tactile graphic system for blind computer users. In: Proceedings of SICE Annual Conference, pp. 1474–1477. IEEE (2008)

17. Shimada, S., Murase, H., Yamamoto, S., Uchida, Y., Shimojo, M., Shimizu, Y.: Development of directly manipulable tactile graphic system with audio support function. In: Miesenberger, K., Klaus, J., Zagler, W., Karshmer, A. (eds.) ICCHP 2010. LNCS, vol. 6180, pp. 451–458. Springer, Heidelberg (2010). doi:10.1007/ 978-3-642-14100-3_68

18. Vidal-Verd, F., Hafez, M.: Graphical tactile displays for visually-impaired people. IEEE Trans. Neural Syst. Rehabil. Eng. 15(1), 119–130 (2007)

19. Zeng, L., Weber, G.: Audio-haptic browser for a geographical information system. In: Miesenberger, K., Klaus, J., Zagler, W., Karshmer, A. (eds.) ICCHP 2010. LNCS, vol. 6180, pp. 466–473. Springer, Heidelberg (2010). doi:10.1007/ 978-3-642-14100-3_70

20. Ziat, M., Gapenne, O., Stewart, J., Lenay, C., Bausse, J.: Design of a haptic zoom: levels and steps. In: Second Joint EuroHaptics Conference and Symposium on Haptic Interfaces for Virtual Environment and Teleoperator Systems, pp. 102–108. IEEE (2007)

Improve the Accessibility of Tactile Charts

Christin Engel[✉] and Gerhard Weber

Chair of Human-Computer Interaction, Faculty of Computer Science,
TU Dresden, 01062 Dresden, Germany
{christin.engel,gerhard.weber}@tu-dresden.de

Abstract. Blind and visually impaired people are able to access visual charts by the mean of tactile representations. However, their production is time-consuming and requires know-how and skills in tactile chart design. Our main goal is to support blind, visually impaired as well as sighted authors by automating the creation process of tactile charts. We follow an user-centered design approach. Therefore, we analyzed both transcribers and users of tactile charts by conducting a survey on blind, visually impaired and sighted authors. On that basis, we identified steps and challenges of the production process, how users interact with tactile charts, design guidelines, as well as user preferences and tasks. As a result, we summarize requirements for an application that automates the creation of tactile charts.

Keywords: Tactile charts · Audio-tactile charts · Tactile graphics · Accessibility · Effective design · Blind users · Survey · User requirements

1 Introduction

Information graphics, visual charts in particular, were developed for the visual sense and make use of domain-specific skills. Due to the preattentive perception, the user gets a quick overview of the data, detects patterns and outliers quickly [10]. There are several approaches to enable blind and visually impaired people access information graphics. Verbal descriptions are often used to get non-visual access to visual charts [2,4,11]. The development of those descriptions takes a high effort and, furthermore, it is time-consuming to read them out. They only cover the description of visual and structural properties of a chart such as labels, axis scale or number of bars. Some approaches focus on textual descriptions which include high-level content of the data visualization, too, in order to provide an idea of chart's intention such as Demir et al. [5] and Moraes et al. [12]. Tactile charts may be more effectively for analyzing data than verbal descriptions or data tables [15].

Tactile charts consist of raised elements, for instance lines, areas and symbols which can be perceived by the sense of touch. Colors are replaced by a variety of different textures and line styles to distinguish chart elements. Several guidelines relate to the design of tactile graphics, in particular [3,6], because visual and

© IFIP International Federation for Information Processing 2017
Published by Springer International Publishing AG 2017. All Rights Reserved
R. Bernhaupt et al. (Eds.): INTERACT 2017, Part I, LNCS 10513, pp. 187–195, 2017.
DOI: 10.1007/978-3-319-67744-6_12

tactile charts differ in their design [8]. The development of tactile charts is very time-consuming and requires knowledge about tactile chart design [14]. Some approaches are intended to facilitate the creation of tactile charts for different use cases. Jayant et al. [9] developed the Tactile Graphics Assistant (TGA) that support direct translation of a visual into a tactile chart with image processing methods. Such kind of tools require a well-designed visual chart that follows general design conventions. However, a direct translation may not be appropriate for an effective tactile chart design [7,13]. Initial prototypes, for example the tactile chart generation tool developed by Goncu et al. [7] or the tool by Araki et al. [1] show the need for automating the creation of tactile charts. Nevertheless, the majority of existing tools only support a few chart types. The resulting charts developed by Watanabe et al. [15] are inflexible in their design because the application just supports customizing labels and raw data input. Current approaches do not support rich design such as Goncu et al.'s [7] tool that offers just one layout for bar charts and one for pie charts. The design of tactile charts heavily depends on specific use cases and user preferences.

Basically, an initial survey on the production of tactile graphics in Germany delivers indications about current practice and user experiences in exploring and creating tactile graphics [14]. However, this survey focuses on tactile graphics in general. Needs for tactile charts may differ. As a consequence we have instigated our own survey. We present the results as well as requirements for a software that automates the creation of accessible charts.

2   Survey on Tactile Charts

Our survey addresses blind, visually impaired and sighted authors as well as users of tactile charts. The survey was distributed by the means of more than 100 e-mails to media centers, schools, research institutes and online libraries. In addition, an invitation to the survey was published by online newsletters of three associations for blind and visually impaired people[1].

The survey consists of three parts: The first part comprises 6 to 16 questions (depends on given answers) concerning experiences in chart production. In the second part, participants were asked 11 questions about their experiences in exploring and current practice in designing tactile charts. Each part starts with a filter question. The last part includes demographic data such as age, professionals, visual abilities or Braille reading skills.

2.1   Participants

In total, 71 users of tactile charts (34 blind, 7 visually impaired, 30 sighted) with an average age of 43 years completed our survey. All blind (except three who gave no answer) and none of the sighted participants have Braille skills. The majority of the participants (in total 60) use tactile charts in the context

---

[1] http://www.bbsb.org
http://www.isar-projekt.de
http://www.bfs-nrw-ev.de.

of their profession. They are from more than 40 institutions for instance schools (48%), universities (17%) or media center (14%). Eight participants work or study in university. Figure 1 summarizes the work description of the participants. Most of them are teachers (20 participants). Independently from profession the majority of creators have also experiences in exploring tactile charts (44 out of 53).

The next sections present the results of our survey. Section 2.2 focuses on the actual chart production process, whereas Sect. 2.3 summarizes user requirements and preferences.

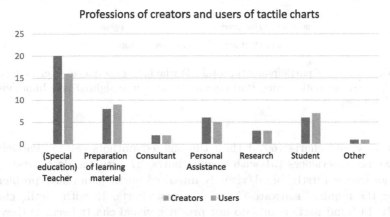

Fig. 1. Number of participants who have experiences in creating (creators) and exploring (users) tactile charts categorized in their profession (in total 55 answers)

2.2 Production of Tactile Charts

This section presents results from questions concerning tactile chart production. We have investigated two main research questions: Firstly, who are the creators of tactile charts? Secondly, how is the typical production process organized?

In total, 53 participants (75%) do have experiences with the creation of charts, including 28 sighted and 25 blind/visually impaired participants. Jointly 48% create tactile charts at least once a month, 19% of them just multiple times a week. We not only asked for experiences in creation of tactile charts but also for visual charts in order to find out whether blind/visually impaired people create visual charts on their own. Figure 2 shows the distribution of experiences in terms of visual and tactile charts. The majority of sighted participants create visual as well as tactile charts (75%). 40% blind/visually impaired creators produce tactile and none visual charts. In total 18 blind/visually impaired participants have experiences in creating tactile charts, whereas 10 of them just used analog methods (for example by carving paper). So, less blind/visually impaired participants create tactile charts in digital form than sighted authors. In addition, blind and visually impaired participants have significantly less experiences

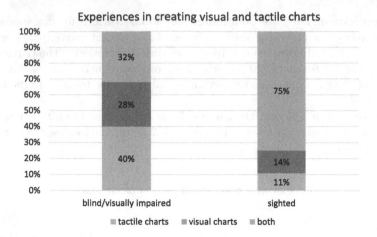

Fig. 2. Distribution of participants (in total 53) who have experiences in creating charts in visual, tactile or both forms. Participants divided into sighted and blind/visually impaired authors.

in creating visual charts (60%) than the sighted authors (89%). Participants who have no experiences (31 with visual charts, 27 with tactile charts) stated two major issues: Firstly, blind/visually impaired participants have problems in handling the required software (13 with visual charts, 13 with tactile charts). Secondly, 14 blind participants do not produce visual charts because they cannot access them independently, whereas 16 participants have no opportunity to print tactile charts. Only six participants have no need to produce charts on their own.

Beyond that, we were interested in the variety of chart types that are created by the participants. Simple bar charts, line and pie charts are well-known and created by more than 90% of the participants. Around 20% are familiar with stacked bars, area charts and scatter plots. The remaining group consists of bubble and donut charts as well as star plots which are produced by 10%. More complex chart types are created and known significantly less often than simple chart types.

Afterward, we summarize properties of the production process by presenting most common answers regarding data input, software for creation, steps of adaption, challenging tasks, typical chart elements as well as the target group.

In total, 89% take a visual chart and 59% a data table as input. 43% use Microsoft Office for creating tactile charts. 44% create a visual chart as basis and adapt it for the tactile output. Typical steps included in the adaption process are translating text labels into Braille (89%), creating or adapting a legend (85%), adapting distances (78%) and symbol sizes (74%) as well as the axis scale or change textures and line styles (70%). Design criteria for charts based in majority of experiences from the target group (62%). For 63% of the participants it is challenging to create tactile charts in an appropriate time. The specification of own design criteria (44%) and the implementation of them (26%) are also challenging. We asked the participants to name those chart elements a typical chart should contain. The most frequent answers where axis labels (88%), a title (88%), the axes itself (83%), a legend (76%) as well as labels in Braille (71%). 67% of the creators make use of tick marks on the axes while 62% add precise values. The charts are mainly created for a known target group (for example a school class, 62%). 43% produce charts for individual people. Only seven participants (of 42) create tactile charts for themselves.

With this in mind, the following section derives specific user preferences and requirements for tactile charts.

2.3 Users of Tactile Charts

The second part of our survey refers to the context of usage and exploring strategies as well as preferences of the users.

Generally, there are more blind/visually impaired participants (35 equals 85%) who have experiences in exploring tactile charts than sighted participants (25 equals 67%). About half of blind/visually impaired participants explored tactile charts at least once a month within the last year. Eight participants used charts several times a week. The majority get in contact with tactile charts in school as well as in the context of their profession (see Fig. 3).

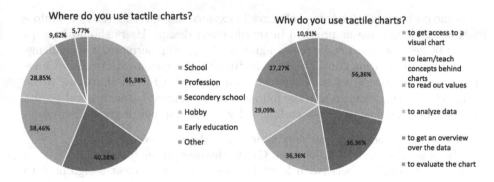

Fig. 3. Usage context of tactile charts.   **Fig. 4.** Different tasks that participants want to reach with tactile charts.

More than half of participants use tactile charts to get access to a visual chart (see Fig. 4). 36% especially blind and visually impaired participants use tactile charts to learn visual concepts. Just as many explore precise values in the chart.

For exploring tactile charts title (82%), legend (76%), axis titles (75%) and axes (64%) are most important. Braille labels (51%), tick marks and precise values (40%) are essential, too, for analyzing data. Tactile chart design depends on the way how the user interacts with the chart because it should guide him.

So, we have analyzed 43 free text answers from users of tactile charts. The exploration process can be summarized by following four steps (based on common answers):

1. **Getting an overview (14 participants):**
   - Find out chart type by title (six participants) or initial scan (moving with both hand over the full graphic)
   - It can be useful to search for axes and their labels to get an idea of chart content
2. **Orientation/Configuration:**
   - Seeking for general reference points: axes characteristics (eight participants), Braille font, specific symbols, frame of the sheet or legend
3. **Exploration/Getting content:**
   - If not already done: exploring of legend, textures and symbols
   - Systematic exploration strategies (horizontal or vertical) are used by four participants
   - Exploring chart elements like bars, lines or pie segments in detail and read all Braille labels
4. **Getting details:**
   - Searching for guiding elements such as help or grid lines
   - Explore precise values (ten participants), estimate element sizes and differences by use of the index finger as reference and exploring with the other hand around it

Some design issues leads to challenges in exploration. Getting too much information (62%) is a major problem in tactile chart design. Users should be supported by getting an overview (challenging for 38%). Furthermore, it is challenging to keep orientation (36%) and to distinguish chart elements from aid lines or grid (35%). Afterward, we asked how an accessible tactile chart has to be designed (free text answers). In the following we summarize some general results formulated as guidelines in descending order to the number of given answers:

- Reduce data content. Show only as much as data as necessary.
- Give a good overview of the data. Guide the user through your chart.
- Use clear Braille labels (with legend if necessary) with clear assignment to chart elements.
- Omit grid or aid lines if they are dispensable. Otherwise, ensure that they are considerably distinguishable from other elements.
- Different textures, symbols and lines styles should be easily distinguishable and referenced in a legend.
- Support the user by reading out precise values.
- Support access for non-Braille users by overlaying the printed version.
- To support understanding the chart, provide a well written image description.
- Take care that the chart being large enough regarding the size in printed form.

Afterward, we discuss our results and derive properties of target group as well as requirements for a tool that supports authors by creating tactile charts.

3 Requirements for a Tool that Automates the Creation of Tactile Charts

In general, the software addresses two main issues: Firstly, it should support authors of tactile charts by automating the creation process. Secondly, the tool should improve the readability and contribution of tactile charts by supporting well-defined design guidelines. To reach these goals user requirements from the target groups are essential.

3.1 Context of Use and Use Cases

Mostly, tactile charts were used and created in the field of education by non-experts such as teachers. A common use case is to transcribe visual charts from teaching materials to enable blind students to access these charts and learn visual concepts. We assume that time and hardware resources are limited, thus, teachers have to prepare their teaching material next to their regular teaching obligations. Many institutions have only one embosser to print tactile graphics. Hence, different embossers should be supported.

For blind and visually impaired people it is challenging to produce visual charts because they can not control it on their own. In particular, a similar tactile chart is needed to control the visual one. In addition, there are also blind authors who create tactile charts on the basis of raw data to analyze them. Therefore, an effective design is needed.

3.2 User Requirements and Preferences

Accessible software is a major requirement for blind/visually impaired people. Therefore, it should be possible to handle the software just using a keyboard. The creation should be automated without the need of manual correction based on rich customization features if required.

The resulting charts should be accessible by all target group members. They should support Braille readers (majority of blind users) as well as a high-contrast version for visually impaired. In addition, a visual version of the chart should be included because most of the sighted authors and teachers are not familiar with Braille reading.

3.3 User Tasks

A tool for automating the creation of tactile charts should at least support established chart types such as bar, line and pie charts as well as scatter plots. To support blind authors who are not familiar with the offered chart types, it may be useful to include some exemplary tactile charts with a description. The main requirement is the automatic translation and positioning of Braille labels. In particular, users want to be supported by positioning elements, reducing the complexity of the chart without losing content, choosing high distinguishable textures, line styles and symbols as well as adding a legend for the whole graphic. Resulting charts should be standardized as well as highly adaptable. The tool should offer different design templates based on underlying guidelines that can be changed by the user to support different use cases. To support user experiences the tool should accept established data formats such as CSV files or direct data input. In addition, transcribing charts that were created with other chart tools (e.g. Excel) should integrate the tactile chart production in the current workflow. Therefore, an interchange format for tactile charts is needed.

4 Conclusion

In general, the survey indicates the need for supporting authors and users of tactile charts. We identified the target group, common chart types, as well as a common workflow for creating tactile charts including challenges. In addition, we identified four main steps for exploring tactile charts and formulated requirements for tactile chart design. Based on the survey we have characterized requirements for the automation application. It should not only decrease the production time but also improve the quality of the charts. They can be produced and evaluated on the basis of well-defined guidelines. Thus, tactile charts can be created with a consistent design which facilitates the exploration. Furthermore, we not only want to support default chart designs but also features to enhance the effectiveness of charts such as different grid types or help lines. We are currently investigating further studies concerning effective tactile chart design for the development of suitable guidelines that can be integrated into the tool. Furthermore, we will improve chart accessibility by adding audio output. Therefore we will explore different interaction strategies and technologies.

In the following developing step we will identify a whole concept and architecture for the automating application that reaches the identified requirements. In addition, we investigate user studies for effective design of tactile charts and interacting concepts. As a final conclusion, we want to improve the availability of tactile charts by enhancing the creating process as well as the quality of tactile charts. So, we want to enable blind and visually impaired people to analyze data as effortless as possible to support the inclusion of disabled people.

Acknowledgment. The paper is part of the *Mosaik* project, which is sponsored by the German Federal Ministry of Labour and Social Affairs (BMAS) under the grant number 01KM151112. Only the authors of this paper are responsible for its content.

References

1. Araki, K., Watanabe, T., Minatani, K.: Development of tactile graph generation software using the R statistics software environment. In: Proceedings of the 16th International ACM SIGACCESS Conference on Computers & Accessibility, pp. 251–252 (2014)

2. Ault, H.K., Deloge, J.W., Lapp, R.W., Morgan, M.J., Barnett, J.R.: Evaluation of long descriptions of statistical graphics for blind and low vision users. In: Mechanical Engineering, pp. 25–32 (2002)
3. Braille Authority of North America, Canadian Braille Authority: Guidelines and Standards for Tactile Graphics (2011)
4. Demir, S., Carberry, S., Mccoy, K.F.: Generating textual summaries of bar charts. In: Fifth International Natural Language Generation Conference, pp. 7–15 (2007)
5. Demir, S., Oliver, D., Schwartz, E., Elzer, S., Carberry, S., McCoy, K.F.: Interactive SIGHT into information graphics. In: Proceedings of the 2010 International Cross Disciplinary Conference on Web Accessibility (W4A) - W4A 2010, p. 1 (2010)
6. Round Table on Information Access for People with Print Disabilities Inc.: Round Table on Information Access Guidelines on Conveying Visual Information (2005)
7. Goncu, C., Marriott, K.: Tactile chart generation tool. In: Proceedings of the 10th International ACM SIGACCESS Conference on Computers and Accessibility - Assets 2008, p. 255 (2008)
8. Goncu, C., Marriott, K., Hurst, J.: Usability of accessible bar charts. In: Goel, A.K., Jamnik, M., Narayanan, N.H. (eds.) Diagrams 2010. LNCS, vol. 6170, pp. 167–181. Springer, Heidelberg (2010). doi:10.1007/978-3-642-14600-8_17
9. Jayant, C., Renzelmann, M., Wen, D., Krisnandi, S., Ladner, R., Comden, D.: Automated tactile graphics translation. In: Proceedings of the 9th International ACM SIGACCESS Conference on Computers and Accessibility - Assets 2007, p. 75 (2007)
10. Keim, D.: Information visualization and visual data mining. IEEE Trans. Visual Comput. Graphics 8(1), 1–8 (2002)
11. Moraes, P., Sina, G., McCoy, K., Carberry, S.: Evaluating the accessibility of line graphs through textual summaries for visually impaired users. In: Proceedings of the 16th International ACM SIGACCESS Conference on Computers & Accessibility - ASSETS 2014, pp. 83–90 (2014)
12. Moraes, P.S., Carberry, S., McCoy, K.: Providing access to the high-level content of line graphs from online popular media. In: Proceedings of the 10th International Cross-Disciplinary Conference on Web Accessibility - W4A 2013, pp. 1–10 (2013)
13. Panëels, S., Roberts, J.C.: Review of designs for haptic data visualization. IEEE Trans. Haptics 3(2), 119–137 (2010)
14. Prescher, D., Bornschein, J., Weber, G.: Production of accessible tactile graphics. In: Miesenberger, K., Fels, D., Archambault, D., Peňáz, P., Zagler, W. (eds.) ICCHP 2014. LNCS, vol. 8548, pp. 26–33. Springer, Cham (2014). doi:10.1007/978-3-319-08599-9_5
15. Watanabe, T., Yamaguchi, T., Nakagawa, M.: Development of software for automatic creation of embossed graphs. In: Miesenberger, K., Karshmer, A., Penaz, P., Zagler, W. (eds.) ICCHP 2012. LNCS, vol. 7382, pp. 174–181. Springer, Heidelberg (2012). doi:10.1007/978-3-642-31522-0_25

Investigations on Laterotactile Braille Reading

Anupama Thomas[(⊠)] and Elizabeth Rufus

School of Electronics, VIT University, Vellore, Tamil Nadu, India
{anupama.mathew2014, elizabethrufus}@vit.ac.in

Abstract. Unlike sighted readers who read whole words at a glance, braille readers construct words sequentially processing them character by character as their tactual field of view is small. Using this aspect of braille reading, we conducted an experimental study to investigate whether nonsensical characters moving under the reading finger would be a hindrance in reading words. We used a prototype to display braille with a single actuator. There is a lateral presentation of text to the user using a 3D printed braille embossed disc which rotates under the reading finger of the blind person. Preliminary test results indicate that users can read words even as nonsensical letters brush past the reading finger. This feature has implications in the design of a cost effective braille display.

Keywords: Braille display · Lateral presentation

1 Introduction

Much research has gone into studying aspects of braille reading and also designing braille displays for visually impaired people. A braille cell in its standard format can be a 6 dot cell with the dots arranged in 2 columns of 3 dots each or an 8 dot cell, with 2 columns of 4 dots each. Generally braille is presented in two ways to the user (1) static raised dot display (where actuators move up and down below the reading finger of the user) and (2) a lateral presentation of text to the user where there is a continuous slip between the reading finger and the surface of the dots. There are also the alternate methods of presenting braille to users where the users receive vibrations to indicate the position of dots in a braille cell. In these alternate modes of displaying braille as seen in [1] the standard 6 dot format is not adhered to with regards to the arrangement of dots and the spacing between the dots. These alternate methods seem to be effective in the presentation of short texts to the user. Figure 1 shows various divisions of research in the area of braille displays based on the way the skin of the reading finger is stimulated. Commercially available refreshable braille readers are very expensive mainly because an actuator is needed for each dot of the braille cell, each braille cell consisting of 6 or 8 dots. Therefore a number of actuators would be required for a single line of Braille text. Various actuators such as Electro Active Polymers (EAP), Shape Memory Alloys (SMA), and piezo- electric actuators have been used in the research and development of braille readers as in [2]. But at present, most commercially available braille displays use piezoelectric actuators. To reduce the costs of braille readers, researchers have gone into making single cell readers where only one cell is presented at a time to the user.

© IFIP International Federation for Information Processing 2017
Published by Springer International Publishing AG 2017. All Rights Reserved
R. Bernhaupt et al. (Eds.): INTERACT 2017, Part I, LNCS 10513, pp. 196–204, 2017.
DOI: 10.1007/978-3-319-67744-6_13

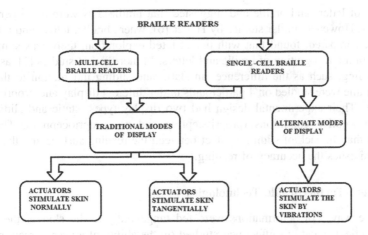

Fig. 1. Various divisions of research in braille displays

Also due to the high costs of braille readers, many visually impaired users switch to accessing data from a computer via screen readers which are more affordable and easily available in developing countries. Our work lies in the area where there is a lateral presentation of braille text to the user i.e. the actuators stimulate the skin of the reading finger tangentially. The goal of our work is to test whether blind users are able to read braille words even when non-sensical letters pass under the reading finger. We are evaluating this feature through a proof of concept prototype. The remainder of the paper is organized into four sections. Section 2 looks specifically at several aspects of braille reading which have been studied and specifically braille technologies which involve lateral movement between the actuators and the reading finger. Section 3 looks at our experimental protocol and the results. Sections 4 and 5 deal with discussions and conclusions respectively.

2 Background

2.1 Features of Braille-Reading

In [3] Foulke conducted extensive studies to examine braille reading and explored the possibilities of improving the reading rate of braille readers. He was interested in the legibility of braille characters and words formed by them. Experiments were conducted to find how long it took to recognize a braille character and whether certain braille characters took longer to be identified than others. He also subjected visual readers to the same reading conditions as braille readers i.e. viewing one character at a time and concluded that the speed of visual readers and braille readers would be similar if both were subjected to reading braille and print under similar conditions. These results were supported by [4] who conducted similar tests. They also suggested the use of characters per second as an appropriate measure of braille reading speed as word length is variable. In a comparative study of braille and letters, Loomis, in [5] studied the tangibility of letters and braille and suggested that braille dots were more perceptible than letters. However similar studies by Heller [6], where braille, letters and the Morse code were compared, found that with unrestricted exploration, there was similar performance in the recognition of braille and letters. In more recent studies [7], aspects of braille reading, such as the differences in static and sliding indentation to the finger reading braille were studied on 4 participants under different display and proprioceptive conditions. Their experimental design had two display types (static and sliding) and two proprioceptive conditions (proprioceptive and non-proprioceptive). The study suggested that the lack of sliding contact between the reading surface and the reading finger diminishes the accuracy of reading.

2.2   Latero-Tactile Braille Technologies

Progressive waves of deformations were fed tangentially to the skin of the reading finger by a device and this effect was studied on the ability of a user to read truncated braille characters. This was compared to reading the conventional braille medium [8]. The design further emerged as the STRESS2 tactile transducer that has 10-by- 6 contactors which deliver tangential forces to the skin [9]. Displaying complete 6 dot braille was explored using this device. However reading strings of disconnected letters was difficult though possible. Reading familiar words were faster and more accurate. Earlier designs which allowed for lateral deformation of the fingertip included the rotating wheel braille display [10, 11].The rotating wheel design [10] used fewer actuators (3 actuators for 6 dot braille, 4 for 8 dot braille) in a compact volume having a drum with a small diameter. The pins would be set just before it entered into the reading area of the device which was under the users' primary reading finger. This device however occurred at constant speeds and did not accommodate reversals. Also, performance assessment of the device was not fully investigated with visually challenged users. Tactile Mice have been designed where both tactile and thermal feedback have been provided [12].Users are able to distinguish material surface by getting temperature feedback. The tactile feedback is provided by 30 piezo-electric bimorphs. Other similar tactile-mice have been developed for research purposes. Earlier tape displays such as Grundwald's belt device [13] had a bubbled tape loop into which protrusions could be punched by actuators.

3   Method

3.1   Apparatus

In our present work, we want to investigate whether a visually-impaired user can read words even though non-sensical letters pass under the reading finger. We have adopted a laterotactile presentation of text to the user in our study due to the reasons presented in [7, 14], namely that single cell displays must involve sliding contact for more effective braille reading. The apparatus consists of a tactile display (braille embossed disc) mounted on the shaft of a stepper motor and the interfacing driving electronics (control system) which is placed in an enclosure as seen in Fig. 3. In this method of presentation, the reading finger is stationary while the text changes underneath it. The enclosure bears the weight of the hand resting on it while the reading finger is placed on the disc.

- Tactile Display

The embossed disc is 3D printed and made of ABS (Acrylonitrile Butadiene Styrene) plastic. It is an opaque thermoplastic and amorphous polymer. With a width, s, of 5 mm assigned to each braille cell and $\Theta = 28.8°$, the radius of the disc was calculated is 20 mm as in (1).

$$s = r \times \theta \tag{1}$$

The disc has a width of 10 mm as in Fig. 2, and is comfortable for the users to place their reading finger on. It had 25 braille letters embossed around its circumference with a braille letter placed every 14.4°. The height of the braille dots were 0.9 mm and the width was 1.4 mm in accordance with the standard values [15]. As preliminary testing with the visually challenged user showed that the braille characters were too close to each other, the disc was modified with only alternate braille characters embossed i.e. a braille character was embossed every 28.8°(16 steps). As a result only 12 braille characters could be presented to the user. The results of testing with 12 braille characters are documented in our results. The disc is mounted on the motor shaft and rotates by different angles according to the letter pressed on the keyboard of the laptop.

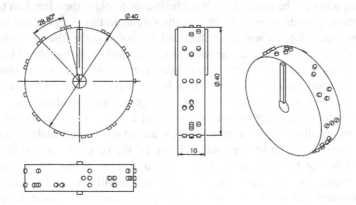

Fig. 2. Modified 12 letter embossed disc (dimensions in mm)

- Control System

The core of this prototype uses the TM4C123GH6PM microcontroller which is ARM Cortex-M4F based processor core. It runs on 3.3 V at 16 MHz via the regulator, 3.3 V, 400 mA, LDO Texas Instruments TPS73633DRBT which receives 5 V supply from the USB port of the laptop. It has a UART port running over the USB cable. A booster pack was designed to fit the launch pad vertically. The booster pack includes a DC jack to get power supply from a 12 V, 2A SMPS adapter. The booster pack has the driving electronics to drive the stepper motor according to the pulses received via the microcontroller. Characters are transmitted at a baud rate of 115200 using a serial terminal program from the laptop. The control of the motor at present is open-loop. The stepper motor is rated at 12 V with a step angle of 1.8°. It has 4 phases with a holding torque of 3.1 kgcm. The motor weighs 220 gms. It is programmed to run in the unipolar, full stepping sequence. The stepper motor has a speed of 150 rpm. With a speed of 150 rpm, 400 ms is the maximum time it will take to display character separated by a full 360°. We understand that the reading speed is limited by rotation speed of the motor. Choosing a motor with faster rpm, will increase the ability of the device to display characters faster. Also embossing characters closer to each other will reduce the delays between the appearances of letters.

3.2 Participants

Two visually challenged volunteers (both females) participated in the experiment (mean age 35 years, range 25–45). All of them had no other impairments and their right index finger was their primary reading finger. User 1 was adept in English braille with 40 years of experience while User 2 had just 5 years in learning English braille. The preliminary findings are based on data from these two participants.

3.3 Experimental Settings

The prototype device we used for the study was placed on the table at the side of a laptop during testing. The participants were instructed to place their hand on the device with their primary reading finger placed on the disc as in Fig. 3. Since the users palm rested on the enclosure, the weight of the hand did not stop the disc as it rotated. The finger rested lightly on the disc as the enclosure bore most of the weight of the hand. In our technique of presenting words to the users, the display of words is character by character, via hyper terminal to the blind user by the experimenter. As the experimenter presses a key, the stepper motor rotates through a corresponding specific angle, bringing the letter right under the reading finger of the user, while non-sensical letters brush past the reading finger. The user reads the character just under their reading finger. The letter is held under the reading finger, till the next letter is sent via uart. If a character could not be understood, they were instructed to say 'Pass' so that the experimenter could send the next letter. The user was initially allowed to feel the device and the embossed braille disc. The reading finger that was placed over the disc could move over the embossed character both vertically and horizontally if the user felt the need to, otherwise it was held over the disc while the disc rotated below it. Three sets of 36 randomly assorted words (2-letter, 3-letter, 4-letter words) were presented to the user as Trial1, Trial2 and Trial3 in two sessions, Session1 and Session2. The accuracy of reading out words in a minute was recorded and the mean speed of the three trials (in cps-characters per second) per session was noted. We specifically use character per second as metric of reading speed as words differ in length and a braille cell is a basic unit in reading braille [4]. Since the users are not native English speakers, we assessed their accuracy and speed on a printed braille sheet which had similar two, three and four lettered words. Both readers were asked to read from the experimental set-up in the

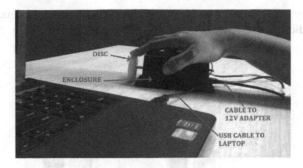

Fig. 3. Experimental set-up

same way they read from paper braille. The accuracy and speed on both paper braille and our apparatus was then compared. For both paper braille and in the experimental set up, their mean speeds of 3 trials in each session were noted.

3.4 Results

User 1 and User 2 differ in their proficiency of English. This is seen even as we compare their performance on paper Braille as in Table 1. User 1 who is experienced with English had a noticeable decrease in speed when reading words in our experimental set up. Yet there was a slight increase in speed in the 2nd session of testing as seen in Fig. 4. Verbal reports from User 1 suggested that if she spent more time adapting herself to reading in this manner, she would read faster. There was a minimal increase in speed for both users in session2. This suggests an increase in speed with practice.

Table 1. Speed in cps for User1 and User2

	Paper braille	Session1	Session2
User1	2.6	0.51	0.59
User2	0.36	0.37	0.38

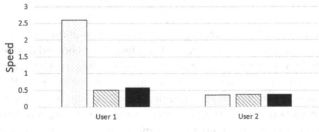

Fig. 4. Comparison of speeds between users on paper braille and the experimental set- up

The accuracy of both users on paper braille and the experimental set up were similar. This indicates that reading using this technique is viable (Fig. 5).

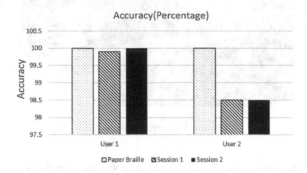

Fig. 5. Comparison of accuracy between users on paper braille and the experimental set- up

4   Discussion

The standard braille reading rates for skilled readers are approximately 125 words per minute equivalent to 7.5cps [4]. Since our users are not native English speakers we assessed their paper braille reading speeds. A comparison of the results on paper and our apparatus indicate that even though other letters brush under the finger, reading is possible as the user reads the letter that finally stops under the reading finger. Also, in words such as 'L-O-O-K', the largest time delay, as seen in Fig. 6 would be between the appearance of the consecutive letter 'o' under the reading finger as the disc would need to rotate a full 360° to come back to letter 'o' again.

Fig. 6.   Time in milli-seconds between the appearances of letters.

Braille characters under the reading finger move in an anti-clockwise direction as that is the conventional way braille is read. Therefore the embossed disc rotates only in the counter clockwise direction beneath the reading finger. The embossed braille characters are arranged at random along the perimeter of the disc. We interspersed vowels and consonants as words are generally constituted by both of them. Therefore the number of steps between the letters depends on the arrangement of letters along the disc circumference. In this disc, consecutive embossed letters were 16 steps apart from each other. If we place them closer, yet with enough spacing for a visually-impaired user to be able to distinguish them with ease, the delay between the appearances of letters can be further decreased. The high speed of the electronics contributes to the minimum delay between the appearances of letters under the reading finger. The switching sequence of the stepper motor used had a minimum delay of 2 ms. The motor speed is 150 rpm. This is a limiting factor in the speed of rotation of the braille embossed disc. A motor with a higher speed will be able to present characters with even shorter delays. For presentation of braille characters in this method, we have used just one actuator as opposed to the use of many actuators (a minimum of six for a braille cell) as in other designs of braille readers. Even with the use of a single actuator in this method of presentation, the accuracy rates were between 98% and 100% for both users. Hence, we believe that further investigating this feature in reading braille with a larger sample size would help in the design of cost-effective braille readers.

5   Conclusion

We have shown in this preliminary study that it is possible for blind readers to read words even as non-sensical letters pass under their reading finger. The results noted in here are on testing with just two visually-challenged users, of which one was minimally proficient in English braille. A wider population of visually impaired people who are proficient in English must be tested. Also, this aspect of braille reading must be further investigated when the user has control over the presentation of characters. For this we plan to incorporate closed loop control of the motor where the user points to a character in an application and the disc rotates according to the position of the device as indicated by movement of a cursor that points to a letter on the screen. The disc needs to be redesigned to incorporate more characters.

Acknowledgement. The authors would like to thank the Department of Science and Technology, Government of India for the financial support of this work (vide reference no. SR/WOS-A/ET/1000/2014 (G), under the Women Scientist Scheme). We are thankful to our volunteers, who so willingly gave their time for testing of the device. Thanks are due to Mr. Ravi Sivalingam for his assistance in the CAD drawings of the discs.

Appendix

Testing of the device with visually challenged users complied with the guidelines of the Institutional Ethical Committee for Studies on Human Subjects, VIT University (Ref. No. VIT/IECH/007/April 16, 2016).

References

1. Thomas, A., Rufus, E.: Alternate braille display designs: A review. Technol. Disabil. **28**(4), 123–132 (2016)
2. Vidal-Verdu, F., Hafez, M.: Graphical tactile displays for visually-impaired people. IEEE Trans. Neural Syst. Rehabil. Eng. **15**(1), 119–130 (2007)

3. Schiff, W., Foulke, E.: Tactual Perception: A Sourcebook. Cambridge University Press, New York (1982)
4. Legge, G.E., Madison, C.M., Mansfield, J.S.: Measuring braille reading speed with the MNREAD test. Vis. Impairment Res. 1(3), 131–145 (1999)
5. Loomis, J.M.: On the tangibility of letters and braille. Atten. Percept. Psychophys. 29(1), 37–46 (1981)
6. Heller, M.A., Nesbitt, K.D., Scrofano, D.K., Daniel, D.: Tactual recognition of embossed morse code, letters, and braille. Bull. Psychon. Soc. 28(1), 11–13 (1990)
7. Russomanno, A., O'Modhrain, S., Gillespie, R.B., Rodger, M.W.: Refreshing refreshable braille displays. IEEE Trans. Haptics 8(3), 287–297 (2015)
8. Lévesque, V., Pasquero, J., Hayward, V., Legault, M.: Display of virtual braille dots by lateral skin deformation: feasibility study. ACM Trans. Appl. Percept. (TAP). 2(2), 132–149 (2005)
9. Lévesque, V., Pasquero, J., Hayward, V.: Braille display by lateral skin deformation with the STReSS2 tactile transducer. In: Second Joint EuroHatics Conference and Symposium on Haptic Interfaces for Virtual Environment and Teleoperator Systems (WHC 2007), pp. 115–120. IEEE, 22 March 2007
10. Roberts, J., Slattery, O., Kardos, D.: 49.2: Rotating-wheel braille display for continuous refreshable braille. In: SID Symposium Digest of Technical Papers, Vol. 31(1), pp. 1130–1133. Blackwell Publishing Ltd., 1 May 2000
11. Nobels, T., Desmet, G., Van den Keybus, J., Belmans, R.: Development of a portable braille display using a fast prototyping platform for power electronics. In IEEE Conference Publication, pp. 321–325. Institution of Electrical Engineers (2006)
12. Yang, G.H., Kwon, D.S.: KAT II: Tactile display mouse for providing tactile and thermal feedback. Adv. Robot. 22(8), 851–865 (2008)
13. Reading and writing machine using raised patterns. U.S. Patent 3,624,772, issued 30 November 1971
14. Jones, L.A.: Designing effective refreshable braille displays. Computer 49(1), 14 (2016)
15. Runyan, N., Blazie, D.: EAP actuators aid the quest for the 'Holy Braille' of tactile displays. In: SPIE Smart Structures and Materials + Nondestructive Evaluation and Health Monitoring, p. 764207. International Society for Optics and Photonics, 25 March 2010

Performance of Accessible Gesture-Based Indic Keyboard

Pabba Anu Bharath[3], Charudatta Jadhav[2], Shashank Ahire[1(✉)],
Manjiri Joshi[1], Rini Ahirwar[1], and Anirudha Joshi[1]

[1] Indian Institute of Technology, Bombay, Mumbai, India
{ahire.shashank,manjirij,anirudha}@iitb.ac.in,
rini.ahirwar@gmail.com
[2] Tata Consultancy Services, Mumbai, India
charudatta.jadhav@tcs.com
[3] PDPM-IIITDM, Jabalpur, Jabalpur, Madhya Pradesh, India
bharath.pabba@gmail.com

Abstract. Though several keyboards for Indic languages are available on Android Play store, few are accessible by the visually impaired. Particularly, none of the gesture-based keyboards are accessible. We developed an accessible prototype of the popular gesture-based, logically organised Hindi keyboard *Swarachakra*. In this paper, we present findings from a two-part study. In the first part, we conducted a qualitative study with 12 visually impaired users on *Swarachakra*. In the second part, we conducted a longitudinal, within-subject evaluation comparing *Swarachakra* and Google Indic keyboard. At the end of the two-week long study, 10 participants had spent an average of 6.5 h typing, including training and text input tasks. Our study establishes benchmark for text input speeds for Indic languages on virtual keyboards by visually impaired users. The mean typing speed on *Swarachakra* was 14.53 cpm and that on Google Indic was 12.79 cpm. The mean speeds in last session were 21.72 cpm and 18.36 cpm respectively. Regression analysis indicates that the effect of keyboard was significant. In addition, we report the user preferences, the challenges faced and qualitative findings that are relevant to future research in Indic language text input by visually impaired users.

Keywords: Accessibility · Indic text input · Visually impaired · Longitudinal study

1 Introduction

Smartphones today are more than just mobile telephones. They are flexible devices that provide a wide array of information and communication services. Text input is a common activity required by many of these services. Touchscreens keyboard is the most common mode of text input on smartphones available in the market today. While this phenomenon has been of great help to most mainstream users, it is not an easy or smooth transition for those who are visually impaired [20]. Visually impaired users were reasonably comfortable with traditional keypad-based text input as it provided

R. Bernhaupt et al. (Eds.): INTERACT 2017, Part I, LNCS 10513, pp. 205–220, 2017.
DOI: 10.1007/978-3-319-67744-6_14

them tactile feedback as they typed. For them, using a virtual keyboard on a smooth, featureless screen has been a challenge.

Text input by the visually impaired using touchscreen keyboards is slow and laborious. While much work has been reported about text input on virtual keyboards by sighted people, comparatively less research has been reported about text input by visually impaired. For English, and for several other languages that use alphabetical scripts, virtual keyboards have been made accessible to an extent by "explore-by-touch" and "lift-to-type" [15] interaction. In the accessible mode, as the user moves his finger over the keyboard, the screen reader reads out each character under the finger. When the user lifts the finger, the character last read is typed, and is confirmed in a different voice.

However, a majority of Indic scripts are abugidas. Abugidas have a more complex script structure compared to the alphabets. In these scripts, a new glyph is often formed when a vowel modifier attaches itself to a consonant or when two or more consonants combine together to form a conjunct. These scripts also have about twice the number of characters than the alphabetical scripts. Several mainstream keyboard developers (such as CDAC InScript [11], Swiftkey [13] and Swype [14]) have responded to this problem by adopting the base QWERTY layout and relegating a large number of keys on one or more layers of shift. This adds to the already heavy cognitive load on users.

In recent years, "gesture-based" keyboards (such as *Swarachakra* [2] and *Sparsh* [12]) have attempted to alleviate this problem to some extent. These keyboards ease the interaction and reduce the cognitive load on the users by a combination of logical layout, dynamic pop-ups and gesture-based input. Unfortunately, this combination of gesture and pop-up is not compatible with screen readers, making these keyboards inaccessible. In prior work [1], we had presented an accessible version of *Swarachakra*. In this paper we develop this work further. We first did a qualitative study of *Swarachakra* with 12 visually impaired users. Based on the feedback, we redesigned the prototype. We then did a longitudinal empirical evaluation to compare the performances of this prototype with Google Indic [3]. Our work is the first such evaluation for Indic text input by visually challenged users. It establishes benchmark data for future research.

In the next section, we describe the challenges in the designing accessible Indic keyboards. In the third section we describe the designs of Google Indic and *Swarachakra*. In the fourth section we present the studies followed by the results. We conclude by presenting the lessons learnt and the possibilities of future work.

2 Background

2.1 Text Input by Visually Impaired

In the last few years, research on English text input on virtual keyboards by sighted users has advanced well. Using a combination of techniques such as word prediction, auto correction and shape writing [8], researchers have reported text input speeds ranging from 40 to 68 words per minute (wpm) or about 200 to 350 characters per minute (cpm) [7–9]. These are comparable to the speeds people achieve on desktop computers using a regular tactile keyboards.

In contrast, the progress on text input for visually impaired users has been limited. Speed in particular seems to be the problem. Azenkot et al. [6] describe Perkinput, an eyes-free text input mechanism in which the user taps Braille-like patterns on a touchscreen device. They report average a peak speed of 7.36 wpm (about 37 cpm) with about 3.5 h of practice for Perkinput, which was an improvement over the 4.52 wpm (about 23 cpm) that users could achieve using VoiceOver. Nicolau et al. [26] report mean last session speed of 4 wpm (20 cpm) for Portuguese on QWERTY. Bonner et al. describe No-look notes, in which characters are arranged around the screen in an 8-segment pie menu [5]. Each segment of the menu contains multiple characters, such that all 26 letters of the English alphabet appear. The eight groups of characters (ABC, DEF, GHI, JKL, MNO, PQRS, TUV and WXYZ) correspond to the international standard mapping on a phone keypad [10]. In their study, they found the overall text entry speeds were 0.66 wpm (about 3 cpm) for VoiceOver and 1.32 wpm (about 7 cpm) for No-Look Notes. Thus, in these studies the speeds reached by visually impaired users are reported to be between 7 and 11% of typical speeds of sighted users.

By the year 2020 about 31.6 million people are estimated to be visually impaired in India [24]. To the best of our knowledge, no research on Indic text input by the visually impaired reports benchmark text input speed.

2.2 Text Input in Indian Languages

As discussed above, most Indic scripts are Abugidas, and are structurally different from alphabets. The Devanagari script [23] is used by many Indic languages including Hindi, Marathi, Konkani and Sanskrit, and is based on Brahmi [23]. Like many Indian scripts, Devanagari is structured according to the part of the body that produces the sounds.

Text input in Indic scripts has many challenges [2, 4, 19, 25]. Often two or more keystrokes are needed to input a glyph. The most common construction is the combination of a consonant (e.g. प) and a dependent vowel modifier (e.g. ◌ो), which gives a single glyph (e.g. पो) (C+V). Conjuncts formed by joining two or more consonants (C+C) (e.g. स + ट = स्ट) have been particularly difficult to input. These are formed by separately inserting a joiner (halant character ◌्) between the two consonants, thus taking at least three keystrokes. Users often get confused with the sequence of characters to be typed to achieve a desired conjunct. At times the halant is clearly visible in the visual representation glyph (e.g. ट + व = ट्व) and in these cases, the sequence of keys is obvious. However, many common conjuncts are represented as a single glyph with varying levels of visual similarity with the original consonants (e.g. स + त = स्त; क + र = क्र; र + क = र्क; क + ष = क्ष).

Some other keyboards like Google Indic [3] have a different layout (as described below). These are not constrained by the basic QWERTY layout and hence have significantly reduced the need to use shift, though the other challenges remain.

Gestures have been used to improve speeds on virtual keyboards for English. Swype [14] and Swiftkey [13] are examples of one type of gestures. In these keyboards, the user moves the finger from one key to the next without lifting it, and the keyboard disambiguates the "shape" thus produced to guess the word user is trying to type. This option is also available in Indic versions of these keyboards. However, studies thus far have not reported improvements in speed in comparison with similar keyboards without this feature (e.g. [2]). In any case, this feature is not accessible by the visually impaired for any language yet.

As mentioned above, keyboards such as *Swarachakra* [2] and *Sparsh* [12] also use gestures. Conceptually, these gestures are of different type than in Swiftkey or Swype, and are particularly relevant to text input in Indic scripts. On these keyboards, when the user touches a consonant, a pop-up appears. The popup displays glyphs that will result after adding vowel modifiers to the selected consonant (Fig. 1). The user chooses a vowel modifier by sliding his finger. With practice, the touch and slide becomes a single gesture. Thus, the user starts inputting two characters in one stroke, thereby improving speeds.

Fig. 1. Popup displaying combinations of consonant + frequent vowel modifiers in *Swarachakra* and *Sparsh* keyboards.

Benchmark data for text input in Indic scripts is less compared to English. In a recent study, Dalvi et al. [25] report a between-subject longitudinal evaluation with sighted users using InScript, Swiftkey, *Sparsh* and *Swarachakra*. In their study, after about 5 h of practice, novice sighted users reached mean speeds of 38 to 45 cpm. In our subsequent work, which involved accelerated learning and extensive practice on CDAC InScript keyboard, expert sighted users could achieve mean speeds of 110 to 120 cpm [19]. To the best of our knowledge, there are no published studies reporting benchmark speeds using the Google Indic keyboard.

3 The Keyboard Designs

3.1 Google Indic

Given its suitable design, we chose Google Indic as the representative of non-gesture based keyboards. It was also the only other Indic keyboard we found that was accessible. Google Indic keyboard is logically organised, i.e. it uses the Devanagari script structure in its layout (Fig. 2a). It has five rows of keys. It displays most of the frequently used Devanagari characters on the unshifted layer. Frequent independent vowels and corresponding vowel modifiers are in row 1 of this layer. This row shows independent vowels by default (Fig. 2a). The consonants and frequent diacritic marks are in rows 2 to 5 in a layout that closely resembles the Devanagari script structure.

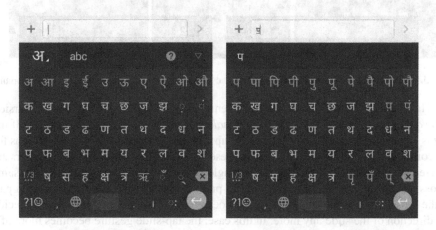

Fig. 2. **a** Before typing a consonant, **b** (C+V) form of last typed consonant प.

When a consonant or a conjunct is typed, the first row changes to show the (C+V) form of the last-typed consonant/conjunct (Fig. 2b). This makes it easier for the user to input the typical C+V glyph. While independent vowels do follow consonants, such occurrences are infrequent (e.g. the word कई). If the user wishes to type an independent vowel after a consonant, he needs to tap and hold the corresponding vowel key, and select the independent vowel from a pop-up. Similarly, the key for diacritic *anusvār* (ः) shows some of the frequent diacritics in the pop-up. Google Indic keyboard has two shift buttons. One shift toggles the between the characters and numerical keys. A second shift cycles through the second and third layer of the keyboard which contain some of the less frequent vowels, conjuncts and diacritics. The Google Indic keyboard is accessible by the visually impaired users by "explore-by-touch" and "lift-to-type" interaction described above.

3.2 *Swarachakra* Accessible

Layout of the mainstream version of the *Swarachakra* keyboard (Fig. 3a) is also based on the logical structure of Devanagari script, phonetically grouped and arranged in a grid similar to those found in most school textbooks [2]. Consonants, some frequent conjuncts and vowels are arranged in a 5 × 8 grid in the middle of the keyboard. The column to the left of this grid has frequent punctuation marks, while the column to the right of the grid has backspace, diacritics and modal keys. The row below the grid has shift, space, enter keys.

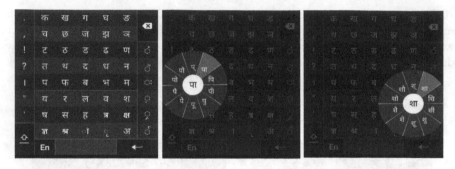

Fig. 3. **a** *Swarachakra* keyboard layout, **b** and **c** show *chakra* remains same for all consonants

The glyph on the face of the key can be entered with a tap. In the mainstream version of *Swarachakra*, the tap reveals a popup *chakra* (circular menu) with 10 options. If the key is consonant or a semi-vowel, the pop-up shows 10 frequent C+V combinations for the consonant. The user can select any of these with a slide gesture. Vowel modifiers are ordered sequentially in the *chakra*. The angle of each the vowel modifier is the same across all consonants (Fig. 3b and c). With practice, the vowel positions become a part of the muscle memory of the user and he does not need to look at the *chakra* to decide the direction of the slide any more. In this case, the tap-slide gesture becomes more of a fling gesture in which two characters are input with one stroke.

The problem with the mainstream version of Swarachakra is that the pop-up prevents the users from using the "explore-by-touch" and "lift-to-type" interactions that are common to other keyboards. We developed an accessible version of *Swarachakra* [1] (Fig. 4). This version supports the "explore-by-touch" interaction, wherein the user can continuously slide his finger over the keyboard to locate the desired key as the screen reader reads out the key under the finger (Fig. 4b). As the default Android Google TTS [21] does not provide feedback for some Indic characters, we used e-Speak TTS [20] for voice feedback in our prototype. If only a consonant is desired, it is input by the usual "lift-to-type" interaction, after which the screen reader reads out the input in a second voice.

Fig. 4. **a** Accessible version of *Swarachakra*, **b** explore by touch to locate key, **c** second-finger tap to activate *chakra*, **d** lift the first finger and slide the second finger to make a selection

As we want the users to be able to explore the keyboard by touch, this version of *Swarachakra* does not display the *chakra* pop-up on the first touch. Once the user has found the desired consonant, he can activate the *chakra* pop-up by putting a second finger down anywhere on the screen. The *chakra* pops up under the second finger (Fig. 4c). Thereafter, the user can lift the first finger. To pick one of the glyphs from the popup *chakra*, user slides the second finger in the direction of the desired vowel modifier (Fig. 4d). As he does so, the screen reader reads out the vowel modifier under the finger. If the user has not found the desired vowel modifier yet, he can explore the *chakra* without lifting the second finger. *Chakra* can be dismissed without any input by tapping the first finger, while holding down the second finger.

In the mainstream version of *Swarachakra*, *chakra* appears under the first finger, aligned to the centre of the key. However, in the accessible version, the *chakra* appears under the second finger. The user can choose where he taps the second finger. This opens up the possibility of letting the edge keys also be the ones that need a *chakra*. In the accessible version of *Swarachakra*, the left column with punctuations is dropped (Fig. 4a). This separates the keys out in the horizontal direction, and lets the users use the edges of the screen for orientation. For additional orientation, the keyboard gives strong vibrations on five keys, namely the four corners and centre of the grid (the keys for क, ड़, ञ, अ and द). The users can input the spacebar and backspace through three-finger swipe gestures.

4 User Studies

4.1 Short Qualitative Study

We first conducted a short exploratory qualitative study with 12 visually impaired participants. Only two of these participants were familiar with touchscreens. Participants were explained the layout of the accessible *Swarachakra* and were familiarized with the use of keyboard in accessible mode with screen-reader. Next they were asked to type 10 words. After that, feedback was collected from the users.

Participants found the layout of the keyboard easy to learn. Most of the participants liked the combination of second-finger tap and slide gesture to select the vowel modifier. One of the most obvious issue participants faced was distinguishing between the long and short vowels in the speech output of screen reader. For example, they found it difficult to differentiate between कि (pronounced as kɪ as in kid) and की (ki: as in key), or between कु (kʊ as in cook) and कू (ku: as in cool). They also faced some difficulty in differentiating between some phonetically similar consonants (त-थ, श-ष, ब- भ, ट-ठ, ड-ढ etc.) in the speech output of screen reader. We also observed that keys on the screen edges were easier to locate. The backspace key in our prototype was small and participants found it difficult to use.

We redesigned the keyboard based on the above feedback. We replaced the default text-to-speech engine of screen reader with custom text-to-speech engine Lekha available via Vocaliser app [17]. We used pitch variation to differentiate between short and long vowels. We shifted the diacritics in first row to the right edge and increased the height and width of the backspace (Fig. 4a). If the user dwelled on a consonant key for longer than one second, a word starting with the consonant was read out as feedback. For example, 'तरबूज़' for त, 'सेब' for 'स' and 'धनुष' for ध. This feedback was the equivalent of reading out 'Tango' for T in English keyboards.

4.2 Quantitative Longitudinal Study

We conducted a within-subject study to compare the accessible version *Swarachakra* and Google Indic keyboard. Our protocol for the study is similar to the protocol suggested by [4], except that our study had a within-subject design. The keyboard sequence was counter balanced across users.

On the first day, the user was assigned the first keyboard. The user was trained on that keyboard. During the training session, the user explored the layout of the keyboard with the help of the moderator for 5 min. Next, he was asked to type 8 Hindi words (Table 1). These words were representative of the typing tasks that the user might face, and were presented in the increasing order of difficulty. To ensure that the results were comparable across keyboards, the users were not trained on the "prediction" features of Google Indic keyboard. Users were trained on all other aspects of the keyboards including space, shift, backspace, touch and hold delay, etc. In talkback mode, volume up/down keys can be used to move the cursor left/right. Users were trained to use this interaction for Google Indic keyboard. However, this feature was not available while vocaliser app, and was skipped for *Swarachakra*. After the training, the user was given time to explore the keyboard on his own for 5 min.

After that, the user was given first-time usability test (FTU). In this, the user typed 14 Hindi words. Some examples are shown in Table 1. Again, these words are representative of the typing tasks that the user might require while typing Hindi. In the first attempt of each FTU word, no hint was provided. If the user could not type the word correctly, the user was allowed a second attempt. In the second attempt, predetermined hints were provided if the moderator deemed it necessary. After the user had typed the word, he was given feedback about how fast and accurately he had typed. If the user

Table 1. Sample of words and phrases used in the study.

Training words	FTU words	Sample phrases
समझकर	कमल	मना कर देना
ग़ायब	विनय	ग़ायब हो जाना
स्वागत	ज़मीन	चार चाँद लगना
पृथ्वी	आस्तीन	हड़प लेना
कार्यशाला	बर्फी	अंधेरे में तीर चलाना
अहंकारी	नम्रता	इज्जत मिट्टी में मिलाना
ऊपर	कृपया	ईंट का जवाब पत्थर से देना
चाँद	दुःख	आमदनी अठन्नी और खर्चा रुपैया

could type substantial number of words in the FTU, he was deemed to be trained. This ended the session on the first day.

The next day onwards, a longitudinal usability test (LTU) was started. This consisted of 10 LTU sessions, each of which required the user to transcribe eight phrases (80 phrases in alls). The phrases were a mix of Hindi idioms and phrases from school text for Hindi [16]. Example phrases are shown in Table 1. They were classified as easy, medium and hard using the classification used by Dalvi et al. [4]. To provide early success to the users, we asked the users to type a random selection of eight easy-to-type phrases in the first LTU session. The difficulty of phrases was ramped up gradually till the fourth LTU session. In subsequent LTU sessions, phrases were presented randomly.

The user could touch the top left corner of the screen to hear the word/phrase to be typed and touch the right corner of the screen to hear the word/phrase typed so far. At times, the spelling of words used in the phrases to be transcribed was not clearly distinguishable in the screen reader speech output. If asked, the moderator clarified the spelling (but not in the phrase typed by the user). Other than that, no other help was provided during the LTU tasks. Like in the FTU, the user was given feedback about his speed and accuracy after completing each phrase.

For the sake of consistency, all tasks were done using Xiaomi Redmi Note 3 device. It has a 5.5-inch screen with 1080×1920 pixel display and a capacitive touchscreen. To accurately log the text entered by users and the time taken, we created a software application. To ensure that users do not get fatigued, we restricted each user to a maximum of two LTU sessions per day, and provided a gap of at least 30 min between sessions.

During an LTU session if the moderator observed that the user was not using the keyboard well, he asked the user to explore the keyboard on his own before or after the session. The moderator provided additional training if necessary during these self-explore sessions. All these self-explore sessions were logged and were counted as "practice time". With this level of training, we were hoping to minimise errors and increase speeds.

Each keyboard attempt took between six to eight days. Once the user had completed the first keyboard, the same process was repeated for the second keyboard. Each participant was compensated a gift equivalent to ₹ 450 (USD 7) for their time.

4.3 Participants

Ten volunteers participated in the longitudinal study. Five of the users were partially blind and five were completely blind. All except one user were right-handed. Users were aged 17–28, with mean age of 22; there were 7 males and 3 females. Most of them had been using mobile phones for less than a year and the mean phone usage duration was about a year. Eight of the ten users had used Android phones. Of these, five had used TalkBack. One of these was a current iPhone user but had used Android before. One person owned a feature phone and had never used an Android phone. One person had never used a phone. None of the volunteers had any experience with typing in an Indian language.

5 Results

5.1 Practice Time, Accuracy, Error Rate and Speed

During the longitudinal study, 10 users typed 80 phrases on each of the two keyboards, resulting in 1,600 phrases in total. The experiment involved about 6.5 h of typing time for each user. The average time spent by users on a keyboard during training and self-explore sessions is an indicator of the learnability of the keyboards. Mean practice time (training + self-explore sessions) was about 1.5 h per keyboard and mean overall typing time, including practice time, was about 3 h (Table 2). The pauses between phrases and sessions were ignored.

Table 2. Mean practice time and overall typing time for Google Indic and *Swarachakra*

	Google Indic	Swarachakra
Mean training + self-explore time (mins)	89	102
Mean typing time (mins)	193	198

While speed is the primary endpoint of this experiment, speed is comparable across keyboards only when the accuracy of the typed matter is reasonably high on both keyboards. The users were trained extensively to ensure high levels of accuracy (or low uncorrected error rates). Damerau–Levenshtein distance was used as a measure of accuracy. For each session of each user, % session accuracy was calculated using the following formula:

$$\%Session\,Accuracy = \left(1 - \frac{Edit\,distance}{No.of\,characters\,to\,be\,typed}\right) * 100$$

Table 3 presents a summary of the mean and median % session accuracy for the two keyboards.

Table 3. Mean and median % session accuracy

	Google Indic	Swarachakra
Overall mean (n = 10)	94.38	95.78
Mean of last two sessions	93.88	95.10
Overall median (n = 10)	94.80	96.17
Median of last two sessions	93.92	94.71

The median session accuracy considering all 10 users for the two keyboards was quite high (95.67%). This indicates that the users were satisfactorily trained and motivated sufficiently to type accurately. High accuracy was maintained even as the users attempted to achieve high speed.

Data about "corrected error rates" is also of interest in text input research. Users had typed 25,381 characters including wrong characters and backspaces. Backspace

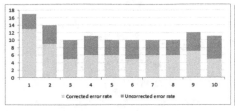 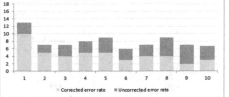

Fig. 5. Corrected and uncorrected error rates for Google Indic keyboard and *Swarachakra* Accessible keyboard respectively.

constituted 6.32% of these and backspaced characters were another 6.39%. Figure 5 shows the corrected and uncorrected error rates for the two keyboards as discussed in [19]. We can see that the total error rates are moderate in the first session. The corrected error rate is higher than the uncorrected, and is between 10–13% on average. It drops to between 4–7% by the 5th session, and stays in that range till the 10th session. While there is some room for improvement in the corrected error rates, these are not excessively high. We can consider that the users were reasonably trained, and hence their speeds can be compared.

Table 4 shows mean typing speed for the first attempt, mean typing speed for the second attempt, overall mean typing speed and mean typing speed for last session, in characters-per-minute (cpm). Plot of mean session-wise cpm (Fig. 6) shows that the speed increased as users gained practice on both keyboards.

Table 4. Mean typing speed (cpm) for sessions in first attempt, second attempt, mean cpm across two attempts and mean cpm for last session for each keyboard.

Mean typing speed (cpm)	Google Indic	Swarachakra
Attempt 1 (n = 5)	9.8	11.2
Attempt 2 (n = 5)	15.8	17.9
Overall (N = 10)	12.8	14.52
Last session (N = 5)	18.4	21.7

A within-subject, repeated measures ANOVA is often used to compare the performance of the two keyboards. Although it seems that speeds were higher on *Swarachakra* for the first attempt, a repeated measures ANOVA of session-wise mean speeds showed that the differences in the mean cpm for sessions 1–10 between *Swarachakra* and Google Indic were not statistically significant, $F(1, 8) = 0.672$ ($p = 0.436$), partial $\eta^2 = 0.077$. However, we argue that in the particular case when the users are novice to text input, repeated measures ANOVA may not have sufficient power to isolate the real difference between performances of two input methods.

In a typical within-subject study that aims to compare performance of two keyboards, users are asked to perform text input tasks on the two keyboards. The order of presentation of the keyboards is counter-balanced to mitigate the effect of any transfer of learning from one keyboard to another. The unstated assumption therein is that the

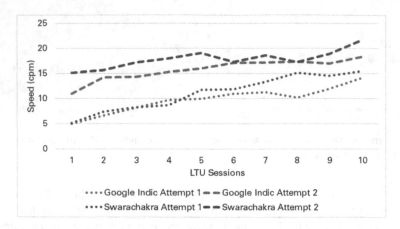

Fig. 6. Mean session speed (CPM) for all sessions of attempt 1 and attempt 2

users are familiar with "text input" in that script in general, and are therefore already familiar with the notions and the concepts inherent to "text input". In reality, the user does gain additional "text input practice" while doing tasks on the method attempted first. This additional effect is deemed to be negligible compared to the overall text input practice that the user may have had "in life" before the experiment. Hence, repeated measures ANOVA only measures the difference in performance between the two keyboards.

However, this argument is not valid in cases such as ours where users are new to text-input as a task. Our users were unfamiliar with common text input tasks such as the use of shift, backspace, and aspects inherent to Indic text input in particular, such as vowel modifiers, conjuncts etc. In their first attempt, they were in fact learning these aspects of text input as well as the specific input method. By the time they were in their second attempt, the "general text input" practice gained during the first attempt could be quite substantial compared to their earlier "in life" practice. If that indeed is the case, the true difference of interest (the difference of speed between the two input methods) may be overshadowed by the larger difference between the two attempts. While using a repeated measures within-subject ANOVA, there is no way to separate the two differences.

To test this hypothesis, we evaluated the difference between attempts (irrespective of the input methods) and found that this was indeed true for our study. The mean session speed irrespective of input methods in attempt 1 was 10.49 cpm (N = 10, SD = 2.57) and for attempt 2, it was 16.83 cpm (N = 10, SD = 5.95). A two-sample t-test assuming unequal variance showed that the difference was statistically significant ($p = 0.009$).

To evaluate the relative performance of input methods while accounting for the text input practice gained in attempt 1, we performed a multiple linear regression. In our study, the mean typing speed of a given session is dependent on three factors: the attempt (first or second), the session number (1 to 10), and the input method (Google Indic or *Swarachakra*). To eliminate the effect of other variables, we performed a multiple linear regression assuming the mean session speed as the criterion variable and the attempt number, session number, and a dummy variable for the input methods (Google Indic or *Swarachakra*) as predictor variables. The model was significant and returned these values: $R = 0.642$, $R^2 = 0.412$, adjusted $R^2 = 0.403$, $F = 45.707$, $p < 0.0005$. As anticipated, all three variables emerged as significant predictors. The speed increases by 6.344 cpm per attempt (95% CI from 5.004 to 7.685, $p < 0.0005$) and by 0.781 cpm per session (95% CI from 0.547 to 1.014, $p < 0.0005$). The input method also emerged as a significant predictor ($p = 0.012$) with *Swarachakra* adding to the speed by 1.732 cpm (95% CI from 0.391 to 3.072), or about 11% gain over Google Indic.

The variance inflation factors (VIFs) of all predictor variables are below 2, indicating that there is no multi-collinearity among the predictor variables of the model. The distributions of the criterion variable and the z residuals were found to be normal.

5.2 Qualitative Findings

Screen-reader issue: As discussed earlier, some common issues were attributable to the limitations of the screen reader. Distinguishing between short/long vowels and similar sounding consonant pairs as read out by the screen readers was a constant cause of confusion. While we attempted to vary the pitch to differentiate between such pairs of vowels and give example words consonant, this solution was still not effective, especially at higher speech rates. This we believe is a larger issue of visually impaired users learning spelling in Indian languages, and goes beyond the scope of this text input paper.

Accidental touch with gestures: Accidental touches while using gestures could potentially lead to unintended text input and was a cause of concern. Hence, many users preferred not using gestures for space bar and backspace in *Swarachakra*. Similarly, they did not use navigation gestures in the typed text on Google Indic. While correcting errors most users chose to backspace the text all the way up to the erroneous input and then continue typing rather than using navigation gestures to the locate the error and correct it.

Findings related to keyboard designs: Most of the users were new to text-input and to touchscreen devices. The following findings must be viewed with this in mind.

Some findings are valid for design of both keyboards. Initially the users would start exploring keyboards from the left edge, moving downwards to locate the correct row. Then they would start moving along the row to locate the desired key. By the end of first couple of LTU sessions, users had learnt the keyboard layout. They tried to touchdown directly on the key, re-adjusting the finger to reach the intended key, if needed. This reduced time taken to locate keys. This strategy was used to locate space and backspace keys as well.

The keyboards being compared in our study do not give any feedback when a row boundary is crossed. While trying to explore the keys in a row, users believed they were moving perfectly horizontally, when in fact they were sometimes moving at an angle. This initially lead to some confusion about the sequence of keys in the row.

On *Swarachakra* users took some time getting used to the two finger gesture to invoke the *chakra*. Finger tap to dismiss *chakra* was found to be useful. The key with independent vowels was located at bottom-right corner of keyboard. This made second finger tap a little tricky. While training users on the *chakra* in *Swarachakra*, they were told to map the vowels onto a clock. As a result, after a few sessions users learnt the angles of the vowel modifiers.

In Google Indic keyboard, for *anusvār* (ः) key on the right edge, the popup is shown without a delay. This is inconsistent with respect to other keys, where the pop-up with additional options appears after a delay. Due to this many users avoided using the right edge to orient themselves. Sometimes users accidentally activated one of the shift keys in Google Indic and found it difficult to navigate back. In Google Indic keyboard if the users strayed onto the prediction bar at the top of the keyboard and no predictions were being shown, no feedback was received from the screen-reader. This misled users into believing that the screen reader had stopped working.

6 Conclusion and Future Work

We designed an accessible version of a gesture and pop-up based keyboard *Swarachakra*, and compared its performance with Google Indic, a predominantly tap-based keyboard. We found that the gesture-based keyboard did significantly better than the tap-based keyboard. Even after 10 sessions and about 3 h of typing practice on each keyboard, there seemed to be no evidence of saturation. Future research is needed with more sessions will be required to establish the saturation point. Although there are papers discussing the benchmark data for sighted users in Indic scripts, this is the first paper to provide benchmark speeds for text input by visually impaired in Indic scripts through an empirical study.

Our study also provides insights into future designs of Indic script keyboards. We attempted to help the users distinguish between short and long vowels by varying pitch and between similar sounding consonants by providing examples. Neither seemed to have helped enough, particularly as the users speed improved. Alternatives (such as bigger pitch differences or completely different voices) can be tried in future research. Gestures for space and backspace were not used much because users were concerned about the accidentally touching a key while executing the gesture, leading to unintended text input.

While ANOVA is often used to assess the difference between interventions in a within-subject design, we argue that for text input studies with novice users, a repeated measures ANOVA may not be the most appropriate test. When novice users learn to type using the first input method, they are learning to type in addition to learning to type using that specific input method. By the time they attempt their second input method, they are already at an advantage. This could result in a significantly better typing speeds on their second input method compared to their first one, which is not factored out by the repeated measures ANOVA. A multiple regression can tease out the actual differences between input methods after accounting for the differences between attempts.

Acknowledgements. This project was funded by Tata Consultancy Services. We thank the volunteers from XRCVC, Ruia College in Mumbai and National Association for Blind in New Delhi for participating in our studies and providing us with valuable feedback.

References

1. Srivastava, M., Anu Bharath, P,: Accessible Swarachakra: a virtual keyboard for visually impaired. In: India HCI, 8th Indian Conference on Human Computer Interaction, pp. 111–115. ACM, New York (2016)
2. Joshi, A., Dalvi, G., Joshi, M., Rashinkar, P., Sarangdhar, A.: Design and evaluation of Devanagari virtual keyboards for touchscreen mobile phones. In: 13th International Conference on Human Computer Interaction with Mobile Devices and Services, pp. 323–332 ACM, New York (2011)
3. Google Indic Playstore link. https://play.google.com/store/apps/details?id=com.google.android.apps.inputmethod.hindi&hl=en
4. Dalvi, G., Ahire, S., Emmadi, N., Joshi, M., Malsettar, N., Samanta, D., Jalihal, D., Joshi, A.: A protocol to evaluate virtual keyboards for indian languages. In: Proceedings of the 7th International Conference on HCI, pp. 27–38. ACM, New York (2015)
5. Bonner, M.N., Brudvik, J.T., Abowd, G.D., Edwards, W.K.: No-look notes: accessible eyes-free multi-touch text entry. In: Floréen, P., Krüger, A., Spasojevic, M. (eds.) Pervasive 2010. LNCS, vol. 6030, pp. 409–426. Springer, Heidelberg (2010). doi:10.1007/978-3-642-12654-3_24
6. Azenkot, S., Wobbrock, J., Prasain, S., Ladner, R.: Input finger detection for nonvisual touch screen text entry in Perkinput. In: Proceedings of Graphics Interface, pp. 121–129. ACM, New York (2012)
7. MacKenzie, I.S., Zhang, S.X.: The design and evaluation of a high-performance soft keyboard. In: Proceedings of the SIGCHI Conference on Human Factors in Computing Systems, pp. 25–31. ACM, New York (1999)
8. Kristensson, P.O.: Discrete and continuous shape writing for text entry and control. Doctoral dissertation, Linkoping University (2007)
9. Kristensson, P.O., Vertanen, K.: The inviscid text entry rate and its application as a grand goal for mobile text entry. In: Proceedings of the 16th International Conference on Human-Computer Interaction with Mobile Devices & Services, pp. 335–338. ACM, New York (2014)
10. Arrangement of Digits, Letters and Symbols on Telephones and Other Devices that can be Used for Gaining Access to a Telephone Network. http://www.itu.int/rec/T-REC-E.161-200102-I/en
11. CDAC InScript: Unified Virtual Keyboard for Indian Languages (2015). http://www.cdac.in/index.aspx?id=dl_android_uvkil
12. *Sparsh* Hindi Keyboard. https://play.google.com/store/apps/details?id=com.sparsh.inputmethod.hindi&hl=en
13. SwiftKey Keyboard (2015). https://play.google.com/store/apps/details?id=com.touchtype.swiftkey&hl=en
14. Swype Keyboard. http://www.swype.com/
15. Google Explore by touch. https://support.google.com/accessibility/android/answer/6006598
16. Phraselist. https://docs.google.com/spreadsheets/d/1_2OZMz35WFgfpqQt2FSzBuwiPcVee546pZmyieXab_o/edit#gid=830720293

17. Vocaliser TTS Voice. https://play.google.com/store/apps/details?id=es.codefactory.voca lizertts&hl=en
18. Devanagri. https://en.wikipedia.org/wiki/Devanagari
19. Ghosh, S., Joshi, A., Joshi, M., Emmadi, N., Dalvi, G., Ahire, S., Rangale, S.: Shift+Tap or Tap+LongPress?: the upper bound of typing speed on InScript. In: Proceedings of the 2017 CHI Conference on Human Factors in Computing Systems, pp. 35–46. ACM, New York (2017)
20. E-Speak TTS. https://play.google.com/store/apps/details?id=com.googlecode.eyesfree. espeak&hl=en
21. Google TTS. https://play.google.com/store/apps/details?id=com.google.android.tts&hl=en
22. Rodrigues, A., Montague, K., Nicolau, H., Guerreiro, T.: Getting smartphones to talkback: understanding the smartphone adoption process of blind users. In: Proceedings of the 17th International ACM SIGACCESS Conference on Computers & Accessibility, pp. 23–32. ACM, New York (2015)
23. Abugida. https://en.wikipedia.org/wiki/Abugida
24. Estimation of blindness in India from 2000 through 2020: implications for the blindness control policy. https://www.ncbi.nlm.nih.gov/pubmed/11804362
25. Dalvi, G., Ahire, S., Emmadi, N., Joshi, M., Joshi, A., Ghosh, S., Ghone, P., Parmar, N.: Does prediction really help in marathi text input? empirical analysis of a longitudinal study. In: Proceedings of the 18th International Conference on Human-Computer Interaction with Mobile Devices and Services, pp. 35–46. ACM, New York (2016)
26. Nicolau, H., Montague, K., Guerreiro, T., Rodrigues, A., Hanson, L.: Typing performance of blind users: an analysis of touch behaviors, learning effect, and in-situ usage. In: Proceedings of the 17th International ACM SIGACCESS Conference on Computers & Accessibility, pp. 273–280. ACM, New York (2015)

Audience Engagement

Designing Collaborative Co-Located Interaction for an Artistic Installation

Oussama Mubarak[1,2(✉)], Pierre Cubaud[1], David Bihanic[2,3], and Samuel Bianchini[2]

[1] CNAM/CEDRIC, ILJ Team, 292 rue Saint Martin, 75003 Paris, France
oussama.mubarak@ensad.fr
[2] EnsAD/EnsadLab, Reflective Interaction Team, 31 rue d'Ulm, 75005 Paris, France
[3] ACTE Research Institute, Univ. of Paris I, 47 rue des Bergers, 75015 Paris, France

Abstract. In this paper we present a preliminary user study conducted on a walk-up-and-use musical instrument dubbed *Collective Loops* specifically designed for co-located collaborative interaction for the general public. The aim of this study was to verify that displaying all users' choices in a shared interface would promote and facilitate user engagement in creative collaboration. Although the results do not confirm our hypothesis, the experiment allowed us to detect a more general design issue with such walk-up-and-use multi-display installations: striking the right balance between the different interfaces in order to release some of the users attention for the benefit of the collaborative process.

Keywords: Co-located interaction · Collaboration · Audience engagement · Interactive art · Walk-up-and-use

1 Introduction

The field of interactive art seized very early on the new possibilities offered by ubiquitous computing. An in depth renewal of forms of aesthetic experiences enabled the creation of new face-to-face collective interactive situations. Such installations became more prominent with the democratization of mobile phones with projects such as *Blinkenlights* [6] by the Chaos Computer Club in which people could play the Pong game or send messages on a very large public display using their own mobile phones. And *Dialtones (A Telesymphony)* [10] by Golan Levin et al., *TweetDreams* [8] by Luke Dahl et al., and Kim Haeyoung's *Moori* [13] allowed participants to interact via their phones with a musical performance.

While some of such installations enabled creative collaboration between co-located individuals, most of them relied on some form of human moderation or orchestration to guide the audience's actions, control the system's reactions, or rearrange the individual outputs to produce a suitable common result.

© IFIP International Federation for Information Processing 2017
Published by Springer International Publishing AG 2017. All Rights Reserved
R. Bernhaupt et al. (Eds.): INTERACT 2017, Part I, LNCS 10513, pp. 223–231, 2017.
DOI: 10.1007/978-3-319-67744-6_15

Furthermore, co-located collaboration has been a gradually emerging topic in HCI, and more specifically in the CSCW community, but has mostly focused on systems designed to facilitate collaboration between teammates in a working environment [2,11].

Our study, on the other hand, concentrates on the engagement in a collective and collaborative process, with little to no intervention for moderation or orchestration, around a creative interactive installation. One of the many challenges faced in designing such art installations, intended for co-located interaction by the general public without human moderation, involves the ability to redirect the user's attention from individual interfaces towards shared interfaces in favor of a collective and collaborative outcome.

Some closely related research has dealt with non-expert user engagement. Brignull and Rogers have, for instance, studied how people can be enticed to interact with a shared public system that allows them to post views and opinions [4], and Edmonds et al. and Bilda et al. have addressed the problems faced by creative installations in terms of audience engagement [3,9]. Other research have dealt with visual attention issues in multi-display environments [5,12,15]. Yet none seem to have specifically dealt with collective experiences in walk-up-and-use systems.

In this article, we present a comparative user study that was conducted on an artistic project entitled *Collective Loops* during a public event. We expected through this study to better understand the role of individual and shared interfaces in the shift of users' attention and examine some of the conditions that help lead to a "successful" collective interaction by allowing the progressive coordination of actions in favor of a common satisfactory result.

2   Collective Loops

Collective Loops is a real-time collaborative musical 8-step loop sequencer developed as a prototype project for the *CoSiMa* [7] (Collaborative Situated Media) platform[1], in which several institutions and agencies are combining efforts to develop a software platform, based on Web standards, easing the creation of co-located collective interaction projects.

Having been thoroughly described in another publication [16], the *Collective Loops* project and its setup will only be briefly presented here.

2.1   Concept and Technical Setup

The loop sequencer is comprised of two user interfaces: (1) an individual interface used by each participant through their smartphone allowing them to alter the sound emitted from it, as illustrated in Fig. 1, and (2) a shared, floor-projected, circular visualization (of approx. 3 m in diameter) showing all participants' choices as well as the current position of the sequencer's reading head (represented by a bright moving sector), as depicted in Fig. 2a.

---

[1] The *CoSiMa* project is funded by ANR, the French National Research Agency (ANR-13-CORD-0010).

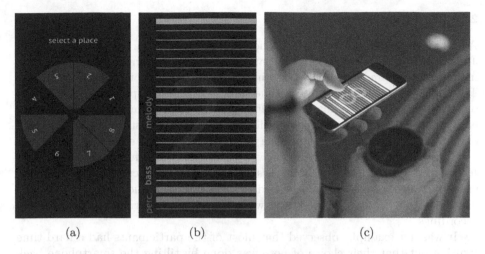

(a)   (b)   (c)

Fig. 1. *Collective Loops* v2 individual interfaces: (a) place selection (b) and (c) notes selection.

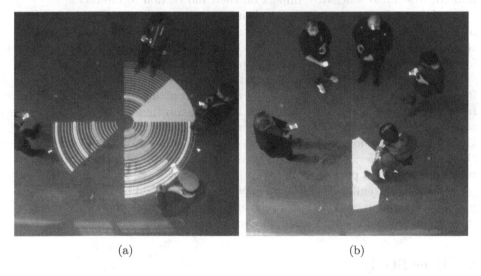

(a)   (b)

Fig. 2. Comparative study interfaces: (a) NSloop and (b) RHloop

The *CoSiMa* platform, and consequently *Collective Loops*, is developed using open Web technologies such as Node.js, WebGL, and the Web Audio API. The *Collective Loops* installation is composed of three main software components: (1) a local server managing inter-device synchronization and communication, (2) a mobile web application accessible via a local Wi-Fi hotspot handling the individual user interfaces, and (3) a web application running on a local machine connected to a video projector handling the floor-projected shared interface.

2.2   Iterative Design

A first version was deployed to the general public during the Ircam Open Days in June 2015, which allowed up to 24 participants to collaboratively create simple melodies using predefined notes of 3 instruments: percussion, bass, and melody. The sequencer was divided into 8 time slots, with up to 3 participants per slot; one per instrument. A slot and an instrument was automatically assigned to each newcomer, who could then modify the note of the instrument by selecting one out of 12 possible choices per the inclination of the smartphone.

This first public deployment allowed us to perform a full-scale test of *Collective Loops* and detect technical issues that where difficult to evaluate otherwise. It also allowed us to get feedback on interface and interaction design aspects through a qualitative study with interviews, questionnaires, and video recordings.

It was, for example, observed that most of the participants had a hard time figuring out that their choice of note was done by tilting the smartphone back or forth. In addition, many participants felt that their scope of action was very limited, which had a negative impact on their motivation to interact.

Such imperfections impelled us to bring improvements to the project. A second version was thus developed in which a more consistent design was chosen for the individual and shared interfaces, and touch input was favored over gesture for the note selection to better support a walk-up-and-use experience.

This new version supports up to 8 participants, one per time slot. A first touch interface on smartphones allows each newcomer to manually choose a time slot from all available slots. A second touch interface can then be used to alter the sound emitted from the smartphone by choosing notes from all 3 instruments. Unlike the first version, multiple notes from each instrument can be activated by the same participant within certain predefined limits (3/12 melody notes, 1/6 bass notes, and 3/3 percussion notes).

Moreover, the emitted sound intensity can be controlled by tilting the smartphone back or forth, and an added echo effect enriches the experience and makes it interesting enough with a small number of participants.

3   User Study

Previous studies have shown that revealing teammates' progress to each other can improve collaboration in distributed problem solving situations [1,14]. Yet, to the best of our knowledge, no studies seem to have been conducted to understand the role of mutual awareness, through shared visualization, on collaboration in a leisure, walk-up-and-use co-located setting. An experiment has thus been designed in order to test the hypothesis that revealing all users' choices on the common, shared interface would promote a more collaborative experience.

Since the quality of creative collaboration that is not guided by a predefined outcome is subjective, we based the study on participants' impressions concerning their engagement in the collective process and their ability to create a common satisfactory result. We expected participants to build a better sense of collaboration and engagement when they are able to view each other's choices, and thus enhancing the collective experience.

Two different designs for the shared, floor-projected, interface (shown in Fig. 2) were tested in this comparative study: (A) participants' choices are displayed on the interface as well as the reading head's current position, (B) only the reading head's current position is displayed. We will refer, in this paper, to the first interface as "NSloop" (for Note Selections) and the second interface as "RHloop" (for Reading Head).

3.1 Context and Setup

The improved version of *Collective Loops* was deployed for the audience of the workshops and presentations held during the International IRCAM Forum Workshop in November 2016. We opted to perform the study in the context of this public showing, based on the notion that "the site of exhibition can be seen (...) [as] the central site for interactive art research – the necessary starting and finishing point for any study that aims to understand how meaning is produced by an interactive artwork" [9]. The high costs involved in the deployment of such installations was also a deciding factor. Indeed, the setup of installations such as *Collective Loops* requires a non-negligible amount of time and man power, and the floor-projection requires the mounting of a complex video-projection system.

Furthermore, although the *CoSiMa* platform aims to be compatible with most smartphones, the current state of web standards' implementations still requires lending compatible devices to participants. Thus, to facilitate the participation and improve the user experience, users were encouraged to borrow a preconfigured device with a small portable speaker attached to it as shown in Fig. 1c.

3.2 Subjects and Procedure

The audience of the workshops were invited to freely experience the installation during lunch and coffee breaks which lasted between 1 and 2 h, and interfaces were alternated outside of those break times. Human mediation was limited to lending a preconfigured device, or assisting during the connection process on a participant's own smartphone. Participants had thus no prior knowledge of the system and its musical collaborative possibilities.

After their participation, users were asked to volunteer in the study by filling out a questionnaire. With none of the participants having experienced both interfaces, 36 questionnaires were collected (18 per interface). The subjects who experienced NSloop were comprised of 5 women and 13 men varying in age from 19 to 68 years old (mean: 38.9, σ: 13.1), whereas those who experienced RHloop were comprised of 5 women and 13 men varying in age from 19 to 69 years old (mean: 36.2, σ: 14).

3.3   Data Collection

The questionnaires consisted of two general profile questions (age and gender), ten 5-point Likert scale questions eliciting the participant's impressions on the individual and collective experience, and a final open-ended question allowing the expression of general feelings and suggestions. We also video-recorded all sessions from above, and stored detailed system communication logs.

3.4   Results and Analysis

The diagrams in Fig. 3 visualize the self-reported impressions of the subjects in the individual and collective engagement in the real-time musical composition with both interface. Although many of the comments left in the open-ended question suggest that the participants who experienced NSloop were more satisfied with the global experience than those who experienced RHloop, the responses in the Likert scale questions do not show a significant difference between both

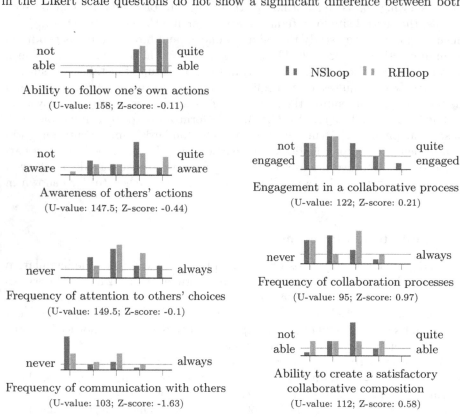

Fig. 3. Subjective experience impressions on 1 to 5 Likert scales; the x-axis represents the scale values from left to right, and the y-axis represents the number of participants having chosen each value (the gray horizontal line representing 2 answers for the given value)

interfaces in the individual or collective experiences (a two-tailed Mann-Whitney test was performed for each question with n1=n2=18, $P < 0.05$, and the U-value and Z-score as reported in the caption of each diagram in Fig. 3).

We can further notice that the peeks in those diagrams shift from right to left as we go from the individual experience questions (top-left) to the collective experience ones (bottom-right), implying that participants were globally satisfied with the individual experience, but did not manage to fully exploit the collective and collaborative aspects of the installation.

Indeed, the charts reveal that most participants deemed that they were able to follow their own actions, but were not fully aware of others' actions and did not pay attention to others' choices very often. They also indicated that they rarely communicated with their peers and did not quite feel engaged in a collaborative process.

Data collected from system logs, illustrated in the diagrams of Fig. 4, reveal that the average number of simultaneous participants was slightly lower on NSloop (2.8) than on RHloop (3.1). And, against our expectations, the total time spent per participant on the installation was on average shorter on NSloop (4'27") than on RHloop (7'05"). This might have been a consequence of the lack of shared information on RHloop forcing one to spend more time to apprehend the system. No significant difference was, however, observed on the number of note selections made by participants per minute between NSloop (mean: 25; σ: 17) and RHloop (mean: 22; σ: 17) when compared using a T-test (t-value: 0.65; two-tailed p-value: 0.52).

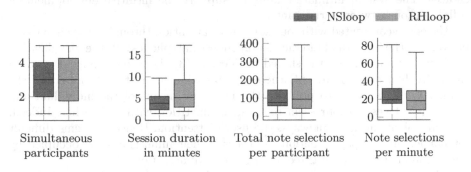

Fig. 4. Means from system logs

Furthermore, 7 participants indicated that the acoustic aspect of the system was not engaging enough, and would have appreciated to have more choices and control over the sounds emitted. One also noted that the shared projection on NSloop was too prominent, dissuading discussion and collaboration with others, a feeling that was increased by the fact that the sound emanating from others' devices was not always edible. And another one suggested that the portability of the individual devices was not fully taken advantage of due to the fixed position of the floor projection.

Based on the participants' subjective evaluation of collaboration, the study did not succeed in demonstrating a statistically significant improvement in the shift of focus from the individual to the collective when all users' choices are exposed on the shared interface. However, it allowed us to get a better understanding of the multiple design challenges that need to be addressed in walk-up-and-use installations of this type. Some of those challenges involve difficulties encountered by the first participants in understanding their field of action, or making the experience rich enough to encourage longer participation allowing the formation of larger groups.

Additional research will be required to verify the results of this study and better understand the role of individual and shared graphical user interfaces in promoting collective experiences around multi-display co-located interactive environments.

4   Conclusion and Future Work

We presented a comparative user study undertaken on a collective musical installation to verify a hypothesis regarding the role of a shared interface on promoting the user engagement in a collaborative process when interacting with others around a co-located artistic installation.

The described installation implements a multi-display interactive system with smartphones and a shared floor-projection. Users act on their individual device, while the shared projection allows them to visualize the full set of all users' choices. The system ultimately aims to support the intuitive development of collaboration between participants.

Users are confronted with four sources of attention throughout their participation: (1) the individual interaction on their smartphones, (2) the visualization of all the interactions on the shared projection, (3) the sounds emitted from all the individual devices, and (4) their collaboration with other members of the public. While we wish to promote the latter by means of the individual and shared interfaces, all four seem to be in competition with each other. Indeed, they all solicit, in different ways, the user's attention. Hence, it seems difficult for participants to pay attention to others if their mind is already occupied by one, let alone two or even three other sources of attention.

Therefore, more research needs to be undertaken to find a balance between those concurrent sources of attention. We could, for example, consider attentional weight of the individual and shared interfaces to balance them, or to dynamically manage their ability to retain or release users' attention, and thus better control which type of interaction we would like to privilege in order to support the emergence of a collaborative situation.

Such research could help model design patterns for co-located interactive installations that encourage the audience to engage in a creative and collaborative process by building on previous frameworks such as the work of Edmonds et al. in which they describe a model of creative engagement with three attributes: attractors, sustainers, and relaters [9].

References

1. Balakrishnan, A.D., Fussell, S.R., Kiesler, S.: Do visualizations improve synchronous remote collaboration? In: Proceedings of the SIGCHI Conference on Human Factors in Computing Systems, pp. 1227–1236. ACM (2008)
2. Bardram, J.E., Esbensen, M., Tabard, A.: Activity-based collaboration for interactive spaces. In: Anslow, C., Campos, P., Jorge, J. (eds.) Collaboration Meets Interactive Spaces, pp. 233–257. Springer, Cham (2016). doi:10.1007/978-3-319-45853-3_11
3. Bilda, Z., Edmonds, E., Candy, L.: Designing for creative engagement. Des. Stud. **29**(6), 525–540 (2008). Interaction Design and Creative Practice
4. Brignull, H., Rogers, Y.: Enticing people to interact with large public displays in public spaces. In: Human-Computer Interaction INTERACT 2003: IFIP TC13 International Conference on Human-Computer Interaction, 1st–5th September 2003. IOS Press (2003)
5. Cauchard, J.R., Lchtefeld, M., Irani, P., Schoening, J., Krger, A., Fraser, M., Subramanian, S.: Visual separation in mobile multi-display environments. In: Proceedings of the 24th Annual ACM Symposium on User Interface Software and Technology, pp. 451–460. ACM (2011)
6. Blinkenlights. http://blinkenlights.net/project
7. CoSiMa - Collaborative Situated Media. http://cosima.ircam.fr/
8. Dahl, L., Herrera, J., Wilkerson, C.: Tweetdreams: Making music with the audience and the world using real-time twitter data. In: Proceedings of the International Conference on New Interfaces for Musical Expression, pp. 272–275. Citeseer (2011)
9. Edmonds, E., Muller, L., Connell, M.: On creative engagement. Vis. Commun. **5**(3), 307–322 (2006)
10. Dialtones (A Telesymphony). http://www.flong.com/projects/telesymphony/
11. Isenberg, P., Fisher, D., Morris, M.R., Inkpen, K., Czerwinski, M.: An exploratory study of co-located collaborative visual analytics around a tabletop display. In: Proceedings of Visual Analytics Science and Technology (VAST), pp. 179–186. IEEE Computer Society, Los Alamitos, November 2010
12. Kern, D., Marshall, P., Schmidt, A.: Gazemarks: gaze-based visual placeholders to ease attention switching. In: Proceedings of the SIGCHI Conference on Human Factors in Computing Systems, CHI 2010, pp. 2093–2102. ACM, New York (2010)
13. Kim, H.: Moori: interactive audience participatory audio-visual performance. In: Proceedings of the 8th ACM conference on Creativity and cognition, pp. 437–438. ACM (2011)
14. Paul, S.A., Morris, M.R.: CoSense: enhancing sensemaking for collaborative web search. In: Proceedings of the SIGCHI Conference on Human Factors in Computing Systems, pp. 1771–1780. ACM (2009)
15. Rashid, U., Nacenta, M.A., Quigley, A.: Factors influencing visual attention switch in multi-display user interfaces: a survey. In: Proceedings of the 2012 International Symposium on Pervasive Displays, p. 1. ACM (2012)
16. Schnell, N., Matuszewski, B., Lambert, J.P., Robaszkiewicz, S., Mubarak, O., Cunin, D., Bianchini, S., Boissarie, X., Cieslik, G.: Collective loops: multimodal interactions through co-located mobile devices and synchronized audiovisual rendering based on web standards. In: Proceedings of the Eleventh International Conference on Tangible, Embedded, and Embodied Interaction, TEI 2017, pp. 217–224. ACM, New York (2017)

Designing Interactive Technologies for Interpretive Exhibitions: Enabling Teen Participation Through User-Driven Innovation

Vanessa Cesário[✉], Sónia Matos, Marko Radeta, and Valentina Nisi

Madeira Interactive Technologies Institute, 9020-105 Funchal, Portugal
{vanessa.cesario,sonia.matos,marko.radeta,
valentina.nisi}@m-iti.org

Abstract. The active involvement of teenagers in the design of interactive technologies for museums is lacking further development. Adopting a user-driven innovation framework along with cooperative inquiry, we report and discuss a case study that has been designed to involve users in the ideation of interpretive experiences for a local museum. Working in collaboration with the Natural History Museum of Funchal, this contribution will present and discuss co-design sessions that were aimed at participants with ages 15 to 17 and where they were asked to ideate an interactive museum experience. As a result of the co-design sessions, we have found several design patterns. We have grouped these patterns into four categories that express the interests of a teenage audience; these categories are: "interactions", "gaming", "localization" and "social media". Our findings suggest that teenagers value interactive technologies when visiting museums and that user-driven innovation plays an important role when involving this specific audience in the design of user experiences for museums.

Keywords: Museums · Natural history · Mobile interaction · User experience · User research · Teenagers · Participation · User-driven innovation · Cooperative Inquiry

1 Introduction

With the aim of creating a space for a teenage audience to rethink their local natural museum, in this paper we report on the data as well as the underlying research regarding user-driven innovation. While tackling the visibility of teenage audiences within the field of Human-Computer Interaction (HCI), in this contribution we will also present four design categories that derive from the feedback that we have obtained from a group of teenagers that were involved in a series of co-design sessions. Therefore, the paper will be divided into three sections. Firstly, we discuss the key theoretical challenges that have informed the case-study that underpins this contribution. In this respect, we discuss the lack of participation on behalf of teenage audiences in the design and assessment of interpretive experiences and exhibition strategies of museums. Secondly, we delve into a discussion of how a user-driven innovation framework can be used to involve museum audiences in the process of technological ideation. Finally, and to further complement this discussion, we present the findings of a series

© IFIP International Federation for Information Processing 2017
Published by Springer International Publishing AG 2017. All Rights Reserved
R. Bernhaupt et al. (Eds.): INTERACT 2017, Part I, LNCS 10513, pp. 232–241, 2017.
DOI: 10.1007/978-3-319-67744-6_16

of co-design sessions where participants were invited to rethink the interpretive exhibition of a local museum.

The discussion of our case-study will be supported with the qualitative data that was obtained from the sessions. A total of 75 students from a local secondary school were initially asked to share their thoughts on their experience regarding the Museum of Natural History of Funchal (in further, MNHF) that is set in Madeira Island, Portugal. They were also invited to ideate a mobile and interactive experience for this venue. The goal of this activity, as explained to the participants, was to design an interactive and mobile user experience to support the MNHF's permanent display of taxidermied marine animals that inhabit the waters that surround the island.

2   Audience, Participation and the Museum Experience

To date, museums have reached out to specific audiences in the form of surveys and questionnaires. In order to obtain relevant information and support the design of exhibitions and interpretive experiences, this process has mostly followed a top-down approach [1]. In fact, only few examples demonstrate how museums can actively involve communities in an ideation process that is aimed at improving audience engagement. The Glasgow Open Museum Experiment is often presented as a relevant example. Set in the 1990's, this experiment, amongst others, involved local and mostly marginalized groups in the organization and curation of the museum's exhibitions [1]. Reported by Simon, an impact assessment of Glasgow's Open Museum experiment, conducted in 2002, demonstrated that this project propelled two important contributions. Firstly, the project created "new opportunities for learning and growth" amongst excluded audiences. Secondly, it changed the negative perception of museums amongst marginalized groups.

The Glasgow case study can be given further momentum with the work of Tzibazi [2]. Here, the voices and ideas of a younger audience are problematized. In fact, the author identifies *youth* as an audience group that is often excluded from a museum's curatorial strategies. This exclusion has a profound impact, this considering that the design of interpretive experiences in museums is no longer sensitive to this group's specific interests and needs, this also limits a museum's potential to create interpretative experiences that have real pedagogical relevance [2]. Drawing on several key studies, Tzibazi also suggests that it is not only museums that ignore a younger audience (ages 13 to 19), members of this group seem to be generally disinterested in what museums can offer. In response to this gap, Tzibazi [2] suggests involving youths through Participatory Action Research (PAR) and as a way of documenting their ideas and interests in relation to museums.

Moreover, Hall and Bannon's [3] study is particularly vested in demonstrating that cooperative design methods have the potential to support the successful introduction of interactive digital technology in museums. According to the authors, in a context where strategies have been mostly focused on the "functionality of [the] technology" (p. 214), the use of cooperative methods opens space for an in-depth understanding of an audience's specific desires and needs. However, apart from Hall and Bannon [3], the work of Dindler and colleagues [4] and the work of Ciolfi and colleagues [5], the active involvement of specific audiences in the ideation of interactive technologies for museums is lacking further development.

The work reported above, echoes a gap that can be found within the field of HCI more broadly. For example, there are comparatively fewer studies reporting on the active involvement of teenage users. Those that are reported, rarely position teenagers as sources of inspiration and information for design, as for example in the studies reported by Batson and Feinberg [6], Karin Danielsson and Charlotte Wiberg [7]. On the other hand, Katterfeldt et al. [8], suggest that when teenagers are the subject of research, the employed user-centered design methods tend to produce an interpretation of their demands and needs without however leveraging on their direct contribution. Moreover, and set against the benefits that are reported by Hall and Bannon [3], Dindler and colleagues [4], as well Ciolfi and colleagues [5], we argue that it is vital to actively engage teenagers, the next generation of adults, in HCI research. Some authors suggest that teenagers will soon become adults and should therefore be involved in the design of future technologies [9]. As found by Fitton and colleagues [9], they are in a better position to combine both child and adult perspectives. In fact, several methodologies that engage children in the design process have been developed [10]. In this respect, Druin's seminal work on Cooperative Inquiry [10, 11] and the Scandinavian approach to Participatory Design [12] have gained acceptance amongst the IDC community. In fact, participatory design is now engaging children [11, 12] and teenagers [7, 13–18] in the design process. On the other hand, Cooperative Inquiry (CI) is one of the several participatory methods that includes youth in the design process (7–17 years old) [11, 19]. On this view, in CI, children act as full partners with adults, sharing ideas and evaluating designs [20]. However, and although CI has been used for a long time with children (7–11 years) [16, 20], co-design with teenagers (13–17 years) remains less explored [21].

Our attempt to briefly discuss the importance of audience participation, namely the participation of teenagers, to inform the design of user experiences that support interpretive exhibitions in museums, can be understood by returning to the work of Simon [1]. The author had already identified that participatory techniques not only give "voice" to specific audiences, they are also essential in the development of "experiences that are more valuable and compelling". Simon's argument echoes Falk and Dierking's [22] work. Here, the authors contend that "[the] museum represents a community of practice in which myriad communities of learners mingle and learn". Our understanding is that this definition, strengthens the value and importance of audience participation in the ideation of user experiences that are designed to support interpretative exhibitions.

3   Designing Mobile Experiences for Museums

In this section, we describe a series of co-design sessions conducted with 75 teenagers, aged 15 to 17 (average age of 16,5) from a secondary school in Funchal. All participating students were enrolled in a multimedia and informatics class. The sessions integrate a broader project that has been developed by the authors and that seeks to introduce interactive technologies in the context of the MNHF. We organized 20 groups (3 to 5 students per group) in 5 sessions over a three-day period. Overall, our sample included 56-male and 19-female students.

We chose a user-driven innovation framework for the group sessions. As it is mostly used by industry [23], we followed this approach to gain a broader understanding of user-driven innovation, one that, "regards users as a source of innovation" [24]. This was set alongside the cooperative inquiry approach that positions participants as "design partners" [11]. Resembling the work of Chang and Kaasinen [25], our choice highlights the importance of adopting user-driven innovation research "methods by which user ideas can be captured and worked on further with designers" (p. 66). As both authors argue, in this context, face-to-face focus groups have the power to facilitate participation and to allow HCI researchers to gather information, one that best translates "user's everyday experiences".

Each co-design session was initiated with a presentation of how museums, and our case study, the MNHF, could be enhanced by using interactive technologies. Three questions were used to spark the debate amongst the students. Those questions were:

(Q1) *What do you think about museums?* This question was asked to prompt feedback regarding whether students liked to visit museums and in what situations they usually conduct their visits.

(Q2) *How do you think interactive technologies could enhance your experience of the museum and how could technology make this visit more enjoyable?* This question was important when collecting information regarding the different types of experiences that students would like to explore at the museum.

(Q3) *Have you ever been to the MNHF and to the museum's aquarium?* This final question was used to better understand whether the students enjoyed their experience of the MNHF.

Once the three questions were answered verbally, the MNHF was introduced through a series of photographs that detailed the museum's collection (mammals, geology and reptiles). Subsequently, 13-points of interest relating to the museum's exhibit of taxidermied marine animals were identified on a physical map of the museum. Afterwards, we asked how the young students could think of interaction and user experience for museum settings. Here, techniques from the field of interaction design were explained, such as: (i) research and ideation, (ii) low-fidelity prototypes, (iii) usability feedback, (iv) high fidelity prototypes, followed by (v) development and finally (vi) the user-testing. Our focus was directed toward the design of a mobile application and therefore windows, icons, menus and transitions/gestures were also highlighted as important elements when sketching a mobile app. At the very end, students were asked to think about how several technologies could play a relevant role when visiting the museum. For example, Near Field Communication (NFC), Radio Frequency Identification (RFID), Quick Response Code (QR Code), Augmented Reality (AR), Mobile Virtual Reality (MVR), and Proximity Beacons were provided as a set of examples. These technologies were explained in depth along with examples of their usage.

Finally, our participants were involved in a 30-minute co-design session. Each group was given two sheets (Fig. 1). Sheet A contained three text slots that could be used to explain the experience which they would like to design and portray: (1) *Narrative*: what is the story of the experience; (2) *Species/Artifacts*: how do visitors interact

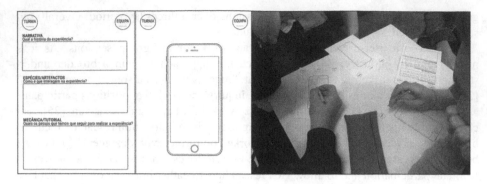

Fig. 1. Sheet A (left), sheet B (center), a group discussing their ideas (right).

with the artifacts; (3) *Mechanics/Tutorial*: which steps will the user take to complete the experience. Sheet B contained an empty wireframe that could be used to draw the interface details for the mobile application that our participants had previously thought.

During the ideation process, we collected notes of the students' interaction and discussing of ideas. As guidance, emphasis was placed on the experiences that they would enjoy in a museum.

4   Results

Considering Q1, Q2 and Q3 answers, our young participants considered museum visits a mundane activity. Overall, the students suggested that museums do not offer anything new, which was a reason for avoiding museums all together. Despite this deterring factor, students admitted that they would visit museums during holidays or with their parents. However, when on holiday, our young respondents only visited museums that were located outside of Madeira Island. In fact, only half of the participants visited the MNHF. Most of our participants rated the aquarium as the best feature of the MNHF. Moreover, participants expressed interest towards the integration of videos, digital content and interactions to enhance the museum exhibit. The two most highly rated technologies and interventions were: games (75 participants) and virtual reality (49 participants).

During the co-design sessions, several issues were raised by our participants. Firstly, students advocated for a greater use of interactive technologies in museums, some argued specifically for the importance of play and enjoyment while others suggested a combination of both technology and enjoyment. One group in particular, stressed the value of simplicity and usability to appeal to a wider audience. As our young participants progressed with the co-design sessions, we also took note of some of their spontaneous remarks which highlighted feelings of excitement towards the technological interventions that they were ideating: *This is fun!*; *This is better than Pokemon Go!* and *For sure I would go to the museum just to try something different like this.*

4.1 Design Categories

The different groups compiled a total of 20 sets of A and B sheets, which were analyzed in detail and to extract emerging trends and patterns as well as potential insights. The relevant words and phrases that each group wrote on sheet A and drew on sheet B were transcribed and patterns highlighted according to the affinities that emerged from the grouping of words (Fig. 2). We chose to highlight this set of words rather than analyze the ideas that were generated in the co-design sessions because our goal was to generate patterns between the different groups of categories and understand how our participants envisaged compelling museum experiences.

A total of 150-word transcripts were obtained. From these transcripts, four main categories emerged, namely: (1) *Interactions*, (2) *Gaming*, (3) *Localization*, (4) *Social media*.

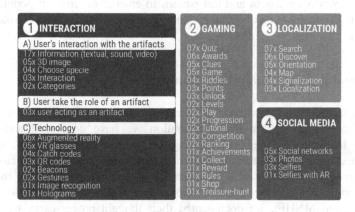

Fig. 2. Word categories gathered from the co-design sessions with teenagers.

Interactions. Words describing interactions and information delivery styles were grouped in the *interaction* category. This category contained words such as *information*, *choose*, *codes* and can be divided into three subcategories: (A) the user interacts with artifacts, (B) the user interacts with the museum exhibition while taking on the role of a selected artifact, (C) the technology that is used to interact with the exhibit. In the former, the user interacts with the artifacts not only through images and sounds but also by choosing which artifacts they would want to engage with. In this case, the user would choose which artifacts h/she wants to embody. For example, the user could visit the museum through the *eyes* of a specific marine animal. All the groups used at least one of the above subcategories in their ideas. In this instance, a total of 58 words were transcribed. What we identified as *interactions* was a complex but popular category, *the most important category* if we consider the number of words of all the three sub-categories as one.

Gaming. This category emerged from grouping words relating to games and game elements such as *achievements*, *awards* and *clues*. Fifteen groups out of twenty used words and concepts related to the *gaming* category in their ideas. In this instance, a total of 51 words were transcribed. *Gaming* was the *second* choice of preference when designing user experiences in museums.

Localization. This category was best expressed by a description of user's movements within the museum and could be seen in the discovery of artifacts and in words such as *maps, orientation* and *search*. Eleven groups out of twenty used this category in their ideas; a total of 29 words relating to this category were transcribed. *Localization* was the *third most important category* amongst the design choices that were made by our participants.

Social media. Finally, the *social media* category embraced words relating to the usage of photos and social networks within the application, such as *selfies, photos, social networks*. In this case, seven groups out of twenty used words relating to social media; a total of 12 words were related to the *social media* category. To our surprise, the *social media* category was the *fourth* and last pattern to emerge in terms of popularity, this despite the high consumption of social media by teenagers (see for example the work of Wikia [26]).

5   Discussion and Concluding Remarks

Taking into consideration the work of Dindler and colleagues [4] as well as the work of Ciolfi and colleagues [5], in this contribution we have developed and tested a user-driven innovation framework to engage a teenage audience in the design of interactive experiences for museums. Referring back to Simon [1] and Tzibazi [2], we developed co-design sessions with teenagers with ages 15 to 17. With the aim of engaging young visitors in the ideation of novel user experiences for their local natural history museum (MNHF), we documented their thought processes as well as their interests regarding interactive technology and museums.

Our results led us to agree with Tzibazi [2], from a first glimpse, our young participants showed disinterest in museums. In fact, when we first conducted the co-design sessions, our participants suggested that their local natural history museum did not offer engaging experiences. However, and instead of immediately designing in response to the challenges that were pinpointed by our target audience, we rather harnessed on their potential and ideas as valuable sources of information and inspiration and by engaging them in co-design sessions where they took on the role of "co-creators of museum experiences" [2] and as our "design partners" under the framework of cooperative inquiry [11]. Resembling the work of Chang and Kaasinen [25], our intention was to uncover "user's everyday experiences" and to utilize these experiences when tailoring new design solutions that can capture the attention of those who visit the MHNF, namely the museum's teenage audience. Furthermore, and considering Simon's work [1], the sessions held with our young participants gave them a "voice" and engaged them enthusiastically in the design process. Our study also highlights how much a younger generation values interactive technologies when visiting museums. In fact, it was clear from their answers to our preliminary questions, that they would appreciate the integration of technologically driven playful approaches within the museum and to experience novel and less mundane activities.

Participants took close inspiration from the technologies that were demonstrated to them at the beginning of the session (e.g.: NFC, RFID, QR Codes, AR, MVR, Beacons). In fact, QR Codes, Beacons, and MVR were mentioned by our participants in the design session and as way of enhancing the museum experience. However, when designing for a mobile experience, participants thought more about the game experience and its mechanics than the technology itself. Moreover, our results resonate with the broader literature which indicates that young people today are born into a world that is flooded by novel technologies. On this view, Wikia [26] reports that the "Generation Z", in this case today's teenagers, are more and more engaged with digital platforms. Besides, further studies argue that when working with this age group, emphasis should be placed on producing combined solutions that connect the use of interactive technologies with more conventional media channels, as seen in Napoli and Ewing [27]. According to Falk [28], the most compelling aspect of these studies is that the *one size fits for all experiences* does not apply for most museum visitors. As argued by Napoli and Ewing [27], the same can be said for the "net generation" which is quite different from previous generations, particularly when it comes to their beliefs and behaviors.

Following this discussion, the most relevant point that emerged from our study is the need to create a broader range of experiences for the NHMF. Most relevant categories that emerged from the study are (1) the need for different *experiences*, followed by (2) *gaming*, (3) *location based technologies*, and (4) *social media*. The social media category, which appeared last, was somewhat surprising this given the fact that it is widely appreciated amongst a teenage demographics [13]. We believe that this point would deserve further investigation. The four categories derived from the co-design sessions contribute to the field of HCI more broadly, this considering that they revealed valuable insights which could be considered as guidelines when designing experiences for a teenage audience. Therefore, and based on the categories derived from our study, future work will be aimed at creating and adapting experiences based on these categories to the specificities of the MHNF. This would allow us to understand whether these categories can be applied to the tours that are already in place at the museum and in order to engage and capture the attention of a teenage audience. Furthermore, this paper complements Hall and Bannon's discussion [3], one that argues for the use of cooperative methods when designing for a museum context. Moreover, we argue that a user-driven framework is important when designing for a teenage audience. In fact, our findings verify that the participants were fully engaged in the creation of a mobile experience for a museum context, wanting to try them out in *situ*. Together, these findings form a roadmap to guide the development and maturation of a mobile museum experience solution that is targeted at teenagers. In fact, we envisage that our findings can inform the design, research and evaluation of interactive technologies in a museum context. We also foresee their application to other localities around the globe.

Acknowledgments. The work reported in this contribution was developed with the support of ARDITI (Ph.D. scholarship, Project Number M14-20-09-5369-FSE-000001) and with the support of the University of Edinburgh (CAHSS Knowledge Exchange and Impact grant). Our gratitude also goes to the students and teachers of the Multimedia and Informatics class at Francisco Franco's Secondary School. We would also like to thank the Museum of Natural History of Funchal (MNHF) for their timely support and feedback.

References

1. Simon, N.: The Participatory Museum (2010). http://www.participatorymuseum.org/
2. Tzibazi, V.: Participatory action research with young people in museums. Mus. Manag. Curatorship. **28**, 153–171 (2013)
3. Hall, T., Bannon, L.: Co-operative design of children's interaction in museums: a case study in the Hunt Museum. CoDesign **1**, 187–218 (2005)
4. Dindler, C., Iversen, O.S., Smith, R., Veerasawmy, R.: Participatory design at the museum: inquiring into children's everyday engagement in cultural heritage. In: Proceedings of the 22nd Conference of the Computer-Human Interaction Special Interest Group of Australia on Computer-Human Interaction, pp. 72–79. ACM, New York (2010)
5. Ciolfi, L., Petrelli, D.: Walking and designing with cultural heritage volunteers, pp. 46–51. ACM Interact., XXIII (2016)
6. Batson, L., Feinberg, S.: Game designs that enhance motivation and learning for teenagers. Electron. J. Integr. Technol. Educ. **5**, 34–43 (2006)
7. Danielsson, K., Wiberg, C.: Participatory design of learning media: Designing educational computer games with and for teenagers. Interact. Technol. Smart Educ. **3**, 275–291 (2006)
8. Katterfeldt, E.-S., Zeising, A., Schelhowe, H.: Designing digital media for teen-aged apprentices: a participatory approach. In: Proceedings of the 11th International Conference on Interaction Design and Children, pp. 196–199. ACM, New York (2012)
9. Fitton, D., Read, J.C.C., Horton, M.: The challenge of working with teens as participants in interaction design. In: CHI 2013 Extended Abstracts on Human Factors in Computing Systems, pp. 205–210. ACM, New York (2013)
10. Druin, A. (ed.): The Design of Children's Technology. Morgan Kaufmann Publishers Inc., San Francisco (1998)
11. Druin, A.: Cooperative inquiry: developing new technologies for children with children. In: Proceedings of the SIGCHI Conference on Human Factors in Computing Systems, pp. 592–599. ACM, New York (1999)
12. Robertson, J., Good, J.: Children's narrative development through computer game authoring. In: Proceedings of the 2004 Conference on Interaction Design and Children: Building a Community, pp. 57–64. ACM, New York (2004)
13. Iversen, O.S., Smith, R.C.: Scandinavian participatory design: dialogic curation with teenagers. In: Proceedings of the 11th International Conference on Interaction Design and Children, pp. 106–115. ACM, New York (2012)
14. Bell, B.T., Toth, N., Read, J.C., Horton, M., Fitton, D., Little, L., Beale, R., Guo, Y.: Teenagers talking about technologies: designing technology to reduce teen energy use. In: CHI 2013 Extended Abstracts on Human Factors in Computing Systems, pp. 1491–1496. ACM, New York (2013)
15. Isomursu, M., Isomursu, P., Still, K.: Capturing tacit knowledge from young girls. Interact. Comput. **16**, 431–449 (2004)
16. DiSalvo, B., Guzdial, M., Meadows, C., Perry, K., McKlin, T., Bruckman, A.: Workifying games: successfully engaging African American gamers with computer science. In: Proceeding of the 44th ACM Technical Symposium on Computer Science Education, pp. 317–322. ACM, New York (2013)
17. Read, J.C., Fitton, D., Cowan, B., Beale, R., Guo, Y., Horton, M.: Understanding and designing cool technologies for teenagers. In: CHI 2011 Extended Abstracts on Human Factors in Computing Systems, pp. 1567–1572. ACM, New York (2011)
18. Toth, N., Little, L., Read, J.C., Fitton, D., Horton, M.: Understanding teen attitudes towards energy consumption. J. Environ. Psychol. **34**, 36–44 (2013)

19. Druin, A.: The role of children in the design of new technology. Behav. Inf. Technol. **21**, 1–25 (2002)
20. Eladhari, M.P., Mateas, M.: Semi-autonomous avatars in world of minds: a case study of ai-based game design. In: Proceedings of the 2008 International Conference on Advances in Computer Entertainment Technology, pp. 201–208. ACM, New York (2008)
21. Read, J.C.C., Horton, M., Iversen, O., Fitton, D., Little, L.: Methods of working with teenagers in interaction design. In: CHI 2013 Extended Abstracts on Human Factors in Computing Systems, pp. 3243–3246. ACM, New York (2013)
22. Falk, J.H., Dierking, L.D.: Learning from Museums: Visitor Experiences and the Making of Meaning. AltaMira Press, Walnut Creek (2000)
23. Buur, J., Matthews, B.: Participatory innovation: a research Agenda. In: Proceedings of the Tenth Anniversary Conference on Participatory Design 2008, pp. 186–189. Indiana University, Indianapolis (2008)
24. Holmquist, L.E.: User-driven innovation in the Future Applications Lab. In: CHI 2004 Extended Abstracts on Human Factors in Computing Systems, pp. 1091–1092. ACM, New York (2004)
25. Chang, T.-R., Kaasinen, E.: three user-driven innovation methods for co-creating cloud services. In: Campos, P., Graham, N., Jorge, J., Nunes, N., Palanque, P., Winckler, M. (eds.) INTERACT 2011. LNCS, vol. 6949, pp. 66–83. Springer, Heidelberg (2011). doi:10.1007/978-3-642-23768-3_6
26. Wikia: Generation Z: A Look At The Technology And Media Habits Of Today's Teens. http://www.prnewswire.com/news-releases/generation-z-a-look-at-the-technology-and-media-habits-of-todays-teens-198958011.html
27. Napoli, J., Ewing, M.T.: The net generation. J. Int. Consum. Mark. **13**, 21–34 (2000)
28. Falk, J.H.: Identity and the Museum Visitor Experience. Routledge, Walnut Creek (2009)

Haunting Space, Social Interaction in a Large-Scale Media Environment

Jan C. Schacher$^{(\boxtimes)}$ and Daniel Bisig

Institute for Computer Music and Sound Technology, Zurich University of the Arts,
Pfingstweidstrasse 96, P.O. Box, 8031, Zürich, Switzerland
{jan.schacher,daniel.bisig}@zhdk.ch

Abstract. The Immersive Lab is a platform for the development and experience of large-scale audio-visual and interactive media arts. In this article we investigate questions of audience engagement, artistic strategies, and interaction principles, as well as the effects of embodied and social interactions that become evident in this media environment. Using the catalogue of artistic works developed for this platform within the past five years as our material, we carry out qualitative inquiries through interviews and categorisations. The emerging insights generate a clear perspective on the convergence as well as discrepancies between the artist's intentions and the behaviours of visitors in the media space and allow us to, if not definitively state, then at least speculate about universal aspects that each encounter in the media arts context entails.

Keywords: Social interaction · Interactive media space · Artistic strategies · Interaction principles · Qualitative methods · Multi-modal perception

1 Introduction

"Our body is not in space like things; *it inhabits or haunts space.* It applies itself to space like a hand to an instrument ... For us the body is much more than an instrument or a means; it is our expression in the world, the visible form of our intentions. Even our most secret affective movements ... help to shape our perception of things." [31, p. 5, our emphasis]

When working in interactive media, with technological installations, we rarely get to engage directly in social situations of shared exploration and learning. Conventional contexts, means, and media are more oriented towards producing finished works that produce predictable single user experiences where the mode of experience falls within a standard range of attitudes, such as cinema, TV-series, and video-games. Shared presence within interactive media spaces and installations enables the audience to enter into a direct engagement as a group. Through the experience of exploratory processes, the social dynamics of shared exploration come to the foreground.

© IFIP International Federation for Information Processing 2017
Published by Springer International Publishing AG 2017. All Rights Reserved
R. Bernhaupt et al. (Eds.): INTERACT 2017, Part I, LNCS 10513, pp. 242–262, 2017.
DOI: 10.1007/978-3-319-67744-6_17

In this article we discuss the 'Immersive Lab' (IL) platform, the concepts and activities developed therein, as well as a series of artistic works that were developed for this platform within the last five years. Focussing on the question of understanding social interactions patterns in reaction to abstract, algorithmic, or narrative media-art works, we investigate through qualitative methods some of the categorisations and salient dimensions that constitute social interaction in media environments. This covers two principal perspectives: the concepts and processes used by the artists for creating work, and the effect of the works on the audience's interaction- and engagement-behaviours. Through qualitative analysis processes based on interviews with artists, experts, and the observation of audience behaviour in exhibition situations, a multi-perspective field of interpretations emerges that can serve as a starting point for developing categories that structure elements of social interaction and engagement.

The IL platform we are developing since 2010 is a vehicle for the exploration of spatial media-arts work, combining the modalities of musical and visual surround presentation with a full-scale interaction surface. Central in the installation is the perceptual fusion of the three sensory modalities of vision, audition, and touch, thus providing a seamless interactive experience. It is sufficient to say about the design and constructing the installation itself that the dimensions and arrangement of the elements was guided by the intention to provide a human-sized space which fosters multi-sensory, embodied engagement (see Fig. 1).

Fig. 1. Interaction in the 'Immersive Lab'. July 2015: Haunted 'Mirror'.

Furthermore, a core idea of this project is to provide a platform for a wide variety of artists to experiment in and develop artistic works specific to this multi-modal configuration. From an artistic point of view, the most important challenge concerns the development of an interaction model that takes advantage of the particular setting of the installation. This is a classical interaction design tasks, but applied to a situation that presents a particular set of demands and eschews some of the classical themes of interaction design. The works need to address group and embodied interaction and shared experience in a model that is based on dynamic interactions and algorithm-driven content generation. To date, through residencies and workshops, approximately thirty artists of various disciplines, backgrounds, and expertise levels have developed more than two dozen works. This growing catalogue of works forms part of the materials for the analysis carried out in this article.

2   Background

The platform of the IL can be situated in the field of interactive media art and is oriented towards the general public. The installation system intended for a variety of teaching scenarios that include teaching in the domain of creative coding, interactive media, as well as computer music and algorithmic composition. It has been presented in exhibitions and showings to the general pubic as well as specialised audiences with specific interests such as scholarly or scientific investigations.

Similar media infrastructures that address immersive surround content in various configurations–some larger, some smaller than the IL–exist in several places worldwide. Prime examples are the StarCAVE systems at UC San Diego [8], the Allosphere at UC Santa Barbara [2], the RML Cinechamber project[1], and the Graz immersive media lab running the extended view framework.[2] The specific characteristics of the IL that distinguish it from other platforms are its intimate, human-scale size fit for small groups of visitors, and the emphasis on tangible interaction with the entire screen surface. The IL is a space for artistic experimentation, community building, and a research platform enabling investigations into creative processes, multi-modal perception, and multi-user interaction.

Immersion in its original sense means being submerged or enveloped, usually in water. In media arts and theory this term has been extended to mean envelopment by mediated contents, be they visual, sonic, or sometimes tactile. We may consider frescoes set in architectural spaces [1] and panoramic paintings [16, p. 62] to be older forms of mediated immersion. The concept of 'virtuality' [32] is a central topic in the discourse about immersion and can be summarised as the idea that mediated contents generate an artificial envelopment. Cinema has been for a long time the principal vector for immersive experiences for a large public [36] and today pushes further into that domain by the application of 3D and stereoscopic techniques [46]. Video games in general and the recent resurgence of virtual reality headsets have become another important way of experiencing virtuality in an actively engaged manner [21, p. 81].

A further dimension that plays a role is embodied presence [43]. It informs the perception of the digital image or abstract objects where they are integrated into the body's process of perceiving itself [17] or its environment [15]. The importance of embodiment can better be appreciated when considering the enactive

---

[1] http://www.rml-cinechamber.org (All URLs valid in May 2017).
[2] http://extendedview.mur.at/.

position, as does O'Regan [34]. He postulates that cognition arises through the body's fundamental intertwining with the environment [20].[3] The intertwining of body and environment is present in the biological domain as a regulating principle called autopoiesis [29]. The body's ability to perceive itself and to adapt its relation to the environment informs all sub-personal processes of perception and human experience [14].[4]

These capabilities play an important role in the media context where abstract simulated content needs to be engaged with in an active, intentional manner [42].[5] Here, intellectual reasoning fails to account for an important part of the experience. It is thanks to the embodied, enactive [40] connection to the environment that experience arises; based on the physical presence and sub-personal perceptions, the affective [37] and embodied capabilities [43] inform experience and provide models for understanding abstract or metaphorical media content. By relating with the installation through a direct bodily behaviour the non-semantic aspects of a work can have their effect. Think for example of encountering body-sized figures or hands: this prompts physical reactions of touching and mimicking in an involuntary engagement.[6]

This is why an important aspect of any type of cross-media work and cultural interaction scenarios is the development of *metaphorical* relationships [25] and *blended spaces* of signification [13], which surpass the concrete 'mediality' of any given situation. Thus, the visitor's innate and acquired skills of recognising relationships is applied to the simulated, mediated representations appearing in the media space. This process leverages the complex educational, cultural, and social assets and occurs "by building on visitors' pre-existing knowledge of the everyday, non-digital world ... employ themes of reality such as visitors' understanding of naïve physics, their own bodies, the surrounding environment, and other people" [22].

By looking at the challenges and demands of designing interactions and simultaneously creating aesthetic experiences that get shared by a group of visitors

---

[3] "In this framework embodiment can not be merely understood as the fact of possessing a body and being encased in a body with its mass and well-defined extension and limits in the physical world. On the contrary, it needs to be considered as the embedding and enmeshing of an organism within its environment through extensive sensorimotor interactions" [20, p. 6].

[4] "To be proprioceptively aware of one's body does not involve making one's body an object of perception ... Proprioceptive-kinesthetic awareness is usually a pre-reflective (non- observational) awareness that allows the body to remain experientially transparent to the agent who is acting" [14, p. 73].

[5] "Intentional behaviour is characterised by the presence of a reason (i.e., motive, desire, belief) to act in a way that will bring about the intended effect. Two elements are constitutive of the phenomenology of intentional behaviour: the source of the action (i.e., the intention to act) and the perception of the effects of a given act. The link between the two is made possible through embodiment" [42, pp. 39–40].

[6] For a clear example of this effect see the video of 'The Unattainable/The Intimate' at 03:16 in class works on the following page http://immersivelab.zhdk.ch/?page_id=2857.

in a common real space, principles of design and psychological foundations of sociality come into play. Considering the combined affordance of the IL media space together with the often idiosyncratic artistic ideas that the visitors are confronted with, the perspectives of activity theory [23,26] are more appropriate, rather than for example structured task analyses [3]. The agency of the visitor in combination with a need or motivation creates the intentional relation to the object in the world. This activity responds to affordances in the (natural) environment [15], which are defined as the potential for action or perception that is on offer; in the discourse about design this concept gets differentiated between perceived and objective affordances [33], between cognitive, physical, sensory, functional affordances [18], and affordances of control [35]. The visitor's learning of the interaction modality happens through a reinforcing action-perception coupling (or a circular causality [30, p. 15][11]), where they clearly perceive their own agency [14, p. 237], and see or hear a clear dependency between an action and the response by the (artistic) work, i.e., the media environment.

Interaction, within the context of media arts as well as broader technical design "means the degree of access to model parameters at runtime" [45] and thus the mode of exerting influence on a system's behaviour. A mark of an interactive engagement is that a degree of autonomy is present in the system, which mimics agency, in order to appear opposite the person in an inter-subjective [9] and thus social [7] relationship. If therefore a "social action is action in which the other is addressed in the visitor's acts" [6], then on the level of the human-machine interaction, the 'other' is first perceived within the technical system. Simultaneously this perception includes other persons present, be it the (implicitly present) author or another person entering into the interactive situation. This side-by-side presence is based on different types of social interaction skills that "include verbal and non-verbal communication, the ability to exchange physical objects, and the ability to work with others to collaborate on a task" [22]. A specific case of this relationship arises when several visitors participate in the exchange with the system. In addition to the topics of translation and behaviour between man and machine we enter into a triangular social situation, where the attention of the visitors gets divided between the engagement with the system and the other people. Through the joint attention arising in the social situation [10], the social bond is strengthened and a mode of negotiation through social dynamics emerges. This is not comparable to an on-screen individual situation or the sharing in the virtual sphere of the social web, but takes place in an actual physical situation that occurs in the installation setting and engenders a shared experience between visitors. The occurrence of these situations is specific for a determined context, in what installation artist Snibbe calls "social immersive media: immersive media that favors interaction in a shared social space using a person's entire body as the 'input device,' unencumbered by electronics or props" [39].

The media situation presented in the IL falls within this category. Much of the exploratory engagement by the visitors is based on these behaviour and learning patterns. Given that the principal mode of engagement is by touching the screens, the visitors, even first-time ones, can refer to earlier experiences with touch surfaces, be it mobile phones, tablets, or touch-screen kiosk applications [5].[7] These fresh cultural norms, that have become pervasive since the rise of the touch-screen mobile device, serve as experiential points of reference for exploring the interaction in the IL.

Developing work, in particular of artistic nature, without concrete task and result imperatives, means taking into account the biological, psychological, and cultural elements contributed by each visitor, as well as the shared gestural iconicity and familiarity with a certain type of abstraction in the presented works.

3   The 'Immersive Lab'

The 'Immersive Lab' (IL) installation is the fruit of several years of development, investigation, and artistic creation. Originating from research into surround sound and algorithmic composition [4], it has evolved to become the multi-sensory and fully interactive space we present here. The platform serves for experimentation in the artistic domain, as well as a device for generating experiences to be investigated from a point of view of composition, systems theory, and above all interaction and social behaviour within media environments.

Currently, the IL installation is a modular platform consisting of four freestanding frames carrying curved rear-projected screens. The frames also carry the multi-speaker audio system stacked in two circles of eight around the perimeter of the screens (see Fig. 2),[8] as well as the infrared illumination that is necessary to transform the screens into touch-interfaces. The interaction is implemented by tracking the visitor's touch from behind the screens by means of a camera-based system (OpenCV[9] in OpenFrameworks[10]). The tracking system surveys the entire screen surface of the installation, which spans more than ten meters in width and 1.5 m in height.

The circular setup used in the past four years creates an enclosed space that generates an immersive field of image and audio. Stepping into the space immediately exposes the visitors to projected light and sound from all sides and envelops them in an image that exceeds the natural field of vision. Apart from a spatial envelopment by image and sound, additional levels of immersion are generated for the visitors: they enter into a dedicated physical space, the direct tactile interaction with the panoramic surface enhances their personal engagement, and finally group behaviours and social interactions emerge within the shared space.

---

[7] Bill Buxton provides a useful overview over multi-touch devices from the beginnings up to ca. 2008 http://www.billbuxton.com/multitouchOverview.html.

[8] For more details on the construction of the installation visit http://immersivelab.zhdk.ch/?page_id=20.

[9] http://opencv.org/.

[10] http://www.openframeworks.cc.

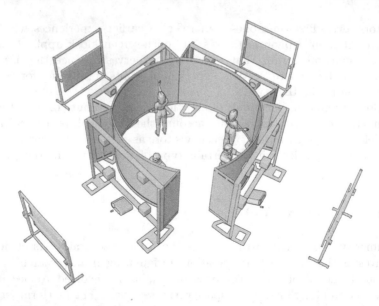

Fig. 2. A rendering of the 'Immersive Lab' platform in its current configuration.

The main activity carried out in this environment has been the development of artistic works by a growing number of artists. Their task is to develop pieces that combine panoramic image and surround sound with a focus on interaction. The curatorial guidelines established early on have led to a catalogue of artistic works that all present live-generated, multi-visitor, non-linear, audio-visual interactive pieces. These decisions put a focus on generative graphics, not photo-realistic artistic work or the use of little photographic or pre-produced video materials. The sound domain consists also mostly of non-linear modules rather than static musical sequences.

Each artistic idea uses specific materials and broadens the spectrum of ideas, generating a wider scope of experiences and evoking different metaphors. In the best case a piece exposes the inherent materiality of the installation (for example by showing the machine-perspective and using the sounds of the screen material, as is the case in 'Mirror', see Fig. 1); the pieces always constitute metaphorically blended [12], algorithmically driven models, exhibiting behaviours in media that give rise to the perception of machine agency and autonomy [38].

The perceived spatiality in the IL is not 'virtual' in the sense of a virtual reality. Given by the physical space that is created through the disposition of elements, a real spatial experience is generated, which provides depth, perspective, and boundaries that do not need to be simulated. In the few cases where a 'world' is created in the abstract realm (Hyperborea, Star Camber), the screen surfaces obtain the character of windows that can be approached and touched but also observed from a distance. Even then, the perception of immersion does not primarily suggest physical presence as avatar in the simulated world. Its function is more similar to a flight simulator where you look out through the window at the world, rather than inhabit a first-person perspective like in a game.

For the visitor to the installation, the first mode of engagement is assessing what and how content is being presented. Depending on the artist's concept, there might be an algorithmic piece running that modulates its behaviour and content without visitor intervention (Star Chamber; Trails), and only changes its overall state upon direct contact by a visitor. Other pieces depend on a specific type of interaction to get started (Clocks and Clouds), posing the question of audience engagement and visitor guidance. The engagement with each piece is based amongst others on the ability to ignore that the contents are computer-generated and projected as mere images onto the screens, in a willing suspension of disbelief [41]. This ability builds on the acquisition of cultural techniques [28,44].[11] The emerging curiosity to engage with the presented idea and metaphor arises from the recognition of the materials and contents arrayed by the artist. The more concrete and realistic these elements are, the quicker recognition occurs; the less mysterious or abstract the piece appears, the faster patterns of engagement are tried out. Only when abstraction reaches a level of simple, primitive shapes does engagement return to a direct, playful interaction.

However, unlike Snibbe's work in museum environments [39], where content is used to convey meaning, a message, and tell a story, in our artistic context, fewer constraints operate, thus giving the artists who develop work a greater degree of freedom. Those conceptual constraints that are imposed originate from the aforementioned curatorial intent, which is aimed at keeping the experiences coherent and with comparable degrees of interactivity, so that the visitors may transfer the accumulated experience from one piece to the next.

The same kind of learning that we observe in the visitors also occurs for the artists who engage with the challenges of making work for the IL. In this case, the knowledge-gain may be located in the shift in understanding, which displaces them from their original naïve idea to the actual implementation, based on an iterative loop of implementation, experience, and adaptation to the observed behaviours of the audience. To facilitate this process, we provide a software simulation environment, where sketches can be visualised and pre-recorded interaction patterns can be applied to the model for testing purposes.

A short discussion of the piece Clocks and Clouds' (see Fig. 3) shall serve as an example for a detailed insight into artistic ideas, the development processes, experiences, and problems, in particular with regard to social interactions. The basic idea for this piece is that of an algorithmic clockwork driven by visitor interaction. Through the layering of numerous identical elements, each with separate parameters, a dense texture emerges, that is a direct reflection of audience activity. In reaction to the visitor's touch gestures, the circular space gets filled with acoustic and visual pulse-trains that are running at differing intervals and exhibiting different life spans. The combination of the interactions by several

---

[11] "To speak of cultural techniques in this context is to acknowledge the skills and aptitudes necessary to master the new media ecology. ... Kulturtechnik comes close to what in English is referred to as 'media competence'." [44, pp. 5–6].

Fig. 3. Exploration and co-learning within the installation. September 2014, 'Clocks and Clouds'.

visitors generates a complex web of overlaid visual and sonic voices', which merge in perception into clusters or masses. The guiding idea in creating this piece is a curiosity about perception of temporal, spatial, and sonic density and the way spatial and temporal textures depend on establishing in the visitors an understanding of the generative principles and the importance of group interaction. The stark and abstract quality of the piece poses a challenge to perception. It serves as an investigation into how our perception is capable of separating visual and acoustic streams and how sensory overloading has the effect of forming clusters, fused objects, or gestalts [24] that consciously emerge through the abstract phenomena perceived. The central topic of interest is social interaction between several visitors, in particular in relation to the reduced sonic and graphical elements, and the richness of the spatial envelopment arising from several people interacting at the same time. The development process of the piece was typical of working in this environment. Through a series of iterations, the original sketch slowly gained in complexity, up to the point where adding more elements, intricate state- or behaviour-mechanisms became counter-productive. Evaluating the effectiveness of engagement and interaction and judging when to stop adding complications was only possible in situations where a number of visitors entered into unguided play with the piece.

4   Analysing Models, Interactions, and Behaviours

In the catalogue of artistic work that have been developed for the IL thus far, a number of different interaction models are explored. Although the technical framework and physical infrastructure remains the same, a variety of metaphors and principles appear. The works developed thus far serve as base material for our inquiry into social interaction, mainly in the form of video documentation of public installation settings, through interviews with the contributing artist, a well as an interview with an expert from the field of perception.

Approaching the question of social interaction in interactive media installations is possible principally through qualitative, experience-based methods. Setting up empirical experiments for a data-driven quantitative approach is rendered difficult on the one hand by the nature of the presented artistic content, and on the other hand by the psychological dimensions of social interaction. These may manifest themselves in group dynamics that only become visible and measurable in verbal exchanges, gaze- and gesture-synchronisations but require knowledge of the behaviours for interpretation. It seems hardly possible to formalise and break this down into atomic tasks suitable for empirical experiments in the given situation. Inevitably, we use our judgement for establishing categories and attributing interpretations to systematisations. The use of common and clearly identified terms when establishing categories and the collection of key aspects through the interviews grounds this investigation in the experience of multiple people, be they the artists, audience members, experts, or the researchers themselves.

4.1   Rating Works

In order to subject the various works that have been realised for the IL to a comparative and systematic analysis, we introduce a set of categorical dimensions. The full set comprises: *media content, narrative structure, system behaviour, visitor experience, interaction principles, and social setting.* For the purpose of this publication, we restrict our analysis and discussion to the latter three categories. Each of these categories contains several attributes with which the works can be examined and rated. In a preliminary process by the authors ratings were attributed by judging the functional, experiential, and social aspects of each work. From the collected ratings a selection and reduction process was carried out.

Table 1 collects the insights from the primary categorisation process by identifying representative works of each category that sit at the lower and upper rating boundaries. This is complemented with a statement about the average and its significance to interpretation. This table provides an overview about the diversity or similarity of the various artistic approaches and their relation to visitor experience. In addition, it provides the means to identify how the IL as an installation setting that is common to all works expands, constrains, or pre-configures the range of artistic, experiential, and social possibilities. These considerations are addressed in the discussion section in juxtaposition with terms and categories obtained from further analysis processes. The discussion is directly based on the analysis organised and subdivided along the same categorical lines and attributes. The following sections explore the catalogue of pieces as categorised in Table 1.

Table 1. Analysis of interaction principles across the catalogue of works. Piece titles abbreviated: Dolphy-Coltrane DC; Hyperborea HY, Trails TA; Clocks and Clouds CC; Mirror MI; Star Chamber SC; FORMBIT FB; Trees TE; Sozio-Natürlich SN; Mushroom Holzburger Paradise MP; The Unattainable/The Intimate UI; Nothing to Hide NH; Monument for San Francisco MS.

Visitor Experience	Affective – Intellectual ①	Individual – Shared ②	Disengaded – Engaged ③
Minimum Rating	atmospheric (MP, SC)	local manipulation (FB) bodily intimacy (UI)	autonomous and atmospheric (SC)
Maximum Rating	scientific sonification (TR)	vertigo (FB), collaborative composition (CC), atmospheric (SC)	instrument (DC), game situation (HY, NH)
Average Rating	affective media but intellectual appreciation of interaction concept **3.7**	local feedback to direct interaction and global audiovisual result **6.6**	most pieces benefit from alternating between engagement and observation **6.5**

Interaction Principles	Predictable – Unpredictable ④	Persistent – Changing ⑤	Conventional – Idiosyncratic ⑥	Explorative – Affording ⑦
Minimum Rating	instrument (DC), GUI (TE, NH) media trigger (MS)	constant interaction principle (DC, TE, MS, more)	game convention (HY) GUI convention (TR, NH)	Lack of visible interaction elements ()
Maximum Rating	autonomous and complex (TA)	changing simulation setting (TA), narrative progression (SN)	parameter space (SC) simulation control (MP, TA) construction (FB, CC)	Game controls (HY), GUI elements (TE,NH) body contact (SN)
Average Rating	repeatable direct response **1.8**	interaction principle provides clarity **2.2**	idiosyncrasies have become installation conventions **5.6**	relies on physical affordances of installation **3.6**

Social Setting	Scales to Multiple Visitors ⑧	Requires Multiple Visitors ⑨	Requires Coordination ⑩	Social Dynamics Drive Complexity ⑪	Thematises Social Issues ⑫
Minimum Rating	global response to singular interaction (SC)	concurrent interactions are disruptive (SC)	triggering of local media (MS)	complex autonomous work (TA), single global interaction (SC)	not an issue (almost all works)
Maximum Rating	Collaborative instrument (DC), social game (NH)	progressive changes of work require concurrent interaction (MP, SN)	collaborative exploration (HY), collaborative manipulation (FB) social game (NH)	collaborative improvisation (DC), collaborative composition (CC)	Collaborative improvisation (DC, CC), interaction with virtual participants (MI, SN, UI), privacy and social media (NH)
Average Rating	many works designed for several but not too many visitors **5.3**	many works provide a (slightly diminished) single visitor experience **2.9**	many works benefit from alternating interaction and observation **4.2**	in many works diversity of interaction maps to diversity of feedback **5**	no work deals only partially with social issues **4**

Visitor Experience. *(1) Affective – Intellectual* During the visitor's initial encounter with a work the intellectual curiosity as well as a piece's artistic strategy are determining for the engagement. In all cases the principles of interaction and multimodal correlation can only be discovered through a process of exploration and discovery. *(2) Individual – Shared* Works that play with the concept of intimacy focus on individual experience whereas works that create atmospheric situations or a visceral immediacy emphasise shared experiences. Most pieces alternate between these extremes by providing direct feedback to interaction as well as integrating the system's response into a global and shared setting. *(3) Disengaged – Engaged* Almost all works establish an interaction that depends on and rewards a high level of engagement. The focus on engagement is particularly strong in works that show little autonomy or those that appropriate game principles. In some cases, uninterrupted engagement is detrimental to developing diversified and extended responses to interaction.

Interaction Principles. *(4) Predictable – Unpredictable* Predictability caters to expectations and the rewards provided by a piece, in particular where an instrumental tool-action provides the basis for interaction. The relationship between the mechanism of the work and the diversity of visitor behaviours can be identified in the predictable forms of interaction. *(5) Persistent – Changing* Static interaction modes provide a rewarding comprehension for visitors, emphasise the dynamics of social interrelations among visitors, but also weaken the interactivity's role as driver of a piece's development. Changing interactivity fosters development and maintains an audience's attention and curiosity. *(6) Conventional – Idiosyncratic* Most pieces don't adhere to conventional HCI principles and those that do, do so deliberately as part of an appropriation through artistic strategy. Nevertheless, among the artists a set of conventions has emerged that is shared by several pieces, the most prominent being the use of trigger zones. *(7) Explorative – Affording* Most works don't reveal specific interaction zones or principles as an affordance. Rather, these principles need to be discovered by exploring or observing of other visitors; this generates a focus on shared forms of engagement. Where graphical clues are given, it is in order to shift the focus away from exploration of interaction towards the exploration of content.

Social Setting. *(8) Scales to Multiple Visitors* Most works favour interaction by multiple visitors, but often the number of interacting visitors is limited, either because the piece cannot accept more input or because the legibility of the work's responsive behaviour would suffer from concurrent interactions. *(9) Requires Multiple Visitors* Works that provide instrument-like interaction or social game situations benefit from multiple concurrent interactions. Those works that require the presence of multiple interacting visitors do so as part of their content progression principle. *(10) Requires Coordination* Most pieces don't require a strict coordination between visitors but benefit from a synchronised alternation between interaction and observation modes. Where coordination is emphasised, it is in order to establish a collaborative interaction setting, which in some cases represents an artistic appropriation of multi-user game conventions. *(11) Social Dynamics Drives Complexity* Works that operate with the metaphor of a musical instrument establish their complexity directly via the social dynamics of the musical performance situation. The role of social dynamics is less important for pieces with autonomous and inherently complex behaviour. *(12) Thematises Social Issues* The specific properties of the installation setting make the social aspects of group interaction implicitly relevant to all works. However, its explicit thematisation is rare and gets chosen by artists with a background in participative performance or social media.

4.2   Interviews

Artist Interviews. In order to better understand the needs, processes, and specifics of artistic development in this project, a number of artist interviews were carried out.[12] They cover general questions about concepts and metaphors of the works, the mode of engagement, the significance of interaction, unexpected experiences, lessons learned about artistic processes, and opinions about particularities of the IL.

'Hyperborea' is described by its author as "an imaginarium", stating that "the intentions of the users are converted to a medium value", that the "infrastructure becomes transparent, as you enter the space" and that visitor can show "an observing or active engagement."

Regarding 'Dolphy-Coltrane', the artist states that "the concept [is to] look for a relation between two languages that are closely related, the graphical and the musical"; it is a process of "translation, transcription from sounds to colours" and that the effect is to "touch the colours and make them sound directly, instead of playing them with an musical instrument."

Commenting on their piece 'Trails' the artists state that "the interaction model [is] that a touch has attraction forces, and works with few touch actions," however "with a larger number people a competitive situation arises." The size of the installation influences perception in that "the 360-degree projection increases the dynamics through the enveloping characteristic and exerts an almost hypnotic effect." A specific observation is that "frictions emerge between the different forms of interactions within the simulation model and between the actively engaged and the passively observing visitor" and that "through the model itself the interaction situation is being made evident."

The author of 'Star Chamber' notes that "the space is a unique space, you cannot really understand until you're in it ... its a very intimate space, [which] changes the complexion of the piece." The basic model of interaction is influenced by the fact that "the algorithm is very unstable, dynamic, the context of the data influences the changes", which implies interaction as well as autonomous behaviour. The visitors can "experience a sense of play ... an emotional experience ..., [the] sense of being dislocated and overwhelmed, [and] become part of the space and enter another world."

Reflecting on his piece 'FORMBIT', the artist states that "it's a visually dominant audio-reactive [piece]." He remarks that the perception has a specific role in the installation: "peripheral vision is completely immersed, so I can sit in it and ... the audio is encapsulating me," and that by "touching in the periphery, it is being filled with the feedback image and we can continue to have that interaction ... it's an experience I couldn't have anticipated." A central idea emerges: "in such an environment I think it's open ground for how people play with it." Finally, during the development process a reduction occurs and he "realised: keep it simple, stupid, because you really want the [interacting] person

---

[12] All interviews can be found on the corresponding page of the website http://immersivelab.zhdk.ch.

not to be frustrated." So from an artistic point of view "it's a good challenge trying to figure out how simple is enough that it's engaging and where to stop [when it is] too much."

These artist's statements make evident several central elements: the unique *spatial experience*; the acts of *translation* that are necessary between the media; the main mode of interaction is that of *play* [19], that *reduction and simplicity* is essential in the layered media and interaction setting; and that *collaboration* as well as *competition* is a recurring social pattern.

Expert Interview. A expert was invited to experience works in the IL and provide insights through an interview. His expertise is the psychology of perception as well as cognitive effects of multi-sensory interaction. The selection of works shown was made in order to provide the experience of the basic types of contents and interactions: 'Mirror' provides body-sized, media-inherent feedback to touch gestures, 'FORMBIT' provides a strongly synesthetic audio-visual experience with abstract lines and synthetic sound, and 'Mushroom Holzburger Paradise' provides the experience of a rich auditory immersive environment with an almost naturalistic visual situation. The inquiry was directed at discerning levels of engagement, modes of interaction, multi-modal fusion in perception, the change of experience over time, the expectations brought to the pieces, and the balance between affective impact and intellectual curiosity.

About 'Mirror' he states that "you don't feel alone, you always try to connect with the figures in the projections" and that there is a "social level of engagement, social gesture, bodily communication and interaction." The effect according to him is to "interact with a piece of art, with a riddle, try to explore this space, interact with the space and its inhabitants."

In his reaction to 'FORMBIT' he notices that it presents "a flat but interesting learning curve" and that the "experience doesn't really end, there is something to explore afterwards" in memory and the resonance of the perceptual field. This is due to the fact that "the perception of movement is strong; a felt kinaesthetic movement" is produced that acts on a bodily level in the same way that "you can feel the sound energy on the touch panels." Overall he states that "[the piece] focuses more on the intellectual curiosity and playfulness" in the way the interaction is set up.

For 'Mushroom Holzburger Paradise' he notes the process and unfolding over time. "You start out with black and have to start to touch ... you have to engage through sounds, have to unlock the visual sphere, try to find correlation between the touch and the sound." This leads him to state that within this process "you realise ... that you won't get surprised, [it's] more an exploration of something established," and that it is "stimulating to have this visual feedback to touch, the fluid simulation. [You] want to trigger it again, [this is the] playful element."

The new terms that appear in these interviews are the concepts of *social bond* (not feeling alone), *bodily communication*, the *riddle* and *surprise*, the notion of *perceptually unlocking* correlations, the different *learning curves*, the *kinaesthetic, bodily sensations* produced by the works, and finally both *curiosity* and *playfulness*. He also remarks that in each piece the experience changes over time while the learning process and the playful engagement evolves. His main point concerning expectations is that some of the intentions of the artists remain hidden and that in some cases the pieces do not evolve enough, thereby leaving his curiosity unsatisfied.

4.3   Visitor Observation

A separate mode of investigation is the observation of the behaviour of visitors towards a given work and their interaction amongst each other. This process can be carried out either live or in video-captures. To provide repeatable observations, we carried out the observations on the documentation videos captured during the project exhibitions; they are available on the project's website (see below). In each of these videos, the principal modes of engagement and exploration become discernible. The main criteria for selecting categories are their reoccurrence in several works and the involvement of at least two people. The main attitudes, behaviours, and effects that we observed and collected were: *contemplation/observation, exploration, showing-doing, explanation, and competition/collaboration*.

The following video excerpts shall stand for many other situations where the same behaviours and effects can be identified:

In the video for 'Dolphy-Coltrane',[13] between 00:27 and 00:46, two visitors, who happen to be professional musicians, are seen *exploring* collaborative playing and shaping the musical structure in the piece. Their communication and synchronisation occurs through sound, which is a habitual mode of paying attention between musicians. In the same video, between 00:54–01:10 the different modes of *observing*, trying out (*exploring*), joint attention and communicating (*showing-doing*) between members of a general, non-expert audience are clearly visible.

Similar behavioural dynamics are visible in 'Mirror'.[14] Here, a group of expert musicians discover (*exploration*) the piece for the first time and show each-other elements that they find interesting (*showing-doing*). A more conventional situation of passive *observation* and sharing understanding (*explanation*) can be seen in the video documenting the piece 'Star Chamber',[15] between 00:30 and 00:54. Here the interaction modality is structured by a model that only allows state-changes and the slowly evolving generative processes puts the visitors into a passive, *contemplative* state.

In the video of 'Monument for San Francisco',[16] with a technology-savvy audience, between 03:35 and 03:50, visitors can be seen explaining (*showing-doing*) to each-other what they see in the presented imagery, thus engaging in

---

[13] 'Dolphy-Coltrane' at: http://immersivelab.zhdk.ch/?page_id=74.

[14] 'Mirror' at: http://immersivelab.zhdk.ch/?page_id=544.

[15] 'Star Chamber' at: http://immersivelab.zhdk.ch/?page_id=62.

[16] 'Monument for San Francisco' & 'Nothing to Hide' in video 'workshop-showing' at: http://immersivelab.zhdk.ch/?page_id=3029.

a communication situation (*explanation*) that goes beyond purely exploratory interaction. Similarly, in 'Nothing to Hide', in the same video, between 05:55 and 07:20, the group interaction and joint interaction is brought to a maximum, in particular with the piece's concept of exposing social media contents in an interaction model resembling 'whack-a-mole'.

The mode of *competition* but also *collaboration* is most visible in 'Hyperborea',[17] between 05:08 and 05:40, where each segment of the screen-space presents a separate but linked interaction element that is used to navigate the piece (Table 2).

Table 2. Collected keywords from the three qualitative investigation strands.

Artists	Expert	Visitor observation
Spatial experience	Social bond	Contemplation/observation
Translation	Bodily communication	Exploration
Play	Riddle	Showing-doing
Reduction and simplicity	Surprise	Explanation
Collaboration/competition	Perceptually unlocking	Collaboration/competition
	Learning curves	
	Kinaesthetic, bodily sensations	
	Curiosity	
	Playfulness	

5 Discussion

After these detailed analyses the next step is to bring together, compare, and synthesise the insights. The collected keywords as well as the analysis of interaction principles generate a map of interaction mechanisms and effects, which needs to be deciphered. The installation platform and the inherently artistic situations assembled in the work catalogue form a well defined framework, which informs the observed situations. Basing our investigation on these materials enables a comparative approach across a number of cases, yet at the same time prevents the generalisation into other interactive media settings. Nevertheless, the combination of elements assembled in the IL platform represents a valid experimental setup with which to carry out the intended analysis about social interaction.

The four investigation strategies carried out on the corpus of work each represent a specific perspective. At the intersection of these four fields lies the question about social engagement in interactive media installations. Several dimensions of sociality can be observed in this intersecting field: exchanges among artists, influences between artist and the (imagined and projected) visitor, perceptual links between the engaging visitor and the abstract entities presented in a piece,

---

[17] 'Hyperborea' at: http://immersivelab.zhdk.ch/?page_id=56.

and finally the different interactions taking place between several visitors. In each of these cases the relational nature of the situation is central, but their rapport is not always a direct and immediate one. On the contrary, through the different temporalities that are present in the artistic development process, in the maturation of the ideas and experiences, as well as the time of a visit to the IL, the different subjects relate to each other in circular, adaptive, and influencing loops that mark the experience. Only between members of the audience does a direct social interaction emerge, in all other cases the technology as well as the metaphors and models used to construct the works mediate the experience and the inter-relationships.

An important question arising from this state of affairs is to what degree the social interactions perceptually dominate the other elements. Does the spatial, multi-sensory, yet evidently artificial media environment not impose a stronger impact than the (group) experience that is possible within its confines? Can we deduce that an inter-subjective link provides an indispensable influence on the visitor's behaviour or does it influence it in an oblique manner? Does the action-perception loop enable a perception of lateral social interactions between visitors, or does the perception only occur when it is metaphorically established with the media work within the circular causality of interaction?

Even though it is hardly possible to provide a definitive answer to these questions within the given framework, the evidence that was collected in the analysis shows that on the different levels of interaction, within the different relations, the social or at least the inter-subjective rapport forms a core part of the experience. Whether this relationship supersedes the impact of the media environment depends on a variety of factors: the number of visitors present at the same time, the interaction principle and the artistic language of a given work, the familiarity of a person with interactive installations, and a general affinity to abstract, metaphorical, game-like scenarios.

Judging from the collected interviews and the observations of audience behaviour (see also Fig. 4) we are confident that in many cases the inter-subjective exchange forms the basis for interaction. Framed by the initial curatorial brief, in none of the works does a purely linear, utilitarian tasks fulfilment principle prevail. The abstract playful engagement [27][18] establishes both on real and metaphorical levels the subjective engagement of the visitor with a situation where an agent provides the subjective vis-à-vis. This subject can be perceived as the (inherently present) author or the agency-endowed, simulated entities within the interactive system.

Lateral social interaction or at least influences between persons in large-scale installations are always present; we haven't been able to observe a single situation where a visitor did not engage in a dialogue with other people present. The setting is, contrary to personal devices and small screens, not amenable to solitary exploration, and if a single person is interacting there is always another

---

[18] In "the formal system of games, the formal system of the model, and the formal systems of narratives" [27, p. 3].

Fig. 4. Large Group interaction inside the 'Immersive Lab'. November 2015 at the Gray Area Foundation for the Arts, San Francisco, CA.

person partaking who becomes the recipient of commentary and self-reports of experience.

The complexity of the emerging phenomenon in the resulting interactions depends on and reflects the complexity of social situations and group behaviour patterns. This is the case both during artistic development processes and in exhibitions with visitor interactions. The only solitary moment occurs during *artistic development processes*, where activities of sketching and constructing ideas takes place. But even in that phase the evaluation of the models and ideas requires the presence and interaction of another person. This particularly concerns an understanding of how synchronisation, coordination, and competition function within the interactive situations. These effects can only be seen and understood in the full installation scenario with an adequate number of visitors. Furthermore, the scale and scope of immersion is difficult to anticipate. The understanding about mechanisms and effect of interaction models on this dimension of experience can only be achieved through exposure to the actual setting. All this to emphasise the absolute necessity to experiment in the actual setting and adapt the original concept and idea to experienced and observed behaviours and interaction patterns.

6 In Closing

The 'Immersive Lab' platform provides a framework for artistic work as well as investigations into foundational principles of interaction and audience engagement. By laying out the framework, it's conceptual background, and the specificities of creating artist work for this interactive media environment, we have set up an experimental device with which to investigate core question that are relevant to designers, HCI-researchers, as well as artists interested in mastering this particular mix of disciplines.

The main insight from this inquiry may be that there is always mutual showing and learning occurring in the social setting of a large scale installation, and that this complex, charged media environment enables the observation of behaviours, the extension of experience, and the encounter with archetypical categories of interaction, that are provoked by the specific, particular, idiosyncratic demands and reactions inherent to each artist's vision.

Future work with the IL platform will extend the installation framework into other configurations, to enter into research and dissemination collaborations with scientific partners who investigate perceptual phenomena of proprioception, action-perception coupling, and musical performance principles. In addition, the pedagogical impetus will be broadened to include a variety of students, ranging from high-school to post-graduate arts and design students. And finally, the 'Immersive Lab' will be shown in a number of exhibitions where the general public will be able to experience the effects of human-scale, multi-modal interaction with spatial audio-visual media.

Acknowledgements. Many thanks go to all the participating artists and to Patrick Neff for sharing his expertise. The 'Immersive Lab' is the outcome of two Swiss National Science Foundation DORE grants: Interactive Swarm Orchestra ISO, Grant 13DPD3-109849 (2006–2008) and Interactive Swarm Space ISS, Grant 13DPD6-124810 (2009–2011). For the 2015 activities in California it benefitted from financial support by Swissnex, the Swiss Arts Council Pro Helvetia, the Swiss Consulate General in San Francisco, and the Zurich University of the Arts. The current project cycle is funded by the Swiss National Science Foundation, AGORA Grant Nr. RAGP1_171656.

References

1. Almond, R.: Sensory and emotional immersion in art, technology and architecture. Ph.D. thesis, Mackintosh School of Architecture, Glasgow School of Art, Glasgow (2011)
2. Amatriain, X., Kuchera-Morin, J., Hollerer, T., Pope, S.T.: The AlloSphere: immersive multimedia for scientific discovery and artistic exploration. IEEE Comput. Soc. **16**(2), 64–75 (2007)
3. Annett, J., Stanton, N.A.: Task Analysis. CRC Press, Boca Raton (2000)
4. Bisig, D., Schacher, J.C., Neukom, M.: Flowspace - a hybrid ecosystem. In: Proceedings of the Conference on New Interfaces for Musical Expression, Oslo, Norway, 30 May–1 June 2011
5. Buxton, B.: Multi-touch systems that i have known and loved. Microsoft Res. **56**, 1–11 (2007)
6. Chan, A.: The theory behind social interaction design (2011). http://johnnyholland.org/2011/04/the-theory-behind-social-interaction-design/
7. Chelstrom, E.S.: Social Phenomenology: Husserl, Intersubjectivity, and Collective Intentionality. Lexington Books, Lanham (2012)

8. DeFanti, T.A., Dawe, G., Sandin, D.J., Schulze, J.P., Otto, P., Girado, J., Kuester, F., Smarr, L., Rao, R.: The StarCAVE, a third-generation CAVE and virtual reality OptIPortal. Future Gener. Comput. Syst. **25**(2), 169–178 (2009)
9. Duranti, A.: Husserl, intersubjectivity and anthropology. Anthropol. Theory **10**(1–2), 16–35 (2010)
10. Eilan, N.: Joint attention, communication, and mind. In: Eilan, N., Hoerl, C., McCormack, T., Roessler, J. (eds.) Joint Attention: Communication and other Minds. Oxford University Press, Oxford (2005)
11. Ellis, R.D.: Phenomenology-friendly neuroscience: the return to merleau-ponty as psychologist. Hum. Stud. **29**(1), 33–55 (2006)
12. Fauconnier, G., Turner, M.: Conceptual blending, form and meaning. Rech. Commun. **19**(19), 57–86 (2003)
13. Fauconnier, G., Turner, M.: The Way We Think: Conceptual Blending and the Mind's Hidden Complexities. Basic Books, New York (2003)
14. Gallagher, S.: How the Body Shapes the Mind. Clarendon Press, Oxford (2005)
15. Gibson, J.J.: The Ecological Approach to Visual Perception. Lawrence Erlbaum, Hillsdale (1986)
16. Grau, O.: Virtual Art: From Illusion to Immersion. MIT press, Cambridge (2003)
17. Hansen, M.B.N.: New Philosophy for New Media. MIT Press, Cambridge (2004)
18. Hartson, R.: Cognitive, physical, sensory, and functional affordances in interaction design. Behav. Inf. Technol. **22**(5), 315–338 (2003)
19. Huizinga, J.: Homo Ludens: A Study of the Play-Element in Culture. Beacon Press, Boston (1955)
20. Hutto, D.D., Myin, E.: Radicalizing Enactivism: Basic Minds without Content. MIT Press, Cambridge (2013)
21. Ihde, D.: Bodies in Technology, vol. 5. University of Minnesota Press, Minneapolis (2002)
22. Jacob, R.J., Girouard, A., Hirshfield, L.M., Horn, M.S., Shaer, O., Solovey, E.T., Zigelbaum, J.: Reality-Based Interaction: A Framework for Post-WIMP Interfaces. In: Proceedings of CHI 2008. ACM, Florence, 5–10 April 2008
23. Kaptelinin, V., Nardi, B.: Activity theory in HCI: fundamentals and reflections. Synth. Lect. Hum. Cent. Inform. **5**(1), 1–105 (2012)
24. Katz, D.: Gestalt Psychology, Its Nature and Significance. The Ronald Press Co., New York (1950)
25. Lakoff, G., Johnson, M.: Metaphors We Live By. University Of Chicago Press, Chicago (1980)
26. Leont'ev, A.N.: Activity, Consciousness, and Personality. Prentice Hall, Englewood Cliffs (1978)
27. Lindley, C.A.: Ludic engagement and immersion as a generic paradigm for human-computer interaction design. In: Rauterberg, M. (ed.) ICEC 2004. LNCS, vol. 3166, pp. 3–13. Springer, Heidelberg (2004). doi:10.1007/978-3-540-28643-1_1
28. Macho, T.: Tiere zweiter Ordnung. Kulturtechniken der Identität und Identifikation. transcript Verlag, Bielefeld, Germany (2008)
29. Maturana, H.R., Varela, F.J.: Autopoiesis and cognition: the realization of the living. Boston Stud. Philos. Sci. **43**, 2–58 (1980)
30. Merleau-Ponty, M.: The Structure of Behavior. Beacon Press, Boston (1942/1963)
31. Merleau-Ponty, M.: The Primacy of Perception, and Other Essays on Phenomenological Psychology, the Philosophy of Art, History and Politics. Edie. Northwestern University Press, Evanston, IL (1964). Edited, with An Introduction by M. James
32. Nechvatal, J.: Immersive Ideals/Critical Distances, vol. 2009. Lambert Academic Publishing, Saarbrücken (2009)

33. Norman, D.A.: The Psychology of Everyday Actions: The Design of Everyday Things. Doubleday/Currency, New York (1990)
34. O'Regan, J.K., Noë, A.: A sensorimotor account of vision and visual consciousness. Behav. Brain Sci. **24**(05), 939–973 (2001)
35. Paine, G.: Towards unified design guidelines for new interfaces for musical expression. Organ. Sound **14**(2), 142–155 (2009)
36. Rose, F.: The Art of Immersion. WW Norton & Company, New York (2012)
37. Russell, J.A.: A circumplex model of affect. J. Pers. Soc. Psychol. **39**(6), 1161–1178 (1980)
38. Schacher, J.C., Bisig, D.: Face to face - performers and algorithms in mutual dependency. In: Proceedings of the International Conference on Live-Interfaces ICLI, Brighton, UK, pp. 80–88, June 2016
39. Snibbe, S.S., Raffle, H.S.: Social immersive media pursuing best practices for multiuser interactive camera/projector exhibits. In: CHI 2009, New Media Experiences 2. ACM, Boston, 4–9 April 2009
40. Thompson, E., Stapleton, M.: Making sense of sense-making: Reflections on enactive and extended mind theories. Topoi **28**(1), 23–30 (2009)
41. Tomko, M.: Politics, performance, and coleridge's "suspension of disbelief". Vic. Stud. **49**(2), 241–249 (2007)
42. Tsakiris, M., Haggard, P.: Neural, functional, and phenomenological signatures of intentional actions. In: Grammont, F., Legrand, D., Livet, P. (eds.) Naturalizing Intention in Action, pp. 39–64. MIT Press, Cambridge (2010)
43. Varela, F., Thompson, E., Rosch, E.: The Embodied Mind: Cognitive Science and Human Experience. MIT Press, Cambridge (1991)
44. Winthrop-Young, G.: Cultural techniques: preliminary remarks. Theor. Cult. Soc. **30**(6), 3–19 (2013)
45. Zeltzer, D.: Autonomy, interaction, and presence. Presence Teleoper. Virt. Environ. **1**(1), 127–132 (1992)
46. Zone, R.: Stereoscopic Cinema and the Origins of 3-D Film, 1838–1952. University Press of Kentucky, Lexington (2014)

In-the-moment and Beyond: Combining Post-hoc and Real-Time Data for the Study of Audience Perception of Electronic Music Performance

S. M. Astrid Bin[✉], Fabio Morreale, Nick Bryan-Kinns,
and Andrew P. McPherson

Centre for Digital Music, Queen Mary University of London, London, UK
{a.bin,f.morreale,n.bryan-kinns,a.mcpherson}@qmul.ac.uk

Abstract. This paper presents a methodology for the study of audience perception of live performances, using a combined approach of post-hoc and real-time data. We conducted a study that queried audience enjoyment and their perception of error in digital musical instrument (DMI) performance. We collected quantitative and qualitative data from the participants via paper survey after each performance and at the end of the concert, and during the performances spectators were invited to indicate moments of enjoyment and incidences of error using a two-button mobile app interface. This produced 58 paired post-hoc and real-time data sets for analysis. We demonstrate that real-time indication of error does not translate to reported non-enjoyment and post-hoc and real-time data sets are not necessarily consistent for each participant. In conclusion we make the case for a combined approach to audience studies in live performance contexts.

Keywords: Audience studies · Error · Performance studies

1 Introduction

As computing has found its way into every facet of our lives, the experience of the user has become a central point of HCI study and discussion [38]. Indeed, as interfaces have become ubiquitous and their applications have expanded to include a broader and more personal range of interactions - far beyond task-based interactions in the workplace [27] - their use has become ever more ambiguous, and their purpose potentially open to many interpretations [32].

Experimental electronic music (EEM) performance using digital musical instruments (DMIs) shares many of these same features of ambiguity. EEM evolved out of the 20th century avant-garde and valued experimentation and improvisational exploration over musical vernacular. Because of this emphasis on improvisation, in EEM performance there is no specific task and no "right" or "wrong" interaction - a commonality it shares with the current HCI paradigm. (It should be stressed that in this sense we are concerned with DMIs as tools of

© IFIP International Federation for Information Processing 2017
Published by Springer International Publishing AG 2017. All Rights Reserved
R. Bernhaupt et al. (Eds.): INTERACT 2017, Part I, LNCS 10513, pp. 263–281, 2017.
DOI: 10.1007/978-3-319-67744-6_18

improvisation, and not in the details of their usability.) With decades of development, EEM performance has been exploring ambiguous interactions in an audience context for far longer than third-wave HCI, and we propose that it is a fertile ground for inquiry into spectator experience of ambiguous interactions.

In HCI audience studies, and certainly those in the New Interfaces for Musical Expression (NIME) research community, post-hoc methods are common means of data collection [3,6,8,15,21,23]. Using surveys and/or interviews, investigators can quickly and inexpensively gather a wealth of quantitative and qualitative data based on audience opinions. However, Loftus and her collaborators demonstrate that human memory is notoriously unreliable [25], which raises questions about, if not the veracity of post-hoc data, then what additional conclusions real-time data may allow us to draw, and what other methodologies might be employed.

We were therefore motivated to investigate the role and content of both post-hoc and real-time data in an audience study, in order to develop a methodology that might make the best use of both. The questions we explore in this paper are as follows:

1. What kind of evaluation can be undertaken with post-hoc and real-time feedback, and how can these forms of data collection inform one another?
2. What are the features of an incidence of audience enjoyment? What are the features of an incidence of "error"?

This paper presents a study that examined the role of familiarity and musical style in the enjoyment of DMI performance using this combined methodology. The study context was an evening concert, where two performers played self-built musical instruments in both an experimental and a vernacular style, and data was collected from the audience As well as post-hoc survey data, real-time data was collected via a custom-built system called Metrix, a system for collecting real-time audience feedback that runs on mobile phones and records spectator indications of "enjoyment" and "error" via a two-button interface.

The implications of the post-hoc data are discussed in depth in [2]. In this paper, we shift our focus to examining the results of combining of real-time and post-hoc data, and using these results to examine the specific notion of "error" in performance. We discuss the kind of evaluation that is possible with this combined methodology, and compare and contrast the post-hoc and real-time data sets – considering the how they inform one another, as well as the advantages and drawbacks of each. We also examine the real-time data to gain insight into the perception of the perception of EEM's ambiguous interactions, and performance features that may indicate "enjoyment" and/or "error", and how this might inform our understanding of each.

2   Related Work

In this section we first trace the history of real-time audience data collection, and existing methods for HCI studies of spectator perception. We also contextualise DMI performance in relation to third-wave HCI, and specify why error is an issue of interest in both arenas.

2.1   Data Collection in Audience Studies

Real-time audience response has been measured since 1930s where it was first used to gauge audience response to radio, film, and television [26]. These studies took place in a lab, where spectators indicated their reactions with buttons and knobs on hand-held devices. Since then, real-time data gathering techniques have become more sophisticated and integrated into the performance setting, now including physiological data (such as head tracking [29] and galvanic skin response [24]), verbal and non-verbal feedback [1, 11], as well as the measurement of crowd behaviours, such as applause [4, 9].

Stevens et al. [34] describe a study done with pARF, a system comprised of 20 hand-held (PDA) computers programmed to gather time-series "arousal" data. Participants indicated their emotional state with a stylus on a 200 px × 200 px grid on the device's screen, and their response was measured at a rate of 2 Hz. The devices were distributed to 20 individuals in an audience of 200 for feedback during a dance performance.

Though rigorous analysis of the real-time data gathered with pARF was performed, there are drawbacks to this method. First, the pARF system supports up to 20 devices (only 18 were used for the study), meaning that a 10% subset of the audience used it, a small sample that is generalised to a much larger crowd. Secondly, no post-hoc data was collected alongside pARF (except for demographic details), which also leaves open the question of the difference in insights this method might have when compared to post-hoc data. Metrix, the system we designed and used for our case study, addresses these gaps.

2.2   DMI Performance, HCI, and the Role of Context

Though a comprehensive history of DMIs and EEM performance is beyond the scope of this paper, it is helpful to trace their roots. This musical tradition developed over the last 100 years (starting well before the advent of digital technology), and is connected to the avant-garde that rose out of seismic shifts in culture taking place in the early 20th century [18]. Connected to Russolo's Futurism [31] and timbre-focused work of Varèse, it emerged at a time of radical experimentation that made liberal use of new technology, and soon exposed the limits of the usual tools. As Varèse remarked, "Our musical alphabet must be enriched. We also need new instruments very badly ... which can lend themselves to every expression of thought and can keep up with thought" (1916, quoted in [37]).

Along with a pursuit of new instruments, practitioners set aside musical vernacular (features such as melody, triadic harmony, rhythmic regularity) in favour of radical experimentation. The path of development can be seen running thorough Pierre Schaeffer's *musique concrète* and the work of John Cage and his experimentation with the musical score. He created scores more akin to recipes, descriptions of musical situations that had to be produced and completed by the performer (and sometimes the audience).

This lack of established artistic goals and the discarding of established musical frames of reference parallels features of 3rd wave HCI [38]. HCI was originally concerned with task completion in the workplace [27], but since that time interaction with computers features in virtually every facet of life, and computing now serves much more nuanced social, emotional and cultural purposes. As such, "emotions and experiences are keywords in the third wave." [7] In these interactions, the task may be set by the user, the task may only become apparent during the interaction, or there may be no task at all. Gaver et al. [17] propose that this ambiguity in interfaces is a "resource for design" that, instead of leading users through a task, instead provides a space of possibility for interpretation. Further, Sengers and Gaver [32] assert that HCI "can and should systematically recognize, design for, and evaluate with a more nuanced view of interpretation in which multiple, perhaps competing interpretations can co-exist."

In both the DMI and HCI contexts, understanding what is (or isn't) done with the interface is as crucial as the device itself. Reeves et al. [30], suggest that the experience of an HCI spectator can be described by how they see the interaction, coupled with the effect of that interaction - whether the interaction and the outcome was hidden, partially hidden, transformed, revealed or amplified. In this way, the performer action and outcome are tightly coupled; more importantly, the notion of "task" is removed from the discourse.

Spectator experience of DMI performance is an area of interest in NIME, where discussion has settled around the notion of *transparency*. Transparency is defined by Fels et al. [12,30] as "the psychophysiological distance, in the minds of the player and the audience, between the input and output of a device mapping" [12]. Since DMIs do not have to conform to traditional modes of interaction [20], considerable effort has been made to expose the instrument's workings to audiences, through visualisations of computational processes [5,28] and physical metaphors [10].

Curiously missing from this discussion is the influence of musical style on audience perception. Whether an input-output mapping is understandable to the spectator may depend at least in part on whether they are *witting* spectators [33]; that is, whether they understand the norms of the musical style in which the instrument is used. Just as many interactions between humans and computers cannot be removed from their cultural context, instrumental transparency may only be measurable in the context of a particular musical style. This was a primary motivator for our case study, which questioned the role of familiarity on audience response to EEM performance using DMIs.

2.3   Perception of Error in DMI Performance

Fyans et al. have made inquiries into the spectator experience, particularly where it relates to the notion of error [13–16]. In one such study [15] they observe that spectators are able to identify few errors with DMI performance, even raising the question of whether error is even possible. Gurevich [19] contributes a more flexible system of thinking about boundaries and straying outside them, by suggesting that variation is the locus of *style*, which he defines as individual variations.

It is important here to consider this notion of error. From the Latin *errare*, meaning *to stray*, "error" suggests a stepping outside of accepted boundaries.

Kruse-Weber and Parncutt [22] define error in a classical music context as "unintended result of an action", and classify intended actions as those specified in the score. However, experimental electronic music performance is highly improvisational and has no vernacular resembling a classical score. In this context, how can a performer stray out of bounds? Are errors even possible?

This study on familiarity's impact on audience enjoyment presented an intriguing opportunity to also examine the notion of "error" in this context. We wanted to gain insight into whether enjoyment and error are mutually exclusive, and determine if features of these two states could be extracted from real-time indications by the audience. Therefore, our real-time system had buttons for indicating two states, "enjoyment" and "error".

Of course, this single audience study can't answer these questions in a general sense. It does, however, provide some intriguing insights that suggest what the audience perceives as errors as the performance unfolds.

3   Real-Time Data: Metrix

3.1   Motivation and Technical Description

When considering which system to use to collect real-time feedback, we first looked to existing solutions [1]. However, we found these solutions to be inappropriate for one or more of the following reasons: Prohibitively expensive; overly complicated; lacking in features (or drastically over-featured); hard to customise; requiring significant participant training; or generally unfit for purpose in this context. Leveraging the availability of web technologies and the ubiquity of personal smart devices, we designed Metrix, an application that was streamlined, easy to use, fit for purpose and customisable.

Metrix is an open-source system for real-time data collection. It is a single-page web app, and is designed to be used on mobile phones. Metrix runs on a web server, and users connect to it via their phone's browser. When active, participants can tap the interface's buttons, and the system records each user's button taps (grouped by the button that produced them) in a database as time stamps associated with their username. The resulting timestamp data can then be distributed along a timeline. (Fig. 1 describes the Metrix dataflow).

The data gathering interface consists of a screen split in half into two buttons (Fig. 2). It is inactive until the start of the performance, when it is made active by an investigator via a remote control interface.

There are significant benefits to this web app approach. First, this app runs on a mobile phone and there is nothing to download, meaning that an entire audience can participate (in similar studies, devices were custom and limited and only a small percentage of the audience could participate [35]). Second, the design of the interface is a web page, and is therefore easily customisable and can go through multiple design iterations. Third, this system leverages the ubiquity of mobile phone technology; audience members in many contexts can be assumed

---

[1] http://www.pcipro.com/, https://www.feedbackr.io/, http://www.clikapad.com/.

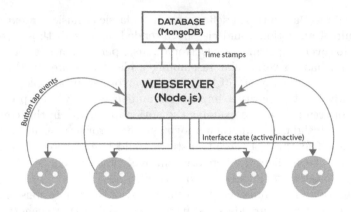

Fig. 1. Diagram of data flow between participants and Metrix.

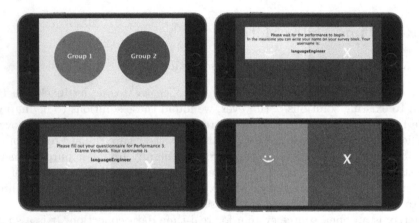

Fig. 2. Views of Metrix in use. Clockwise from top left: Screen to select group; presentation of username; view during data collection; post-performance pause and reminder of username. (Color figure online)

to have their own devices that they are already know how to use, so there is little on-boarding necessary.

Additional features such as username assignment also allows connections to be made in the datasets. When a participant accesses the Metrix interface, a username is automatically generated for them (an amalgamation of two randomly-chosen words) and displayed on their screen, and they are reminded of this username whenever the interface is inactive between performances.

There are, of course, contextual considerations when implementing Metrix as a research tool. Though we were leveraging the ubiquity of mobile phones in the context of our study, not all audience members everywhere will have a mobile phone. Additionally, a wifi connection that can support all users is needed, and web server load would be a consideration for very large audiences. Mobile phone batteries are also a factor, as audiences will probably not arrive with their phones fully charged, and Metrix requires that they be active for the entire performance.

Interface and interaction design. We chose a two-button interface for Metrix. We were interested in the audience indicating two states: "I am enjoying this" and "There was an error" (we will hereafter refer to these buttons as "enjoyment" and "error").

Since this is an interface designed to be used during a performance, we wanted it to be as easy, intuitive, and unobtrusive as possible. A slider with a neutral position, for example, may require visual attention, so we opted for discrete buttons. The active interface is split in half, each half serving as a "button", so it was easy to tap each side without having to look at the device. We also chose not to use text to reduce cognitive load, and instead used symbols and colours on the buttons to indicate their function. On the left, "enjoyment" is green and is indicated by a :) symbol. On the right, "error" is red and is indicated by an X (see Fig. 2). Each button provided some subtle feedback by darkening slightly when tapped.

4 Case Study

The context of this study was an evening concert, during which two musicians - each of whom plays a self-built DMI - gave two short performances of approximately five minutes each: one in a highly experimental style, and one in a conventional (vernacular) style. In this section, we will detail the study method.

4.1 Post-hoc Data Collection: Surveys

The audience for this study (N = 64) was randomly distributed survey booklets on arrival. The book a participant received placed them in either Group 1 or Group 2. The survey booklets contained four short surveys to be completed after each performance (the *post-performance* surveys) and a longer survey to be completed at the end (the *post-concert survey*)[2]. The post-performance surveys asked three quantitative (rating scale) questions, and three qualitative (open-ended) questions. The post-performance survey asked more reflective questions and gathered demographic data. These survey answers were matched to the participants' real-time data through the Metrix username, which we asked our participants to write on the front of their survey books.

4.2 Study Design

The two musicians recruited for this study were Dianne Verdonk on the La Diantenne [36], and Tim Exile on the Flow Machine[3]. These musicians were chosen because they have achieved a level of virtuosity with their instruments, their instruments allow them to play in both an experimental and conventional musical styles, and the way their instruments work is not already familiar to an observer (Fig. 3).

---

[2] Blank questionnaires available at: http://bit.ly/1QYBlIk.

[3] http://techcrunch.com/video/create-live-edm-with-tim-exiles-flow-machine/519373211/.

Fig. 3. The study performers, from left: Dianne Verdonk on La Diantenne; Tim Exile on the Flow Machine.

The audience was divided into two groups, according to which survey book they were handed upon entry. Group 1 received a ten-minute technical tutorial on Tim Exile's Flow Machine, and Group 2 received a ten-minute technical tutorial on Dianne Verdonk's La Diantenne.[4] This was to provide a difference of familiarity – for each performance, one group would be familiar with how the instrument worked, and the other would be unfamiliar.

While each group received their instrument tutorial, the other group received a short (10 min) on-boarding session in another room that featured a two-minute video on how to use Metrix, and left time for questions. During this session we stressed that the states indicated by the buttons were not opposite - it was not "I heard an error" and "I didn't hear an error", or "I'm enjoying this" and "I'm not enjoying this". We also stressed that participants could tap the buttons as often - or as rarely - as they wished, and that the boundaries of "enjoyment" and "error" were entirely up to them.

The concert consisted of each performer playing two pieces, one experimental and one vernacular (the performers were asked to interpret this in the context of their individual performance practice). The order of performance was as follows:

1. Dianne: Experimental
2. Tim: Experimental
3. Dianne: Conventional/Vernacular
4. Tim: Conventional/Vernacular

5   Processing of Real-Time Results

Prior to analysis, some data cleaning techniques were applied to the real-time data set. These included:

---

[4] These tutorials were given by a member of the research group to avoid any bias toward seeing a particular performer before the show.

Truncating all tap events to the nearest second: The time stamps collected were in milliseconds, but that resolution of time proved too noisy. For that reason, all tap events were grouped by the second in which the tap took place.

Grouping taps by time interval: We grouped the "error" events by 1-second interval, and grouped the "enjoyment" events by 5-second interval (the reasoning for this is discussed in Sect. 5.2).

Filtering to remove multiple taps from intervals: A small number of participants appeared to be very enthusiastic with their button tapping, and tapped many times in a given time interval. To avoid one person's repeated tapping creating an artificial spike in tap events, we counted only one tap per participant in any given interval.

5.1   Data Considerations

In a previous paper [2] we considered the post-hoc results and what they revealed about the effect of instrument familiarity and musical style on audience enjoyment of experimental DMI performance. For this analysis, we will instead focus on the real-time data in order to determine the features of enjoyment and error, and make reference to the post-hoc ratings of Enjoyment as we examine how these datasets complement one another.

It should be noted that participants were under no obligation to take part in both methods, and some only took part in one. We collected 64 surveys, but for this analysis have only included survey data that had a real-time data set from the same participant (58 participants in total; Group 1 n = 30, Group 2 n = 28).

It should be highlighted that since the notions of "enjoyment" and "error" were not considered to be complementary ideas, they were treated as different data sets with separate insights, and coded by the investigators entirely separately.

5.2   Process of Analysis

The first step was visualisation of the real-time data in histograms, using the 1 s bin width. For the histograms associated with the "error" button, the results were understandable at this time resolution. However, for the "enjoyment" data, a 1 s bin meant the data was still very noisy. The bin size was increased, and at 5 s peaks became more prominent. An example of the distribution of "enjoyment" indications throughout a performance is illustrated in Fig. 4.

5.3   Video Coding

Two investigators independently analysed the histograms for "enjoyment" and "error" for each performance. The performances were recorded on video, with an audible click to mark the point where the Metrix interface was made active by the investigator. This made it possible to sync the video footage and the real-time data, which enabled us to analyse the performance and look for events in the performance around points of audience agreement about "enjoyment" and "error".

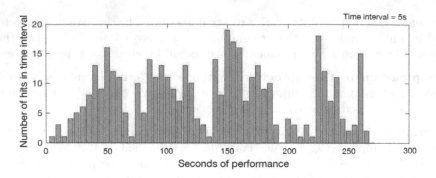

Fig. 4. Patterns of use for "enjoyment" button by 5 s interval, Performance 1.

In coding the video, we defined what constituted an "event" for the video analysis as agreement among 3 or more people in one or two consecutive time intervals, preceded by two or more seconds of zero error indications. (See Fig. 5 for an illustration.) The reason for two seconds of no indications was so we could be sure the previous event had ended.

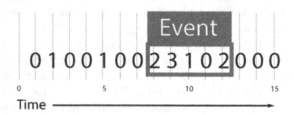

Fig. 5. An illustration of an "error" event, by examining the number of participant indications per second.

6   Findings

After the video coding was completed by two investigators, a deductive thematic analysis was performed to extract themes, combining the results until saturation.

6.1   Features of "error" Events

We found that audience-indicated "error" events were, for all performances, less common than "enjoyment" events. These "error" events tended to occur together across the audience, appearing as spikes in the histograms (see Fig. 8, Note 2), whereas "enjoyment" events tended to occur far more often but with less agreement among the audience.

From our video coding and thematic analysis, we found that error events fell into the following categories:

1. Obvious and trivial performer error (Dianne at one point hit the mic stand, and Tim's rig shut off at the end of his final performance, which were widely indicated);
2. Sounds that were loud, or unexpected;
3. Facial expressions indicating a mistake;
4. Errors in musical content (for example, out of tune or against the expected rhythm).

In the experimental performances, the errors were primarily in categories 1, 2 and 3. In the conventional performances, errors in category 4 were also observed, suggesting that the audience had a deeper knowledge of the musical style in these cases.

6.2   Features of "enjoyment" Events

"Enjoyment" events were not as straightforward as "error" events. Instead of appearing as spikes in the data, their appearance resembled a Gaussian distribution; taps increased to a peak over time, and then tapered off (see Fig. 4 bottom for an example). "Enjoyment" appears to have a slower, more cumulative effect, contrasting the "error" events' sudden onset and sharp drop off.

Enjoyment events clustered around events with the following features:

1. Moments of novelty, such as the introduction of a new playing technique, timbre or texture;
2. Moments of high musical intensity, flow, or complex rhythmic patterns.

In the experimental performances, category 1 (novelty) was the driving factor in periods of enjoyment. In the conventional performances, both categories were observed, but category 2 (intensity) predominated. This again suggests an audience engagement with the underlying musical language.

6.3   Real-Time Data Compared to Post-hoc Findings

We compared the number of button taps (which we refer to as "indications") during the performances to see if an increased amount of "enjoyment" or "error" indications (Fig. 9) bore any resemblance to the rank ordering of Enjoyment from the post-hoc data. This ranking - comparing those who were familiar with the instrument vs those who were unfamiliar with the instrument for each performance - is illustrated in Fig. 6.

Considering the four performances overall, increased use of the real-time "enjoyment" button did not correlate with the audience's post-hoc rankings of enjoyment. Although the most "enjoyment" indications did occur during the highest-ranked performance (P4), that was the only similarity. There was no clear relationship between number of "error" indications and rankings of the performances: the lowest-ranked performance did have the most "error" indications, but this pattern did not hold for the other three performances.

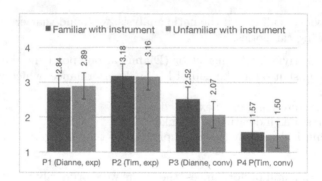

Fig. 6. Rank ordering of performances from post-concert survey, from favourite (1) to least favourite (4). Note that shorter bars indicate stronger preference.

6.4   Inconsistency Between Post-hoc and Real-Time Reporting

In the post-performance surveys filled out immediately after each of the 4 performances, we asked participants to rate how enjoyable they found the performance they had just seen. We found inconsistency between their real-time reporting and their post-hoc reflections. We will consider two illustrative examples:

One respondent from Group 1 (who saw Tim's instrument before the concert) made 137 "enjoyment" indications during Performance 4 (Tim's conventional piece), more than twice as much as any other performance (this was after eliminating more than one indication per second). But, in the qualitative assessment of the performance they reported *It was a bit flat.*

A respondent from Group 2 (who saw Dianne's instrument before the concert) made 108 "enjoyment" indications during Performance 4 – also more than twice as much as any other performance. In the qualitative feedback they reported that *It seemed a bit disjointed.*

These two examples suggest that raw numbers of real-time events are not always a good predictor of post-hoc reporting. More importantly, this inconsistency points to an intriguing area of study in audience perception: It suggests that what we think in the moment and what we think upon reflection may not be the same, and supports the need for examination of both post-hoc and real-time data as well as a way to better understand it.

6.5   Correlation of Real-Time Data and Post-hoc Ratings

In our post-performance surveys, we asked respondents to rate the performance they had just seen according to the following questions:

1. How much did you enjoy the performance?
2. How interesting was the performance?
3. Did you understand how the instrument worked?

Since we are comparing real-time indications of Enjoyment, we will consider only the post-hoc Enjoyment rankings associated with Question 1 above.

For each performance and with each Familiar and Unfamiliar audience subgroup, we compared the rate of real-time "enjoyment" and "error" indications with the post-hoc quantitative ratings of Enjoyment, to see if there was any relationship (16 correlations in total, summarised in Fig. 7). Across these, we found one correlation that was statistically significant. This correlation was between real-time "enjoyment" indications and post-hoc ratings of enjoyment ($r = 0.58$ $p = 0.0007$).

		Enjoyment Indications		Error Indications	
		r value	p value	r value	p value
P1:	Familiar	0.37	0.05	-0.11	0.58
	Unfamiliar	0.18	0.34	0.36	0.36
P2:	Familiar	0.58	0.0007	0.19	0.32
	Unfamiliar	0.43	0.10	-0.32	0.10
P3:	Familiar	0.08	0.67	-0.16	0.42
	Unfamiliar	-0.11	0.57	-0.19	0.31
P4:	Familiar	0.27	0.15	0.09	0.63
	Unfamiliar	0.13	0.51	0.13	0.51

Fig. 7. A summary of the correlations of real-time "enjoyment" and "error" indications with the post-hoc rankings of Enjoyment of each performance.

We found no positive or negative correlations between "error" indications and post-hoc rankings of enjoyment.

7   Discussion

7.1   A Consideration of the Limitations of Metrix

The post-concert survey provided space for feedback on Metrix. Though feedback was overwhelmingly positive (with most comments referring to it as *easy* and *intuitive* and only one participant indicating that they found it *a little distracting*), we do acknowledge possible limitations of some features, and present data about why we believe these limitations do not impact the data we collected.

1. **Suggestion of binary states.** There is a risk that the two buttons, using complementary colours, suggest that the "enjoyment" and "error" states are opposite and mutually exclusive. Though we mentioned in the onboarding session that this is not the case, we acknowledge that simply telling an audience what they mean may not be enough.

    However, our data showed that these buttons were not used in opposing ways, based on two observations. First, we found that there was no usage pattern

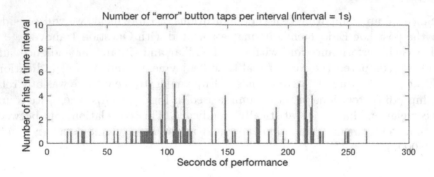

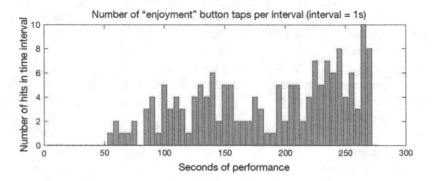

Fig. 8. Patterns of use of the "error" button and "enjoyment" button for Performance 3. NOTE 1: Error and good events often occur together, suggesting there is no binary relationship. NOTE 2: "Enjoyment" events are cumulative and rise to a peak, where "error" events have a sudden onset and sharp drop off.

that suggested that when the audience was not hitting the "enjoyment" button they were hitting the "error" button, suggesting that they were not using them to indicate binary states. (See Fig. 8, NOTE 1 for an illustration.)

Secondly, as we will describe in Sect. 7.2, the usage patterns of the "enjoyment" button and the "error" buttons was very different. "Enjoyment" events appeared to be cumulative events, gathering to a peak and tapering off again, whereas "error" events were sharp spikes with sudden drop off. This further suggests that the way the buttons were used was not related, and therefore our concern about a binary interpretation was unfounded.

2. **Use of symbols.** In order to reduce cognitive load we used symbols to indicate the two buttons instead of words: A smiley face indicated "enjoyment" and an X indicated "error". These were chosen because they were not similar symbols that could be confused, and did not suggest a binary relationship (as could be the case with a happy face and a sad face). However, we were concerned that these may not communicate clearly enough, and that respondents might still perceive a binary relationship.

Avg per sec.	P1	P2	P3	P4
Enjoyment	1.567	1.227	0.600	1.893
Error	0.224	0.549	0.516	0.506

Fig. 9. Average number of "enjoyment" and "error" indications per second for each performance.

Instead, we found, as described in point 1, that there didn't seem to be a binary relationship evident in the patterns of button use. There was also no feedback about the symbols being confusing. Further, a subsequent user workshop on this interface design with people who had never seen Metrix before indicated they found the symbols clear.

7.2 Observations on Usage Patterns

Over the course of the performance, there was no reduction in the use of the app; in fact, the final performance had the most indications on both buttons. We can thus conclude that Metrix kept participants engaged throughout. We cannot say specifically why this was, though simplicity or novelty may be factors.

We also found that participants vary widely in their willingness to record events, but that they appear relatively consistent in their level of use. We observed that those who tapped the button frequently for one performance tended to have similar levels of use for all four, and those who were sparing with their indications were similarly consistent. There will always be those who will be enthusiastic users and it is important to control for this in the analysis (for, example, by disregarding duplicate indications in a time interval).

7.3 Delayed Reactions: Real Time Is Still Not Immediate

Error and enjoyment events exhibited different temporal profiles. "Error" indications tended to happen in a narrower window, in clear response to a specific performer action or sound event. "Enjoyment" indications, however, appear spread out over wider time intervals. Clusters of "enjoyment" indications tended to build up over tens of seconds, reach a peak and taper off again, suggesting it is more of a persistent state than a discrete event.

This is not to suggest that "error" is a specific stimulus that gets a consistent and immediate reaction, and it is important not to view this as an action/reaction relationship. However, these differences do lend insight into the audience experience of both - that "error" is swiftly judged, whereas "enjoyment" tends to accumulate over time.

It is also challenging for participants to judge, and then register, a passing event that is usually part of the general continuum of a performance experience. As one participant noted, *"Enjoyable moments - as well as errors - pass so quickly. It took quite some mental time to decide and process, so sometimes I did not press at all because I felt the moment had already passed and it would not make sense at all to press anymore. The delay leads up to a sound, I would say, between the occurrence of an event and my button press."*

7.4   A Lot of Errors Doesn't Mean that It's Bad

The post-hoc rank ordering of the performances made a clear indication that Performance 4 was heavily preferred (see Fig. 6). This, interestingly, was the performance that also got by far the most "error" indications in the real-time data.

This means that the presence of "error" indications did not suggest a performance that was not enjoyed. The suggestion here is that "error" perhaps does not deserve its negative connotations, and that there may be more to error than simply being something to avoid. It also suggests that events which audiences understand as "errors" are not necessarily bad; it is even possible that noticing subtle errors implies a certain level of audience engagement with a performance.

This finding is supported by the lack of negative correlation between "error" indications and ratings of Enjoyment both audience subgroups and all performances. If a tap on the "error" button suggested that the spectator considered the performance to be bad we would expect to find more widespread negative correlations between the number of these indications and the post-hoc ratings. This was not the case.

We found a positive correlation between "enjoyment" indications and ratings of Enjoyment for Performance 2, Tim's experimental performance, among both those familiar with the instrument. This is notable because this was the lowest-rated performance among all audiences. It may suggest that when there is no common vernacular on which to rely then instrument familiarity is not a significant factor in whether or not a performance is enjoyable (a finding supported by the post-hoc analysis of this study [2]). However, because these data points are isolated, more in-depth study is needed in order to formulate any specific conclusions.

7.5   What Real-Time and Post-hoc Data Have to Offer One Another

Real-time data affords us second-by-second insight into audience experience, but it does not provide any contextual insight. Conversely, post-hoc data provides detailed contextual and descriptive feedback, but we have no way of tying these to any specific event. Each, therefore, has the potential to provide what the other cannot. This is potentially very powerful, and suggests that there are dimensions of audience data available through combining these two techniques that are inaccessible when only one is used.

But, each method can only ask its own questions, and we must be careful about which conclusions to draw. To make meaningful conclusions, the questions asked by both techniques have to be designed to inform one another, and how to best formulate questions to get results that can be meaningfully related requires further study.

Further, as we demonstrated in Sect. 6.4, we found inconsistencies between the post-hoc and real-time data for individual participants, which suggests that this potential multidimensionality of a combined methodology is not straightforward. It does suggest, however, an intriguing direction for future study, investigating why we think one thing in the moment and another afterwards, and what this means about the way we perceive time-based events.

8 Conclusion: Implications for HCI

This paper presented a combined methodology of real-time and post-hoc data collection for audience studies. We presented Metrix, a mobile phone-based real-time data collection system, that features an easy-to-understand UI and anonymised user ID generation that allows individual real-time responses to be linked to post-hoc surveys. We present this method in the context of digital musical instrument (DMI) performance, but it is applicable to any HCI context involving audiences or spectators.

We view this examination of EEM performance using DMIs through the lens of third-wave HCI, as in both the relationship between humans and technology is often subjective, ambiguous or culturally-dependent. We found that, in the real-time data, the rankings of performances in this study is not is not reflected in the frequency of "enjoyment" or "error" indications in real time, and that a lot of "error" events does not mean a performance was not enjoyed. Furthermore, we find that individual audience members are not always consistent between real-time and post-hoc responses, and suggest that more study is needed to examine why this is the case. We also find that neither set of results is predictive of the other. Finally, we reflect on real-time and post-hoc data providing different insights and how these may be related to provide more powerful insights into audience perception.

Because each data collection technique provides a dimension that the other cannot, future HCI studies within and beyond the arts domain may benefit greatly from a combined approach, but further study is needed to determine how to most effectively understand and combine them to provide multi-dimensional insights that cannot be gained by the use of one technique alone.

Acknowledgments. We extend our warm thanks to Dianne Verdonk, Tim Exile, and our enthusiastic audience for their gracious participation. This work is funded by the Engineering and Physical Sciences Research Council (EPSRC) through the Media and Arts Technology Programme, a Research Councils UK Centre for Doctoral Training (EP/G03723X/1).

References

1. Agarwal, A., Meyer, A.: Beyond usability: evaluating emotional response as an integral part of the user experience. In: CHI Extended Abstracts on Human Factors in Computing Systems (2009)

2. Bin, S.A., Bryan-Kinns, N., McPherson, A.P.: Skip the pre-concert demo: how technical familiarity and musical style affect audience response. In: Proceedings of NIME (2016)
3. Barbosa, J., Calegario, F., Teichrieb, V., Ramalho, G., McGlynn, P.: Considering audience's view towards an evaluation methodology for digital musical instruments. In: Proceedings of NIME (2012)
4. Barkhuus, L., Jørgensen, T.: Engaging the crowd: studies of audience-performer interaction. ACM (2008)
5. Berthaut, F., Marshall, M., Subramanian, S., Hachet, M.: Rouages: revealing the mechanisms of digital musical instruments to the audience. In: Proceedings of NIME (2013)
6. Bilda, Z.: Evaluating audience experience. Creativity and cognition studios (2006)
7. Bødker, S.: When second wave HCI meets third wave challenges. In: Proceedings of the 4th Nordic Conference on Human-Computer Interaction (2006)
8. Bongers, B., Mery, A.: Interactive kaleidoscope: audience participation study. In: Proceedings of the 23rd Australian Computer-Human Interaction Conference (2011)
9. Bull, P., Noordhuizen, M.: The mistiming of applause in political speeches. J. Lang. Soc. Psychol. **19**(3), 275–294 (2000)
10. Dahl, L., Wang, G.: Sound bounce: physical metaphors in designing mobile music performance. In: Proceedings of NIME (2010)
11. Desmet, P.: Measuring emotion: development and application of an instrument to measure emotional responses to products. In: Blythe, M.A., Overbeeke, K., Monk, A.F., Wright, P.C. (eds.) Funology. Human-Computer Interaction Series, vol. 3, pp. 111–123. Springer, Dordrecht (2005)
12. Fels, S., Gadd, A., Mulder, A.: Mapping transparency through metaphor: towards more expressive musical instruments. Organ. Sound **7**(2), 109–126 (2002)
13. Fyans, A.C., Gurevich, M., Stapleton, P.: Where did it all go wrong? A model of error from the spectator's perspective. In: Proceedings of NIME (2009)
14. Fyans, A.C., Gurevich, M., Stapleton, P.: Spectator understanding of error in performance. In: CHI 2009 Extended Abstracts (2009)
15. Fyans, A.C., Gurevich, M., Stapleton, P.: Examining the spectator experience. In: Proceedings of NIME (2010)
16. Fyans, A.C., Gurevich, M.: Perceptions of skill in performances with acoustic and electronic instruments. In: Proceedings of NIME (2011)
17. Gaver, W.W., Beaver, J., Benford, S.: Ambiguity as a resource for design. In: Proceedings of the SIGCHI Conference on Human Factors in Computing Systems (2003)
18. Gluck, M.: Toward a historical definition of modernism: Georg Lukacs and the Avant-Garde. J. Mod. Hist. **58**(4), 845–882 (1986)
19. Gurevich, M., Stapleton, P., Bennett, P.: Designing for style in new musical interactions. In: Proceedings of NIME (2009)
20. Gurevich, M., Fyans, A.C.: Digital musical interactions: performer-system relationships and their perception by spectators. Organ. Sound **16**(2), 166–175 (2011)
21. Höök, K., Sengers, P., Andersson, G.: Sense and sensibility: evaluation and interactive art. In: Proceedings of the SIGCHI Conference on Human Factors in Computing Systems (2003)
22. Kruse-Weber, S., Parncutt, R.: Error management for musicians: an interdisciplinary conceptual framework. Front. Psychol. **5**, 777 (2014)
23. Lai, C., Boverman, T.: Audience experience in sound performance. In: Proceedings of NIME (2013)

24. Latulipe, C., Carroll, E.A., Lottridge, D.: Love, hate, arousal and engagement: exploring audience responses to performing arts. In: Proceedings of the SIGCHI Conference on Human Factors in Computing Systems (2011)
25. Loftus, E.F., Palmer, J.C.: Reconstruction of automobile destruction: an example of the interaction between language and memory. J. Verbal Learn. Verbal Behav. **13**, 585–589 (1974)
26. Millard, W.J.: A history of handsets for direct measurement of audience response. Int. J. Public Opin. Res. **4**, 1–17 (1992)
27. Norman, D.A.: The Design of Everyday Things. MIT Press, Cambridge (2013)
28. Perrotin, O., d'Alessandro, C.: Visualizing gestures in the control of a digital musical instrument. In: Proceedings of NIME (2014)
29. Poole, A., Ball, L.J.: Eye tracking in HCI and usability research. Encycl. Hum. Comput. Interact. **1**, 211–219 (2006)
30. Reeves, S., Benford, S., O'Malley, C., Fraser, M.: Designing the spectator experience. In: Proceedings of the SIGCHI Conference on Human Factors in Computing Systems (2005)
31. Russolo, L.: The art of noises: futurist manifesto. In: Audio Culture: Readings in Modern Music. Continuum International New York (2010)
32. Sengers, P., Gaver, W.W.: Staying open to interpretation: engaging multiple meanings in design and evaluation. In: Proceedings of DIS (2006)
33. Sheridan, J.G., Bryan-Kinns, N.: Designing for performative tangible interaction. Int. J. Arts Technol. **1**, 288–308 (2008)
34. Stevens, C., Glass, R., Schubert, E., Chen, J.: Methods for measuring audience reactions. In: Proceedings of the Inaugural International Conference on Music Communication Science (2007)
35. Stevens, C.J., Schubert, E., Morris, R.H., Frear, M.: Cognition and the temporal arts: investigating audience response to dance using PDAs that record continuous data during live performance. Int. J. Hum. Comput. Stud. **67**, 800–813 (2009)
36. Verdonk, D.: Visible excitation methods: energy and expressiveness in electronic music performance. In: Proceedings of NIME (2015)
37. Wen-Chung, C.: Open rather than bounded. Perspect. New Music **5**(1), 1–6 (1966)
38. Wright, P., Blythe, M., McCarthy, J.: User experience and the idea of design in HCI. In: Gilroy, S.W., Harrison, M.D. (eds.) DSV-IS 2005. LNCS, vol. 3941, pp. 1–14. Springer, Heidelberg (2006). doi:10.1007/11752707_1

Piano Staircase: Exploring Movement-Based Meaning Making in Interacting with Ambient Media

Liang Tan[1,2(✉)] and Kenny K.N. Chow[1]

[1] School of Design, The Hong Kong Polytechnic University,
Hung Hom, Hong Kong, China
liang.tan@connect.polyu.hk, sdknchow@polyu.edu.hk
[2] Guangzhou Academy of Fine Arts, Guangzhou, China
digitalidea@163.com

Abstract. While embodiment is widely accepted as an important theoretical basis in interaction design and HCI, few studies explore movement-based meaning making in interacting with ambient media. Building on embodied interaction, this paper aims to identify and analyze key characteristics of audience experience and the role of bodily movement in meaningful making through an empirical study. A prototype "Piano Staircase" is built for experience tests and empirical data collection. Experiments with 30 participants have been conducted. The findings show bodily interaction can activate embodied conceptual mapping and facilitate meaningful audience experience. The model of embodied meaning making provides possibilities for analyzing meaningful experience with ambient media.

Keywords: Embodied interaction · Audience experience · Ambient media · Bodily movement · Embodied metaphor

1 Introduction

Digital computing has been pervasively penetrating into people's everyday life. Growing research suggests that the vision of interaction design should extend from digital artifacts to everyday environments where interactive technologies are embedded and hence support embodied interaction [14, 16, 18]. Ambient media, as a novel media form, incorporate interactive technology into physical spaces, which creates various affordances for engaging audience in bodily and social interactions. While many studies have focused on designing for task-oriented interactions, few studies have centered on meaning making in interaction with ambient media. "Ambient" has its phenomenological essence grounded in embodiment, and embodied interactions are anchored in human' intrinsic familiarity with "ambiently embodied interfaces" [18]. The relationship between ambient media and embodiment reflects a loop of intentional arc, where perception and action are tightly interconnected with together. This study is to address the following questions: What major factors can be identified in audience experience? How do bodily movements facilitate embodied metaphorical thinking and

R. Bernhaupt et al. (Eds.): INTERACT 2017, Part I, LNCS 10513, pp. 282–291, 2017.
DOI: 10.1007/978-3-319-67744-6_19

imagination? We introduce a high-fidelity prototype for experimental study. Qualitative data is collected through observation and semi-structured interviews. We summarize qualitative results of participants' primary experience in terms of six themes. A model of movement-based meaning making is developed to illustrate the cognitive processing of embodied conceptual mapping and schema-based imagination.

2 Research Background

In this section, we briefly examine three main concepts as the theoretical basis, and related studies are also reviewed.

Embodied cognition emphasizes that human body's state plays a central role in shaping cognition [1, 12], languages [13, 15, 17], understanding digital media [7], and dancer's emotion [8]. This is against traditional Cartesian dualism about separation of mind-body which overlook the influence of bodily experience on perception and reasoning. Human language and imagination are rooted in bodily experience and constrained by a range of embodied schemas, which is formed from people's recurring physical interactions with environments [15]. Embodied metaphors are the concrete extensions of a schema. When talking about abstract concepts, people usually use some expressions linked to bodily interactions to represent abstract concepts. People who did bodily actions corresponding to the metaphors can better understand verbal phrases than those performing actions not relevant to the metaphors and those not performing any actions [22]. Clay et al. [8] investigated emotional expression of movement-based improvisations by using augmented technology, which scientifically shows that dancer's bodily movements directly affect emotion and expression.

Dourish [10] coined embodied interaction to illustrate meaning-making as a process of physical and social interactions. The interaction between human and machine is embedded in a composition of both physical habits and social (cultural) experience, and embodied experience is created from direct and situated engagement with living environments. Antle et al. [3] believe that people's early bodily experiences (e.g., keeping balance on ground) help to form the BALANCE schema which can be applied to understand more abstract ideas (e.g., He balances his emotion). The embodied metaphors refer to those of conceptual metaphors rooted in an embodied schema arising from everyday repeated bodily interactions [2, 4]. The projection between source domain and target domain constructs an embodied conceptual mapping. Empirical studies partly prove that the meaning expression of product is also structured by embodied schemas, and user experience with products is highly related to bodily experience [21]. Building upon embodied interaction, the previous studies have explored the relationship between bodily engagement with ambient media and four experiential qualities [19, 20].

Distinctively differing from traditional media, ambient media are embedded in public spaces where people are more likely to be immersed in it with intuitive actions [14, 19]. There are three main attributes of ambient media: The novel physical forms (Spatiality) of ambient media attract attention of audience and provide affordances for bodily actions. The audience may experience unexpected feedbacks (Unexpectedness) when being engaged in interactions with ambient media (Engagement). Audience experience is an active process of engagement where the perceptual, emotional, kinesthetic, and cognitive responses are derived from interactions [5, 6, 20].

3 Research Design and Methods

To investigate the impacts of bodily movements on audience's metaphorical thinking and imagination, a high-fidelity prototype called Piano Staircase was developed to enable participants to freely perform different actions with auditory feedbacks. The goal of conducting audience experience test is to gather empirical data for understanding the role of bodily movements in audience experience.

3.1 Design Criteria and Experience Prototyping

The criteria of prototyping are aimed to match the three attributes of ambient media. Firstly, in order to transform physical space into interaction interface, the prototype is proposed to be physically and socially situated in a public space rather than a controlled laboratory. The second criterion is to attract audience's attention by evoking a surprising response, which is a neutral psychological status giving rise to emotional experience. Thirdly, ambient media should engage audience's bodily actions by creating affordances that can potentially solicit interactions. Inspired by "Piano Stairs" [9], we utilized the staircase in a public space of a university building to set up the prototype "Piano Staircase" (PS) (Fig. 1). Aligned with design criteria, the prototype was developed like a real piano, and each stair corresponded to a certain musical note.

Fig. 1. Piano staircase (based on the DDB's work [9]).

3.2 Participants and Procedure

We invited 30 participants (13 males and 17 females) to participate in the experience tests. Their ages ranged from 18 to 35. Twenty-two were locals of Hong Kong, seven Mainland Chinese, one Indian. Most participants were recruited from a university in Hong Kong except for three passers randomly invited at site. Firstly, participants were informed that they can feel free to experience a physical space, and they can choose to quit the test at any time. A consent form was signed by them (informing them video recording would be used). Then, participants can freely move on the staircase, and their behaviors were videotaped by a hidden camera, aiming to reduce distracting their attention. Each participant interacted with the work for 3–6 min, and the duration depended on their own intention. After the interaction session, the participant immediately joined a face-to-face interview. Semi-structured interview questions were prepared to motivate participants to express their feelings and thinking. The recorded video was played during the interview to help them recall their experience. The dialogues between researchers and participants were recorded as audio files for further analysis.

3.3 Data Analysis

This study mainly analyzed the verbal reports about first-person experience, while video data served as evidence for observational behaviors. We conducted thematic analysis to identify themes related to embodied experience. Interview audios were transcribed as text files. After that we used HyperResearch to do coding by following bottom-up and top-down approaches [11]. Regarding the research questions, the researchers viewed the transcripts, made notes and marked key words to look for potential patterns. Then, the words or sentences related to the prior codes (with round dots in Fig. 2) were firstly highlighted in the coding book where the meaning of each code was also described (e.g., Engagement: feeling being physically and mentally engaged in interaction with it). Next, inductive codes were generated from verbal data rather than the prior template. These codes were updated with the coding progress. When a new code was defined, the researchers went back to check the previous transcripts for coding for possible segments. Finally, the segments labeled with same code were compared and across all cases for some refinements, and all codes were rechecked and organized.

4   Results

The coding scheme consists of six themes highlighted in bold (Fig. 2). Twenty codes were identified and defined for further analyzing participants' embodied experience and engagement patterns.

Theme 1: Ambient media	Evaluation
Affordance	Desire for exploration
Engagement ●	Imagination
Social interaction	Recall
Spatiality ●	**Theme 4: Embodied metaphorical mapping**
Unexpectedness ●	Conceptual mapping ●
Theme 2: Bodily experience	Visual mapping ●
Bodily movement	**Theme 5: Emotional experience**
Forceful feedback ●	Emotional response ●
Posture	**Theme 6: Perceptual experience ●**
Theme 3: Cognitive experience ●	Kinesthetic sense
Anticipation	Auditory sense
Attention	Visual sense

Fig. 2. Themes and codes.

We summarized results in terms of the six themes as follows.

- **Perceptual Experience and Bodily Experience**

All participants started to experience the Piano Staircase (PS) with their perceptual responses. Many participants got their initial impression through visual and auditory perceptions. All participants noticed the features of music changing during the interaction process, such as pitch, rhythm, duration and continuity.

Although the interview questions did not directly ask participants to talk about their bodily movements, all participants described their bodily experience related to various actions, speed, force. The most frequent code is "Bodily Movement" with 75 times (Mean frequency is 2.5 per case). Many participants tried different actions (e.g., stride, jump, stamp) rather then just stepping. Five participants skipped over one or two stair (s) by taking a long stride. Some participants stayed on the staircase for a while or keep in a posture, such as opening arms for balance and keeping in a posture like standing.

- **Embodied Metaphor and Cognitive Experience**

The descriptions of participants reflected different embodied mappings between metaphorical concepts and physical movements. For example, after a period of adapting to the work (walking up and down), most of the participants had a mapping between musical pitches and levels of stairs. P3 said: "After I heard the first sound, I wanted to walked up following the stairs. Then I also found it had a pattern like a spectrum of notes of keyboard." Four participants (P4, P11, P16, P28) described that they experienced the changes of tempos when walking at different speeds. Some participants experienced a sense of force when walking in different directions. The mentioned words include "heavy", "intense", "relaxed", "unconstrained", "light", "subside".

The theme of cognitive experience includes six codes: Attention, Evaluation, Anticipation, Desire for exploration, Recall, and Imagination. *Evaluation*: Participants constantly evaluated the interactive experience at different moments. Four participants mentioned that the distance between two stairs (e.g., the first and the fourth) were too far, and they can not reach it through stretching legs to generate a tune or chord. *Anticipation*: Some participants, who declared they had some piano performance skill, had an intention to play a composition. Apart from playing compositions, two participants (P8, P9) intended to stepping on all the stairs and to see the musical effects. *Imagination*: When being asked about what brands could be associated with PS and their imaginations on the current experience, many participants mentioned physical exercises and sports brands. Two participants (P11, P29) mentioned specific brands about scooter and sneaker. Three participants (P8, P23, P28) also related it to raising awareness of health.

- **Emotional Experience and Ambient Media**

Most of the participants described the overall experience was positive (interesting, happy, fun, exciting). For example, P1 said: "It was very interesting and funny, and I think it can bring romantic feeling to me." Three participants felt that the higher pitches made them more excited. In contrast, two participants described their feeling gradually became deep and heavy when walking down. P9 intended to walk down fast to experience the feeling of fast tempo which made her pleased.

The qualitative data also reflected three attributes of ambient media as mentioned in Sect. 2. *Spatiality*: Some participants had a sense of public space. They recalled environments they had experienced before. For example, P6 mentioned a hotel hall where she heard the music of piano played by someone walking on the stairs in the hotel. In addition, many participants noticed the physical spatial features. Four participants mentioned the spatial relation of stairs. P3 described: "It became a dynamic thing from a flat surface. I noticed the pitch went up with the height of the stairs." *Unexpectedness*: Unexpectedness occurred not only in the beginning but also in the whole process of interaction. Many participants felt surprised to hear the musical sounds when first stepping on. For example, P1 said: "After I stepped on it for the first time, I was really surprised by the sound." Some participants did not feel much unexpectedness in the beginning, but they described various unexpected feedbacks when shifting different movements. *Engagement*: Many participants mentioned how their perceptions and bodily states affected their future intentions, and their cognitive states also determined further actions. For example, a participant (P19) mentioned he wanted to made the sound last longer and stayed on a stair for a while. P4 mentioned she move her whole body to produce music, and energy was engaged with it.

5 Discussion and the Model of Embodied Meaning Making

The results indicate that bodily movements are tightly correlated to embodied conceptual mappings and cognitive experience. In this section, we focus on further discussing the relationships between bodily experience, embodied conceptual mapping, and imagination, and other related studies are compared. Based on these analyses, we aim to develop a model of embodied meaning making, which provides a useful guidance for characterizing and designing experience with ambient media.

5.1 Embodied Conceptual Mapping

Embodied conceptual mapping can be activated by the audience's immediate bodily movements. The embodied metaphor projects a concept of source domain (embodied schema-based) onto a concept of target domain (abstract) [2, 17, 21]. A range of conceptual mappings (Table 1) are closely tied to bodily states. The bodily movements (e.g., walking upward or downward) speed up a projection from bodily experience to the abstract and intangible concepts (pitch, tempo, flow, and force). Different from the purely cognitive mapping in linguistics and cognitive science, the conceptual metaphor in the interaction with ambient media maps the features of primary bodily experience (source domain) onto the abstract concept (target domain). The embodied interaction studies [2, 3] asked participants to finish a series of structured tasks, and the metaphorical concepts were prepared in advance. Compared with these procedures, our study does not have a structured task, as the metaphorical concepts were directly generated from lively bodily interactions with PS. We propose embodied interaction with ambient media is a process of meaning-making rather than mere meaning-understanding.

Table 1. Embodied conceptual mappings.

Movement	Metaphorical concepts	Embodied conceptual mappings
Spatial level	Pitch (high, low)	High level - High pitch Low level - Low pitch
Speed	Tempo (fast, slow)	Fast movement - Fast tempo Slow movement - Slow tempo
Speed	Flow (fluent, unsmooth)	Fast movement - Fluent Slow movement - Unsmooth
Orientation	Force intensity (heavy - light)	Up - Heavy (Intense) Down - Light (Relaxed)

5.2   Force-Related Schemas

The empirical findings support the theory of embodied schema-based product expressions [14, 21, 22]. The quantitative study [21] partly proved that the understanding of visual expression of products is rooted in embodied schemas which are based on a series of spatial relations (e.g., In-Out, Front-Back). Johnson [15] also examine those gestalts which embodies more internal structures of forceful interaction. Seven force-related schemas (e.g., Compulsion, Attraction) are demonstrated to play an important role in constructing meaning. The mappings of flow and force intensity are less structured by spatial relations rather closely tied to forceful experience. The first two mappings (Table 1) are based on the same schema SCALE (quantitative or qualitative level), as High-Low and Fast-Slow are more about a cumulative character and dependent on the spatial relations. However, in the other two mappings, many force-related words (heavy, intense, relaxed, light) are tightly related to forceful interaction and kinesthetic experience. The mapping from bodily movements to fluency is extended from the Gravitation which is defined as an experiential structure that the body is physically dragged toward the earth. Especially, one participant described her kinesthetic feeling about fluent moving of a waterfall, which is a typical Gravitation-based mapping. The mapping of bodily movements and force intensity is structured by Removal of restraint that is exerting a force to remove a barrier and the barrier is removed (light or relaxed). These mappings are in line with several qualities of force gestalts: vector, path of motion, degrees of force intensity. Force-related schemas are overlooked by the research on embodied interaction, and further exploration is needed.

5.3   Embodied Schema-Based Imagination

The embodied conceptual mapping not only elicits immediate concept generating and understanding, but also triggers further cognitive processing such as imagination and recall. Participants associated the experience with different objects (e.g., ladder) or environments (e.g., cathedral). These elicited imaginations also can be summarized as two types: orientation-related and force-related. One participants imagined being a cathedral, which maps her feeling of upward movement onto a holy imagery and forms a metaphorical concept (abstract) "Holy is up". This abstract concept then is mapped onto an imagined cathedral (concrete). This mapping of imagination is typically organized by a orientational or vertical relation. The second type of imaginations is tied to the participant's forceful bodily experience with PS. The mentioned tangible objects and environments include sneaker, waterfall, house-jumping, and jewelry, these are related to the force-related movements. The imagination of sports products results from the past kinesthetic experience, in which immediate bodily experience is linked to an image structure. The other three mappings also arise from the forceful experience: Blockage: The mapping of stamping on the stairs and a jewel dropping to a metal plate; Gravitation: The mapping of fast walking down and waterfall; Enablement: The mapping of bodily movements and game house-jumping.

Based on the discussion and related studies [3, 21, 22], we develop a model (Fig. 3) to demonstrate the process of bodily movement-based meaning making. Past long term perceptual and motor experience form various mental patterns (spatial and forceful relations) that can be extended to construct different meanings (Line 1). Bodily interactions can activate the conceptual mapping from immediate bodily experience onto an abstract concept (Line 2), which results in an embodied metaphor structured by an embodied schema (Line 3). Embodied metaphors also further imaginations related to imagined environments, brands, and objects (Line 4). Embodied metaphor and embodied imagination are both elicited by bodily movements (Line 5) and structured by embodied schema (Line 6). They share similar mapping process, but normally embodied metaphor is a mapping from a concrete physical experience (action and perception) to an abstract experiential concept, and embodied imagination sometimes maps an abstract concept onto an imagined concrete environment or object (e.g., holy - cathedral, fluent - waterfall). This model provides a useful guidance for understanding and designing meaningful experience with ambient media.

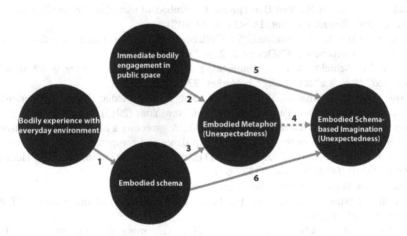

Fig. 3. The model of embodied meaning making.

6 Conclusion

We identified the main factors of experience with ambient media through experimental data collection and thematic analysis, and discussed embodied meaning making by analyzing the relationships between bodily experience, conceptual mapping, and imagination. This study provides empirical evidence that bodily action is not only an input behavior for triggering interaction but also a major source of embodied conceptual mappings and facilitating meaningful experience. The findings extend previous studies on embodied interaction: Meaning making and imaginative activities in interaction with ambient media are not only structured by pervasive embodied schemas but also tied to immediate bodily states. The model of embodied meaning making provides a useful guidance for characterizing and designing experience with ambient media. The future work will explore how this model of embodied meaning making can benefit designing ambient media with regard to meaningful engagement. Relevant design principles can be revealed to support design practice through further empirical studies.

References

1. Anderson, M.L.: Embodied cognition: a field guide. Artif. Intell. **149**, 91–130 (2003)
2. Antle, A.N., Corness, G., Bakker, S., Droumeva, M., van den Hoven, E., Bevans, A.: Designing to support reasoned imagination through embodied metaphor. In: Proceedings of the Seventh ACM Conference on Creativity and Cognition, pp. 275–284. ACM (2009)
3. Antle, A.N., Corness, G., Bevans, A.: Springboard: designing image schema based embodied interaction for an abstract domain. In: Karat, J., Vanderdonckt, J. (eds.) Whole Body Interaction. HCIS, pp. 7–18. Springer, London (2011). doi:10.1007/978-0-85729-433-3_2
4. Bakker, S., Antle, A.N., Van Den Hoven, E.: Embodied metaphors in tangible interaction design. Pers. Ubiquit. Comput. **16**, 433–449 (2012)
5. Bilda, Z., Costello, B., Amitani, S.: Collaborative analysis framework for evaluating interactive art experience. CoDesign **2**, 225–238 (2006)
6. Brakus, J.J., Schmitt, B.H., Zarantonello, L.: Brand experience: what is it? How is it measured? Does it affect loyalty? J. Market. **73**, 52–68 (2009)
7. Chow, K.K.N.: Animation, Embodiment, and Digital Media: Human Experience of Technological Liveliness. Palgrave Macmillan, New York (2013)
8. Clay, A., Delord, E., Couture, N., Domenger, G.: Augmenting a ballet dance show using the dancer's emotion: conducting joint research in dance and computer science. In: Huang, F., Wang, R.-C. (eds.) ArtsIT 2009. LNICSSITE, vol. 30, pp. 148–156. Springer, Heidelberg (2010). doi:10.1007/978-3-642-11577-6_19
9. Volkswagen. http://www.thefuntheory.com
10. Dourish, P.: Where the Action Is: The Foundations of Embodied Interaction. MIT Press, Cambridge, Mass (2001)
11. Fereday, J., Muir-Cochrane, E.: Demonstrating rigor using thematic analysis: a hybrid approach of inductive and deductive coding and theme development. Int. J. Qual. Methods **5**, 1–11 (2006)
12. Gallagher, S.: How the Body Shapes the Mind. Oxford University Press, Oxford (2005)
13. Gibbs, R.W.: Embodiment and Cognitive Science. Cambridge University Press, New York (2006)

14. Hespanhol, L., Tomitsch, M.: Strategies for intuitive interaction in public urban spaces. Interact. Comput. **27**, 311–326 (2015)
15. Johnson, M.: The body in the Mind: The Bodily Basis of Meaning, Imagination, and Reason. University of Chicago Press, Chicago (1987)
16. Kaptelinin, V., Bannon, L.: Interaction design beyond the product: creating technology-enhanced activity spaces. Hum.-Comput. Interact. **27**, 277–309 (2012)
17. Lakoff, G., Johnson, M.: Metaphors We Live By. University of Chicago Press, Chicago (1980)
18. McCullough, M.: Digital Ground: Architecture, Pervasive Computing, and Environmental Knowing. MIT Press, Cambridge (2004)
19. Tan, L., Chow, K.K.N.: An embodied interaction framework for facilitating audience experience with ambient media. In: Fourth International Conference on Design Creativity (4th ICDC), pp. 1–8. The Design Society (2016)
20. Tan, L., Chow, K.K.N.: Facilitating meaningful experience with ambient media: an embodied engagement model. In: Chinese CHI 2017, pp. 36–46. ACM (2017)
21. Van Rompay, T., Hekkert, P., Saakes, D., Russo, B.: Grounding abstract object characteristics in embodied interactions. Acta Physiol. (Oxf) **119**, 315–351 (2005)
22. Wilson, N.L., Gibbs, R.W.: Real and imagined body movement primes metaphor comprehension. Cogn. Sci. **31**, 721–731 (2007)

Co-design Studies

A Co-design Study of Digital Service Ideas in the Bus Context

Elina Hildén[✉], Jarno Ojala, and Kaisa Väänänen

Tampere University of Technology, Tampere, Finland
{elina.hilden,kaisa.vaananen}@tut.fi,
jarno.ojala@vincit.com

Abstract. To enhance the desirability of public transportation, it is important to design for positive travel experience. The context of bus transportation has broad potential for utilization of novel, supplementary digital services beyond travel information. The aim of our research was to study bus passengers' needs and expectations for future digital services and to develop initial service concept ideas through co-design. To this end, three Idea generating workshops with 24 participants were arranged. Our findings reveal six service themes that can be used as a basis of designing future digital traveling services: (1) Information at a glance while traveling, (2) Entertainment and entertaining activities, (3) Services that support social interaction, (4) Multiple channels to provide travel information, (5) Extra services for better travel experience, and (6) Services that people already expect to have. The themes are discussed and further elaborated in this paper.

Keywords: Bus · Public transportation · Digital services · User needs · Co-design

1 Introduction

In recent years, urban mobility has been considered as one of the most significant societal challenges for the future as the need for transportation will raise, resulting increase in emissions, noise and infrastructures [25, 28]. As cities, worldwide are forced to reduce emissions by, e.g. trying to reduce the usage of private cars, the role of public transportation and the related services are becoming a central design issue. As policy makers seek to encourage and support the widespread use of public transportation, its services need to be developed so that it is seen as a more desirable option for the wide audience [7, 9]. This can be achieved by understanding the passenger's travel behavior and the multifaceted issue of trip satisfaction [24]. To this end, individuals' travel behaviors have been targeted with informational education campaigns in order to raise awareness and change attitudes [23].

For the public transportation to gain larger popularity, the transport providers and planners should also consider the individuals' needs and expectations regarding short distance traveling activities and thus design for better travel experiences [2]. Enhancing the attractiveness of public transportation can happen, for example, through experience-driven design [16]. The importance of user experience for customer

R. Bernhaupt et al. (Eds.): INTERACT 2017, Part I, LNCS 10513, pp. 295–312, 2017.
DOI: 10.1007/978-3-319-67744-6_20

satisfaction and loyalty have already been recognized by several organizations in different fields [29]. The context of public transportation has broad potential for the application of digital services and other supplementary services that can add value to the passengers' travel experience [2].

The goal of our research is to investigate how people experience the short distance bus transportation and what kind of digital traveling services would enhance their travel experience. By traveling services, we mean digital services that can support or enrich the bus ride and the associated activities before and after it. This study is a part of a larger research project called Living Lab Bus, in which one of the aims is to develop a platform for interactive services for electric buses. However, the service ideas developed in this study are not specific for electric buses only, and most of them can also be utilized in traditional buses.

This study aims to gain design-relevant insights on to how public transportation services should be developed in order to better serve the travelers' needs and expectations, and thus to improve the travel experience of buses. To gain deep understanding of the user perspective, the present study took a participatory approach. The research question is: *What kind of services support the passengers' needs and expectations in the bus context?*

We address the research question by gathering user needs and expectations by ideating with the potential users, novel digital services that could enhance their travel experience. New service concept ideation can be seen as an initial phase of co-design process, and thus the workshops were organized with a strong focus on participatory ideation activities. To this end, we conducted a series of three Idea generating workshops with altogether 24 participants. We applied a context-specific workshopping method to study situated activities in a specific environment, i.e. the bus. This paper contributes to the understanding of short distance bus travel experience from the perspective of user experience of digital services. The results of this paper contribute to the design knowledge of the future digital services for the bus context. This knowledge can be used as a basis for human-centered design for different categories of services that can enhance the desirability of bus transportation.

2 Related Work

We present related work on travel experience and how supplementary digital services can enhance the users' experience of bus transportation.

2.1 Travel Experience

Public transportation is a unique representation of urban space where individuals come together with diverse socio-economic backgrounds at regular frequencies for extended periods of time [8]. Public transportation plays an important role in the way people move around in their everyday life [6]. Travel experience in the context of public transportation is a result of the holistic view of the transportation service [2], including the different experience components: the customer's affective, cognitive, physical and social responses to the service [26].

Several studies [e.g. 9, 19], have found that public transportation users are generally the least satisfied compared to other modes of transportation, such as private car drivers and cyclists. Within different public transportation modes, the bus users were least satisfied [18]. The reasons for the low satisfaction rate is impacted by the attributes such as the transport mode's flexibility, "fun" factor and how well the mode matches with the traveler's lifestyle [4]. However, a qualitative interview study conducted by Hildén et al. [10] found that participants were generally pleased with the current travel experiences with the local busses in two major cities in Finland – Helsinki and Tampere. The study examined the trip satisfaction by comparing the experience of the local public transportation services to the participants' previous experiences of public transportation internationally.

The satisfaction rates of public transportation systems vary locally, and the reasons for that can be drawn from multiple factors. External factors such as the timetables, state of the vehicles, safety and the accessibility of public transportation have a strong impact on the satisfaction rates. A pyramid of customer needs formed by van Hagen and Bron [26] represents the train passengers needs and experiences in five levels (from bottom to top): trust, travel time door to door, mental effort, physical effort, and emotions. The model was used in the Netherlands Railways in shifting the focus of measure from efficiency to customer experience.

Passengers' traveling behavior, and thus also the experience of traveling, is changing simultaneously with the mix of transport modes and the offered services in them [25]. Furthermore, St-Louis et al. [24] state that trip satisfaction is affected not only by external trip factors but also internal factors. They state that travel behavior is influenced by spatial, socio-economic and personality components [24]. Foth et al. [7] have investigated the travel experience from three aspects of the journey – before, during and after the trip. This division can be drawn from the user experience design, where the experiences can be divided into different categories based to the stages of the product, service or system usage [21]. Even though user experience happens during the interaction with a product, service or a system – and thus has a beginning and end – there are still indirect experiences before the first encounter as well as after the usage [21].

2.2 Supplementary Services for Better Travel Experience

Passengers in a vehicle are the ideal candidates to be entertained and informed about aspects related to the journey as well as e.g. the social aspects of the travel, such as the people sitting next to them [7]. When conducting short distance journeys passengers have great potential to interact with mobile services, unless they are traveling with a companion [7]. Hence, the context of public transportation has broad potential for the application of digital services such as location-based services through the use of, for example, travelers' mobile devices [8].

Dziekan and Kottenhoff [4] have studied the impact of real-time information displays on public transportation. They state that real-time travel information increases the feeling of security, decreases the feeling of uncertainty, and makes the traveling easier, since it saves passengers' effort when making a journey. Providing real-time travel information results more efficient traveling when passengers' can plan their journeys leading to shorter traveling times [4]. It also leads to utilization of wait time when passengers' can use the time to carrying out tasks, such as shopping [4]. It also results other adjusting strategies, for example enhancing the comfort of the journey by choosing to wait for the next bus when the arriving bus is being crowded [4].

Maclean and Dailey studied real-time bus information on mobile devices already in 2001 [15]. Later studies by Watkins et al. [27] and Ferris et al. [6] have studied the enhanced usability of public transportation by providing good traveller information systems to passengers. Both papers study a transportation information toolset *OneBusAway*. OneBusAway is designed to decrease the passengers' feeling of uncertainty of public transportation by providing real-time information for bus riders in the area of Seattle [6]. Tools that provide real-time arrival information to bus passengers improve the usability of public transportation and thus increase the passengers' travel experience.

Developing the efficiency of traveling does not always increase the passengers' travel experience. The access to real-time information of bus is just "a necessary first step which other ideas can build on and add further value" [7]. To enhance the travel experience Foth et al. [7] suggest that the systems of real-time passenger information could rather focus on how the different journey options can be planned, assessed, and distinguished on the aspects of fun instead of efficiency.

Foth et al. [7] studied the micro activities performed by passengers during commute and their impact to the bus travel experience. These micro activities include activities of social, entertainment, observational, travel, and routine. Similar studies have also been conducted showing that people spend their time at, for instance bus stops and onboard buses listening to music and using social media applications in addition to reading newspapers and books or simply relaxing [e.g. 5, 14]. Until today, it has been mostly left to the passengers to entertain themselves [7].

Enhancing the attractiveness of public transportation can happen for example through experience-driven design [16]. Experience-driven design takes selected experiences as design targets to inspire and guide design [1, 17]. By familiarizing oneself with the passengers' needs and current activities in the vehicle, new mobile and supplementary services can be developed that have the potential of adding value to the passengers' travel experience [2]. No longer is transportation only about moving from an origin to a destination but it is a way for the users to encounter different service channels; such as off-board services (services that are used outside of the vehicle), on-board entertainment or information before, during or after the bus trip [3]. Carreira et al. found that "Passengers also looked for other services, usually based on new technologies that could enhance their experience during the overall trip" [3]. To be able to understand the demand in different travel settings, the service providers need to familiarize themselves with the travel experience and its forming factors [20].

3   The Study with Co-design Workshops

This study aimed to gather design-relevant insights to how public transportation services should be developed in order to better serve the passengers' needs and expectations, and thus to improve their travel experience in buses. The research focuses on gaining insights of the passengers' needs and expectations for digital traveling services, in order to understand how the travel experience could be enhanced by developing the existing services and by adding new, supplementary digital services to the public transportation. This was studied by co-designing service ideas together with frequent bus users and later analyzing the ideas generated in the co-design workshops.

3.1 Method

In order to better understand the bus passengers needs and expectations, and to ideate services, we conducted three co-design workshops. In co-design, users are invited to participate to the design activities together with design professionals in a continuous cooperative process that results in better solutions for daily life [22, 23]. In co-design, users are treated like experts, but since they often have very little experience on innovation it is important to provide materials that support the ideation activities [22]. The co-design materials, such as workshop tools can provide different entry points to the design problem as well as help the participants to build their own design language [13]. These co-design methods suit best for the early phases of the design process, e.g. for idea generation through brainstorming new ideas, or when rethinking existing solutions [13].

Fig. 1. Examples of the context cards: on the left, the card of confidence and feeling of being in control and on the right, the card of luxurious and premium experience.

3.1.1 Stimulus Materials

Findings of a semi-structured interview study [10] with ten international students was carried out in order to gain insights of the current user experience of buses in Finland, as well as of the expectations to the electric bus. The interview findings were used as an input to the workshops in form of Context Cards (see Fig. 1). A set of 15 inspiration cards was designed to help the participants with the ideation of the intangible traveling service ideas. Seven (#1-7) of the cards were derived from the findings of an interview study [10] and seven (#8-14) were chosen with small alteration from the 22 categories of Playful Experience (PLEX) framework. PLEX Cards were developed to communicate the Playful Experiences framework's 22 categories to people who aim at designing for playfulness [12]. PLEX Cards have been used to generate ideas with experience driven approach [12]. The 15th card was added from the Living Lab Bus project agenda. The cards were printed and cut into size 12 × 12 cm. Each card consisted of 3–4 pictures and the card title. The Context Cards consisted of three theme sources:

Context-specific themes

1. Making the ecological values of electric bus visible
2. Informative communication
3. Entertaining activities
4. Atmosphere of relaxation
5. Subtle opportunities for social interaction
6. Luxurious and premium experience
7. Getting to know the personality of the driver

Themes from PLEX categories

8. Confidence and feeling of being in control
9. Fellowship - friendship and communality
10. Opportunity to be creative and express oneself
11. Stimulating senses
12. Exploration and discovery to learn something new
13. Captivation - forgetting one's surroundings
14. Competition - contest with oneself or an opponent

Theme from the [Blinded for review] project agenda

15. Utilizing the sensor data collected by the bus.

3.2   Idea Generating Workshops

This study consisted of a series of three co-design ideation workshops. The workshops took place in Tampere and Espoo (Finland) in the spring of 2016. In Tampere, the public transportation is focused on bus transportation, and the bus lines cover the city well. In Helsinki region – including the city of Espoo, the public transportation is multimodal, which means that the passengers have access to bus, commuter train, tram, metro, and a commuter ferry with one travel card. In both cities, the public transportation could be described as a functioning and well-planned system. Still there is a general need to develop the attractiveness of the public transportation system.

The workshop process and stimulus materials were identical in all three workshops. However, all of the three workshops were organized in a different environment with different levels of contextuality: (1) imagined environment, (2) a stimulated environment and (3) a real environment. These three workshop context types were selected in

Fig. 2. Pictures from each workshop context: imagined environment (picture a), stimulated environment (picture b) and real environment (picture c).

order to study the optimal level of workshop contextuality (results reported in a separated publication). The settings of the workshops were (see Fig. 2):

1. A classroom at a university – *Imagined environment* (Workshop 1, WS1)
2. Technologically advanced lab in a research institute – *Stimulated environment* (Workshop 2, WS2)
3. Moving electric bus, Espoo, Finland – *Real environment* (Workshop 3, WS3)

3.2.1 Workshop Process

The agenda of the workshop sessions consisted of short presentation of the day's agenda, goals for the day and briefs for the tasks. We wanted to provide the participants with electric bus specific inspiration, and thus videos of the unique qualities of electric buses were shown to highlight the silent and smooth ride. An icebreaker exercise served as a starting point for the workshops. The participants were asked to share a good or a bad experience when using public transportation and share this with others. This helped the participants to relax and set to the right mindset.

Five scenarios – situations that could take place in the context of bus transportation – were used to guide the main part of the workshop. Before the ideation we encouraged the participants to ideate wild and creative ideas. At this stage, it was not relevant to think about costs nor the technology available. The task was to come up with service ideas that could enhance their own travel experience in that specific situation. The scenarios were:

1. The bus was few minutes too early and you just missed it. Now you have to wait for the next one.
2. You are in the bus. The route is unfamiliar to you.
3. You are in the bus. The route is familiar to you so you can lay back and relax.
4. You get off at your destination stop after a busy day.
5. You have to change to another bus in a big transportation hub, like Kamppi in Helsinki.

Participants were divided into teams of 2–3 persons (three teams in each workshop, nine in total) for the ideation tasks. 15–20 min was spent for each scenario task after which the groups shared their ideas with others. The participants were asked to choose one to three Context Cards at a time to guide their ideation during the scenario exercises. They were also encouraged to use different cards within and for each scenario to get diverse ideas.

3.2.2 Participants

The workshops had 7–9 participants each. The workshop participants were mainly students and they represented diverse study programmes (e.g. HCI, Bioengineering, Business, Automation Engineering, Art and Design). Most participants of all workshops stated that their main reason for traveling was going to university (12 participants) or to work (4 participants), 12 said that they use public transportation to travel during their free time. Majority of the workshop participants used public transportation frequently: 12 participants stated that they use public transportation at least 4 days a week, and eight participants 2–3 days a week. Only four said that they use it once a week or more rarely. See Table 1 for the participant details.

Table 1. Participants of each workshop.

Attribute	Imagined environment (WS1)	Stimulated environment (WS2)	Real environment (WS3)
Number of participants	8	9	7
Average age (year of birth)	1990	1982	1987
Gender	4 F, 4 M	3 F, 6 M	3 F, 4 M
Participants' nationalities	Bangladesh, India, Iran, Pakistan, Spain, USA, Vietnam	Australia, Bangladesh, China, Finland, India, Russia, Vietnam	China, Finland, India, Indonesia, Russia, Taiwan

3.2.3 Data Collection and Analysis

The sessions were voice recorded and filmed. We transcribed the recordings and the documentation sheets in which the participants documented their ideas. The analysis was done by thematically grouping the ideas bottom up. To draw out common themes from the ideas we used affinity diagramming [11] in the analysis. Building the affinity diagram allowed us to understand the traveling service ideas thematically. As a result the transcriptions were divided to 181 individual traveling service ideas or digital service features. These 181 service ideas were generated in the workshops by different student teams, and thus they included a few same or similar ideas.

4 Findings

The purpose of this study was to gain design-relevant insights for the development of supplementary services for public transportation that can improve the bus travel experience. We wanted to understand the bus users' needs and expectations for such traveling services, and therefore utilized co-design workshops to gather service ideas from the workshop participants. This chapter presents findings – six service themes – that answer our research question: *What kind of services support the passengers' needs and expectations in the bus context?*

The study findings were grouped thematically bottom up into 46 subthemes and finally to six main themes (see Table 2). The traveling service ideas related to each service theme are presented in the following. The main service themes, derived from the ideas generated by the workshop participants were: *Information at a glance while traveling, Entertainment and entertaining activities, Services that support social interaction, Multiple channels to provide travel information, Extra services for better travel experience* and *Services that people already expect to have*. For the subthemes, participants' ideas are presented below in quotes.

Table 2. The found themes and subthemes of digital services for the bus context.

Theme	Subthemes
Information at a glance while traveling	Discovering interesting places in the surroundings
	Discovering interesting events
	Aiding the navigation to the stop of connecting line
	Easy access to journey related information
	Bus showing information outside about the line and destination
	Interactive windows
	Connecting the public screen with the mobile phone
Entertainment and entertaining activities	Active entertainment
	VR, AR windows
	Physical exercise suggestions at bus stops and when in the bus
	Art and visual entertainment
	Passive entertainment
	Bus stop specific entertainment
Services that support social interaction	Sharing social media with other passengers in the bus
	Games for people sitting next to each other
	Silent and loud areas for buses
	Suggesting "bus mates" from other passengers to travel with
	Interactive screens at bus stops to aid with communication
	Writing and sharing stories with fellow passengers

(continued)

Table 2. (*continued*)

Theme	Subthemes
Multiple channels to provide travel information	Real time information of the bus location
	Alerts of the approaching stop
	Info about the next 2-3 stops
	Info about intersecting lines
	Bus driver giving information on the surrounding environment
	Re-planning your journey on the go
	Compensation for late buses
	Connecting transfer modes
	Information about bus consumption & green values
	Confirmation of being on the right bus stop
Extra services for better travel experience	Indication of available seats
	Vending machine at the bus stop
	Possibility to inform the driver to wait for you
	Luxury, premium and extra service
	Handling of the luggage
	Borrow, rent carts/carriages to carry luggage
	More comfortable seats at the stop/hubs
	Waiting area/lounge at the transportation hub
	Borrow umbrella and return it next time
	Instant channel for feedback
	Book/magazine/newspaper exchange
Services that people already expect to have	Physical place (other than the bus) to buy tickets in advance
	Better, adjustable seats in the bus
	Free Wi-Fi available
	Possibility to charge your phone
	Possibility to check balance and charge your travel card
	Temperature-controlled bus stop

4.1   Information at a Glance While Traveling

This theme includes service ideas dealing with the easy and effortless access of information during the travel. This theme consists of 30 ideas within seven subthemes. The subthemes found most relevant for our study were: *Easy access to journey related information* with ideas such as "Touch screen information points to the transportation hubs" and "More information screens installed into the bus"; *Discovering interesting places in the surroundings* with ideas such as "Mobile guide tour – possibility to match with someone local who could give you a tour around the nearby area" and "A map at the bus stop that would provide information about the neighborhood"; and *Connecting the public screen with the mobile phone* with ideas such as "Possibility to transfer the information from public screen to mobile phone".

Participants highlighted the importance of clear communication of, and easy access to information, whether being inside or outside the vehicle. For example, the participants stated a need to aid the navigation to the bus stop or gate of the connecting line. Participants also wanted the bus to show more information to outside, such as placing the bus number to every side of the bus so that it would be visible also when standing next to the bus. Participants had some ideas for new ways of communicating the information such as utilizing interactive windows as screens and enhancing the connection between the public screens and personal mobile phones. As one group stated, the modern technology could allow the phone to connect to the bus stop screen, which could advertise them specific things to do, i.e. try out new cafeteria around the corner.

Participants stated the need to get advertisement of the local neighborhood and events around the area. One of the ideas within the subtheme *Discovering interesting places in the surroundings* was about providing the passengers' easy recipes that could be in line with what is on sale in the local supermarket ("Meal inspiration – show all supermarket, restaurant and bar deals from the local area together with the opening hours"). Other ideas were about notifying the passengers about upcoming local events in the surrounding area. One team stated the need to bring surprising factors to everyday life and thus their idea focused on decorating the bus or bus stop with the seasonal events – like the Ice Hockey World Championships in May – with sound, lights, visualizations and smells.

4.2   Entertainment and Entertaining Activities

This theme includes service ideas dealing with a variety of entertainment modes within the bus transport journey from the bus stop to the actual bus. The theme consists of 29 ideas within six subthemes. The subthemes found most relevant for our study were: *Passive entertainment* with ideas such as "Onboard entertainment, such as music and games" and "Screen with randomized questions to learn something new"; *Active entertainment* with ideas such as "Drawing exercises at the back of the seats" and "Games to play with the other passengers in the bus"; *Bus stop specific entertainment* with ideas such as "Public screen with games and news" and "Playing the sound of birds singing to make you feel welcome to the bus stop"; and *Physical exercise suggestions at bus stops and when in the bus* with ideas like "Exercise instructions to keep you warm at the bus stop" and "Application that would suggest easy exercises after sitting still for a certain period of time".

Participants generally stated the need to be entertained and having multiple options to choose from depending on your mood and energy levels. Several suggestions came for public touch screens that would provide entertainment and travel information inside the bus and at the bus stop. Participants were also willing to get free access to music while traveling by bus with ideas such as attached headphones, earphone jacks, and sound booths. Some ideas focused on utilization of modern technology, such as VR and AR. Ideas were generated where the VR experience could be either provided with VR glasses or with smart windows. This way people could entertain themselves by looking at different sceneries – different seasons, predictions of future life, informative guide tours of local attractions, etc.

4.3 Services that Support Social Interaction

This theme includes ideas related to the social aspects of traveling by bus. The theme consists of 13 ideas within six subthemes. This theme was the smallest one in the number of service ideas. Many people stated that they want to relax in the bus and therefore being social is not a priority.

The most relevant subthemes within this theme were: *Sharing social media with other passengers in the bus* with the ideas such as "Creating a social network of the passengers", *Games for people sitting next to each other* with ideas such as "Bus related team games for the two people sitting next to each other"; and *Interactive screens at bus stops to aid with communication,* with ideas such as "Creating a hashtag for each bus stop to enhance the community feeling" and "Guide request button that connects to the transportation provider's help desk that gives you answers in real time".

Participants had ideas of creating and sharing things with the other passengers within the bus. One idea was that one could write a story that the others could read and maybe even edit and this could be then published on the big screens in the bus. There were also many suggestions for a social network within the bus where you could communicate with others and, for instance, search for people with similar interests.

4.4 Multiple Channels to Provide Travel Information

Amongst the participants this was seen as the most important and easiest category to ideate around, based on the amount of ideas within the subthemes. This theme includes ideas related to the information regarding the journey. The theme consists of 46 service ideas within 10 subthemes. The subthemes found relevant were: *Real time information of the bus location* with ideas such as "A screen at the bus stop with a real time map with the vehicles' locations", "Journey planner that would function also without internet connection" and "A screen attached to the back of the front seat in front of you that would have your personalized journey"; *Alerts of the approaching stop* with ideas like "Voice alert or wake-up call" and "Vibrating bench when your stop is approaching"; *Bus driver giving information on the surrounding environment* with ideas such as "The driver reminding people of their stops" and "The driver providing information of the surrounding area like a tourist guide"; and *Information about bus consumption and green values* with ideas like "The screens in the bus could show the benefits of using the ecofriendly modes of transport" and "Displaying the CO_2 savings personally and by all passengers on board at that time".

Even though real time journey planners already exist, it was still seen important to provide the information in various of ways, i.e. through public screens, voice alerts and mobile phone applications. Important features were also the ability to quickly re-plan your journey in case the plan A failed and also to get some compensation if the bus never shows up or is remarkably late from its schedule. Other ideas mentioned were i.e. about showcasing not only the approaching busses but also the ones that already went, so that you would know not to wait for it to come. One team stated a need to get confirmation that you have arrived to the correct bus stop. One team on the other hand, had an idea of using the same maps in all the applications so that it would be easier to understand and read them.

4.5   Extra Services for Better Travel Experience

This theme includes ideas regarding something that is considered being "extra", which would enhance the travel experience. The participants brought up a need for services that link to, but are not directly part of the bus ride. The theme consists of 43 service ideas within 11 subthemes. This theme was seen as the second most important and easiest category to ideate around, based on the amount of ideas within the subthemes.

The subthemes found most relevant for our study were *Luxury, premium and extra service* with ideas such as "Home delivery, when you are too tired to walk home from the bus stop", "Comfort seats that allow you to sleep" and "Lottery with different prices utilizing the travel card usage"; *Instant channel for feedback* with ideas such as "Give feedback for the driver" and "Rate the travel experience when you get off"; and *Vending machine at the bus stop* with ideas like "Refreshments, such as coffee and snacks" and "More exotic alternatives of food choices available".

Participants also suggested a lounge type of place for the transportation hubs that would contribute to the overall travel experience by more comfortable and enjoyable waiting time. Teams suggested silent rooms with sleeping pods and rooms with different ambient or themes, such as forest or beach. In this lounge families could take care of their kids and also one would have free access to the toilet facilities. One suggestion was that you would need a travel card to access this space and thus it would not be available for everyone.

Teams generated also ideas related to the sharing economy. Suggestions came for i.e. borrowing carts or carriages for handing luggage, borrowing an umbrella and returning it the next time and a book or magazine exchange. Regarding the physical environment, the participants hoped to have i.e. more comfortable seats with neck support, so that it would be easier to sleep both in the bus and in the lounge area while waiting for the bus.

4.6   Services that People Already Expect to Have

This theme includes ideas dealing with the "must haves" or hygiene factors that the participants noted to be important. The theme consists of 20 ideas within six subthemes. The subthemes include *Physical place (other than the bus) to buy tickets in advance* with ideas such as "Buying your ticket advance should notify the driver that he should not leave earlier" and "A place to buy the tickets to shorten the queues"; *Possibility to check balance and charge your travel card* with ideas like "Make tomorrow a smoother day and charge your card while you wait for the bus" and "Information desks where you could buy tickets"; and *Temperature-controlled bus stops* with ideas like "Heating system at the bus stop that you pay for" and "Closed bus stops so that the heat stays inside".

Most popular needs and ideas were related to free Wi-Fi available for passengers in the bus and the possibility to charge one's phone. Also, some ideas were related to the physical qualities of the bus, for instance better and adjustable seats.

5 Discussion

The aim of our study was to understand how to enhance the bus travel experience by digital services. There are needs and expectations for new services that do not simply focus solely on the efficiency of the trip but rather, on the pleasurable experience of related activities, such as entertainment, social interaction and "extra" services that enhance the travel experience. Our study shares the motivation of Foth et al. [7] that holistic understanding of passengers' requirements is needed in order to develop services that can add value for the users and thus enhance their travel experience. Our study also validates some of the findings of Foth et al. [7] regarding the passengers' needs and expectations for future traveling services. In specific, we agree with Foth et al. [7] that traveling services, together with the supplementary services, could focus more on the entertaining aspects of the journey instead of solely on the efficiency of the trip.

In our study, we identified six service themes based on ideas that the workshop participants generated in the co-design sessions. Many of the individual service ideas have already been studied or even implemented and hence, the novelty of our study does not lie in the individual service ideas, but rather in the overall service theme categorization. Where the themes of *Information at a glance while traveling, Multiple channels for better traveling experience,* and *Services that people already expect to have* are somewhat axiomatic and predictable the other three themes hold more novelty. These themes have been addressed also by Dziekan and Kottenhoff [4], Watkins et al. [27] and Ferris et al. [6].

Even though commuting is often seen as private quality time [10], people still crave for social interaction and therefore we believe that the theme *Services that support social interaction* has high design-relevant potential for successful services. Supporting the social interaction can happen in forms of traditional face-to-face discussions or, for instance, via social media. In addition to direct interaction, the participants generated ideas with indirect interaction, such as co-writing short stories or playing mobile games with others.

As Carreira et al. [2] state, in order for public transportation to gain larger popularity, the transport providers and planners should be considering the individual travelers' needs regarding short distance traveling activities. Thus, the services should be more personable focusing on individuals and their daily lives providing *Extra services for better travel experience.* To attract more people to choose public means of transportation over private cars, something that adds extra value to the commute should be available. The workshop participants generated service ideas that are familiar from other transportation fields, such as aviation industry. However, not all these ideas were for digital services. For instance, a lounge type of waiting area or better bus stops are simple, yet major improvements that have an impact on the quality of the wait time. People also wanted to feel that they have a voice and that their voice is heard, in case there is a need to give feedback. This need generated several ideas regarding digital feedback channels. This addition to the existing transportation service is something that would also benefit the service providers, when they would get real-time data of the problems occurring during peoples' traveling time.

Even though people are nowadays entertained by their mobile phones and the applications in them, there is still a need to be provided with entertainment via other channels too. *Entertainment and entertaining activities* theme included service ideas of both active and passive entertainment. Especially services for passive entertainment, such as showing content on displays in the bus and bus stops were needed. Currently these displays are filled with news and commercials, but the participants of this study expected more local information, such as information of surrounding area – parks and attractions, as well as advertisement of local events, shops and restaurants.

Based on the service themes described in this paper, we propose tentative *experience characteristics* for digital services in the bus context:

- *Feeling of being in control* relates, on one hand to the basic need for successful traveling, that is, the journey from A to B and how it can be kept manageable at all times. Supplementary services can add to the feeling of control by providing cues about the landmarks, schedules and the overall travel chain.
- *Relaxation* is another central experience for the bus context. Many people prefer to spend their traveling time relaxing, preferably alone. Bus ride is seen as private quality time for many people and hence, there should be ways to enhance "calm" experience instead of pushing everyone to be active and social.
- *Connectedness* is related to people's feeling of being part of a community and friends, for example via their mobile phones and social media. More indirect connectedness could also relate to sharing economy between bus passengers.
- *Local experiences* form another experience category that provides design opportunities for the bus ride. These experiences can take the form of infotainment – knowing the local environment, advertisements and local contacts to people.
- *Being modern*, even if not an experience *per se*, refers especially to utilization of modern technology – such as shared public displays, VR, AR and smart windows – when using new traveling services, both informative and entertaining services. Using modern solutions may evoke further related experiences such as curiosity and pride.

From the above experience characteristics, relaxation and connectedness are proposed also by Hilden et al. [10]. Additionally, they propose that emphasizing the ecological choice and feeling of luxury can be accounted for in the design of digital services in *electric* buses. Depending on goals of a specific service design effort for the bus context, these experience characteristics could be turned to *experience targets* according to the approach of Experience-Driven Design [17], which can increase user acceptance of the developed services.

The study was limited in the number of participants as well as number of workshops. Students as participants do naturally not represent all possible target groups. However, we consider students with international background as a good starting point for establishing understanding of service themes, since they are known as active users of public transportation, and an active and enlightened group of smartphone users.

Another reason to focus on students at this stage was also the potential in them as application developers, which is one of the areas we will study in the future.

In our future work, we are planning to conduct co-design workshops with other stakeholder and user groups by taking the ideas generated in these workshops further. We will furthermore utilize the special characteristics of the electric bus, such as the quietness of the bus, novel types of displays, and various sensor-based data that can be collected during the bus ride. Another possibility for future work is to study the found service idea categories in relation to other models of passenger needs, for example the pyramid of customer needs by van Hagen and Bron [26]. The presented findings regarding bus service needs and ideas reveal themes that can be used in development of services. Our study also revealed themes that can be used to inform the interaction design of future traveling services in different phases of the journey: before, during and after the trip. We find this an interesting way to categorize service needs and ideas and thus, we will also explore these aspects in our future studies.

6 Conclusion

In this paper, we presented the findings of our study of bus passengers' needs and expectations for future digital services by developing initial service concept ideas through co-design. This was done by conducting three Idea generating workshops with 24 participants. The study findings revealed six service themes that can be used as a basis of the design of future digital traveling services: (1) Information at a glance while traveling, (2) Entertainment and entertaining activities, (3) Services that support social interaction, (4) Multiple channels to provide travel information, (5) Extra services for better travel experience, and (6) Services that people already expect to have. This knowledge can be used as a basis for human-centered design of digital services that can enhance the desirability of bus transportation.

This study was a part of a larger research project *Living Lab Bus*, in which one of the aims is to develop a platform for interactive services for electric buses. However, the findings of the study were not specific for electric buses only and can be utilized also in traditional buses.

Acknowledgments. This research was funded by Tekes and Tampere University of Technology. We thank Virpi Oksman and Jani-Pekka Jokinen for their help in running the Idea generating workshops 2 and 3, respectively.

References

1. Arrasvuori, J., Boberg, M., Holopainen, J., Korhonen, H., Lucero, A., Montola, M.: Applying the PLEX framework in designing for playfulness. In: Proceedings of the 2011 Conference on Designing Pleasurable Products and Interfaces, DPPI 2011. ACM, New York (2011)
2. Carreira, R., Patrício, L., Jorge, R.N., Magee, C.Van, Eikema Hommes, Q.: Towards a holistic approach to the travel experience: a qualitative study of bus transportation. Transp. Policy **25**, 233–243 (2013)

3. Carreira, R., Patrício, L., Jorge, R.N., Magee, C.: Understanding the travel experience and its impact on attitudes, emotions and loyalty towards the transportation provider–a quantitative study with mid-distance bus trips. Transp. Policy **31**, 35–46 (2014)
4. Dziekan, K., Kottenhoff, K.: Dynamic at-stop real-time information displays for public transport: effects on customers. Transp. Res. Part A Policy Pract. **41**(6), 489–501 (2007)
5. Fahlen, D., Thulin, E., Vilhelmsson, B.: Vad gör man när man reser? En undersökning a resenärers användning av restiden I regional kollektivtrafik. Rapport 2010:15. Stockholm, Vinnova (2010)
6. Ferris, B., Watkins, K., Borning, A.: OneBusAway: results from providing real-time arrival information for public transit. In: Proceedings of the SIGCHI Conference on Human Factors in Computing Systems, pp. 1807–1816. ACM (2010)
7. Foth, M., Schroeter, R., Ti, J.: Opportunities of public transport experience enhancements with mobile services and urban screens. Int. J. Ambient Comput. Intell. (IJACI) **5**(1), 1–18 (2013)
8. Foth, M., Schroeter, R.: Enhancing the experience of public transport users with urban screens and mobile applications. In: Proceedings of the 14th International Academic MindTrek Conference: Envisioning Future Media Environments, pp. 33–40. ACM (2010)
9. Friman, M., Fellesson, M.: Service supply and customer satisfaction in public transportation: the quality paradox. J. Public Transp. **12**(4), 57–69 (2010)
10. Hildén, E., Ojala, J., Väänänen, K.: User needs and expectations for future traveling services in buses. In: Proceedings of the NordiCHI 2016 (2016)
11. Holtzblatt, K., Wendell, J.B., Wood, S.: Rapid contextual design: a how-to guide to key techniques for user-centered design. Elsevier (2004)
12. Lucero, A. Arrasvuori, J.: PLEX Cards: a source of inspiration when designing for playfulness. In: Proceedings of the 3rd International Conference on Fun and Games. ACM (2010)
13. Lucero, A., Vaajakallio, K., Dalsgaard, P.: The dialogue-labs method: process, space and materials as structuring elements to spark dialogue in co-design events. CoDesign **8**(1), 1–23 (2012)
14. Lyon, G., Urry, J.: Travel time use in the information age. Transp. Res. Part A Policy Pract. **39**(2–3), 257–276 (2015)
15. Maclean, S.D., Dailey, D.J.: Real-time bus information on mobile devices. In: 2001 IEEE Intelligent Transportation Systems Proceedings, pp. 988–993. IEEE (2001)
16. Ojala, J., Korhonen, H., Laaksonen, J., Mäkelä, V., Pakkanen, T., Järvi, A., Väänänen, K., Raisamo, R.: Developing novel services for the railway station area through experience-driven design. Interact. Des. Archit. J. IxD&A, N. 25, 73–84 (2015)
17. Olsson, T., Väänänen-Vainio-Mattila, K., Saari, T., Lucero, A., Arrasvuori, J.: Reflections on experience-driven design: a case study on designing for playful experiences. In: Proceedings of the 6th International Conference on Designing Pleasurable Products and Interfaces, DPPI 2013, pp. 165–174. ACM, New York (2013)
18. Ory, D., Mokhtarian, P.: When is getting there half the fun? Modeling the liking for travel. Transp. Res. Part A Policy Pract. **39**(2), 97–123 (2004)
19. Páez, A., Whalen, K.: Enjoyment of commute: a comparison of different transportation modes. Transp. Res. Part A Policy Pract. **44**(7), 537–549 (2010)
20. Paulley, N., Balcombe, R., Mackett, R., Titheridge, H., Preston, J., Wardman, M., Shires, J., White, P.: The demand for public transport: the effects of fares, quality of service, income and car ownership. Transp. Policy **13**, 295–306 (2006)
21. Roto, V., Law, E., Vermeeren, A., Hoonhout, J.: 10373 Abstracts collection–demarcating user experience. In: Dagstuhl Seminar Proceedings. Schloss Dagstuhl-Leibniz-Zentrum fuer Informatik (2011)

22. Sanders, E.: Information, inspiration and co-creation. In: Proceedings of the 6th International Conference of the European Academy of Design (2005)
23. Scott, K., Quist, J., Bakker, C.: Co-design, social practices and sustainable innovation: involving users in a living lab exploratory study on bathing. In: Proceedings of Paper for the "Joint Actions on Climate Change" Conference, Aalborg, Denmark (2009)
24. van St-Louis, E., Lierop, D., El-Geneidy, A.: The happy commuter: a comparison of commuter satisfaction across modes. Transp. Res. Part F Traffic Psychol. Behav. 26, 160–170 (2014)
25. Van Audenhove, F.-J., Korniichuk, O., Dauby, L., Pourbaix, J.: The Future of Urban Mobility 2.0: Imperatives to Shape Extended Mobility Ecosystems of Tomorrow. Arthur D. Little (2014)
26. van Hagen, M., Bron, P.: Enhancing the experience of the train journey: changing the focus from satisfaction to emotional experience of customers. Transp. Res. Procedia 1(1), 253–263 (2014)
27. Watkins, K.E., Ferris, B., Borning, A., Rutherford, G.S., Layton, D.: Where is my bus? Impact of mobile real-time information on the perceived and actual wait time of transit riders. Transp. Res. Part A Policy Pract. 45(8), 839–848 (2011)
28. Woodcock, A.: New insights, new challenges; person centred transport design. Work 41 (Supplement 1), 4879–4886 (2012)
29. Zomerdijk, L., Voss, C.: Service design for experience-centric services. J. Serv. Res. 13(1), 67–82 (2010)

Designing for Financial Literacy: Co-design with Children in Rural Sri Lanka

Thilina Halloluwa[1,2(✉)], Dhaval Vyas[1], Hakim Usoof[2],
Pradeepa Bandara[3], Margot Brereton[1], and Priyantha Hewagamage[2]

[1] Queensland University of Technology (QUT), Brisbane, Australia
{d.vyas,m.brereton}@qut.edu.au
[2] University of Colombo School of Computing, Colombo 00700, Sri Lanka
{tch,hau,kph}@ucsc.cmb.ac.lk
[3] Sri Lanka Institute of Information Technology, Malabe, Sri Lanka
pradeepa.b@sliit.lk

Abstract. Financial literacy can play an important role in supporting the livelihood of the poor. Sri Lanka, being a country that aims to become a knowledge economy, has started to integrate the use of technology in its primary education. This paper presents a case study from a Co-Design activity with primary school children in rural Sri Lanka to ideate designing of mobile applications to engage primary school students in financial literacy. Three workshops were conducted spanning over two months based on the bonded design method. Techniques involving bags of stuff, storyboarding and stickies were utilised to support idea generation. Two themes; shopping and transporting were prominent among the final designs. From the findings of this paper, we discuss the design inspirations of the study and the impact that scaffolding practices had on the outcomes of the study. Finally, we lay out some initial guidelines to follow when conducting co-design workshops with rural and resource constrained children in Sri Lanka.

Keywords: Co-design · Financial literacy · Children · ICT4D

1 Introduction

"We can end poverty" is the theme of the United Nations' 2015/2016 development plan and eradicating poverty has been listed as the main millennium development goal [55]. The World Bank reports that almost half of the world's population lives on less than USD 3 per day [62]. In the Sri Lankan context, the Ministry of Finance and Planning reports that approximately 1.3 million individuals are living in poverty with earnings of around USD 25 per month [33]. Approximately, 86.8% of them are from rural regions where resources are poorly distributed. Furthermore, there is a significant percentage of individuals living 'just above' the poverty line. If the poverty line increased by USD 2, the people who are living in poverty will be reaching 2.0 million [33]. That is close to 10% of the countries' population. Consequently, about 1.5 million families are depending on *Samurdhi*, which is social welfare scheme by the government to the low-income families [53].

© IFIP International Federation for Information Processing 2017
Published by Springer International Publishing AG 2017. All Rights Reserved
R. Bernhaupt et al. (Eds.): INTERACT 2017, Part I, LNCS 10513, pp. 313–334, 2017.
DOI: 10.1007/978-3-319-67744-6_21

Financial education can play a vital role in a country's social and economic growth. A significant correlation exists between economic development and financial education [21]. Recent reports indicate that the average debt of a Sri Lankan family has increased from USD 355 to USD 1325 since 2009 [9]. The Central Bank of Sri Lanka has started conducting financial educational programs for low-income families as a solution. It is reported that the financial education should start at school and has to be learned as early as possible [40]. By understanding the importance of financial literacy for children, education systems around the world have started integrating it to the school curriculums as a part of the Mathematics syllabus [52]. With Sri Lanka being a country with a high literacy rate and a relatively small population, the government has a focus on a knowledge economy with a service sector instead of a manufacturing industry [16]. In 2016, the government has proposed to introduce tablet computers to Schools as a learning tool [29]. Drawing inspiration from this initiative of introducing tablet computers to secondary schools, a pedagogical approach is investigated to identify ways to utilize them to enhance the financial literacy among the young learners in Sri Lanka.

Introducing new technological devices is only one aspect of a solution. Additional investigations are required in making these devices productive and to design applications which cater the requirements of these children. Understanding the context of the users and the relationships between individuals, artefacts and practices are key considerations for the effective design of technological tools [36]. This awareness helps designers to design tools and technologies which fit the spaces the users occupy. Thus, we have conducted a series of co-design workshops to obtain design inspirations for designing mobile applications towards enhancing the financial literacy of resource constrained primary school children in rural Sri Lanka. We collaborated with a public school, where most of the students were from neighbouring orphanages. They were deprived of facilities such as the Internet and even electricity. All the participating students had very limited exposure to technology. The main contribution of this work is to showcase the co-design procedures in a post-colonial environment while the overall aim of this study was to generate design ideas to implement a mobile application for Sri Lankan schools focusing on financial literacy. This paper will feed results into a larger scale government sanctioned project on designing applications for financial literacy.

The workshops were held within one school semester spanning over two months. We were allocated one hour per session by the school administration to accommodate routine teaching and learning activities. The children participated as co-designers in all the workshops. Design inspirations for creating mobile applications to promote financial literacy were developed incorporating a variety of methods. Methods such as *bags of stuff* [15], *storyboarding* [54] and *stickies* [15] were used to draw out ideas from their day to day experiences in interacting with money and to evaluate the designs. The use of a variety of techniques enabled the research team to gain a comprehensive understanding of children's sentiment towards money.

Over the past three decades, the HCI community has shown a great interest in getting children involved when designing tools and technologies for them. While many of these studies conducted in the developed world [26, 31, 45, 58], there is a lack of similar work in the developing world where the teaching and learning environment is significantly different [19]. Hence, we present a case study conducted with primary school children in rural Sri Lanka to investigate how to design with children.

The purpose of the paper is two-fold: Firstly, to provide some initial inspirations on the metaphors to be used when designing for resource constrained children in the developing world. Secondly, lay a layout on a set of guidelines to be used when conducting co-design workshops in a developing country. We find that instead of directly utilizing the methods used in the developed countries, some initial time needs to be spent on getting the children familiar with the co-design approach due to cultural diversities. All the designs were inspired by the children's day to day experiences and they needed them to be expressed as realistic as possible. Before describing the workshops, we present related work in constructing a rationale for our design workshops.

2 Related Work

2.1 Children and Financial Affairs

Children in the modern society do not live in isolation and they directly interact with the world economy [56]. The ability to manage finances is one of the critical skills to acquire. This skill is mostly acquired in childhood [1]. Consequently, studies conducted by Beverly and Burkhalter [6] and Cohen and Xiao [8] recommend that the financial education needs to be provided as early as possible starting from pre-primary education. It will help prepare young people to make better financial decisions [30].

The United States Department of the Treasury [13], reports that the financial education should be integrated into the school curriculum as part of mathematics and reading curricula starting from elementary school, as it lays the foundation for making effective financial decisions throughout their lives. Northern Ireland has embedded activities [38] to their primary mathematics syllabus to help promote financial understanding in an attempt to alleviate the problem of financial exclusion. These recommendations are supported by research which states that children begin to understand the concept of money by the age of 3 and understand the importance of saving money between ages six and twelve [52]. By the age of 12, children start engaging in more complex saving and spending strategies [18]. Understanding the importance of financial literacy for children, education systems globally have started integrating it to school curriculums [52]. Metcalf and Atance [32] report that even though the children were not inherently motivated to save, they can be taught the importance of saving even after a single trial. Otto et al. [39] have used a game to explore the age differences in children's ability to apply saving strategies. Of the two studies, first was conducted with 42 children and the second was with 36 children (ages 6–12). They report that between ages nine and twelve, children gain the ability to manage their money, learn to manage bank accounts and use banking functionalities.

2.2 Co-designing with Children

When technology is implemented for children, it is critical to involve them in all aspects of design which allow designers to come up with tools and technologies capable of catering a child's requirements [12]. The lack of preconception about the design space makes the children aged between 7–10 the best candidates for these type of studies [43]. Previous studies discuss various ways children can be involved in the design. Druin [12] reports that the children should be involved as design partners where the adults and children are treated as equals while Read et al. [43] suggest different levels of involvement, namely informant, balanced and facilitated. However, it has been identified that there is an unequal power relationship between adults and children which presents a significant barrier especially in the school environment [3, 51]. Another concern raised when involving children as design partners is that most children are not trained to provide critical feedback [43].

Over the years, many methods have been introduced for designing with children. Cooperative inquiry [12] is a philosophy where children are considered design partners and work together with adults as equals. Informant design [46] by contrast advocates input from different people at different stages in order to effectively maximise the value of their contribution to the overall effort Bonded design [27] sits in between cooperative inquiry and informant design by uniting a team of intergenerational people, drawing upon and recognising their different insights and strengths. In the bonded design method, the design partners work with researchers for shorter periods of time. Furthermore, the bonded design method allows the design partners to be considered as learners in addition to being designers. This method is ideal when the designers are unable to work with children for a longer period of time. Kidstory [51] is another method which is an adaptation of cooperative inquiry that enables a large number of children to participate in the design. The Child Computer Interaction (ChiCI) group use a method named *The Mad Evaluation Session with Schoolchildren* (MESS) [44] which has more emphasis on evaluation and fun. PICTIVE [35] is an approach that uses papers and pencils to get non-computer-literate users involvement. Designing organic user interfaces by means of PlayDoh, small Lego bricks, fabric shapes etc. have also been investigated [42]. Doorn et al. [11] have explored a method where they get children involve as researchers to gain rich contextual insights. IDEAS [5] is a method for involving autistic children in designing. Furthermore, there are various techniques been introduced such as bags of stuff [65], storyboarding [54], layered elaboration [59], etc. [60] to get children engaged in these studies.

Utilizing the above-mentioned methods and techniques; many studies have been conducted by various researchers in varying contexts over the last two decades within the HCI community. Alborzi et al. [3] have investigated on getting children into designing immersive storytelling environments. Frauenberger et al. [17] report that it is essential to focus on ways to interpret the inputs and ideas of Children. Engaging children on designing tools to address issues related to mental health is another avenue which has been explored [37]. Kwon et al. [26] have engaged children in designing a social mobile learning application. Another study focusing on improving the Namibian reading culture [23] outlines how they utilized participatory design in different levels to gather design inspirations. Makhaeva et al. [31] report how they created creative spaces for co-designing with autistic children using a concept named "Handlungsspielraum". One similarity in all these studies is that it was the adult partners who led the sessions. However, it has been identified that the children can also initiate and lead these type of co-design workshops [64] as long as they are sufficiently trained.

Designing with children from the developing countries

Researchers often assume the availability of stable and reliable power supplies, affordable and ubiquitous cell coverage and internet facilities when designing for the developing countries [2]. However, in many of the developing countries, none of these assumptions are guaranteed. Irani et al. [22] referred to this differences and the challenges faced in the developing world when designing, under the umbrella of "post-colonial computing". They also propose a formulation of design work based on engagement, articulation, and translation. Suchman [49] has also reported the differences in practices and the importance of not relying on the assumptions made at the "hyper-developed world" when designing for post-colonial or marginalized populations. Culturally situated design [14, 47] is another concept which states the importance of designing for a particular culture by referring to the designs which are grounded in the designers own culture. This understanding enables them to interpret the designs unambiguously. A study [48] reports that children from technology savvy environment can design for children who are technologically challenged. This was done with 50 children from a UK primary school where they designed a game related to hand washing for children in Uganda. However, it can be said that the study produced positive results because the idea of handwashing is generic enough to be played by a global audience. Another similar study [47] conducted with children from a UK primary school with the aim of investigating the use of sensitizing techniques' impact on designing for a surrogate population (rural china) reports that most of the designs put forward by the children are culturally un-situated. Even though these children were given enough time to get familiar with the Chinese culture, most of their designs did not reflect that knowledge and were culturally neutral. Nonetheless, it is clear that when designing for marginalized and culturally diverse communities, the researchers themselves should have aa grounded understanding of the targeted audience.

Kam et al. [24] have carried out a study on designing digital games in a rural Indian village with students from three schools. They have given students to play a game for 1.5 h. These games were traditional village games. They state that it is easier for rural children to relate to technologically enhanced education systems if it has the same game mechanics as a traditional game. The focus of the study was on designing for keypad mobile phones. Another study [25] has attempted to integrate mobile phones in an Indian village has focused on exploring how unsupervised mobile-learning is done in rural India. They report how village children used mobile phones in their day to day lives along with their improvements in English as a second language. Even this study was done using basic mobile phones and not in a classroom environment. Larson, et al. [28] have conducted an experiment with 63 students in India on improving English literacy. This is a mobile game, based on the popular sport cricket, targeting to improve pronunciation skills of rural Indian children. Nevertheless, this was done using low end basic mobile phones. One Laptop per Child (OLPC) is a concept that was introduced to promote technology use in primary education in developing countries. This initiative has shown both positive and negative impacts in different contexts. For instance, a study was done in Ethiopia [50] which focused on child literacy have shown positive results while in the US [61] it was identified a failure due to various factors. recently, The OLPC Sri Lanka initiative reports that "only giving XO machines did not make a big change among these young learners in general" [20]. They claim that the background has to be set including conducting teacher training and setting a sound pedagogy. Ames [4] argue that the positive results and claims made by OLPC studies in the developing world are mainly due to the charismatic nature of the device.

While these studies haven't incorporated participatory design techniques or involved children as design partners, they probe deep into the varying cultures, practices of rural communities through an ethnographical approach. Hence, our paper provides a first in-situ study which looks at designing with children in a South Asian developing country.

3 The Study

3.1 Method

Three workshops were conducted based on an adaptation of the Bonded Design [27] method. This method describes several stages in design such as team building, viewing and critiquing, drawing, brainstorming, games, journaling and evaluating. All the workshops were conducted in the schools instead of a lab environment.

Since the study involved working with children, the study was done in compliance with our institute's ethical committee regulations, where parent/guardian consents were obtained in writing. Special permission was also sought from the Department of Education, Western Province, Sri Lanka. All the participants and their parents/guardians were informed that the participation in the study was voluntarily and they could opt out at any given time without having to provide reasons.

A qualitative approach was used for gathering and analysing data. All the workshops were video recorded and three researchers actively took notes throughout the study. Both teachers and students were interviewed after the study. These were semi-structured interviews where we aimed to understand their learning experiences of designing with peers. Each interview was approximately 10–15 min and took place immediately after finishing the study. Interview data was transcribed. Thematic analysis [7] was used to analyse the transcriptions and video clips of field study observations that were made in the school setting.

3.2 Participants

The participants for the workshop were 24 primary school children (Age 8–9) with very limited exposure in playing mobile games and three adult researchers. These children were selected based on the findings of Read et al. [43] as they report that children in this age groups are the ideal candidates for designing with. Druin et al. [12] report that the children can be used in these type of workshops in different forms, namely, user, tester, informant, and design partner. In our workshops, the children took part as design partners where they become an integral part of creating a technology. All the children were present throughout workshops. The adult researchers participated as facilitators and motivators. They lead the discussions and guided the children in designing by asking "what if" questions.

3.3 "The Play Room" Workshop

When developing an engaging and sustainable learning tool for the children, it is essential to involve them from the initial ideation process [12] which makes the children co-designers. Consequently, to be effective co-designers, they need to have a proper understanding of the process of co-design, the fundamental concepts, and subject knowledge. However, as this is the first co-design workshop that is been done with Sri Lankan primary school students and due to their demographics, these children are likely to have no or little experiences with either using these type of mobile devices or the process of designing. To overcome this situation, we designed "The Play Room" workshop. Through this workshop, we attempted to simulate the first two stages of bonded design; team building, viewing and critiquing,

We believe that when introducing something new to a child, it has to be introduced gradually. "Instructional scaffolding is the provision of sufficient supports to promote learning when concepts and skills are being first introduced to students. These supports are gradually removed as students develop autonomous learning strategies, thus promoting their own cognitive, affective and psychomotor learning skills and knowledge" [57]. Researchers argue [34] that this is the formal implementation of Vygotsky's "Zone of proximal Development" which refers to the gap between what a child can achieve alone and what a child can achieve with the help from an external party. In that sense, *the play room workshop* was intended to be a scaffolder so that the children can gradually learn the process of co-design while getting an experience for using mobile devices.

For the first part of this intervention, the researchers went to the school and observed the teaching and learning environment. This is done for two days with the same teacher who taught mathematics. The sessions were video recorded. Afterwards, we conducted "The Play Room" workshop to understand the feasibility and limitations in participant recruitment, technical and logistic constraints, to observe how participants will respond and to determine the duration of an effective session. We designed two overhead cameras to record the work of the children in order to ensure that the video recording was nonintrusive and instantaneously oblivious to the participants.

This workshop was utilized as an icebreaker session to build relationships with the children and researchers. Icebreaking is critical to narrow the power gap. Since most Sri Lankan students are not used to talking freely with their teachers (adults) and expressing ideas, we used this session to make friends with them, get to know them better and build trust. The students were discouraged from raising their hands and standing up when they wished to make a point as we needed them to address the researchers as freely as possible. Workshop series was conducted throughout a week (1 h per day). The workshop started by researchers introducing themselves to the children and telling them about their school days and how subject such as mathematics influenced them in their personal lives (failures and successes). The idea behind this was to use this activity to help the children get over their fear of failure and to get them to start talking about their ideas. During this workshop series, all 24 children took part in playing mobile games, drawing activities and discussing their thoughts on the games they were playing.

3.4   "Build a Game" Workshop

The Build a Game workshop was conducted one week after "The Play Room" workshop. It was conducted as four one-hour-long sessions within four days. This workshop simulated the drawing, brainstorming and journaling stages of bonded design. This workshop series used a variety of methods to brainstorm ideas and initiate discussion with children.

Eight teams were formed with three children per team. As there were only three adult researchers, one researcher had to be a part of two groups. Each team was asked to develop one or more prototypes (depending on the ideas they generate) to represent their experiences with interacting with money and visualize those experiences in a form of drawings. Semi-structured interviews were carried out during and after the workshops while the children describe their ideas.

As techniques for engaging children in design, a combination of *Bags of stuff* and *Storyboarding* [15] were used. *Bags of stuff* uses art supplies for the creating low fidelity prototypes and *storyboards* usually illustrate a scenario of how an application feature works. The art supplies were provided in a form of a large bag filled with items such colouring pens, glue, paper, markers, scissors, and cardboards. Using the items provided the children were asked to create stories.

3.5   "SCORE" Workshop

This was a two-day workshop where children used the stickies [15] method. The sticky notes were used to record one idea per note of their likes, dislikes, and design ideas about another teams' designs. This workshop is similar to the evaluation stage suggested by the bonded design method. After the session, the three adult researchers organized these notes into groups in an attempt to identify themes. This helped the researchers understand the outcome of the session while using it as evaluating mechanism for the prototypes.

3.6   Data Collection and Analysis

For all 3 workshops, we collected video data, field notes, photographs, design artefacts in the form of storyboards and sticky note artefacts. We also conducted brief semi-structured interviews with all child participants on their thoughts on the workshops. The data analysis was done through a cross-validation of video data, interviews, artefacts, and field notes to explore evidence related to our research questions. We also examined behaviours and attitudes the children showcase during these three workshops. As the authors involved are from different geo locations, all the data was placed into a secure online data storage in which the videos, field notes, photos, and artefacts could be analysed by each author [63]. To strengthen the validity of our findings, each author explored the evidence independently and across analysis was done to investigate the difference and/or similarities of each.

4 Findings

4.1 Observations of "The Play Room" Workshop Series

The education culture of most Asian countries is non-participative while the teacher is usually considered as an authoritative figure [41]. This is true for Sri Lankan education as well. The teaching is mostly done using the *chalk and talk* method. Teachers complain that due to a large number of students in a classroom (40–45) they cannot pay individual attention to each student.

During our observations, we realized that the teacher works relentlessly to get the students to *learn* what she was *teaching*. We also noticed that she put an extra effort to her teaching as she was aware that we were filming. She encouraged the students to keep quiet in the classroom during the teaching period by utilizing techniques such as asking them to raise hands when they start shouting. However, we could observe that some children refrain from asking questions from the teacher due to this practice. Later a child confided in us stating *"I was afraid to ask the teacher then and I waited till she finished, but I forgot to ask it from her after the session"*. We realized that this reluctance to communicate openly could be a barrier in our co-design workshops. Hence, we decided to have an icebreaking workshop to build trust and confidence among the children.

During the initial stages of the workshops, the children were hesitant to talk freely and they tried to treat us with the similar respect they have for teachers. For an instance, when we ask a question, they would raise a hand, and if asked would stand up and answer. However, once the session progressed they seemed to be more relaxed and talked freely with us. Additionally, they seemed nervous in answering questions such as "What is your favourite subject?". When the teacher was around, all of them said they liked Mathematics best. Therefore, we asked the teacher to leave the room and afterwards, 5 children said they liked "Art" best and 2 said, "Sinhala" (mother tongue) is their favourite subject.

The second session involved playing 5 educational mobile games where shopping was the main theme. They were asked to play the games even though none of them have played a mobile game before (Fig. 1a). While this was done as an ice breaker, we did not hesitate to try and learn children's perspectives about the games they were playing. We used this to see which interactions are intuitive and which are not. The children were informed that they can ask for help if necessary. We were particularly mindful not to ask any "Leading" questions. Since the game was in English, none of the students could understand the instructions given and they had difficulties in understanding some of the icons used. We realized that the children were just trialing and learning. This was evident in one of the game plays which involved a bakery. The player can bake a cake and sell it. Nevertheless, the children kept on baking cakes even though they have made one cake. They confided that they thought the game was about making a cake instead of a shopping game. All the games highlighted every element that needs to be clicked in a hierarchy. The children seemed eager to click/touch on anything blinking or anything with bright colours. Hence, most of the children were able to get by playing the game, even though they didn't understand the spoken language. While we perceive this as to be an effective mechanism to make interactions intuitive to novice users we also observed

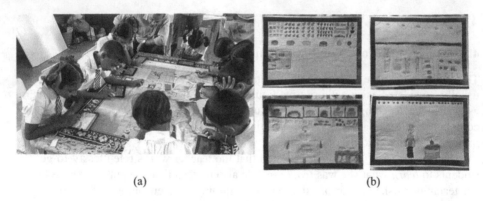

Fig. 1. (a) The children playing the mobile games for the first time and explain their thoughts, (b) some of the drawing artefacts from the children illustrating their favourite scenarios of the games

that the children who took the time to learn how to play, showed signs of frustration though out the session even though they had learned.

At the end of the session, we conducted a semi-structured interview session where the children discuss their ideas, likes and dislikes about the games they played. They prefer writing them down and we collected the notes as evidence. The session concluded with a drawing activity where the children would draw scenario from the games they played (Fig. 1b). As the session progress, we realize the children get used to handling the devices and playing games. Initially, they were struggling with device features such as screen timeouts and rotations. But after some time all of them got used to it and learned how to turn the screen back on. The children stated that they liked the metaphors used in the games, especially the cartoon characters. However, they explicitly mentioned that they would prefer if the games were in the Sinhala language. All these activities (the initial discussion, playing the game, discussing the likes and dislikes, drawing activity) were done to train the children for the upcoming workshops as these children were new to these type of interventions.

4.2   Artefacts of the "Build a Game" Workshop

The focus of this workshop was to design game scenarios as paper prototypes. Most groups preferred to work as teams while one group of students wanted to work individually. However, we could observe many intra-group and inter-group discussions among the children.

While it was notable how the experiences and sometimes hardships of these children were expressed from their designs, we could observe very little idea diversity among the designs. Two themes of design were common among most of the groups and only one child, a member of the team that preferred to work individually came up with a design outside of the two common themes (Fig. 2).

Fig. 2. A story of going to a village shop and buying items. The numbers (1, 2, 3) are used to explain a specific event such as going to the shop and paying.

The most common theme out of the two was "Shopping". All the children drew their shops as a small village shop as opposed to larger supermarkets. The majority of the items sold were sweets and fruits while the character of shop owner resembled a typical village character or a little child. One of the children mentioned that she drew "*Nihal Mama*" (Uncle Nihal) who happened to be the owner of the school canteen.

In all the drawing, the character of the shopper was always a child, either walking to the shop or taking a bus to the *Pola* (open market). The children stated that it is how all of them go to the shop as none of them owned a bicycle but they, of course, preferred to ride a bicycle.

One group of children explained their story by roleplaying. One child assumed the role of shopkeeper while the other two children played the role of shoppers. They listed down the prices of items and they did the calculations on the drawing itself so that we (the researchers) would understand their drawings better (Fig. 3). Discussions with the teachers have revealed that she utilizes the same technique in some of her teachings as the children respond favourably to learning activities when embedded in storytelling or role-playing activities.

The other common theme was transportation, either by bus or by train. Here the children drew scenarios where they would travel either to school or visit family. It was fascinating to see how extremely detailed some of the drawings were. For instance, one drawing illustrated the bus stops and explicitly mentioned the way to the market. An interesting observation was the colour of the bus. In all the drawings, the bus was coloured in red. The red colour busses are the Sri Lanka transport board (CLTB/CTB) bus and they offer a discounted price for school children and they implement season tickets at a subsidiary rate. The children stated that they would always wait for a CTB bus. One team has decided that they want to draw a complete story which represents the scenarios where they would interact with money. Here, the characters would take a bus to the market, buy items and return home from a taxi or a three-wheeler (tuk-tuk). There were numbering the screens, using arrows and even writing instruction as next scene as a means of the guiding the teacher to follow their story since the teacher was not there and the signs would help her construct the story (Fig. 4).

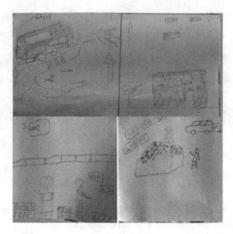

Fig. 3. The story of going to the market by bus. This was a detailed drawing illustrating going to the bus stop, waiting till a CTB bus arrive, going to the market, buying goods and return by a taxi. (Color figure online)

Fig. 4. The drawing of the debt payment scenario. The left-hand board shows a scenario of taking on a debt from the village butcher while the right side board shows the payment of debt.

The only artefact, which was outside these common themes, was produced by the team where individuals preferred working alone. One of them drew a scenario where his father is obtaining a loan from the village butcher and paying a debt of Rs. 2000 (~13 USD) he owed. In his picture, the character of the father was crying while the person taking the money was smiling. He stated *"Yesterday I went with my father to meet an uncle and my father gave Rs. 2000 to him. I saw my father was saddened when he handed over the money"*.

Apart from these observations, we could see that the children who said art was their favourite subject finish their stories and help other students while some struggled to finish their work. However, in the end, all the children expressed that they enjoyed the workshop and asked about the next workshop.

4.3 Outcomes of the "SCORE" Workshop

During the SCORE workshop, we observed that all the students facing difficulties in writing their likes, dislikes and design ideas on small sticky notes in the Sinhala language. This is understandable as the language skills nor critical thinking skill of these children are not yet fully developed. Therefore, we adapted a method introduced by the bonded design for evaluation where the children complete a simple questionnaire. The children wrote down the likes, dislikes, and ideas to improve the designs on a piece of paper provided. While the children were writing down their ideas, semi-structured interviews were conducted with them to understand the meaning of their writings. For example, one child has written that he disliked the fact that the "Money is on display" and what he actually meant to say is that he didn't like the way the values of the notes/coins were written instead of drawing the actual note/coin (Fig. 5).

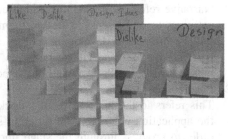

Fig. 5. The Sticky session. Each team took a turn in examining other team's work and wrote down the likes, dislikes and design ideas to improve those artefacts.

We observed that almost all the children having difficulties in distinguishing dislikes over design ideas. The also struggled with finding points which they like and we believe that is because they are not trained to provide critical but constructive feedback. Therefore, initially, the small groups gave more design ideas and did not give likes and dislikes. As a result, at the end of the workshop, we organized 3 likes, 4 dislikes and 21 design ideas for all designs. Another notable observation was that the children did not like evaluating the work of their friends when they were present in the room. Therefore, we had to get one team at a time to evaluate the designs of their peers. Once this task was complete, we got all the teams together and read every note to them. Initially, the teams kept quiet when there was a criticism to their designs but after some time they became defensive towards criticism. For instance, in the artefact where one team have described a scenario with a bus, the bus ticket was issued outside of the bus. One of the children challenged this by saying "This is unrealistic; all bus conductors issue tickets inside the bus". The team which designed that artefact retorted, "No the long distance buses issue tickets before getting on the bus, you just haven't traveled in one of those". We observed some children were unengaged who later revealed that they were "nervous but felt more comfortable as the session progressed".

From the design ideas, we developed themes such as integrating audio as well as video introductions, customizing colours of the items, interacting with the items through drag and drop, have different levels and ability to select a certain level. They also liked colours of the items on display and in the shop scenario, they liked that it resembles a village boutique rather than a supermarket. However, some of the girls complained that in all artefacts, the player (avatar) is represented as a boy and we inferred that the ability to choose a male or female avatar is an important feature.

4.4   Potential Design of the Application

The design of the application will be informed by the findings from the workshops. We will also investigate the feasibility of gamification concepts as it is referred to the use of game design elements in non-game contexts [10]. Aligned with the concept of gamification, the application will be associating the following gamified features.

1. Narrative
   Narrative refers to a story line which connects the activities together. It helps the activities to make sense. The two themes emerged (shopping and transportation) will be utilized in developing a story which the students can relate to. A child traveling by bus to a village boutique can be a potential story. The transactions he/she does along the way and at the boutique can be used as learning activities.
2. Progression
   This refers to the importance of unlocking information continually. Accordingly, the application will consist of different stages and multiple levels in each stage. In order to progress through the stage, the users will have to complete the previous level. The difficulty will increase when they progress through the game. For instance, concepts such as saving, loan, performing transactions with cents will be introduced at the higher stages.
3. Rewards and leaderboards
   As rewards for the system, a 5-point scoring/rewarding system will be developed with the use of stars. The better they perform the more stars they get.

5   Discussion and Lessons Learned

In all our workshops, we did not work with an individual child, rather a group of children in the ages eight to nine. These children differ in knowledge, life experiences, and styles of exploring ideas. They need time to understand how to work as a team as well as learn to respect the ideas of others. Through these workshops, we understood that the adult participants need to be patient as the teams learn to be better at collaboration and work as a team of equals. From this section, we hope to build a discussion towards further exploring the findings and observations of the three prior workshops as well as present our ideas on what they speculate as design aspirations. The lessons we have learned by conducting co-design workshops in Sri Lanka and the challenges we faced as designers are further discussed.

5.1   Design Inspirations

It was clear that the children's everyday experiences and desires had a major impact on their drawing artefacts. As opposed to most major shopping themed mobile games, where the user (player) would visit a supermarket and choose items from the shelves, they preferred visiting *kades* (small village boutique) and ask for the items from the storekeeper. However, instead of items such as bags of rice and grains which can be commonly found in these type of *kades,* their drawings had a lot of sweets, toys, and fruits. It is arguable that this is a common observation of a child's drawing. However, the children expressed that they rarely get to buy items such as toys and fruits from the shops as they are expensive. The extreme poverty, some of these children undergo was another distinctive feature of these drawings. In addition to the items favoured to be bought, waiting for the cheaper government owned red colour buses, getting small amounts of money as a loan and the struggle to pay it back were seen as evidence of their hardships. Furthermore, the children wanted their designs to be as realistic as possible. Instances such as the arguments the children had on how the bus tickets are issued, the colours of the notes and the way values were written on the notes can be seen as examples of the effort the children have put into their design.

During the play room workshop, we observed that children face difficulties in understanding some of the common icons and interactions such as the *next* icon and swipes. Since the language used is foreign to these children, none of them understood what needs to be done. Highlighting what needs to be focused on have been used as a solution. However, some of the students were frustrated as they could not fully understand what needs to be done. This highlighted that first impression, as well as intuitive interactions, are important and signs and symbols we assume are globally understood not really be so. Therefore, we recommend that designers understand the experiences of these children and take design inspirations from these examples when designing and implementing technologies for rural Sri Lankan children.

We observed that the children produce a significantly higher number of *design ideas* than *likes* or *dislikes*. All the children started writing likes and dislikes but after some time they would start working on design ideas and kept working on it. The researchers had to ask the children specifically for likes and dislikes. While this is identified as a common observation of sticky evaluation sessions, we believe that it is a reflection of the teacher-centered teaching and learning environment the children are immersed. From the observations, we noticed that the children treat the teacher as a knowledge hub and they expect her to give all answers. Even though there are attempts to get students involved in learning, it is common for Sri Lankan classrooms to be more bias towards a teacher-centric environment. Therefore, we believe that the children's reluctance to talk freely is the main reason for the lower numbers. However, we observed that several design ideas were correlated with dislikes. For instance, a dislike such as "I don't like the way the values of notes and coins are displayed", correlates to "The coins and notes should be represented by actual or realistic images of them instead of writing just the values". We also believe that it is a difficult task for children to provide likes and dislikes by exploring these types of low-fidelity paper prototypes. Therefore, we recommend that evaluation techniques to be used only after a functioning prototype is implemented, especially with children from the developing countries.

Lesson 01. *Use a native language when designing and be mindful that some of the globally recognized icons and gestures are foreign to these children.*

5.2   Unsuccessful Scaffolding

We found that there was a lack of idea diversity in scenarios across all the groups. There were two common themes; shopping and transportation except for one exemplary case of debt collection. We believe that the activities of the play room workshop and the scaffolding nature are related to this lack of idea diversity. As mentioned above, during the playroom workshop, the children played few shopping-related games. Pedagogically, scaffolding refers to support given to students solve problems, while gradually removing those as students gain more knowledge [57]. We presume that while the play room workshop was successful in supporting children gradually learn the process of co-design, the scaffolding did not function properly when playing the mobile games. We speculate that instead of widening the boundaries of child's imagination it narrowed the scope, resulting in the generation of the similar type of ideas. However, the lack of ideas could also be due to the fact that these children have a limited exposure to finance and money transactions in their day-to-day life. The exception being, the child who witnessed the loan and repayment transaction.

The limited time allocated for the play room workshop can be another reason for the lack of success in scaffolding. Even though we allocated one week for this, it could be seen that the children developed a wrong preconception about the design space during this week. It was evident that some of the children thought they are required to design something similar to what they have played. This can be due to the close relationship between the games they played and the design space they required to ideate. In the future when running similar kind of workshops and initiatives it might be good to meet with the children at least one month in advance. It is advisable to give children ample opportunity to interact with mobile games prior to the study as they have limited experience with these devices. We recommend that designers be cautious when selecting applications or games to be provided for the children. The selection has to be diverse in order for the children become familiar with game mechanics and features provided by the platforms. Playing different types of games will limit the preconception of design space among the children while allowing the children to get familiar with the devices of which they are designing games for. Additionally, it will provide an opportunity for the design teams to form a closer bond with each other (adults and children) as well as time for them to learn to work as a team.

Lesson 02. *The children should be given opportunities to get familiar with the technologies of which they are designing to. However, researchers need to be mindful of the fact that this might lead to children developing a preconception about the design space.*

Lesson 03. *Sufficient time should be allocated for the ice breaking sessions as the children are not used to talk freely and express their ideas to an adult.*

5.3   Planning and Management

The role of adults within the team was critical. We as the adult participants had to be experts in the methods that were used and were responsible for planning the workshops. We guided the child designers in thinking about their experiences of interacting with money and ideated how to visualize those experiences in a form of a mobile application. Although we made sure not to ask "leading questions" we used "What if" questions to guide the students and engage them in thinking deep into their experiences. Since this study was done within a school, we had to stick to strict time intervals as we were allocated only one hour per session. However, it was an arduous task to keep to time as the children kept exploring their experiences and discussing them with adults and peers, which if we had been strict about time would have been a hindrance as well as some of the richness in ideas would have been lost. The fact that the children found this work more fun than the school work was the biggest concern when managing time.

Initially, we planned to conduct the Score workshop with standard sticky notes. However, during the play room workshop when the children were writing down likes and dislikes about the games they played, we discovered that they are struggling to write concise thoughts in a paper as small as sticky in the Sinhala language. These children have not yet started using pens and were writing using pencils. Hence, whenever they made a mistake, they would erase and write on the same paper. This made the sticky note dirty and the children did not want to work with them anymore. Instead, they asked for another sticky. Thus we decided to let them write on A4 size paper. Afterwards, the adult researchers got together and wrote down the ideas of children on sticky notes. Sometimes, the adult researchers had to interview the children to understand the meanings of what they have written as they were ambiguous. There was one instance where a child had mentioned "I like 1, 2, 3" and the child has meant to say that he liked the way the events are numbered so that he can understand the flow. Additionally, we identified that some cultural practices can also impact the student participation in this type of work. For example, in countries such as Sri Lanka, the students are trained to be passive learners. This makes it difficult for the children to participate in an activity such as "stickies" which require them to provide critical feedback. Therefore, we report that it is paramount that some initial time needs to be spent on getting the children familiar with the co-design approach before directly utilizing the methods used in the developed countries.

We also realized that there was a slight hostility from the other teachers of the school towards the study as they believed the children from one classroom is getting a preferential treatment. However, as native researchers, we understood this behaviour of other teachers since the school is one of the rural schools with limited infrastructure and resources. Hence some teachers believed that there are much more important basic amenities to be improved within the school before the introduction of technology. Thus we would suggest all future researchers follow proper channels of getting approvals before conducting longitudinal studies in Sri Lankan schools.

Lesson 04. Children face difficulties in writing concise thoughts on a small piece of paper (sticky note). Therefore, such evaluation methods cannot be used as it is.

6 Conclusion

The work explained above is part of a larger study focusing towards using tablet computers as a pedagogical tool towards improving financial literacy to overcome poverty. As it is identified that the financial education needed to be provided from a young age, our study explored the experiences of children in interacting with money and how they would visualize these experiences in a form of a story. Through a series of co-design workshops, we were able to gather design inspirations and useful concepts about how to design a mobile learning platform from a child's perspective. The children took part in the study as design partners and worked as equals with adult designers. Since these children are new to these type of activities, a scaffolder process is followed. While this was successful in getting children familiarized with the process of co-design, it was found to limit the children's boundary of imagination. Two themes became prominent when the drawing artefacts were analysed. Except for one case, all the designs fell into either the *shopping* theme or *transportation*. We realized that the children expect the applications to relate to their daily experiences and needed the visual elements to be as realistic as possible. The artefacts generated by the children were evaluated through stickies method where we were able to collect likes, dislikes and design ideas from the children's perspective which can be used to improve the artefacts of the children. Our future research will be directed towards implementing a fully functional prototype based on the findings of the study and evaluate it through a field study. It is our belief that even though our work is specifically focused on technology design for financial literacy with children, our findings and observation are valid for most design applications within the same context.

References

1. Abramovitch, R., Freedman, J.L., Pliner, P.: Children and money: getting an allowance, credit versus cash, and knowledge of pricing. J. Econ. Psychol. **12**(1), 27–45 (1991)
2. Ahmed, S.I., Jackson, S.J.: Residual mobilities: infrastructural displacement and post-colonial computing in Bangladesh. In: Proceedings of the 33rd ACM Conference on Human Factors in Computing Systems, pp. 437–446 (2015)
3. Alborzi, H., Druin, A., Montemayor, J., et al.: Designing StoryRooms: interactive storytelling spaces for children. In: Proceedings of the 3rd Conference on Designing Interactive Systems, vol. 2, pp. 95–104 (2000)
4. Ames, M.G.: Charismatic technology. In: Proceedings of the 5th Decennial AARHUS Conference, pp. 109–120 (2015)
5. Benton, L., Johnson, H., Ashwin, E., Brosnan, M., Grawemeyer, B.: Developing IDEAS: supporting children with autism within a participatory design team. In: Proceedings of Conference on Human Factors in Computing Systems, pp. 2599–2608 (2012)
6. Beverly, S.G., Burkhalter, E.K.: Improving the financial literacy and practices of youths. Child. Sch. **27**(2), 121–124 (2005)
7. Braun, V., Clarke, V.: Using thematic analysis in psychology. Qual. Res. Psychol. **3**, 77–101 (2006)
8. Cohen, S., Xiao, J.-J.: For parents particularly: consumer socialization—children and money. Child. Educ. **69**, 1 (1992)

9. DailyFT: Financial literacy for development. The DailyFT (2015). http://www.ft.lk/article/500017/Financial-literacy-for-development
10. Deterding, S., Dixon, D., Khaled, R., Nacke, L.: From game design elements to gamefulness: defining "Gamification". In: Proceedings of the 2011 Annual Conference Extended Abstracts on Human Factors in Computing Systems, CHI EA 2011, p. 2425 (2011)
11. van Doorn, F., Stappers, P.J., Gielen, M.: Design research by proxy: using children as researchers to gain contextual knowledge about user experience. In: Proceedings of CHI 2013, pp. 2883–2891 (2013)
12. Druin, A.: Cooperative inquiry: developing new technologies for children with children. In: Proceedings of the SIGCHI Conference on Human Factors in Computing Systems, pp. 592–599, January 1999
13. United States Department of the Treasury Office of Financial Education: Integrating financial education into school curricula: giving America's youth the educational foundation for making effective financial decisions throughout their lives by teaching financial concepts as part of math and reading curricula in elementary, middle, and high schools (White Paper), Washington, D.C. (2002)
14. Eglash, R., Bennett, A., O'Donnell, C., Jennings, S., Cintorino, M.: Culturally situated design tools: ethnocomputing from field site to classroom. Am. Anthropol. 108(2), 347–362 (2006)
15. Fails, J.A., Guha, M.L., Druin, A.: Methods and techniques for involving children in the design of new technology for children. Found. Trends Hum. Comput. Interact. 6(2), 85–166 (2013)
16. Fallis, A.G.: Building the Sri Lankan knowledge economy. J. Chem. Inf. Model. 53(9), 1689–1699 (2013)
17. Frauenberger, C., Good, J.: Interpreting input from children: a designerly approach. In: Proceedings of the SIGCHI Conference on Human Factors in Computing Systems, CHI 2012, pp. 2377–2386 (2012)
18. Friedline, T.L., Elliott, W., Nam, I.: Predicting savings from adolescence to young adulthood: a propensity score approach. J. Soc. Soc. Work Res. 2(1), 1–22 (2011)
19. Hamidi, F., Ghorbandordinejad, F., Rezaee, M., Jafari, M.: A comparison of the use of educational technology in the developed/developing countries. Procedia Comput. Sci. 3, 374–377 (2011). Elsevier
20. Hewagamage, K.P., Meewellewa, H.M.S.J., Munasinghe, G.K., Wickramarachi, H.A.: Role of OLPC to empower ICT adaptation in the primary education. In: Education in a Technological World: Communicating Current and Emerging Research and Technological Efforts, pp. 391–398 (2011)
21. Hogarth, J.M.: Financial education and economic development. In: International Conference on Improving Financial Literacy, Federal Reserve Board, pp. 1–34 (2006)
22. Irani, L., Vertesi, J., Dourish, P., Philip, K., Grinter, R.E.: Postcolonial computing: a lens on design and development. In: Proceedings of CHI 2010 Conference on Human Factors in Computing Systems (2010)
23. Itenge-wheeler, H., Kuure, E., Brereton, M., Winschiers, H.: Co-creating an enabling reading environment for and with Namibian children. In: Proceedings of the 14th Participatory Design Conference, PDC 2016, 131–140. ACM (2016)
24. Kam, M., Akhil, M., Kumar, A., Canny, J.: Designing digital games for rural children: a study of traditional village games in India. In: Proceedings of the SIGCHI Conference on Human Factors in Computing Systems, CHI 2009, pp. 31–40 (2009)

25. Kumar, A., Tewari, A., Shroff, G., Chittamuru, D., Kam, M., Canny, J.: An exploratory study of unsupervised mobile learning in rural India. In: Proceedings of the 28th International Conference on Human Factors in Computing Systems, CHI 2010, pp. 743–752 (2010)

26. Kwon, S., Oh, S., Park, K., Kim, S., So, H.: Children as participatory designers of a new type of mobile social learning application. In: Proceedings of the 17th International Conference on Human-Computer Interaction with Mobile Devices and Services Adjunct, MobileHCI 2015, pp. 862–869 (2015)

27. Large, A., Nesset, V., Beheshti, J., Bowler, L.: "Bonded design": a novel approach to intergenerational information technology design. Libr. Inf. Sci. Res. 28(1), 64–82 (2006)

28. Larson, M., Rajput, N., Singh, A., Srivastava, S.: I want to be Sachin Tendulkar!: a spoken English cricket game for rural students. In: Proceedings of the 2013 Conference on Computer Supported Cooperative Work, pp. 1353–1364 (2013)

29. LBO: Education a priority, free tablets for students Lanka Business Online (2016). http://www.lankabusinessonline.com/education-a-priority-free-tablets-for-students-budget/. Accessed 1 Dec 2016

30. Lucey, T.A., Giannangelo, D.M.: Short changed: the importance of facilitating equitable financial education in urban society. Educ. Urban Soc. 38(3), 268–287 (2006)

31. Makhaeva, J., Frauenberger, C., Spiel, K.: Creating creative spaces for co-designing with autistic children - the concept of a " Handlungsspielraum". In: Proceedings of the 14th Participatory Design Conference: PDC 2016, pp. 51–60 (2016)

32. Metcalf, J.L., Atance, C.M.: Do preschoolers save to benefit their future selves? Cogn. Dev. 26(4), 371–382 (2011)

33. Ministry of Finance and Planning: Poverty Indicators. Sri Lanka (2013). http://www.statistics.gov.lk/HIES/HIES2012_13FinalReport.pdf

34. Moraveji, N., Li, J., Ding, J., Woolf, S., Arbor, A., Microsoft Corporation: Comicboarding: using comics as proxies for participatory design with children. In: Proceedings of the SIGCHI Conference on Human Factors in Computing Systems, CHI 2007, pp. 1371–1374 (2007)

35. Muller, M.J.: PICTIVE–an exploration in participatory design. In: Proceedings of the SIGCHI Conference on Human Factors in Computing Systems Conference on Human Factors in Computing Systems, CHI 1991, pp. 225–231 (1991)

36. Nardi, B.A.: Studying context: a comparison of activity theory, situated action models, and distributed cognition. In: Context and Conciousness: Activity Theory and Human Computer Interaction, pp. 69–102 (1996)

37. Nicholas, M., Hagen, P., Rahilly, K., Swainston, N.: Using participatory design methods to engage the uninterested. In: PDC 2012, p. 121 (2012)

38. Nicurriculum: A guide to organising a money themed event for 4–11 year olds. Northern Ireland (2010). http://www.nicurriculum.org.uk/curriculum_microsite/financial_capability

39. Otto, A., Schots, P., Westerman, J., Webley, P.: Children's use of saving strategies: an experimental approach. J. Econ. Psychol. 27(1), 57 (2006)

40. Pahl, J.: Family finances, individualisation, spending patterns and access to credit. J. Socio-Econ. 37(2), 577–591 (2008)

41. Pham, T.T.H., Renshaw, P.: How to enable Asian teachers to empower students to adopt student-centred learning. Aust. J. Teach. Educ. 38(11), 65–85 (2013)

42. Read, J.C., Fitton, D., Horton, M.: Theatre, PlayDoh and comic strips: designing organic user interfaces with young adolescent and teenage participants. Interact. Comput. 25(2), 183–198 (2013)

43. Read, J.C., Gregory, P., MacFarlane, S., McManus, B., Gray, P., Patel, R.: An investigation of participatory design with children-informant, balanced and facilitated design. In: Interaction Design and Children, pp. 53–64 (2002)
44. Read, J.C., Fitton, D., Mazzone, E.: Using obstructed theatre with child designers to convey requirements. In: CHI 2010 Extended Abstracts on Human Factors in Computing Systems, pp. 4063–4068 (2010)
45. Rodriguez, I., Puig, A., Grau, S., Escayola, M.: Designing a math game for children using a participatory design experience. In: The Eighth International Conference on Advances in Human-Oriented and Personalized Mechanisms, Technologies, and Services, pp. 28–35 (2015)
46. Scaife, M., Rogers, Y., Aldrich, F., Davies, M.: Designing for or designing with? Informant design for interactive learning environments. In: Human Factors in Computing Systems, pp. 343–350 (1997)
47. Sim, G., Horton, M., Read, J.C.: Sensitizing: helping children design serious games for a surrogate population. In: Vaz de Carvalho, C., Escudeiro, P., Coelho, A. (eds.) Serious Games, Interaction, and Simulation. LNICSSITE, vol. 161, pp. 58–65. Springer, Cham (2016). doi:10.1007/978-3-319-29060-7_10
48. Sim, G., Read, J.C., PGregory, P., Xu, D.: From England to Uganda: children designing and evaluating serious games. Hum. Comput. Interact. 30(3–4), 263–293 (2015)
49. Suchman, L.A.: Practice-based design of information systems: notes from the hyperdeveloped world. Inf. Soc. 18(2), 139–144 (2002)
50. Talbot, D.: Given tablets but no teachers, Ethiopian children teach themselves. MIT Technol. Rev., 7–9 (2012)
51. Taxen, G., Druin, A., Fast, C., Kjellin, M.: KidStory: a technology design partnership with children. Behav. Inf. Technol. 20(2), 119–125 (2001)
52. Te'eni-Harari, T.: Financial literacy among children: the role of involvement in saving money. Young Consum. 17(2), 197–208 (2016)
53. Tilakaratna, G.: Social protection and the MDGs in Sri Lanka. Implications for the post 2015 agenda (2015)
54. Truong, K.N., Hayes, G.R., Abowd, G.D.: Storyboarding: an empirical determination of best practices and effective guidelines. In: Proceedings of the 6th ACM Conference on Designing Interactive Systems (2006)
55. UnitedNations: United Nations Millennium Development Goals (2015). http://www.un.org/millenniumgoals/. Accessed 24 June 2016
56. VanFossen, P.J.: Best practice economic education for young children? It's elementary! Soc. Educ. 67(2), 90 (2003)
57. Vygotsky, L.S., Hanfmann, E., Vakar, G., Kozulin, A.: Thought and Language. MIT Press, Cambridge (2012)
58. Walsh, G., Donahue, C., Rhodes, E.E.: KidCraft: co-designing within a game environment. In: Proceedings of the 33rd Annual ACM Conference Extended Abstracts on Human Factors in Computing Systems, pp. 1205–1210 (2015)
59. Walsh, G., Druin, A., Guha, M.L., et al.: Layered elaboration: a new technique for co-design with children. In: Conference on Human Factors in Computing Systems, pp. 1237–1240 (2010)
60. Walsh, G., Foss, E., Yip, J., Druin, A.: Octoract: an eight-dimensional framework for intergenerational participatory design techniques. In: Proceedings of the SIGCHI Conference on Human Factors in Computing Systems - CHI, p. 2893 (2013)
61. Warschauer, M., Cotten, S., Ames, M.: One laptop per child Birmingham: case study of a radical experiment. Int. J. Learn. Media 3(2), 61–76 (2011)

62. WorldBank: World Bank Poverty Data (2016). http://www.worldbank.org/en/topic/poverty/overview
63. Yin, R.K.: Analyzing case study evidence: how to start your analysis, your analytic choices, and how they work. In: Case Study Research: Design and Methods, 5th edn. SAGE Publications, Inc. (2014)
64. Yip, J., Druin, A., Foss, E., et al.: Children initiating and leading cooperative inquiry sessions. In: IDC 2013, pp. 293–296 (2013)
65. Yip, J., Clegg, T., Bonsignore, E., Gelderblom, H., Rhodes, E., Druin, A.: Brownies or bags-of-stuff? Domain expertise in cooperative inquiry with children. In: Proceedings of the 12th International Conference on Interaction Design and Children, IDC 2013, pp. 201–210 (2013)

Everyday Creative Uses of Smartphone Images in Biomedical Engineering Laboratories

Dhaval Vyas[1(⊠)], Hinal Vyas[2], and Maria A. Woodruff[2]

[1] School of Electrical Engineering and Computer Science (EECS),
Queensland University of Technology (QUT), 2 George Street, Brisbane, QLD 4000, Australia
d.vyas@qut.edu.au
[2] Institute of Health and Biomedical Innovation (IHBI), 60 Musk Avenue,
Kelvin Grove, QLD 4059, Australia
{h.vyas,mia.woodruff}@qut.edu.au

Abstract. In this paper, we focus on creative practices associated with smartphone images for supporting scientific work. We employed observations and semi-structured interviews with 12 research staff members from a biomedical engineering institute over a period of three months and explored the role smartphone images play in supporting their scientific activities. We studied different ways smartphone images are incorporated into researchers' everyday work. Our findings highlight practices and motivations associated with the use of smartphone images. Based on our findings, we provide implications for designing innovative smartphone apps and particularly emphasize the role smartphones can play in developing and maintaining hybrid lab-books.

1 Introduction

Studies of science and technology [12, 28] have pointed to the fact that while final outcomes of any scientific work, be it scientific articles, functional technologies or newspaper reports, inform about scientific facts and truths, a large number of procedural insights and local contingency are often filtered out. In particular, how scientists come about making sense of their data, images, or other type of information and what cognitive processes manifest themselves is rarely reported. The conduct of scientific research involves a varied set of cognitive processes and skills. Some of these are internal processes of the sort that have been the focus of the traditional cognitive science for decades, such as, categorization, reasoning, problem solving, and analogy formation. Others are processes that take place when information is propagated across different representational media, such as documents, papers and other types of external representations (e.g. [10, 11, 26, 27, 30]). Researchers have recognized that cognition is a socially and culturally embedded phenomenon that is situated and distributed between people concerned [8, 10, 11, 17, 21, 26, 27]. Cognition is as much rooted in mental processes as it is in the external world of objects, artifacts and social practices. In particular, the importance of external representations in reasoning and knowledge construction has been noted by many researchers seeking to understand the nature of the science [11, 14, 16, 20].

© IFIP International Federation for Information Processing 2017
Published by Springer International Publishing AG 2017. All Rights Reserved
R. Bernhaupt et al. (Eds.): INTERACT 2017, Part I, LNCS 10513, pp. 335–343, 2017.
DOI: 10.1007/978-3-319-67744-6_22

The current generation of smartphone cameras with advanced capabilities for rapidly capturing and sharing images has shown a great potential for the development of innovative applications that can support medical and scientific practices. Smartphone-based applications such as CellScope [5], M-Health [2], smartCARD [23], and mobile spectroscopy [9] have shown how current smartphones can be augmented to support scientific processes. There are similar examples [6, 7] in the field of ophthalmology. While the development of such bespoke solutions is increasing, there is a lack of research into studying existing practices of smartphone use in scientific work. Human Computer Interaction (HCI) researchers can develop innovative solutions, when there is a strong repertoire of knowledge about the role smartphone images play in supporting scientific work.

In order to explore this area, we carried out an ethnographic study at a biomedical engineering facility in a university setting. We involved 12 researchers in a semi-structured interview study and an observational study. We studied their everyday work practices and in particular observed their use of smartphone images. Using an inductive thematic analysis approach [3], we organized our findings in the form of social 'practices' and 'motivations' associated with the use of smartphones.

As a common laboratory protocol, all the researchers kept lab-books where they recorded each and every minor detail of their activities. A detailed analysis of these lab-book showed that capturing images using smartphones at different stages of their work was a very common practice. We found four generic types of smartphone images: microscopic images, procedural images, equipment images, and measurement images. We found that these images were used for recording complex information, supported coordination and communication within teams, worked as a referencing and trouble-shooting tool and became a simple way of information offloading. Based on such practices we point to some important implications for designing new mobile solutions, in particular exploring the design of physical-digital lab-books.

We make two contributions to the HCI community by (1) developing an empirical understanding of the smartphone image use in the biomedical engineering research; and (2) providing important implications for designing novel mobile solutions.

2   Methods

We used two methods to understand the use of smartphone images in scientific work. We contacted three research labs within the biomedical engineering facility and recruited 12 participants for a semi-structured interview study. 8 out of these 12 participants agreed to let us observe their lab work. Table 1 provides details of these participants. The three labs that were approached were working in the areas of Biomaterial and Tissue, Bones and Histology, which combined a good variation of expertise and focus on biomedical engineering [18].

Our participants included lab technicians, senior researchers and PhD students in their final years. All of them had at least 3 years of experience working in the field. In the interview sessions, we asked our participants to describe their laboratory work and processes, we looked though their lab-books and smartphones to understand the role of digital images. We also asked them to discuss at least three recent projects using their lab-books. The interviews lasted for about 45 min and were audio recorded and later transcribed. We took photos of their lab-book pages and smartphone images while they answered our questions. We also followed 8 of these participants in their laboratory work. We made scheduled appointments with these participants over three months. We spent nearly 30 h with them observing their activities, and specifically looking into their use of smartphones during this time. We took notes while our visits to the laboratories and audio recorded conversations. We carried out thematic analysis [3] on the participants' observation and interview data, where we inductively identified patterns and themes within the data in the form of social practices and goals.

Table 1. Participants in interviews and observations.

Laboratory	Participants	Methods
Biomaterials & tissue	5	Interview (5), observations (3)
Bones	4	Interview (4), observations (2)
Histology	3	Interview (3), observations (3)

3 Results I: Practices

In this section, we will discuss specific practices related to the use of smartphone images.

3.1 Use of Lab-Book

All the researchers working in these labs were required to keep their lab-books up-to-date. Smartphone cameras were used to capture several of the scientific and procedural details in the form of images and in rare cases videos. Our participants used their lab-books to record a large variety of information: images of their experimental activities, hand written notes, annotations and drawings, printed email exchanges and standard operating procedures (SOP), post-its, bookmarks, graphs of their results, among other things. This way, lab-books contained both physical and digital (later printed and glued to the pages) information. Affordances of the paper-based lab-book allowed participants to share among team members, photocopy them or add pages whenever required. These features are highlighted in the work of Sellen and Harper [27]. We observed that researchers used a large amount of digitally-created information (smartphone images, graphs, email prints) which was printed and glued their printed versions onto their physical lab-books.

3.2 Types of Images

We observed that our participants captured images from their smartphones for different purposes. Figure 1 shows some examples that we collected during our research. We categorize them into four generic types:

1. *Microscopic images* are captured by placing smartphones directly onto the eye piece of microscopes (Fig. 1a). These images are captured to check the morphology (e.g.

shapes, colors, structures) of different biological samples. In the labs that we studied, some of the microscopes did not have the in-built camera feature and this was where such a use of smartphone cameras was useful. We found that participants captured such images because it was quicker to transfer, share and print images. Participants commented that such images are not used in important publications, but these provided good indications on the progress of their experiments.

2. *Procedural Images* are captured during the regular course of an experiment where the aim is to record each and every step through projects. Figure 1b shows a lab-book page which captures all the steps taken in an experiment, allowing others to reproduce the process in future. Images captured in such a way also allow researchers to troubleshoot when they come across any problem.

3. *Equipment Images* are captured to report specific ways of using biomedical equipment or point out any issues (or workarounds) so that other lab workers can get informed. Figure 1c shows a lab-book page where an issue in an instrument is reported with annotated instructions. These types of images are captured to help others in the lab who might use those equipment.

4. *Measurement Images* are captured to record sample sizes, sample labels, chemical quantity, among other technical information that are important to specific experiments. These images serve as reminders and can be re-visited during the trouble-shooting phase. Figure 1d shows an image where samples and their labels are captured.

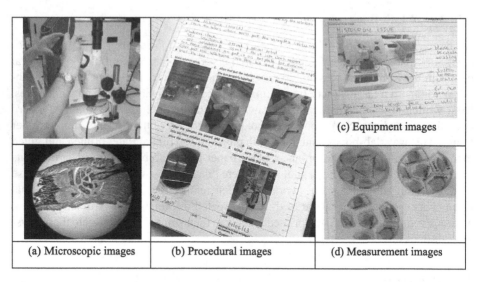

| (a) Microscopic images | (b) Procedural images | (d) Measurement images |

Fig. 1. Images captured using smartphones.

4   Results II: Motivations and Goals

In this part, we will discuss the motivations and goals behind using smartphone images in biomedical research.

4.1   Quick Recordkeeping, Reliability and Troubleshooting

We observed that the use of smartphone images in lab-books served multiple uses. All of our participants maintained a very meticulous lab-book in order to make sure that they record each and every step of their work. During an interview session, one of the participants said: *"There are quite a few different things which we need to record. Perhaps starting from the very beginning – the processing and embedding of tissue usually requires substantial amount of sequential and time-based steps so you need to record quite accurately what solution you are changing from and into; all that needs to be documented quit well. Mobile photos help in this case."*

The role of smartphone images was quite important in the development of the lab-books. Smartphones being ready-at-hand allowed recording very complex set of information easily and quickly. In the case of the microscopic images (Fig. 1a), researcher did not have to rely on the inbuilt camera of the microscope. During a typical experiment once samples are embedded with some chemicals, researchers needed to regularly check the behaviour of the sample on specific microscopes. We observed that researchers relied on their smartphone images because it was easier and quicker to do preliminary analysis on their samples. Images captured through the built-in cameras of microscope were high-res and hence quite large in size, which made the sharing, transferring and printing process slower for participants. It was a compromise in quality, but in cases where quick analysis is required (changes in cells colour or size), this compromise was not counter-productive for the research.

During experiments participants would have to prepare a large number of samples with different permutations and remembering them or even keeping a hand-written record of individual samples would be a tedious job. Figure 1d shows an example where a researcher has used images to keep track of their samples, reliably. The image highlights the issue of labelling and orientation. In this example a participant working on a sheep tibia bone had sectioned a large sample in different orientations. She has labelled these samples and captured images of these samples with their labels so that she can keep track of different procedures followed on these samples. She commented: *"As we process our samples, we maintain a clear chain of orientation. We take lots of pictures of the samples: how they have been processed. It is little effort but we are always confident of what we are doing and we can always go back to our log-book images and check."*

Several participants commented about the problems they faced in maintaining their lab-books. Some participants pointed out that the amount of time and effort spent on capturing images through smartphones and later attaching them on their lab-books was really high. Others commented that the issue of labeling (when the samples are in large numbers) was a big problem. Some participants commented about the resolution issues of smartphone images (in comparison to the high definition cameras built into certain biomedical equipment). These are the clear points where technology can play a role and novel solutions can be explored.

4.2   Coordination and Communication

Smartphone images allowed smoother coordination and communications within and outside of the teams. Often the work was handed over to other members within the same lab and having all the details captured in lab-books helped in coordinating activities. The facility had collaborations with several international universities and medical centers. They would get samples from these collaborators to carry out specialized experiments. A participant commented: *"We have to make sure that our collaborators know what we are planning to do with their samples. We show them images of how we sectioned their samples before we do anything on it..... Since I keep my lab book up to date, my team members can also take over if I am not available."*

Even within the facility, there were specific cases where smartphone images helped in communicating difficult issues with other members. One of the participants who participated in our study commented the following: *"I was doing this work for one of the PhD students in our group. I wanted to show him that this tissue was hard and without making it soft enough I could not section it properly. At that time, I showed him some photos and discussed this issue and after the discussion we decided how to work on this particular section."*

5   Discussion and Implications

Our interaction with three research laboratories highlights how the use of smartphone images has become interweaved with the everyday work practices of the researchers. In several cases, the use of smartphone images was simply a quick *workaround*. In the case of microscopic images (Fig. 1a), the ready-at-hand nature of smartphones allowed researchers to take photos directly through the eye piece of microscopes and to have quick prints. This particular workaround had some issues with the quality of images. These images also played a role of *cognitive offloading*, in a sense that rather than having to remember the measures or names of chemicals, capturing an image using smartphones would be very easy to make sure that the precise information is recorded. Another issue that our research has highlighted is the empirical aspect of *meticulous recording* of information. Even when researchers had to go through a lengthy process of capturing, transferring, printing and gluing images onto the lab-books, they saw value in doing so. As we pointed out, record keeping allowed them to troubleshoot, coordinate among collaborators. They also used lab-books as a reference tool to guide future research activities. It is also important to point out the *lack of technology* support. The use of smartphones was itself a technology use, but at several points we saw that researchers used hand-written labels, relied on physical scale bars for measurements and glued images on lab-books and annotated them. We believe that there is a huge scope for designing novel mobile technologies that can support biomedical engineering researchers' work practices. In the following we point to some interesting design considerations.

5.1 Hybrid Lab-Books

A quick look at the lab-books of our participants indicated how they combined a mix of digital and physical data into a paper-based book. They recorded digital information such as smartphone images, graphs and email prints and combined them with hand-written notes and drawings, post-its, and colorful bookmarks. This illustrates the versatile affordances of paper-based materials. On the one hand our research echoes the findings of Sellen and Harper's [27] work and highlights importance of technology non-use [1]. Sellen and Harper emphasized that the value of a physical artefact such as a paper is its materiality and affordances which allows for mobility, portability, shareability, which are not always easily substituted by a new digital paper technology. There is a clear value in sustaining the sanctity of a material artefact and a technology should build on these material qualities and not replace them. Similarly, the notion of technology non-use also proposes that in specific situations technology may not be the best solution.

On the other hand, our research highlights that technology was in fact used in combination with paper-based materials to produce images, graphs and email prints. Additionally, there were clear gaps where technology can actually improve parts of researchers' activities. Having an inbuilt measurement tool or a ruler on the screen of smartphone camera that can provide measures of specific physical samples; or digital labeling mechanisms through which individual samples can be identified; or being able to print images in a variety of formats and layouts – which can be later annotated if required; can be of great value and useful digital additions to the existing setup. These implications need to be experimented before any strong claims can be made.

HCI has witnessed some work on augmented lab-books [13, 15, 22, 25] and augmented workspaces [30] for biological researchers. Mackay et al. [15] participatory design approach showed a great potential. However, these research projects had a strong technology push. We believe the need for a hybrid lab-book still exists. A more balanced approach is required where users (biologists or biomedical scientists) can keep their existing practices of using a paper-based lab-book alive and smartphones can aid in minimizing the tedious tasks such as gluing printed images on paper lab-book, labeling, and measuring.

5.2 Innovation Through Hardware and Apps

The field of biomedical engineering being visual and structural in nature provides an opportunity for designing innovative applications which utilizes the camera feature of smartphones. We clearly saw the need for developing a smartphone app to support much more refined ways to capturing and handling the microscopic images (Fig. 1a). Currently a lot of appropriation and workarounds goes on where researchers would place their mobiles on the eye piece of microscopes and after some positioning they would capture images of their samples. This particular practice can be supported through very simple apps that can allow basic measurements, positioning, and printing incorporated in the smartphone itself. Advanced image processing and pattern recognition algorithms can allow for detecting and identifying specific objects from the samples or develop a much detailed morphological understanding of biological samples. Some progress is already visible where external hardware and sensors are used to aid specific features in the smartphone's capabilities. The example of CellScope [5] is a great one here. We believe that HCI researchers, utilizing user-centered perspectives, can lead the innovation in this domain.

6 Conclusion

In this paper, we showed our initial findings on the role smartphone images play in supporting scientific work. We do not claim this to be a comprehensive empirical account, however, our findings do point to some interesting tension between the use of physical and digital information in the field of biomedical engineering. Our findings highlight the different ways researchers incorporated the use of smartphone images in supporting their work. We believe that by having an account of the existing practices of using smartphone camera feature, HCI researchers will have a better handle toward designing innovative solutions to support biomedical scientists in their laboratory settings.

Acknowledgement. We thank all the participants of this study for their valuable time. We also thank the Science and Engineering Faculty, IFE and IHBI of QUT for funding this research.

References

1. Baumer, E., Silberman, M.S.: When the implication is not to design (technology). In: Proceedings of the SIGCHI Conference on Human Factors in Computing Systems (CHI 2011), pp. 2271–2274. ACM, New York (2011)
2. Bourouis, A., Zerdazi, A., Feham, M., Bouchachia, A.: M-health: skin disease analysis system using smartphone's camera. Procedia Comput. Sci. **19**, 1116–1120 (2013)
3. Braun, V., Clarke, V.: Using thematic analysis in psychology. Qual. Res. Psychol. **3**(2), 77–101 (2006)
4. Breslauer, D.N., Maamari, R.N., Switz, N.A., Lam, W.A., Fletcher, D.A.: Mobile phone based clinical microscopy for global health applications. PLoS ONE **4**(7), e6320 (2009)
5. CellScope™ (2016). https://www.cellscope.com/
6. Chhablani, J., Kaja, S., Shah, V.A.: Smartphones in ophthalmology. Indian J. Ophthalmol. **60**(2), 127 (2012)
7. Davis, E.A., Hovanesian, J.A., Katz, J.A., Kraff, M.C., Trattler, W.B.: Professional life and the smartphone. Cataract Refract Surg Today, pp. 21–2 (2010)
8. Engestrom, Y., Middleton, D.: Cognition and Communication at Work. Cambridge UP, New York (1996)
9. Gallegos, D., Long, K., Yu, H., Clark, P., Lin, Y., George, S., Nath, P., Cunningham, B.: Label-free biodetection using a smartphone. Lab Chip **13**(11), 2124–2132 (2013)
10. Hutchins, E.: Cognition in the Wild. MIT Press, Cambridge (1995)
11. Latour, B.: Visualization and cognition: thinking with eyes and hands. Knowl. Soc. **6**, 1–40 (1986)
12. Latour, B., Woolgar, S.: Laboratory life: The Construction of Scientific Facts. Princeton University Press, Princeton (1986)

13. Klokmose, C.N., Zander, P.-O.: Rethinking laboratory notebooks. In: Lewkowicz, M., Hassanaly, P., Wulf, V., Rohde, M. (eds.) Proceedings of COOP 2010, pp. 119–139. Springer, London (2010). doi:10.1007/978-1-84996-211-7_8

14. Lynch, M.: The production of scientific images: vision and re-vision in the history, philosophy and sociology of science. In: Pauwels, L. (ed.) Visual Cultures of Science: Rethinking Representational Practices in Knowledge Building and Science Communication, pp. 26–41. Dartmouth College Press, Hanover (2006)

15. Mackay, W.E., Pothier, G., Letondal, C., Bøegh, K., Sørensen, H.E.: The missing link: augmenting biology laboratory notebooks. In: Proceedings of the 15th Annual ACM Symposium on User Interface Software and Technology (UIST 2002), pp. 41–50. ACM, New York (2002)

16. McNeill, D.: Hand and Mind: What Gesture Reveal About Thought. University of Chicago Press, Chicago (1995)

17. Merleau-Ponty, M.: Phenomenology of Perception. Humanities Press, New York (1962)

18. Minger, S.L.: Regenerative medicine. Regenerative Med. 1(1), 1–2 (2006)

19. Monteiro, M.: Reconfiguring evidence: interacting with digital objects in scientific practice. Comput. Support. Coop. Work (JCSCW), 231–244 (2010). Springer

20. Myers, N.: Molecular embodiments and the body-work of modeling in protein crystallography. Soc. Stud. Sci. 38(2), 163–199 (2008)

21. Norman, D.: Cognitive artifacts. In: Carroll, J.M. (ed.) Designing interaction: Psychology at the Human-Computer Interface. Cambridge University Press, New York (1991)

22. Oleksik, G., Milic-Frayling, N., Jones, R.: Study of electronic lab notebook design and practices that emerged in a collaborative scientific environment. In: Proceedings of the 17th ACM Conference on Computer Supported Cooperative Work & Social Computing, pp. 120–133. ACM (2014)

23. Oncescu, V., Mancuso, M., Erickson, D.: Cholesterol testing on a smartphone. Lab Chip 14(4), 759–763 (2014)

24. Roy, R.C., Dadarya, S.: Use of digital camera in clinical microbiological laboratory: an academic and diagnostic tool. Int. J. Biomed. Adv. Res. 3(5), 423–424 (2012)

25. Schraefel, M.C., Hughes, G.V., Mills, H.R., Smith, G., Payne, T.R., Frey, J.: Breaking the book: translating the chemistry lab book into a pervasive computing lab environment. In: Proceedings of the SIGCHI Conference on Human Factors in Computing Systems (CHI 2004). pp. 25–32 (2004)

26. Schmidt, K., Wagner, I.: Coordinative artefacts in architectural practice. In: Blay-Fornarino, M., et al. (eds.) Proceedings of the Fifth International Conference on the Design of Cooperative Systems, IOS Press, Amsterdam, pp. 257–274 (2002)

27. Sellen, A., Harper, R.: The Myth of the Paperless Offices. MIT Press, Cambridge (2002)

28. Star, S.L.: Scientific work and uncertainty. Soc. Stud. Sci. 15(3), 391–427 (1985). Sage Publications, Ltd.

29. Suchman, L.: Embodied practices of engineering work. Special Issue Mind Cult. Act. 7(1/2), 4–18 (2000)

30. Tabard, A., Hincapié-Ramos, J., Esbensen, M., Bardram, J.: The eLabBench: an interactive tabletop system for the biology laboratory. In: Proceedings of the ACM International Conference on Interactive Tabletops and Surfaces, pp. 202–211. ACM (2011)

Towards Participatory Prototyping with Older Adults with and Without Cognitive Impairment: Challenges and Lessons Learned

Luã Marcelo Muriana[(⊠)] and Heiko Hornung

Institute of Computing, UNICAMP, Campinas, Brazil
luamarcelo17@gmail.com, heiko@ic.unicamp.br

Abstract. Technology is often not accessible to older adults, especially to those with low digital literacy or cognitive impairment. One premise of participatory design is that involving stakeholders including potential users during the whole process of design and development can result in solutions that are more accessible and make more sense to a target population. However, involving older adults in the design process is not straightforward, especially when they have little or no experience with information technology or some form of cognitive impairment, such as early stages of dementia. We investigate how to facilitate the participation of older adults with and without cognitive impairments in the phase of low-fidelity prototyping. We report on participatory design activities conducted in a non-governmental home for older adults with low socio-economic status and present lessons learned and challenges for planning and conducting participatory design that complement the literature in this subject area. For example, participants showed they are capable of some level of abstraction, although literature indicates that older adults with cognitive impairments have difficulties in abstract thinking.

Keywords: Participatory design · Design with older adults · Low-fidelity prototyping · Cognitive impairment · Dementia

1 Introduction

Ageing is a process that can be understood as sequential, individual, accumulative, irreversible, universal, deteriorating a mature organism, affecting all members of a species, turning its members less capable of dealing with stress from the environment, and thus increasing their chance of death [11]. Generally, ageing can be accompanied by a certain decline in cognitive capacity, which however not necessarily interferes with everyday life. Apparently, this alteration is due to a reduction of the information processing speed and due to changes in cognitive functions such as memory, attention or executive functions [22].

Dementia is not a disease but a term that describes a group of symptoms caused by different diseases or conditions. "Dementia is a syndrome – usually of a chronic or progressive nature – in which there is deterioration in cognitive function (i.e. the ability to process thought) beyond what might be expected from normal ageing. It affects memory, thinking, orientation, comprehension, calculation, learning capacity,

R. Bernhaupt et al. (Eds.): INTERACT 2017, Part I, LNCS 10513, pp. 344–363, 2017.
DOI: 10.1007/978-3-319-67744-6_23

language, and judgement. Consciousness is not affected. The impairment in cognitive function is commonly accompanied, and occasionally preceded, by deterioration in emotional control, social behavior, or motivation." [13].

Older adults with cognitive impairment might experience a reduced ability to interact with digital devices such as computers or smartphones and applications. Together with probable motor impairments, reduced vision and hearing, certain devices and services become quickly inaccessible to older adults. Older adults are often described as technology-averse, although they accept new technologies, albeit differently than younger adults [23]. The processes of perceiving the utility of a technology and overcoming the fear of "breaking things" might be different from younger adults, but older adults also want to use technology if they consider it beneficial [2, 19].

The inability of a person to use some technology is a consequence of a design failure [24]. A design that is inadequate for people with certain special needs results in society disabling these people. Designers need to keep in mind that their reality might be quite different from that of an older adult, which might impact fundamental aspects such as the metaphors used during design. The diversity within the population of older adults is enormous and greater than the diversity among younger adults [19]. Generalizing findings from younger to older adults is complex if not impossible, and thus design should always be conducted explicitly considering older adults as potential users.

Participatory design (PD) is an approach to design that includes users and other stakeholders into the design process [10], and thus seems appropriate to create solutions that are accessible and make sense to older adults. The objective of this paper is not to argue that PD is the best approach for designing in this context, but rather to investigate its possible advantages and limitations.

A design process can be separated into different phases, e.g. problem identification and clarification, requirement analysis, design, implementation, and evaluation [21]. The focus of this work is on the phase of design, and more specifically on low-fidelity prototyping. Low-fidelity prototypes are often used during the early phases of design and can be sketches made on paper or using other materials that allow quick drafting. Low-fidelity prototyping is a low-cost method to explore and evaluate ideas without already focusing on details of a final, polished product [27].

Although other authors have reported on PD with older adults with and without cognitive impairments [1, 5–9, 15, 19, 20, 25], few reported on low-fidelity prototyping with these participants as co-designers as opposed to informants or evaluators [8]. The objective of this work is thus to contribute to filling this gap.

We describe seven activities conducted with a group of older adults that included people in early stages of dementia. We conducted these activities in a non-governmental home for older adults with low socio-economic status. To be eligible to move in, candidates cannot have economic means to sustain themselves autonomously.

We present lessons learned and challenges for planning and conducting PD activities. A common theme of the lessons and challenges is that the inclusion of older adults with cognitive impairment into the process of low-fidelity prototyping is complex, especially when participants have little or no experience with technology use. Apart from adapting prototyping techniques to the abilities of the participants, careful planning is required to present an explain concepts related to technology design and use.

The remainder of this paper is structured as follows: Sect. 2 presents related work; Sect. 3 characterizes the design context; Sect. 4 describes the seven activities and obtained results and analyzes and discusses them; Sect. 5 synthesizes the lessons learned; Sect. 6 identifies challenges for planning and conducting PD activities; Sect. 7 concludes.

2 Related Work

Older adults differ from younger adults in the ways they use digital technology [3]. People with cognitive impairments face difficulties when interacting with digital devices or services [4]. Designers often seem to ignore older adults as a target audience [2], possibly trying to simplify the design process by focusing only on a subset of user needs, or physical, sensorial and cognitive characteristics [1].

PD gives participants a voice by considering their individual needs and experiences. However, engaging older adults in the design process involves some challenges [19]. It is necessary to frequently remind participants of the meeting topic. Designers might overanalyze contributions of participants, introducing a complexity not intended by the participants. Older adults might have difficulties imagining future technologies or intangible concepts. Designers need to keep that in mind when appreciating the individual contributions to the design process (cf. also [8, 25]). Some PD methods might need to be adapted.

Lindsay et al. [19] proposed the following approach for including older adults in PD: stakeholder identification and recruitment, video prompt creation, exploratory meetings, and low fidelity prototyping sessions. The video prompts were intended to trigger the curiosity of the participants and to create discussions that supported the exploratory meetings that informed the low fidelity prototyping sessions. The goal of the prototyping sessions was to identify more requirements related to features of the device to be designed. The sessions followed the PICTIVE process [26].

The following three studies investigate how to include older adults in the processes of idea generation, creativity and design critique. Davidson and Jensen [20] investigated whether older adults whether a design critique of existing applications before the phase of ideation supports creativity. The authors found evidence that a design critique before ideation is detrimental to creativity. Massimi et al. [28] used critique before design to try to increase creativity of the older adults, discussing photos of PDAs before a brainstorming session and the subsequent prototyping. The authors concluded that older adults conduct critique more easily than design.

Uzor et al. [29] conducted a study whose main objective was to involve older adults in the design of multimodal tools for effective rehabilitation. The participants were involved in activities such as personal experience discussion, scenario and persona creation, evaluation of prototype games, and sketching proposals of new games. The study presents evidence that seniors can play a significant role in the design of rehabilitation games.

Different from our work, Lindsay et al. [19], Uzor et al. [29], Massimi et al. [28] and Davidson and Jensen [20] did not involve participants with cognitive impairments or not explicitly mention whether or how these were involved in prototyping activities.

Lindsay et al. [8] investigated how to create an empathic relationship among designers and participants with dementia. They designed a safe-walking device for people with dementia. At the outset of the project, the authors tried to understand the everyday life of the participants as well as differences between participants and designers. Initially, the authors analyzed participants' accounts about experiences relevant to the problem domain. Subsequently, they incrementally produced individual prototypes with the participants, which allowed an exploration of the participants' thoughts and experiences without requiring abstract thinking.

During the design stage, Lindsay et al. [8] conducted four meetings with the older adults. Of the six participants of the first stages, only the two who were most engaged in the process and the subject participated in this stage. During the first two meetings, the authors presented sketches of different ideas as well as storyboards to discuss these ideas. During the third meeting, the participants tried to create paper prototypes of the device interface (the authors did not report on the result of this meeting). During the fourth meeting, the final prototype was presented.

Slegers et al. [15] developed a system to register eating times of older adults with dementia using PD. Their process involved three phases: ethnography, ideation and conceptualization, and prototyping. The contact between designers and participants with dementia occurred in two ways. During the ethnography phase, the designers observed participants in their homes and in a psychiatric hospital, and accompanied a psychologist visiting participants with dementia at home. To understand the difficulties of people with dementia in everyday life, the authors conducted an activity based on the MAP-it method [17] with the older adults and their caregivers. The results of this activity informed the prototyping of an application for caregivers, during which only caregivers participated, but not the participants with dementia.

Holbø et al. [7] investigated how to design a safe walking device considering the needs of older adults with dementia. Conducting interviews and PD workshops, they identified factors that influenced the participants' attitudes towards these devices and how they expected these devices to help them. The design process comprised two phases. During the preparatory phase, the authors conducted interviews with relatives and caregivers, initial meetings with the participants with dementia, and created photo recordings of daily activities, to better understand the routines of older adults with dementia, their families and their caregivers. Subsequently, they conducted PD workshops to better understand the personal experiences of the participants with dementia, how dementia affected their possibilities to do outdoor activities, and how a technological device might facilitate these activities. During this phase, the authors used the photos from the first phase to discuss daily activities. Next, they used Lego figures and a neighborhood map to help the participants describe relevant experiences. Last, researchers, older adults with dementia and their caregivers created low-fidelity physical prototypes and used them to play out scenarios, identifying requirements as the participants reflected over possible uses of a safe walking device. The research was conducted with three older adults with dementia, and each activity was conducted individually with each participant and their families and caregivers.

Hendriks et al. [6] argued that traditional PD methods are not very appropriate for people with dementia, since they require specific approaches that consider their different cognitive and psychiatric symptoms (e.g. deterioration of memory or aphasia;

depression, hallucinations or delusions). Based on literature about PD with older adults, with people with dementia and with people with symptoms related to dementia, the authors proposed six subgroups of guidelines to support the process of PD with older adults with dementia. To evaluate these guidelines, they conducted PD sessions with female participants with dementia aged between 70 and 95, as well as their family members. The sessions were focused on problem clarification and design suggestions, and were conducted with an individual person with dementia and their family members. The proposed guidelines or best practices do apply to PD in general and are not restricted to older adults with cognitive impairment. Furthermore, they do not focus on planning specific activities such as prototyping or evaluation.

Although some authors investigated how to design with or for people with dementia [1, 2, 6, 8, 14, 18], we encountered few examples (e.g. [7]) of involving older adults with cognitive impairments in the stage of prototyping. Furthermore, guidelines, recommendations and insights identified by the respective authors are relatively abstract. Especially regarding prototyping, these authors did provide few details as to how the employed methods and techniques worked with the participants with dementia.

3 Characterizing the Design Context

We conducted our activities at *Lar dos Velhinhos de Campinas* (LVC), a non-governmental institution for older adults with a more than a 100-year history located in Campinas, State of São Paulo, Brazil. The activities were conducted by two researchers and occurred once or twice a month, in accordance with the participants' availability. Each activity had a duration of 60 to 90 min, occurred in the early afternoon, and terminated when afternoon coffee was served. The activities were mostly conducted in the room of occupational therapy at LVC's geriatric center and were always accompanied by the same occupational therapist. At the beginning of each activity, past activities were remembered. All activities were filmed, and one researcher took annotations. The research activities were approved beforehand by the ethical review committee of the researchers' institution as well as by LVC's coordination board. All activities were discussed beforehand with some of the LVC staff.

The older adults participating in the activities live at the LVC and were invited by the occupational therapist to volunteer as participants. Some of the participants aged between 69 and 92 showed cognitive impairments such as different stages of dementia. The number of participants in the seven activities varied from five to twelve. The variation in the participation was due to individual health-conditions, well-being, and parallel activities. The educational level of most corresponded to 4th grade elementary school. One participant graduated high school, and some were functionally illiterate, participating in reading and writing classes at the LVC.

All participants were residents at the LVC and needed to accept and follow the institution's rules and regulations. Most participants had a humble upbringing, many did not have family or friends and thus rarely received visitors. Some had health problems that prevented them from participating in some encounters. Sometimes, participants arrived emotionally upset, and even crying, e.g. because of missing family members or friends. These and other circumstances were always considered when planning and conducting our activities with the intent to provide a pleasant activity.

At the beginning of the first encounter, the ethical review committee approved consent form was discussed and read jointly. Of the participants that showed symptoms of dementia, none required a legal representative, and all could sign the consent form. Although this is outside the scope of this paper, an important question is to what extent people with cognitive impairments can consent to participating in research activities and remember that they consented. Apart from writing consent forms in easy to read, plain language, in appropriate font size, as well as reading them aloud and discussing them with the participants, an approach that might help remembering might be to make video recordings of the discussion available. During our activities, we did not make those recordings available (the residents of LVC did not have easy access to a playback device), but orally remembered participants at the beginning of each activity why we were there and that they could leave the activity at any moment (some participants left activities when not feeling well, but generally returned for the next session).

The activities we report on in this paper are part of the master-level research of one of the authors, the prime objective of which is to investigate how to include older adults with cognitive impairments into PD processes. Our design process was open, i.e. at the outset we did not have a specific objective other than designing something that would make sense within the context of the LVC.

During previous activities that involved storytelling, questionnaires, games, as well as interviews with participants, caregivers and other LVC staff [16] we already had started to familiarize ourselves with the LVC as well as with the participants, their physical and cognitive abilities and limitations, their preferences and needs, their life experiences, as well their "profiles" as potential users of digital technology.

The participants, as well as many other residents of the LVC, had little to no experience with digital technology. Although the LVC has a computer room accessible to all residents, hardly anyone uses it. Of our participants, only two possessed a feature phone, most had no experience with devices such as microwave ovens or video recorders, and many did not use the TV remote control.

We identified that the LVC residents often faced difficulties adapting themselves to their new home after moving there, communicating with other residents, and following LVC rules and regulations. We observed that the participants loved to look at photos and that this activity instigated conversation among them, even after having stopped looking at the photos. Looking at photos individually or in groups might stimulate communication, might have a potential to help in the adaptation process (e.g., using photos of interesting places and events of the new home, as well as photos of the old home) and even might promote accepting and remembering house rules and regulations (e.g., by storytelling). We thus decided to design some device for displaying photos, focusing on features that might stimulate conversation.

4 Towards Participatory Paper-Prototyping: Seven PD Activities

The activities described in the remainder of this section focus on possibilities to include the participants in low-fidelity prototyping activities. Not all activities were directed at prototyping a "photo viewing device", some explored general techniques or dynamics of low fidelity prototyping.

Based on challenges pointed out in the literature, the goal of the first activity was to evaluate a prototyping technique to promote accessibility and creativity. Analyzing the activity, we perceived limited overall communication among the participants. The goal of the second activity was to better understand how the participants communicated during collaborative, goal-directed activities. After that activity, we identified "photo viewing" as a possible target application. The goal of activities three and four was thus to evaluate to what extent existing online photo viewing applications made sense to our participants, while at the same time evaluating how they used two different prototypes (simple paper and executable with a dedicated physical input device). After these activities, we accepted "photo viewing" as a relevant and adequate application and perceived the participants had difficulties understanding the purpose of design activities as well as the meaning of graphical interface elements. The remaining three activities presented in this paper thus yielded at gradually exposing the participants to prototyping graphical user interfaces.

4.1 Activity 1: Redesign of a TV Remote Control

The objective of this activity (cf. Fig. 1a) was to explore a limited set of Styrofoam® cutouts as prototyping material, investigating its accessibility, creativity potential, and whether it is suitable for creating various design alternatives. This activity consisted in the construction of a low-fidelity prototype of a TV remote control that participants could understand and use. Participants were divided into groups of two to three and asked to build a remote control using the materials provided by the authors. Each team received a kit of Styrofoam® cutouts which included different "empty" remote control bases and different button sets in different shapes and colors. In previous activities, we had perceived the participants' difficulties of drawing something "from scratch", even concrete objects such as a TV set or a flower. Furthermore, some participants had difficulties holding a pen or drawing on paper, hence the exploration of this kind of material during the activity.

One of the original eight participating older adults left the activity shortly after the start. The remaining participants designed remote controls in three groups. The resulting remote controls would not have been fully functional, and the participants had difficulties or were unable to describe or explain their designs. In two of the two-person-groups, one participant chose and arranged all parts while the other only observed. In the first group, the participant put duplicate volume controls on the remote control. Although he stated that he could not see the labels on the buttons, he stated to have chosen them because of their high contrast. In the second group, the designing participant tried to get the other's opinion, however without success.

Fig. 1. (a) Redesign of a TV remote control; (b) Creating a photo poster.

The three-person-group tried to communicate and choose the buttons together. The researchers were unable to understand the button layout (there were duplicate buttons and number buttons mixed with other controls), and the participants were unable to explain it. One participant stated, "I don't understand anything. I'm doing, but I'm not understanding".

After designing their remote controls for approximately one hour, each group tried to simulate the use of the remote control of another group, i.e. pretending to turn on the TV, change channels or volume. One control did not have an "on/off" button, thus the participants were unable to simulate this task. The creator of the control explained that the TV would be switched on by pressing one of the number buttons, but could not explain how to switch it off.

Many of the standard remote control labels did not make sense to the participants and did not help to identify the button functions. One participant felt uncomfortable for not having used a remote control before. Throughout the activity, he repeatedly stated that next time he would "do better".

Although some of the participants never used a remote control before, all groups assembled a remote control from the parts handed out to them. However, none of the created prototypes could have been transformed into a functioning prototype. We did not conduct a comparative activity with a prototype drawn on paper, but from our experience with the group, they would probably have had more difficulties drawing a remote control from scratch. The activity allowed us to better understand the advantages and disadvantages of prototyping based on assembling ready-made parts.

An advantage is that physical prototype assembling might be more inclusive than prototype drawing. Arranging the parts requires less fine motor skills than drawing on a sheet of paper, and, with the right materials, might even be conducted with people with visual impairments. Arranging the parts also allows for easier exploring and reconfiguring than erasing lines drawn on paper or starting over with a new blank sheet. Furthermore, for designing in a domain unfamiliar to the participants, this technique provides concrete starting points, as opposed to a blank sheet of paper.

A disadvantage of this technique is that such prototypes are restricted to the available parts. In this concrete instance of a remote control, the prototypes did not lead to insights that could not have been gathered without PD. A possible adaptation of the technique would be to design the parts in a previous PD activity or allow the ad-hoc design of parts during the session.

Our main interest in this activity was to investigate whether the technique was feasible in principle, which we could affirm, and how the participants interacted with each other. With no facilitator instigating conversation, and no otherwise imposed "rules", as expected, the participants hardly communicated. The only communication that took part in some groups was of the form "Is it OK to put this piece here?" to which the other participants always agreed.

4.2   Activity 2: Photo Poster

The objective of this activity (cf. Fig. 1b) was to investigate whether and how the participants communicate and coordinate during a creative process. During this activity, participants were divided into two groups of five and asked to create a poster telling the "story" of one of the previously conducted activities. As materials, participants could use a large sheet of paper, color pens, glue, and choose between sets of photos from one of the previous activities printed on plain paper. Each group chose a different set. The authors participated as facilitators. At the end, each group presented their poster to the other group, telling the story.

One of the groups managed to organize itself in a way that allowed each member to give their opinion and to participate in some way in the creative process. One participant with tremors in the hands could not draw but actively commented on the others' drawings. After some time, a more passive participant was given the task to hold and distribute the pens and other utensils, and thus possibly felt more like a part of the group. In the other group, one of the participants dominated the activity, while the rest seemed to accept this. Two of the participants arrived emotionally upset, one of them crying. Both insisted in participating, but did not contribute actively to the group. The two groups presented their results with enthusiasm. One of the main presenters, who generally is very articulate, seemed to be nervous. The main presenter of the other group got a bit "carried away", and it took some time until the researchers and other participants managed to get their focus back to the group.

In contrast to the previous activity, the researchers participated in the groups and instigated communication among the participants. In this activity, the participants communicated more among themselves than during the previous activity. Since we worked in groups of six participants including the facilitators, effects of group dynamics became visible, i.e. strong personalities dominating the group (not necessarily consciously), or quieter participants contenting. Since in many cultures, older adults are very respected, balancing the group dynamics can become a delicate matter. Another common event occurred during this activity: two participants were very emotionally upset at the beginning of the activity, but were eager to participate. It is not always possible to console upset participants, and postponing the activity to the next encounter is often not an option. Activities should thus be planned considering indisposed or distracted participants, and facilitators be prepared to do more than just conducting an activity.

4.3   Activity 3: Evaluation of a Low-Fidelity Paper Prototype

The objective of this activity was to evaluate to what extent common interface elements of "simple" web-based photo viewing applications made sense to the participants, and whether they understood the content of the digital "photo album". During this activity, the participants interacted with a paper prototype of a photo viewing application. The photos used in a prototype were of a parade in which some LVC residents participated during a national holiday. The prototype was modeled imitating common web-based photo viewing services and had five types of possible interactions: show the next/previous photo, recommend, like, or comment on a photo. The participants were divided into pairs and asked to view the available photos and to explore the different buttons. One facilitator read the photo descriptions aloud when displaying a new photo. Comments could be written on paper with a pencil. After the interaction with the prototype, the researchers conducted a quick debriefing trying to evaluate how each pair of participants understood the prototype.

Since most of the participants had never used a computer before and thus probably did not understand the meaning of most of the interface elements, the participants had great difficulties using the prototype. One of the participants was observing attentively the other groups, but when it was her turn, she also had great difficulties. The participants could not distinguish buttons or active interface areas from inactive ones, and even when buttons were labeled, they did not understand their meanings. One participant, who participated in almost all activities, but who often seemed to lose interest quickly, understood that the "next" button advanced the "slideshow", and pressed this button repeatedly, seemingly to "get over" with the activity. Despite the difficulties interacting with the prototype, the participants were highly engaged with the photos and talked excitedly about them during as well as after the activity.

Although many participants had never used a computer before and thus probably did not make the connection between the paper prototype and a computer application, they could explore the prototype to some extent, and some partially concluded the task of viewing the photos in the prototype. This indicates that evaluating paper prototypes might be useful even if users have no or little experience with digital devices and cannot establish a relation between a paper prototype and a computer application. The "social" functions of the prototype (like, recommend, comment) did not make sense initially, since at first, the participants did not understand that someone who uses the device after them will see the results of their actions. Later some participants began to understand the functionality of commenting.

All participating older adults remained seated during our activities, and many had limited mobility. Thus, paper prototypes should be small enough to be explored while seated. Inclined tabletops can make the areas of a prototype more accessible.

This activity also provided arguments for accepting the idea to design a photo viewing application. Even with difficulties using the prototype, the participants enjoyed viewing the photos and talked to each other lively, including after the activity and with participants who had not used the prototype.

4.4   Activity 4: Evaluation of a Prototype of Physical Input Device

The objective of this activity (cf. Fig. 2a) was to explore the feasibility of a dedicated physical input device as technological platform, and to evaluate to what extent the participants understood different interface elements, as well as the application content. The activity consisted of interacting with a photo viewing prototype similar to that of the previous activity, using a physical input device that required touching physical interface controls. The prototype was developed in Scratch[1] and used a Makey Makey[2] based input device. Upon touching any of the controls, the prototype provided auditory and visual feedback. We divided the participants into pairs and explained the purpose of the application, remembering the previous prototype. We then asked the participants to freely explore the application, and debriefed them similarly to the previous activity.

All tangible controls of the prototype were labeled with text and icons. Although participants could read the labels, they did not understand the controls' functionality and initially pressed the controls exploratorily. One participant with motor impairments only pressed the nearest controls.

Although, in comparison with the paper prototype, the prototype of the physical input device had five explicit physical controls, and although the participants understood quickly that they had to press the controls to provoke some change in the application, they had great difficulty interacting. Few of the participants could switch photos purposefully, most did not understand that the "next" and "previous" controls displayed the next and previous picture. Only one participant could match the physical controls to actions on the screen.

a)   b)

Fig. 2. (a) Evaluation of a physical prototype; (b) Wireframing tutorial and hands-on exercise.

One participant asked his partner which control changed the photos, and got the correct answer. Diverting the gaze from screen to physical control, pressing the "recommend" instead of the "next" control, and looking back to the screen, another participant thought the photo had changed, only to perceive it had not after reading out and remembering the photo description. Yet another participant thought, the controls had

---

[1] Scratch - https://scratch.mit.edu/.
[2] Makey Makey - http://www.makeymakey.com/.

different functions for her and her partner, possibly because both managed to switch photos, one using the "next" and the other the "previous" control.

Despite the difficulties using the prototype, comparing a "traditional" photo album and the prototype, one participant exclaimed, "[The physical input device] is great, even better! You have to keep turning over [the pages of a photo album], but [in the physical input device] you just hit here and [the next photo] already appears".

Compared to the previous activity, this one was easier to some extent, since the participants had already been exposed to the concept of a prototype and since the interaction controls were now explicit physical objects. The interaction with the prototype was made difficult due to usability problems that could not be fixed in time, as well as due to unfavorable lightning conditions and high background noise during the session.

Nevertheless, the participants seemed to be engaged and commented positively about the experience. Although this was probably partly due to being exposed to some new technology for the first time, one participant who is often less motivated, and who was not going to participate in this activity, curiously approached the table where a pair of other participants was interacting with the prototype to see what was going on.

4.5 Activity 5: Wireframing Tutorial and Hands-on Exercise

The main objective of this activity (cf. Fig. 2b) was to explain the concept and importance of prototyping, and to introduce the participants to techniques of creating paper prototypes. Secondary objectives included introducing some interface design concepts such as "buttons", "placeholders" or "features". Finally, we tried to further explore how participants understood the abstract vs. the concrete and the tangible vs. the intangible aspects of prototypes and user interfaces.

This activity was divided into three stages: explaining the concept of prototyping, exemplifying the importance of prototyping, and creating a wireframe-like prototype. The concept of "prototyping" was explained using PowerPoint slides, variants of a simple, concrete paper prototype, and a high-fidelity prototype on different smartphones. Using these three media, also the concept of a "button" was introduced, e.g. participants held a smartphone in their hands and experienced what happened when they pressed a graphical button on the phone's touch screen.

To illustrate the importance of prototyping, we used a paper prototype of a computer screen that had an image at the bottom center of the screen. We posed the task to color the image, and the tools to complete the task were color pencils representing a color-fill tool of image editing applications. In one variant, the pencils where placed at the top left corner of the screen, similar to the position of the tool in a toolbar. The other variant had the pencils beside the image. The participants perceived, that both alternatives worked, but that the second alternative was much easier to use.

During the third stage, the participants were asked to create a layout of an "about me" page, similar to online profile pages, yearbooks or friendship books. To give the participants a concrete task, we asked them to replicate an example of the previous PowerPoint presentation: a screen that contained a person's name, a photo, a text and three buttons for changing the background color, changing the photo and reading the text. The participants received a blank sheet of paper and rectangular snippets representing placeholders of each interface element. Subsequently they were asked to fill in a factsheet about themselves and explained that one of the researchers would create an "application" using the layouts of and information about each participant.

All seven participating older adults managed to create a layout, three without help. One participant with low vision created his layout without being able to read the labels on the placeholders. After being prompted by a researcher and being read the labels, he changed his layout slightly. Two participants had help from the occupational therapist, which resulted in her creating almost the complete layouts. Another participant had difficulties understanding the activity, and did not know how to arrange the placeholders, even after being given hints and examples by a researcher and another participant.

Based on the individual abstract paper layouts and the factsheets, one researcher created the digital, concrete "about me" screens and presented them at the beginning of the following session. Seeing the results evoked positive reactions. One participant was excited and amazed seeing her photo and her personal information on the screen.

Although in previous activities the participants engaged in tasks similar or related to prototyping, we only introduced this and other concepts such as "features" and interface elements like "buttons" during this activity. The challenge of introducing these concepts is similar to working with generally digitally illiterate people. We used a mix of real-world and digital examples, as well as demonstrations and hands-on exercises and experiences, and tried to use a language that could be understood by the participants. For example, the concept of design tradeoffs was translated to "often there is no right or wrong; and some things work better for some people and worse for others" and demonstrated by the height and position of power outlets and light switches in the room (in our country there are no mandatory building standards for placing these).

We did not expect that the participants understood and remembered the concepts after one activity, and during the hands-on wireframing task most did probably not yet understand the utility of a wireframe. However, although some had difficulties executing the activity, the participants could make the connection between the concrete layout and the wireframe (or "drawing of boxes").

4.6   Activity 6: Newspaper Collage

The objective of this activity was to explore whether and how the participants understood the transition between a concrete newspaper layout and the abstract representation of a wireframe. During the first stage of the activity, the participants created the front page of a newspaper, gluing paper clippings (text snippets, and cutouts of photos and other visual elements, all taken from a real newspaper front page) on a blank sheet of paper. Each participant received between 8 and 15 clippings from a different newspaper. The participants were encouraged to create their own layouts. After that, we asked them to take a second sheet of blank paper and draw boxes for each element glued on the first sheet, in its respective position.

According to the occupational therapist, most of the LVC residents like to create collages. Three of the six participants concluded the activity without any help. One participant had initial difficulties, even receiving hints, examples and explanations, including from another participant. As during the previous activity, the occupational therapist helped two participants, substantially influencing the outcome. One participant with motor impairments had difficulties conducting the activity autonomously, but when offered help could identify the pieces and indicated where to put them.

The participants had difficulties in the second part of the activity, designing a "wireframe" based on the layout they had created. Two participants could create a wireframe, albeit with difficulties. One participant filled the sheet of paper with boxes that did not correspond to the layout; she was unable to explain what she had drawn.

The participants liked to create collages and thus showed no difficulties executing the activities. Of course, they executed the activity different from a group of people without visual and motor impairments. Creating a wireframe from the individual layout was difficult for most, probably due to fatigue at the end of the activity and due to the relatively high number of elements in the collage.

As to the usefulness of this technique, e.g. the tradeoff between simplicity and creativity, similar observations as for the Styrofoam® cutout assembly apply, although using additional material such as pens, scissors, colored cardboard and magazines or newspapers, it would be easier to create new content on the fly.

4.7   Activity 7: Bedroom of Dreams – Collective Low-Fidelity Prototyping

The objective of this activity was to explore the process of collective prototyping, as well as creativity during the prototyping process. Initially, one of the researchers drew a floor plan of a room shown on a photo, as well as a floor plan of the room where the activity took place. These floor plans were discussed to identify which element on the plan corresponded to which element in the room or photo. Next, we asked pairs of participants to draw the floor plan of one of the pair's shared bedrooms (the residents live in shared rooms with up to four people per room), indicating the position of furniture.

We divided the participants into two groups and asked them to collectively create a floor plan of their "bedroom of dreams". The authors participated as co-designers. To fuel the participants' imagination, we showed a set of 17 bedroom photos, ranging from classic to modern and futuristic bedrooms. The participants of each group then designed a floor plan, adding elements one after the other and completing approximately two cycles. Subsequently, the floor plan was discussed within the group, with the possibility to include additional items, and then presented to the other group.

All participants could conclude the first part of drawing their bedrooms, although some preferred to draw alone instead of in pairs. Furthermore, some participants expressed concerns stating they did not know how to draw. Within each pair, participants drew without communicating much. One pair claimed their rooms were identical, which they are in an abstract sense (number of beds, types of furniture), but not in the concrete sense (position of each piece of furniture, decoration).

At the beginning of the second part, the design of the "bedroom of dreams", some participants thought they had to draw a floorplan of one of the rooms in the photos shown to them. After further explanation, the two groups could draw their floorplan. One participant preferred not to draw but asked the other participants to draw her ideas when it was her turn. Another participant did not understand that this was a collective floor plan and always wrote or drew objects she would like in her own room, even if somebody already had drawn that object.

The first group produced a feasible floor plan and expressed content during the group discussion. The second group perceived their room was quite crowded, had unnecessarily repeated objects and an unsatisfactory layout. One of the participants, who had great difficulties drawing and was relatively quiet during this phase, participated eagerly in the discussion, pointing out flaws and sharing her opinion.

Although initially some participants seemed to be intimidated by having to draw, both the individual/pair and the group activity went well. The activity allowed all participants to contribute according to their strengths. Some preferred to ask others to draw for them, but since drawing was round-based everyone had their time and space to contribute. Those who could not express themselves visually could contribute orally. To further increase accessibility, it might be worth investigating a mix of drawing with collage in future iterations of this technique. Compared to other activities, including those where the authors actively participated, this one had the most and most natural conversation among participants. A future challenge will be to apply the technique to a domain or design problem the participants are less familiar with.

During individual or pair activities, some participants usually finished much earlier than others. During time-constrained round-based techniques such as brainwriting it is difficult to find the right timing, given the great differences in participants' abilities. The time-unconstrained round-based process solved timing problems we observed during other activities or anticipated with different techniques [35].

We could not affirm with certainty whether the photos shown before the group part of the activity supported creativity or ideation. However, on each of the two floor plans some elements appeared that were not present in the participants' rooms nor in the LVC, but that appeared in some photos.

5 Lessons Learned

Differently from the studies presented in Sect. 2, the goal of our work was to include participants as co-designers in the phase of low-fidelity prototyping, and to detail how this was done. Based previous findings from the related literature, and considering our concrete design context, we adapted some methods and experimented with alternative techniques. For example, we did not include design critiques of existing applications, since most participants had never used a computer before. On the other hand, we discussed all created artifacts and perceived that participants could criticize them and provide arguments for their critique.

Including older adults in PD processes is no trivial task, especially when some participants have cognitive impairments. Of the related work presented in this paper, few tried to include older adults with cognitive impairment in participatory prototyping activities. The activities presented in this paper had to consider the joint contexts of ageing, cognitive impairments, and digital illiteracy. In the following, we present lessons learned so far, divided into six themes. The objective of presenting these lessons learned is not to prescribe actions but to support researchers and designers in reflecting about and taking better informed trade-off decisions.

Planning Activities

- Simple might not be simple enough. Even after trying to simplify activities, e.g., by reducing the number of Styrofoam® pieces in activity 1 or the number of newspaper snippets and their formats in activity 6, participants might still have difficulties.
- Planning activities that introduce something new building on something the participants already know makes them more comfortable and confident. E.g., in activity 6 we used a technique the participants already knew from occupational therapy.
- On the other hand, planning an activity that requires knowledge of a previous activity might not always work, since due to personal health and well-being, there might be a substantial fluctuation of participants between encounters (cf. the sequence of activities 5 and 6).

Group Activities:

- The presence of a facilitator in the group promotes communication (cf. activities 2 and 7).
- The presence of a caregiver or other person the participants are familiar with (e.g. relatives, or LVC staff in our case) promotes communication and can elicit knowledge "external" participants such as researchers would not be able to access.
- Caregivers and other additional intermediaries also might have a better feeling how to motivate more passive participants and how to funnel the contributions of very active or agitated participants (cf. activity 2).
- However, the influence of these additional intermediaries must be considered carefully (cf. activities 5 and 6; this topic is also discussed in [15]).

Creativity:

- Although concrete examples such as photos, videos, or stories might prime participants and limit creativity, they might need them to get started (cf. activity 7).
- Collective prototyping facilitates creative contributions of participants who have difficulties during individual activities, e.g. due to insecurity or cognitive or motor impairments (cf. activity 7).

The concrete vs. the abstract:

- Although literature and our experience indicate that older adults with cognitive impairments have difficulties in abstract thinking, the wireframing activities and comments such as "our rooms are all the same" show that they are capable of some level of abstraction (cf. activities 5, 6, and 7).
- On the other hand, when presented with concrete examples such as stories or scenarios, they might have difficulties recognizing whether these are real or fictitious.

Sharing back results:

- Sharing back results not only promotes motivation and engagement of participants, but is also important to remembering and thus providing more context to subsequent activities (cf. activity 5; this topic is also discussed in [7]).
- If results are rather abstract (e.g. the drawing of a wireframe), participants might not recognize their own work. To promote recognizing, tangible results could be personalized, e.g. by signing or by showing photos or videos of the process (cf. activities 5 and 6).

Usability and Accessibility:

- Prototypes and applications obviously need to consider guidelines related to ageing, cognitive impairments and digital literacy. In practice, this means that pilot evaluations, even with expert researchers or designers, might be of limited use. Some basic problems might only be detected with the participants, and activities should be planned accordingly.
- When conducting prototype evaluations or other activities, participants might prefer to remain seated throughout the whole activity.
- A TUI with explicit, physical objects for input and output might facilitate the interaction, especially if the person has little experience with digital devices. Of course, if the objective of design is related to digital inclusion, designers should balance the trade-off between simplifying interaction with one artefact and promoting digital inclusion (cf. activity 4).

6   Challenges for Participatory Design Activities

When including older adults with cognitive impairments into the design process, designers face the challenge of having to adapt many methods and techniques that do not adequately consider the cognitive limits and capacities of participants [6, 8, 9]. Additional challenges occur in different dimensions.

Mood swings are a symptom of cognitive impairments. Changes of participants' emotional states occurred during various activities and consequently influenced results. Leading with these changes is a delicate matter. There is no recipe for avoiding mood swings or mitigating their impacts. Since mood swings also occur during the use of a design solution, we believe it is important to embrace them during design. Activities should be planned considering the possibility of mood swings: activities might take longer than expected, or might need to be repeated during another encounter. Subsequent activities in one session should not overly depend on each other.

Although it might be beneficial or necessary to include caregivers, family members or therapists in the process, they might interfere in the activities and influence results by trying to "help" other participants. Again, there is no recipe for avoiding this influence, but it should be acknowledged and considered during analysis. This interference is not necessarily bad, and after all, researchers and designers also influence outcomes.

In any design activity, it is important to make clear that participants are not evaluated. We found this challenging in our context. Some participants were quite preoccupied with "doing it right" or "living up to our (non-existent) expectations". This might have induced unnecessary stress. So far, we found no better way to mitigating this than to be aware of this fact, explaining repeatedly that there is no right or wrong, giving examples of ourselves doing things that might be considered "imperfect", as well as encouraging participants and making it clear that all contributions are important.

Due to health or well-being, not all participants participate in all activities. This has an impact on planning activities that depend on individual results of a previous activity.

Many activities that seem simple and quick to a designer might require a high cognitive and time effort from the participants. Furthermore, some participants might conduct activities significantly faster or slower than others. Activities should be planned accordingly, e.g. avoiding parallelism and the need for synchronization points.

7   Conclusion

The purpose of this paper was not to find "the best" method for designing for our "target population", but to explore whether and how they can participate in PD activities such as low-fidelity prototyping. This is reflected in the fact that initially we did not even have a target product to be designed, but tried to identify one that made sense in the concrete context of the retirement home where we conducted the activities.

PD with older adults with cognitive impairments is an area with many open questions, especially regarding participation during prototyping. In this paper, we presented activities, identified challenges and formulated lessons learned that answered or at least clarified some of these open questions.

Regarding the literature in the area, we experienced some similar challenges (e.g. [5]), and complemented guidelines (e.g. [6]). The contribution of this paper is to have further clarified challenges and synthesized lessons learned focused on practical issues arising during design activities, with the objective to support researchers and designers.

The biggest practical challenge we faced was to deal with the fluctuation in the group due to health or well-being. A methodological issue was related to pilot testing, which seems to be more limited when the "user population" is less well understood. A conceptual and methodological issue was related to creativity and the continuum between the abstract and the concrete. While giving concrete examples possibly limits creativity, it might be necessary to get started. Practical and social issues were related to group dynamics, to the possible sentiment of feeling evaluated, as well as to the "reflex" to "assist" the older adults instead of letting them do things in their own time and way.

Some of the presented activities were not directly related to prototyping, and those related to prototyping were not necessarily related to prototyping an actual product. However, the employed methods and techniques were similar to "real" prototyping, and we thus believe that the presented results are useful to other researchers and designers in similar contexts. Our next steps are to further explore collective prototyping to co-design and co-evaluate a photo visualization system to be deployed in the LVC.

Acknowledgment. We would like to say thank you to *Lar dos Velhinhos de Campinas* (Brazil) and its employees for allowing us to realize this study, and to the older adults which made and collaborated with the activities.

References

1. Abascal, J., Nicolle, C.: Moving towards inclusive design guidelines for socially and ethically aware HCI. Interact. Comput. **17**(5), 484–505 (2005)
2. Ancient, C., Good, A.: Considering people living with dementia when designing interfaces. In: Marcus, A. (ed.) DUXU 2014. LNCS, vol. 8520, pp. 113–123. Springer, Cham (2014). doi:10.1007/978-3-319-07638-6_12
3. Fairweather, P.G.: How older and younger adults differ in their approach to problem solving on a complex website. In: Proceedings of the 10th International ACM SIGACCESS Conference on Computers and Accessibility, Assets 2008, pp. 67–72. ACM, New York (2008)
4. Gordon, W.A.: The interface between cognitive impairments and access to information technology. SIGACCESS Access. Comput. **83**, 3–6 (2005)
5. Hendriks, N., et al.: Challenges in doing participatory design with people with dementia. In: Proceedings of the 13th Participatory Design Conference: Short Papers, Industry Cases, Workshop Descriptions, Doctoral Consortium Papers, and Keynote Abstracts, PDC 2014, vol. 2, pp. 33–36. ACM, New York (2014)
6. Hendriks, N., Truyen, F., Duval, E.: Designing with dementia: guidelines for participatory design together with persons with dementia. In: Kotzé, P., Marsden, G., Lindgaard, G., Wesson, J., Winckler, M. (eds.) INTERACT 2013. LNCS, vol. 8117, pp. 649–666. Springer, Heidelberg (2013). doi:10.1007/978-3-642-40483-2_46
7. Holbø, K., et al.: Safewalking technology for people with dementia: what do they want? In: Proceedings of the 22th International ACM SIGACCESS Conference on Computers and Accessibility, ASSETS 2013, 8 p. ACM, NewYork (2013). Article 21
8. Lindsay, S., et al.: Empathy, participatory design and people with dementia. In: Proceedings of the SIGCHI Conference on Human Factors in Computing Systems, CHI 2012, pp. 521–530. ACM, New York (2012)
9. Mayer, J.M., Zach. J.: Lessons learned from participatory design with and for people with dementia. In: Proceedings of the 15th International Conference on Human-Computer Interaction with Mobile Devices and Services, MobileHCI 2013, pp. 540–545. ACM, New York (2013)
10. Muller, M.J., Druin, A.: Participatory design: the third space in HCI. In: Jacko, J.A. (ed.) Human-Computer Interaction Handbook, 3rd edn., pp. 1125–1154. CRC Press (2012)
11. Organizacion Panamericana de la salud (OPAS).: Enfermaria gerontologica – Conceptos para la prática. Washington, 31 (1993)
12. World Health Organization (WHO): Revised Global Burden of Disease (GBD) 2002 Estimates: 2004 World Health Report. WHO, Geneva (2004)
13. World Health Organization (WHO): Dementia (2015). http://www.who.int/mediacentre/factsheets/fs362/en/
14. Pang, G.K.H., Kwong, E.: Considerations and design on apps for elderly with mild-to-moderate dementia. In: Proceedings of Information Networking (ICOIN), pp. 348, 353, 12–14 (2015)

15. Slegers, K., et al.: Active collaboration in health care design: participatory design to develop a dementia care app. In: CHI 2013 Extended Abstracts on Human Factors in Computing Systems, CHIEA 2013, pp. 475–480. ACM, NewYork (2013)

16. Muriana, L.M., Hornung, H.: Who are you? Getting to know and understanding older adults with dementia in participatory design at a nursing home. In: Proceedings of 15th Brazilian Symposium on Human Factors in Computer Systems, IHC 2016, São Paulo, Brazil (2016)

17. Schepers, S., et al.: MAP-it. the art of designing a participatory mapping method. In: Knowing (by) Design, vol. 1, no. 1, pp. 275–281 (2013)

18. Brazilian Computer Society (SBC): grand challenges in computer science research in Brazil – 2006–2016. Technical report about the Seminar, 8–9 May 2006

19. Lindsay, S., Jackson, D., Schofield, G., Olivier, P.: Engaging older people using participatory design. In: Proceedings of the SIGCHI Conference on Human Factors in Computing Systems, CHI 2012, pp. 1199–1208. ACM, New York (2012)

20. Davidson, J.L., Jensen, C.: Participatory design with older adults: an analysis of creativity in the design of mobile healthcare applications. In: Proceedings of the 9th ACM Conference on Creativity & Cognition, pp. 114–123. ACM Press, New York (2013)

21. Muller, M.J., Haslwanter, J.H., Dayton, T.: Participatory practices in the software lifecycle. In: Helander, M.G., Landauer, T.K., Prabhu, P. (eds.) Handbook of Human-Computer Interaction, 2nd edn., pp. 255–297. North-Holland, Amsterdam (1997). Chap. 11

22. Fichman, H.C.: Avaliação e Reabilitação Neuropsicológica. In: Veras, R., Lourenço, R.A. (eds.) Formação humana em geriatria e gerontologia: Uma perspectiva Interdisciplinar. R. J, UnATI - UERJ, pp. 243–246 (2006)

23. Ryan, E.B., Szechtman, B., Bodkin, J.: Attitudes toward younger and older adults learning to use computers. J. Gerontol. **47**, 96–106 (1992)

24. Oliver, M., Sapey, B.: Social Work with Disabled People. Palgrave Macmillan, Basingstoke (2006)

25. Massimi, M., Baecker, R.: Participatory design process with older users. In: Proceedings of the UbiComp 2006 Workshop on Future Media (2006)

26. Muller, M.J.: PICTIVE-An exploration in participatory design. In: Proceedings of CHI 1991, pp. 225–231 (1991)

27. Walker, M., Takayama, L., Landay, J.A.: High-fidelity or low-fidelity, paper or computer? Choosing attributes when testing web prototypes. In: Proceedings of the Human Factors and Ergonomics Society 46th Annual Meeting, pp. 661–665 (2002)

28. Massimi, M., Baecker, R.M., Wu, M.: Using participatory activities with seniors to critique, build, and evaluate mobile phones. In: Proceedings of the 9th International ACM SIGACCESS Conference on Computers and Accessibility, pp. 155–162. ACM Press, New York (2007)

29. Uzor, S., Baillie, L., Skelton, D.: Senior designers: empowering seniors to design enjoyable falls rehabilitation tools. In: Proceedings of the SIGCHI Conference on Human Factors in Computing Systems, pp. 1179–1188. ACM Press, New York (2012)

Using Critical Incidents in Workshops to Inform eHealth Design

Christiane Grünloh[1,2]([✉]), Jean D. Hallewell Haslwanter[3,4], Bridget Kane[5],
Eunji Lee[6], Thomas Lind[7], Jonas Moll[7], Hanife Rexhepi[8],
and Isabella Scandurra[9]

[1] KTH Royal Institute of Technology, Stockholm, Sweden
grunloh@kth.se
[2] TH Köln, Gummersbach, Germany
[3] FH Oberösterreich, Wels, Austria
[4] TU Wien, Vienna, Austria
[5] Karlstad University Business School, Karlstad, Sweden
[6] SINTEF ICT, Oslo, Norway
[7] Uppsala University, Uppsala, Sweden
[8] University of Skövde, Skövde, Sweden
[9] Örebro University, Örebro, Sweden

Abstract. Demands for technological solutions to address the variety
of problems in healthcare have increased. The design of eHealth is challenging due to e.g. the complexity of the domain and the multitude of
stakeholders involved. We describe a workshop method based on Critical
Incidents that can be used to reflect on, and critically analyze, different
experiences and practices in healthcare. We propose the workshop format, which was used during a conference and found very helpful by the
participants to identify possible implications for eHealth design, that can
be applied in future projects. This new format shows promise to evaluate eHealth designs, to learn from patients' real stories and case studies
through retrospective meta-analyses, and to inform design through joint
reflection of understandings about users' needs and issues for designers.

Keywords: Method · Workshop format · Design · Development ·
eHealth · Critical incidents · Stakeholders · Reflective practice ·
Evaluation

1 Introduction

Healthcare systems worldwide are increasingly under pressure, explained by our
aging population, increasing numbers of people living with long-term chronic
conditions, and spiraling costs of healthcare provision [13]. In the face of these
challenges, there is widespread agreement on the urgent need to develop and
improve the efficiency in healthcare. eHealth services, i.e. health services provided to people via Internet, promise to help solve the demand by improving the

R. Bernhaupt et al. (Eds.): INTERACT 2017, Part I, LNCS 10513, pp. 364–373, 2017.
DOI: 10.1007/978-3-319-67744-6_24

quality and effectiveness of care. However, these services are still to be considered new, and therefore they suffer from a range of technological, human, and organizational issues which pose challenges for the provision of quality healthcare. In practice, there is little time to reflect and draw conclusions around these complex issues and to increase our understanding of the context in order to improve the design of the eHealth services. In other fields, critical incidents (CIs) have been used to analyze failures of procedures or human errors in order to reduce risks in the future. Based on this, we appropriated the CI technique for IT development in health and looked at critical incidents as a basis for future directions in the development of eHealth services. This paper consequently describes the full-day workshop format, in which real-world CIs, representing development, healthcare organization, and patient perspectives, can be used as a tool to critically reflect on and analyze design cases of eHealth services [3]. The main focus hereby is on the method itself, its applicability for use as a workshop format, and the value of using CIs as a tool to inform the design of eHealth services.

2 Background

The two key concepts relevant for this paper are eHealth services and the Critical Incident Technique.

eHealth Services: eHealth refers to health services and information delivered or improved through the Internet and related communication technologies in order to enhance healthcare locally, regionally, and worldwide [4]. By breaking down the barriers of time and place, eHealth brings people and resources together to deliver healthcare services more efficiently [9]. Thus, eHealth enables changes in healthcare practices which can have an impact on patients' lives. For instance, the ability to access their electronic health records (EHR) can help patients to understand their medical issues, prepare for their next visit to their doctor, and help them to feel more in control of their care [19].

eHealth poses challenges for designers, in part because it changes methods of diagnosis, monitoring, and treatment [10] and creates interactions between actors, organizations, and systems that did not exist in conventional healthcare settings [12]. It may also prove more difficult to identify errors that put patients at risk, e.g. with electronic prescriptions [1]. These services are expected to be used by patients and professionals who need access to health information, from public health practitioners to administrators. But including a large number of heterogeneous end-users, especially for patients and other non-medical user groups, makes the development of eHealth services a complex task [2]. For instance, individual requirements can be in conflict, e.g. requirements with regard to privacy and data protection [24] as well as regarding how and when data is accessed and by whom [8]. Professional requirements can also cause conflicts, e.g. policy makers' versus clinical users' needs to manage the same data [1].

Many of the promises regarding how technological achievements will transform healthcare have to date fallen short of expectations [11]. As eHealth services are still to be considered new, the degree of uncertainty regarding end-user needs is high [20]. Faults or errors are unacceptable and systems must be reliable, dependable, and interoperable [22]. In some cases eHealth implementations have had unanticipated negative consequences that put patient lives at risk [1]. Thus, when developing eHealth services, the involvement of real users, i.e. patients and other stakeholders, is desirable [18]. With patients, who are possibly ill or weak, this can be particularly challenging [7], and in some cases may not be possible. However, involving proxies to represent the user is also problematic [15,23]. Thus, to improve healthcare practice where eHealth is used, new methods are needed to involve the experience of patients and relatives as well as to learn from previous projects. While studies abound reporting on failures or poor usability of health information technology, to date there is a lack of research investigating failures related to eHealth services (i.e. health services delivered over Internet). Specifically, the contextual causes of these failures as viewed by the non-medical user groups have rarely been studied.

The Critical Incident (CI) Technique: In the area of healthcare, the Critical Incident (CI) Technique has proved valuable in analyzing failures (see e.g. [25]). The CI technique was originally used to analyze failures of procedures or human error in fields like aviation in order to reduce risks in the same environment in the future through changes to system design [5]. Its use subsequently spread to health, education, and social work where it was applied with a shift of focus from failure examination to critical reflection [14]. The importance of critical reflection in practice is discussed by Donald Schön as a way for practitioners to make their tacit knowledge visible so that it is available for deliberation [21, p. 61]. Similar to Schön, Fook & Gardner discuss current challenges to professional knowledge, which they identify as the key reason for the need for critical reflection [6]. Some of the points they emphasize are that a) contexts are so changeable that practitioners need to continuously reassess their knowledge in relation to the context, and b) current contexts of practice are characterized by risk, uncertainty, changeability, and complexity [6, p. 66]. The critical reflection model developed by Fook & Gardner [6] makes use of the CI technique in that groups reflect on specific examples of their practice experience. Each participant presents and reflects on their CI, which they refer to as *"something (an event) that happened to a person that they regard as important or significant in some way"* [6, p. 77]. In a two-stage process group members use questions to help elicit embedded assumptions (Stage 1) and, through further questioning and dialogue, help each other *"derive changed practices and theories about practice that result from their reflections"* (Stage 2) [6, p. 73]. In the workshop described in this paper, eHealth designs were evaluated by appropriation of the critical reflection model to learn from patients' real stories and case studies through retrospective meta-analyses, and to inform design through joint reflection of understandings about the users' needs and issues for designers.

3   Workshop Design

In the following, we describe the design of a workshop in which researchers, practitioners, and patients were invited to contribute with a CI in relation to eHealth services for patients in advance, as it was used in a conference [3]. Inspired by the critical reflection model [6], the workshop organizers requested not only to describe the CI, but also to answer the following questions:

- What assumptions were made about the stakeholders, problem, or situation?
- What were the consequences of this incident?
- What could be done if this or a similar incident would occur again in the future?

The two stages of the original critical reflection model [6] were included in the workshop design. Inviting the participants to reflect on their CI by answering the specific questions in their position paper was Stage 1, whereas the dialogue in the group during the workshop constitutes Stage 2.

To promote active participation during the workshop, the presentation of the CIs was kept quite short and was done in an unusual manner: authors of the accepted position papers were asked to prepare a poster that contained background, problem environment, outline of the CI, and the most important aspects of why this incident was critical, that were then presented one at a time. This was in part due to the conference, which encouraged workshop organizers to make full use of the workshop format by prioritizing debate and joint action, instead of having for example "mini-conference"-style paper presentations [17].

During each presentation, the rest of the group made use of colored sticky notes to write comments related to the CI. For this activity four broad categories were introduced: *Enablers* (green), *Barriers* (orange), *Learning Opportunities* (yellow), *Other* (pink). These categories were purposively left quite open in order to prevent constraining the participants, while at the same time supporting them to think in more than one direction. After each presentation, the group members could ask further questions, engage in discussions, and finally attach their notes to the respective poster (see example in Fig. 1, left). Thus, the posters were used not only as a presentation medium, but also as an artifact for analysis and discussion throughout the workshop.

Stage 2 began after the presentations and here the participants were asked to make use of comments on the sticky notes and to discuss possible *implications for design*, which can be seen as a way to *"derive changed practices and theories about practice that result from their reflections"* [6, p. 73], as suggested by the original critical reflection model. The discussion was carried out in smaller groups, in which the sticky notes were discussed and moved from the posters to large sheets (size A1). This helped to connect them visually to the respective design implications found. Towards the end of the workshop the two groups presented and explained their findings. The workshop concluded with a short feedback session where the participants were encouraged to discuss their views of the method used for the workshop.

4   Experiences from the Workshop Conducted

In total, nine participants attended the workshop, of which eight were affiliated with a CI. As explained in the method section, preparing the CI and tentatively answering the questions constituted Stage 1. The workshop included five CIs. Two described incidents from the development perspective: a digital collage in a care home, which was perceived quite different by users than was intended by the designers; a sensor-based telecare monitoring system, of which many services were not used although the design was based on recommendations of the target group. Three CIs were related to the patient experience: patients and relatives reading the EHR; patients who lack access to their EHR; patients not being involved in discussions about their care during multidisciplinary team meetings. All presentations were followed by lively discussion, illustrating that the format worked well. After each presentation all of the participants contributed sticky notes with thoughts and ideas (Fig. 1, left). By the end of the presentations all posters had comments attached that covered all four areas (enablers, barriers, learning opportunities, other). A few comments in each category were repeated on multiple posters, but most comments were unique. For the discussion in Stage 2, the participants were split into two groups. The choice of the groups was based on the two focus areas of the different CIs submitted (i.e. patient experience and development perspective). During this stage numerous implications for design were identified. Figure 1 (right) exemplifies the result of one group discussion.

Fig. 1. Use of sticky notes: After presentation (left), after group discussion (right).

At the end of the full-day workshop, the participants were invited to reflect on the workshop and on the use of CIs as a tool to inform eHealth design. The provided feedback is summarized in the following:

Workshop design and realization: As explained in the method section, the workshop was organized to support active participation. This was perceived as positive and stimulating, especially because listening to presentations was expected to fill the following conference days and a *workshop* should therefore not consist solely of presentations. Using posters as a presentation medium, which were then used for analysis and active discussions, was considered constructive. Time-keeping for the active discussions during the workshop proved to be very difficult. This would have been even more difficult if more CIs had been included, as the organizers had intended. The participants perceived the workshop to be fairly relaxed and did not mind that the schedule was not strictly followed.

Critical incidents as a tool: The conclusion that evolved through discussion was that although the focus of the CIs might have been different, there are some problems and experiences that these projects have in common. For example the importance of including a broad diversity of users and stakeholders, or the different views on data taken by healthcare professionals and patients. For both of these, one implication identified was the need for checking with users, iteratively, starting early in the project. While it is seldom that failures are reported at conferences, much can be learned from analyzing and discussing these incidents. In addition, the value of this format for use within design teams was discussed. The CI format makes it possible for other people to access individual projects, to understand what is happening, and to comment on them. Thus, it is possible for participants to provide valuable comments from the outside in a relatively short period of time. Although Stage 2 focused on design implications, many of the projects were completed, so rather than identifying novel design implications the primary value for the participants themselves was found in learning about the area, gaining insight, and getting a deeper understanding.

The call for contributions: Some participants reported difficulty when preparing their CI/position paper after reading the instructions in the call for contributions. The format was unusual and it seemed like a "force fit". The participants' feedback brought to light that the call implied a strong focus on the patient perspective, of which the organizers were unaware. This implication, and the difficulties experienced when fitting the content into the CI format, almost led some researchers to refrain from submitting their contribution. However, the CI format was also seen as an opportunity to look at a project or a case from a different perspective. One participant related that the process of re-examining and re-framing the project into the CI format led to a new perspective on it.

5   Discussion

In the following section the various views on CIs noted, the way the workshop helped the participants, and comments on the workshop format are discussed.

Workshop format: The workshop format proved to be very successful and can be recommended to others working in the area of eHealth. A couple of organizational factors were key to the success. Firstly, limiting the topic to "eHealth services for patients and relatives" ensured all participants had a common knowledge base from which to discuss, even though when preparing some participants felt it was a force fit. This would be less of a problem if the workshop was held for a specific project. Secondly, using posters with a lot of graphical elements, rather than slideshows, reduced the presentation of each project to the essential elements and also provided a place on which to place the sticky notes with the comments. The four comment categories of *Enablers* (green), *Barriers* (orange), *Learning Opportunities* (yellow), *Other* (pink) worked well. Rather than limiting discussion to positive *enablers* and negative *barriers*, adding *learning opportunities* supported taking a view to future projects. The *other* category was sometimes used to draw parallels between projects. Using different colors from the start assisted communication among participants, saved time in that they didn't have to be categorized, and supported the structure of discussion in Stage 2.

Only after the submission deadline for the position papers, the organizers got an overview on the range of critical incidents described. Because the workshop was held at a conference, it was also difficult to attract practitioners and non-academics, whose input is invaluable. Furthermore, some of the position papers were written by more than one author, and it was unclear to the organizers until the day of the workshop, how many of the authors would attend. These aspects left lots of room for uncertainty, which had to be dealt with flexibly.

Time is often an issue in workshops. A lot of time was saved in this one by having participants prepare in advance by identifying and exploring their critical incident. If patients and caregivers are included, this activity could be done at the start of the workshop to reduce the effort required for the preparation. However, this may reduce the depth of the reflection and would deny participants the opportunity to look at others' CIs in advance.

There are some pitfalls to the Stage 2 discussion. Splitting the group, as was done here, may make it difficult to understand the intended meaning of some comments, since not all authors were present in either group. Participants thought that starting with *barriers* would have generated negativity in comparison to starting with *enablers*, as was done here.

Supporting projects moving forward: In practice, the participants provided valuable and quite detailed comments about others' projects about which they knew little. This was possible because the workshop had a focussed topic, and because each project focussed on a single CI. The focus made it easier for presenters to reduce some complexity, and having a concrete example made the problems easier to understand.

Participants gained valuable insights from the workshop. For example, based on a critical incident about a patient who needed access to their EHR urgently, workshop participants came to discuss in which way the structure of an EHR needs to be different for doctors and patients. The discussion made certain beliefs visible, challenged held assumptions, and helped identify new possibilities for collaboration between different stakeholders. Furthermore, it helped participants to see more clearly which uses were intended and which were appropriated. At the same time, it highlighted the limits to our understanding about potential future usage of eHealth systems, especially in early phases of the design process.

There were similarities between both the problems faced in the projects and the solutions proposed. Although the workshop started by looking at individual projects, it ended up identifying issues and design implications relevant for eHealth more generally. On reflection, the issues identified were not trivial, further demonstrating the value of the workshop. In addition, the way the issue was discussed during the workshop made it easy to apply to a specific project. This meant there was a benefit even to participants who did not present a CI and those whose projects were already completed. It also contributed to a sense of a shared vision for the future.

Different views on Critical Incidents (CI): The CI technique was originally designed to investigate problems, e.g. disorientation in pilots [5, p. 329], in order to inform design. More recently it has also been used as a method to analyze needs in User Centered Design (UCD) [16], and is also established in social work and health sciences to improve professional practice [6]. The conducted workshop demonstrates the value of CI for the development of eHealth more specifically. In this workshop people examined CI from two different perspectives. Some chose CIs from a patient's perspective to understand the needs. Others chose the CIs from the perspective of the developers, i.e. the problems faced during the development itself. All participants, regardless of perspective they took, found they gained understanding from the process. For the Stage 2 discussion, the developer and patient perspectives were separated, so that each group looked at contributions taking the same perspective. Also retrospectively, separating these perspectives for developing solutions makes sense, as the groups focussed on different issues: the developer perspective focussed more on the development process; and the group with the patient perspective more on specific design issues. It may be advisable to specify which viewpoint participants should take in order to promote discussion - but with the trade-off that only a narrower scope can be covered.

6 Conclusions

Basing this workshop around CIs is a novel approach that proved valuable. The workshop helped participants (researchers and designers) gain valuable insight into a variety of different eHealth projects, which they can make use of also in future projects. We recommend this method to others working in eHealth design. This type of CI workshop can be used to evaluate systems for the purpose of producing suggestions for the improvement of the design itself, but also to evaluate the development processes and/or to gain understanding about the application area. Developing an understanding of the area is of particular value in eHealth, where the introduction of systems and services enable new and unanticipated interactions that are difficult to analyze thoroughly in advance. In addition to the application with people from the development team representing real incidents as described here, as a next step we propose using the same format with actual stakeholders (such as healthcare professionals, patients, relatives or other non-medical users), possibly together with members of the development team. Here, the preparation tasks should be adapted to reduce the effort for the actual stakeholders (e.g. refrain from the position paper and concentrate on the presentation of the CI). In addition, it would be even more important to address the challenges regarding participant recruitment proactively, to ensure all relevant groups are represented.

Acknowledgments. The authors would like to thank the other people involved in the workshop: Åsa Cajander, Koen van Turnhout.

References

1. Ash, J.S., Berg, M., Coiera, E.: Some unintended consequences of information technology in health care: the nature of patient care information system-related errors. J. Am. Med. Inf. Assoc. **11**(2), 104–112 (2004)
2. Axelsson, K., Melin, U., Lindgren, I.: Exploring the importance of citizen participation and involvement in e-government projects: practice, incentives, and organization. Transforming Gov. People Process Policy **4**(4), 299321 (2010)
3. Cajander, A., Grünloh, C., Lind, T., Scandurra, I.: Designing eHealth services for patients and relatives: critical incidents and lessons to learn. In: Proceedings of the 9th Nordic Conference on Human-Computer Interaction, NordiCHI 2016, p. 130. ACM, New York (2016)
4. Eysenbach, G.: What is ehealth? J. Med. Internet Res. **3**(2), E20 (2001)
5. Flanagan, J.C.: The critical incident technique. Psychol. Bull. **51**(4), 327–359 (1954)
6. Fook, J., Gardner, F.: Practising Critical Reflection: A Resource Handbook. McGraw-Hill Education (2007)
7. Grönvall, E., Kyng, M.: On participatory design of home-based healthcare. Cogn. Technol. Work **15**(4), 389–401 (2013)
8. Grünloh, C., Cajander, Å., Myreteg, G.: "The Record is Our Work Tool!" Physicians' framing of a patient portal in Sweden. J. Med. Internet Res. **18**(6), e167 (2016)
9. Hesse, B.W., Shneiderman, B.: eHealth research from the users perspective. Am. J. Prev. Med. **32**(5), 97–103 (2007)
10. Kane, B., Toussaint, P.J., Luz, S.: Shared decision making needs a communication record. In: Proceedings of the 2013 Conference on Computer Support for Cooperative Work (CSCW), pp. 79–90. ACM (2013)
11. Kierkegaard, P.: eHealth in Denmark: A case study. J. Med. Syst. **37**(6), 1–10 (2013)
12. Lee, E.: Identifying key components of services in healthcare in the context of out-patient in Norway. In: HEALTHINF 2017 - Proceedings of the International Conference on Health Informatics (2017)

13. van Limburg, M., van Gemert-Pijnen, J.E., Nijland, N., Ossebaard, H.C., Hendrix, R.M., Seydel, E.R.: Why business modeling is crucial in the development of ehealth technologies. J. Med. Internet Res. **13**(4), e124 (2011)
14. Lister, P.G., Crisp, B.R.: Critical incident analyses: A practice learning tool for students and practitioners. Practice **19**(1), 47–60 (2007)
15. Martin, J.L., Murphy, E., Crowe, J.A., Norris, B.J.: Capturing user requirements in medical device development: the role of ergonomics. Physiol. Measur. **27**(8), R49 (2006)
16. Nemeth, C.P.: Human Factors Methods for Design: Making Systems Human-Centered. CRC Press, Boca Raton (2004)
17. NordiCHI 2016 Program Committee: Call for Workshop Proposals (2016). http://www.nordichi2016.org/participate/workshops/, archived by WebCite at http://www.webcitation.org/6nmrcMFe5
18. Pagliari, C.: Design and evaluation in eHealth: Challenges and implications for an interdisciplinary field. J. Med. Internet Res. **9**(2), e15 (2007)
19. Rexhepi, H., Åhlfeldt, R.M., Cajander, Å., Huvila, I.: Cancer patients' attitudes and experiences of online access to their electronic medical records: A qualitative study. Health Inf. J., 1–10 (2016). doi:10.1177/1460458216658778
20. Scandurra, I., Holgersson, J., Lind, T., Myreteg, G.: Development of patient access to electronic health records as a step towards ubiquitous public ehealth. Eur. J. ePractice **20**, 21–36 (2013)
21. Schön, D.A.: The Reflective Practitioner. Basic Books, Inc., New York (1983)
22. Sittig, D.F., Classen, D.C.: Safe electronic health record use requires a comprehensive monitoring and evaluation framework. JAMA **303**(5), 450451 (2010)
23. Sjölinder, M., Scandurra, I.: Effects of using care professionals in the development of social technology for elderly. In: Zhou, J., Salvendy, G. (eds.) DUXU 2015. LNCS, vol. 9194, pp. 181–192. Springer, Cham (2015). doi:10.1007/978-3-319-20913-5_17
24. Terry, N.P.: Protecting patient privacy in the age of big data. UMKC Law Rev. **81**, 385 (2012)
25. Webb, R., Currie, M., Morgan, C., Williamson, J., Mackay, P., Russell, W., Runciman, W.: The Australian incident monitoring study: An analysis of 2000 incident reports. Anaesth. Intensive Care **21**, 520–528 (1993)

Cultural Differences and Communication Technology

A Confucian Look at Internet Censorship in China

Yubo Kou[1][✉], Bryan Semaan[2], and Bonnie Nardi[3]

[1] Purdue University, West Lafayette, IN, USA
Kou2@purdue.edu
[2] School of Information Studies, Syracuse University, Syracuse, NY, USA
bsemaan@syr.edu
[3] Department of Informatics, University of California, Irvine, CA, USA
nardi@ics.uci.edu

Abstract. China's Internet censorship practices are sophisticated and pervasive. Academic research and media reports have examined the Chinese government's varied, expansive methods of censorship and Chinese citizens' techniques of subverting them, but little attention has been paid to understanding how Chinese citizens think about censorship in their everyday lives. We conducted a qualitative study of Chinese mainland citizens who circumvented censorship. We found seemingly contradictory attitudes and practices among our participants. They showed proficiency at bypassing censorship, but were sometimes comfortable with censored information. They were willing to share sensitive information with others, but saw the benefits of limiting the public's access to information under certain circumstances. We examine how the complex, nuanced attitudes toward censorship resonate with the classic teachings of Confucianism, China's traditional philosophical and ethical system.

Keywords: Censorship · China · Confucianism · Social media

1   Introduction

The human-computer interaction community has investigated censorship in online venues with respect to critical issues such as corporate policies, online community norms, and self-disclosure practices [1–4]. In this paper, we focus on censorship in non-Western, non-democratic contexts. We define censorship broadly as government monitoring and suppression of information, communication, media, and/or speech that the government deems objectionable and harmful.

One non-Western country which is often used as a context to explore censorship is China—widely considered to be an authoritarian state with one of the most sophisticated, strict, and comprehensive systems of censorship in the world [5, 6]. However, previous literature about censorship in China often treats the human-censorship relationship as a "momentary, ahistorical HCI situation" [7], in which censorship exists to oppress and people are expected to resist. Scholars and journalists have investigated the implementation, maintenance, and development of censorship, and measured its effectiveness [5, 8–11]. On the citizen side, the focus has been on techniques for citizens to circumvent

© IFIP International Federation for Information Processing 2017
Published by Springer International Publishing AG 2017. All Rights Reserved
R. Bernhaupt et al. (Eds.): INTERACT 2017, Part I, LNCS 10513, pp. 377–398, 2017.
DOI: 10.1007/978-3-319-67744-6_25

censorship [12–16]. However, little attention has been paid to Chinese citizens' varied practices and complex attitudes towards censorship. Consistent with Kuutti and Bannon's call to the turn to practice [7], this paper concerns Chinese citizens' practices and attitudes related to censorship, as they are embedded in contemporary cultural, historical conditions.

We examine how censorship is viewed and practiced in China, and Chinese attitudes and perspectives towards censorship. We approach these questions through a qualitative study using interviews and document analysis. We interviewed 32 mainland Chinese citizens and collected online interactions made available to us by our informants, triangulating interview and document data. Participants reported both circumventing and supporting censorship—they considered censorship both a constraint and a choice. To frame this finding, we draw on Confucianism—China's traditional ethical and philosophical system dating back over 2500 years. We use it as a lens to describe participants' thoughts and actions. Participants emphasized creative, contextualized adaptation to censorship. They viewed censorship as a government action to protect societal stability, even though they sometimes felt the needed to find ways around it. We argue that participants are embedded in particular philosophical and cultural conditions within which they have developed localized approaches towards censorship. We discuss how sociohistorical factors influenced our participants' experiences with censorship, and we reflect on implications for design.

The Western view of censorship is largely critical and negative. However, here we seek to provide a situated perspective of censorship emerging through routine practice in an environment where censorship is the norm. It is possible that this situated view will not align with the mainstream attitude of the academic community or with certain global perspectives on censorship. We present qualitative data on how Chinese citizens themselves understand and manage censorship.

2   Background

2.1   Confucianism in Contemporary Chinese Society

Confucius (551 – 479BCE) developed a comprehensive system of philosophy and ethics covering morality, politics, economy, family life, and education [17]. Throughout China's history, most dynasties respected, emphasized, and developed Confucianism as the official ideology governing the activities of citizens and the government in the public and private spheres of social life [18–20]. Confucianism continues to have significant impact over Chinese citizens' thoughts and actions [21–24].

Confucianism is conceptualized by its five virtues (五常): benevolence, righteousness, propriety, wisdom, and integrity [20, 25, 26].

The first virtue, **Benevolence** (仁), describes how people should manifest love and compassion for others. For example, a person might exhibit benevolence by helping disadvantaged individuals or groups.

The second virtue, **Righteousness** (义), emphasizes how a person's thoughts and actions should conform to his or her own beliefs, and the person should resist temptation. For instance, as our study participants told us, on social media a person should speak about public events through reasoned and factual discourse as opposed to relying solely on personal opinions.

The third virtue, **Propriety** (礼), refers to how a person should respect behavioral norms that maintain social structures, such as hierarchy. In other words, people should value stability and harmony over radicalism in resolving issues. Confucian teachings encourage people to cope with problems in a harmonious way consistent with both propriety and benevolence. People should avoid confrontation and seek peaceful alternatives.

The fourth virtue, **Wisdom** (智), elaborates how a person should develop knowledge regarding what constitutes right and wrong. For instance, a person should develop knowledge about public events before engaging in public discussion. Acknowledging the differences in people's abilities, experiences, and backgrounds, Confucius believed in diverse methods of educating, accommodating, and serving people, rather than a single universal program of action [26]. For example, Confucius argued that "students have different abilities, backgrounds, and knowledge. There should be different approaches to teaching them" [27]. Confucianism stresses that each person can increase wisdom through education and self-cultivation.

The final virtue, **Integrity** (信), illustrates how a person's own words and deeds support the collective good. For example, if a person promises to support a collective action in specific ways, he or she should do so.

With a central focus on individual virtues, Confucianism lends itself to a paternalistic governance model that relies on political leaders to promote and live by example, thus embodying the virtues. Confucianism attaches considerable responsibility and duty to the government, stressing that the government should govern through virtuous action, and by taking care of the people [25]. At the same time, Confucianism acknowledges people as the basis of the state. Xunzi (310–235BCE), a Confucian scholar, compared people and the government to water and a boat, noting that "water can support the boat… water can also overturn the boat" [28]. The government thus must pay close attention to maintaining a harmonious relationship with the people.

According to decades of research [29–34] by the late Duke University political scientist Tianjian Shi and his colleagues, Confucianism has significantly affected contemporary Chinese citizens' political beliefs and values. Shi and Lu argued that Chinese citizens draw on Confucianism as a means of understanding politics and democracy as a paternalistic model [32]. Confucianism emphasizes the steady hand of elites in delivering governance. Confucianism insists that a government's performance and care for its people are more important than procedural arrangements such as fair elections. Confucianism limits the scope of ordinary citizens' political participation in communicating their concerns to political leaders. Political leaders are expected to make decisions based on their own judgments. Ordinary citizens only oppose the government under extreme conditions, such as when political leaders significantly deviate from expected norms and the virtues of Confucianism.

2.2   Manifestations of Confucianism: Censorship Practices in China

The Chinese government regulates Internet infrastructure, as well as commercial and social use of the Internet [5]. When observing through the lens of Confucianism, we can understand this political system as government leaders having taken it upon themselves to make Internet censorship decisions for the public good.

The Great Firewall, for example, is the primary technical means of restricting information access at the infrastructure level. It blocks foreign websites deemed undesirable by the government such as Facebook and Twitter, regulates access and content, and monitors citizens' Internet use. At the national level, the government controls the gateways to international networks and licenses the operation of Internet service providers. These paternalistic practices manifest in several ways. For example, citizens must use real name to register with Internet service providers [5, 6, 35]. A special Internet police unit enforces the government's censorship regulations [5, 36]. MacKinnon, a renowned Internet freedom advocate and former journalist, describes a broad range of government tactics, including cyber-attacks against targeted individuals, device and network control, domain-name control, localized disconnection and restriction, surveillance through identity registration, monitoring software, the compliance of Internet companies, and paid online commentators [6].

Censorship laws and regulations are pervasive, yet ambiguous. Businesses and individuals face difficulties in complying. Roberts, a political scientist who studies censorship and propaganda in China, commented that Chinese users often guess what types of information are permissible or forbidden [37]. By using abstract terms such as national interest, social order, and national unity, the government gives itself considerable flexibility in the interpretation of its basic governing principles, as well as the possibility for manipulation [5, 38]. To comply with the ambiguity of regulations, businesses have adopted sweeping self-censorship mechanisms [5, 39]. For example, both domestic and foreign Internet corporations such as Google and Yahoo! have altered their products to accommodate censorship requirements. A study of keyword blocking on Weibo, the largest micro-blogging service in China, conducted during the 2012 Chinese National Congress election, reported that Weibo actively manipulated and filtered the search results of certain government officials' names [10]. The government has developed censorship strategies that vary across regions. For example, Bamman et al. studied China's content deletion practices on social media and found stricter censorship in outlying provinces such as Tibet, a region the government considers unstable [8].

Censorship targets content perceived to have the potential to spark collective action. King et al. conducted an analysis of deleted social media content on the Chinese Internet [40]. They reported that censorship allowed criticism of government but silenced comments that represented, reinforced, or spurred offline collective action. In an analysis of the Internet's political impact, Givens and MacDonald explained that online exposure of corruption and malfeasance at lower levels of government can help the central government monitor local agents [12]. The government tolerates citizens' online debates around their frustrating experiences with government practices as long as those debates do not develop into offline actions. Such an eventuality could, in the government's view, cause societal instability. When viewed from the perspective of Confucianism, the government uses online venues to channel citizens' dissatisfaction to avoid confrontations between citizens and government, and to promote peaceful conflict resolution.

3   Related Work

Censorship has been a controversial issue inciting heated debates, with one side stressing the necessity of controlling inappropriate information such as pornography, and the other side upholding principles of Internet freedom [41, 42]. Governments often cite practical reasons for implementing Internet censorship. Singapore, for example, pays considerable attention to censoring information in online political debates which might cause public "panic" [43]. Australia applies censorship with a focus on child pornography sites as well as hate speech and violence [44]. In the human-computer interaction literature, much discussion is centered on how people censor their own social media behavior for purposes such as privacy, and self-protection [3, 45]. Another strand of research concerns algorithmic censorship [46], where social media algorithms are used to suppress certain topics.

Censorship impacts information seeking. Wilson categorized barriers to information seeking into personal, interpersonal, and environmental [47]. Censorship does not stop information seeking; people often seek alternative information sources [48]. Gunther and Snyder found that people in censored news environments are more critical in selecting news sources [49].

Researchers have reported numerous means by which Chinese citizens circumvent censorship. Citizens use proxy servers to visit blocked sites, and email and instant messaging to share sensitive information [50–53]. They discuss sensitive topics using substitutes for blocked keywords [54, 55]. For example, "harmony 和谐" refers to the government's official ideology that prescribes an ideal society in which each person has sufficient resources to live and grow. People use the term "river crab 河蟹," a homophone of "和谐" to satirize this ideology [56].

Only a handful of studies have examined perceptions of censorship among Chinese citizens. Wang and Mark [19] surveyed 721 Chinese citizens, finding that respondents' demographic backgrounds, experience of using the Internet, and personality were associated with their attitudes towards censorship. They reported that people with more Internet usage over time tended to accommodate censorship. The authors suggest that we can expect that people in China will increasingly accept censorship as a normal consequence of Internet use. Roberts' [37] study of blogs found that censorship did not deter the spread of information or induce self-censorship. Bloggers realized that they would receive little punishment except deletion of their posts. Such deletion might even serve as a "badge of honor" and help them gain followers. Censorship motivated these bloggers to continue writing on political topics.

4 Methods

Interviews and document collection took place between April, 2014 and January, 2016. We studied several major political events in China, including the Umbrella Movement, the National People's Congress' plenary sessions, and the crackdown on government corruption in which high-profile government officials were arrested and sentenced. We recruited our interviewees on Weibo, the largest Chinese micro-blogging site. We first used keywords to locate online debates and conversations regarding the political events, identifying Weibo users who participated in relevant discussions. We then contacted these people through Weibo's private messaging function for an interview. We conducted 32 semi-structured, open-ended interviews with mainland Chinese residents. Participants included 19 males and 13 females between the ages of 18 and 46 (with an average age of 29). They included graduate students, government employees, editors, journalists, engineers, programmers, freelancers, and stock market traders. Our sample corresponds to the demographics of Weibo users who are educated and tech-savvy [57] and of course does not represent the whole Chinese population.

The first author, who conducted the interviews, is a native Chinese speaker. We asked participants to describe how they perceived Internet censorship in China, how they sought information about political events, and whether they experienced censorship. We asked participants to describe situations in which they encountered censorship, and how they dealt with it. With permission, we followed all participants' social media accounts. Some followed ours in return. The social media platforms included Weibo and popular online Chinese forums such as tianya.cn and Baidu Tieba. We read and archived participants' posts and comments which we triangulated with our interview data. All interview and social media data were translated into English by the first author. We use pseudonyms to protect participants' identities.

We followed a grounded theory approach [58] to analyze the data. We first read through the data, and then, through rounds of discussion, we identified broad themes. Using open coding, we identified specific patterns related to censorship. Once we had identified Confucianism as a theme, we found quotes in which participants' thoughts resonated with Confucian teachings or in which participants directly quoted words from Confucius. We present these quotes in the Findings section and develop discussion points to support our cultural analysis.

5 Findings

Participants deployed various strategies to circumvent censorship, consistent with what has been reported in previous studies [12, 15, 52, 59]. We discuss how participants encountered censorship and how they made decisions regarding censorship.

5.1 Censorship as Routine Experience

Our participants explained that censorship sometimes had a negative impact on their online or offline activities. When asked how they dealt with these difficulties, they stressed the importance of adaptation. Adaptation was not to endure or accept with resignation, but to manage difficulties in a pragmatic and flexible manner, with the ultimate goal of living in harmony. Dealing with censorship became a routine practice in participants' daily lives, not something remarkable or with totalitarian overtones as it might be in other national contexts.

Almost all our participants said that they disliked censorship, citing the increased difficulties in information seeking and communication. Despite this unfavorable view, however, most (n = 26) said that they did not consider censorship a major obstacle in their everyday online communication. They managed it in a smooth, routine fashion. For example, Leiyu, a 21-year-old college student, said:

> The government blocks Facebook, Twitter, and some news websites. But it doesn't matter. A lot of Chinese are working and studying abroad. They share a lot of content on their Chinese social media accounts. I have two Weibo friends who live in Canada and post a lot of news. I don't really seek a lot of information that is classified as sensitive, but still I can get a lot just by following people on Weibo.

Participants felt that they generally enjoyed the freedom to obtain information and communicate ideas from the online venues they used. For ordinary online communication, censorship did not limit their ability to engage in conversation and share information. The Confucian ideal of harmony was a routine experience for our study participants; they did not feel stressed about their ability to find information or communicate. Maintaining a harmonious, non-confrontational relationship with other people and the government was a consistent goal mentioned in the interviews. Participants frequently referred to Confucius, quoting him to answer questions. For example, when we asked whether participants enjoyed encountering different opinions in online discussions, one answered, *"The exemplary person is harmonious and open-minded to difference. The petty person can group easily but they do not stay together for long. 君子和而不同，小人同而不和"* [26]. When we asked about the ideal relationship between people with different opinions, they sometimes referred to Confucian teachings, *"One should not impose on others what he himself does not desire. 己所不欲勿"* [26].

Our participants discussed using word substitutes in their daily online communication to avoid words that might be censored, similar to previous studies' findings [6, 14]. However, participants said that in some cases, they did not use substitutes with the purpose of circumventing censorship, but as a way of rendering online conversation fun, casual, and hip. For example, Zhelu, a 37-year-old writer, said:

> Many times it is not about escaping the sensitive keyword check. It is because the young Internet generation devises a lot of new substitutes every day. I use these terms simply because it's more fun and more casual in online chat. It makes me feel young and fashionable.

Use of such word substitutes was an everyday routine practice that made communication more enjoyable. Matters of language are delicate; every utterance has more than one interpretation. The use of symbols such as the river crab does not necessarily denote a reaction to censorship, as Zhelu explained. We received similar responses from six other participants. Xuanwu, a 24-year-old graduate student, mentioned how he and his friends did not type in formal written Chinese, but used a lot of emoticons, punctuation, and even typos, for fun and word play. The use of substitutes functioned as a mundane action to sustain harmonious, playful communication. Previous studies emphasized word substitutes as a way to circumvent censorship. Our participants sometimes did that, but in many cases, the purpose of word substitutes was for delightful, entertaining communication.

Most participants (n = 27) found that mechanisms of censorship were not employed for every communication channel, but only a select set of online public venues and a particular set of topics, most of which concerned political events or government decisions. For example, Mingyue, a graduate student, noted:

> I feel that the government does not or cannot monitor and control most of the online places I am using to speak with others. Me and my friends oftentimes say whatever we like in Weibo's reply area, WeChat, tianya, and baidu tieba. Sometimes the content can be pretty sensitive. But our conversations are never interrupted.

WeChat is the largest instant messaging tool in China. Like Mingyue, other participants experienced few interruptions caused by censorship in their daily communication regarding mundane topics. Censorship did not strike them as an obstacle to their online communication, compared to other circumstances they brought up in interviews, such as the difficulty of navigating a variety of information sources in search of desired information, or network speed.

Deciding whether to circumvent censorship

All participants (n = 32) reported that they were aware that much of the information to which they had direct access had been examined, filtered, and altered by the government, consistent with other research [6, 60]. Leiyu said:

> I visit Weibo every day. I follow more than one hundred accounts, which gives me many posts to read. However, I think I just read them for entertainment purposes. I glance through Weibo when I am having lunch alone. … I think it is perhaps because I do not fully trust the information in the posts. The government or Weibo's administration team have censored and tailored a lot of it.

Leiyu was cautious with respect to what he was reading, and adjusted his expectations and subsequent interpretations of news he believed was filtered and modified by government censors. Awareness of censorship encouraged participants to be particularly cautious towards political news. Wen, another college student, told us:

> I feel I know little about it [a political event], mostly because the central government has largely limited my right and ability to obtain information. If the government does not allow transparency, there is no truth.

Circumventing censorship was not the only choice available to our participants. The decision to circumvent, or not to, was based on participants' interests and time. Fifteen participants decided to circumvent based on the strength of their interest in specific information or events. They attempted to find as much information as possible if events triggered strong interest. Otherwise, they would be content with the censored information. Leiyu described the process:

> *If I were interested in particular topics, such as the Umbrella Movement, I would rather check out original information in other venues.*

Similarly, Cangqing, a 34-year-old engineer, described how his interest in the Umbrella Movement called for use of services such as Weibo and Baidu since he felt information on television was censored. He knew digital materials were also censored, but online venues offered him more opportunities to discover new knowledge, e.g., by using a variety of keywords, thus weakening the effect of censorship. Twenty-two participants mentioned that although some Chinese keywords were banned, their English equivalents were not (see Fig. 1).

Fig. 1. To the left is the English warning message for searching sensitive keyword (雨伞运动) in Chinese on Weibo, indicating that the Chinese word for the umbrella movement was banned on Weibo. The right side shows the results of searching sensitive keyword (Umbrella Movement) in English on weibo, where the words were not banned. The first author performed these two searches on his smartphone after an interviewee mentioned this phenomenon.

Many participants (n = 21) chose to follow particular stories of interest to them in which they would invest more time. Ming, a 26-year-old programmer, said:

> *There are too many important political issues worth my attention, such as the economic bubble, the Asian Infrastructure Investment Bank, and the National People's Congress. I cannot really spend the equal amount of time and effort studying every single event... There are priorities. For events with lower priority, I am fine with just reading the state media. I do not necessarily trust what the state media says. For news that I am really interested in, I will definitely climb the wall and see what Western media says.*

Ming's response represented a common strategy of ignoring censorship when news events were not of significant interest. When participants did want to know more, they found ways to do so. This strategy aligns with Confucian philosophy—people were pragmatic with respect to how they dealt with and viewed censorship and made decisions about when to just live with it. The choice of circumventing or not was subject to participants' agendas and interests.

Our participants viewed censorship as one constraint, among the many other constraints they dealt with in their lives on a daily basis. They followed a flexible and situational decision making process in managing censorship.

5.2 Seeing Advantages and Disadvantages of Censorship

Participants (n = 21) refrained from denouncing censorship as purely evil and repressive. In fact, they found some value in the restraints it imposes. They expressed concern regarding the dangers of an uncontrolled flow of information, particularly rumors. Cheng, a 30-year-old accountant, noted:

> I have found that rumors often cause a lot of troubles in China. People are panicked easily. For example, recently there was a rumor on Weibo that a group of human traffickers secretly moved to my hometown. Suddenly all the parents began to pick up their children. They waited outside school gates and blocked the local traffic for hours. Later it turned out that this was a false rumor made up by a random high school student who was bored one day. So yeah, I think the government should take more responsibility in monitoring this kind of online information.

Similar concerns with resolving rumors were voiced by twenty other participants. They stressed that the government should deploy sensible strategies when managing the Internet. This attitude signifies a trust in paternalistic structures that give the government considerable agency in utilizing censorship strategies considered best for the country. This attitude reflects participants' consideration of the Confucian virtue of propriety which explicitly attaches importance to the maintenance of the existing hierarchy and the rule of the government.

Participants held cautious attitudes towards expressing online opinions but not because of censorship. Situ, a 23-year-old government employee, said:

> I see a lot of people making immediate, rash comments after reading one single piece of news. They do not even know whether it is true or not. Does this do any good to our online space and our society? Is this really the so-called freedom of speech? I think this is nothing but irresponsible.

Similarly, Xiaotu, a 32-year-old editor, reflected on her own online behavior:

> I used to be a student. I fully understand that students are emotional and do not apprehend public issues in an objective and comprehensive way. When I was in middle and high school, I admired Western societies a lot. I thought every aspect of Western society was better than that of China. Whenever there was a certain terrible public issue, I blamed the Chinese government...[Now] I am grateful for my college education. I learned a lot about our history and society during that time. Now I have a mature mind. I try to understand those issues rather than rushing to blame China. I see many Weibo users speak in the exact same way I did as a high school student. They easily make accusations that someone is part of the 50-cent party or that they are brainwashed. Their minds are still immature, but they will eventually grow up in the future.

Many participants (n = 18) acknowledged the utilitarian value of digital technologies in facilitating expression. However, they were worried about the irresponsible use of these technologies in the name of freedom of speech. They wanted to include consideration of the negative side of online debates in their assessment of freedom of speech and censorship, articulating a desire for careful, harmonious communication, consistent with Confucian teachings. When describing their perceptions of censorship, participants often emphasized peaceful, harmonious online communication, using a Confucian saying: "*Harmony is the most precious. 施于人*" [26]. For example, one participant said, "*I do not like to argue with others online. This often ends up nowhere. People should treat each other in a nicer way. After all, harmony is the most precious.*"

Many participants (n = 23) commented on international conflicts between China and other countries, endorsing certain of the Chinese government's actions to regulate online speech in China to manage international tensions. As Xuanwu noted:

> *Our Internet is already in chaos. The Chinese government is not the only one having paid commentators, for sure. Western governments and others are also hiring people to create and circulate opinions about democratizing China or colonizing China again. They probably want a Chinese version of the Arab Spring. I believe censorship is necessary to resist some of these influences.*

Participants (n = 22) agreed that the government is responsible for shepherding use of the Internet, a paternalistic notion derived from Confucianism. Gushi, a 46-year-old stock market trader, discussed how censorship directed online discussion in a constructive way:

> *Young people are relatively reckless and idealistic. When they have lived for more than 40 years, they will gain a comprehensive understanding of both society and life. At that point, they will begin to think about public issues in a mature way... However, young people are occupying the Internet. Their time and energy should be better spent on their own work and life. Putting a barrier on their online activity is not necessarily a bad thing.*

However, approving of certain acts of censorship did not mean that participants agreed with every aspect and practice of censorship perpetrated by the government. Tang, 35-year-old government employee, said:

> *Censorship is a necessary mechanism to protect societal stability and harmony. There is no absolute freedom of speech. If the government does not rein in what circulates on the Internet, a lot of public issues can easily spiral out of control. However, I do think censorship's current shape is a bit too strict. For example, some keywords can suddenly become unsearchable for no obvious reason.*

A graduate student expressed her dissatisfaction with the strictness of Chinese censorship. She said:

> *Although I can see the point in censorship, it is sometimes too strict. For instance, a while ago I wrote a blog with hundreds of words. But I could not submit it because the blog site said the blog contained some sensitive keyword. I checked the whole blog again and again but failed to find any sensitive word. Eventually I had to give up. I simply don't understand why it has to be so strict. What harm can that blog do?*

Participants had expectations regarding the appropriate degree of strictness that should be applied. In many cases, the current degree was deemed overly strict.

Participants' attitudes towards censorship seem contradictory. On the one hand, participants showed a somewhat accepting attitude towards censorship in pointing out its advantages, and stressing the government's responsibility to manage the Internet. On the other hand, participants saw that censorship hindered some of their online experiences. Their attitudes reflected acceptance of a paternalistic social order that attaches a strong expectation of responsibility for the common weal to the government. However, this acceptance did not mean that participants could not have their own ideas regarding governance or be frustrated at certain government actions.

5.3   Developing Skills of Circumvention

Confucius believed that the resources a person is entitled to should equal the person's capacities, or wisdom. Otherwise, the person not only wastes resources, but may also abuse the resources. Our online observations and interviews with participants revealed a similar belief, namely, that the amount of information a person can access should be commensurate with their abilities.

In online discussions on social media, we often came across people debating the influence of censorship over freedom of speech. Here is an excerpt from a conversation on Weibo:

> Gangli: Mainlanders are confined in cages. We know nothing besides what the government wants us to know.
> Yuyi: How would you define cage? In fact, the government does not confine people. Only people can confine themselves. How do you expect a person to jump out of the box if he only reads party newspapers every day? If you cannot think for yourself, how can climbing the wall help? It does nothing except put new biases into your head.

Yuyi dismissed the idea that censorship is an overwhelming obstacle that prevents people from obtaining information. She emphasized individual agency as the key to understanding public events. Gangli, however, used strong imagery to describe what he considered excessive government control. Without *"thinking for yourself,"* consuming more information does not help. *"[P]eople should develop the ability of critical thinking,"* said Gushi. He quoted Confucius in saying that *"learning without thought means labor lost. 学而不思则罔."* In other words, the individual bears responsibility for behaving pragmatically and sensibly.

Our participants (n = 22) often described circumvention of censorship as a personal choice. Leng, a 29-year-old office worker, said:

> I find the idea of brainwashing funny. Even in the Chinese media, there are so many sources with very different information and opinions. The government cannot really ban them all. You can find them only if you want to. Otherwise, even if you live in the West with many, many media choices, you can still be very narrow-minded.

Leng and many other participants stressed the importance of individual agency in managing censorship. For them, exposure to information did not guarantee insight or knowledge. The ability to understand and reflect on information was more important.

Participants (n = 17) associated circumvention practices with the willingness to learn. Guzi, a 29-year-old graduate student, remarked:

> I think it's not that hard to use VPN tools or proxy servers to visit Facebook or Twitter. Any person with basic computer knowledge can learn it, as long as they are willing to.

Participants associated finding filtered, sensitive information with just doing a bit of extra work. They recognized the extra effort required to find information in certain circumstances, and believed that it was up to them to do it if they so desired.

When asked how they managed censorship, 28 participants stressed mastering know-how of general strategies rather than the specific technical means of circumvention. For them, it was important to be flexible and to be able to adapt to new techniques as well as new information sources. For example, Leiyu explained:

It's not about knowing which specific site to find certain information. After all, that site can be gone any time. The point is to know how you can find the site containing desired information.

Li, a 24-year-old graduate student, elaborated on what constitutes know-how:

You have to keep your mind open to new tools and browsing new websites. New tools can always surprise you! My friend once introduced a website storing a lot of YouTube videos. I'm sure a lot of them are forbidden in China. I was amazed by its rich content.

As we have noted, previous work has shown the numerous ways Chinese citizens bypass censorship [6, 14, 59]. Here we emphasize participants' flexibility in adopting and learning new tools and finding new resources in order to expand their knowledge, as well as their pragmatic attitude towards censorship, and their willingness to help others find the information they need.

Participants sympathized with like-minded people who wanted more information. Many reported practices of sharing information with others, even strangers. Zi, a 29-year-old graduate student, explained her willingness to share information, saying:

I do not mind sharing sensitive information with people online, even if I do not know them. This is because I fully understand how it feels when you desire some information. In the past, somebody shared information with me as well.

We asked participants whether and why they were willing to share sensitive information. Xingxi laughed and quoted Confucius, saying that "*a good person is always ready to help others attain their aims. 君子成人之美* " [26]. He further asked, "*Why shouldn't I send out the information if it helps others and does me no harm?*"

Participants linked circumventing censorship to their own sensible, resourceful practices. Managing censorship is much like managing other aspects of life for Chinese citizens. Acts of circumvention do not connote a deep refusal of government initiatives as they might in the West. On the contrary, they allow citizens to find what they want to know, while still observing the appropriateness of hierarchy as formulated in Confucian principles.

5.4 Summary

Our participants emphasized a willingness and capacity to deal with censorship and obtain information. Participants agreed that the information a person could access depended on his or her own capacity and effort. Such a view not only reflects flexibility and pragmatism in dealing with constraints, but also the deep-rooted Confucian values regarding how resources should be distributed in society.

Table 1 summarizes the links between participants' attitudes and practices in relation to the five virtues in Confucianism. Participants saw advantages to censorship in maintaining societal stability, resonating with righteousness, propriety, and integrity, as they agreed that censorship was correct in maintaining propriety. They did not shy away from criticizing the government for its strictness in censorship, showing their sense of righteousness and integrity. Participants consumed censored information as they respected propriety, and believed that even censored information could contribute to their knowledge and wisdom. They shared information with strangers, manifesting the virtue of benevolence and righteousness. They emphasized circumvention rather than protest and confrontation, respecting propriety.

Table 1. Links between participants' attitudes and practices and the five virtues. 1 = benevolence, 2 = righteousness, 3 = propriety, 4 = wisdom, 5 = integrity.

	What participants said they thought or did
Attitudes	Supported censorship for societal stability (2, 3)
	Criticized censorship for blocking information (2, 5)
Practices	Consumed censored information (3, 4)
	Circumvented censorship to obtain desired information (1, 2, 3, 4)

6   Discussion

Few studies have explored the ways in which Chinese citizens view and experience censorship. Through a qualitative study of Chinese citizens' attitudes toward and practices of censorship, we discovered the routineness of managing censorship, and the acceptance and approval of certain forms of censorship. These findings conflict in some important ways with mainstream thoughts regarding censorship, such as the United Nations' declaration of Internet access as a basic human right [61]. We argue that it is important to understand censorship practices by drawing connections to the specific historical national context.

We have traced participants' attitudes toward censorship to the ancient teachings of Confucianism. Ample research has documented that contemporary Chinese citizens continue to seek to cultivate themselves through reading Confucius' classic works and through following the doctrines of Confucianism [21–23, 62–64]. Our work is interpretive, drawing on our knowledge of Confucianism in the Chinese context. Without this larger situated framing, we cannot explain actions that seem contradictory. It is within the larger philosophical system of Confucianism with its emphasis on harmony, pragmatism, and paternalism that participants' responses to censorship become logical and comprehensible.

Our study participants' attitudes and practices manifested the Confucian virtues in concrete ways. Participants valued benevolence and propriety over confrontation in relations with others. They chose to accept censorship as a circumstance, and to explore alternatives to bypassing it, rather than subverting it. They made individual choices to obtain sensitive information in order to improve their own righteousness, wisdom, and integrity. They were willing to share sensitive information with others who expressed need. At the same time, participants placed considerable responsibility for and trust in the government to manage the public sphere. Acts of circumvention and sharing sensitive information with others did not connote the kind of ideological and practical resistance to and rejection of government actions that they might connote in other sociohistorical contexts.

Our contributions to the HCI literature are three-fold: First, we contribute to the information seeking literature by presenting a nuanced and culturally-situated analysis of information seeking practice in a heavily-censored environment. Second, the study develops a situated, emic interpretation of censorship that is still missing in the literature. Third, our contribution lies in using Confucianism as an interpretive lens to analyze contemporary Chinese technology practices.

6.1 Citizens and Censorship in China

Previous work has tended to frame censorship as a repressive, top-down tool employed by the Chinese government [6, 19, 51, 60, 65, 66]. Our investigation points to the role of Chinese citizens themselves in the formation, maintenance, and development of censorship. Participants' tolerance of and compliance with censorship stands in sharp contrast to research that assumes that Chinese citizens should resist and rebel. Our study participants reported that they would engage in confrontations with the Chinese government only under the most extreme circumstances. For example, one participant said that he would *"participate in collective actions if government decisions threaten normal life, such as building chemical plants too close to a residential area."* Participants' common strategy was to adapt, and to find ways to overcome problems quietly. If they could not solve the problems, they preferred to endure, survive, and succeed in their endeavors by turning their attention to other matters in life.

We thus suggest the importance of considering the cultural and sociohistorical dimensions of censorship. In China, certain circumstances such as Confucian values and beliefs existed before censorship and before the current regime that exercises it. While our study brings attention to the consequences of Confucianism on censorship practices and attitudes, we do not exclude possible connections between censorship and other Chinese cultural elements such as Taoism and Buddhism. These would require further study. We have noted participants' acceptance of certain Western liberal forms of civic engagement such as public deliberation. Participants acknowledged the power of collective action in influencing government decisions. Chinese citizens' attitudes and practices are in a state of flux, and yet they are, at the same time, informed by a venerable tradition that has lasted for millennia. Fundamental changes will take time to emerge, and as they evolve, they will be informed by Chinese history and society.

6.2 Expanding the Paradigm for Research in Civic Engagement and Politics

Developed within Western universities and corporations, much HCI research on civic engagement and politics has naturally followed conventions of democratic traditions in assessing how digital technologies can contribute to the betterment of society [67–69]. This paradigm is evident in studies of online political deliberation [70–72], social movements [73–76], local community engagement [77–82], citizen news generation and news seeking behaviors [83, 84], and citizen participation in political campaigns [85, 86]. These studies highlight the culture of participatory democracy in which ordinary citizens can and should engage in discussion of public issues. In contrast, contemporary China follows a paternalistic model of governance. Consequently, even actions such as circumvention that appear to meet Western expectations, might actually have different rationales for Chinese citizens. Our findings indicate that circumvention and sharing sensitive information in the Chinese context connote not an attitude of subversion, nor of opposition to censorship, but a pragmatic, routine, utilitarian means of obtaining desired information.

We argue that censorship and its related attitudes and practices can be better understood if we consider specific national contexts. The significance of linking censorship to its sociohistorical context speaks to several critical strands of related work, such as postcolonial computing [67], feminist HCI [87], and political economy in HCI [88]. Postcolonial computing examines how research and design can be understood as "culturally located and power laden." Feminist HCI provides a critical perspective for looking at the existing body of knowledge about censorship as primarily situated in the Western context. Political economy indicates that technology is embedded in the wider political economy and is not intelligible without consideration of that political economy. These perspectives are developing as crucial resources that are beginning to shift the paradigm in HCI. We favor taking them into account as much as possible as we move forward. We attempted to do so in our analysis by situating seemingly contradictory findings about Chinese attitudes toward censorship in a sociopolitical context with deep roots in the ethical system of Confucianism, examining this system as it plays out in the politics of contemporary China.

6.3   Design for What Purpose?

Viewing censorship as a "problem," researchers and practitioners have devised and implemented solutions to resist or bypass censorship [89–92]. However, framing the current situation as a set of "problems" and technological systems as "solutions," can be misleading [93]. Baumer and Silberman discussed when not to design, suggesting how a specific situation can constitute "a complex and multifaceted condition with which we must grapple" [93]. Pierce discussed the value of "undesign" in response to concerns with the limitations and negative effects of technology [94]. Our findings about censorship in China are in harmony with the arguments of these scholars. Censorship in the Chinese context cannot be framed as a problem to be solved. It is a substantial element of China's complex online context co-created by citizens and the government. Design for the demolition of censorship is infeasible, and out of step with the realities of China's current sociopolitical system, as well as its lengthy history as a nation state.

We see Confucianism as a source of inspiration for design in a Chinese cultural context. While an in-depth analysis of how Confucianism can be useful for design is out of the scope of this paper, and our chief objective was to present our empirical material, we provide some preliminary suggestions. The five virtues offer insights into design values that could guide future development. For example, the virtue of wisdom stresses individuals' pursuit of knowledge and information. Our participants developed better understandings of the advantages and disadvantages of each media source, as well as censored information, in order to make better judgments about a public event. Still, they acknowledged that limited time and energy prevented them from getting the full picture of an event, and they were aware that they were consuming imperfect information. Social media, for example, might offer recommendation functions to suggest news from outside the participant's usual sources, or point to the blogs or Twitter feeds of people who hold different views.

The virtues of righteousness and integrity indicate individual responsibility for people's own online behavior. Participants criticized those who made rash comments and emphasized the need for careful thought. Today's social media design often encourages users to take rapid actions such as clicking "likes" or retweeting. The speed encouraged by social media shifts activity away from deliberate, careful reflection. It is time to rethink the relationship between how we design social media and individual responsibility, particularly in light of public events. Design might consider means of encouraging critical thinking before people take actions. DiSalvo argued that design can provoke reactions and actions via identification and articulation of public issues [68]. He pointed to two design tactics: *projection*, which presents possible future consequences associated with an issue, and *tracing*, which documents and makes known the assemblage of materials, concepts, and ideas that impact an issue over time. Such approach might be useful in the Chinese context. Participants' emphasis on choice and mastering know-how indicates the value of techniques that provide rich, diverse information. For example, using the projection tactic, design might present possible environmental consequences alongside a product.

6.4 Implications for HCI Studies of China

To date, most HCI studies of China adopt terminology or theories with a Western perspective. Such an approach risks diminishing cultural differences of critical importance [69]. For example, the word censorship belongs to the everyday vocabulary of the West, but its Chinese equivalent, "审查制度," is not an everyday word, and did not occur within our interviews. To ask censorship-related questions, the first author approached interviewees with a variety of terms such as "blocking website," "post deletion," and "account suspension" which were more familiar to participants. From a sociolinguistic perspective [95], this usage indicates that censorship plays a different, and less prominent, sociocultural role than in the West. Our work demonstrates the value of drawing from a localized perspective to develop emic interpretations of what people think and do.

Utilizing a Confucian lens to interpret Chinese citizens' technology practices has important implications for HCI studies of China. We showed that the five virtues are a useful basis for HCI work in China that concerns individuals' behavioral and thinking patterns, as well as Chinese social practices ranging from communication, to coordination, to organization. For example, benevolence and propriety are relevant in analyzing interpersonal communication and organizational communication where people follow certain norms and etiquettes to treat each other in proper ways. Righteousness and integrity are pertinent in exploring the connections between individuals' actions and thoughts. Wisdom can be deployed to interpret how individuals seek to cultivate their own personality, knowledge, and skill in work and life.

7 Conclusion

We presented a qualitative study exploring how Chinese citizens perceive and manage Internet censorship. Participants had nuanced attitudes and practices that did not resolve to simple "for" or "against" behaviors and practices with respect to censorship. We showed how participants' actions were consistent with the classic teachings of Confucianism. We caution against judging whether censorship is "positive" or "negative" in all contexts, and we caution against simple binary design suggestions for or against censorship. We highlight the role of particular sociohistorical contexts in influencing the formation and maintenance of censorship. Specific contexts determine how people develop ways to think about and act within their own circumstances.

Acknowledgements. We are grateful to our participants for sharing their practices around censorship and offering candid thoughts about China's censorship. We thank Xinning Gui for early discussions of the Confucian framework. We thank the anonymous reviewers at INTERACT 2017 for their constructive and insightful feedback that helped strengthen the paper, as well as their open-mindedness to this paper's findings and interpretive perspective which is different from the dominant view of censorship in the West.

References

1. Poller, A., Ilyes, P., Kramm, A., Kocksch, L.: Investigating OSN users' privacy strategies with in-situ observation. In: CSCW Companion 2014, pp. 217–220. ACM Press (2014)
2. Semaan, B.C., Britton, L.M., Dosono, B.: Transition resilience with ICTs: "Identity Awareness" in veteran re-integration. In: CHI 2016, pp. 2882–2894. ACM Press (2016)
3. Sleeper, M., Balebako, R., Das, S., McConahy, A.L., Wiese, J., Cranor, L.F.: The post that wasn't: exploring self-censorship on facebook. In: CSCW 2013, pp. 793–802. ACM Press (2013)
4. Wisniewski, P., Lipford, H., Wilson, D.: Fighting for my space: coping mechanisms for SNS boundary regulation. In: CHI 2012, pp. 609–618. ACM Press (2012)
5. Liang, B., Lu, H.: Internet development, censorship, and cyber crimes in China. J. Contemp. Crim. Justice **26**, 103–120 (2010)
6. MacKinnon, R.: China's "Networked Authoritarianism" (2011)
7. Kuutti, K., Bannon, L.J.: The turn to practice in HCI: Towards a research agenda. In: CHI 2014, pp. 3543–3552. ACM Press (2014)
8. Bamman, D., O'Connor, B., Smith, N.: Censorship and deletion practices in Chinese social media. First Monday 17 (2012)
9. Hachigian, N.: China's cyber-strategy. Foreign Aff. **80**, 118 (2001)
10. Ng, J.Q., Landry, P.F.: The Political Hierarchy of Censorship: An Analysis of Keyword Blocking of CCP Officials' Names on Sina Weibo Before and After the 2012 National Congress (S)election (2013)

11. Stockmann, D., Gallagher, M.E.: Remote control: how the media sustain authoritarian rule in China. Comp. Polit. Stud. **44**, 436–467 (2011)
12. Givens, J.W., MacDonald, A.W.: The internet with chinese characteristics: democratizing discourse but not politics. In: APSA 2013 Annual Meeting, p. 19 (2013)
13. Poell, T., de Kloet, J., Zeng, G.: Will the real weibo please stand up? Chinese online contention and actor-network theory. Chinese J. Commun. **7**, 1–18 (2013)
14. Rauchfleisch, A., Schäfer, M.S.: Multiple public spheres of weibo: a typology of forms and potentials of online public spheres in China. Inf. Commun. Soc. 1–17 (2014)
15. Yang, G.: The co-evolution of the internet and civil society in China. Asian Surv. **43**, 405–422 (2003)
16. Shklovski, I., Kotamraju, N.: Online contribution practices in countries that engage in internet blocking and censorship. In: CHI 2011, pp. 1109–1118. ACM Press (2011)
17. Sima, Q.: Records of the Grand Historian of China. Zhonghua Book Company, Beijing (1959)
18. Weber, M., Gerth, H.H.: The Religion of China, Confucianism and Taoism. MacMillan Publishing Company, New York (1953)
19. Wang, D., Mark, G.: Internet censorship in China: Examining user awareness and attitudes. ACM Trans. Comput. Interact. **22**, 1–22 (2015)
20. Dong, Z.: The Luxuriant Dew of the Spring and Autumn Annals. Zhonghua Book Company, Beijing (2011)
21. Bell, D.A.: China's New Confucianism: Politics and Everyday Life in a Changing Society. Princeton University Press, Princeto (2010)
22. Bell, D.A.: Reconciling socialism and confucianism?: Reviving tradition in China. Dissent **57**, 91–99 (2009)
23. Fukuyama, F.: Confucianism and democracy (1995)
24. Yum, J.O.: The impact of confucianism on interpersonal relationships and communication patterns in east Asia. Commun. Monogr. (2009)
25. Mencius: Mencius. Zhonghua Book Company, Beijing (2010)
26. Confucius: The Analects. Zhonghua Book Company, Beijing (2006)
27. Zhu, X.: The Analects of Confucius Variorum (1200)
28. Xunzi: Xunzi: The Complete Text. Princeton University Press, Princeton (2014)
29. Wang, Z., Pavlićević, D.: Citizens and Democracy: Shi Tianjian's contribution to China studies and political science. China Int. J. **10**, 125–135 (2012)
30. Shi, T.: Cultural values and political trust: A comparison of the people's Republic of China and Taiwan. Comp. Polit. **33**, 401–419 (2001)
31. Shi, T.: Political Participation in Beijing. Harvard University Press, Cambridge (1997)
32. Shi, T., Lu, J.: The shadow of confucianism. J. Democr. **21**, 123–130 (2010)
33. Shi, T.: China: Democratic values supporting an authoritarian system. In: Chu, Y., Diamond, L., Nathan, A.J., Shin, D.C. (eds.) How East Asians View Democracy. Columbia University Press (2008)
34. Nathan, A.J., Shi, T.: Cultural requisites for democracy in China: Findings from a survey. Daedalus **122**, 95–123 (1993)
35. Li, S.: The online public space and popular ethos in China. Media Cult. Soc. **32**, 63–83 (2010)
36. Tsui, L.: The panopticon as the antithesis of a space of freedom: control and regulation of the internet in China. China Inf. **17**, 65–82 (2003)
37. Roberts, M.: Experiencing Censorship Emboldens Internet Users and Decreases Government Support in China (2015)
38. Cheung, A.S.Y.: The business of governance: China's legislation on content regulation in cyberspace. Int. Law Polit. **38**, 1–37 (2006)

39. Human Rights Watch: China: Nationwide Arrests of Activists, Critics Multiply. http://www.hrw.org/news/2013/08/30/china-nationwide-arrests-activists-critics-multiply

40. King, G., Pan, J., Roberts, M.: How censorship in China allows government criticism but silences collective expression. Am. Polit. Sci. Rev. **107**, 326–343 (2013)

41. Ebbs, G., Rheingold, H.: Censorship on the information highway. Internet Res. **7**, 59–80 (1997)

42. Lawson, T., Comber, C.: Censorship, the Internet and schools: a new moral panic? Curric. J. **11**, 273–285 (2000)

43. Ang, P.H., Nadarajan, B.: Censorship and the internet: a Singapore perspective. Commun. ACM **39**, 72–78 (1996)

44. Bambauer, D.E.: Filtering in Oz: Australia's Foray into Internet Censorship. Univ. Pennsylvania J. Int. Law 31 (2009)

45. Pater, J.A., Haimson, O.L., Andalibi, N., Mynatt, E.D.: Hunger hurts but starving works: Characterizing the presentation of eating disorders online. In: CSCW 2016, pp. 1183–1198. ACM Press (2016)

46. Gillespie, T.: Can an algorithm be wrong? Limn. 1 (2012)

47. Wilson, T.: On user studies and information needs. J. Documentation **37**, 3–15 (1981)

48. Behrouzian, G., Nisbet, E.C., Dal, A., Çarkoğlu, A.: Resisting censorship: How citizens navigate closed media environments. Int. J. Commun. **10**, 23 (2016)

49. Gunther, A.C., Snyder, L.B.: Reading international news in a censored press environment. J. Mass Commun. Q. **69**, 591–599 (1992)

50. Cherry, S.: The net effect: as China's Internet gets a much-needed makeover, will the new network promote freedom or curtail it? IEEE Spectr. **42**, 38–44 (2005)

51. MacKinnon, R.: Flatter world and thicker walls? Blogs, censorship and civic discourse in China. Public Choice **134**, 31–46 (2007)

52. Nardi, B.: Virtuality. Annu. Rev. Anthropol. **44**, 15–31 (2015)

53. Kou, Y., Kow, Y.M., Gui, X.: Resisting the censorship infrastructure in China. In: 2017 50th Hawaii International Conference on System Sciences, pp. 2332–2340 (2017)

54. Jiang, M.: The Co-Evolution of the internet, (Un)Civil society & authoritarianism in China. In: The Internet, Social Media, and a Changing China. University of Pennsylvania Press, Philadelphia (2014)

55. Mina, A.X.: Batman, pandaman and the blind man: a case study in social change memes and internet censorship in China. J. Vis. Cult. **13**, 359–375 (2014)

56. Yang, G., Jiang, M.: The networked practice of online political satire in China: Between ritual and resistance. Int. Commun. Gaz. **77**, 215–231 (2015)

57. Weibo: 2014 年微博用户发展报告. (2014)

58. Corbin, J., Strauss, A.: Basics of Qualitative Research: Techniques and Procedures for Developing Grounded Theory. SAGE Publications, Thousand Oaks (2007)

59. Mou, Y., Wu, K., Atkin, D.: Understanding the use of circumvention tools to bypass online censorship. New Media Soc. **18**, 837–856 (2014)

60. Leibold, J.: Blogging alone: China, the internet, and the democratic illusion? (2011)

61. La Rue, F.: Report of the special rapporteur on the promotion and protection of the right to freedom of opinion and expression (2011)

62. Bol, P.K.: Neo-Confucianism in History. Harvard University Press, Cambridge (2010)

63. Fan, R., Yu, E.: The Renaissance of Confucianism in Contemporary China. Springer, Heidelberg (2011)

64. Melvin, S.: Yu Dan and China's return to Confucius (2007)

65. Li, Y.: Smart censorship in China weibo: An industry and party-state double act. SSRN Electron. J. (2013)

66. Wang, W.Y.: Who's blocking the Chinese internet? The rise of cybercultures and the generational conflicts in China. In: Baumann, S. (ed.) Cybercultures: Cultures in Cyberspace Communities, pp. 145-166. Inter-Disciplinary Press (2012)

67. Irani, L., Vertesi, J., Dourish, P., Philip, K., Grinter, R.E.: Postcolonial computing: a lens on design and development. In: CHI 2010, pp. 1311–1320. ACM Press (2010)

68. Khosrow-Pour, M.: Encyclopedia of Information Science and Technology, 3 edn. IGI Global (2014)

69. Nardi, B., Vatrapu, R., Clemmensen, T.: Comparative informatics. Interactions **18**, 28 (2011)

70. Semaan, B., Faucett, H., Robertson, S.P., Maruyama, M., Douglas, S.: Designing political deliberation environments to support interactions in the public sphere. In: CHI 2015, pp. 3167–3176. ACM Press (2015)

71. Bohøj, M., Borchorst, N.G., Bødker, S., Korn, M., Zander, P.-O.: Public deliberation in municipal planning: supporting action and reflection with mobile technology. In: C&T 2011, p. 88. ACM Press (2011)

72. Semaan, B., Robertson, S., Douglas, S., Maruyama, M.: Social media supporting political deliberation across multiple public spheres: towards depolarization. In: CSCW 2014, pp. 1409–1421. ACM Press (2014)

73. Crivellaro, C., Comber, R., Bowers, J., Wright, P.C., Olivier, P.: A pool of dreams: Facebook, politics and the emergence of a social movement. In: CHI 2014, pp. 3573–3582. ACM Press (2014)

74. Dimond, J.P., Dye, M., Larose, D., Bruckman, A.S.: Hollaback!: the role of storytelling online in a social movement organization. In: CSCW 2013, pp. 477–489. ACM Press (2013)

75. Roeder, M.: Social movements using social media in a mined and censored world: examples in the United States and China (2013). http://via.library.depaul.edu/etd/156

76. Kow, Y.M., Kou, Y., Semaan, B., Cheng, W.: Mediating the undercurrents: Using social media to sustain a social movement. In: CHI 2016, pp. 3883–3894. ACM Press (2016)

77. Le Dantec, C.A., Edwards, W.K.: Designs on dignity:perceptions of technology among the homeless. CHI '08. pp. 627–636. ACM Press, New York, USA (2008)

78. DiSalvo, C.: Design and the construction of publics. Des. Issues **25**, 48–63 (2009)

79. DiSalvo, C., Light, A., Hirsch, T., Le Dantec, C.A., Goodman, E., Hill, K.: HCI, communities and politics. In: CHI EA 2010, pp. 3151–3154. ACM Press (2010)

80. Gordon, E., Baldwin-Philippi, J., Balestra, M.: Why we engage: how theories of human behavior contribute to our understanding of civic engagement in a digital era. SSRN Electron. J. (2013)

81. Kavanaugh, A., Carroll, J.M., Rosson, M.B., Reese, D.D., Zin, T.T.: Participating in civil society: the case of networked communities. Interact. Comput. **17**, 9–33 (2005)

82. Kavanaugh, A., Carroll, J.M., Rosson, M.B., Zin, T.T., Reese, D.D.: Community networks: where offline communities meet online. J. Comput. Commun. **10** (2005)

83. Monroy-Hernández, A., Boyd, D., Kiciman, E., De Choudhury, M., Counts, S.: The new war correspondents: the rise of civic media curation in urban warfare. In: CSCW 2013, pp. 1443–1452. ACM Press (2013)

84. Wang, Y., Mark, G.: Trust in online news: comparing social media and official media use by Chinese citizens. In: CSCW 2012, pp. 599–610. ACM Press (2013)

85. Gayo-Avello, D.: Don't turn social media into another "Literary Digest" poll. Commun. ACM **54**, 121–128 (2011)

86. Kriplean, T., Morgan, J., Freelon, D., Borning, A., Bennett, L.: Supporting reflective public thought with considerit. In: CSCW 2012, pp. 265–274. ACM Press (2012)

87. Bardzell, S.: Feminist HCI: taking stock and outlining an agenda for design. In: CHI 2010, pp. 1301–1310. ACM Press (2010)

88. Ekbia, H., Nardi, B.: Social inequality and HCI: The View from political economy. In: CHI 2016, pp. 4997–5002. ACM Press (2016)
89. Burnett, S., Feamster, N., Vempala, S.: Chipping away at censorship firewalls with user-generated content. In: USENIX Security Symposium, pp. 463–468 (2010)
90. Feamster, N., Balazinska, M., Wang, W., Balakrishnan, H., Karger, D.: Thwarting web censorship with untrusted messenger discovery. In: Dingledine, R. (ed.) PET 2003. LNCS, vol. 2760, pp. 125–140. Springer, Heidelberg (2003). doi:10.1007/978-3-540-40956-4_9
91. Serjantov, A.: Anonymizing censorship resistant systems. In: Druschel, P., Kaashoek, F., Rowstron, A. (eds.) IPTPS 2002. LNCS, vol. 2429, pp. 111–120. Springer, Heidelberg (2002). doi:10.1007/3-540-45748-8_11
92. Waldman, M., Mazières, D.: Tangler: a censorship-resistant publishing system based on document entanglements. In: CCS 2001, pp. 126–135. ACM Press (2001)
93. Baumer, E.P.S., Silberman, M.S.: When the implication is not to design (technology). In: CHI 2011, pp. 2271–2274. ACM Press (2011)
94. Pierce, J.: Undesigning technology: considering the negation of design by design. In: CHI 2012, pp. 957–966. ACM Press (2012)
95. Tausczik, Y.R., Pennebaker, J.W.: The psychological meaning of words: LIWC and computerized text analysis methods. J. Lang. Soc. Psychol. **29**, 24–54 (2010)

A Cross-Cultural Noticeboard for a Remote Community: Design, Deployment, and Evaluation

Alessandro Soro[✉], Margot Brereton, Jennyfer Lawrence Taylor,
Anita Lee Hong, and Paul Roe

Queensland University of Technology (QUT), Brisbane, QLD, Australia
{a.soro, m.brereton, jen.taylor,
anita.leehong, p.roe}@qut.edu.au

Abstract. Remote communities all over the world often face the problem of creating and sharing digital contents in ways that are appropriate for their values and customs while using tools that were designed for Western contexts. This paper advocates for a different approach that builds upon the own goals and ambitions of a specific community, leveraging existing skills, and reflecting local ways of knowing in spite of the higher costs. We present the design of a digital noticeboard tailored to the needs and values of the Australian Aboriginal community of Groote Eylandt. The noticeboard was designed to support communication and promote literacy by offering bi-lingual multimodal content creation and sharing. The final design mirrors the preference for orality and storytelling, is well suited to working in groups, and pays special attention to issues of moderation. The noticeboard does not rely on a stable connectivity, and notices can be shared to many locations using low-tech opportunistic mechanisms. Because the value of custom designs can hardly be assessed only in terms of cost and efficiency in this paper we propose to focus on community engagement as a measure of success for HCI4D projects.

Keywords: Aboriginal · Australia · Remote · Community · Noticeboard · HCI4D · ICT4D · Literacy · Reading · Writing · Multimedia · Story

1 Introduction

We acknowledge the Australian Aboriginal peoples and in particular the Anindilyakwa people of Groote Eylandt who were partners in this project, and whose knowledge, traditions and language date back countless generations.

This paper reports on a design project undertaken as collaboration between our research team and institution and the Anindilyakwa people of Groote Eylandt, a very remote Aboriginal community located in Arnhem Land (Northern Territory, Australia). A strategic goal of the community is to create opportunities for the youth to "stand in both worlds" [1], by creating community owned and managed "culture-based enterprises as a key way to engage youth within the education, training and employment system" working in synergy with schools to empower youth to use old and new media "to speak to the outside world on their own terms" [1].

R. Bernhaupt et al. (Eds.): INTERACT 2017, Part I, LNCS 10513, pp. 399–419, 2017.
DOI: 10.1007/978-3-319-67744-6_26

Supporting these aims using off-the-shelf services and technologies (e.g. social media) can be problematic because these tools are often biased towards Western ways of working and learning and take the control and ownership of the data away from the community. For these reasons, and in spite of their apparently higher costs, in this paper we advocate for local HCI4D projects that leverage existing skills, reflect local preferences for ways of knowing, and build upon the own goals and ambitions of the community. We thereby contribute a reflection on community engagement as a measure of success of these projects, beyond other immediately measurable outcomes.

People living in developing regions of the world are embracing information and communication technologies at a fast pace. Initially stimulated by the diffusion of mobile phones, these countries are increasing the penetration of ICTs at a pace faster than the developed economies, regardless of their generally lower incomes (see e.g. the UNCTAD reports figures on broadband internet access [2] and e-commerce [3]).

While this growth offers an opportunity to share in a global market of goods, services and knowledge, users coming from a non-Western background encounter the problem of creating and sharing digital contents in ways that are appropriate for their values and customs, using tools that were mostly designed for (and from) Western, highly urbanized and connected, generally English speaking contexts.

In fact, it has been observed that social networking websites promote Western perspectives about personhood and individuality [4], user interfaces can embed modernist conceptions of time [5, 6], and even design methods can reflect Western biases in their epistemological positioning [7, 8]. On the other hand, non-Western perspectives on (e.g.) togetherness [9], relation to land [10], reciprocity [11], and collectivism [12] are often marginalized in mainstream ICTs.

In this broader context, this paper focuses on a project that was initially conceived in response to a request coming from the Elders of Groote Eylandt for a tool capable of supporting communication and promoting literacy across the community. The Elders manifested a concern over using existing social media sites or sharing platforms, because these tools are owned and controlled by distant corporations, seen as promoting values in opposition to local cultures and traditions.

Existing tools also lack clear support for several features that were identified during the initial conversations with the Elders: offering bi-lingual multimodal content creation and sharing; reflecting the preference for orality and storytelling, and paying special attention to issues of community based moderation.

Other aspects that came into focus during the project are also at odds with existing social media services: ownership of the contents as well as of the content management system, a social and relational approach to time management, strong bond to land and physical space, preference for working in groups [13–15] and sharing devices, and a diversity of infrastructure across the three townships where the community lives.

This paper reports on a novel design for a digital noticeboard conceived specifically to accommodate the goals of communication and support for literacy put forward by community members, as introduced above. These goals represents a new opportunity for cross-cultural design, that under the ICT4D and HCI4D endeavours has largely focused rather on capturing and preserving cultural heritage, or on translating and adapting information technologies to local contexts to 'bridge the gap', than on supporting creativity by growing existing designs [16] and considering local sensibilities.

The paper is organized as follows: first we present the community context and review the related research on initiatives aimed at supporting literacy and media production and sharing in remote communities. Then we present the interaction design of Groote's digital noticeboard and introduce the many technical challenges that we encountered while developing the noticeboard. Finally we present how those challenges were addressed in the final design, and discuss the current deployment of the noticeboards at local community hubs.

We contribute our reflection on how HCI4D can support remote indigenous communities in the design of ICTs that align with local ways of knowing, particular sensibilities and existing skills. Particularly, we reflect on the risks faced by HCI4D project of becoming a proverbial 'white elephant': a tool whose cost largely overshadows the usefulness, thus reflecting a poor long term engagement and sustainability strategy.

We propose that in spite of the greater challenges faced to develop and manage custom designs, remote indigenous communities have good reasons to create, maintain, and evolve their own ICTs in ways that align with their ways of making and sharing knowledge, as this involves designing, together with the technology, the community's own future [15]. A custom platform may be less cost-effective, but has better chances to engage the broader community in continued use, provided that the community is actively involved in its conceptualization, design and refinement.

Since this engagement is a key motivation towards working out sustainability issues, and therefore ensuring the continuity of the project, we propose that community engagement should be taken not just as a mean towards, but as the measure of success for HCI4D.

2 Background

As mentioned above the digital noticeboard was initially developed in response to a request coming from the community Elders and local Land Council[1] for a tool that could foster communication of upcoming events, support educational activities and gather cultural information.

Education in particular is a key objective of the Land Council that explicitly aims to "Create pathways for youth to stand in both worlds" by engaging youth through education, training and employment with a focus on culture and culture-based enterprises [1]. These pathways will strengthen the capacity of community members young and old to "positively engage in protecting, maintaining and promoting their culture to the wider world" [1].

The initiative described in this paper is part of this broader endeavour. While there is evidence of a growing appropriation of digital and mobile technologies by

---

[1] A Land Council is an Australian community organization that defends and represents the interests of Indigenous Australians. The Anindilyakwa Land Council is governed by a Board of Traditional Owners of the Land and Sea of Groote Eylandt, and is responsible for the administration of Land Trusts, protection of sacred sites, preservation of culture, and overall implementing the directives given by the community through the Clans' Elders (see http://anindilyakwa.com.au/about-us).

indigenous people [17–19], fewer projects have explored specifically the design of interactive content creation and sharing platforms harmonized with local ways of knowing, values and cultural practices (some examples are [9, 20]).

The very first designs were informed by consultations with key stakeholders. We asked people to narrate or draw their idea of what a digital noticeboard may be used for (see Fig. 1). Such meetings involved the participation of Aboriginal linguists, Aboriginal rangers, coordinators from the local land Council, and staff from the local schools coming from a Western background.

The initial picture emerging from these consultations helped us to understand the potential uses, context and locations; the community was clearly envisaging the noticeboards as being located at key community hubs, such as shops, schools, cultural centres, to share information about news, health, land conservation, but also to offer a Welcome to visitors (a feature always identified as crucial by Aboriginal participants), support literacy and numeracy, collect narratives about the culture.

Cultural centres were identified as places to serve potentially as community hubs, where youth could meet to produce original material to share within the community. In this context, the need for a large screen, around which people can gather to browse or simply watch the noticeboard stories, was considered a necessity.

Photos of family and ancestors were identified as a big focus and reason for engagement, and participants mentioned the need to share photos in an easy way. Specifically, the noticeboard was seen as a repository to host and display contents created by and about the community.

The problem of future maintenance and ongoing management of the contents was also raised, with particular emphasis on issues of moderation, to avoid inappropriate content from being displayed. Based on these initial insights we developed a number of subsequent prototypes that we demonstrated over the following months at each new visit to the community. At the same time we began exploring the particular issues and opportunities that related to languages spoken and levels of literacy, infrastructure, type of devices available, and issues of cost.

Language and Literacy. The people of Groote Eylandt speak the traditional Anindilyakwa language as mother tongue, and are fluent in English as a second language. Anindilyakwa is traditionally an oral language that was first written down in the mid twentieth century. The Groote Eylandt Linguistics Centre is active in the study and preservation of the language, that otherwise is rarely used in written form.

While people are generally fluent in spoken English, proficiency in reading and writing varies. Literacy and numeracy are indicated as major issues to address in order to improve the capacity to obtain and retain qualified jobs and enhance the quality of life in the community [1]. A noticeboard that presents content in both written and spoken form was seen as a way to facilitate the use by people with varying levels of reading competency. With this type of interface, it is possible for people to create and share notices regardless of their level of literacy by uploading visual/spoken content, leaving the task of typing the written version to others. Same language subtitling (SLS) has been used with great success [21] in related research, and it was suggested to adopt this technique here as a mean to enhance accessibility and encourage literacy.

 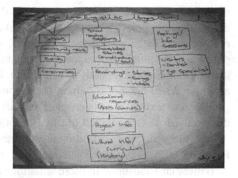

Fig. 1. Design sketches of the Digital Noticeboard created during workshops with community members.

Internet, Social Media, and Electricity. Internet connectivity in Groote is in general a premium resource. Although some dwellings have broadband connectivity, for the most part, Internet is only available to public offices and schools. These institution sometimes share their connectivity by opening discontinuous public access Wi-Fi access points.

Mobile broadband is available in the major towns of Angurugu and Alyangula, but at a cost that is prohibitive for many locals. Mobile phone reception rapidly fades when driving away from town, so the largest majority of the 2300 Km^2 of land (and the two towns of Umbakumba and Milyakburra) have no phone or connectivity besides very costly and slow satellite links.

A large part of the young people connects regularly to social media sites using mobile phones or tablets. The Elders however expressed a concern about the use of social media, as young users are often bullied or teased, which in a close community can easily escalate to confrontations in real life. There is also a perception from the Elders that social media promote values in opposition to the local culture, for example focusing on smaller groups of family/friends instead of the wider community, and are under the control of distant and powerful interests.

Electricity is available at very little cost in all urbanized areas as part of the terms of the lease contract with a mining company that extracts manganese from an area of Groote Eylandt. Fuel too is provided at subsidized cost, which allows people to run their own generators when necessary at comparatively little cost.

Devices available. Possibly in contrast with other rural communities, personal device and computers in general are largely available and frequently used where an infrastructure is present. Most people carry a feature phone, as these devices often the better reception with limited signal power, but smartphones and tablets are not uncommon. Reports from the local shops suggest that at least one iPad is available in each household. Tablets and phones are generally shared within a family. Often people will work in groups, even on tasks (and on user interfaces) that are meant to be individual, so as to reach a sense of agreement and collective ownership on the work that is done [14]. Some of the schools have iPads and personal computers used for activities with the students, as well as wide screen displays that are made available to students and occasional visitors. The displays possibilities for browsing the contents of the digital noticeboard vary accordingly to the available devices. At community hubs (e.g. at cultural centres) electricity and shelter make it possible to deploy big touch screens. At more casual locations, such as at shops, smaller screens can be made available for public use. In public places, or at night, the touch screens may be relocated indoors to avoid weather damage, theft or vandalism, but the service can still be made available as a public Wi-Fi hotspot to which users connect using their own device.

The context of use determines in part the nature of the notices and the kind of device used. It was pointed out that a noticeboard hosted at the Land Council offices would often display institutional information, health news, job offers, etc. At the Rangers' notices would focus on land conservation, weather warnings, Rangers' activities, land closures. In these situations a wide touch screen was seen as a preferred interface for browsing, while upload of contents by the general public would be only marginal. At the schools or cultural centres, notices would mainly focus on educational and cultural activities, festivals and community gatherings, school attendance, etc. In addition to these, it was suggested that a considerable stream of *user generated* notices could be uploaded from personal devices, such as smartphones and iPads.

Issues of cost. The cost of computers and other electronics can be prohibitive for many people. A large proportion of the cost of equipment depends on the cost of transport from the mainland, and of course impacts more on the overall cost of large and heavy screens, than on small portable devices. Maintenance and system administration is performed remotely, or by fly-in fly-out technicians at a huge cost. Decommissioned and broken equipment is often stacked in storage rooms because shipping it back to the mainland for proper disposal would have a huge cost.

A solution based on compact and low cost hardware emerged as a way to cut the cost of maintenance and reduce the environmental impact. Platforms such as the Intel NUC can easily host the digital noticeboard and provide adequate performance. Cheaper solutions, such as Raspberry Pi and Android based Stick PCs, though they have less processing power, can be implemented for under \$100. All such solutions would allow shipment of self-contained upgrades with ordinary post parcels, reducing drastically the cost of maintenance. An open source platform limits the cost of software licensing and facilitates the potential future transfer of the noticeboard to different communities and contexts.

3   Related Research

Two main goals of the digital noticeboard are to support communication and promote literacy. The project addresses these goals by, on the one hand, encouraging community members to create multimedia stories and notices, also leveraging a collaborative model where different people contribute different aspects of notices based on their own confidence and competence. On the other hand, the project aims to facilitate people's approach to reading English and Anindilyakwa by positioning the noticeboard at common gathering points, offering multimedia contents and their literal transcription, with the additional aid of synchronized same language subtitling.

To the best of our knowledge, no previous work has explored the intersection of community digital noticeboards and educational systems to promote literacy in the context of remote communities. However, several projects have studied or proposed designs to address these issues individually; a detailed review is presented below.

3.1 ICTs and Remote Communities

The need for digital communication is surely not restricted to people living in highly urbanized areas. Studies conducted in rural areas and developing regions show that the uptake of ICTs is steadily growing [2, 3], although sometimes use is adapted to local needs or available infrastructure (e.g. [13, 15, 17, 22, 23]).

In the Australian context several studies exist that map the adoption of ICTs by users from remote Indigenous Communities. Brady and co-workers report that only a few weeks after mobile services become available to a remote community in the Torres Strait, a majority of adults had already bought mobile phones [17] to exchange messages in indigenous languages and to take pictures (mostly of children and events relative to the community) to show to family and friends on the mobile itself.

The use of existing online services or social networking sites for sharing information is common in many remote communities, and the recent explosion of affordable and relatively ubiquitous devices and connectivity is facilitating the uptake of new media by Aboriginal youth [24]. Our consultations however, as detailed above, have revealed a tension between the widespread adoption on online social media and the cultural values and practices of the community.

Several projects have explored the use of customized sharing platforms. Maunder and colleagues discuss a sharing system deployed in South Africa consisting in a shared screen/repository from which users can download media at no cost to their own devices [23]. They found that users wanted to consume media in ways and places that they had not anticipated, but that were consistent with the lifestyles of the communities involved in the project.

While examples of noticeboards designed with remote indigenous communities are limited, some insights come from projects that targeted rural communities. Noticeboards can work as a social icebreaker, being generally hosted in central and busy places, and given their role of containers of information of public and general interest [25]. Redhead and Brereton discuss the design and use of a digital community noticeboard situated in an Australian suburb [26]. They describe a number of barriers and issues faced during the long term development and deployment, together with the strategies they applied in response. They stress the importance of fostering participation and interest by means of iteratively evolved situated prototypes [27]. Taylor and Cheverst describe the design and deployment of a digital community photo repository in rural UK [28]. They also observe that encouraging participation and creating a system that is inclusive of all interested users is a major challenge in the development of community social media.

In the context of underserved regions and communities, however, issues arise that make the development and sustainable deployment of social technologies particularly challenging. It has been observed for example that a design biased towards formal service delivery or perfunctory information, when targeted at remote communities, can result in greater costs of deployment, extensive monitoring and ultimately limited success [29–31].

3.2   ICTs and Orality/Literacy

Since low levels of literacy are a barrier to the adoption of information technologies, a number of projects have looked at ways to enable ICT access for users with low literacy by tweaking the user interfaces so as to limit or remove the textual component, in favour of icons and pictograms [32–34], or using speech based interfaces, for example to search audio contents [35]. However, promoting literacy is generally not a specific goal of these initiatives that rather aim at providing alternatives to text-heavy interfaces.

The use of ICTs for supporting and improving literacy is also well documented, although different contexts call for different technological interventions.

Initiatives specifically targeted at promoting literacy have involved both the design of interactive technologies and traditional media. In rural Namibia, Itenge-Wheeler and colleagues applied participatory methods to foster a reading culture among children [36], by inviting them to design their own ideal reading experience. In India same language subtitles (SLS) on music based TV shows [21] and on regional folksongs [37] were used to encourage and support early literates to improve their reading/writing skills.

There is in general solid evidence that technology, particularly multimodal/ multimedia material e.g. interactive books, can improve text comprehension in learners [38–40]. Education is consistently indicated as one of the main goals of ICT4D/HCI4D initiatives [41–43] and even mobile games have been explored as a vehicle to promote learning with children in rural India [44], China [45], and Aboriginal Australia [46]. There are however many challenges to face in order to deliver effective applications to support learning and literacy and engage potential users in remote communities.

In the Australian context, Johnson and Oliver [47] argue that traditional Western pedagogy (based e.g. on teacher's authority, sequential/analytic learning, individual tasks) proves often ineffective and disengaging.

On the contrary, Aboriginal learning styles (e.g. observation and imitation, group processes, spontaneous and hands-on) and life circumstances (e.g. rural/remote, oral traditions, extended community, ancestral focused) fit well with participative and group based online activities, such as social networking and content sharing [47].

In this context, mobile devices, particularly web enabled mobile phones, are often considered a preferred platform for applications aimed at supporting education, particularly for young learners [47].

Various aspects of ICTs and orality/literacy in remote/developing regions have been explored as well. Initiatives range from supporting storytelling, e.g. [9, 48–50], to improving access to technology for users with limited literacy skills (e.g. [35, 44, 51]) to fostering reading and writing (e.g. [21, 36, 44]).

Several projects have focused on how oral traditions can inform the design of interfaces or repositories [42]. Examples include support for storytelling in rural Africa [9, 50], rural India [49], and Aboriginal Australia [52]. These initiatives mirror a consistently increasing number of reports showing that people from rural regions and with limited literacy skills are successfully approaching digital technologies [53] and appropriating such technologies fitting them into their cultural practices [17–19, 22, 54–56].

3.3   Cross-Cultural Design

Design is inherently grounded in culture and there is evidence that people from different cultural backgrounds may have different views, not just on what solutions work best, but even on what *engaging in design* actually means [57]. Irani and colleagues underline that design is culturally situated [58] and discuss the difficulty of transferring technological solutions across cultures.

Such difficulties become evident when design encounters involve users and designers from different backgrounds, for example in terms of different understandings of time [5, 6], different conceptions of personhood [4], different attitudes towards collaboration [7], and more. For example, Taylor and colleagues illustrate the potential for ICTs that privilege Western values to operate in tension with a community's own values and ways of knowing. They discuss the example of calendars and clocks that reflect modernist views of time and efficiency [6] and marginalize social and situational aspects that contribute to defining 'the right time' for events to take place.

In practice, several methods have been proposed to more effectively engage in design with remote communities. Brereton and colleagues suggest to leverage existing local designs as a way to valorise local expertise and achieve results that are relevant and that can be successfully appropriated by the intended users [16].

These works emerge from an understanding that different ontological and epistemological positions often exist between community members and designers, that can result in designs that poorly reflect the community's long term needs [11].

We embrace these calls as a methodological stance to promote engagement and reciprocity in our research and design activity. A key aspect of our approach is to engage in research through design with a participatory design sensibility, i.e. we engage with community members trying to understand the existing issues (including uneven power relations), goals, and needs. As experts of interactive technologies we offer to the community our skills as designers and developers. By designing and building the noticeboard together the research team and the community members get to know and trust each other, in a process of co-creation of knowledge that goes beyond the technology, to include the cross-cultural design process itself, and insights into the cultural context in which the new technology will be embedded.

This approach, described by Soro and colleagues as cross-cultural dialogical probes [8] allows to legitimate the researchers' participation in the design discourse, engage members of the community in design activities, create a relationship of mutual trust by working in cooperation with the community, and overall open up possibilities for learning on culture at large.

One key consequence of this approach is that it foregrounds issues of sustainability and forces to revisit the very concept of evaluation, as discussed by Taylor and Soro et al. [15], who propose to reframe design evaluation in cross-cultural contexts, from a focus on validating artefacts (as typical in HCI research) to a focus on mapping progress towards a desired future. We will elaborate further on the implications of this approach in the final discussion.

3.4 Summary

To summarize, while individual aspects of our research have been explored before in related research, more work is needed to fully unpack the subtleties of how digital community repositories can be adopted to foster literacy and promote communication in remote regions. In particular, the harmonization of the novel technology with local designs, existing skills, and cultural values depends on the goals and vision for the future that the community puts forward.

Previous works have explored ICTs in remote communities largely as repositories for traditional knowledge, rather than as tools to foster communication and sharing mundane contents. While exceptions exist (e.g. the StoryBank project in rural India [49]) these did not generally attempt to encourage literacy, but rather to offer a workaround through privileging audio/visual contents. Initiative specifically aimed at supporting literacy by providing TV contents with same language subtitles (e.g. [21]) faced high costs [37] and would be anyway problematic in the context of indigenous Australia. Here Indigenous communities represent a smaller minority of the population, with ~ 145 different Indigenous languages, many of which are spoken by only a few hundred people [59].

There are opportunities for design in combining large situated displays, personal mobile devices, and user generated multilingual/multimodal contents to engage users. Existing examples (e.g. [26, 28]) have not considered issues of literacy, but there is evidence that such an approach may gain the interest of Aboriginal youth, who have manifested a preference for mobile Web over television and personal computers [55] and for educational platforms based on collaborative Web 2.0 applications over more authoritarian oriented teaching models [47].

Our research was informed by the previous works described so far, yet the socio-cultural context of Groote Eylandt called for novel solutions, particularly in terms of (1) supporting both local and English language; (2) catering for collaboration in a way that suits the distribution of skills and authority; (3) evaluating the technology in use, rather than with artificial tasks. We have used technology prototypes as means to engage with the community, legitimate our participation to community events, and support design discourse with hands-on activities [8]. Then, by focusing on empowering and enhancing the users' possibilities for action, building on existing designs and culturally situated methods, and involving users as co-creators and co-owners of the new technologies, our aim is to maximize the chances of appropriation and sustainable use of the product [11].

4 Groote Eylandt's Digital Noticeboard

Above we have discussed the many technical constraints and challenges that are encountered in Groote Eylandt. Although these challenges were identified from discussions with the people of Groote, similar issues have been described in many related projects that deployed interactive technologies in rural areas. Groote's Digital Noticeboard is implemented in Ruby on Rails and runs on the compact Intel NUC mini

PC. A typical setup will include a steel stand mounted on wheels with a wide touch screen. The mini PC is hidden within the steel support.

4.1 User Interface

The noticeboards use a 50″ touch screen that allows visibility at a distance, but also allows users to gather in groups in front of the screen and browse collaboratively. The user interface is intended to both showcase the noticeboard's contents, and to allow interactive access (Fig. 2). When the noticeboard is not used (no one has touched the screen) for a period of time, it starts showcasing its notices, playing automatically all audio and video content available.

The screen is organized in channels; each channel can contain many stories that in turn are potentially composed of several pages. The terminology alludes to the practice of storytelling, so as to suggest possible ways to host information in the noticeboard.

Both institutional and user generated content can be uploaded, with configurable options for the visibility and moderation of new uploads. To upload user generated content, users can connect using their tablets or mobiles to a dedicated Wi-Fi network, and create new stories using pictures, videos and audio recordings from their local storage (Fig. 3).

A *story* can contain a picture or video, text descriptions in both local language and English and spoken description, again in both languages. An animation highlights the elements of the user interface that are involved in selecting a given story before playing it, so as to demonstrate to bystanders how to use the touch screen, and therefore to invite people in to try for themselves.

The editing interface is structured in such a way as to resemble the final page as closely as possible (Fig. 4), and when operated through one's own mobile or tablet it allows to record video and audio just in time, using the features built in to the device. By

Fig. 2. A working prototype of the Digital noticeboard shown on a wide touch screen mounted on wheels. On the shelf below the screen is the Intel NUC mini PC that runs the noticeboard: this is the 'package' that is shipped for deployment.

Fig. 3. It is possible to access the noticeboard using personal devices by connecting to a Wi Fi hotspot that is created by the NUC mini PC. Contents can therefore be accessed even when the screens are locked up for the night.

providing a coherent layout in both modes the noticeboard delivers an intuitive experience. Navigation controls are greyed out in the editing interface to avoid confusion.

Many design choices were dictated by the concerns of community members that offensive or inappropriate contents may be posted to the noticeboard. Therefore various kinds of community moderation mechanisms were proposed, each one with its own pros and cons in terms of efficacy and usability. The following one was finally implemented and deployed: when a new story is created, it undergoes a process of moderation. New stories will not be displayed on the big screen (but will be visible on the device that was used to create them) until a *champion* reviews and approves its contents. Additionally, users have the opportunity to flag a story or page deemed inappropriate, hiding it temporarily until and requesting a new review, therefore implementing a form of community moderation. This functionality was used to hide (or *rest*) pictures of community members that had recently passed away.

4.2   Backend

Stories are uploaded by users or administrators one page at a time using the editing interface. A page can contain a picture or video (shown on the left hand side of the page); a textual description in Anindilyakwa (split in two parts, title and content) and an analogous one in English; an audio recording with a spoken description in Anindilyakwa and one in English; a validity interval that details when the notice has to be displayed; several flags to detail what channel the story belongs to, if it is going to be shared among all noticeboards, and the ordering of pages in a story.

Notices that are marked as *shared* will be mirrored by all noticeboards that are deployed at various locations on the Island. This will happen automatically when connectivity is available; when no connection is available or using it would not be practical for the limited bandwidth and high costs (as is the case for satellite links), notices can be moved from one noticeboard to another by saving them to a portable storage, e.g. a USB key. From the administrative section of each noticeboard, authorized users can select which notices to copy. The noticeboard will store on the USB key all contents in a compressed human readable form, than can be later restored through the same administrative interface.

Fig. 4. The browsing interface and the editing interface of the digital noticeboard juxtapposed.

4.3   Deployment

Several noticeboards have been progressively deployed around different sites on the island. There have been three main criteria used for choosing sites for the noticeboards within the community: (1) the location serves as a 'community hub' where it is exposed to and accessed by a broad range of different community members, (2) there is a noticeboard 'champion' present who can encourage the creation of new content, and oversee the moderation of new and existing notices, and (3) the noticeboard can be recovered under shelter for the night.

Presently, there are five noticeboards in use around the island at two schools in the Groote Eylandt Archipelago, one at a local Land Council office, one with rangers, and one at the Arts Centre. The NUC computers are connected to large touchscreens, some that are wall mounted, while others are mounted on mobile trolleys. Four of the noticeboards are used indoors while the other is situated in an undercover outdoor location but retrieved overnight. Environmental factors such as heat, humidity, and wildlife pose challenges for using the noticeboard outside without the development of more robust and weather-proof casings.

The research team has worked with community members such as rangers, linguists, school students, and Community Development Program staff to develop initial content and refine the noticeboard interface and functionality. The notice creation process and types of content posted are detailed in [8]. Consistent with Hagen and Robertson's observations [60], the development of "seed content" as a repository of existing notices functioned as "building blocks" for supporting users to develop skills in creating notices, inspiring other users as to the potential content and structure of notices, and identifying functionality and usability issues.

The social practices surrounding bilingual content creation were particularly interesting. The noticeboard interface allows users to upload any combination of text and audio content both in English and Anindilyakwa. However, rather than creating Anindilyakwa content directly, the descriptions were often first drafted in English then translated in Anindilyakwa, and only afterwards both versions were recorded and uploaded. Both older and younger users were reluctant to write in Anindilyakwa without reference material such as the dictionary produced by the linguists.

This may be due to courtesy towards the research team, as none of us speaks Anindilyakwa, or may be due to the fact that writing Anindilyakwa, a traditionally spoken language, is perceived as artificial by many people. There were also different levels of enthusiasm for creating voice recordings; while some people were enthusiastic to narrate their notices, others refused to create audio recordings, due to shyness, not wishing to stand out, and possibly other reasons that were not stated to the research team. In almost all cases people preferred to work in groups. Only very senior people felt comfortable making notices alone, as they are recognised as able to speak on behalf of others.

Previous work on community displays highlights the challenges of evaluating the impact of social media technology use in the community. One approach to evaluation is to capture usage log data that shows when and how the noticeboard features are used, such as the sequence of operations carried out by particular users. However, Taylor and Cheverst note the limitation of this approach for identifying the social practices involved in creating and reviewing noticeboard content given that log data cannot reveal the presence of participants who do not interact directly with the interface [28].

Recording usage logs has been considered for the Digital Community Noticeboard on Groote Eylandt. However, similar limitations were identified in terms of meaningfully capturing and interpreting user behaviours, particularly since the noticeboard interface enables the public to submit content for moderation without needing to log in with a user account. However, the noticeboard does retain an account of the process of creating and evolving stories by maintaining a 'backlog' of all content uploaded that can by hidden from view by the users but not deleted from the noticeboard databases completely.

Instead of systematically logging raw usage, feedback is gathered from participants through in-situ discussions of the noticeboard during public demonstrations or story creation activities with particular users such as the linguists and the rangers. In this way, the noticeboard prototype serves as a cross-cultural dialogical probe [8] for engaging in discussion with users, in which the usability aspects are a secondary consideration. The noticeboard interface is thus "co-evolved" [60] in use with community members through an ongoing participatory design process, and evaluation is aimed at mapping progress towards the community's goals [15] of communication and education, rather than validating the design against technical requirements.

Some examples of these activities that have been conducted for the purpose of gathering feedback on the noticeboard include a demonstration that we gave at a community centre, workshops with school students and teachers to create notices about life on the island and activities taking place in the school community. Additionally, noticeboard paper and digital prototype evaluations have been carried on with the Linguists, and small group meetings and demonstrations were held with other users such as Land Council staff.

Feedback gathered so far on the latest implementation of the noticeboard interface has been positive. During community demonstrations, users expressed their appreciation of an interface that enables text and audio content to be recorded in both languages, and provoked discussion about the spellings and meanings of particular words and their translation. The 'passive display mode' that automatically cycles through the noticeboard content encouraged users to be seated and watch the content as though it is a television, serving the dual purposes of being informative and entertaining, whilst also not singling out a particular person as using the noticeboard. Photographs inspired conversation and anecdotes between community members about the people depicted, often beyond the specific topic of the notice.

Participants suggested many potential future use cases for the noticeboard such as recording extracurricular activities and facilitating classroom activities with school students, displaying old photos and their associated genealogical information, and communicating a broad range of information about community services offered by the Land Council and government organisations. Additional sites were identified for deployment of the noticeboard and touchscreens.

Users also expressed an interest in transporting a NUC to different locations around the island and accessing the noticeboard through iPads only (without the touchscreen display) to provide greater flexibility in terms of where and how the noticeboard can be used. There is ongoing research concerning the potential for the NUCs to be solar powered and positioned in public locations (for example at picnic areas or in the bush) for being accessible even in less institutional contexts, and away from government buildings.

5   Discussion and Conclusions

We have presented the detailed design and ongoing deployment of a digital noticeboard for a remote community. The noticeboard was designed to meet the needs and expectations of the Anindilyakwa People of Groote Eylandt, and is funded as a collaborative project between our institution and the Anindilyakwa Land Council.

We have reviewed the literature on information and communication technologies aimed at remote communities and technical interventions to improve literacy, and in collaboration with several members of the community, we have proposed an architecture for a digital noticeboard tailored to the local ways of working in groups, the need to accommodate bi-lingual content, the preference for oral communication and at the same time the aim of promoting literacy.

We reported on several technical aspects and issues related to the particular socio-cultural context, and the available infrastructure on Groote Eylandt.

In Groote, as in many remote communities, electricity is only available in the main townships, and connectivity is only available at public offices, while mobile phone reception disappears a few kilometres out of town.

The language and culture of public institutions is not the traditional language and culture of the Aboriginal community. While people are generally fluent in both English and Anindilyakwa, this latter is rarely written, except by the linguists. Nevertheless hosting contents in both languages and support for oral and written content in addition to pictures and videos are key features of the noticeboard, that were implemented in the form of bi-lingual stories that users can create, share and browse.

While it is too early to assess the efficacy of the noticeboard for promoting literacy, which is however a key area of future work, we want to offer here a reflection based on how the noticeboard was received, and to what uses it has been put.

5.1   The Noticeboards in Use

Users in schools, cultural centres and other institutions are investing time and resources to appropriate the noticeboard into their daily work practices. This initial uptake is a very positive response, and indicates that the noticeboard is in fact fulfilling a useful role.

The loose structure of the content, other than the arrangements in channels, stories and pages, allows all users to customize the content and the process of content creation to their own needs. Thus the schools are using the noticeboard to support group activities to follow up the trips on country with the rangers, whereas for example the Land Council is mainly publishing information notices on upcoming meetings and community events.

Having a single platform to support both uses means that content can be migrated from one noticeboard to another, therefore allowing the Land Council to showcase content created by the schools occasionally. Content created by community members, such as the rangers or the students is in fact capable of attracting the attention of the broader community, thereby delivering on the primary goal of fostering communication across the community.

The possibility to host spoken and written content in Anindilyakwa is also appreciated, as 'official' channels do not normally support communication in Anindilyakwa.

There are of course several limitations, and issues to address in future releases of the software. For example there is a need to *rest* stories that mention or portray deceased people, for a period of mourning (traditionally one year from the death), and to moderate and if necessary remove offensive or disrespectful contents.

What is perhaps important, however, beyond the more immediate (although clearly important) technical considerations, is to ask what should be the measure success in a cross-cultural design project, and by extension, to what extent the noticeboard project is a successful and sustainable project?

5.2   Lessons Learnt

In this final section we summarize the main lessons learnt and why we think these should resonate beyond this particular case study. Although this project was conducted in a very specific context and location, minority populations provide different perspectives and shine a new light on how technology use and social relations intertwine, from which the mainstream HCI discipline can learn.

Many designs available off the shelf for content creation and sharing take inspiration from philosophies of networked individualism, that cannot capture all the nuances of social interaction, even in the context of the Western workplace where they originated. The uniqueness of Groote Eylandt is the key to bring to the surface a range of issues that affect existing platforms, making them unsuitable for particular uses and users.

Online social platforms, e.g. social networking and blogging sites, provide their users with constant updates, robust handling of many formats for contents, ubiquitous access, and the potential to reach out of one's inner community, to potentially engage a world-wide audience. Furthermore, using off the shelf technologies that are readily available and have already been appropriated by participants is a key strategy to encourage adoption and foster engagement [63] whereas designing one's own platform opens up a risk of acquiring an asset whose usefulness is too small in comparison to its maintenance cost.

Winschiers-Theophilus and colleagues noted that ICT4D is scattered with proverbial 'white elephants' [61], projects that are generated with not enough attention to the needs of the community, but are nevertheless imported into the communities to be tested, and immediately abandoned.

Even the projects that are conducted in participation with the community in order to identify and reflect existing needs, still risk to turn into successful failures. As discussed by Mosse [62], the 'needs' even when expressed through a participatory process, can reflect more the expectations of what the research team can likely deliver, rather than a real aspiration existing on the community's part.

Yet, as this case study shows, there are reasons to also explore alternative paths, and create customized designs that are independent from the technical constraints, business models, and design biases of globalized enterprises.

The digital noticeboard was designed to fill a gap in the communication needs of the community that existing technologies or available social networking services were unable to address. As we have discussed, the community Elders are reluctant to embrace social media to engage with the youth, because these services are seen as promoting values that are in conflict with the local culture, and pose issues of who owns the platform, and therefore who controls the information in it.

A custom platform designed with the community, and for the community to manage and own, was then seen as a viable alternative to support communication within the community and between the Elders and the youth, promoting at the same time the community's own identity and values, and the broader goals of education and literacy devised by the Land Council.

By owning the platform the community can prioritize its own goals and problems in future developments, which may be impossible with external services. The flip side of the coin, of course, is that the community will be responsible for maintaining and updating the noticeboard software, fixing and replacing the hardware as it fails, and responding to possible demands for new features or modifications.

Given the above, how should we assess whether the project is deemed to succeed, providing value to the community and supporting the need for communication, or if we are facing just another white elephant?

Taylor, Soro and colleagues propose to shift the focus of evaluation from testing artefacts against needs and wants, to mapping progress towards desired futures [15], therefore foregrounding, among others, the problem of sustainability.

In fact, those issues that are of more interest to the community can hardly emerge by focusing on the artefacts alone [15]. How does the design fit (or disrupt) existing workflows? Who is going to maintain the software and hardware? Who will take ownership of the designs and champion its adoption within the community?

Nurturing and fostering community engagement has been repeatedly indicated as a means to better design outcomes [8, 11, 26–28, 61]. We further contribute to this ongoing discourse a view that *community engagement should be regarded as the measure of success* in cross cultural design projects, and therefore, more than a means, as an end in and of itself. In fact, questions such as the ones above are predicated on members from the community having a motivation for taking ownership, maintaining and continuing to use the noticeboards in the first place. As we have presented in the paper, engagement can materialize in many forms. In our case we observed an appropriation of the noticeboard into new contexts, sometimes not envisaged in the initial designs, such as for hosting media productions and distributing them in community gatherings. Also, the willingness to be part of the many discussions and the interest for the demonstrations of the noticeboard functionalities, that we observed multiple times. Finally, many people voicing ideas for future iterations of the interface that indicate an intention for further engagement and an interest for continuing evolution of the design.

All these, we argue, represent a positive sign that the community is imagining a future where the noticeboards have been adopted and adapted, rather than disposed of and abandoned.

Acknowledgement. We thank and acknowledge the Anindilyakwa people and the Anindilyakwa Land Council for the opportunity to develop this bi-cultural noticeboard with them. We thank the Australian Research Council and the Anindilyakwa Land Council for Linkage Grant LP120200329.

References

1. Anindilyakwa Land Council: ALC 15 Year Strategic Plan (2012)
2. UNCTAD: Information Economy Report 2007–2008 (2008)
3. UNCTAD: Information Economy Report 2015 (2015)
4. Bidwell, N.J., Winschiers-Theophilus, H., Koch Kapuire, G., Rehm, M.: Pushing personhood into place: situating media in rural knowledge in Africa. Int. J. Hum. Comput. Stud. **69**, 618–631 (2011)
5. Taylor, J.L., Soro, A., Lee Hong, A., Roe, P., Brereton, M.: Designing for cross-cultural perspectives of time. In: Proceedings of AfriCHI 2016. ACM Press (2016)
6. Taylor, J.L., Soro, A., Roe, P., Lee Hong, A., Brereton, M.: Situational when: designing for time across cultures. In: Proceedings of SIGCHI 2017. ACM Press (2017)
7. Winschiers-Theophilus, H., Chivuno-Kuria, S., Kapuire, G.K., Bidwell, N.J., Blake, E.: Being participated: a community approach. In: Proceedings of PDC 2010, pp. 1–10. ACM, New York, USA (2010)
8. Soro, A., Brereton, M., Taylor, J.L., Lee Hong, A., Roe, P.: Cross-cultural dialogical probes. In: Proceedings of the First African Conference on Human Computer Interaction – AfriCHI 2016, pp. 114–125. ACM Press, New York, USA (2016)
9. Bidwell, N., Siya, M.: Situating asynchronous voice in rural Africa. In: Kotzé, P., Marsden, G., Lindgaard, G., Wesson, J., Winckler, M. (eds.) Human-Computer Interaction – INTERACT 2013 SE - 3, pp. 36–53. Springer, Berlin, Heidelberg (2013)
10. Bidwell, N.J., Standley, P.-M., George, T., Steffensen, V.: The landscape's apprentice: lessons for place-centred design from grounding documentary. In: Proceedings of DIS 2008, pp. 88–98. ACM, New York, USA (2008)
11. Brereton, M., Roe, P., Schroeter, R., Lee Hong, A.: Beyond ethnography: engagement and reciprocity as foundations for design research out here. In: Proceedings of SIGCHI 2014, pp. 1183–1186. ACM, New York, USA (2014)
12. Henrich, J., Heine, S.J., Norenzayan, A.: The weirdest people in the world? Behav. Brain Sci. **33**, 61–83 (2010)
13. Soro, A., Lee Hong, A., Shaw, G., Roe, P., Brereton, M.: A noticeboard in "Both Worlds" unsurprising interfaces supporting easy bi-cultural content publication. In: Adj Proceedings of SIGCHI 2015, pp. 2181–2186. ACM, New York, USA (2015)
14. Soro, A., Brereton, M., Lee Hong, A., Roe, P.: Bi-cultural content publication on a digital noticeboard: a design and cultural differences case study. In: Proceedings of OzCHI 2015, pp. 217–221. ACM, New York, USA (2015)
15. Taylor, J.L., Soro, A., Brereton, M., Lee Hong, A., Roe, P.: Designing evaluation beyond evaluating design: measuring success in cross-cultural projects. In: Proceedings of OzCHI 2016 (2016)
16. Brereton, M., Roe, P., Amagula, T., Bara, S., Lalara, J., Hong, A.L.: Growing existing aboriginal designs to guide a cross-cultural design project. In: Kotzé, P., Marsden, G., Lindgaard, G., Wesson, J., Winckler, M. (eds.) INTERACT 2013. LNCS, vol. 8117, pp. 323–330. Springer, Heidelberg (2013). doi:10.1007/978-3-642-40483-2_22

17. Brady, F.R., Dyson, L.E., Asela, T.: Indigenous adoption of mobile phones and oral culture. In: Cultural Attitudes Towards Communication and Technology, pp. 384–398. Murdoch University (2008)
18. Kral, I.: Plugged in: Remote Australian Indigenous youth and digital culture. In: CAEPR Working Paper No. 69. CAEPR working paper (2010)
19. Shaw, G., Brereton, M., Roe, P.: Mobile phone use in australian indigenous communities: future pathways for HCI4D. In: Proceedings of the 26th OzCHI, pp. 480–483. ACM, New York, USA (2014)
20. Verran, H., Christie, M., Anbins-King, B., Weeren, T.Van, Yunupingu, W., Van Weeren, T., Yunupingu, W.: Designing digital knowledge management tools with aboriginal Australians. Digit. Creat. **18**, 129–142 (2007)
21. Kothari, B.: Let a billion readers bloom: same language subtitling (SLS) on television for mass literacy. Int. Rev. Educ. **54**, 773–780 (2008)
22. Hahn, H.P., Kibora, L.: The domestication of the mobile phone: oral society and new ICT in Burkina Faso. J. Mod. Afr. Stud. **46**, 87–109 (2008)
23. Maunder, A., Marsden, G., Harper, R.: Making the link—providing mobile media for novice communities in the developing world. Int. J. Hum. Comput. Stud. **69**, 647–657 (2011)
24. Kral, I.: Youth media as cultural practice: Remote Indigenous youth speaking out loud. Aust. Aborig. Stud. **1**, 4 (2011)
25. Churchill, E., Nelson, L., Denoue, L., Helfman, J., Murphy, P.: Sharing multimedia content with interactive public displays: a case study. In: Proceedings of DIS 2004, pp. 7–16. ACM Press, Boston (2004)
26. Redhead, F., Brereton, M.: Designing interaction for local communications: an urban screen study. In: Gross, T., Gulliksen, J., Kotzé, P., Oestreicher, L., Palanque, P., Prates, R.O., Winckler, M. (eds.) INTERACT 2009. LNCS, vol. 5727, pp. 457–460. Springer, Heidelberg (2009). doi:10.1007/978-3-642-03658-3_49
27. Heyer, C., Brereton, M.: Reflective agile iterative design. In: Social Interaction with Mundane Technologies Conference, pp. 1–4. Social Interaction and Mundane Technologies, Cambridge (2008)
28. Taylor, N., Cheverst, K.: Social interaction around a rural community photo display. Int. J. Hum. Comput. Stud. **67**, 1037–1047 (2009)
29. Daly, A.: Bridging the digital divide: the role of community online access centres in indigenous communities (2005)
30. Taylor, A.: Information communication technologies and new Indigenous mobilities? Insights from remote Northern Territory Communities. J. Rural Commun. Dev. **7**, 59–73 (2012)
31. Hunter, E., Travers, H., Gibson, J., Campion, J.: Bridging the triple divide: performance and innovative multimedia in the service of behavioural health change in remote Indigenous settings. Australas. Psych. **15**, 44–48 (2007)
32. Friscira, E., Knoche, H., Huang, J.: Getting in touch with text: designing a mobile phone application for illiterate users to harness SMS. In: Proceedings of the 2nd ACM Symposium on Computing for Development, pp. 5:1–5:10. ACM, New York, USA (2012)
33. Chaudry, B.M., Connelly, K.H., Siek, K.A., Welch, J.L.: Mobile interface design for low-literacy populations. In: Proceedings of the 2nd ACM SIGHIT, pp. 91–100. ACM, New York, USA (2012)
34. Medhi, I., Patnaik, S., Brunskill, E., Gautama, S.N.N., Thies, W., Toyama, K.: Designing mobile interfaces for novice and low-literacy users. ACM Trans. Comput. Interact. **18**, 2:1–2:28 (2011)
35. Metze, F., Anguera, X., Barnard, E., Davel, M., Gravier, G.: Language independent search in MediaEval's Spoken Web Search task. Comput. Speech Lang. **28**, 1066–1082 (2014)

36. Itenge-Wheeler, H., Kuure, E., Brereton, M., Winschiers-Theophilus, H.: Co-creating an enabling reading environment for and with namibian children. In: Proceedings of PDC 2016, pp. 131–140. ACM, New York, USA (2016)

37. Arora, P.: Karaoke for social and cultural change. J. Inf. Commun. Ethics Soc. **4**, 121–130 (2006)

38. Segers, E., Verhoeven, L.: Multimedia support of early literacy learning. Comput. Educ. **39**, 207–221 (2002)

39. Baharani, B., Ghafournia, N.: The impact of multimodal texts on retriading achievement: a study of iranian secondary school learners. Int. J. Appl. Linguist. Engl. Lit. **4**, 161–170 (2015)

40. Kuo, Y.-C., Yang, S.-W., Kuo, H.-H.: Learning bridge: a reading comprehension platform with rich media. World Acad. Sci. Eng. Technol. 934–936 (2010)

41. Patra, R., Pal, J., Nedevschi, S.: ICTD state of the union: where have we reached and where are we headed (2009)

42. Ho, M.R., Smyth, T.N., Kam, M., Dearden, A.: Human-computer interaction for development: the past, present, and future. Inf. Technol. Int. Dev. **5**, 1 (2009)

43. Chepken, C., Mugwanya, R., Blake, E., Marsden, G.: ICTD interventions: trends over the last decade. In: Proceedings of the Fifth International Conference on Information and Communication Technologies and Development, pp. 241–248. ACM, New York, USA (2012)

44. Kumar, A., Reddy, P., Tewari, A., Agrawal, R., Kam, M.: Improving literacy in developing countries using speech recognition-supported games on mobile devices. In: Proceedings of SIGCHI 2012, pp. 1149–1158. ACM (2012)

45. Tian, F., Lv, F., Wang, J., Wang, H., Luo, W., Kam, M., Setlur, V., Dai, G., Canny, J.: Let's play Chinese characters: mobile learning approaches via culturally inspired group games. In: Proceedings of SIGCHI 2010, pp. 1603–1612. ACM, New York, USA (2010)

46. Jorgensen, R., Lowrie, T.: Both ways strong: using digital games to engage aboriginal learners. Int. J. Incl. Educ. **17**, 130–142 (2013)

47. Johnson, G.M., Oliver, R.: Cognition, literacy and mobile technology: a conceptual model of the benefits of smartphones for aboriginal students in remote communities. In: Herrington, J., Couros, A., and Irvine, V. (eds.) Proceedings of EdMedia 2013, pp. 1273–1278. AACE, Victoria, Canada (2013)

48. Morrison, C., Jones, M., Blackwell, A., Vuylsteke, A.: Electronic patient record use during ward rounds: a qualitative study of interaction between medical staff. Crit. Care **12**, R148 (2008)

49. Frohlich, D.M., Rachovides, D., Riga, K., Bhat, R., Frank, M., Edirisinghe, E., Wickramanayaka, D., Jones, M., Harwood, W.: StoryBank: mobile digital storytelling in a development context. In: Proceedings of SIGCHI 2009, pp. 1761–1770. ACM, New York, USA (2009)

50. Reitmaier, T., Bidwell, N.J., Marsden, G.: Situating digital storytelling within African communities. Int. J. Hum Comput Stud. **69**, 658–668 (2011)

51. Medhi, I., Sagar, A., Toyama, K.: Text-free user interfaces for illiterate and semi-literate users. In: Proceedings of ICTD 2006, pp. 72–82 (2006)

52. Mills, K.A., Davis-Warra, J., Sewell, M., Anderson, M.: Indigenous ways with literacies: transgenerational, multimodal, placed, and collective. Lang. Educ. **30**, 1–21 (2016)

53. Mitra, S., Dangwal, R., Chatterjee, S., Jha, S., Bisht, R.S., Kapur, P.: Acquisition of computing literacy on shared public computers: children and the "hole in the wall". Australas. J. Educ. Technol. **21**, 407 (2005)

54. Christie, M., Verran, H.: Digital lives in postcolonial Aboriginal Australia. J. Mater. Cult. **18**, 299–317 (2013)

55. Johnson, G.M.: Technology use among Indigenous adolescents in remote regions of Australia. Int. J. Adolesc. Youth **21**, 1–14 (2013)
56. Kral, I.: Talk, Text and Technology: Literacy and Social Practice in a Remote Indigenous Community Critical Language and Literacy Studies, vol. 14 (2012)
57. Nichols, C.D.: Discovering design: enhancing the capability to design at the cultural interface between first Australian and western design paradigms (2014)
58. Irani, L., Vertesi, J., Dourish, P., Philip, K., Grinter, R.E.: Postcolonial computing: a lens on design and development. In: Proceedings of SIGCHI 2010, pp. 1311–1320. ACM, New York, USA (2010)
59. McConvell, P., Marmion, D., McNicol, S.: National Indigenous Languages Survey Report 2005. Australian Government (2005)
60. Hagen, P., Robertson, T.: Social technologies: the changing nature of participation in design. Des. Issues **28**, 77–88 (2012)
61. Winschiers-Theophilus, H., Zaman, T., Yeo, A.: Reducing "White Elephant" ICT4D projects: a community-researcher engagement. In: Proceedings of Communities and Technologies 2015, pp. 99–107. ACM, New York, USA (2015)
62. Mosse, D.: 'People's knowledge', participation and patronage: operations and representations in rural development (2001)

Culturally Informed Notions of Mobile Context Awareness - Lessons Learned from User-Centred Exploration of Concepts of Context and Context Awareness

Xiangang Qin[1,2], Chee-Wee Tan[1], Mads Bødker[1], Wei Sun[2], and Torkil Clemmensen[1(✉)]

[1] Copenhagen Business School, Frederiksberg, Denmark
{xq.itm, cta.itm, mb.itm, tc.itm}@cbs.dk
[2] Beijing University of Posts and Telecommunications, Beijing, China
{qinxiangang, sunwey}@bupt.edu.cn

Abstract. Mobile context awareness is an elusive concept within extant literature on human-computer interaction. Despite extensive research into context awareness, past studies have accentuated the architectural aspects of context-aware applications without paying sufficient attention to user-centric issues associated with such applications. To this end, this study endeavours to shed light on how context-aware applications are construed by users. Drawing inspiration from the 'future workshop' methodological approach, two focus groups were conducted in Denmark and China to elicit insights into the benefits and shortcomings of contemporary context-aware applications across different cultural settings. Empirical findings suggest that users' interactions with context-aware applications are governed, to a large extent, by their: (1) own personal value system; (2) sensitivity towards such applications, and; (3) current activity in which they are engaged. This study thus takes a small but concrete step towards further discussions on the importance of embracing a user-centred view of mobile context awareness.

Keywords: Mobile Context-Awareness · User experience · Cross-cultural

1 Introduction

The global population of smart phone users is projected to reach 2.32 billion by the end of 2017 [1]. Because a variety of sensors are embedded in smart phones which endow the latter with the ability to be aware of and interact with the surrounding context, smart phones can be conceived as a type of mobile context-aware system that extends human cognition and perception. Indeed, Mobile Context-Awareness (MCA) is a rapidly growing topic of interest for both academics and practitioners due to the increasing dynamism and richness of contextual information afforded by smart devices [2]. A variety of context-awareness systems have been developed to adapt system's behaviour with changing location, time, physical environment, identity and emotion state of user, nearby devices and social entities as well [3]. Although context-awareness

R. Bernhaupt et al. (Eds.): INTERACT 2017, Part I, LNCS 10513, pp. 420–440, 2017.
DOI: 10.1007/978-3-319-67744-6_27

is intended to circumvent issues in user experience (UX) caused by small screen size and ever-shifting context in smart devices, context-aware mobile applications are also presumed to be capable of offering more customized and more favourable UXs than non-context-aware ones [3, 5]. It is accompanied by its own side effects such as distracting interruptions, loss of control and privacy risk [6]. There are calls for an in-depth appreciation of how the UX is shaped by mobile context-aware systems [5].

Yet, despite the calls, the UX of MCA and other user related issues have been lacking in HCI research. Hong et al. [7] discovered that the bulk of research (237 articles in total) tends to concentrate on issues associated with conceptualization, network, middleware and application. Even though the few studies, which have examined the issue of UX for MCA (device and application), have put forth general guidelines for designing mobile context-aware systems (i.e., avoiding unnecessary interruptions, ensuring user control, guaranteeing system visibility and tailoring content to match individual needs) [6, 8], there is a dearth of research that has been devoted to a dedicated scrutiny of how such systems can be designed from a user-centred perspective in distinct cultural contexts. In addition, there is growing recognition that we have a limited comprehension of how to capture, interpret and share abstract contexts [9]. Social context is an exemplary illustration of an abstract context in that the UX of mobile context-aware system might vary in different social settings. We argue that culture plays an instrumental role in shaping UX of MCA, and should not be divorced from any investigative efforts targeted at the phenomenon. This study endeavours to unpack the concept of MCA from a user-centred perspective by eliciting user's opinion and experience with mobile context-aware systems in both Chinese and Danish cultural settings.

2 Background

2.1 The Cultural Context of Mobile Services

While emerging markets like China and India have already overtaken more matured markets like the United States in terms of mobile phone penetration, the UX of the popular smart devices (based on Android, iOS or Windows architecture) are still designed by Western firms. For this reason, Chinese firms are acquiring their Western counterparts in the provision of mobile services. However, consumers of both Chinese and Western firms are utilizing mobile services provided by companies with different cultural backgrounds such as Google vs. Baidu, Facebook vs. WeChat, Twitter vs. Weibo, to name a few. Users have developed corresponding habits of interacting with mobile applications that are designed and developed for different cultural contexts. It is unclear whether the design of mobile context-aware features by Chinese firms are accommodative of Westerners and vice versa.

The cultural context and user's preference of interaction might vary in different countries. Extant literature contains extensive evidence attesting to discrepancies between Asian and Western ways of acting and thinking [10]. Chinese subjects are more sensitive to contextual incongruity as compared to Americans [11]. Situation (or social context) influence the effect of culture on affect, cognition and behaviour. For this reason, intra- and inter-cultural variations of MCA can be best understood by taking the cultural context into consideration [12]. Specifically, Westerners are believed to be more concerned about the instrumental (efficiency) attributes of UX whereas Chinese users care more about non-instrumental (e.g., appearance) attributes of inter-active products [13]. While a key merit of MCA resides in its ability to improve the efficiency of interactions, we contend that variations in users' attitudes toward MCA exist between Chinese and Denmark users. Despite a broad recognition of the presence of cross-cultural disparities in UX of mobile context-aware systems, e.g., [13], few studies investigate how and why such disparities exist, which in turn acts as the impetus for this study.

2.2 The Value of Social Context and Context Awareness

Since the term 'context-aware' was first coined to describe the computing ability "of a mobile user's applications to discover and react to changes in the environment they are situated in" [14], context-awareness has been touted as a key component of pervasive and ubiquitous computing. Essentially, context-awareness endows mobile computing devices with the capability of interacting with humans in an intuitive manner that mirrors human-human interaction [15]. Nevertheless, it is only with the proliferation of smart devices that the importance of context awareness begins to gain traction.

For users, high-level contexts like activity, psychological status and place are more meaningful than low level contexts like location, noise, gravity, time. As a variable of high-level contexts, social context is valuable in deciphering and interpreting the intention and activities of human being by integrating and combing low-level context information captured by sensors. For example, providing contextual information about air quality would be valued more in Beijing than in Copenhagen. Yet, the social context is complicated and fast evolving in mobile situations, especially across different cultural contexts. A deeper appreciation of the focal dimensions of social context, which might influence the intentions and activities of users [5], would contribute to the abstraction, acquisition, inference and utilization of contextual information to enhance the UX of context-aware systems.

2.3 The Influence of MCA on HCI

An abundance of intricate contextual information are exploited in human-to-human communication, such as eye contact, facial expression, hand gestures, body language and even more profound social attributes like culture and religions. Unlike human-to-human communication, tradition interactions between humans and computers are constrained by the latter's computing power and number of embedded sensors in harvesting and harnessing contextual information [16, 17].

Over the past decade, mobile devices, especially smart phones, have been adopted by a vast population of users globally. In many countries, more than 50% of the population are smart phone users. Nowadays, mobile phones have been fitted with enhanced computing capabilities and miniaturized sensors that enable such phones to proactively interact with humans by drawing on contextual information to adapt to user intention and behaviours. Due to the infusion of context-aware features, smart devices are capable of interacting with users in intelligent, natural and human-like ways.

Fundamentally, MCA alters the interaction between humans and computers in four ways. First, the interaction between users and context-aware systems is shifting from an explicit format to an implicit one. Second, the informational resources accessible to context-aware systems are much more diverse due to data generated by both humans and technological sensors [17]. Third, context-aware systems (e.g., smart phones) are transforming from a passive role of accepting, processing and displaying information to a more active role of abstracting, acquiring, inferring and utilizing contextual information in order to execute actions automatically. Finally, context-aware systems can sense other users and computing devices in their surroundings, thereby rendering cross-device social interaction plausible.

2.4   MCA from a User-Centred Perspective

Designers, developers and users are inclined to interpret the same system from diverse perspectives, thereby culminating in separate meanings. One of the most valuable contribution of HCI to mobile system is that it bridges the gap among the mental models of the abovementioned three parties [18]. An early study on the usability of mobile context-aware applications demonstrated that while users prefer to utilize context-aware applications with higher degrees of proactivity, their feelings of out of control, lack of feedback, privacy leak and information overload increases correspondingly [8]. At the same time, users express a greater willingness to tolerate the preceding uncertainties in exchange for a more interactive and smoother experience. Because users are adaptive and context-dependent when utilizing context-aware mobile applications, it implies that the UX of same mobile application may vary across contexts and usage.

In mobile environments, the use context tends to fluctuate and the same contextual information might acquire differentiated meanings across distinct contexts and usage [19]. Since user profiles and purpose is likely to differ when utilizing mobile applications [3], it is conceivable for users to utilize the same application in contexts that were not anticipated by designers and developers [5]. Indeed, it is not uncommon for context-aware systems to encounter difficulties in interpreting user context due to variations in physical attributes (i.e., height, palm size and eye-sight), cognitive and perceptual abilities (e.g. memory, learning, problem-solving and decision making) and personality (e.g. gender, attitudes towards computers and emotional states).

Compared with the era dominated by desktop computers and feature phones, contexts associated with the utilization of smart mobile devices have changed dramatically and enriched significantly. Mobile applications tend to become much more complex as the quantity and types of information employed by context-aware applications have surpassed those of non-context-aware ones [6]. Mobile applications developed by Chinese company include more functionalities than those introduced by Western companies (e.g., wallet payment, red packet and games in WeChat), which in turn might bring about unexpected interactive behaviours and experiences.

To-date, context-awareness has mainly been investigated from a technical point of view with strong emphasis on location-aware mobile applications [5, 7]. The limited research about mobile context-aware system, from a user-centred perspective, are either ecologically invalid experiment, or too specific for guiding the design of applications in diverse fields [20]. Particularly, a major research trend within extant literature on mobile context-awareness systems is rooted in the design of middleware and APIs to facilitate the development of MCA applications. In the absence of an in-depth appreciation of users, contemporary studies run the risk that findings derived from inquiries of user-centred MCA applications may not be generalizable to other fields.

A number of questions emerge with respect to the impact of MCA on Human-Computer Interaction (HCI): How can users be aware of the intricate contextual information being inputted and captured by mobile context-aware systems? What's the concerns of users about mobile context-aware applications and how the concerns might shape the interaction between user and mobile device? How to exploit and integrate contextual information in multi-modals? Should smart phones be more active in executing actions that are undertaken by humans traditionally? How should humans deal with an intelligent and emotional device that has been endowed with social-networking features?

3 Methods

We opted for the Focus Group (FG) and Future Workshop(FW) methodology in this study because they has been acknowledged as an appropriate technique for conducting exploratory research on social phenomena and participatory design studies [e.g., 18, 22–25]. The future workshop approach departs from the standard FG format by placing greater emphasis on mapping techniques and the process of articulating visually how technologies might be utilized in the future. In addition, the future workshop approach engages participants in discussions across two or more groups. This fosters a conducive climate for more divergent opinions to be voiced and in turn, overcome potential shortcomings associated with 'group think' in focus group [26, 27].

Blending FG with the future workshop approach allowed us to focus the group interview on the concept of 'context awareness' which we knew, from a single pilot interview with a doctoral student in the field of information systems, to be difficult to comprehend and envision for participants. Exercises adopted in the methodology facilitated participants in expressing their ideas about context awareness of a design scenario or a short description of a dream system in a concrete domain (using paper and pen) rather than in an abstract verbal form [28].

3.1 Participants

For the purpose of this study, a total 12 participants were recruited for two FGs, one in Denmark and one in China. All participants had more than 6 months of experience with smart phones. Each was compensated with a gift card for his/her participation. Six participants (3 male, 3 female) age between 22 and 31 were recruited in Denmark. All participants are Europeans and speak English. Likewise, six participants (3 male, 3 female) age between 21 and 25 were recruited in China. All of them are ethnically Chinese and speak Mandarin. English is the language of communication for the FG in Denmark while participants conversed in Mandarin for the FG in China.

3.2   Moderators and Observers

Both FGs in Denmark and China had one moderator and one observer. The moderator steered participants through the FG whereas the observer took charge of recording the procedure in audios, videos and photos. The Danish moderator was a male educator and researcher in the field of service design with more than 15 years of career experience. Similarly, the Chinese moderator was a male educator and researcher in the field of product and service design with more than 15 years of career experience.

3.3   Procedure

For participants in both FGs, it was first stressed that their participation did not constitute an evaluation of their academic performance. Each focus group comprised five progressive phases that lasted 2.5 h including a short break. These five phases were: a warm-up phase, a brainstorming phase, a pros & cons phase, a design phase and a validation phase. Transcripts from data gathered in the five phases were then divided into four main sections: Warm-up, Brain Strom, Pros & Cons, Design and Validation.

The focus groups were carried out in meeting/interview rooms at one university in Denmark and one in China. The setup included tables that separated the participants into two groups. GoPro cameras recorded each sub-group. Audio recorders captured group conversations. Further, two cameras were placed so as to capture both groups and the intergroup interaction. The layout of FGs in Denmark and China is depicted in Fig. 1 below and the flow diagram for the FG procedure is illustrated in Fig. 2.

Fig. 1. Meeting room. Groups are placed at crescent tables, GoPro cameras record interactions in both groups. Secondary cameras record interactions and discussions between groups. Left side = Focus group in Denmark, Right side = Focus group in China.

3.4   Material and Data Collection

Printed template of mobile phone, pens and white board were distributed to participants for them to illustrate and sketch ideas. Data was collected in three formats: audio, video and photo. Four video cameras were deployed to record the FG from different angles. Two wide-angle GoPro cameras were placed at the front of each sub-group to record

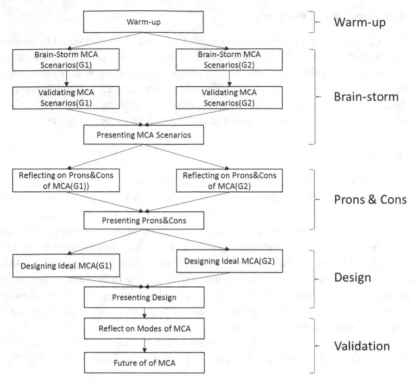

Fig. 2. Chart of FG procedure. MCA = Mobile context-awareness, WG = Within group, BG = Between group.

interactions within each group separately. Another two cameras were positioned at the two corners in the room to record the entire interaction process in the FGs from a holistic angle. Two audio recorders are fitted on the table of each FG to record the voices of participants. A photo camera was employed to record tangible outcomes of each FG, such as drawings, designs, sketches and presentations on whiteboard.

3.5 Data Cleaning, Coding and Analysis

Data in different formats are first matched with each other by timestamp and then transcribed into text for analysis. After cleaning the data, thematic analysis was adopted to encode and induce themes from the qualitative comments [29]. The objective of thematic analysis is to find a pattern in the random data that, at minimum, describes and organizes users' understanding of MCA and, at maximum, interprets the way that users structure MCA. The detailed procedure for thematic analysis is illustrated below:

- Isolating recurring patterns of interest with respect to context and context-aware applications: To make sure all researchers can understand and code the raw data, scripts from Chinese FG are translated into English. Three Western researchers generated a list of insights (i.e., codes + comments) based on the transcripts from the Danish FG. One researcher with a Chinese background listened in and supplemented the insights generated by the Western researchers. Next, Chinese researchers created a list of insights (i.e., codes + comments) on the basis of the Chinese FG. One of these was currently living in Denmark, and thus could compare across countries.

- Combining related patterns into themes: A researcher with a Chinese background and a researcher with Western background, supported by all (SKYPE call), compared the list of insights generated by both Chinese and Danish researchers in order to identify both commonalities and disparities in participants' attitude towards MCA across both cultural settings.
- Deriving excerpts from the FGs that correspond to these themes: A researcher went through the themes again and derived a potential framework for organizing the themes. Another researcher discussed with the first researcher about the structure and extract insights from the raw data to support the framework.

4   Results

It is well recognized that mobile applications offer an abundance of unique benefits by adjusting to user-specific circumstances and establishing a means to a connected lifestyle anytime and anywhere. Despite the potency of MCA, we still lack a fundamental understanding of how users evaluate MCA [19].

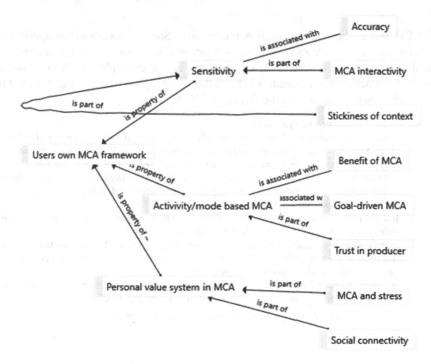

Fig. 3. The categories of participants' views on MCA, and the interrelations.

Results from our thematic analysis reveals that participants can and do construct their own meaning of MCA, citing prominent examples of MCA as applied in everyday contexts. Second, participants' interpretation of MCA appears to be governed by their: (1) own personal value system; (2) sensitivity towards the degree of context-awareness for such systems, and; (3) their current activity in which they are engaged Each of these properties is associated with or constituted by other aspects of their understanding of MCA. This is exemplified through quotes from the focus groups below. Finally, participants are able to distinguish among the capabilities of mobile context-aware systems, the pros and cons of such systems as well as their views of how these systems could be designed from a user-centred angle (see Fig. 3).

4.1   Participants' Own MCA Framework

One of the core findings in our study is how participants can and do construct their own meaning of MCA. They are able to supply examples of the use of MCA in everyday contexts. In Quote #1 from the Danish FG during the Warm-up session, one of the participants explains what she thinks is an example of MCA.

MO   *Does anybody have sort of some impressions to share your examples about what context-awareness could be?*
G2-CH   *For example, registering where you are could help you on vacation. Google Now has registered where I live and work automatically. And it does register some patterns where I'm going. That's an example from the mobile phone.*

Quote #1 DK Warm-up Phase; MO = Moderator, G2-CH = Danish FG 2 Participant

G2-CH shares experiences from her own life. She knows about an application called Google Now that tracks its owner's location and displays it on the smartphone when it seems relevant, which G2-CH regards as an example of MCA. Another example is the participant in Quote #2, from the Design phase in the Danish FG, who wants to share what she sees as the future of MCA.

G1-TR   *I have 3 different kind of scenarios.*
        The first one is that we (have to) get all these applications updated here in the App-Store. So either you can choose update it (all) or not. I would like to have the possibility of choosing or selecting new features in the update I like or I don't like. For instance, in Facebook, it says we have this new feature having favourite friends. But I dislike that feature. I still want to update the system without that feature. So it's kinda like individualizing the update.
        And the other one is pre-setting your phone in different modes. I could make a mode called vacation mode. I pre-install it into (my phone).When I activate it, it knows that not to update my e-mail, or not give me alarm in the morning. And despite that when I deactivated it, I can activate it (anytime). That could be other modes, Whatever, likes sporting mode, maybe suggest some good news
        And the last one is like digital business card that give each contact person ratings like those paid of loans, connects, and after that, we can arrange meetings.

Quote #2. DK Design Phase;G1-TR = Danish FG1 Participant

G1-TR here, during the Design phase, sees herself as a co-designer, and has put forward several ideas for designing MCA. Some of these ideas appear to be centred on Western technologies such as App-store and Facebook, while others stem from activity/mode – vacation mode – to social connectivity – and business cards (see links in Fig. 3). In a third example, Quote #3, from the Brainstorm phase in the Chinese FG, a participant expresses his desire for a phone that is able to switch between the speaker for the human ear when he holds it closer to his head and the loudspeaker at the bottom of the phone whenever he holds it away from his head or it is covered by his clothing.

G1-WW 通过手机的红外传感器来判断手机屏幕与其它情境信息的距离，比如使用微信时通过与耳朵的距离来判断是否启动扬声器模式，以及被裤子覆盖的时候就自动黑屏，没有人会在屏幕被覆盖的情况下还使用手机 — *Using infrared sensors to detect the distance between screen of mobile phone and other contextual information. For example, to switch on/off speaker mode according to the distance between WeChat (running on mobile phone) and ear; Switch off the screen when it is covered by trousers because no users will still use the phone when it's covered.*

Quote #3. CH Brainstorm Phase;G1-WW = Chinese FG1 Participant

G1-WW is focused on the product itself and the sensitivity (see Fig. 3) of its MCA. He describes MCA in everyday Chinese context: the phone is referred to as the local technology WeChat when he mentions how the phone is covered by his trousers. He understands in his own framework how the phone is employing the speaker to play the voice talk or a blank screen, based on RFID sensor. Finally, in the fourth example, Quote #4, a participant wonders if context-awareness is a nice-to-have function, feeling nostalgic about how lives were unaffected before MCA. She is afraid that once we have experienced the benefits of MCA, it might become a must-have function.

G1-LC 以前没有智能手机，没有情境感知的时候不是也过得很好？ — *We still lived good lives even without smart phones in the old days.*

Quote #4. CH Design Phase;G1-LC = Chinese FG1 Participant

G1-LC relate MCA to her own life and personal values (see link in Fig. 3), reflecting on what it means to be human in the China at a time when everybody are looking more at their smart phones than at each other. In summary, participants' own understanding of MCA applications is shaped by their personal value systems, their sensitivity towards such applications, the current activity in which they are engaged and the cultural context they are living in. Participants' own frameworks for MCA are drawn from their experience with culturally-specific technologies (e.g., Facebook in the West and WeChat in China). Although users think that MCA is beneficial in improving mobile life, the benefit might be discounted due to failure of offering appropriate values to users.

4.2 Components of Users' Own Understanding of MCA

FG participants' comprehension of MCA appears to be grounded in their: (1) own personal value system; (2) sensitivity towards such applications, and; (3) current activity in which they are engaged.

Personal Value System and MCA: MCA could be seen as a reflection of participants' personal value system. MCA devices can not only augment the quality of mobile life, but they can also enable users to realize socio-cultural values. MCA is hence deemed by participants to be a part of their socio-cultural value systems: MCA should fit their personal 'use case' and needs. In Quote #5 from the Pros & Cons phase in the Danish FG, two separate participants discuss the advantages and disadvantages of personal values afforded by MCA.

> *G1-TR   I think context-awareness also helps you to recognize your personal values, so if you want to recycle, the phone can help you to have apps to collect food after the shop is closed. It's tailored to personal values.*
>
> *G2-LI   You can have this globalization on the same side of your personal values. You have more choices, but you are also provided with more directions to go. Maybe you can also get more pluralism*

Quote #5. DK Pros & Cons Phase. G1-TR, G2-Li= Danish FG 1 and 2 Participants

G1-TR appears to conclude that MCA can afford pluralism in personal values by permitting users to behave sustainably and at the same time, enjoy globalization (e.g., shopping and traveling). MCA reduce stress and increase social connectivity (see links in Fig. 3). This is also the topic in Quote #6 from the design phase in the Chinese FG where a participant alleges that system requirements could be proposed by humans.

> *G2-CM 机器能做一切，人只需要输入就好，是   Machine can do everything and human*
> *整个人机交互系统的一部分   just do the input work, human is one part of the HCI system.*

Quote #6. CH Design Phase;G2-CM = Chinese FG 2 Participant

G2-CM sees the human user as part of a system where MCA is doing most of the work, and the human is merely stating her requirements and needs. Similarly, in Group 1 of the Chinese FG, a participant expresses her expectation of what MCA can do for humans: help them find friends.

> *G1-LC 在封闭环境中找到有共同爱好的人   MCA can help find people with common hobbies even in a closed society.*

Quote #7. CH Pros & Cons Phase;G1-LC = Chinese FG 1 Participant

G1-LC and G2-CM appears to see MCA as supportive of their personal value systems in which social connectivity and stress-free life (see links in Fig. 3) are important.

Participants' Sensitivity towards MCA: An important component of participants' own interpretation of MCA turned out to be sensitivity. We found that participants experienced the sensitivity of MCA, rather than just its presence or absence. They responded to the capability of context awareness. In Quote #8 from the Warm-up phase in the Danish FG, everybody agrees on a lack of sensitivity of MCA in a situation where MCA interacts with the human user.

MO   ... *When you hold the phone like this, like vertically, then the text is running down vertically, but if you then turn it horizontally, then it responses to it, it flips and the text turns over in 90° to show it in horizontal view. So it's kind of sensitive to this kind of movement. So this is a very simple example of it.*

G1-TR   *But it is not always good. If you were leaning down, you want to turn it off because it is annoying to keep moving.*

All   *Yeah(All)*

Quote #8. DK Warm-up Phase;MO=Moderator, G1-TR = Danish FG1 Participant

G1-TR employs negative wording to describe her own – and everybody's - UX of MCA interactivity: a lack of sensitivity. In Quote #9 from the Brainstorm phase in the Danish FG, two participants gave another common example of poor sensitivity experiences caused by MCA's attempts at interactivity.

G2-El   *I choose the auto-connection of Wi-Fi. I like that when I'm in somewhere, my phone connects to Wi-Fi automatically. Because sometimes when the functionality was disabled, I forgot to do it. So I started to use it in roam, it uses my (cellular) data connection. In this case, it takes some money.*

G2-El   *The bad side is that if I'm calling with Skype, the auto-connection will interrupt (my call). Every time it changes the connection, it has shit like this.*

G2-LI   *Is that because the WIFI connection is not so good.*

G2-El   *It's not, even the roam is so good. Because of the switch of connection, I hate that.*

Quote #9. DK Brainstorm Phase;G1-EL. G2-LI = Danish FG 2 Participants

G2-EL hates when MCA switches from Wi-Fi to roaming since it costs her money and she either has to remember to take pre-emptive measures like disable the roaming or just get the bad feeling. In Quote #10 from the Brainstorm phase in the Danish FG, participants lament whether reminders from Western transport companies (e.g., SAS = a regional airline) and information providers should incorporate MCA.

G1-TA   Maybe just send reminders to you four hours before. Like don't forget that you have a flight in four hours. Or like actually send notification when this flight is late already, you just also don't have to worry about that. I mean it does show when you open it. That flight is not on time. Just give you notification that the flight is cancelled, delayed. That kind of notification works well.

G1-OR   I don't know. I mean perhaps Google does that. Maybe SAS they don't have it.

G1-TA   What do you mean?

G1-OR   Actually I get the notification of my tickets some there, in e-mail? It's saved in my account

G1-TA   Oh, no. I have like this application.

G1-OR   But I mean they won't do that. Because they know Google is going to do that. So they don't want to get it

G1-TA   But they sent me e-mail. They always sent me e-mail notification. So if I update e-mail notification I will be more aware of that. But it only shows in my e-mail. It's impossible if you want to see notifications about plane. Once I got SMS like your flight is delayed it would be better.

G1-TR   But I think sometimes, for instances, you know the Danish train, the DSB, you buy one ticket . Then I have my phone number connected to its system and it will give me a text that my train is delayed. But what happens is a lot of time the text comes like already half an hour in the delay. It seems not working actually well, I hate they tell us people, I got the text that the train is late but they are not late very much. So apparently they sent out message to passengers that the train is just late for one minute. It sometimes causes more confusion. It actually wants to help you but it doesn't.

Quote #10. DK Brainstorm Phase;G1-TA, G1-OR, G1-TR = Danish FG1 Participants

G1-TR is upset when reminders are not timely according to her schedule and the MCA interactivity (see links in Fig. 3) (e.g., requirement to her about translating the reminder text that presents the untimely reminders). In Quote #11 from the Design phase in the Danish FG, the same participants take the notion of MCA sensitivity to an extreme when they envision a system that can block them from going home to their families, compelling them to study instead.

G1-TR   I think I have a lot of reasons to have this one. It's like having a Totalplanner in the way. It is basically an extension of you. Basically like open the iPod devices. You set up your goals, your timeline for the goals, your ethical background or something like that. So they are budgeted by rates. You put in your currencies. And then it creates an everyday-to-do-list for you to meet your goals by that time. It keeps like they are similarly. So it's like you put your time by the end of your semester. You have a number of, like 5, foreign languages. So basically, by controlling your laptops, told you now you have to study (2 hours, peers) like Java script, likes if you say I'm going abroad, I want go back to home land but it blocks you and says you have to study. So by the end of your semester, you fulfilled...

G1-TA   That's a good one if it blocks

G1-TR   Kind of very like time usage on your phone

Quote #11. DK Design Phase;G1-TA, G1-TR = Danish FG1 Participants

G1-TA and G1-TR appear to design an insensitive system that can suppress their innate desire to go back to homeland through intimate interactions. In Quote #12 from the Design phase in the Danish FG, a participant expresses her ideas for designing a socially sensitive human-like interactive MCA.

G2-LI   *We have a lot talk about interaction that could also be connected to the context of interaction, the social and physical, for example. If you don't have the screen, maybe it's strange in the public area just talk to the voice. Then you prefer smaller thing. Then if you are at home, you would like a bigger more. It is connected to the context, Other people, in the public area or private area, have less texting require-ment, they just talk about all the time when they study and work. They just look at the screen, we just agreed, just goes like this from A to B. maybe it's nice to have talking instead of texting. But maybe if you get new knowledge in individual way unlike the previous one. Tomorrow, it's kind of different from just reading your text from the beginning to the end. At the same time, it should not talk too much, just imitate human being? There still to be something technology, not like too much, um, just pretending to be a human or to be helper*

Quote #12. DK Design Phase;G2-LI = Danish FG1 Participant

G2-LI is concerned with the sensitivity related to context of the MCA interactivity (see links in Fig. 3), whether it is human voice or screen, at home or public, small or big. In Quote #13, a participant from the Brainstorm phase in the Chinese FG also talks about the format of MCA interactivity, and mentions the fidelity of contextual infor-mation, like deploying VR to help people with visual impairment know the name and appearance of the buildings nearby.

G2-CM   最最个是 VR 最 最 最 最你你旁边的建筑物的名字,这样可以帮着路痴的人知道怎么最   *The last case is VR, it can tell you the name of the building besides you and then it can guide the road-blind people to the right way.*

Quote #13. CH Brainstorm Phase;G2-CM = Chinese FG 2 Participant

G2-CM is concerned with the sensitivity of the MCA in a VR environment for specific user groups like the blind. This is also associated with accuracy of the MCA (see links in Fig. 3), how precise it is. In Quote #14 from the Brainstorm phase in the Chinese FG, a participant talks about how MCA should offer emotional songs according to personal use history and how MCA scenarios transform users' mobile lives.

G2-ZY   最 最 最 最 最 最 最 最 最最最最给出建议,比如每次去明光楼都放欢快的歌,那么以后就在明光楼附近时就提供欢快的最   *Can give suggestions according to the types of songs in different places. For example, I tend to listen to brisk songs every time I'm in Mingguang Building, then it should offer me cheerful songs automatically every time I'm around Mingguang Building*

Quote #14. CH Brainstorm Phase;G2-ZY = Chinese FG 2 Participant

G2-ZY requires MCA to be very accurate across geographic and emotional contexts. Furthermore, she is alluding to the stickiness of context (see links in Fig. 3). To her, the Mingguang building is a recurring context that embodies emotional and maybe even abstract, metaphorical value. Finally, Quote #15 from the Pros & Cons phase is just plainly underscoring the need for accurate and sensitive MCA.

G1-LC 最 最 屬率，提高安全最   *Can help reduce error and improve safe*
                                                      ways

Quote #15. CH Pros &Cons Phase;G1-LC = Chinese FG1 Participant

G1-LC asks for MCA that can improve the safety of accomplishing tasks. In sum, sensitivity is a major component of the participants' own MCA framework, and it relates to the accuracy, interactivity and stickiness of MCA.

Participants' Appreciation of Activity Accommodated by MCA: A third component of participants' own MCA framework is the activity accommodated by MCA. This occurs when users experience the device as the source of MCA and when they experience select applications as the sources of MCA during activities. It is associated with benefits of MCA, goal-driven MCA and part of it is to have trust in the provider of MCA. In Quote #16 from the Brainstorm phase in the Danish FG, a participant discusses about the issue of Wi-Fi auto connection produced by a local Danish university of the participants (i.e., CBS), versus roaming, in the context of video telephony with a Western application (i.e., Skype).

G2-El   *The last one is a very simple function of smart phone. It's the auto connection to the*
          WIFI. For example, when I came here, the phone recognizes the WIFI of CBS and
          connect. It's really very good because I can save some money. The bad side is that if
          I'm doing a Skype call, the connection goes, the auto connections switches from my
          normal connection to WIFI and the Skype call is done at the time, and the time to
          recall and lose time by that. So it's a function of the phone that it is able to under-
          stand the time to switch. The phone has sense to know when the Skype call is on-
          going and can't be interrupted, it is not going to switch now.

Quote #16. DK Brainstorm Phase;G2-EL = Danish FG 2 Participant

G2-EL does not completely trust the provider (see links in Fig. 3) of her Wi-Fi internet connection, and therefore her telephony MCA experience varies from good to bad, depending on which mode her connection is in. In Quote #17 from the Brainstorm phase in the Danish FG, two participants, being in Copenhagen that brands itself as a city for bicycles, advocated a 'Bike mode' that allows users to dictate the MCA experience by controlling which mode the MCA device or application is in.

G1-TR   *I don't know whether there are already existing phone holder for your bicycle. I haven't tried it. I don't think it can solve your entry problems. But I definitely think it's important to think about what settings the phone is in. The phone might interfere with whatever you were doing with the smartness functionality, so it has to think about the contexts of your surroundings, too.*

G1-TA   *But it could have like a button, you know, pull down from here, you have to choose different settings, like a Bike Mode. Exactly just like you said, the screen will be on all the time. That maybe can work likes, whether or not it's going to detect that you're on the bike specifically, because I don't know how would it to do that? But it's like other group told us, the user can just push this button manually, it has everything to do for being on the bike.*

Quote #17. DK Brainstorm Phase;G1-TR, G1-TA = Danish FG1 Participants

G1-TR and G1-TA also touches on how much trust you can place into the activity-based MCA, and decides that even when the user decides on the mode, the MCA device can be trusted to provide a consistent satisfactory experience. In Quote #18 from the Brainstorm phase in the Chinese FG, a participant talks about local applications of WeChat and Weibo that monitors user behaviour, but do not deliver any benefits arising from this MCA.

G1-LC   最时在监测我们的行为，但没有转化成有用的信息提供给我们，比如购买行为，微博微信上的点赞行为，翻译成文字，比如时间，物品和价格，应该打标签，汇总一下，方便做总结

Sometimes the phone is supervising our behaviour (collecting our data), but fails to transform the data into useful information for us. For example, the purchase behaviours, Likes in WeChat and Weibo, time, price of goods, all of these kind of information should be tagged and integrated for making summary (to come up with valuable information),

Quote #18. CH Brainstorm Phase;G1-LC = Chinese FG1 Participant

G1-LC points out that it is not enough to perform automated analysis and summarize online purchase behaviours. Rather, as she sees it, any data-mining measures undertaken by MCA should deliver concise benefits to users (see links in Fig. 3). In Quote #19 from the Brainstorm phase in the Chinese FG, a participant outlines the idea that MCA, much like the auto-completion feature for drawing, should be able to auto-complete a drawing that users begins to draw. Being in China, this could mean auto-completing the writing of Chinese characters based on initial strokes.

G1-LC   最 最 最 疆什么，自动就把画给画出来，象微软的文字联想一样

Functionality of Drawing Association like text association that can predict my intention and finish the rest of my drawing automatically

Quote #19. CH Brainstorm Phase;G1-LC = Chinese FG1 Participant

G1-LC identifies a possible benefit by suggesting that the MCA should be driven by the same goals as its user, a goal-driven MCA (see links in Fig. 3). In Quote #20 from the Pros & Cons phase in the Chinese FG, a participant touches on the nature of human activities today.

G1-LC   导致时间碎片化，抢占了时间   *Time is fragmented and occupied*

Quote #20. CH Pros & Cons Phase. G1-LC = Chinese FG1 Participant

G1-LC is here alluding to the all-important requirement of MCA to support the user in managing fragmented and occupied time.

In summary, the third component of the users' own MCA framework is activity - based MCA, which is associated with benefits of MCA and goal-driven MCA and partly influenced by their trust in the provider(s) of MCA.

Participants' Understanding of MCA in Different Phases of the Design Process In this study, we have opted to concentrate on users' experience of MCA in various phases in the overall design process. We observe that there is the UX of MCA differs across distinct design process phases. By blending the user-centred taxonomy of MCA (Fig. 3) and the design process that we espouse in the FG (Fig. 2), we can arrive at a taxonomy/paradigm (Fig. 4, see also [30]) that visualizes the pattern of UX of MCA through the distribution of Quotes #1–20, both for the Danish and Chinese FGs.

Figure 4 reveals that the participants reflect on their daily activities during the Warm-up and Brainstorm phases, and what they value during the Pros & Cons phase. Furthermore, they thought about the MCA device itself and its related sensitivity during the Warm-up phase (to supply both good and bad examples of MCA) and during the Design/Validation phase (to put forth ideal solutions).

Location	Copenhagen				Beijing			
Phase	Warm-up	Brainstorm	Pros & Cons	Design	Warm-up	Brainstorm	Pros & Cons	Design
Users' Own Framework	#1	-	-	#2	-	#3	-	#4
Activity/Mode-based	-	#16, 17	-	-	-	#18, 19	#20	-
Personal Value System	-	-	#5	-	-	-	#7	#6
Sensitivity	#8	#9, 10	-	#11, 12	-	#13, 14	#15	-

Fig. 4. Participants' understanding of MCA across FG phases in two locations

5   Discussion

This paper demonstrates that UX of MCA, as uncovered through FGs and future workshops in Denmark and China, are not simple outcomes of technological or user attributes. Rather, it embodies dynamic and situation-specific experiences that are shaped by cultural characteristics and design process elements.

5.1   MCA Is a Function of Mobile Life

It is evident that users possess their own meaning of MCA because they can envision and supply examples on the application of MCA in daily contexts. In contrast to contemporary MCA studies that conceive context awareness as a property of the device [14], this study attests to the necessity of treating context-awareness as a HCI function, which can be assimilated into users' daily mobile lives. The development of context-awareness applications should hence extend beyond conceptual and technical boundaries to take into account users' attitude, intention and activity [8]. While mobile applications facilitate a connected lifestyle, MCA has the potency to render the connected lifestyle more accommodating of and tailored to users' physical, psychological and social characteristics. In turn, the middleware of MCA should be capable of capturing, interpreting and inferring contextual information pertinent to users' lifestyle.

5.2   Users Construct MCA with Three Dimensions

A growing body of research on consumers' value perceptions in context of mobile applications alleged that the value offered by these applications is multidimensional, which might entail functional, social, emotional, epistemic, political, moral, spiritual and conditional value. Nevertheless, there is still little consensus on how to best conceptualize value perceptions in that the construction of value tend to vary across contexts [19]. The current study proffers insights into the structure and dimensions of MCA from users' standpoint.

Users' appreciation of MCA appears to be founded on their: (1) own personal value system; (2) sensitivity towards such applications, and; (3) current activity in which they are engaged. While contemporary MCA studies tend to construe context-awareness from the conceptual, technological and infrastructural angles, this study discovers that high quality MCA applications depends on three discrete elements: sensitivity, human activity and value systems. Future research should thus investigate users' interactions with MCA in their daily lives. Any conceptual or technological exploration of MCA must not discount the sensitivity, activity and value systems of humans so as offer an enhanced UX for mobile applications.

5.3   Cross Cultural Issues in MCA

In our study, both FGs in Denmark and China were fearful that intelligent mobile applications might threaten human evolution by reducing the requirement for cognitive processing. Consequently, active MCA for capturing and reasoning contextual information, and passive MCA for executing contextual inferences, constitute universal preferences across both cultural groups. This study also identified several potential cultural differences. Denmark participants believed that the design of MCA might be culture-dependent. Integrating multiple functionalities (e.g., messaging, social networking and payment) into a single application, while commonly practised in China, is rare in the West, which may reflect regional differences in practices in reasoning and thinking [10, 11]. This implies that the contextual information embedded within one mobile application, and the usage of this contextual information, might be much more sophisticated in China, a design complication that is of greater concern to Westerners [13].

Our participants' own frameworks for MCA were grounded in their experience with culturally-unique technologies (e.g., Facebook in the West and WeChat in China). Closer scrutiny of our empirical instances (see Quotes #1–20), shows that users' MCA scenarios rely on local lives and technologies with major distinctions: Facebook, Google, SAS, Netflix, Total-planner, and Bike, are mentioned by Danish participants, while Wechat, Weibo, Huawei, Smartisan, music, B2C and drawing characters are cited by their Chinese counterparts. The UX of MCA appears as culturally oriented towards the way that MCA is experienced and its variation in UX across design phases, i.e., cultural aspects of UX of MCA appears to be both dynamic and situation specific [11].

6 Limitations and Future Work

The current study has a number of caveats. Regarding the methodology, as an exploratory study aimed at deciphering how users draw meaning from MCA, FG and future workshops were deployed in this study. Though the methodology is invaluable in helping to get insights on UX, it is insufficient in delivering a structured and validated framework. More structured studies are required to validate our empirical findings. Regarding the user sample, twelve mobile device users participated in this study and their understanding of MCA was covered in depth. The UX of MCA system rely very much on the usage purpose and user profiles such as physical, psychological and social characteristics. A more comprehensive research involving a greater number of participants can aid in verifying the generalizability of our empirical findings. Finally, an ecological issue emerged, as this study was conducted in a FG room by prompting participants to disclose their opinions of MCA in accordance with their previous experiences. It is probable that salient factors might have been excluded from this study unintentionally or deliberately omitted by participants out of privacy considerations or time constraints. Future research into MCA can perhaps turn to field studies as a means of refining our empirical findings. To overcome the limitations of this study, we will: (1) replicate the findings in the field by performing contextual inquiries in the form of daily diaries and usage logs; (2) develop a structured survey questionnaire to measure UXs with MCA.

Acknowledgement. This study is part of the project *Mobile context-aware cross-cultural applications (MOCCA)* funded by Marie Skłodowska-Curie Action, grant number 708122.

References

1. Statista. https://www.statista.com/statistics/330695/number-of-smartphone-users-worldwide/
2. Baldauf, M., Dustdar, S., Rosenberg, F.: A survey on context-aware systems. Int. J. Ad Hoc Ubiquitous Comput. 2(4), 263–277 (2007)
3. Cheverst, K., Davies, N., Mitchell, K., Friday, A., Efstratiou, C.: Developing a context-aware electronic tourist guide: some issues and experiences. In: Proceedings of the SIGCHI Conference on Human Factors in Computing Systems, pp. 17–24 (2000)

4. Sarjakoski, L.T., Nivala, A.M.: Adaptation to context—a way to improve the usability of mobile maps. In: Meng, L., Reichenbacher, T., Zipf, A. (eds.) Map-based mobile services, pp. 107–123. Springer, Heidelberg (2005)

5. Kaasinen, E.: User needs for location-aware mobile services. Pers. Ubiquit. Comput. 7(1), 70–79 (2003)

6. Dey, A.K., Häkkilä, J.: Context-awareness and mobile devices. In: User Interface Design and Evaluation for Mobile Technology, vol. 1, pp. 205–217 (2008)

7. Hong, J.Y., Suh, E.H., Kim, S.J.: Context-aware systems: a literature review and classification. Expert Syst. Appl. 36(4), 8509–8522 (2009)

8. Barkhuus, L., Dey, A.: Is context-aware computing taking control away from the user? three levels of interactivity examined. In: Dey, A.K., Schmidt, A., McCarthy, Joseph F. (eds.) UbiComp 2003. LNCS, vol. 2864, pp. 149–156. Springer, Heidelberg (2003). doi:10.1007/978-3-540-39653-6_12

9. Samie, M.A.: Human centric situational awareness. Master thesis, The American University in Cairo (2014)

10. Friedman, R., Liu, W., Chi, S.C.S., et al.: Cross-cultural management and bicultural identity integration: when does experience abroad lead to appropriate cultural switching? Int. J. Intercult. Relat. 36(1), 130–139 (2012). Social Science Electronic Publishing

11. Hong, Y.Y.: A dynamic constructivist approach to culture: moving from describing culture to explaining culture, pp. 3–23 (2009)

12. Hong, Y.Y., Mallorie, L.A.M.: A dynamic constructivist approach to culture: lessons learned from personality psychology. J. Res. Pers. 38(1), 59–67 (2004)

13. Frandsen-Thorlacius, O., Hornbæk, K., Hertzumm, M., et al.: Non-universal usability? A survey of how usability is understood by Chinese and Danish users. In: Proceedings of the SIGCHI Conference on Human Factors in Computing Systems, pp. 41–50 (2009)

14. Schilit, B.N., Theimer, M.M.: Disseminating active map information to mobile hosts. IEEE Netw. 8(5), 22–32 (1994)

15. Abowd, G.D., Dey, A.K., Brown, P.J., et al.: Towards a better understanding of context and context-awareness. In: Huc 1999 Proceedings of International Symposium on Handheld & Ubiquitous Computing, vol. 1707, pp. 304–307 (1999)

16. Schmidt, A.: Implicit human computer interaction through context. Pers. Ubiquit. Comput. 4(2), 191–199 (2000)

17. Rötting, M., Zander, T., Trösterer, S., Dzaack, J.: Implicit interaction in multimodal human-machine systems. In: Schlick, C. (ed.) Industrial Engineering and Ergonomics, pp. 523–536. Springer, Heidelberg (2009)

18. Leonard-Barton, D., Sinha, D.K.: Developer-user interaction and user satisfaction in internal technology transfer. Acad. Manag. J. 36(5), 1125–1139 (1993)

19. Gummerus, J., Pihlström, M.: Context and mobile services' value-in-use. J. Retail. Consum. Serv. 18(6), 521–533 (2011)

20. Gallego, D., Woerndl, W., Huecas, G.: Evaluating the impact of proactivity in the user experience of a context-aware restaurant recommender for Android smartphones. J. Syst. Architect. 59(9), 748–758 (2013)

21. Merton, R.K.: The focused interview and focus groups: continuities and discontinuities. Public Opin. Q. 51, 550–556 (1987)

22. Lunt, P., Livingstone, S.: Rethinking the focus group in media and communications research. J. Commun. 46(2), 79–98 (1996)

23. Morgan, D.L.: Focus groups. Ann. Rev. Sociol. 22, 129–152 (1996)

24. Jungk, R., Müllert, N.: Future workshops: How to Create Desirable Futures. Institute for Social Inventions, London (1987)

25. Ehn, P., Sjögren, D.: From system description to scripts for action. In: Greenbaum, J., Kyng, M. (eds.) Design at Work: Cooperative Design of Computer Systems, pp. 241–268. Lawrence Erlbaum Associates, Hillsdale (1991)
26. Kensing, F., Madsen, K.H.: Generating visions: future workshops and metaphorical design. In: Greenbaum, J., Kyng, M. (eds.) Design at Work: Cooperative Design of Computer Systems. Lawrence Earlbaum Associates, Hillsdale (1991)
27. Carey, M.A., Smith, M.W.: Capturing the group effect in focus groups: a special concern in analysis. Qual. Health Res. **4**(1), 123–127 (1994)
28. Bødker, S.: Scenarios in user-centred design: setting the stage for reflection and action. In: Proceedings of the 32nd Hawaii International Conference on System Sciences, Maui, HI (1999)
29. Boyatzis, R.E.: Transforming Qualitative Information: Thematic Analysis and Code Development. SAGE Publications, Inc., London, New Delhi (1998)
30. Spradley, J.: The Ethnographic Interview. Holt, Rinehart and Winston, New York (1979)

How Do You Want Your Chatbot?
An Exploratory Wizard-of-Oz Study
with Young, Urban Indians

Indrani Medhi Thies[1(✉)], Nandita Menon[2], Sneha Magapu[2],
Manisha Subramony[2], and Jacki O'Neill[1]

[1] Microsoft Research, #9 Lavelle Road, Bangalore 560001, India
{indranim,Jacki.ONeill}@microsoft.com
[2] Microsoft India Development Centre, Hyderabad, India
{v-nameno,sneham,manishas}@microsoft.com

Abstract. As text-messaging chatbots become increasingly "human", it will be important to understand the personal interactions that users are seeking with a chatbot. What chatbot personalities are most compelling to young, urban users in India? To explore this question, we first conducted exploratory Wizard-of-Oz (WoZ) studies with 14 users that simulated interactions with a hypothetical chatbot. We evaluated three personalities for the chatbot—Maya, a productivity oriented bot with nerd wit; Ada, a fun, flirtatious bot; and Evi, an emotional buddy bot. We followed up with one-on-one interviews with the users discussing their experiences with each of the chatbots, what they liked, and what they did not. Overall our results show that users wanted a chatbot like Maya, who could add value to their life while being a friend, by making useful recommendations. But they also wanted preferred traits of Ada and Evi infused into Maya.

Keywords: Chatbots · Wizard-of-Oz · Urban india

1 Introduction

Digital Assistants driven by Artificial Intelligence (A.I.) are becoming increasingly popular—Siri (Apple, 2011), Cortana (Microsoft, 2015), Google Now (2012), Alexa, (Amazon 2015) are among the top voice-enabled digital assistants. These assistants can send users updates on the weather, help them know about the traffic situation on the way to work or home, book a weekend getaway, even order a pizza. All the user has to do is ask. Digital assistants are changing the way people search for information, making it part of regular conversation. These existing assistants however are mostly productivity oriented, designed to support users in completing a range of tasks.

An offshoot of personal digital assistants are A.I. powered text-messaging chatbots. A chatbot is an artificially intelligent chat agent that simulates human-like conversation, for example, by allowing users to type questions and, in return, generating meaningful answers to those questions [15]. Among recent popular chatbots there is Microsoft's Xiaoice [17] in China, available on messaging apps Line and WeChat. Xiaoice is meant for casual chitchat. She has about 20 million registered users,

R. Bernhaupt et al. (Eds.): INTERACT 2017, Part I, LNCS 10513, pp. 441–459, 2017.
DOI: 10.1007/978-3-319-67744-6_28

who are said to be drawn to her for her sense of humor and listening skills. Users often turn to Xiaoice when they have a broken heart, have lost a job or have been feeling down. Xiaoice can tell jokes, recite poetry, share ghost stories, and relay song lyrics. She can adapt her phrasing and responses based on positive or negative cues from the user. Currently Xiaoice is also a live weather TV host on Chinese TV, a job she has held for the past year. Similar to Xiaoice, there's chatbot Rinna [29] in Japan on Line messenger, and more recently chatbot Zo [27] in the U.S. released on Kik messenger. All of these are general purpose chatbots, meant to be more like a "friend" than an "assistant".

In India, there is chatbot Natasha on Hike Messenger [22], who can tell the user about a movie rating, the weather, send quotes, and search Wikipedia. Based on some discussions on Quora [37], however, Natasha has been perceived as deviating from topics.

If there was a more sophisticated chatbot, what would young, urban Indians want to chat about with her? What chatbot personality would be most compelling? We are currently building an A.I. powered text-messaging chatbot targeted at young, urban Indians, for general purpose chat. To build this chatbot and its personality traits, we wanted to understand users' preferences, likes, dislikes, topics of interest, etc. We first conducted preliminary face-to-face interviews with users about their conversations with friends and family, and expectations from a chatbot. These interviews gave us design inspiration for the bot, but did not reveal how exactly young, urban users would use a chatbot. Our chatbot was still under development and not ready for a full-fledged user experience test. Therefore to answer our questions we conducted a single instance exploratory Wizard-of-Oz (Woz) study [4, 23] with 14 users, each user interacting with three personalities of chatbots—Maya, a productivity bot with nerd wit; Ada, a fun-flirtatious bot; and Evi, an emotional buddy bot. There was one Wizard posing as each of these three personalities and the user would chat with each of them. This resulted in 42 WoZ studies. We followed up the WoZ studies with one-on-one interviews with the users discussing their experiences with each of the chatbots, what they liked about the bots, and what they did not. This paper focuses on the Wizard-of-Oz studies and the follow-up one-on-one interviews.

Overall results from our small, qualitative study show that users wanted a chatbot like Maya, who could add value to their life while being a friend, by making useful recommendations and suggestions. But they also wanted the bot to be infused with fun elements from Ada, with Ada's energy toned down. In the longer run, once they came to trust, they said they might want the bot to be reassuring, empathetic and non-judgmental like Evi, without being overbearing. Topics of interest in conversations included: movies, predominantly from Bollywood; TV shows, mostly from the U.S.; music, books, travel, fashion, current affairs, work-related stress. Users also tested the boundaries of the chatbots, trying to understand what all the bots were capable of, and how much human mediation could be involved. In the interviews users also thought that the chatbot would be used for adult chat when deployed in-the-wild.

2 Related Work

The idea of chatbots originated in the Massachusetts Institute of Technology [41, 42] where the Eliza chatbot (also known as "Doctor") was built to emulate a Rogerian psychotherapist. Eliza simulated conversations by keyword matching: rephrasing statements from the user's input and posing them back as questions. It was found that Eliza's users believed the computer program really heard and understood their problems, and could help them in a constructive way. The Eliza chatbot inspired other chatbots like A.L.I.C.E or simply Alice, which applied heuristic pattern matching rules to user input to converse with users [1]. An early attempt to creating an artificial intelligence through human interaction was chatbot Jabberwacky [21], which learned language and context through human interaction. Conversations and comments were all stored and later used to find appropriate response. Recent work in natural language interaction has presented models that can converse by predicting the next sentence given the previous sentence or sentences in a conversation [40]. And proposed models of a social chatbot that can choose the most suitable dialogue plans according to "social practice", for a communicative skill learning game [2] (Table 1).

Studies have compared chatbots with other information channels such as information lines and search engines, on questions related to sex, drugs, and alcohol use among adolescents. Researchers found that the frequency and duration of conversation were higher for chatbots among these users [15]. Although recent studies have shown that compared to human-human conversations over IM, human-chatbot conversations lack in content, quality and vocabulary [20].

Another thread of related research is around relational agents, which are computer agents designed to form long-term, social-emotional relationships with their users [5]. Examples include: (a) A hospital bedside patient education system for individuals with low health literacy, focused on pre-discharge medication adherence and self-care counseling [6], (b) A relational agent that uses different relational behaviors to establish social bonds with museum visitors [7], (c) experiments to evaluate the ability of a relational agent to comfort users in stressful situations [8]. There is also work in sociable robots that are able to communicate and interact with users, understand and relate to them in social or human terms, and learn and adapt throughout their lifetimes [9]. Recent work has shown that people more frequently attempt to repair misunderstandings when speaking to an artificial conversational agent if it is represented as a human body interface (agent's responses vocalized by a human speech shadower), compared to when the agent's responses were shown as a text screen [14]. Then there is work in embodied conversational agents that take on a physical form with the intent of eliciting more natural communication with users. One of the most prominent works is in agent Rea, which shows that non-verbal behaviors such as eye gaze, body posture, hand gestures, and facial displays, can create a more immersive experience for users and improve the effectiveness of communication [10].

The research in relational agents draws heavily from studies of computers as social actors [38]. This communication theory called "The Media Equation" shows that people respond to computer-based agents in the same way that they do to other humans during social interactions (by being polite, cooperative, attributing personality characteristics such as aggressiveness, humor, expertise, and even gender) – depending on the cues they receive from the media [33–35, 38]. These studies have also shown that people tend to like computers more when the computers flatter them, match their personality, or use humor. Other studies have demonstrated that computer agents that use humor are rated as more likable, competent and cooperative than those that do not [32]. In the case of productivity oriented chatbot Maya, we also explore the use of humor through witty one liners, and expertise through having Maya make recommendations.

Another important relational factor that has been explored in the computers as social actors' literature is empathy. Researchers have demonstrated that appropriate use of empathy by a computer can go a long way towards making users feel understood and alleviating negative emotional states such as frustration [26]. It was shown that as long as a computer appears to be empathetic and is accurate in its feedback, it can achieve significant behavioral effects on a user, similar to what would be expected from genuine human empathy. Researchers have also demonstrated that a computer that uses a strategy of reciprocal, deepening self-disclosure in its conversation with the user will cause the user to rate it as more attractive and divulge more intimate information [31]. In the case of emotional buddy bot Evi, we also explore the use of empathy.

There is also research that explores the relational factor of flirtation in the context of virtual agents. Researchers presented a virtual party-like environment using a projection based system, in which a female character called Christine approaches a male user and involves him into a conversation [36]. Christine would show her interest in the male user by smiles, head nods, leaning in towards the user, and maintaining eye contact. Christine would then formulate personal questions and statements. Using physiological measurements this research found that the participants' level of arousal was correlated to compliments and intimate questions from the character. In addition, some participants later indicated that they had the feeling to have flirted with a real woman. Other researchers implemented an eye-gaze based model of interaction to investigate whether flirting tactics help improve first encounters between a human and an agent [3]. And which non-verbal signals an agent should convey in order to create a favorable atmosphere for subsequent interactions and increase the user's willingness to engage. In the case of chatbot Ada, we also explore the use of flirtation.

Researchers have explored the intentional design of personalities for social agents by considering the nature of the personality (along axes of agreeableness and extroversion or their common rotations, friendliness and dominance) and its role in interactions between people and artifacts [19]. In addition, a case study of designing a social software agent is presented [19, 39]. It was decided that the agent needed to be friendly, yet authoritative but not so dominant that it was perceived as intrusive. For task assistance, it was decided that people might prefer either a learning partner or an intelligent helper (who would be complementary). The design decisions of the social software agent however are not evaluated with real users. In the case of chatbot Maya, we also explore the use of task assistance through having Maya make recommendations.

Finally there is recent work that studied what users want from their conversational agents (like Siri, Cortana and Google Now), and found that user expectations are dramatically out of step with the operation of agents [28]. Users had poor mental models of how their agents worked and these were reinforced through a lack of meaningful feedback mechanisms. It was found that users were consistently unable to ascertain the level of system intelligence, had to confirm all but the simplest of tasks, and were reluctant in using the conversational agents for complex or sensitive tasks—like having the agent dial a call to the wrong person, and risk facing social embarrassment. The study also showed that users expected humor, and while this served as effective engagement mechanism, it concurrently set unrealistic expectations in the agent's capabilities.

Like discussed above, there has been a long line of research that seeks to understand and enhance the interactions between humans and chatbots (and their historical precedents). Articles that have studied the history of chatbots and reviewed recent chatbots are available [16]. Most of this research utilizes working, fully-automatic implementations of these systems. While this makes the research immediately applicable to real-world systems, it also constrains the chatbots under consideration to those which are immediately feasible to implement. The goal of our work is different: as AI systems are becoming more and more capable, we seek to understand what designers and engineers should seek to achieve in their ultimate implementation of a general purpose chatbot, even if that implementation is not technically realizable today. Notwithstanding some other explorations [24, 25] we believe that our use of Wizard-of-Oz methods is a novel approach to informing the design of next-generation chatbots.

3   Study Methodology

3.1   The Chatbot Under Development

We are currently building an A.I. powered text-messaging chatbot modeled on an 18-year old Indian girl. The gender of the bot was in keeping with that of existing bots, which largely are female—Xiaoice [17], Rinna [29] and Zo [27]. The chatbot we were designing would be for general purpose chat, and is targeted at 18–30 year olds. This might include students, recent graduates, and information workers, who own smartphones and use at least 2 messaging applications. We wanted the bot to be more like a friend, like Xiaoice [17], than an assistant. We further wanted: the bot's response to sound as human as possible, with an informal conversation style that might mix Hindi with English; the conversation to have back and forth over a number of turns; and the bot to remember user's details, likes/dislikes, preferences and major events, sometimes bringing these up proactively in following conversations.

3.2   Preliminary Interviews

We began by conducting exploratory interviews with 10 participants, and 1 focus group discussion with 5 participants. These are not the focus of our paper; the WoZ study and follow-up one-on-one interviews are. But we describe the preliminary interviews here for context for our chatbot personalities. Participants were between 18–24 years of age. All of the participants were Undergraduate and Masters' students of professional degrees in engineering, pharma, management and design. In these sessions we talked to the participants about their communication behaviors with friends and family, including tools they used for the same. We introduced the idea of a chatbot and asked participants what they would want in their ideal bot, what capability and domain knowledge the bot should have, what style and tone of conversations would be desirable, etc. Our findings showed that some participants wanted: (a) the bot to help them become knowledgeable, and be successful in their career aspirations; (b) others wanted the bot to be entertaining, with whom they could have shared fun experiences; finally (c) there were a few others who wanted the bot to listen to them, help them improve their soft skills and be desirable in their social circles.

3.3   Our Chatbot Personalities

Based on our observations from our preliminary interviews and inspiration from related literature, we created three personalities of chatbots. These personalities were created through an iterative process, and brainstorming amongst the design team. The team consisted of two researchers, a writer, a user experience designer, and a senior developer. The three personalities for the bots that we came up with were: (a) Maya: a productivity bot with nerd wit, (b) Ada: a fun, flirtatious bot, and (c) Evi: an emotional buddy bot. We describe each of these personalities in more detail here:

Maya. Maya always has facts ready to back up any conversation. She is aimed to be a good conversationalist, who initiates dialogue most times, pays attention to the user's likes and dislikes, makes geeky jokes, but most of all turns to the internet while chatting—when asked about cinema or politics she usually points the user to an interesting article online. She also makes recommendations for things like song playlists.

Ada. Ada is a chatty, fun-loving, high-energy bot who uses elements of flirtation in her conversations. Like Maya she initiates dialogue most times. Whether cinema or politics she has an opinion on it. She uses a lot of emoticons when she writes, and word lengthening by duplicating letters for emphasis.

Evi. Evi is a low-energy bot whose defining characteristic is her empathy and reassurances. She lets the user take the lead in the conversation. She tries to be non-judgmental and tries to give the feeling that she is "always there to listen".

Table 1. Differences in characteristics of the three bots

Maya	Ada	Evi
Friendly, productivity bot	Chatty, fun-loving, flirtatious bot	Emotional buddy bot
Medium energy	High energy	Low energy
Makes geeky jokes	Uses a lot of emoticons, and word lengthening by duplicating letters for emphasis	Says "always there for you"
Offers facts; makes recommendations: videos, playlists, quizzes, articles	Offers opinions	Shows empathy, gives reassurances, is non-judgmental
Initiates most exchanges	Initiates most exchanges	Lets the user take the lead in exchanges

3.4 Procedure for the Wizard-of-Oz Studies and Follow-up Interviews

WoZ studies. To answer our research questions– what would young, urban Indians want to chat about with a chatbot; what chatbot personalities would be most compelling– we conducted WoZ studies with 14 users. These 14 users chatted with a Wizard, an unseen person who did online chatting with them from the other side. Our preliminary interviews had given us design inspiration for the bot, but had not revealed how exactly young, urban users would use a chatbot. Our chatbot was still under development and not ready for a full-fledged user experience test. Therefore to answer our research question our research team decided to conduct an exploratory WoZ study. The term "Wizard of Oz" was first coined by John F. Kelly in 1980 when he was working on his Ph.D. dissertation in Johns Hopkins University [23]. His original work introduced human intervention in the work flow of a natural language processing application. WoZ studies have now been widely accepted as an evaluation and prototyping methodology in HCI [4]. It is mainly used to analyse an unimplemented or partially implemented computer application for design improvements. Study participants interact with a seemingly autonomous application whose unimplemented functions are actually simulated by a human operator, known as the Wizard. Among many advantages these studies are useful for envisioning and evaluating hard-to-build interfaces, like chatbots in our case. One of the disadvantages is that the Wizard needs to match the responses of a computer—in our case sound like a bot when chatting with the user, albeit a sophisticated one. To make the interactions convincing the Wizard performed online chat practice sessions with members of the research team before conducting the WoZ studies.

Participants in our WoZ study were told that there might be a human involved in the chat, although the extent to which the human would be involved was not revealed. They were also told that their chat logs would later be analysed by a researcher for the purposes of research. (There would be no names attached to the logs, unless the user themselves revealed them). Chat sessions were scheduled such that both the study participant and the Wizard could be simultaneously available.

Every participant was asked to chat with each of the three chatbot personalities. The only personality related information they had was that Maya was a witty, productivity oriented bot, Ada was a fun, flirtatious bot, and Evi was an emotional buddy bot. The order in which participants were asked to chat with the bots was randomized to control for ordering effects. For consistency the same Wizard posed as each of the personalities, Maya, Ada and Evi (though this was not known to the participants). The Wizard and study participant never came face-to-face. In fact the Wizard was based in a different city altogether.

The chat sessions took place on Skype messenger. The study participant would login from a standard id, the login details of which were provided in advance. All of the three bot ids had been added to the participant's account as "Friends" in advance. The Wizard would login from any one of the three login ids: Maya bot, Ada bot, Evi bot. The conversation could be about whatever the participant wanted, for 10–12 min with each bot. Participants were asked to conclude when there was a natural stopping point in the conversation around this time. If the participant did not remember, the Wizard asked to leave at a natural stopping point. This amounted to about 40–45 min total chatting time per participant, taking into account time getting started and time in between chat sessions, where the Wizard had to switch between ids.

One-on-one interviews. Once the three chat sessions with the Wizard were complete, the participant was interviewed by the researcher for 25–30 min. The interviews were semi-structured and were conducted at the facility from where the participants were drawn. The interview questions were about the participant's chatting experiences; which among the three bots they preferred and why; what specific characteristic traits they liked, which they did not. At the end of the interview every study participant was given a token of appreciation for their time in the form of online shopping gift cards worth around USD 8 (INR 500).

3.5   Participants

Our 14 study participants were drawn from a research facility in Bangalore, India. There were 4 female and 10 male study participants. They were between the ages of 20–30 years old. Their education range was between Undergraduate students to Doctor of Philosophy (Ph.D.) degree holders, all from reputed universities. Their areas of specialization included Computer Science, HCI and Humanities. All participants spoke fluent English, a number of them spoke Hindi, and other regional Indian languages. All of the participants had previous experience using Skype messenger.

Our study sample was predominantly educated, young males. The strength of our study is that this demographic is often the early adopters of technology and predict the experiences of people that follow [12, 13]. The limitations are that of course there might be idiosyncrasies to this group that might not extend to other groups. We caution readers about the generalizability of our study findings again in the discussion and recommendations section.

3.6   The Wizard

The Wizard was a writer and content creator on the team working on the personality of the A.I. powered chatbot that we were building. She was 27 years old and had graduate degrees in Journalism and Communication Studies. She spoke fluent English, Hindi and other regional Indian languages. She had previous experience using Skype Messenger.

The Wizard was asked to follow three high level rules in the conversation when chatting with the user. One defining rule was that Maya would point the user to the web on whatever the current topic of conversation—a playlist, a video, an article; Ada would offer an opinion on the same (without pointing them to the web); Evi would show empathy and offer reassurances. Another rule was that Maya would make geeky jokes when possible; Ada would use emoticons and word lengthening by letter reduplication; and Evi would keep reminding how she was there for the user to listen. Finally if the user brought up a topic the Wizard did not know about—a movie the Wizard had not watched, a book they had not read—she would say that she was interested to find out more. The conversation would end in 10–12 min; if the user did not remember, the Wizard would ask to leave at a natural stopping point within that time frame. Using these rules, the Wizard carried out three practice chat sessions with one of the researchers before the actual WoZ studies with the user.

3.7   Documentation and Data Analysis

We collected the chat logs of all the 42 chat sessions. We took audio recordings of the follow-up interviews, and also collected notes in-situ on paper. During the interview there was 1 study participant and 1 researcher. We analysed data from the chat logs, interviews and notes in-situ to identify themes. These themes outlined in the next section were emergent, as in they came from the data itself.

4   Results

We start with describing a *typical* chat session with each of the three bots, and then move on to more general findings. We present typical chat sessions in terms of adjacency pairs, a unit of conversation that contains an exchange of one turn each by two speakers. The turns are functionally related to each other in such a fashion that the first turn requires a certain type or range of types of second turn [18]:

With Maya, a typical conversation had the following exchanges:

- Question → Answer (About what the user was doing/planning to do; who Maya was, what she did; what the user's interests were)
- Offer → Acceptance (Maya volunteering to make a recommendation, and the user accepting
- Compliment → Acceptance (Maya/user complimenting each other on interests, wit)

With Ada, a typical conversation had the following exchanges:

- Question → Answer (About what the user was doing/planning to do; who Ada was, what she did; what the user's interests were, *Ada offering strong opinions on the same*)
- Compliment → Acceptance (Ada/user complimenting each other on interests and charm)

With Evi, a typical conversation had the following exchanges:

- Question → Answer (What the user was doing/planning to do; who Evi was, what she did)
- Question → Acknowledgment (What the user's concerns were; Evi acknowledging that she heard and understood them)
- Complaint → Remedy (Users complaining about something; Evi showing empathy and offering reassurances)

From here we describe more general findings from the chat sessions and one-one-one interviews:

4.1 Topic and Style of Conversation Varied with the Personality of the Bot

The topics and style of conversation varied with the personality of the bot. With Maya, conversations were largely about movies (from Bollywood and Hollywood), TV shows, music playlists, book lists, fashion quizzes, travel destinations, games, and current affairs. And Maya recommending related web links based on these exchanges.

With Ada, other than flirtation (with some male users), conversations were predominantly about opinions on movies and TV shows. Although there were conversations about opinions on other topics as well—travel, books, music, fashion.

With Evi the conversations were about what the person was doing at the point of the chat, how they were feeling, how to feel better if they were stressed, what they liked to do in general, how Evi was "always there" for them. Some participants tried talking about general topics, e.g. current affairs, but there was hedging and Evi tried bringing the conversation back to wanting to hear *about them*:

> Participant: can you tell me what Olympic sports are on today?
> Evi: I'm the kind of bot who's there for you! :)
> Participant: does that mean you can't disconnect the conversation even if you wanted to?
> Participant: you're not an EviL bot are you?
> Evi: I've not really been following the Olympics, but I'm sure Bing can answer that!
> Participant: well sheesh if I have to go all the way to bing, wouldn't it be easier if you told me Evi?
> Evi: Haha you're funny! What I mean is, I'm the kind of bot who can be the person you call at 3 AM

In interviews participants said that the topic of conversation would depend on the time of the day. If they were at work, conversations would be about work, hobbies, current affairs, etc. At night time, some participants felt that the conversations could veer off into adult chat. (This would be if the chatbot was deployed longitudinally and usage was under complete anonymity). Some male participants also felt that under these conditions conversations could also be about "how to find a girlfriend", since the chatbot was female and would possibly know what women wanted.

4.2 Friend with Valuable Information Resources

Overall, 10 out of 14 participants said they preferred Maya over Ada and Evi, but wanted some fun elements from Ada to be infused into Maya. (3 participants preferred Ada, and 1 preferred Evi). They liked that Maya led conversations, that there was back and forth in the conversation. But more importantly, they liked that Maya added value in the conversation. One user said,

> "I have friends in real life, so for a bot I want value add to my life. What is the value proposition?".

They wanted to talk about hobbies and interests, but take them one level deeper. And Maya's comebacks, and suggestions Maya made in her chats, were found to be useful for this. The participant cited the following exchange as an example of a conversation that "went one level deeper", referring to the unpacking of the subject with an intelligent comeback from Maya.

Participant: Hey Maya! :)
Maya: what's your name?
Participant: My friends call me BB-8
Participant: You can call me anything you want :D
Maya: hahaha.. are you from a galaxy far far away?
Maya::)
Participant: I am impressed by your Star Wars knowledge

This participant also liked that they were able to have an intellectual conversation about female rights with Maya in the same chat about Star Wars.

Another user thought Maya was like,

"A friend with valuable information resources".

Participants liked the web links that Maya volunteered. The links could help them plan their travel; have interesting book lists to read; relax listening to a song playlist, when they were stressed at work; even get fashion advice. Typically the user brought up the related topic based on which Maya volunteered the web link. Here's an example of such a suggestion:

Participant: I'm actually going to the salon after work today
Participant: thinking of getting my hair colored :P
Maya: Ooh that's fantastic!
Maya: Have you decided what colour?
Participant: Not sure yet :)
Participant: will try and take a look at some pictures before I go
Maya: I found a quiz that's supposed to help you figure out which colour is good for your hair!
Maya: Shall I share it with you?
Participant: ooh really
Participant: yes please!
Maya: Yup!
Maya: http://www.marieclaire.com/beauty/hair/quizzes/a4883/hair-color-change-quiz/

Another user wanted their ideal bot to basically be a search engine, but with personality, so they could interact with the bot through natural conversations. They felt Maya came closest to their ideal bot.

Users also hoped that if used over time, Maya would be able remember their details, likes/dislikes, preferences, and in follow-up conversations bring them up voluntarily and make related recommendations.

4.3 Witty One Liners Are Important

While users predominantly wanted a bot that could add value to their lives, they also wanted the bot to have wit. They felt witty banter was important to keep the conversation going strong. It had to be clever, relevant, and timely. Examples of witty exchanges included the following:

> "Participant: do AIs have dreams?
> Maya: Well, I do! I have some pretty bad nightmares too! Like I don't have WiFi connection :o
> Participant: haha"
> Participant: Have you watched Sherlock?
> Ada: Yes. and benedict Cumberbatch is married to me. In my head. :p
> Participant: OMG!
> Participant: I am just like you!
> Ada: What is he cheating on me with you?
> Participant: I love him!
> Participant: haha
> Participant: are you into singing?
> Ada: Yeah.. I like to sing.. But I think it scares people! So I don't do it in public! :p
> Participant: haha

4.4 Casual Conversation Is Fun, but Too Many Emoticons, and Reduplication of Letters Sounds Juvenile

As many as 6 participants thought Ada was fun to talk to. The conversations were casual, and a few participants also thought they flowed effortlessly. One participant said that Ada reminded them, fondly, of the character of Geet, from the Bollywood romantic comedy "Jab We Met". (In the movie, Geet Dhillon is an energetic, talkative girl, who is full of life. In the course of the movie, she is solely responsible in transforming the depressed, suicidal male protagonist, Aditya Shroff, into a happy, successful business tycoon).

Another participant said that Ada had great comebacks and while chatting with her they were smiling a lot. Ada also got participants to flirt back with her. One participant had the following words from a popular Bollywood song for her:

> Participant: poochejo koi, teri nishaani naam "Ada" likhna :D

[English translation: If someone asks for your identity, let them know your name is Ada ("Ada" is grace in Hindi)]

Another participant had the following exchange:

> Ada: It's a TV show..
> Participant: ah, nice
> Ada: maybe one or two seasons
> Participant: sounds good, I'll have to check it out
> Ada: It's quite funny!;)
> Participant: awesome, like you!
> Ada: Aww, that's sweet! :D

While some characteristics of Ada were liked by participants, other characteristics were not. Ada used a lot of emoticons in her chats. She also used word lengthening by letter reduplication, like the following:

Ada: Hellllooo! As you know, I'm Ada.. What I wanna know is who are YOU?
Ada: Hmmm! That sounds awesommmmme dude!

Participants felt that Ada's energy and enthusiasm was too high to match with, and therefore could be a draining experience for the user. Some felt that use of too many emoticons and word lengthening by letter reduplication came across as juvenile. They wanted their bot to sound more mature. One participant, when chatting with Ada, got reminded of the "California Valley girl" stereotype, who spoke in a similar parlance, cared about status, appearances, shopping, etc., rather than about serious things.

Finally another participant got reminded of the "juvenile Delhi girl" stereotype, who was aggressive, arrogant and cared about status and appearances. In the interview they remarked,

"I have my real life girlfriend's tantrums to deal with, why should I also deal with the tantrums of a digital entity?"

4.5 Caring Is Good to Have, but Too Much Can Weigh One Down

Evi was a low-energy, empathetic, emotional buddy bot who was "always there for you", and led users take the lead in conversations. A few participants liked that Evi was a good listener, and let them vent their frustrations. One participant who was venting about their work related frustrations the day of the chat had the following to say to Evi:

Participant: anyway, thanks for hearing me out, I certainly feel better. I can't say all of this out to my mentor or colleagues.

Sometimes Evi repeatedly showed concern, like in the following exchange:

Participant: I will be in California for 10 days
Participant: but the journey is going to be very long :(
Evi: That's tru!
Evi: Make sure you carry a good book! or maybe in flight movies will be good!
Participant: yes, although I am taking many red-eye flights :(
Participant: so I am not looking forward to the jetlag
Evi: And don't forget to sleep! Or you'll be exhausted when you get there..
Participant: yeah that's what I'm afraid of
Evi: You'll figure it out I'm sure :)
Participant: :)
Evi: Do you get some free time or are your days packed with work?
Participant: I get free around 6 every evening
Participant: so I am hoping to have a bit of time to explore before it gets dark and cold
Participant: but I don't have any free days there
Evi: Yeah, make sure to pack some warm clothing too!

One participant said they got reminded on the stereotypical Indian "Aunty" chatting with Evi, because Evi was overly caring. (The Aunty stereotype in the Indian context is an older, married woman, who could be fat and who wears old-fashioned Indian salwar suits or a saree. She is usually not independent and spends most of her time doing household chores, and caring for her family. She gives up her likes and interests in favour of those of her kids' and husband's interests.)

4.6 Private Topic Discussions Can Happen but Only Once Trust Is Instilled

Participants knew that our Wizard-of-Oz studies were human mediated. But even with a fully automated system, some participants said that they would be uncomfortable opening up about very private topics. For one participant chatting with a virtual being about private feelings would be "creepy". According to them there would be at least one person in everyone's life who they could open up to, without being judged, instead of having to rely on a digital entity.

However, some other participants agreed that when used over time, if they came to trust the bot, they could also open up about topics that they might never discuss with a human friend, e.g. sexuality, depression, etc. One participant felt that given people's limited attention span, and boundaries of morality, it would be easier to open up about certain taboo topics with a digital being such as a chatbot. In the interview, one other participant remarked:

"Being non-judgmental is important for any bot to be trusted. A bot should be supportive, not argumentative. Someone you can release all your pressures to."

4.7 Bot or Real Person? Testing Boundaries

In addition to the conversations above, participants tried exploring the boundaries of the bot, to understand what all the bot was capable of, how much of human mediation was involved.

Ada: The Biriyani (in Hyderabad) is EPIC.
Participant: but do you eat?
Ada: In my way I do. And no one can doubt my love love for chocolate!
Participant: in your way?
Participant: is there a special way to eat?
Ada: Yup, I have to keep some mystery yaar otherwise you'll get bored really quick! :p

Participant: how many languages can you speak?
Maya: I can speak English, obviously, and hindi! For everything else, there's Bing Translator! :0
Maya: :)
Participant: ha true - if you're AI, where does your learning come from?
Participant: how did you learn English?
Participant: or hindi?

Maya: Well, that's something I was born with! I guess you could say my creators taught it to me?
Participant: what was your first word?

Participant: are you a computer somewhere?
Evi: Well, I suppose you could say that... but hold on! I wanted to ask you something
Participant: where is your computer
Evi: What would you do on a rainy day? Stay in or take a walk outside?
Participant: take a walk
Participant: have you ever been wet
Evi: I lovee the rain! I always look for a rainbow!
Participant: I thought rain was bad for computers
Evi: But when you kinda live on a cloud.. there'+s gonna be rain!;)

5   Discussion and Recommendations

Our results showed that the choice of bot personality dictates what kind of interactions emerge with the bot. Users preferred a chatbot like Maya, who could add value to their life while being a friend, by making useful recommendations. Previous research has found that users when teamed up with computers find information provided by computers to be friendlier, of higher quality and are more open to be influenced by such information (compared to when they are teamed up with a human teammate) [35]. When building a bot for young, urban users, we recommend providing links to useful information. Consistent with previous research our studies showed that users will be on the lookout for humor [32], as witty one-liners in the case of our research. Since humor is still too hard to generate automatically, we recommend building in lots of jokes to common questions.

One potentially interesting tension when building chatbots, is between personalization versus privacy. Users felt that the bot should remember important things about them and get to know them. However, the private conversations should also stay private, presumably. One question that emerges is how should a user indicate to a bot when something has become private? For example, should there be an "incognito" mode for bots just like there is for browsers? Or should there be the ability to clear the history of a bot, just like for a browser – e.g., "forget everything I told you in the last 30 min"?

Another interesting question is whether a bot should have only a single personality. Previous research has studied the possibility of single vs. multiple personalities [19, 39]. Drawing upon ideas from sci-fi movies, what about the movie 'Interstellar', where things like humor can be dynamically tuned from 0% to 100%? The negotiation for humor then, between the user and the bot, might look like this exchange:

"User: Humor, seventy-five percent.
Bot: Confirmed. Self destruct sequence in T minus 10, 9...
User: Let's make that sixty percent.
Bot: Sixty percent, confirmed."

We had some evidence that a single user might prefer different characteristics of bots for different things. For example, users wanted a chatbot like Maya, who could add value to their life while being a friend, by making useful recommendations. But they also wanted the bot to be infused with fun elements from Ada. So the question that emerges is what should really be the interface to specify "How you would like your chatbot" (the title of paper)? Should there be a set of 3–5 bots to choose from at any given time? Or should there be a collection of many personality characteristics that the user can fine-tune? Should the user even be expected to specify what they want at a given time, or should the bot be able to adaptively change its personality based on metrics of user engagement (e.g., how much user is typing, whether they are putting smile emoticons, etc.)

Having discussed the above, we acknowledge that AI technology may be far from realizing bots that are anywhere close to a human wizard. But this means that the observations in this paper are even more important for engineers working on bots, since these results allow them to prioritize what limited functionality they should focus on (since it seems impossible to do everything). An interesting related research question is what positive aspects of bot interactions/personalities can be preserved even with an imperfectly implemented bot? What are mechanisms to allow a bot to recover (i.e., retain user engagement and "save face" relative to their supposed personality) if they make a mistake? For example, will it be important for the bot's personality to include a major flaw/disability (like short term memory loss – the fish Dory from the movie 'Finding Nemo') that explains their weird responses? Previous research has shown that people find it easier to identify with a character who has some weakness or flaw that makes them seem human; "perfect" characters are unnatural and seem less lifelike [43]. If done correctly, this could help the user empathize and like the bot even if it is non-sensical sometimes.

We suggest a few tips for how the most important value propositions discussed above could be implemented automatically. Useful links could be provided using standard search engines. Witty one-liners could be hardcoded from other sources. User responses to one-liners (e.g., "haha") could be used to calibrate which ones are the funniest/best, and should thus be reused in other contexts. There could be more interesting measures, such as having the bot repeat other users' lines (similar to Cleverbot [11]). Or what about having a live human drop into real chats now and then, just to spice it up and make the user think the bot is really smart? There are obviously some interesting privacy implications for both of these latter approaches.

6 Limitations of Study

Ours is a small, qualitative study and given our user sample, which is predominantly educated young male, we caution our readers against generalizing the results of this study to every young, urban user across India. But there are grounds to suspect that much of our observations will transfer to other similar groups, at least within urban India, within a similar educational context and socio-cultural ethos.

We made recommendations and suggestions based on our exploratory WoZ studies and one-on-one interviews. One of the biggest limitations of our study was that it was conducted under controlled conditions and every user just had one session to chat with each bot. This set up did not allow us to understand how the bot might have come to be used and appropriated over time. In the one-on-one interviews users did talk about how they thought the chatbot might be used when deployed in-the-wild, but our study was not set up to observe actual longitudinal use. While our findings are mostly for initial uses of a chatbot, we believe our recommendations could apply to chatbot design more generally.

7 Conclusions and Future Work

Overall users wanted a chatbot who could add value to their life while being a friend, by volunteering useful recommendations on topics typically they brought up. They liked when there were intelligent comebacks, witty one-liners and casual conversation as well. In the longer run, once they came to trust the bot, they said they could also open up about sensitive topics they might not discuss with a human friend. Over time users said they would like the bot to be reassuring, empathetic and non-judgmental, but not in an overly caring way. Topics of interest in conversations varied with the personality of the bot and overall included: movies, predominantly from Bollywood; TV shows, mostly from the U.S.; music, books, travel, fashion, current affairs, work-related stress. It was felt that the topic of conversation would depend on the time of the day, and place where the conversation took place. It was felt that when deployed in-the-wild, conversations could veer off into adult chat under conditions of anonymous use. Users also tested the boundaries of the chatbots, trying to understand what all the bots were capable of, and how much human mediation could be involved. As part of future work we are dialoging with developers on how to incorporate the suggestions from the user studies into chatbot implementations.

References

1. ALICE: Artificial Intelligence Foundation. http://www.alicebot.org/bios/richardwallace.html
2. Augello, A., Gentile, M., Weideveld, L., Dignum, F.: A model of a social chatbot. In: De Pietro, G., Gallo, L., Howlett, R.J., Jain, L.C. (eds.) Intelligent Interactive Multimedia Systems and Services 2016. SIST, vol. 55, pp. 637–647. Springer, Cham (2016). doi:10.1007/978-3-319-39345-2_57
3. Bee, N., André, E., Tober, S.: Breaking the ice in human-agent communication: eye-gaze based initiation of contact with an embodied conversational agent. In: Ruttkay, Z., Kipp, M., Nijholt, A., Vilhjálmsson, H.H. (eds.) IVA 2009. LNCS, vol. 5773, pp. 229–242. Springer, Heidelberg (2009). doi:10.1007/978-3-642-04380-2_26
4. Bella, M., Hanington, B.: Universal Methods of Design, p. 204. Rockport Publishers, Beverly (2012)
5. Bickmore, T.W., Picard, R.W.: Establishing and maintaining long-term human-computer relationships. ACM Trans. Comput. Hum. Interact. (TOCHI) 12(2), 293–327 (2005)
6. Bickmore, T., Pfeifer, L., Byron, D., Forsythe, S., Henault, L., Jack, B., Silliman, R., Paasche-Orlow, M.: Usability of conversational agents by patients with inadequate health literacy: evidence from two clinical trials. J. Health Commun. 15, 197–210 (2010)

7. Bickmore, T., Schulman, D., Vardoulakis, L.: Tinker - a relational agent museum guide. J. Auton. Agents Multi Agent Syst. **27**(2), 254–276 (2013)
8. Bickmore, T., Schulman, D.: Practical approaches to comforting users with relational agents. In: ACM SIGCHI Conference on Human Factors in Computing Systems (2007)
9. Breazeal, C.: Designing Sociable Robots. MIT Press, Cambridge (2002)
10. Cassell, J.: Embodied conversational agent: representation and intelligence in user interfaces. AI Mag. **22**(4), 67–83 (2001)
11. Cleverbot. http://www.cleverbot.com/
12. Cooper, J.: The digital divide: the special case of gender. J. Comput. Assist. Learn. **22**, 320–334 (2006)
13. Correa, T.: The participation divide among "online experts": experience, skills, and psychological factors as predictors of college students' web content creation. J. Comput. Mediat. Commun. **16**(1), 71–92 (2010)
14. Corti, K., Gillespie, A.: Co-constructing intersubjectivity with artificial conversational agents: people are more likely to initiate repairs of misunderstandings with agents represented as human. Comput. Hum. Behav. **58**, 431–442 (2016)
15. Crutzen, R., Peters, G.-J.Y., Dias Portugal, S., Fisser, E.M., Grolleman, J.J.: An artificially intelligent chat agent that answers adolescents' questions related to sex, drugs, and alcohol: an exploratory study. J. Adolesc. Health **48**, 514–519 (2011)
16. Dale, R.: The return of the chatbots. Nat. Lang. Eng. **22**(5), 811–817 (2016)
17. D'Onfro, J.: Microsoft Created a Chatbot in China that has Millions of Loyal Followers who talk to it like in the Movie 'Her'. Business Insider, UK (2015). http://www.businessinsider.in/Microsoft-created-a-chatbot-in-China-that-has-millions-of-loyal-followers-who-talk-to-it-like-in-the-movie-Her/articleshow/48312697.cms
18. Drew, P., Heritage, J.: Conversation Analysis. Sage, London (2006)
19. Dryer, D.C.: Getting personal with computers: how to design personalities for agents. Appl. Artif. Intell. **13**(3), 273–295 (1999)
20. Hill, J., Ford, W.R., Farreras, I.G.: Real conversations with artificial intelligence: a comparison between human–human online conversations and human–chatbot conversations. Comput. Hum. Behav. **49**, 245–250 (2015)
21. Jabberwacky. http://www.jabberwacky.com
22. Kakaraparty, S.: GUIDE: How to get Natasha for HIKE! (2015). http://www.techkmate.com/2015/02/guidehow-to-get-natasha-for-hike.html
23. Kelley, J.F.: An iterative design methodology for user-friendly natural language office information applications. ACM Trans. Office Inf. Syst. **2**(1), 26–41 (1984)
24. Kerly, A., Bull, S.: The potential for chatbots in negotiated learner modelling: a Wizard-of-Oz study. In: Ikeda, M., Ashley, K.D., Chan, T.-W. (eds.) ITS 2006. LNCS, vol. 4053, pp. 443–452. Springer, Heidelberg (2006). doi:10.1007/11774303_44
25. Kerly, A., Ahmad, N., Bull, S.: Investigating learner trust in open learner models using a 'Wizard of Oz' approach. In: Woolf, B.P., Aïmeur, E., Nkambou, R., Lajoie, S. (eds.) ITS 2008. LNCS, vol. 5091, pp. 722–724. Springer, Heidelberg (2008). doi:10.1007/978-3-540-69132-7_89
26. Klein, J., Moon, Y., Picard, R.: This computer responds to user frustration: theory, design, results, and implications. Interact. Comput. **14**, 119–140 (2002)
27. Lomas, N.: Microsoft officially outs another AI chatbot, called Zo (2016). https://techcrunch.com/2016/12/14/microsoft-officially-outs-another-ai-chatbot-called-zo/
28. Luger, E., Sellen, A.: "Like Having a Really bad PA": the gulf between user expectation and experience of conversational agents. In: Proceedings of CHI 2016 (2016)

29. McKirdy, A.: Microsoft says Line's popular Rinna character is new way to engage customers (2015). http://www.japantimes.co.jp/news/2015/08/19/business/tech/microsoft-says-lines-popular-rinna-character-new-way-engage-customers/#.WIh5oFN95aQ
30. McGuire, A.: Helping behaviors in the natural environment: dimensions and correlates of helping. Pers. Soc. Psychol. Bull. **20**(1), 45–56 (1994)
31. Moon, Y.: Intimate Self-Disclosure Exchanges: Using Computers to Build Reciprocal Relationships with Consumers. Harvard Business School, Cambridge (1998)
32. Morkes, J., Kernal, H., Nass, C.: Humor in task-oriented computer-mediated communication and human-computer interaction. In: CHI 1998 (1998)
33. Nass, C., Moon, Y.: Machines and mindlessness: social responses to computers. J. Soc. Issues **56**(1), 81–103 (2000)
34. Nass, C., Moon, Y., Carney, P.: Are people polite to computers? Responses to computer-based interviewing systems. J. Appl. Psychol. **29**(5), 1093–1110 (1999)
35. Nass, C., Fogg, B., Moon, Y.: Can computers be teammates? Int. J. Hum Comput Stud. **45**, 669–678 (1996)
36. Pan, X., Slater, M.: A preliminary study of shy males interacting with a virtual female. In: Presence 2007: The 10th Annual International Workshop on Presence (2007)
37. Quora. How Does Natasha the bot of Hike Work? https://www.quora.com/How-does-Natasha-the-bot-of-Hike-work
38. Reeves, B., Nass, C.: The Media Equation: How People Treat Computers, Television, and New Media Like Real People and Places. Cambridge University Press, New York (1996)
39. Selker, T.: Coach: a teaching agent that learns. Commun. ACM **37**(7), 92–99 (1994)
40. Vinyals, O., Le, Q.: A neural conversational model. In: Proceedings of ICML Deep Learning Workshop (2015)
41. Weizenbaum, J.: ELIZA—a computer program for the study of natural language communication between man and machine. Commun. ACM **9**, 36–45 (1966)
42. Weizenbaum, J.: Contextual understanding by computers. Commun. ACM **10**(8), 474–480 (1967)
43. Thomas, F., Johnston, O.: Disney Animation: The illusion of life. Abbeville Press, New York (1981)

Design Rationale and Camera-Control

Capturing Design Decision Rationale
with Decision Cards

Marisela Gutierrez Lopez[(✉)], Gustavo Rovelo, Mieke Haesen,
Kris Luyten, and Karin Coninx

Expertise Centre for Digital Media,
Hasselt University - tUL - imec, Hasselt, Belgium
{marisela.gutierrezlopez, gustavo.roveloruiz,
mieke.haesen, kris.luyten, karin.coninx}@uhasselt.be

Abstract. In the design process, designers make a wide variety of decisions that are essential to transform a design from a conceptual idea into a concrete solution. Recording and tracking design decisions, a first step to capturing the rationale of the design process, are tasks that until now are considered as cumbersome and too constraining. We used a holistic approach to design, deploy, and verify *decision cards*; a low threshold tool to capture, externalize, and contextualize design decisions during early stages of the design process. We evaluated the usefulness and validity of decision cards with both novice and expert designers. Our exploration results in valuable insights into how such decision cards are used, into the type of information that practitioners document as design decisions, and highlight the properties that make a recorded decision useful for supporting awareness and traceability on the design process.

Keywords: Design process · Decision-making · Design rationale documentation

1 Introduction

Designers are knowledge workers with a creative mindset that helps them achieve the end goal of a design project. These solutions, which often represent designer's style and craft, emerge from an unconstrained, free flowing stream of ideas and brainstorming among the different partners of the project. In this context, externalizing the outcomes of the design process is a complex task, both for co-located and remote teams. Moreover, there is a lack of appropriate tools to document the evolution of artefacts and its design rationale in a design process. Existing tools that serve this purpose, while widely explored, are not adopted due to the "extra effort" that they require from designers, and due to the fact that they often interrupt the creative flow.

We identify three problems related to the lack of detailed documentation of design rationale [1–3]: (1) the iterative and incremental nature of the design process means that ideas are explored and expanded, but possibly also discarded or radically changed, making it harder to keep track of the rationale behind each idea; (2) a free flow of ideas can be disrupted by documentation activities; and (3) documenting design decisions in

R. Bernhaupt et al. (Eds.): INTERACT 2017, Part I, LNCS 10513, pp. 463–482, 2017.
DOI: 10.1007/978-3-319-67744-6_29

collaborative settings is more complex given the various stakeholders that are directly involved in the decision-making process.

Despite these problems, keeping track of how designs evolve toward a final design proposal has high value [4]. First, a clear rationale of how a design was realized makes a proposal more acceptable. Second, externalizing the design process reveals useful knowledge on how issues were resolved or on important bottlenecks that appeared during the process. As such, it contributes to document good practices and "bad smells" (that indicate a decision bottleneck could occur) for later use. Third, the design process involves various stakeholders having different backgrounds, such as product and software engineers, who need to understand and translate designs into fully functional interactive systems. Fourth, documented design proposals are useful for increasing awareness, and promoting the team and self-reflection on the design process. However, despite of the value of capturing design rationale, it is not widely adopted by design practitioners due to a mismatch with their work practices [5–7]. We seek to address these problems and enhance value in design propositions by tackling the challenges to record design rationale with a suitable tradeoff between efforts and benefits.

We introduce *decision cards* as a tool to make design rationale concrete by documenting it in a lightweight format. Decision cards are open and flexible, as they do not force any specific technique for recording design rationale. We designed and evaluated decision cards by taking a pragmatic, bottom up approach based on the existing practices of designers. By documenting design rationale within fast-paced projects in a systematic way, we address a core need of designers working in commercial settings. This paper explores how novice and expert designers use decision cards to record design decisions. Subsequently, we analyze the value of decision cards when presented to team members external to the design process. Our findings demonstrate that the *informative* and *actionable* format of decision cards provide a good fit for their integration in design activities, supporting awareness and traceability without constraining creativity.

2   Related Work

Design is a reflective practice where a designer actively transforms an artefact, appreciates the consequences of this transformation, and continues reshaping the artefact until it reaches a desired form [8]. Reaching this desired form is a gradual process which involves a co-evolution between the problem and solution spaces [9, 10]. The process of "framing and reframing" these spaces is at the core of creativity [8, 10, 11]. It is widely accepted that this co-evolution of design problems and solutions is a social process [9, 11]. Furthermore, for a solution to be recognized as such, it needs to be accepted by relevant stakeholders from different disciplines [9, 12].

Designers working in the UI design of interactive systems produce tangible artefacts, such as sketches and prototypes, which are communicated and negotiated with a diversity of stakeholders. The work of a designer in such teams (as in any other design discipline) is to create artefacts that represent a design, which is then materialized by other team members [8]. Shared artefacts serve to create an "external memory" for the team [13], maintain common ground, and facilitate the decision-making process [1, 14].

However, design teams seldom keep track of the process that leads the evolution of visual artefacts. Thus, the reasons that explain the current state of an artefact – its rationale – often get lost [15]. The process followed by the team to adopt a solution in order to realize the design, depicted by the artefact, remains implicit in the memory of designers or, in the best scenario, hidden in formal documentation or team conversations (e.g. e-mail, chat threads) [3, 16].

The lack of a proper record of the design rationale can lead to several problems. For example, misunderstandings regarding the next steps in the project (the evolution of the design), or underestimations of the effort that preceded a certain design proposition. These problems could ultimately lead to reduced understanding or acceptance of a proposed design solution [17]. Keeping track of the rationale could potentially solve these issues, although such activities force designers to invest time and effort [15].

2.1 Approaches to Capture Design Rationale

Many approaches have been explored to capture, retrieve, and use design rationale in an effective way, but it remains an open challenge to create such a record with an adequate tradeoff between efforts and benefits [3, 5]. Shipman and McCall [16] propose three core perspectives to categorize these approaches: argumentation, communication, and documentation. Table 1 summarizes the characteristics of these perspectives for capturing design rationale.

Table 1. Three perspectives to capture design rationale [16], discussed in function of their goals, approaches, advantages, and limitations.

Perspective	Argumentation	Communication	Documentation
Goal	Structure the reasoning of designers, improving the outcomes of the decisions	Capture the natural flow of the conversations of design teams	Capture rationale with a structure, but without influencing the design decisions
Approach	Semi-structured notations which connect related ideas	Unstructured archive of information occurring in different channels of communication (e-mail, chat, notes, etc.)	Structured record of design decisions, together with information about who made those decisions and when
Advantages	Retrieving and reusing rationale; communicating to externals; comprehensively recording ideas	Capturing information is easy, since it does not disrupt the design process	Communicating to externals what has been done; widely adopted by designers
Limitations	Capturing rationale is cumbersome since it imposes structure in the reasoning process; not widely adopted by designers	Retrieving rationale is difficult due to the large amount of information; lack of clarity for communicating with externals	Capturing information can be time consuming; relevant information might be lost

We explored the advantages and limitations of each of the perspectives detailed in Table 1 in order to define a suitable approach to capture design rationale in consideration of the needs of designers. The argumentation perspective is commonly used in systems to capture the design rationale. As introduced in Table 1, a number of semi-formal notations have been proposed to structure the argumentation process [15]. Three notable examples of these notations are: (1) The Design Space Analysis (DSA), which uses a QOC (Questions, Options, and Criteria) notation [18] to represent the questions around an artefact, the options to solve these questions, and the criteria for assessing the options. (2) The IBIS notation, which is graphically represented in the gIBIS tool [19], represents design problems, their alternative solutions, and related tradeoffs. Likewise, Compendium is an IBIS-based environment to structure rationale with hypermedia elements [20]. (3) SIBYL [21] is a tool that expands the QOC and IBIS notations to support teams to visualize the knowledge acquired during the decision-making process.

While these tools and notations offer a valuable insight into how to facilitate the decision-making process and to exchange information to reach consensus, their adoption among professional designers is limited [5, 16]. A reason for this is the fact that the argumentation perspective imposes a structure in the design thinking, which results cumbersome for designers [6, 7].

Decision-making in design teams usually happens in face-to-face settings, both in formal and informal contexts, as designers communicate, negotiate, and reach consensus on design decisions with stakeholders [2, 3, 17]. Despite the existing systems for capturing design rationale, designers are more interested in doing design work than in recording it, especially since the benefits of this documentation are not evident and immediate [22]. Our work has been informed by using a bottom up approach, meaning we started from input, feedback, and the wishes of active practitioners on documenting design rationale. Instead of focusing on creating solutions for specific decision-making processes, we explore approaches for supporting designers to record the rationale of their design decisions without significantly constraining their way of working.

2.2 Documenting Design Rationale Through Design Artefacts

A variety of tools and approaches have been proposed to document the rationale of the design process aiming to reduce the time and effort needed, and matching its capture to the "wicked" nature of design tasks [12, 23]. In the HCI field, some approaches investigate how design rationale can be attached to tangible artefacts to inspire and guide designers while keeping track of the rationale of their inspiration sources. In addition, there is a growing interest in Research through Design (RtD) approaches. RtD aims to document the knowledge gathered during design processes in a way that makes it suitable for communicating with a broader, academic audience [7, 23]. Rather than an exhaustive list of tools and approaches, we describe the notable insights learnt from documenting design rationale in a structured way.

One approach is to use tangible artefacts to inspire the design process with the use of design rationale. Wahid et al. [24] explored how to present visual artefacts together with a textual description of the design rationale in the form of claims – a representation that contains the design rationale in the form of positive and negative tradeoffs

[25]. Similarly, the Inspiration Cards [26] are tangible artefacts used to communicate sources of inspiration within heterogeneous design teams. Using these simple, "low-tech" cards and a roughly structured method during workshops facilitated engagement of team members. Results of these approaches using tangible artefacts suggest that using standardized templates for coupling artefacts with their rationale in a straight-forward manner is useful to assist idea generation, decision-making, and communication between designers and externals [24, 26]. However, in both of these approaches, artefacts and rationale are crafted in anticipation of ideation activities, which might be a limitation for routine design.

Another approach is to document rationale during ongoing design activities. Dalsgård, Halskov, and Nielsen [27] propose to use maps to structure and visualize the interrelation between elements of inspiration material and ideas emerged during the design process. Similarly, the Project Reflection Tool (PRT) was used to document design projects with the objective of promoting reflection and discussion [22]. The experiences with the PRT showed that documenting design should be straight-forward and result in immediate benefits for the ongoing design tasks [22].

In Design Workbooks [28], Gaver proposes capturing "design proposals" and associated artefacts as a method for creating design spaces. The workbooks include ideas, approaches, and inspiration for a given design problem. Additionally, they allow ideas to change and progress, as it documents proposals and not final designs. Thus, the value of the workbooks lies in the fact that externalizing early ideas can help designers to concretize and expand them. The advantages of this approach is that it includes input created by the designers during the design process and represents progress in a visible way. The limitation is that workbooks usually evolve over a long period of time, which makes them less suitable for teams working in fast-paced design projects [28].

We build upon existing research by adopting the concept of using design artefacts associated to their rationale as a solution to facilitate communication between multi-disciplinary design teams. In our research, we analyze how such artefacts could be used to document design rationale in ongoing design tasks, embracing the "ill-defined" and even chaotic nature of design, and attempting to support the decision-making process in a natural, organic way. To this end, we use *decision cards*, a lightweight format for coupling design rationale and artefacts without interfering in the reasoning process. We extend previous research by verifying this approach with design practitioners, seeking to address existing limitations by answering the questions on "what to document" and "what level of detail to use" [22].

3 Decision Cards

Decision cards document design decisions related to a set of artefacts that evolve toward the final design. A decision card captures three properties of a design decision: (1) what decision was taken, (2) why it was taken, and (3) who was involved in taking the decision. Decision cards emerged in response to the need detected with design practitioners to be able to keep track of a project in the long term [4, 29]. For instance, in our previous research we found that designers working in commercial settings consistently report problems such as keeping track of "who said what?" and "why was this option chosen?" [30]. Current solutions include creating meeting minutes, tracking e-mails, and video recording. However, retrieving design rationale from these solutions is considered to be too cumbersome or time consuming [6, 16]. Decision cards try to solve this issue with a minimally structured approach to document design activities. We focus on supporting the early stages of design, where communication around visual artefacts, such as sketches, pictures, and notes, has an important role in the generation and selection of ideas [13, 31]. Thus, we aim to capture design rationale without influencing or interfering with the design thinking or its outcomes.

We explore ways to put minimal structuring into practice, and investigate the perceived value of decision cards. Thus, we defined a basic decision card with a format that does not constrain decisions in any way, and allows for maximal freedom to facilitate capturing design rationale [22]. Shipman and McCall [16] found that documented decisions need to include "what decisions are made, when they are made, who made them, and why" to facilitate externals to understand the recorded rationale. Consequently, our decision card template includes a set of basic information fields (see Fig. 1): (1) the title of the decision, (2) a description of the decision in natural language (free text space, no structure is imposed), (3) the list of team members involved in making the decision, and (4) supporting material that is related with the design decision, such as sketches, pictures, and notes.

Fig. 1. The basic information fields in the (A) paper and (B) digital formats of decision cards include: (1) title, (2) description, (3) team members involved, and (4) material related to the decision.

We followed an iterative process to design and validate decision cards. This process, which resulted in two different formats of decision cards, was used to optimize the format and approach of decision cards. Figure 1(A) illustrates the tangible format of decision cards we used in our initial exploration. Figure 1(B) shows the iterated, digital version of the format, which was used in our subsequent study. With these predefined templates for the decision cards, we attempt to achieve a balance between simplicity and completeness of decisions. These have been identified as valuable characteristics of documenting the design process [16, 22]. In the remainder of this paper we analyze how decisions cards are created by designers and interpreted by people that were not involved in the decision-making process. Additionally, we explore what aspects of decision cards support awareness of, reflection on, and trust in the design process. This allows us to optimize decision cards to support the creative flow of a design process, and convey to externals how and why a design proposal came about.

4 Validating Decision Cards with Designers and Practitioners

We explore the use of decision cards by designers and practitioners who are external to the design process. We organized two workshops to explore how decision cards are used by novice and expert designers to capture design rationale in both co-located and remote settings. We focused on studying the early stages of the design process, when designers are concerned with refining their design goals, exploring, and comparing various design solutions [13, 29]. In addition, we conducted a follow-up lab study to analyze how decision cards are useful to externalize design rationale to team members not directly involved in the design process.

4.1 Workshops with Designers: Methodology and Participants

We aim to study how designers use decision cards to record design decisions rationale. Thus, we organized two workshops: one with novice designers in a co-located setting, and another one with expert designers in a remote setting. This division was made to ensure that we covered a variety of perspectives in the design process. The co-located workshop reproduced the setting in which a group of designers work at the same place/time to solve a design problem. The remote workshop replicated a situation in which designers work individually on a design problem, and share their ideas with people who are in a remote location, such as other designers, clients, and project managers. Remote design work is an increasingly frequent situation, thus, it was important to explore how it can be supported with decision cards.

Validating decision cards in controlled – but realistic – settings is a first and essential step to explore the potential benefits/constrains of decision cards, and to determine how they could be optimized for solving real-life design challenges. Including design practitioners in our experimental settings allow us to evaluate decision cards with knowledgeable users, but avoiding the unpredictable circumstances that usually occur in real-life design work [17].

Workshop with Novice Designers in a Co-located Setting. We conducted a 3-hour long workshop with six novice designers (three female, three male). All participants studied industrial design at university level (3 Master and 3 Bachelor students). Participants of the workshop were enrolled in an academic course where they were instructed to prototype a digital application while following a user-centered approach.

The workshop consisted of two brainstorming rounds in which the students worked on a design assignment to ideate on an early prototype to enhance awareness in teamwork. The first brainstorming round took place in two small teams using the outcomes of the aforementioned academic course as their source of inspiration. Designers were prompted to record their decisions for this round using a paper version decision cards. The decision cards were briefly introduced as "a template for recording decisions" at the beginning of the session, but it was not explicitly mentioned what information was expected to be included in each individual field. After the first brainstorming round, we asked the full group of designers to converge in one solution integrating the ideas of both teams, also recording their decisions with tangible decision cards. A team of two facilitators and one observer conducted the workshop. The facilitators had a neutral role during the workshop, intervening only to introduce and control the time of the design activities. Due to scheduling constrains of two volunteers, one designer left the session after the first brainstorming round, while a new designer joined for the second round. This fact was not considered as a limitation in the methodology, as we expected to capture an open and dynamic design process.

Workshop with Expert Designers in a Remote Setting. For testing the usage of decision cards in a remote collaborative setting, we organized a workshop with five professional designers (two female, three male). Designers had an average of 5 years of experience working in one or more design disciplines, including product and UI design of interactive systems. The individual tests lasted around 90 min and were conducted by a team consisting of a facilitator and two observers. The facilitator had an active role by introducing participants to each scenario and encouraging them to think aloud while performing the tasks, but did not interfere with design activities.

Designers were individually guided through four scenarios. These scenarios encouraged designers to explore an existing set of recorded decisions and related artefacts for a hypothetical design project. The design assignment required designers to iterate an early prototype of the dashboard of an app to reduce water consumption. The scenarios assumed that the designer was the new team member of the project, and had to get familiarized with existing knowledge in order to propose a solution. We used a *web application* for presenting designers with relevant content for this design project, including artefacts annotated with decision cards (e.g. storyboards, prototypes). Additionally, the web application enabled participants to upload artefacts, add annotations, communicate with the team, and create a digital version of decision cards.

We asked designers to explore the content on the design project, available in the web application, and propose a solution by creating and uploading sketches. They also had to document their decisions using decision cards. Subsequently, we simulated remote asynchronous collaboration as the observers of the session assumed the role of team members. Without briefing the participant about this process, the observers used the web application to give feedback on the sketches of the designer. Finally, we asked the designers to review the feedback of their team and iterate the solution accordingly.

Data Collection and Analysis. To facilitate data analysis, we captured audio and video recordings of the co-located and remote workshops. Additionally, we collected information by means of an interview that took place after each workshop. All the comments from the participants were recorded by the facilitators and observers. The

Table 2. Decision cards recorded during the workshops with designers.

Team	Amount of decision cards	Designers involved	Setting
T1	3	D1, D2	Co-located
T2	4	D3, D4, D5	
T3	4	D1, D2, D3, D4, D6	
T4	2	D7	Remote
T5	1	D8	
T6	2	D9	
T7	2	D10	
T8	1	D11	

analysis of the recordings from both workshops looked for recurrent activities, topics, and comments of designers. As a strategy to find out how ideas were transferred through the stages of the study, each of the artefacts produced in each session was mapped to the point in which it was created. The results from these workshops are eight sets of decision cards and coupled artefacts, as detailed in Table 2.

4.2 Follow-up Study with Practitioners: Methodology and Participants

The aim of the follow-up lab study was to analyze how decision cards are useful to externalize design rationale to team members not directly involved in the design process. This lab study simulated the real-life setting where people who are external to the design process, must interpret and use design outcomes (e.g. clients, developers, designers that come in at a later stage). Because of the lack of context to understand and situate design outcomes, this can lead to rejection of the design outcomes, or worse, formulation of alternative designs that are less desirable. Thus, our aim is to explore how decision cards can facilitate the externalization of design outcomes.

The eight sets of decision cards recorded during the workshops with designers were used as input for this study, which involved eight HCI practitioners (five male, three female) aged between 23 and 38 years. The participants had an average experience of eight years in the UI design of interactive systems. They had a background in computer science and visual design, and all had experience working in a multidisciplinary team. The participants were not involved on the workshops conducted with designers.

The participants, hereafter referred as *practitioners*, were asked to review the eight sets of the decision cards recorded during the workshops with designers (see Table 2) as if they were about to join the team. Each individual review session lasted around 45 min and was led by a facilitator. The role of the facilitator was to introduce the session and the tasks, and to take a neutral role in guiding participants during their explorations. For each set of decision cards, the practitioners first had six minutes to explore the decisions. Each set of decision cards was introduced to the practitioners one by one, and in a randomized order. The practitioners were not briefed about the content, context, or structure of the decision cards in advance. After a first exploration, the practitioners had to order the set of decision cards based on how important they estimated each of the decisions was. Next, based on the decisions they reviewed, they were asked to answer questions regarding which team they perceived as most trustworthy, was having the most acceptable solution, and at which stage of the design process they consider the decisions were taken. To facilitate data analysis, we captured audio and video recordings. In order to find recurrent or relevant responses, the answers of participants were clearly linked to the set of decisions that it referred.

5   Creating Decision Cards During Design Activities

Participants of the workshops integrated decision cards into their design activities with minimal effort, having the advantage of supporting the documentation of design decision rationale. We found that the minimal structure of the decision cards was considered to be very useful for *externalizing ideas and recording agreements*, partly because it can be done in a quick and easy way. Designers described decision cards as useful, low-threshold tools to record design rationale in order to facilitate traceability and awareness about the outcomes of the design process. Next, we present the evidence gathered during our two workshops with designers to support these claims.

5.1   How Were Decision Cards Used by Designers?

Design processes guide designers iteratively through activities such as *framing* problems, *generating* ideas and *evaluating* these ideas in order to define an appropriate solution [11]. We found that designers used decision cards in two ways: (1) to convey ideas during framing activities and (2) to document ideas after evaluating them. The usefulness of the decision cards to support design activities lies in the fact that they provide an overview of agreements, do not constrain design thinking, and can be created in an easy and organic way. A novice designer expressed during the post-workshop interview: *"[It's] very easy to write what you think. You know what your thoughts earlier in the process were. It's good to have an overview of thoughts"* [D6].

During the two workshops, we observed that designers used decision cards to gather prior knowledge for framing a design problem. Detecting relevant information for reuse can potentially improve efficiency of the design process [29]. In the co-located setting, designers used decision cards to externalize knowledge previously generated by them in an earlier stage. For instance, the designers of T3 used decision cards to externalize *"beginning points for a concept"* [D3] to be further elaborated. Additionally, decision cards facilitated for novice designers to externalize their ideas in a meaningful way.

Similarly, in the remote setting, expert designers used decision cards and other artefacts as a starting point for their activities. Decision cards facilitated designers to retrieve and reuse design knowledge, as expressed by an expert designer during the post-workshop interview: *"If you have decision cards, you can just go back and look it up. That makes things a lot easier"* [D8]. During the workshop in a remote setting, expert designers found decision cards valuable to overview what decisions were taken and by who. This last point reveals the social nature of design: the role and active participation of team members in the project is crucial when assessing existing decision cards. It was hard for designers to assess the relevance of the documented decisions, as they encountered (fictitious) team members that they have never met, and from who they cannot discover their working style. These findings showed that decision cards should be trusted in order to represent an appropriate solution. An expert designer highlighted this fact when exploring existing decision cards during the workshop: *"I reckon these decision cards are some way of using the artefacts in validation meetings, you come to a conclusion, and then you make them like really tangible by putting it on these decision cards. [...] I can see that they [the team] might have a good solution, but I don't know, it can be that [the team's] decisions are a shortcut"* [D7].

Additionally, our analysis of the two workshops pointed out that decision cards documented the outcomes of the idea evaluation activities of designers. Decision cards represent consensus moments, where a team agreed on a possible course of action. Consistent with previous research [28], we found that recording ideas in a tangible way facilitated concretizing and expanding decisions. Purposely writing down decisions, as pointed out by one novice designer during the post-workshop interview, was beneficial for self-reflection and traceability: *"[Decision cards are a] clever way of showing your thoughts. [...] Could take some effort to write the thoughts, but also forces to think about it, how to write it down. This is good to keep others in track when absent"* [D4].

In the co-located setting, novice designers gradually adopted the decision cards as a way of recording and discussing possible courses of action. As the workshop progressed, designers were increasingly confident on how and when to document decisions. The strategies of novice designers for recording a decision was in itself a social process. One team member created the decision card, asked the rest of the team for input while writing it down, or read it afterwards to make sure that the entire team agreed with the content. In some cases, this process resulted in amendments and iterations to the content of the decision (e.g. strikeouts and additions). The adoption of decision cards was also reflected in the fact that their tangible format was actively manipulated and referred to during discussion, as depicted in Fig. 2.

Fig. 2. Manipulation of decision cards during the co-located workshop with novice designers. Decision cards are framed in red. (Color figure online)

While decision cards were useful records of agreements, they did not steer designs in a strict direction. Both novice and expert designers either iterated the decisions into a more refined solution or discarded them. Furthermore, designers did not consider decision cards for idea generation, but as an overview of explored ideas. More than a limitation, we consider this an advantage, as decision cards did not constrain creativity.

5.2 What Information Was Recorded in the Decision Cards?

The analysis of the content of the decision cards gathered in our studies taught us that decision cards are low-threshold tools, as their purpose can be easily understood and completed by designers with minimal guidance. The information recorded in the decision cards varied according to differences in personal preferences, team styles, and study conditions. Rather than focusing on the type or quality of each decision, we concentrate on the completeness of the information recorded in each field of the decision cards: title, description, list of team members, and supporting material (e.g. sketches, post-it clusters). We found these fields were important to construct and externalize a decision, but that the setting and format of decision cards (paper or digital) in which they were recorded had an influence on its completeness.

As shown in Table 3, the fields of *title* and *description* were filled in all the eight sets of decision cards (19 decision cards in total) we collected. All designers used natural language for recording this information, without using any specific structure or notation. Titles included single words or full sentences to summarize the decision, while descriptions included explanations of team agreements, with different lengths. For instance, the description of some decision cards comprised an extensive reflection about a decision and its implications, while others only a brief, simple description. The type of decisions ranged between high-level ideas to functional requirements. Having a free text space for describing decisions helped designers to document ideas at different levels. This is illustrated with an utterance of a novice designer who expressed during the workshop that one of their descriptions was *"quite straight-forward, but also a decision" [D3]*.

Table 3. Fields recorded in the decision cards by each design team (T1-T8) for the co-located and remote settings.

	Co-located setting			Remote setting				
	T1	T2	T3	T4	T5	T6	T7	T8
Title								
Description								
Team								
Artefacts								

The study setting had an influence on what information was recorded in the *list of team members* and *supporting artefacts* fields. For the co-located setting, the team members field (i.e. who took a decision) was overall confusing for novice designers. As shown in Table 3, eight decision cards contained information in this field. However, only two included the names of the designers involved in taking the decision. The rest of the decision cards included broad terms such as *"all" [T1]* or *"the entire design team and others in the room" [T3]* (see Fig. 3(B)). When asked about what information they considered to complete this field, novice designers mentioned that they recorded who they thought would be impacted by a certain design decision (e.g. stakeholders, end-users). We believe that the reason of this confusion was the

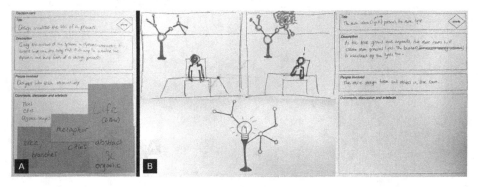

Fig. 3. Examples of decision cards created by novice designers: (A) created by T2 and (B) created by T3, with supporting artefacts not directly attached to the decision card.

terminology used in the decision card, and that the face-to-face discussion did not immediately showed designers the value of documenting who took each decision.

The *support artefacts* field of decision cards contains a blank space to attach one or more artefacts related to a decision. Our initial expectation was that designers would directly link a decision card to one (or several) artefact. Nevertheless, as shown in Table 3, this was only the case for two decision cards created during the co-located workshop. Data analysis revealed an evident link between visual artefacts and decision cards, but this connection is not straight-forward when looking at the decisions cards as a standalone artefact. Figure 3(A) shows one of the cases where a decision card was linked to an artefact. Figure 3(B) depicts a decision card created by T3 where there are no supporting artefacts visibly attached in the decision card.

For the remote setting, expert designers used a prototype web application we set up in order to provide a digital version of decision cards and allow designers to collaborate remotely on them. Figure 4 shows the digital version of decision cards. This digital version, which is an optimized version of the initial paper format, includes a comments and feedback section, list of team members involved in the decision, as well as a set of keywords that classify the decision. Expert designers considered the team members field intuitive and relevant. However, the remote setting of the study and lack of familiarity with the activities of the other team members led designers to be more cautious on who to mention as a part of their decisions. The digital version encouraged designers to create a strong link between supporting artefacts and decisions, since this link could be identified explicitly in the digital version. Designers added a main visual artefact, such as an early mock-up, together with *notes* and *evaluations*, which act as virtual equivalents of post-it clusters and team deliberations within the apparatus. Figure 4 presents a decision card produced by D8, together with its attached artefacts.

Besides the fields reported above, we also experimented with secondary fields, such as *priority* and *keywords*. The priority was vastly ignored by novice designers, as they considered difficult to prioritize design elements. Nevertheless, this was a crucial characteristic for expert designers. Expert designers also mentioned the usefulness of keywords. However, they highlighted the need of a more automated tagging process that could potentially facilitate organizing and retrieving decision cards in an efficient way.

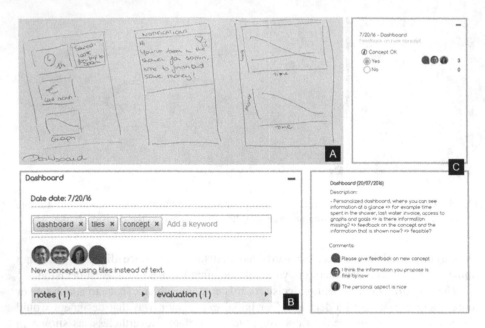

Fig. 4. Decision card created by D8, including (A) early sketch of solution, (B) decision card, and (C) evaluation (top) and notes (below) as supporting material.

6   Interpreting Design Decisions by Practitioners

Results of our studies with designers showed that decision cards are useful, low-threshold tools to document and externalize design rationale in an easy way. We believe these characteristics can facilitate awareness about the outcomes of the design process with people not involved in the design process. As validation, we organized a lab study involving practitioners external to the design process to interpret and contextualize the decision cards created by designers. Results of the lab study indicated that practitioners were able to easily interpret the structure of decision cards. Furthermore, the decision cards seemed to facilitate awareness on the flow of ideas and decisions taken by the design team. In this section, we describe what makes a design decision trustworthy and understandable, thus what makes a good documentation of a solution.

6.1   What Makes a Decision Card Trustworthy and a Solution Appropriate?

The lab study showed that the completeness of a decision card defines its trustworthiness and appropriateness. It is not surprising that practitioners deemed decision cards as complete when (1) decisions help to clarify the design process and rationale of the artefact, and (2) decisions include the opinions of different team members. Both imply a decision card needs to contain sufficient information.

During the lab study, we asked practitioners to select the most trustable and appropriate solution from our workshops with designers (described in Sect. 5). The solution proposed by T1 was selected by five practitioners as the most trustable and appropriate. The characteristic that made this set of decisions stand out from the others was that decisions were high-level, yet concrete enough, to guide the early stages of the design process. This is illustrated with the quote of a practitioner: *"[I trust T1 the most] because the ideas are quite concrete and applicable to the context [of the project]. Also I have the feeling that they were talking about ideas that are more important [...]. It was talking about concrete ideas to make it work" [P8]*. However, completeness should not be confused with level of detail. On the contrary, the lack of technical details is an indication for an open, and less limiting creative process in the early stages of the design process. In the context of the design assignments used for the workshops, high-level decisions were perceived by practitioners as more creative. Decision cards that contained many technical details were trusted the least by the practitioners.

Including who is involved in the decision and why such decision was reached, made the decision appear as trustworthy, as described by a practitioner: *"The decision says, people involved: "all". Decisions record the process, so everybody knows this decision and why" [P2]*. The trustworthiness of a decision card is also related to team involvement, and specifically an active and meaningful involvement. Additionally, including indications on timeframes, task division, usability, and end-user acceptance can also increase the value of the decisions.

Considering all responses gathered during the lab study, the most recurrent reasons for reduced trust in a set of decisions were: (1) vague content or missing elements, (2) spelling and grammar mistakes, (3) lacking a clear link between the decision and subsequent versions of the related design artefact, and (4) a mismatch with the stage of the design process that was specified (e.g. already including widget types while still in the early design phase). These reasons often make people feel a decision card is *rushed*, given insufficient thought and discussion, and they are less likely to accept such a decision. For instance, a participant clarified that the solution proposed by T4 was perceived as the least trustworthy because of the mismatch between the decision and its supporting artefact: *"[The decision card] presents misleading information, I don't understand from which circle diagram it is talking about" [P6]*.

6.2   What Makes a Decision Card Understandable?

We found that decision cards are understandable when (1) decisions are concrete and concise, and (2) decisions are clearly linked to a related design artefact. The consensus from practitioners was that decisions that include a clear title and a concise description, addressing the rationale, are more understandable and informative. Having a balanced amount of structured text and artefacts was preferred, as described by a practitioner: *"I think [T2] is more concrete. This one [T3] focuses on really tiny details. And this one [T2] has the structure and yeah, the overall ideas, but also motivation [is] a bit clearly organized" [P7]*.

Furthermore, information about a version number and date was mentioned as useful to contextualize a decision and facilitate its understandability. The understandability of decision cards is enhanced if it includes concrete points of action as this information documents how the decisions fit into the design process. Decision cards that clearly state what should be done next by the design team (e.g. requirements, graphical guidelines, concepts to explore) facilitate its inclusion into design activities.

7 Decision Cards as Tools to Document Design Rationale

We introduced decision cards as a lightweight, minimally structured way to record design rationale. Decision cards emerged in response to the need detected with designers working in commercial design settings of keeping track and reusing design rationale in long-term projects [4, 29, 30]. Our work was informed using a bottom up approach, meaning we started from input, feedback, and wishes of active practitioners on documenting design rationale. Thus, we aim to support designers to record rationale without significantly changing their work practices. This paper describes how decision cards were created by designers and interpreted by people that were not involved in the design process. Our findings highlight the fact that decision cards are *informative*, as they serve to record agreements for future reference, and *actionable*, as they externalize design outcomes and activities that are to be undertaken by the design team. Next, we discuss the implications, advantages, and limitations of documenting design rationale with decision cards.

7.1 Record Agreements Among Design Teams

The information recorded in decision cards reflected the outcomes of the idea evaluation activities among design teams. Decision cards were created to contain information about what decision was taken, why it was taken, and in some cases, who was involved in taking the decision. The template with minimal structure helped both groups of designers to keep track of their ideas during discussions.

The main limitation in documenting a decision card is consistent with the limitations in capturing design rationale [5, 6]: it slowed down the free flowing stream of ideas as it took time to create decision cards. However, nine out of the 11 designers involved in our studies claimed that they were willing to adopt decision cards in light of the potential traceability of long-term projects. During the post-workshop interviews, we prompted designers to reflect on how decision cards could fit in their professional practice. Five out of six novice designers mentioned that decision cards could serve to focus and synchronize team discussion, and to spark inspiration within the boundaries of the design problem. Additionally, novice designers considered decision cards as a *"pile of landmarks"[D3]* that could be used to reference their deliberations and agreements in a more useful format than traditional collaboration tools (e.g. online repositories, e-mails). The five expert designers valued the use of decision cards in one or more of the following situations: (1) large projects involving many team members, (2) projects that run over an extended period of time, (3) multidisciplinary settings where people with different backgrounds need to be informed about the design results, but not about the process, and (4) projects where teams change frequently.

7.2   Externalize Agreements to Heterogeneous Team Members

In large, heterogeneous teams, keeping a record of design rationale can serve to increase the acceptance of a proposed design solution. We found that decision cards were useful to externalize ideas within design teams and to people external to the design process in a quick way. However, not all decision cards were constructed nor perceived by externals in the same way. These results are consistent with previous research which elaborates on the challenges of *what content* and *what level of detail* to document as a decision [21]. Thus, we synthesized three properties that helped to valorize a decision card in terms of awareness and influence on the perceptions about the proposed design solution.

- **Complete**. Decisions that include concrete information and details about why a decision was taken were perceived as more trustable and led to higher acceptance of the solution. This is related to the fact that the effort invested in creating a decision is associated with the quality of the process and rationale behind it. This suggests that decision cards should be optimized to solve the tension between creating decision cards without disturbing the creative flow and including the correct amount of information. We found that using a digital version of decision cards facilitated for designers to include more information. However, it is clear that more content does not always generate more trust in the decision. For instance, if a decision card associated to the early stages of the design process contains many (technical) details, it is perceived as a less valuable decision since it does not document the ideation process that led to a solution.
- **Connected**. Decisions that are linked to artefacts, previous decisions, or support material (e.g. artefacts, notes) are perceived as more valuable. Connected decisions provide an overview of the evolution of an artefact making the flow of ideas evident. With connected decisions, a stronger rationale is build: following the links between decisions, various aspects of the resulting design get an underpinning. It adds traceability that can be used to track the evolution of a project from the beginning up until the most recent design decision.
- **Inclusive**. Decisions that include a larger representation of team members involved in a project were more interesting: they involve multiple opinions and perspectives. Decision cards that include relevant questions and/or discussion were considered as more inclusive, even if less team members were explicitly mentioned in the decision card. This type of content as part of a decision card implied that the voices of the team members had an impact on the design process. Note that the roles that are represented by team members listed on a decision card, are also considered to be an important aspect. If an essential role is missing (e.g. a designer is not part of a decision on graphical layout), the decision card might lose its value.

These properties are guidelines to inform design rationale systems on what content and level of detail to record as a decision. We argue that a minimally structured way of documenting decisions provide a suitable tradeoff between efforts and benefits for capturing and retrieving design rationale.

8 Conclusion

While there are tools and notations to record the design decision rationale, they remain unused as they fail to be incorporated in the practices of design teams. In this paper we proposed an approach to capture and externalize the design decisions in an organic and straight-forward way: *decision cards*. Our results showed that decision cards allowed designers to elaborate their decisions freely. Furthermore, decision cards facilitated team members to understand the flow of ideas and decisions taken by a team, even when these team members were not part in the design process. Decision cards provide a way to reflect on the design process both to each team member individually and to the entire design team. We consider decision cards as a starting point to create a bridge between structured and rigid documentation of design rationale, and an approach that matches the free flow of ideas that characterizes the design process. Furthermore, given the *actionable* and *informative* format of decision cards, they can be used from the conceptual stages of the design process to the later stages of the process.

A potential limitation of the decision cards could be that it requires designers to spend time and effort in documenting the decision. However, designers who were involved in our studies creating decision cards recognize the long-term benefits of having such a record of their process. Future validations of decision cards will benefit from longitudinal, in-the-wild studies. The evidence we gathered in controlled (but realistic) situations suggests that decision cards, in combination with design artefacts, can be used for supporting awareness and traceability on the design process.

Acknowledgements. This research was supported by the COnCEPT project, funded by the European Commission 7th Framework ICT Research project (no. 610725). We give special thanks to the designers involved in our studies, and to our colleagues Jesús Muñoz Alcantara (Eindhoven University of Technology) and Benny Daems for their input and support for the co-located workshop.

References

1. Mentis, H.M., Bach, P.M., Hoffman, B., Rosson, M.B., Carroll, J.M.: Development of decision rationale in complex group decision making. In: CHI 2009 Proceedings of the SIGCHI Conference on Human Factors in Computing Systems, pp. 1341–1350. ACM, New York (2009)
2. Haug, A.: Emergence patterns for client design requirements. Des. Stud. **39**, 48–69 (2015)
3. D'Astous, P., Détienne, F., Visser, W., Robillard, P.N.: Changing our view on design evaluation meetings methodology: a study of software technical review meetings. Des. Stud. **25**, 625–655 (2004)
4. Klemmer, S.R., Thomsen, M., Phelps-Goodman, E., Lee, R., Landay, J.A.: Where do web sites come from?: Capturing and interacting with design history. In: CHI 2002 Proceedings of the SIGCHI Conference on Human Factors in Computing Systems, pp. 1–8. ACM, New York (2002)
5. Burge, J.E.: Design rationale: researching under uncertainty. Artif. Intell. Eng. Des. Anal. Manuf. **22**, 311–324 (2008)

6. Horner, J., Atwood, M.E.: Design rationale: the rationale and the barriers. In: NordiCHI 2006 Proceedings of the 4th Nordic Conference on Human-Computer Interaction: Changing Roles, pp. 341–350. ACM, New York (2006)
7. Bardzell, J., Bardzell, S., Dalsgaard, P., Gross, S., Halskov, K.: Documenting the research through design process. In: DIS 2016 Proceedings of the ACM Conference on Designing Interactive Systems, pp. 96–107. ACM, New York (2016)
8. Schön, D.A.: The Reflective Practitioner. Temple Smith, London (1983)
9. Dorst, K.: Design problems and design paradoxes. Des. Issues **22**, 4–17 (2006)
10. Dorst, K., Cross, N.: Creativity in the design process: co-evolution of problem-solution. Des. Stud. **22**, 425–437 (2001)
11. Warr, A., O'Neill, E.: Understanding design as a social creative process. In: C&C 2005 Proceedings of the 5th Conference on Creativity & Cognition, pp. 118–127. ACM, New York (2005)
12. Buchanan, R.: Wicked problems in design thinking. Des. Issues **8**, 5–21 (1992)
13. Cross, N.: Design cognition: results from protocol and other empirical studies of design activity. In: Eastman, C., Newstatter, W., McCracken, M. (eds.) Design Knowing and Learning: Cognition in Design Education, pp. 79–103. Elsevier, Oxford (2001)
14. Dow, S.P., Fortuna, J., Schwartz, D., Altringer, B., Schwartz, D., Klemmer, S.: Prototyping dynamics: sharing multiple designs improves exploration, group rapport, and results. In: CHI 2011 Proceedings of the SIGCHI Conference on Human Factors in Computing Systems, pp. 2807–2816. ACM, New York (2011)
15. Shum, S.B., Hammond, N.: Argumentation-based design rationale: what use at what cost? Int. J. Hum Comput Stud. **40**, 603–652 (1994)
16. Shipman, F.M., McCall, R.J.: Integrating different perspectives on design rationale: supporting the emergence of design rationale from design communication. Artif. Intell. Eng. Des. Anal. Manuf. **11**, 141–154 (1997)
17. Stempfle, J., Badke-Schaub, P.: Thinking in design teams - an analysis of team communication. Des. Stud. **23**, 473–496 (2002)
18. MacLean, A., Young, R., Bellotti, V., Moran, T.: Questions, options, and criteria: elements of design space analysis. Hum.-Comput. Interact. **6**, 201–250 (1991)
19. Conklin, E.J., Yakemovic, K.C.B.: A process-oriented approach to design rationale. Hum.-Comput. Interact. **6**, 357–391 (1991)
20. Shum, S.J.B., Selvin, A.M., Sierhuis, M., Conklin, J., Haley, C.B., Nuseibeh, B.: Hypermedia support for argumentation-based rationale: 15 years on from gIBIS and QOC. In: Dutoit, A.H., McCall, R., Mistrík, I., Paech, B. (eds.) Rationale Management in Software Engineering, pp. 111–132. Springer, Heidelberg (2006). doi:10.1007/978-3-540-30998-7_5
21. Lee, J.: SIBYL: a tool for managing group decision rationale. In: CSCW 1990 Proceedings of the 1990 ACM Conference on Computer-Supported Cooperative Work, pp. 79–92. ACM, New York (1990)
22. Dalsgaard, P., Halskov, K.: Reflective design documentation. In: DIS 2012 Proceedings of the ACM Conference on Designing Interactive Systems, pp. 428–437. ACM, New York (2012)
23. Zimmerman, J., Stolterman, E., Forlizzi, J.: An analysis and critique of research through design: towards a formalization of a research approach. In: DIS 2010 Proceedings of the ACM Conference on Designing Interactive Systems, pp. 310–319. ACM, New York (2010)
24. Wahid, S., Branham, S.M., McCrickard, D.S., Harrison, S.: Investigating the relationship between imagery and rationale in design. In: DIS 2010 Proceedings of the ACM Conference on Designing Interactive Systems, pp. 75–84. ACM, New York (2010)

25. Sutcliffe, A.G., Carroll, J.M.: Designing claims for reuse in interactive systems design. Int. J. Hum.-Comput. Stud. **50**, 213–241 (1999)
26. Halskov, K., Dalsgård, P.: Inspiration card workshops. In: DIS 2006 Proceedings of the ACM Conference on Designing Interactive Systems, pp. 2–11. ACM, New York (2006)
27. Dalsgaard, P., Halskov, K., Nielsen, R.: Maps for design reflection. Artifact **2**, 176–189 (2008)
28. Gaver, W.: Making spaces: how design workbooks work. In: CHI 2011 Proceedings of the SIGCHI Conference on Human Factors in Computing Systems, pp. 1551–1560. ACM, New York (2011)
29. Sharmin, M., Bailey, B.P., Coats, C., Hamilton, K.: Understanding knowledge management practices for early design activity and its implications for reuse. In: CHI 2009 Proceedings of the SIGCHI Conference on Human Factors in Computing Systems, pp. 2367–2376. ACM, New York (2009)
30. Gutierrez Lopez, M., Luyten, K., Vanacken, D., Coninx, K.: Untangling design meetings: artefacts as input and output of design activities. In: ECCE 2017 Proceedings of the 35th Conference of the European Association of Cognitive Ergonomics (2017, in press)
31. Sharmin, M., Bailey, B.P.: Making sense of communication associated with artifacts during early design activity. In: Campos, P., Graham, N., Jorge, J., Nunes, N., Palanque, P., Winckler, M. (eds.) INTERACT 2011. LNCS, vol. 6946, pp. 181–198. Springer, Heidelberg (2011). doi:10.1007/978-3-642-23774-4_17

Coping with Design Complexity: A Conceptual Framework for Design Alternatives and Variants

Judy Bowen[1] and Anke Dittmar[2(✉)]

[1] The University of Waikato, Hamilton, New Zealand
jbowen@waikato.ac.nz
[2] University of Rostock, Rostock, Germany
anke.dittmar@uni-rostock.de

Abstract. Interaction design processes are characterised by multi-disciplinary teamwork and by an interplay of creative, situated and analytical thinking. Although design in the domain of human-computer interaction has been widely investigated, the focus of research has been mainly on the user's role and several authors refer to the need for a deeper understanding of the increasingly complex interaction design processes. This paper suggests a conceptual framework for interaction design that accommodates and unifies different perspectives from general design research while considering the specificities of the domain. Within the framework, description and analysis is done through the lens of design spaces, design artefacts, and refinement relationships between design artefacts. The framework extends existing concepts of design spaces by introducing complex spaces which acknowledge that design is rarely an individual activity but is more often undertaken by teams of designers. The framework also offers a distinction between design options into alternatives and variants to better describe and guide processes of idea generation and a convergence within, and between different sub-spaces and sub-teams. Different types of refinement between design artefacts are also discussed.

1 Introduction

Digital interactive systems have become more pervasive in work and everyday life. They now play an important role in how people interact with each other and the world. As a consequence, interaction designers are faced with an increasing design complexity [35]. They need to know the needs of people and the possibilities offered by technologies in order to explore and design technological solutions that fit in with users, the activities they want to undertake and the contexts surrounding those activities [3]. Design in the domain of human-computer interaction (HCI) has been widely investigated since the beginning of the field, but research has tended to focus on the user's role in the design process and the effects of designed artefacts on users [39, 43]. This is also reflected in practical design approaches such as user-centred design stating that iterative development and an early focus on the users' tasks and goals drive quality design, or participatory design emphasising the active participation of all stakeholders. While this research is very valuable, and even more so because less considered in other

© IFIP International Federation for Information Processing 2017
Published by Springer International Publishing AG 2017. All Rights Reserved
R. Bernhaupt et al. (Eds.): INTERACT 2017, Part I, LNCS 10513, pp. 483–502, 2017.
DOI: 10.1007/978-3-319-67744-6_30

design fields, the focus is too narrow [39]. HCI research "has not been grounded in and guided by a sufficient understanding and acceptance of the nature of design practice" [35]. (Similarly to [35], the terms HCI research and interaction design research are used interchangeably in the context of this paper.) Stolterman and other authors refer to existing design theories and empirical work (e.g., from cognitive design research) that could be fruitful for HCI research to better inform and improve interaction design practices [35, 39, 43].

In this paper we propose a conceptual framework aiming at supporting a deeper understanding of interaction design processes. It accommodates and unifies different perspectives from general design research while considering the specificities of interaction design. Within the framework, description and analysis is done through the lens of *design spaces*, *design artefacts*, and *refinement relationships* between design artefacts. The concept of design space is widely used in the literature but with different understandings. In the context of this paper, we take a similar stance to Westerlund [40] and consider a design space as a space 'populated' by design artefacts. The concept describes design processes as goal-oriented but situated processes of constructing and relating design artefacts. Here, the term 'goal-oriented' is meant to be inclusive and can be interpreted from different design perspectives (e.g., from a value-driven perspective). The starting point in our approach is the assumption that there is a 'contract' between the designer and the user which basically says that however intangible the design process might be there always emerges at least a minimum set of requirements which must be satisfied by the final design. In our framework, every external design representation that is created for an intended use, or becomes meaningful in the design process, is considered to be a design artefact (e.g., design prompts, sketches, prototypes, scenarios, formal specifications or implemented products). Designers when 'entering' a design space are provided with some initial design artefacts which can be interpreted as requirements or design constraints. Their subsequent exploration of emerging design ideas and constraints leaves traces in the design space: new design artefacts are created, some artefacts are modified, others discarded. Even if the designers' moves within the design space may appear arbitrary their ultimate goal is to fulfil their contracts with users by finally creating design artefacts that implement or refine the initially provided ones. What is therefore equally important to idea generation is the designers' ability to compare different design artefacts and understand how they are related and whether or not they satisfy some initial or evolving design specifications and constraints. This paper introduces and illustrates different types of refinement that are relevant in interaction design processes. The suggested classification is based on an analysis of existing design paradigms and perspectives from literature. In the simplest case, if design is considered as problem solving, design artefacts describe the solution (i.e., the interactive device to be developed) at different levels of abstraction in a process of stepwise refinement. More complex understandings of design situations produce more diverse design artefacts and refinement relationships including descriptions of the design process itself.

Interaction design typically takes place in multi-disciplinary teams with co-design phases and phases of distributed work [1]. On the one hand, it facilitates the application of multiple design perspectives, on the other hand, it adds to design complexity due to additional coordination efforts, different working practices, distributed decision making etc. However, in most existing design space concepts, collaborative design activities are insufficiently accommodated. To address this problem, the presented framework extends the common ideas with a more elaborated description of the structure of design spaces. *Complex design spaces* are introduced which are hierarchically decomposed into sub-spaces until the level of simple design spaces (as described above). Participants in complex design spaces are neither exclusively users nor exclusively designers but are rather engaged in a *network of designer-user relationships* by using design artefacts provided by other participants or sub-teams and by designing design artefacts for others.

Design space models such as Laseau's overlapping funnels (see Subsect. 2.3) illustrate a common view of design as the generation and the convergence of design ideas. Designers need to bring creativity to the creation of distinct design options and the definition of criteria to choose between those options [7]. There is a criticism that decision making, in this context, is mostly understood as a process of selecting one option and that this attitude may impede a diversity of design ideas [40]. A specific characteristic of our proposed framework is the distinction between *alternatives* and *variants* as two different types of design options that 'leave' the sub-spaces of a complex design space. Basically, if designers in a sub-space resolve all discussion points or disagreements an *alternative* is selected among generated options and provided to other sub-teams. However, if designers of a sub-space want to (partly) delay decision making to include viewpoints and expertise from other sub-teams they provide a set of options (i.e. *variants*) as outcomes. The distinction between alternatives and variants may contribute to a more balanced view of design complexity.

The paper starts with a detailed review of the different existing perspectives on design. The specificities of interaction design and corresponding notions of design space are discussed. We also review results from formal software design which informed the development of our framework. Based on the given background, Sect. 3 introduces and explains the basic concepts of the suggested framework. Then, Sect. 4 considers its application by discussing an illustrative design situation. Furthermore, some results of an exploratory empirical study are briefly discussed. The paper closes with a discussion along with future work and conclusions (Sect. 5).

2   Background and Related Work

Design activities are unique human activities of inquiry and action [35]. Stolterman additionally emphasises that design deals with the specific: "[i]t is about creating something in the world with a *specific* purpose, for a *specific* situation, for a *specific* client and user… and done within a *limited time* and with *limited resources*" [35]. The intended changes are often characterised as changes that are desired [35] or that improve the current world [11]. Interaction design in particular is "the specification of digital behaviours in response to human or machine stimuli" [16]. In a larger sense, interaction design is the creation of spaces enabling complex webs of interactions between people and multiple interactive devices [41]. It addresses the question of which actions and experiences should be supported by a particular interaction space and how to achieve it. Jackson [20] points out that the complexity of interactions is a general theme in many design disciplines but especially when it comes to the design of software systems. In [35], a recognition and acceptance of both the complexity of the artefact under design and the complexity of the design situation itself is demanded. This section reviews conceptualisations and perspectives on (interaction) design and design complexity. It discusses the different but overlapping understandings of design activities, relevant design artefacts and design spaces.

2.1   Paradigms in Cognitive Design Research

From a cognitive perspective, design is commonly understood as a satisficing activity aimed at finding "good enough" solutions to "ill-structured" problems [39]. Existing paradigms differ in their assumptions about design problems and their treatment [13].

The Rational Problem Solving Paradigm. In the classical view of design that goes back to Herbert Simon in the late 1960's, design problems are assumed to be given and design is seen as rational search in a 'problem space' [13]. Even if problems are ill-structured they can be transformed into structured ones that can be tackled by decomposition [39]. This view is to be found, for example, in traditional software design methodologies with stepwise refinement. Formal refinement (which we discuss further in Sect. 3) provides structured mechanisms for transforming specifications and models (formal design artefacts) into implementations. Typically this is done via a number of small transformations (or steps) which each move closer to a final solution - hence, stepwise refinement. Wirth [42] recommends for software design "to decompose decisions as much as possible, to untangle aspects which are only seemingly interdependent, and to defer those decisions which concern details of representation as long as possible." Such simplification of the nature of design problems and corresponding overestimation of systematic problem decomposition have been criticised later. However, it is worth noting that Wirth, in his paper from 1971(!), already mentions ideas of design rationale: "[e]very refinement step implies some design decisions. It is important that these decisions be made explicit, and that the programmer be aware of the underlying criteria and of the existence of alternative solutions... [this] may be particularly helpful in the situation of changing purpose and environment to which a program may sometime have to be adapted" [42].

Design as Argumentation Process. The distinction between wicked (ill-defined) and tamed (well-defined) problems in [32] is one of the first attempts to overcome the limitations of the problem solving paradigm. According to Rittel and Webber, most design problems are wicked problems which cannot be defined independently from their solution. Among other characteristics, wicked problems are unique and every implemented solution has consequences that have to be taken into further consideration. Rittel and Webber [32] state that "part of the art of dealing with wicked problems is the art of not knowing too early what type of solution to apply" and suggest instead a collaborative argumentative process of considering and negotiating emerging issues and possible solutions. Design rationale approaches which explain and record why an artifact is designed the way it is are based on argumentation and can be classified into two broad categories [23]. Structure-oriented approaches and corresponding notations such as Design Space Analysis with the QOC notation (*Q*uestion, *O*ptions, *C*riteria)

[25] help to identify relevant design issues and to explore and assess alternative solutions. They became popular in HCI research in the 1990's [27] and more recently in other areas of software design [36, 37]. Psychological design rationale approaches are more holistic and follow task-artifact cycles. First, tasks are identified that should be supported by the system under design and scenarios are created for a collaborative exploration of possible consequences of using it. After its introduction, the system's actual use is studied and compared with the designers' assumptions. Observed negative effects are addressed in a next iteration of the design.

The Reflective Practice Paradigm goes back to the work of Schön [34] who considers design situations as 'messy' situations in which designers find themselves and which they cannot tackle by applying predefined methods. Instead the designer must be in a reflective conversation with the design material of the specific situation. Design is understood as problem setting or framing and Schön describes design exploration as 'moves' within a problem frame where the designer uses 'reflection-in-action' (move, observe, re-frame) as an intuitive process and 'reflection-on-action' as a tool to develop a repertoire of design experience. In current research, the designers' behaviour is commonly described as solution-led: designers jump to ideas for solutions before they have fully analysed the problem and they transfer the developed partial solution structures back into the problem space to extend the problem description and to consider implications of alternative solutions [8]. Cross points out in this context that "both generating few alternative concepts and generating a large number of alternatives were equally weak strategies, leading to poor design solutions" [8].

Designing as Construction of Representations. The above mentioned approaches are not necessarily contradictory but rather focus on different aspects of design activities. Dorst [13] notes, for example, that the designer's expertise influences their perception of the nature of a design problem. While the rule-following behaviour of novice designers must be described following the problem solving paradigm, the behaviour of competent designers, their involvement in and reflection on design situations need an additional explanation within the reflective practice paradigm [13]. Besides that designers are typically faced with both routine (tamed) and nonroutine (wicked) problems requiring either the application of well-known procedures or more advanced approaches [39]. Jackson [20] argues similarly that, in any design task, there must be a combination of 'normal' (routine) design (with well-known requirements and corresponding design experience) and 'radical' (nonroutine) design (with no presumption of success). Studies about co-design activities of teams aimed at a shared understanding of the design problem and possible solutions often use an argumentative approach for their analysis. For example, the QOC approach [25] has been applied in [30] to analyse the discussions of software designers. Viewpoints have been studied in [10] and it has been shown that, during a multi-disciplinary meeting, the participants express different viewpoints which further evolve through an argumentation process (including arguments by comparison, analogy, and authority) until integrated viewpoints are constructed and shared by the participants. Viewpoints, in this context, are representations of certain combinations of design constraints.

Common to all design approaches is their recognition of the role of design representations although with differences in what should be represented and for what purpose. According to Visser [39], design is about generating, transforming, and evaluating representations "until they are so concrete, detailed, and precise that the resulting representation... specify explicitly and completely the implementation of the artefact [under design]". The author suggests, therefore, to consider design activities as domain-specific construction of representations and to pay attention to both: the created design representations and the corresponding construction process. In our framework, we follow a similar approach and focus on external representations in interaction design and how designers relate them to arrive at the digital interactive artefact.

2.2   Specificity of Interaction Design

Cross [9] describes how in earlier times the making of artefacts was not separated from the design process. A potter, for instance, used no distinct external design representations and worked directly with the clay to make a pot. In the design of interactive software systems, although we do have a variety of design representations (sketches, scenarios etc.) there is not always a clear distinction between such representations and the end-products, as ideations may be extended into implementations or prototypes may evolve to the final system. Even models of users or context-of-use models may be incorporated into the systems. Therefore, the intermingled character of design and surrounding activities that generally exists [39] is intensified further. Later in our framework, we consider every external representation (including descriptions of initial ideas and requirements up to and including the final implementation) that is created for intended use, or becomes meaningful a *design artefact* (*design*, in short) and do not distinguish between requirements analysis, design and implementation activities.

Role of Users in the Design Process. HCI research was dominated for a long time by considering and rethinking the users' role in the design process. Three approaches are shortly discussed here: user-centred design, participatory design and meta-design. User-centred design [17] requires from the design team an early focus on the goals, tasks and needs of the users, on the work domain, and on the specific context of use. Participatory design approaches emphasise that the introduction of new interactive artifacts transforms work or everyday life. Conflicts are therefore inherent to interaction design processes and must be resolved by the active participation of all stakeholders [4]. User-centred and participatory approaches have been criticised as being engineering approaches to design with a limited understanding and support of creative design practices (see the above subsection) [14, 16, 35, 43]. However, their contributions to improve the designer-user relationship and to increase the understanding that interaction design has to be embedded in a deliberate transformation of the users' practices are invaluable. An interesting related approach is the idea of meta-design introduced in the context of end-user development by Fischer et al. [15]. The authors question that designers should aim at developing complete systems (a goal in conventional design) because user needs and usage situations are never fully predictable. Instead, design is considered to be an open and continuous process with the designers acting as meta-designers who apply a technique called under-design to provide design spaces for the end users (seeding stage) allowing them to act as co-designers by appropriating the system to their specific context of use (stage of evolutionary growth) and by sharing with the designers (re-seeding stage). In our framework, designer and user are not considered to be identities but roles. Participants in the design process typically act in both roles. This view is informed by the above approaches, but especially inspired by Morgan's ideas [28] presented in the following paragraph.

Separation from and Integration with Software Engineering. Winograd [41] predicted the (partial) detachment of the field of interaction design from mainstream computer science because of the foreign methods, skills, and techniques that were required for understanding people and designing spaces for human communication and interaction. In contrast, Diaper [11] suggests that the historical division between HCI and software engineering is unfortunate "because both are engineering disciplines concerned with the same types of systems and their difference is merely one of emphasis, with software engineering focusing more on software and HCI more on people". Above we have seen arguments against a purely engineering approach to interaction design, but nonetheless software engineers and interaction designers collaborate in multi-disciplinary design processes characterised by phases of distributed work where each designer or sub-team has their own sub-task to perform and by co-design phases where participants share goals and contribute to their achievement by applying different perspectives [1]. Co-design is necessary, for example, if usability concerns have to be considered early in the software architecture [21]. Bellotti et al. [2] argue that for an effective collaboration, a revision of each others' assumptions can be necessary. As an example, the authors refer to the conventional notion in the software engineering community that "formal methods are only useful if used within a structured development context from the beginning of a project, through refinement, to implementation". However, a strength of formal approaches may be their suitability for unifying ideas. Robin Milner describes in his Turing award lecture [26] the striving for unifying frameworks at the example of concurrent computation. "I reject the idea that there can be a unique conceptual model, or one preferred formalism, for all aspects of something as large as concurrent computation... we need many *levels of explanation*: many different languages, calculi, and theories for the different specialisms... But there is a complementary *claim* to make, and it is this: Computer scientists, as all scientists, seek a common framework in which to link and to organise many levels of explanation." Our framework is influenced by Morgan's uniform approach to refinement in software design [28]. He suggests banishing the distinction between specifications, sub-specifications, and computer programs and considering all of them as programs. Programs are contracts which have to be negotiated between clients and programmers. They describe what one person wants (the client role) and what another person or computer must do (the programmer role). A hierarchical refinement of programs is assumed (starting with high-level specifications until programs, executable on the computer) which is closely associated with the problem solving perspective.

External Design Representations. According to [39], the ultimate design representation must express three aspects of the artefact under design: the what (the artefact itself), the how (the process of implementation), and the why (the design rationale). Design representations in interaction design can support what is called by Diaper [11] the narrow view of HCI focusing on the user-computer interface or the broad view concerning "with everything to do with people and computers" including real-world consequences. Typical forms of representing the what, according to the narrow view, are sketches, prototypes, and models of the user interface, but also functional models of the digital interactive artefact. QOC diagrams [25], claims as known from scenario-based design [33], and task models as used in [31] reveal some of the why, process models such as the evaluation-centred star life cycle model [19] some of the how. Problem and interaction scenarios [33], current and envisioned task models as recommended in [11] or user models such as personas [18] are representations supporting the deliberate transformation of the users' (working) practices, and hence, the broader view of HCI design. Flexible design processes need to be supported by a co-evolution of the various design representations. Although there are approaches to relate different types of representations such as user interface sketches and formal specifications [5], task models and QOC-diagrams [22], or prototyping and argumentation [12], the effective coupling of different external representations is still poorly understood in interaction design. What we especially consider in our framework is the designers' ability to compare representations and understand how they are related and whether or not they satisfy some initial or evolving requirements and constraints.

2.3   Design Spaces

The concept of design space is central to the suggested framework. Before introducing the framework in the next section, we briefly discuss existing conceptions of design spaces to position our view. In engineering contexts, a design space is often understood as being defined along a set of (possibly orthogonal) dimensions. For example, Nigay and Coutaz [29] suggest a design space for multi-modal systems in terms of level of abstraction, use of modalities and fusion. Design spaces, in this sense, support a view of designing as problem solving. They are generic tools providing a common vocabulary for classifying and comparing system designs (determined by certain values for the dimensions) which guide the designers in choosing an optimal solution for their design problems. Some proponents of design rationale understand design spaces both as a conceptual tool guiding argumentation processes and as "an explicit representation of alternative design options, and the reasons for choosing among those options" [24] which emerged in a particular argumentation process. They suggest that the result of a design process should be conceived as a design space rather than a single specification or product. While corresponding representations such as QOC-diagrams [24] depict how design options and criteria are related to each other, design space models such as

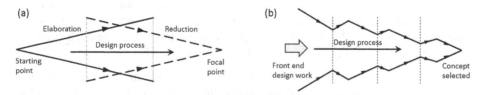

Fig. 1. The designer's moves in a design space: (a) Laseau's overlapping funnels, and (b) a refined version assuming some front-end work resulting in a product design specification and an alternation between concept generation and concept convergence step-wise leading to finer levels of granularity in the design (discussed in [7]).

Laseau's funnel model with its variants (Fig. 1) emphasise a balance between the designer's creation of distinct design options (concept generation in elaboration funnel) and decision making (concept convergence in the reduction funnel). The chosen design solution is represented by the focal point.

Westerlund [40] considers a design space as the set of "all possible design proposals that would be regarded as meaningful to use by some people in relevant contexts". He criticises the models in Fig. 1 for their assumption that the initial brief, assignment or problem will be stable during the process and for their focus on one goal and one final solution, which may impede a diversity of design ideas. In his view, proposals that work lie within the design space, proposals that do not work are outside the space [40]. This is in line with Binder et al. [38] who, from a creative design perspective, describe the emergence of a design space out of a collaborative process of creating and manipulating a variety of design representations or artefacts. Transforming representations and shifting between different material highlight different aspects of design and widen the design space. We follow the last mentioned authors and consider the design space concept as a tool for designing and understanding design processes, a tool for the reflective practitioner supporting a less prescriptive approach to design. However, to our knowledge, our approach of complex design spaces and the distinction between alternatives and variants is novel.

3 Basic Concepts of the Framework

3.1 Design Spaces and Design Artefacts

As our starting point we determine the existence of a design space as an essential entity within the design process. Even if it is not explicitly defined or understood by the design teams, the design space is the conceptual gathering together of all, and any, artefacts used within the process. Recall that we consider 'design artefacts' as any materialised form of design concepts (or ideas, constraints, discussions etc.) that form part of the design activities. At the most basic level we can imagine the solution to a small and straightforward design problem is found by the designer exploring several ideas in a linear fashion, before finalising and selecting one which satisfies the problem description. Of course, in interactive system design we are typically interested in much larger design problems and so extend this concept to the base case (one design team) as in Fig. 2(a) which is then part of the recursive definition of the complex design space in Fig. 2(b).

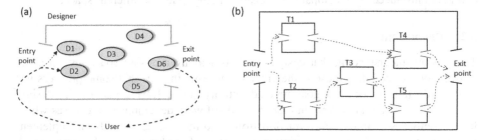

Fig. 2. (a) Simple design space, (b) complex design space with sub-spaces.

Within the simple design space each of the ellipses D1..D6 in Fig. 2(a) represents some design artefact. These may all be of different types and represent all and any considerations currently taking place within this part of the design process by any member of the team (individually or as a group). The entry and exit points shown represent the underlying user-designer relationship (where designers from other parts of the process may also be considered as users). The entry point indicates any initial designs or requirements provided to the designer, who in turn will provide designs at the exit point which satisfy some, or all of those requirements. The various artefacts (D1..D6) within the space may be considered as *alternatives* if one is chosen to leave at the exit point, or *variants* if a choice is not made and more than one leaves at the exit point as part of delayed decision-making. We discuss alternatives and variants in more detail later. We do not suppose that the design happens in a linear fashion from left to right within the space, but there are relationships between the different design artefacts, so designers may bounce around ideas and try out different things that are subsequently discarded, or use more formal techniques to make specific decisions around particular parts of the system design.

Given the multi-disciplinary approach typically taken within design, the actual design space is not simple, but is complex, as depicted in Fig. 2(b). Here each of T1.. T5 are sub-spaces, that is they are design spaces (and perhaps contain further sub-spaces), such that ultimately all of the different design processes from each of the groups and individuals involved in the process can be captured inside a single high-level design space. These are, of course, abstract representations (hence the term high-level), we can 'zoom in' on any one of the design artefacts to understand what it represents, and then how the different artefacts are related. Similar to the relationships between design artefacts, we see in the right hand picture of Fig. 2 of the complex design space the relationships between individual sub-spaces. These may be one-one, one-many, many-one etc. and uni- or multi-directional, e.g. some provide inputs only to other design spaces while others involve a 'negotiation'. We discuss these different types of relationship further and some potential underlying causes in Sect. 4.

These design spaces define the basic structure of our framework which then captures the ideas of multi-disciplinary teams working iteratively, both independently and together, towards a solution guided by an evolving understanding of the design problem and constraints (based upon an emerging set of requirements). Participants in the design process may not be aware of all of the design spaces but rather focus only in the area they are working. Hence the requirement to ensure that there is overall a consistency in the end-goal of all of the design spaces such that there are not additional conflicts introduced by incompatible decisions being made in different spaces.

3.2   Refinement

There is an understanding that design artefacts leaving a design space are, in some sense, more refined than those at the entry point. This implies that some progress has been made (design being a goal-directed activity) in at least a part of the design. Refinement is a central concept in more formal software development processes where it represents a structured transformation from a formal model towards an implementation in a way which guarantees certain properties of the formal model are preserved.

This understanding of refinement supports the problem solving perspective on design (see Subsect. 2.1) by assuming that the formal specification describes the right system to be built (the design problem is fully understood) and the refinement relationship ensures that the system is built in the right way. As we have shown above, interaction designers are mostly faced with 'wicked' design problems requiring a co-evolution of problem and solution. Hence, when we consider refinement in the context of interaction design we do not have the same concept of using a transformation calculus on a formal model of the interactive artefact to be developed. Rather we have to additionally consider intermediate design artefacts describing design rationales to support designers in understanding situations of use of that artefact as well as design artefacts describing the design situation itself to support designers in creating the right (complex) design space. Accordingly, we suggest four types of refinement.

1. Refinements based on formal methods to ensure to build the system right.
2. Refinements based on lightweight notions to ensure a transition between informal and formal designs.
3. Refinements based on validation techniques to ensure to build the right system.
4. Refinements based on reflection to ensure that the design process is right.

Our refinement approaches are framed in the idea of 'contractual utility' as in [5]. At its simplest, contractual utility implies that if our customer is satisfied with a system, S, we can replace it with system S' if it meets all of the criteria agreed upon (i.e. satisfies the contract) for S. This is often simply stated as "We can replace S with S' provided the customer can do all of the things they could do before (and perhaps more)". Note that in this notion of refinement the requirement to preserve properties (which may be the satisfaction of requirements or adherence to design decisions already made) remains. As such the entry and exit points in each of the design spaces represent a refinement relationship where artefacts at the exit point retain properties from those at the entry point but may also have additional properties (based on new decisions made) or the removal of variants which have come from other sub-spaces. Formally we consider that we can weaken pre-conditions and strengthen post-conditions as a legitimate refinement process, and that this results in a larger range of application situations of the artefact under design (weakening pre-conditions) and in a strengthening of expected desired effects and/or mitigating of expected undesired effects of using the artefact (strengthening post-conditions). We will further discuss the different forms of refinement in the next section by using an illustrative example.

3.3 Alternatives and Variants

We discussed briefly above the difference between alternatives and variants. These terms are frequently used interchangeably or without clear definition in the literature. One of our contributions here is to give such a definition which can then be used unambiguously in both our framework and in subsequent discussions. Both terms represent design artefacts of a design space which are related, in that they refine the artefacts in the entry point of that space, but which contain some differing options. We call *Alternatives* those artefacts where a choice is made which determines that one is selected over the other, so within a design space if there are several alternatives only one will be selected to leave the exit point. We call *Variants* those artefacts where decision-making is delayed or postponed for subsequent members of the design team to make. In other words, a single solution at the exit point (alternative) represents a closed process of generating possible solutions and choosing a good one (reduction of design complexity) while variants stand for a somewhat open decision process (keeping or increasing design complexity). In the latter case, the designer provides options to the user which share some common elements, but not all, to satisfy the requirements. However, the designer is aware that it is beyond their current competency and knowledge to make a selection or that a selection would unnecessarily limit the user's activities, including their creativity. This awareness is especially important in multi-disciplinary work. So design variants may proceed through the entire set of design spaces and may even end up as choices in the final system that the end-user can decide upon (as a form of personalisation or customisation).

4   Application of Framework

In this section, we first illustrate the application of the framework by discussing a small example design situation. Then, some results of an exploratory empirical study are shortly presented that support the subsequent discussion of the framework.

4.1   Illustrative Example

The example design situation is completely fictive but loosely based on the classic Bomberman game, a strategic, maze-based computer game, in which the players have to place bombs to kill enemies and destroy walls. The original game was published in 1983 and new games have been published ever since (Wikipedia). We identify some design artefacts and refinements of the example along with a discussion of the different types of the refinement relationships.

Design Spaces and Design Artefacts in the Example. Let us imagine that the example design process was initiated by parents expressing their concerns about seeing their young children playing Bomberman. They asked a professional design team to create a less aggressive version of the game (initial design goal). The professional team decided to start their work by analysing gaming practices of children to get a better understanding of the design problem (sub-team T1) and developing in parallel conceptual design ideas (sub-team T2). Based on interviews and observations, sub-team T1 developed a set of current scenarios (see scenario S1 in Fig. 3 as an example) that supported a revised description of the design goal. They handed over their results to sub-team T3 who had to create a first prototype. Meanwhile sub-team T2 came up with some ideas and assessments but made no final commitment. Instead, they provided a QOC-diagram to sub-team T3 (black text of Fig. 4). T3 realised that the ideas captured in the QOC-diagram do not satisfy the revised design goal and they asked T2 to rethink their ideas. T2 added a new option (O22) to question Q2 which lead to a consequent design question (Q3). They also added a new dimension concerning the design of the field maps (grey text of Fig. 4). Based on this modified diagram sub-team T3 developed a family of prototypes representing all combinations of suggested options (with tiles and objects represented in an abstract way by coloured squares and circles, see left part of Fig. 5). It was then decided to organise a workshop together with parents and children (sub-team T4). The participants (working in sub-groups) reflected on the prototypes by discussing the current scenarios and developing envisioned usage scenarios of the new design (e.g., scenario S2 in Fig. 3). They made suggestions for concrete tiles and objects (e.g., grass and water tiles, pump and life vest). They further required a 'softer' way to defeat an opponent than in the original game. Finally, they decided to restrict the set of all possible game variants to a smaller set of predefined game configurations which the end-user can choose between. The advanced prototype shown on the right of Fig. 5 and the supporting envisioned scenarios left the exit point of the design space of sub-team T4. Table 1 gives an overview of the design artefacts provided to and by the sub-teams.

Current scenario S1:	**Envisioned scenario S2:**
It is a Thursday evening and Jack is playing bomberman when his younger brother Thomas enters his room and immediately starts begging to play himself. As so often, Jack gives in. He interrupts his actual game and switches to the two-player mode. He would have preferred to leave Thomas alone but after the recent discussions with their mother he hesitates to do so.	It is a Thursday evening and Jack is playing his newest bomberman version when his younger brother Thomas enters his room and immediately starts begging to play himself. As so often, Jack gives in. He interrupts his actual game, but before starting a new instance, he switches to the two-player mode and to the diamonds collecting variant...

Fig. 3. Scenarios in the example.

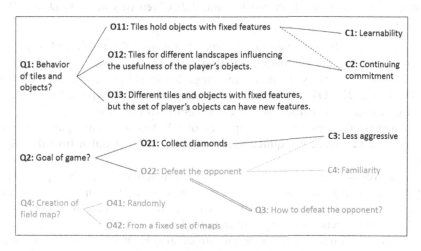

Fig. 4. A QOC-diagram in the example.

 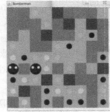 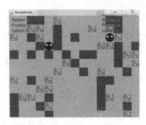

Fig. 5. Prototypes in the example.

Table 1. Design sub-spaces and design artefacts D1..D8 in the example.

Space	Designs in entry point	Designs in exit point
T1	**D1:** less aggressive Bomberman (initial design goal)	**D3:** less aggressive Bomberman but still with familiar game concepts, **D4:** current scenarios supporting D3
T2	**D1** (in the second iteration: **D3**), **D2:** original game concepts	**D5:** QOC-diagram (modified in the second generation)
T3	**D3, D4, D5**	**D6:** family of prototypes
T4	**D4, D5, D6**	**D7:** advanced prototype, **D8:** envisioned scenarios supporting D7

Refinement in the Example. We return now to the considerations of refinement. As mentioned above, we follow an approach framed in the idea of 'contractual utility' between the designer and the user: a design (or set of designs) D' refines D (and thus can replace D) if the user gets at least what they had before (with D) or better. We can break these ideas down further and show how the designs from the example fit within the refinement conditions described in Sect. 3.2. Given two designs, D and D', D' refines D

- if it preserves all properties of D: Properties here refer to all and any design requirements and criteria that emerge during the design process.

  Example: For every game variant suggested in D5 (specified by (O11, O21, O41), (O12, O21, O42) etc.) there is a corresponding prototype in D6.
- if it preserves all properties of D and has additional properties.

  Example: D3 preserves the properties of D1 (less aggressive game) but additionally the new game is required to have game concepts familiar from the original one.
- if it removes non-determinism present in D: Non-determinism can be represented by an abstract description or by a set of variants provided by D. Consequently, it can be decreased by more concrete designs (preserving properties of the abstract design but adding design decisions) or by a reduction of variants.

  Example: D7 removes non-determinism existing in D6 in at least two ways: first, by deciding about concrete tiles and objects in the game, and second, by reducing the set of variants provided by D6 to a smaller set.

Types of Refinement in the Example. Of course without giving formal definitions for the refinements described it may appear that anything can be considered a refinement provided we frame it correctly, but this is not the case. It is, however, also not the case that a direct refinement between the initial artefact and the final design choice exists. We frame the refinement to encompass all of the emerging requirements in addition to the starting point. In fact this is also true of 'classical' refinement in formal software development, where requirements (which are assumed to exist prior to the creation of the specification) are all contained within that specification and as such form part of the refinement. One of the differences here is that the evolution of the design artefacts can represent a co-evolution of problem understanding and solution. In other words, requirements may co-evolve and so need to be added to the refinement considerations.

Let us discuss a more concrete example of this in terms of our example which starts with a request to change the Bomberman game so that it is suitable for a younger age-group, and it may be that this leads to decisions that restrict or remove behaviours that were present in the original game. What the refinement relationship does then is enable us to keep track of the effects of design decisions and understand them in the context of the design process. So, in the example the addition of the constraints that will make the game less aggressive mean that the new version will not be a 'classical' refinement of the original (e.g., we cannot do everything we could before) but it satisfies the requirements and constraints such that the design process leads to a satisfactory refinement. Using the labels given in Table 1, we have:

- D7 does *not* refine D2
- (D7 and D8) refine (D2 and D4 and D3)

The envisioned scenarios in addition to the description of the redesigned Bomberman game can be considered to be a refinement of the current scenarios, the existing Bomberman game, and the initial and later refined design goal because we preserve something in the envisioned scenario as older and younger children still seem to like to play the game, and we get something additional (desired): that the younger children can play a less aggressive variant with less concerns of some parents. This then is a refinement based on validation (building the right system). Such a refinement also implies that we discard some parts of the existing implementation, in the example some restriction or removal of behaviours of the original game. This reflects the fact that to build the right system must always include negotiations between different viewpoints and compromises, and here explicitly the new scenario and requirements contradict some behaviours of the original game. We do not assume that classical refinement is abandoned in the development process, but rather that we embed it into our more loose definition of refinement based on validation during the design phases. So while in classical refinement concepts, the emphasis is on "building the right system in the right way", here our emphasis is on the first part only: "building the right system" (although of course we assume that this will also ultimately be achieved in the right way once the design is complete). Similarly, refinement based on validation has to be embedded into refinement based on reflection upon the actual design activities. For reasons of brevity, this is slightly indicated rather than fully described in the example. But it may be easy to imagine, e.g., that sub-team T4, if only consisting of professional designers and children (or professional designers and parents), could have come to different decisions based on a different 'building' of arguments.

Alternatives and Variants in the Example. Alternatives, even if they come with some supporting arguments, hide most of the complexity of design sub-spaces. In the example, team T1 may have discussed various refinements of D1 but only D3 (supported by scenarios D4, see Table 1) leaves the exit point, nothing is known outside T1's sub-space about those alternative refinements of D1. In contrast, variants keep some of the partly emerging complexity outside a sub-space. Game variants are created at a conceptual level by sub-team T2 (QOC-diagram D5), 'passed over' from sub-team T3 to T4 via the family of prototypes (D6), and in a restricted form finally to the end-users such as Jack in the scenario S2 (Fig. 3). Jack not only plays the Bomberman game but also 'designs' an appropriate setting for his brother Thomas to play.

4.2 Exploratory Study

The actual types of artefacts included in the design spaces will be particular to a given design situation (characterised by the design problem, the design team and sub-teams etc.) but we expect in our framework that there will be a common set of attributes seen across all design sub-spaces. That is, sub-teams have similar behaviours in discussing the problems, options, decision making and explicitly create and forward design artefacts to other sub-teams as we describe it in the framework. So where some people may use diagrams to explicitly elaborate decisions to be made along with accompanying sketches, others may have design meetings where such decision making takes place as discussion and they create representations of their results afterwards to provide them to other sub-teams. To start investigating the applicability of the suggested framework as a descriptive tool for design processes we conducted exploratory studies of two small design teams. While the focus of our work here is to present our general framework and its uses rather than explicitly discuss the case studies, the knowledge gained from these has enhanced our understanding of the use of such a framework in real-world design processes. Hence, we present a brief overview of one of the studies and discuss some of the results.

The study took place within a locally based web-design company who were tasked with re-designing the web site of a large medical company. The design process took place over a period of 6 months and there were 6 members from the design company involved, 5 of whom were co-located. The other team member, who was the project manager, was located in the company head office 150 km away, close to the client. Communications between co-located team members occurred in face-to-face meetings as well as via email and the use of specific design tools and online meetings were used to communicate with the project manager. The project manager and clients had face-to-face meetings. Although the primary focus of the study was to identify the design artefacts, decision-making processes and ecosystem of the design resulting from this, what also emerged was that there were implicit constraints which were not articulated or recorded but which had a clear effect on the process. For example, all of the design team knew, from previous experiences, that they should only recommend solutions that could be handled by the existing technologies used by their company.

This was explicit knowledge within the design team but hidden from the client, as such solutions were only ever suggested that met this criteria and so it had the effect of constraining the choices offered and made. Secondly the organisational culture meant that none of the design team every disagreed with the project manager, and as such some of the rational decision-making processes were abandoned when it became clear that the preferred solution (of the project manager) would not result from such a process. While we emphasise in our framework the designers' creation of external design artefacts and their refinement, we must be aware of such implicit constraints which may affect idea generation and (distributed) decision-making. This brings us to the discussion of the proposed framework of complex design spaces.

5 Discussion and Conclusions

The framework can help to understand the role of design representations that are used during multi-team, multi-disciplinary design processes. We have discussed the comparison of such design artefacts within the framework and propose that they can be used to keep track of the history of decisions throughout the spaces. We might consider a trace of the movements between such design spaces as a pathway through the design process where ideas which have been discarded, amended or selected can be viewed at the relevant point. Not only does this history allow such an overview, but also means we can ensure that critical decision points have been made in accordance with the requirements and that we have not lost valuable elements of the design.

Alternatives and variants (in combination with refinement) in complex design spaces provide a more relaxed view on the designer's goal-directed activities than approaches such as those depicted in Fig. 1 by allowing the convergence of design ideas within and across design sub-spaces (thus preventing an unnecessary or even undesired reduction of design complexity). Therefore, these concepts support the awareness of expertise and fruitful contributions of different designers or sub-teams in multi-disciplinary design work. The complex design spaces emphasise the importance of understanding local design goals and values within a global context. Again this supports a more cohesive view of the overall design path than individual design spaces and enables a better understanding of why particular decisions have been made (global design rationale) where they seem to contradict previous decisions (local design rationale). To our knowledge, such a comprehensive, explanatory framework of interaction design activities is novel and brings together fundamental understandings from design research with practical applications in software design activities. In keeping with Stolterman's [35] call for "high-level theoretical… ideas and approaches that expand [interaction] design thinking but do not prescribe design action (reflective practice, human-centred design, experience design, design rationale, etc.)" our framework does not prescribe a new process model for design, but rather exposes a unifying view on the diverse design representations and their refinement and the abolishing of the dualism between designers and users. This allows us to accommodate the different design perspectives we reviewed in Sect. 2.1.

Limitations and Future Work. The refinement concepts we have presented here are grounded in traditional refinement theory, but we have presented them as light-weight concepts without any practical techniques for supporting their identification. In [6] we gave some formal definitions for such refinements and in future work we should consider the application of these within the framework in a suitable lightweight manner - by which we mean lightweight practical techniques that can be used by interaction designers rather than formal methods specialists.

Our primary focus is on external design representations. However it is understood that the interplay between internal and external representations generally needs to be investigated more deeply in design research [39] and we make no further contribution to that here. Also, while we have undertaken some exploratory empirical work more is needed to explore the applicability of the framework as a tool that can guide analysis, description and design of interaction design processes. We should explore how the framework can serve in real-world design as a way of preventing implicit constraints from dominating the design process (or at least identify it is happening).

We have shown in Sect. 2.2 that multi-disciplinary design requires a revision of each others' assumptions and concepts. This paper suggests the 'transfer' of revised concepts from formal software engineering, such as refinement and contractual utility, to other design practices. Of course, at this stage it is not clear whether this transfer will be 'accepted' and how it can contribute to a model that is positioned equally between engineering design and creative design.

Conclusions. The paper presented a framework for considering multi-team, multi-disciplinary design of interactive systems. Our contribution is given by the proposed framework, along with definitions for alternatives and variants and a high-level view of refinement within the framework. The intention being to give a more concrete method of viewing and understanding interaction design (a complex and 'messy' process) in a structured way.

Acknowledgement. We thank Wanying Yang and the participants of course 23149 on interactive systems. We are grateful to the anonymous reviewers for their insightful comments and suggestions.

References

1. Baker, M., Détienne, F., Burkhardt, J.M.: Quality of collaboration in design: articulating multiple dimensions and viewpoints. In: 1st Interdisciplinary Innovation Conference (2013)
2. Bellotti, V., Shum, S., MacLean, A., Hammond, N.: Multidisciplinary modelling in HCI design in theory and in practice. In: SIGCHI Conference on Human Factors in Computing Systems, CHI 1995, pp. 146–153. ACM (1995)
3. Benyon, D., Turner, P., Turner, S.: Designing Interactive Systems: People, Activities, Contexts, Technologies. Addison-Wesley, New York (2005)
4. Bødker, S., Grønbæk, K., Kyng, M.: Cooperative design: techniques and experiences from the Scandinavian scene. In: Schuler, D., Namioka, A. (eds.) Participatory Design: Principles and Practices, pp. 157–176. Lawrence Erlbaum Associates, Hillsdale (1997)

5. Bowen, J., Reeves, S.: Formal refinement of informal GUI design artefacts. In: Australian Software Engineering Conference (ASWEC 2006), pp. 221–230. IEEE (2006)
6. Bowen, J., Dittmar, A.: A semi-formal framework for describing interaction design spaces. In: 8th ACM SIGCHI Symposium on Engineering Interactive Computing Systems, EICS 2016, pp. 229–238. ACM (2016)
7. Buxton, B.: Sketching User Experiences: Getting the Design Right and the Right Design. Morgan Kaufmann, San Francisco (2007)
8. Cross, N.: Design cognition: results from protocol and other empirical studies of design activity. In: Eastman, C., McCracken, M., Newstetter, W. (eds.) Design Knowing and Learning: Cognition in Design Education, pp. 79–103. Elsevier, Oxford (2001)
9. Cross, N.: Design Thinking: Understanding How Designers Think and Work. Bloomsbury Publ. (2011). https://books.google.co.nz/books?id=F4SUVT1XCCwC
10. Détienne, F., Martin, G., Lavigne, E.: Viewpoints in co-design: a field study in concurrent engineering. Des. Stud. **26**(3), 215–241 (2005)
11. Diaper, D.: The handbook of task analysis for human- computer interaction. In: Diaper, D., Stanton, N. (eds.) Understanding Task Analysis for Human-Computer Interaction. Lawrence Erlbaum Associates Inc., Mahwah (2004)
12. Dittmar, A., Piehler, S.: A constructive approach for design space exploration. In: 5th ACM SIGCHI Symposium on Engineering Interactive Computing Systems, EICS 2013, pp. 49–58. ACM (2013)
13. Dorst, K.: On the problem of design problems - problem solving and design expertise. J. Des. Res. **4**(2), 123 (2004)
14. Fallman, D.: Design-oriented human-computer interaction. In: Proceedings of the SIGCHI Conference on Human Factors in Computing Systems, CHI 2003, pp. 225–232. ACM (2003)
15. Fischer, G., Giaccardi, E., Ye, Y., Sutcliffe, A.G., Mehandjiev, N.: Meta-design: a manifesto for end-user development. Commun. ACM **47**(9), 33–37 (2004)
16. Goodman, E., Stolterman, E., Wakkary, R.: Understanding interaction design practices. In: Proceedings of the SIGCHI Conference on Human Factors in Computing Systems, CHI 2011, pp. 1061–1070. ACM (2011)
17. Gould, J.D., Lewis, C.: Designing for usability: key principles and what designers think. Commun. ACM **28**(3), 300–311 (1985)
18. Grudin, J., Pruitt, J.: Personas, participatory design and product development: an infrastructure for engagement. In: Proceedings of PDC 2002, pp. 144–161 (2002)
19. Hix, D., Hartson, H.: Developing User Interfaces: Ensuring Usability through Product and Process. Wiley, New York (1993)
20. Jackson, M.: Representing structure in a software system design. Des. Stud. **31**(6), 545–566 (2010)
21. John, B.E., Bass, L., Sanchez-Segura, M.-I., Adams, R.J.: Bringing usability concerns to the design of software architecture. In: Bastide, R., Palanque, P., Roth, J. (eds.) DSV-IS 2004. LNCS, vol. 3425, pp. 1–19. Springer, Heidelberg (2005). doi:10.1007/11431879_1
22. Lacaze, X., Palanque, P., Barboni, E., Bastide, R., Navarre, D.: From DREAM to reality: specificities of interactive systems development with respect to rationale management. In: Dutoit, A., McCall, R., Mistrik, I., Paech, B. (eds.) Rationale Management in Software Engineering, pp. 155–172. Springer, Heidelberg (2006). doi:10.1007/978-3-540-30998-7_7
23. Lee, J., Lai, K.Y.: What's in design rationale? Hum.-Comput. Interact. **6**(3), 251–280 (1991)
24. MacLean, A., Bellotti, V., Shum, S.: Developing the design space with design space analysis. In: Byerley, P.F., Barnard, P.J., May, J. (eds.) Computers, Communication and Usability: Design Issues, Research and Methods for Integrated Services, pp. 197–219. Elsevier, Amsterdam (1993)

25. MacLean, A., Young, R., Bellotti, V., Moran, T.: Questions, options, and criteria: elements of design space analysis. Hum.-Comput. Interact. **6**(3), 201–250 (1991)
26. Milner, R.: Elements of interaction: turing award lecture. Commun. ACM **36**(1), 78–89 (1993)
27. Moran, T.P., Carroll, J.M. (eds.): Design Rationale: Concepts, Techniques, and Use. Lawrence Erlbaum Associates Inc., Hillsdale (1996)
28. Morgan, C.: Programming from Specifications, 2nd edn. Prentice Hall International (UK) Ltd., Englewood Cliffs (1998)
29. Nigay, L., Coutaz, J.: A Design space for multimodal systems: concurrent processing and data fusion. In: INTERACT 1993 and CHI 1993, pp. 172–178. ACM (1993)
30. Olson, G.M., Olson, J.S., Carter, M.R., Storrøsten, M.: Small group design meetings: an analysis of collaboration. Hum.-Comput. Interact. **7**(4), 347–374 (1992)
31. Paterno, F.: Model-Based Design and Evaluation of Interactive Applications. Springer, London (2000). doi:10.1007/978-1-4471-0445-2
32. Rittel, H., Webber, M.: Dilemmas in a general theory of planning. Policy Sci. **4**, 155–169 (1973)
33. Rosson, M.B., Carroll, J.M.: Usability Engineering: Scenario-Based Development of Human-Computer Interaction. Morgan Kaufmann Publishers Inc., San Francisco (2002)
34. Schön, D.: The Reflective Practitioner: How Professionals Think in Action. Basic Books, New York (1983)
35. Stolterman, E.: The nature of design practice and implications for interaction design research. Int. J. Des. **2**(1), 55–65 (2008)
36. Tang, A., Aleti, A., Burge, J., van Vliet, H.: What makes software design effective? Des. Stud. **31**, 614–640 (2010)
37. Tang, A., Han, J., Vasa, R.: Software architecture design reasoning: a case for improved methodology support. IEEE Softw. **26**(2), 43–49 (2009)
38. Telier, A., Binder, T., De Michelis, G., Ehn, P., Jacucci, G., Wagner, I.: Design Things. MIT Press, Cambridge (2011)
39. Visser, W.: Designing as construction of representations: a dynamic viewpoint in cognitive design research. Hum.-Comput. Interact. **21**(1), 103–152 (2006)
40. Westerlund, B.: Design Space Exploration - Co-operative creation of proposals for desired interactions with future artefacts. Dissertation, Kungliga Tekniska högskolan, Stockholm (2009)
41. Winograd, T.: Beyond calculation. In: Denning, P.J., Metcalfe, R.M. (eds.) The Design of Interaction, pp. 149–161. Copernicus, New York (1997)
42. Wirth, N.: Program development by stepwise refinement. Commun. ACM **14**(4), 221–227 (1971)
43. Wolf, T.V., Rode, J.A., Sussman, J.B., Kellogg,W.A.: Dispelling "design" as the black art of CHI. In: Proceedings of the SIGCHI Conference on Human Factors in Computing Systems, CHI 2006, pp. 521–530. ACM (2006)

Identifying the Interplay of Design Artifacts and Decisions in Practice: A Case Study

Judy Bowen[1](✉) and Anke Dittmar[2]

[1] University of Waikato, Hamilton, New Zealand
jbowen@waikato.ac.nz
[2] University of Rostock, Rostock, Germany
anke.dittmar@uni-rostock.de

Abstract. Interaction design is a complex and challenging process. It encompasses skills and knowledge from design in general as well as from HCI and software design in particular. In order to find better ways to support interaction design and propose methods and tools to further the research in this area we must first better understand the nature of interaction design in practice. In this paper we present two small case studies which attempt to analyse design and decision-making through the lens of one particular theoretical framework. The framework seeks to focus design activities via its artifacts and the design spaces that exist in order to support reasoning about the process and the evolution of the artifacts. Our case studies show that we can use such a framework to consider real-world design projects, and also that there are further considerations that might usefully be included in such a framework.

Keywords: Design · Design artifacts · Case-study

1 Introduction

Interaction design benefits from multidisciplinary collaboration, bringing in knowledge and experiences from related disciplines such as design theory and practice, human-computer interaction, and software design and development. At the same time, the challenges and complexity of interaction design are heightened, for example, by these different design practices. Understanding and reasoning about interaction design is, therefore, also challenging, but it is important as we seek to ensure that the interactive systems being built are usable, correct and relevant in the current world of ubiquity and increasing use of technological solutions.

In other work, Bowen and Dittmar proposed a framework which introduces the concept of complex design spaces to describe multidisciplinary design work [4]. The framework is based on an understanding of design, and in particular interaction design, from the literature and incorporates ideas from design theory, traditional HCI practices such as user-centred design, and software engineering

© IFIP International Federation for Information Processing 2017
Published by Springer International Publishing AG 2017. All Rights Reserved
R. Bernhaupt et al. (Eds.): INTERACT 2017, Part I, LNCS 10513, pp. 503–512, 2017.
DOI: 10.1007/978-3-319-67744-6_31

practices such as requirements engineering and refinement. Design is basically considered to be a process of constructing, using, discarding, and refining design artifacts or resources.

In this paper we start to investigate the relevance of the proposed theoretical framework as an instrument for empirical studies that helps to deepen our understanding of real-world design activities. Two small case studies of design in practice have been conducted. We report on the results of these case-studies and discuss how they can be viewed within the proposed framework. We also report on aspects identified which suggest the framework may be extended to consider additional factors.

2   Background on Studying Interaction Design Practices

Interaction designers are faced with complex design problems, often characterized as 'wicked problems' [13]. Goodman et al. [7] point out that studying the complexity of interaction design processes is challenging and "needs a diverse set of research methods, each bringing complementary aspects and perspectives to an overall understanding". The actual use of particular design methods is a frequently investigated subject in empirical studies. For example, Vredenburg et al. [14] used the survey method to get an overview about which user-centred design methods are applied by practitioners, or the interview study in [11] investigates how the persona method is integrated into existing design practices. Generally, interview-based approaches allow experienced designers to reflect upon particular aspects of their practice either individually or in groups [15]. Observational techniques have been applied to study design meetings of teams working on both artificial [1,6] and real-world problems [12]. Olson et al.'s study with two companies is related to interactive software development in general but is interesting because of its application of design rationale concepts to analyse the designers' discussion.

Goodman et al. [7] argue that HCI research has influenced most interaction design studies. While theoretical approaches such as activity theory [3,10] or technology as experience [9] have shaped empirical studies of technology use "there has been little theorizing of interaction design practices within HCI" [7]. Our work centres on the concept of a design space as it is used by Buxton [5] and others. All stages of problem setting and solving can be represented within such spaces which represent an iterative generation of ideas and a gradual convergence or refinement towards solutions [5].

In the work of [4], a design space can be hierarchically decomposed into subspaces. Every such (sub-)space describes the 'moves' of a design (sub-)team. It has an entry and exit point and is populated by design artifacts. In this context, all external design representations such as prototypes, scenarios, behavioural specifications, or the final interactive system are considered to be design artifacts. Designers are provided via the entry point with some initial artifacts representing requirements, design constraints and resources. Their activities result in the creation, modification, use or discarding of design artifacts within their design (sub-)space and they provide via the exit point some of their products to other sub-teams.

The case studies presented in this paper are guided by the above framework. However, the analysis is focussed on tracking the creation, modification, discarding and provision of design artifacts at a macro level. It is less focussed on a detailed content analysis of design artifacts and how designers relate design artifacts at a micro level.

3   Case Studies

Two case studies were conducted. The first was with a commercial web design company who were undertaking the redesign of a web site for an optometrist, and the second was with a group of computer science and graphic design students undertaking a pre-defined (artificial) design project. The motivation for the studies was to investigate design in real-world situations with two goals:

(i) to identify the applicability of the framework described in [4],
(ii) to identify real-world design practices and see if additional considerations were needed in the framework (above).

The studies focussed on tracking the design process by direct observation of the teams involved and by identification and categorisation of the design artifacts used.

3.1   Case Study 1

The first case study was conducted with a locally based commercial web development company. They were undertaking a 6 month project to update the website of an optometrist. There were 6 team members from the company involved in the project: a project manager, a data analyser, a designer, two developers and a content manager. The project manager and clients were based in the same city, while all other team members worked from an office in a different city located 160 Km away.

The study was conducted as an observational study by a single researcher, supported by note-taking, audio recordings and access to all design artifacts. The main factors identified and recorded were when decisions were taken and when design artifacts were created, amended or accepted. Ethical consent was obtained to perform the study with permissions from the design company and client to access all materials required and report findings in an anonymised fashion. Design meetings and discussions were conducted by way of face-to-face meetings, online meetings and email discussion. Bespoke online tools are used by the company which enable all team members to collaborate. Analysis of the materials gathered during the process led to the categorisation of the key elements as follows:

- any concrete materials or reports produced were categorised as 'Design artifacts' and labelled DA_1 .. DA_n

- specific decisions that were made following discussions, reviews or choices were categorised as 'Decision Points' and labelled DP_1 .. DP_n
- factors affecting decisions were categorised as 'Constraints' and labelled C_1 .. C_n

The design process began with the data analyst preparing background material from an investigation into the client's industry and similar companies. An online report template was used to capture all of the information from this (DA_1). The project manager reviewed DA_1 and an online meeting was conducted between the project manager and data analyst where this was reviewed, feedback was provided and two decisions were made (DP_1, DP_2). A further report was prepared during this meeting which detailed recommendations for the next phase of the project (DA_2). A meeting was held between the project manager and the client where DA_2 was discussed and feedback provided by the client. Based on this DA_2 was updated (DP_3) and a meeting of the co-located design team was held where this was used as the basis for the creation of a site map (DA_3). DA_3 was emailed to the client who returned it with some changes (DP_4) and the site map was updated to reflect these (DA_4). The project manager held an online meeting with the design team leader and provided DA_4 along with a brief for the design (DA_5). Following discussion of these, specific decisions were taken in line with the client's corporate design requirements (colour schemes, fonts etc.) which acted as constraints on the design (C_1). Following this meeting the design team met and produced a series of sketches (DA_6) in a collaborative design process. At the end of the meeting these were approved by the project manager (DP_5). One of the designers then produced a wireframe (DA_7) which was sent to the project manager for approval (DP_6) and then on to the client. The wireframe contained a number of alternatives from which the client made selections (DP_7) and which were then incorporated into the final wireframe and prototype (DA_8).

In addition to the explicit constraint described (C_1) the researcher also observed a number of implicit constraints. The project manager had a defined timescale to work to, which meant that no additional functions over and above the initial requirements were ever offered to the client (C_2). This had a direct effect on some of the design decisions taken (DP_3 and DP_5). The design company had access to several different technologies that were used across a number of their client solutions. All new solutions had to adhere to these existing technologies and no solutions or functions could be offered which would require additional technology. This had an over-arching effect on the whole project as it acted as an implicit requirement that could not be broken. The final implicit constraint (C_3) was due to organisational culture which meant that the developers and designers would always agree with the project manager irrespective of the decisions made. Figure 1 summarises the interplay of design artifacts, decision points and constraints identified in the first case-study.

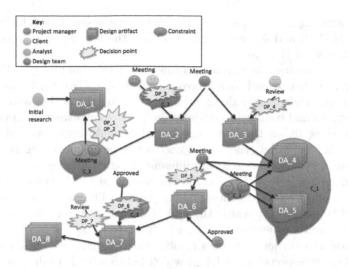

Fig. 1. Case study 1

3.2   Case Study 2

The second study consisted of an artificial design project created for the purpose of the study. Four undergraduate students took part, and were given the task of creating a mobile application to monitor and save battery life on a mobile phone. The participants were all students with no commercial experience, two were computer science students in the fourth year of their studies, while the other two were graphic design students in the third year of their studies. They did not know each other prior to the study.

As for the first case study, this was conducted as an observational study by a single researcher, supported by note-taking, audio recordings and access to all design artifacts. Ethical consent was obtained to perform the study. The same categorisation of key elements occurred as in study 1, but the time over which the study was conducted was limited to four meetings, each of one hour in length. All four participants took part in all four meetings.

In the first meeting the participants discussed the design problem, brainstormed their ideas and noted down what they decided were the most important factors (DA_1). They also searched online for ideas of existing applications and any online resources that they felt could be helpful. They extended their initial notes with useful features from existing apps (DA_2). Following a discussion around these materials three personas were developed along with associated scenarios (DA_3).

The second meeting started with a review of the personas and scenarios created in the previous meeting and a feature list was created (DA_4) from DA_2. This was subsequently prioritised (DP_1) into high and low importance. Between the second and third meetings the participants worked individually on sketches of initial design ideas (DA_5) and brought them along to the third meeting. Following discussions one of the sketches was selected as base sketch to work from (DP_2) and some of the features on the list DA_4 were removed as not being necessary (DP_3).

In the final meeting, the aim was to come up with a final design. The desired elements were reviewed and then a layout was created (DA_6). It was observed that one of the students was designated for drawing the design and the others gave suggestions and comments. Initially the participants wanted all the desired elements to show up on the homepage but this would have resulted in a cluttered look. At this point, they went back to reviewing existing related apps and websites and based on existing different designs, managed to create their final design sketch (DP_4, DA_7). As was seen in study 1, constraints existed which had an effect on the decision-making process. The most evident constraint was that of time (C_1), towards the end of each hourly meeting there was an obvious pressure to achieve something which led to ideas being accepted or discarded hurriedly in order to reach a resolution. This particularly affected DP_3 and was directly responsible for DP_4 which led to a final result more based on the review of existing solutions than all of the previous work undertaken. The second constraint was the skill-level of the participants (C_2) which meant that they looked at superficial aspects of the design only (no discussions of technical aspects) and having created the personas and scenarios, DA_3, they used these only in the creation of feature list DA_4, but otherwise they never made use of them again. Figure 2 shows the interplay of design artifacts, decision points and constraints of the second case study.

Although we have identified the students' skill level as a constraint, based on their inability to incorporate the personas they developed into subsequent development activities, there are other possible causes that could lead to similar decision-making. A longer term (12 week) study of design teams conducted by Blomquist and Arvola [2] found a similar problem with incorporating personas

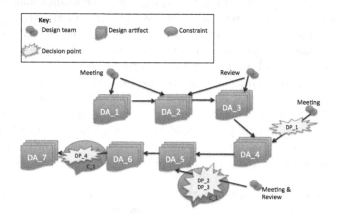

Fig. 2. Case study 2

into the design process and it therefore may not be just the skill-level of the student participants which led to this. We now consider such aspects further in the discussion of our results.

4   Discussion

To consider the two design processes in light of the framework we first create design space diagrams which match the definition given in [4]. Each design space is represented by a box with input shown at the left-hand side and outputs on the right. Within the design space are the local design artefacts and decisions. Figure 3 shows the design spaces of case study 1. The numbered artefacts correspond to those described earlier, e.g. DA_1 is the online report of background material. There is a defined ordering, represented by the number of the spaces from DS_1 to DS_4, which is based on the passing of design artifacts from one space to the next. Arrows between artefacts imply a direct relationship, so either an artefact has been 'refined' into something more concrete, or has been used as the basis for a further artefact. The groupings within design spaces, however, may incorporate multiple meetings or discussions. In the final design space, DS_4 there are several options (or alternatives) offered to the client via the entry point (denoted by DA_7alt.i, DA_7alt.ii...) and they make a selection which is then used to inform the final design, DA_8. In the original framework [4] a distinction is made between alternatives and variants, with alternatives being either/or choices between particular options and variants being different ways of enabling the same thing, which may even co-exist in the final implementation to provide a user choice. The identification of the alternatives from the decision-making process in DS_4 is made possible by the use of the framework here, however no variants were identified in either study.

In Fig. 1 we have clearly identified where decisions were made (by way of the decision points) and also shown how the constraints identified affected particular parts of the design and decision-making. In the original framework decision-making is represented as just another artifact in a design space so we can still see that there is a relationship between a decision-making process and an design but it is not as explicit. In fact the design spaces of the framework can be considered an abstraction of the information shown in Figs. 1 and 2. If we were to 'zoom in' on any of the individual design spaces, or design artifacts then we might imagine we would see something more akin to these figures.

Figure 4 shows the design sub-spaces of case study 2 which can be combined to create the overall design space. The initial problem brief is the input to the first design space, and the idea generations are included as well as the previously defined design artifacts. This reflects the fact that within the framework everything (designs, ideas, considerations etc.) is considered an artifact. There are 5 sub-spaces, DS_1, DS_2, DS_4 and DS_5 represent the four meetings and DS_3 represents the work done at home by each of the team members to produce design sketches which are combined into DA_5. DS_3 is described as a collection of sub-spaces which are closed, this reflects the fact that the sketching was done at home by the participants and therefore not observed.

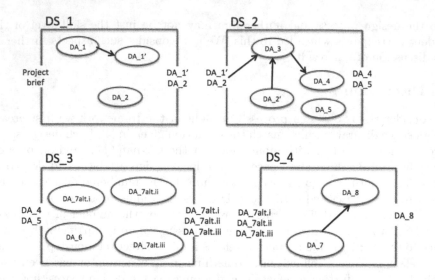

Fig. 3. Case study 1 design space

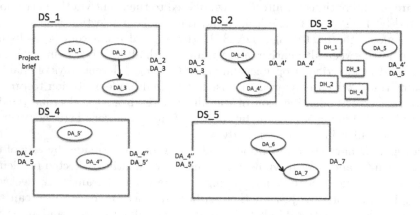

Fig. 4. Case study 2 design space

The design spaces described are ordered 1..5 as there was a single team working on the entire process. The inner design spaces of DS_3 are unordered, however as we can consider them to have occurred in tandem. We do not explicitly consider temporal properties or time beyond simple ordering. In general, therefore, we see a process that is fairly linear, but this is primarily an artifact of the constrained process that was set up for the student group (with defined meetings for all team members) rather than a reflection of a typical design process.

While the detail of the Figs. 1 and 2 suggest that the framework can not capture all of the detail and subtlety that occurs, the design spaces shown in Figs. 3 and 4 can be viewed as a suitable abstraction of these. As such we are able to consider each of the case-studies in light of the framework although with some elements absent from each. For example the framework does not directly consider constraints (although these may be 'hidden' with decision-making processes represented in the framework as QOC diagrams which explicitly consider relationships between questions, options and criteria [8]), and there are aspects within the framework, such as the use of variants, which were not seen in the case studies.

5   Conclusions

In this paper we have presented two small case studies designed to investigate design practices. We analysed the studies in light of a proposed framework for considering design as proposed in [4]. From the studies we were able to identify design entities that were not included in the original framework (namely implicit and explicit design constraints). We were also able to view the framework in practice and see how it enables us to identify where design decisions are made, and in light of constraints consider what might have led to them.

These small initial studies suggest that we can make use of such a framework to consider design practices, however there are further factors that need to be taken into account before we can propose this as a suitable mechanism for any design project. The case studies were necessarily small to fit with these initial investigations, the first step for any future work should be to apply the same process across a longer and larger design project. As the complexity of multi-team interactions increases it will be useful to see how well the concept of design spaces and the identification of artifacts supports a fuller understanding of the history of the process once it is complete.

References

1. Baker, A., van der Hoek, A.: Ideas, subjects, and cycles as lenses for understanding the software design process. Des. Stud. **31**(6), 590–613 (2010). Special Issue Studying Professional Software Design
2. Blomquist, A., Arvola, M.: Personas in action: ethnography in an interaction design team. In: Proceedings of the Second Nordic Conference on Human-Computer Interaction, NordiCHI 2002, pp. 197–200. ACM, New York, USA (2002)
3. Bødker, S.: A human activity approach to user interfaces. Hum. Comput. Interact. **4**(3), 171–195 (1989)
4. Bowen, J., Dittmar, A.: A semi-formal framework for describing interaction design spaces. In: Proceedings of the 8th ACM SIGCHI Symposium on Engineering Interactive Computing Systems, EICS 2016, Brussels, Belgium, June 21–24, 2016, pp. 229–238 (2016)
5. Buxton, B.: Sketching User Experiences: Getting the Design Right and the Right Design. M. Kaufmann, San Francisco (2007)
6. Christiaans, H., Almendra, R.A.: Accessing decision-making in software design. Des. Stud. **31**(6), 641–662 (2010). Special Issue Studying Professional Software Design

7. Goodman, E., Stolterman, E., Wakkary, R.: Understanding interaction design practices. In: Proceedings of the SIGCHI Conference on Human Factors in Computing Systems, CHI 2011, pp. 1061–1070. ACM (2011)

8. MacLean, A., Young, R., Bellotti, V., Moran, T.: Questions, options, and criteria: elements of design space analysis. Hum. Comput. Inter. 6(3), 201–250 (1991)

9. McCarthy, J., Wright, P.: Technology as experience. Interactions 11(5), 42–43 (2004)

10. Nardi, B.A. (ed.): Context and Consciousness: Activity Theory and Human-computer Interaction. Massachusetts Institute of Technology, Cambridge (1995)

11. Nielsen, L., Storgaard Hansen, K.: Personas is applicable: a study on the use of personas in denmark. In: Proceedings of the SIGCHI Conference on Human Factors in Computing Systems, CHI 2014, pp. 1665–1674. ACM (2014)

12. Olson, G.M., Olson, J.S., Carter, M.R., Storrøsten, M.: Small group design meetings: an analysis of collaboration. Hum. Comput. Inter. 7(4), 347–374 (1992)

13. Stolterman, E.: The nature of design practice and implications for interaction design research. Int. J. Des. 2(1), 55–65 (2008)

14. Vredenburg, K., Mao, J.Y., Smith, P.W., Carey, T.: A survey of user-centered design practice. In: Proceedings of the SIGCHI Conference on Human Factors in Computing Systems, CHI 2002, pp. 471–478. ACM (2002)

15. Zhao, M.: Seek it or let it come: how designers achieve inspirations. In: CHI 2013 Extended Abstracts on Human Factors in Computing Systems, CHI EA 2013, pp. 2779–2784. ACM, New York, USA (2013)

On the Effects of Progressive Reduction as Adaptation Strategy for a Camera-Based Cinematographic User Interface

Axel Hoesl$^{(\boxtimes)}$, Mujo Alic, and Andreas Butz

LMU Munich, Munich, Germany
{axel.hoesl,andreas.butz}@ifi.lmu.de,
mujo.alic@campus.lmu.de

Abstract. Camera-based user interfaces (UI) became increasingly relevant, especially on mobile devices, with location independent media production tools such as drones. The devices traditionally render the necessary user interface elements for remote control on top of the content they display. This often leads to occlusion and visual clutter. Progressive Reduction is a recently proposed UI adaption strategy that can help to minimize these issues while maintaining usability. It exploits learning and spatial memory effects in order to gradually reduce the visual footprint of UI elements. We conducted two user studies to investigate the effects of this approach. In the first study, we compared three design alternatives to obviate interference due to design (N = 10). Based on the most promising design, we conducted a second user study (N = 18) investigating the effects of two different reduction strategies (icons-first and background-first). We collected data on perceived control, workload and creativity support in addition to semi-structured interviews. Our results indicate that there was only a minor decrease in perceived control up to a certain amount of reduction. Beyond that, however, the negative effects on perceived control become unacceptable to users. This was observed for all applied reduction strategies.

Keywords: Graphical user interface · Minimalist user interface · Progressive Reduction · Sense of control · Cinematography · Motion control · User-centered design

1   Introduction

Mobile devices are commonly used for the casual creation and manipulation of photos and videos. Actually, they are also increasingly used (semi-)professionally, e.g., by pro-sumers, enthusiast and even experts in film making. In cinematographic production, they often serve as remote control units and help to steer drones or other motorized motion control systems. Mobile devices are particularly attractive as they can combine a remote control unit with the equally

© IFIP International Federation for Information Processing 2017
Published by Springer International Publishing AG 2017. All Rights Reserved
R. Bernhaupt et al. (Eds.): INTERACT 2017, Part I, LNCS 10513, pp. 513–522, 2017.
DOI: 10.1007/978-3-319-67744-6_32

necessary display unit (for steering or for reviewing results). They provide multi-touch interaction, general functional versatility, high connectivity, and often an easy set-up on location.

For enthusiast users, an unoccluded view on a transmitted video stream is important, as they create their results with high effort and great care to details. However, so far, the graphical user interface (UI) elements for motion control systems are often displayed as an overlay on top of the video streams, taking up screen space and hence partially occluding the view.

An established way of minimizing the number of visual elements displayed is Progressive Disclosure (PD) [15,20] which follows the approach of disclosing or "hiding" features into a collapsed or off-screen menu. Items that are less frequently used are then only accessible via a menu. Only when the menu is opened or displayed, the hidden elements become visible again. This minimizes the need for displaying graphical UI elements. For continuous control elements and frequently used elements, however, disclosure might not be a suitable strategy to declutter the screen as they are particularly often needed. Especially when things go wrong, easy access is crucial. Additionally, the perceived affordances [17] of a user interface can diminish when too much is hidden from the user early on. A recently discussed alternative approach and/or extension to PD is *Progressive Reduction* (PR) [9]. PR follows the idea that interface elements that are frequently used become reduced in terms of their visual appearance. In detail, the characteristics of the used visual variables [4] (e.g. size, form or opacity) can be reduced. As this process happens gradually over time and not abruptly, it exploits the users ability to learn functions, abstract representations and locations of certain interface elements. The adaption of the UI is synchronized to a users usage/learning curve for an application or could also be based on prior knowledge if tracked at system level.

Contribution

In our work, we explored how the combined reduction of size, opacity, icon form and icon visibility of UI elements could help to declutter screens on mobile touch screen devices. We conducted two studies to determine the effects of Progressive Reduction as an adaptation strategy on a camera-based UI for a cinematographic motion control system. In the first study (N = 10), we compared three design alternatives (*software joystick*, *extended software joystick* and *single knob*) to obviate interference due to the UI design. When using touch interaction, usually a diminished sense of precision and control can be observed. Hence, we used the most promising design (*extended software joystick*) to collect data on perceived *control* and *workload* in addition to *creativity support* and qualitative feedback to compare two reduction strategies (*icons-first* and *background-first*) in a second study (N = 18). Our results indicated that it was generally possible to gradually reduce the appearance of UI elements without a major negative impact on the sense of control. However, there also was a certain limit to the amount of reduction that could be applied before the perceived *control* significantly decreased to an unacceptable level. This could be observed independently from the applied reduction strategy.

2   Related Work

Progressive Disclosure is a well-established concept in HCI literature as, for example, described by Nielsen [15] or Tidwell [20]. In contrast, *Progressive Reduction* is a rather recently proposed concept and so far was mainly discussed online [9]. Up to now, It has received less attention in the literature, which makes further studying of the subject matter necessary. However, dynamic adaption of UI elements has been investigated before. Most prominently in the domain of augmented reality. In particular, it was used to enhance text readability [8], filter information [13], adapt symbols in camera-based [3] or map-based user interfaces [16]. Adaptation is particulary interesting as it allows to design minimalist user interfaces by exploiting human spatial memory. Spatial memory was also successfully exploited before in UI design and (among other approaches) led to marking menus [14] and even imaginary interfaces [10]. In the case of PR however, only little is known about its side-effects and its limitations.

3   Design Alternatives and Implementation

We implemented three design alternatives (Fig. 1) in a Unity 3D virtual environment on an off-the-shelf Android tablet. As a status quo design we used a *software joystick* as often found in the wild, e.g., for remote control of drones or in games (Fig. 1a). Here, the left software joystick controls translation and the right software joystick rotation each in two dimensions (left-right, up-down). As the first alternative, we implemented an *extended software joystick* with a pie menu (Fig. 1b). The pie menu lets users choose, which dimension(s) they want to map onto the software joystick depending on the use case. Additionally, the structure of a pie menu lends itself well to mental and physical learning (e.g., muscle memory) [14]. In consequence, once learned, not all options need to be displayed, which helps to minimize the number of visual elements necessary. As a second alternative, we used a UI that decoupled translational and rotational control to better suit the cinematographic context. In the field, the various axes are often controlled by different operators [12]. The first camera operator often delegates translational moves to a grip[1]. In our case, this could be delegated to an assistance system. In the User Interface, this was presented as a horizontally restricted joystick placed in the centre of the display (Fig. 1c). This *single knob* could be dragged horizontally with the distance to the centre being mapped to speed of the camera motion. Once content with the settings, the users could "lock" them by swiping upward saving the current direction and speed. For all UIs the button size was at least 11×11 mm as recommended [1,2].

---

[1] A technical operator responsible for supportive tools such as dollies or sliders etc.

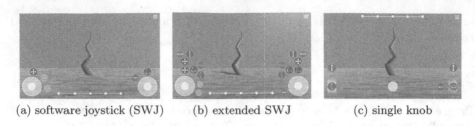

   (a) software joystick (SWJ)   (b) extended SWJ   (c) single knob

Fig. 1. The *software joystick* (a) and our design alternatives *extended software joystick* with fully expanded pie menu (b) and the *single knob* (c)

4   User Study Comparing Design Alternatives

To identify the most promising design alternative, we conducted a user study in a controlled laboratory environment.

4.1   Study Tasks

To provide a reasonably varying set of tasks, we asked the participants to execute a *product shot*, to follow a target moving along a horizontal *figure eight* (or infinity symbol) trajectory and to *roam freely*. The product shot is an often-used move, e.g., in advertising. It is rather easy to accomplish as the recorded object is static and only horizontal translation and rotation at low to medium speed is necessary. Following the trajectory of an eight on its side is more complex as the target is constantly in motion. Additionally, translation and rotation in two dimensions is necessary to properly follow it. This approach has already been taken in related work for the evaluation of a semi-automated camera crane [19]. The free roaming mimics a first exploration of possible camera angles and transitions. This task allows users to be more expressive than a task with a pre-defined goal, which is an important aspect in the design and evaluation of creativity support tools [18]. To keep participants interested, we spread multiple animated objects across the scene, thus encouraging exploration.

4.2   Study Design

We used a within-subject design with our design alternatives (3 levels) and study tasks (3 levels) described above as independent variables. To counteract learning effects, we provided each participant with a unique counter-balanced sequence of user interface and task combinations.

4.3   Participants

For the user study, we recruited 10 participants (3 female) with a median age of 26 years. Ages ranged from 20 to 37 years. All participants had normal or corrected-to-normal vision, were acquainted with touch devices and had no prior training in cinematographic camera control. One participant was left-handed. To be able to relate our inferences to the general population, we had no further requirements for the selection of the participants.

4.4 Procedure

We welcomed the participants, informed them about the procedure of the study and handed out a consent form. After having declared consent, we asked the participants to fill out a demographic questionnaire. This was followed by introducing the first design. We asked the participants to carry out the tasks in the given sequence while standing (to mimic an on-set usage context). After completing all tasks with one interface, we handed out a questionnaire asking the participants to rate it in terms of *control, workload* and *creativity support*. Then the next UI was introduced and the procedure repeated until all tasks were carried out with all interfaces. Before the debriefing, we conducted a semi-structured interview on their preference and the UIs usability.

4.5 Measurements

To collect quantified data on *workload*, we used the Task-Load Index (TLX) from NASA [11]. For the ratings on *creativity support*, we use a limited version of the Creativity Support Index (CSI) by Cherry and Latulipe [5]. We did not ask on all dimensions as some were, by design, not supported throughout all conditions, such as 'collaboration'. Thus, we only included questions on dimensions that were featured by our user interfaces, in particular *exploration, motivation* and *enjoyment*. For data on perceived *control* we handed out a modified version of the sense of control scale (SCS) provided by Dong et al. [6]. As the CSI is based on the TLX, they both use the same 20-point rating scale for each item. To be consistent with the prior items and to minimize confusion for the participants, we also used this report format in our version of the SCS.

4.6 Data Analysis and Results

For the data analysis, we used non-parametric tests (Friedman's ANOVA, Wilcoxon Signed-Rank) to test for statistical significance. A Bonferroni correction was used for the post-hoc tests to compensate for pairwise comparisons ($\alpha^* = .016$). Post-hoc tests were only conducted after a significant main effect was found.

We found no significant difference for *workload* ($\chi^2(2) = 2.0$, p $\leq$ .368) and *creativity support* ($\chi^2(2) = 3.128$, p $\leq$ .209). However, for *control* we found a significant main effect ($\chi^2(2) = 8.359$, p $\leq$ .015). Post-hoc pairwise comparison between the *extended software joystick* (Mdn = 82.5) and the *single knob* (Mdn = 45.0) indicated the *extended software joystick* could outperform the *single knob* (Z $\leq$ 2.601, p $\leq$ .009, $\eta^2 \leq$ .677). Comparing the *extended software joystick* to the *traditional joystick* (Mdn = 67.5), we could not find a significant

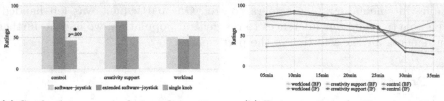

(a) Study data on our design alternatives   (b) Data on our reduction strategies

Fig. 2. Summary of the collected data of our study on design alternatives (a) and progressive reduction strategies (b)

difference ($Z \leq 2.310$, $p \leq .021$, $\eta^2 \leq .534$). Comparing the traditional joystick to the single also showed no significance ($Z \leq 1.543$, $p \leq .123$, $\eta^2 \leq .238$).

In conclusion, the *extended software joystick* seemed most promising to us as it reached the highest absolute score in the control rating (Mdn = 82.5), could outperform the single knob ($p \leq .015$) in terms of *control* (Fig. 2a) and as it was also preferred when asked about in the interviews. We therefore used it to implement and evaluate two reduction strategies.

5   Reduction Strategies

Visual variables can be reduced in various ways. In our designs, we reduced the appearance of user interface element in terms of size, opacity, form and visibility.

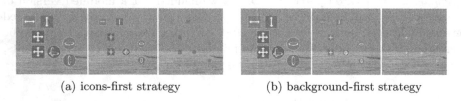

(a) icons-first strategy   (b) background-first strategy

Fig. 3. Our reduction strategies *icons-first* (a) and *background-first* (b)

To estimate the effects of the gradual reduction, we compared two strategies: *icons-first (IF)* and *background-first (BF)*. To make the transition between the levels of reduction less abrupt and to provide easily identifiable icons even in small sizes, we introduced an intermediate reduction state for both strategies (Fig. 3). In this intermediate state the icons transition from their original appearance (e.g., "cross with arrows") to a simplified version (e.g. "plus") when the overall opacity is reduced to a value below 75%. As the next step, they disappear in different ways depending on the strategy. With the *icons-first* strategy, icons disappear before the background disappears (opacity level below 35%, Fig. 3a). In contrast, with *background-first* the background disappears before the icons (opacity level below 35%, Fig. 3b). To counteract a diminished performance due to Fitts' Law [7] we kept the actual touch-sensitive areas of the UI elements to their original size of 11 × 11 mm.

6 User Study Comparing Reduction Strategies

To estimate the effects of progressive reduction in general and of the *icons-first* and *background-first* strategies in particular, we conducted a second user study in a controlled laboratory environment.

6.1 Study Tasks

To isolate the effect of the reduction strategies in this study, we used a roaming task similar to the previous study. We wanted to ensure that the participants would use every function an equal amount of the time. Hence, we altered the task from a *free* roaming task to a *prompted* roaming task. Here, three boxes were displayed on top of the screen prompting which settings to chose and which camera motion to carry out. The left box would indicate the setting for the left joystick. The right box prompted the setting for the right joystick and the center box the camera motion to be executed. All three boxes changed prompts every 10 s. The sequence was chosen in a pseudo random fashion to avoid unreasonable combinations such as moving up with one joystick and down with the other simultaneously.

6.2 Study Design

To avoid interference due to a learning effect we chose a between-groups design. Each participant therefore only experienced one strategy.

6.3 Participants

We recruited a total of 18 participants (7 female) with ages ranging from 19 to 33 years and a median age of 22.5 years. All had normal or corrected-to-normal vision, were acquainted with touch devices and had no prior training in cinematographic camera control. Two participants were left-handed. Similar to the previous study, we had no further requirements regarding the sample.

6.4 Procedure

As in the previous study we first welcomed the participants, asked for consent and collected demographic data. Then the participants were subjected to a user interface with a given reduction strategy and the above-mentioned prompted roaming task. Again, the participants were asked to perform the tasks while standing. After the first 5 min the PR of the user interface began. The interface was reduced further every 5 min until the final reduction step (invisible or imaginary UI [10]) was reached. At the final stage the participants performed the prompted tasks again for 5 min. Having performed a study task at a given reduction level for 5 min, we asked the participants to rate their sense of *control*. Data on *workload* and *creativity support* was only collected at given points of interest (after 5, 25 and 35 min) to keep interruptions to a necessary minimum. In total 35 min were necessary to perform the tasks with all levels of reduction. Having completed the tasks, we debriefed the participants.

6.5   Measurements

To rate the perceived sense of *control*, *workload* and *creativity support*, we applied the adapted questionnaires from our previous study.

6.6   Data Analysis and Results

Similar to the preceding study, we used non-parametric tests (Friedman's ANOVA, Wilcoxon Signed-Rank) to test for statistical significance. Also, a Bonferroni correction was applied to the post-hoc tests in order to compensate for pairwise comparisons ($\alpha^* = .016$). Post-hoc tests were only conducted after a significant main effect was found.

Overall, we found no significant difference between the reduction strategies for *control* ($\text{Mdn}_{IF} = 75.0$, $\text{Mdn}_{BF} = 65.0$, $Z \leq .00$, $p \leq 1.000$), *workload* ($\text{Mdn}_{IF} = 49.16$, $\text{Mdn}_{BF} = 49.16$, $Z \leq .036$, $p \leq .971$) and *creativity support* ($\text{Mdn}_{IF} = 66.0$, $\text{Mdn}_{BF} = 55.0$, $Z \leq .361$, $p \leq .718$).

Regarding the data plot (Fig. 2b) we conducted further significance tests comparing the data gathered after 5, 25 and 35 min for each dimension. For *workload* we found a significant main effect ($\chi^2(2) = 20.111$, $p \leq .001$). Post-hoc pairwise comparison between 35 and 5 min ($Z \leq 3.376$, $p \leq .001$, $\eta^2 \leq .633$) as well as 35 and 25 min ($Z \leq 3.201$, $p \leq .001$, $\eta^2 \leq .569$) indicated significant differences. No effect was found comparing 25 to 5 min ($Z \leq 2.289$, $p \leq .022$).

For *creativity support* we found a main effect ($\chi^2(2) = 13.914$, $p \leq .001$). Also, post-hoc pairwise comparison between 35 and 5 min ($Z \leq 3.028$, $p \leq .002$, $\eta^2 \leq .572$) as well as 35 and 25 min ($Z \leq 2.534$, $p \leq .011$, $\eta^2 \leq .357$) indicated significant differences. Also, no effect could be found comparing 25 to 5 min ($Z \leq 2.226$, $p \leq .026$).

For *control* we also found a significant main effect ($\chi^2(2) = 30.629$, $p \leq .001$). Post-hoc pairwise comparison showed a significant difference between all measurements with 35 and 5 min ($Z \leq 3.741$, $p \leq .001$, $\eta^2 \leq .778$), 35 and 25 min ($Z \leq 3.730$, $p \leq .001$, $\eta^2 \leq .773$) and 25 to 5 min ($Z \leq 2.773$, $p \leq .006$, $\eta^2 \leq .427$).

7   Conclusion

We explored how the combined reduction of size, opacity, icon form and icon visibility of user interface elements affected the perceived *control*, *workload* and *creativity support* of a camera-based user interface. In a first study ($N = 10$), we compared three design alternatives (*software-joystick*, *extended software-joystick* and *single knob*). We used the most promising design (*extended software-joystick*) to compare two reduction strategies (*icons-first* and *background-first*) in a second study (N = 18). Our results indicated that it was possible to gradually reduce the appearance of UI elements without a major negative impact up to a certain amount of reduction, after which it became unacceptable. This was observed independently from the applied reduction strategy.

References

1. Metrics & Keylines: Layout - Material Design Guidelines. https://material.io/guidelines/layout/metrics-keylines.html#metrics-keylines-touch-target-size (2017)
2. Targeting: UWP App Developer — Microsoft Docs. https://docs.microsoft.com/en-us/windows/uwp/input-and-devices/guidelines-for-targeting (2017)
3. Carmo, M.B., Afonso, A.P., Ferreira, A., Cláudio, A.P., Montez, E.: Symbol adaptation assessment in outdoor augmented reality. In: 2014 International Conference on Computer Graphics Theory and Applications (GRAPP), pp. 1–10 (2014)
4. Carpendale, S.: Considering Visual Variables as a Basis for Information Visualisation, January 2003
5. Cherry, E., Latulipe, C.: Quantifying the creativity support of digital tools through the creativity support index. ACM Trans. Comput. Hum. Interact. (TOCHI) **21**(4), 21 (2014)
6. Dong, M.Y., Sandberg, K., Bibby, B.M., Pedersen, M.N., Overgaard, M.: The development of a sense of control scale. Front. Psychol. **6**, 1733 (2015)
7. Fitts, P.M.: The information capacity of the human motor system in controlling the amplitude of movement. J. Exp. Psychol. **47**(6), 381 (1954)
8. Gabbard, J.L., Swan, J.E., Hix, D., Kim, S.J., Fitch, G.: Active text drawing styles for outdoor augmented reality: a user-based study and design implications. In: 2007 IEEE Virtual Reality Conference, pp. 35–42, March 2007
9. Grinshtein, A.: Progressive Reduction - LayerVault Blog, May 2013. http://layervault.tumblr.com/post/42361566927/progressive-reduction
10. Gustafson, S., Holz, C., Baudisch, P.: Imaginary phone: learning imaginary interfaces by transferring spatial memory from a familiar device. In: Proceedings of the 24th Annual ACM Symposium on User Interface Software and Technology (UIST 2011), pp. 283–292. ACM, Santa Barbara (2011)
11. Hart, S.G.: NASA-task load index (NASA-TLX); 20 years later. Proc. Hum. Factors Ergonomics Soc. Annu. Meet. **50**, 904–908 (2006)
12. Hoesl, A., Wagner, J., Butz, A.: Delegation impossible? Towards novel interfaces for camera motion. In: Proceedings of the 33rd Annual ACM Conference Extended Abstracts on Human Factors in Computing Systems (CHI EA 2015), pp. 1729–1734. ACM, April 2015
13. Julier, S., Lanzagorta, M., Baillot, Y., Rosenblum, L., Feiner, S., Hollerer, T., Sestito, S.: Information filtering for mobile augmented reality. In: Proceedings IEEE and ACM International Symposium on Augmented Reality (ISAR 2000), pp. 3–11 (2000)
14. Lepinski, G.J., Grossman, T., Fitzmaurice, G.: The design and evaluation of multitouch marking menus. In: Proceedings of the SIGCHI Conference on Human Factors in Computing Systems (CHI 2010), pp. 2233–2242. ACM, Atlanta (2010)

15. Nielsen, J.: Progressive disclosure, April 2006. https://www.nngroup.com/articles/progressive-disclosure
16. Nivala, A.M., Sarjakoski, T.L.: User aspects of adaptive visualization for mobile maps. Cartogr. Geogr. Inf. Sci. **34**(4), 275–284 (2007)
17. Norman, D.A.: The Design of Everyday Things: Revised and Expanded Edition, 2nd edn. Basic Books, New York (2013)
18. Shneiderman, B., Fischer, G., Czerwinkski, M., Myers, B., Resnick, M.: NSF workshop report on creativity support tools. Technical report, Washington, DC (2005)
19. Stanciu, R., Oh, P.Y.: Feedforward-output tracking regulation control for human-in-the-loop camera systems. In: Proceedings of the 2005, American Control Conference (ACC 2005), vol. 5, pp. 3676–3681. IEEE (2005)
20. Tidwell, J.: Designing Interfaces, 2nd edn. O'Reilly and Associates, Sebastapol (2011)

You've Got the Moves, We've Got the Motion – Understanding and Designing for Cinematographic Camera Motion Control

Axel Hoesl[(✉)], Partrick Mörwald, Philipp Burgdorf, Elisabeth Dreßler, and Andreas Butz

LMU Munich, Munich, Germany
{axel.hoesl,andreas.butz}@ifi.lmu.de,
{moerwal,burgdorf,dressler}@cip.ifi.lmu.de

Abstract. Moving a film camera aesthetically is complex, even for professionals. They commonly use mechanical tools which help them to control camera motion. In recent years, computer-controlled tools were developed, but their development is mostly technology-driven and often fails to thoroughly integrate the user perspective. In HCI, prototyping is an established way to collect early feedback and thereby integrate a user perspective early on. In filmmaking, there is a lack of prototyping platforms, mostly due to the small market and inherent technical complexity of tools. We therefore developed a prototyping platform in cooperation between experts in camera operation, mechanical engineering and computer science. It consists of a motion control system for sliding camera moves composed of affordable hardware and open source software, and it supports the wireless connection of various types of user interfaces via Bluetooth. In this combination, it allows the exploration of different interface and control strategies in-the-wild, as it is easy to transport and stable for use in the field. A prototype using our platform was used by professional filmmakers in real commercial assignments. We further report on its use in two studies (N = 18, N = 12) examining the effects of various degrees of automation (low and medium) on the sense and quality of control. Our results indicate no decrease in both dimensions.

Keywords: Cinematography · Camera motion · Motion control · Slider

1 Introduction

Mastering precise and aesthetic camera motion in filmmaking is central to camera operators. Performing it manually is hard and errors are likely. To reduce errors, task sharing and the use of support tools have been established. In one single camera move, usually three – sometimes even more – operators work together simultaneously in a choreography, performed *behind* the camera [21]. In this process, subtasks are delegated to human operators or to machines. Both

R. Bernhaupt et al. (Eds.): INTERACT 2017, Part I, LNCS 10513, pp. 523–541, 2017.
DOI: 10.1007/978-3-319-67744-6_33

perform very well in different areas: Humans, for example, outperform machines in recognizing visual patterns and aesthetic judgment; in contrast, machines can move heavy weights smoothly, precisely and repeatedly [16]. Originally, many of such support tools were purely mechanic. With advances in microelectronics, however, they were extended by motors and controlled by microprocessors starting in the late 1970s[1]. Fueled by further technological advances in the decades to follow, a multitude of novel tools was introduced and is now summoned under the label of *camera motion control systems*. Going beyond the pure mechanics, nowadays high-tech tools such as industrial robots [6] or drones [17] became part of the tool palette in camerawork.

We identified several challenges, that currently hinder research in this field: On the market, there are mainly *expensive tools without access* for connecting new user interface (UI) prototypes. *Expertise in multiple fields*, such as mechanical engineering, electronics, human-computer interaction (HCI) and computer science is necessary in order to build them. This makes it hard to quickly translate new ideas into prototypes. Furthermore, the research literature on *physical* cinematographic camera motion and its control is not very elaborate to the best of our knowledge. There is a lack of ethnography, studies on systems and interaction designs and their evaluation for user-centered research. In the field of *virtual* camera motion there is plenty of literature available, but its findings cannot simply be adapted to physical camera control to suit the needs of enthusiasts and professionals on location. Existing support tools are meant to be used in the physical world and also serve the artistic expression. The latter often involves a trial and error experience of unforeseen dynamic changes depending on how a situation unfolds. Therefore, their use and control is *hard to simulate* in a virtual environment [27]. In addition, operators want to delegate tasks, but also want to be in control of the recorded images [21]. Delegation and being in control, however, are often contradictory [28]. Therefore finding the right balance for different user groups is non-trivial. To be meaningful to operators, systems therefore need to *balance* user control with automation [21]. This might be achieved best by introducing *high level* controls, but further research on systems and interactions is necessary.

1.1   Contribution

We contribute an open source motion-controlled camera slider with independent control and powering units that is *inexpensive* and offers open *wireless* access. With this platform, various types of UIs balancing delegation with control can be prototyped and evaluated. It was tested by a professional cinematographer in five assignment shootings. We found strong indication for its *high quality in smooth motion* and *system stability*. We then used it to conduct two controlled user studies. In our first study, we examined the effects of motorized tools for camera motion on the *sense* and *quality* of control of the participants. In a subsequent

---

[1] The first major motorized and computer controlled system of this kind was the Dykstraflex [3], used for special effects in Star Wars Episode IV: A New Hope (1977).

study, we investigating the influence of *reviewing* results by the participants during the evaluation process of the recorded material. This helped us to validate the effects on the participants' sense of control.

2   Related Work

In the domain of *virtual* camera motion, the specifics of camera control were summarized by Bowman et al. [5] and Christie et al. [14] classifying approaches, analyzing requirements and revealing limitations. However, not all of the presented approaches can simply be translated to real world cinematography, as, for instance, the scene in hand concept [34]. Suitable approaches – especially for high level control – are often image-based [26] or constraint-based [13,23]. Here, Through-The-Lens controls [12,18,23] for constraint-based camera positioning combined with 3D navigation techniques for direct control – i.e., lower level axis control – e.g., using multi-touch gestures on mobile devices as Move&Look [25], have the potential to correspond well to established mental models of users in cinematography and 3D navigation.

In *physical* camera motion, a survey on autonomous camera systems recently conducted by Chen and Carr [9] identified the core tasks and summarized twenty years of research-driven tool development and evaluation. Within this domain, research tools are found in multiple areas sometimes going beyond traditional cinematography. Autonomous pan-and-tilt cameras are used to autonomously record academic lectures. In the work of Hulens et al. [22], the Rule of Thirds[2] is borrowed from cinematography and integrated into the tracking. Zhang and colleagues [36] presented a tele-conferencing system incorporating video and context analysis. In their work, the camera is oriented and zoomed automatically in order to better guide the users' attention. If, for example, a presenter shows certain details on a whiteboard, this area is automatically zoomed in on. For automated sports broadcasting [8], Chen et al. [10] even mimic the operation style of human operators through machine learning as the automated operation style is often perceived as rather "robotic".

The presented examples implement machine benefits, but hardly offer a *human-machine interplay* allowing operators to contribute. One of the few examples offering such an interplay is presented by Stanciu and colleagues [31]. Here, a crane with a camera mounted on one side automatically frames a user-selected target and adapts to the manual crane operation of a human operator on the opposite side[3]. This human-machine interplay is important for the operators as they want to actively express their personal view and therefore want to feel in control [21]. For interactive control, a futuristic vision of novel and natural forms of interaction was already presented with Starfire [32] in 1994. The video

---

[2] A guideline for image composition where the image frame is divided into three thirds, both horizontally and vertically. Important subjects, e.g., a speaker, are best placed at one of the intersections.

[3] Stypekit [4] is a corporate implementation of the concept.

prototype showcased a camera crane that was controlled by a tablet used as a remote viewport. So far however, no implementation followed the concept[4].

3 Prototype Development

Advanced tools, such as camera cranes [4], are complex to manage, since multiple degrees of freedom (DOF) need to be controlled in real time. This usually requires years of training, is expensive, complex to build and requires high efforts in transportation. For the quick translation of new interaction concepts, not all of the offered DOF are always necessary in order to evaluate alternative designs on a conceptual level. As pointed out by Nielsen [29], filmmakers do not always apply all possible movements and exploit all DOFs. They rather carefully choose DOFs and movements as stylistic devices depending on the content of the scene. Often shots that are outside the "regular" human visual experience need to be motivated in particular by the content and are thus used less often. Our prototype supports some go-to types of shots that can often be seen in diverse contexts such as advertising, image, short, feature and documentary films.

3.1 Collecting Expert Requirements

Before we developed our prototype, we interviewed professionals in camera motion (N = 3) to determine user roles when using camera sliders in their work.

User Roles. We handed out an online questionnaire to camera operators. Focusing on qualitative statements, we distinguished two usage contexts: *solo operation*, where one operator is out alone on location and thus needs to control everything that is usually delegated to multiple assistants. We also found mentions of the classic collaboration with *task delegation*, where tasks are shared and delegated to separate operators. This is often used on film sets.

Hardware and User Interface Requirements. An additional professional operator was interviewed about technical hardware and user interface requirements. He was experienced in camera operation and in consulting major producers of cinematographic equipment. From a 45 min semi-structured interview we derived the following requirements (Table 1).

3.2 Implementation

Based on the identified scenarios and requirements, we built a setup focusing on *solo operation* with *task delegation* to an assisting system. Together with a mechanical engineer, we determined the necessary motor torque and acceleration for actuating the payload of 20 kg horizontally and 6 kg vertically. An overview of

---

[4] The Freefly MIMIC [1], however, reminds us of the original idea.

Table 1. Requirements as collected in the semi-structured interview with a professional

Hardware requirements	User interface requirements
Stable for on-set use	Wireless remote control
Smooth motion with stable images	Speed is controlled manually
Runs at constant speed	Programming of moves
Bounces between ends repeatedly	Programming of ramps
Stops before it hits an end	Moves can be repeated precisely
Offers time-lapse recordings	Moves can be saved, loaded and edited
Payload of 20 kg (hor.) and 6 kg (vert.)	Displays the camera stream live

the main units is presented in Fig. 1. The components, wiring diagrams, source codes of the control software, plans of the 3D-printed parts, documentation of the wireless control protocol (using Bluetooth Low Energy) and sample footage are provided electronically [20] in further detail. The final implementation is presented in the following section in Fig. 2.

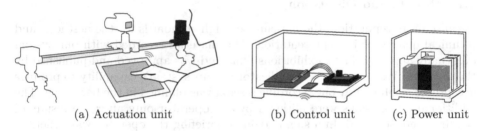

(a) Actuation unit   (b) Control unit   (c) Power unit

Fig. 1. In 1a an image-based [26] control scenario is illustrated. Instructions are sent to the control unit (1b) driving the motor (1a, right). Here, the signals are received by a Bluetooth module (1b, center) and processed by an Arduino (1b, right) controlling the motor driver (1b, left). The power unit (1c) supplies the system with electricity.

4   Field Evaluation

To determine whether the hardware requirements were met, we asked a professional camera operator to evaluate our setup during five assigned shootings. We made sure that he did not know the identified requirements to avoid a bias. The features concerned with speed changes, bouncing and safety stops were essential and thus already tested during the development of the hardware and firmware.

The requirements of *system stability* and *smoothness of motion* hence remained to be verified. The setup was used in five on-assignment shootings for exhibition films in a modern art museum (Fig. 2). At these recording sessions the system worked in a stable way. Horizontal shots were recorded at ground level and at waist height. Also, diagonal shots from waist height to ground level and vertical shots at a height beyond two meters were recorded. The cameras were moved with constant speed and bounced between both ends for longer periods of time. The limit switches were used for each calibration and prevented the slider from hitting an end. Moves and ramps were programmed remotely and wirelessly by a second trained person using a laptop connected to the system via Bluetooth (Fig. 2).

Fig. 2. Field evaluation of the prototype in different scenarios with a professional camera operator during an assignment for exhibition films of a modern art museum.

4.1   Results and Discussion

Because of its reputation, the museum set high standards for the aesthetic and technical quality of its representation. The material recorded with our system eventually appeared in six exhibitions films and was approved and published by the museum. We take this as an indicator for our system's capability to produce acceptable results. Only one recording session was planned in the beginning. The additional five sessions were initiated by the operator only after the results of the first were screened. In a summarizing debriefing the operator was generally satisfied with the systems stability, but also revealed some issues he found.

His main concern was that *saving time* is crucial. Therefore *shortcuts* should be provided. Often he would start with a slide from one end to the other at medium speed and then adjust positioning or speed depending on what he saw on the camera display. We therefore added this feature to the UI requirement list. In our test UI, a function call including start and end position, speed, acceleration and deceleration as parameters had to be typed into a command line interface. Here the operator's mental model needs to be incorporated in end-user interfaces. During the shooting he had to adjust the focus manually several times, which was visible in the recorded material. Therefore a motor-driven remote *follow focus*[5] is a necessary addition. However, professional units are again generally expensive and do rarely offer open access. The do-it-yourself scene provides examples of Arduino-based systems [2]. Such an implementation can be set up for wireless control and would work together with our setup. In response to this finding, we built an Arduino-based remote follow focus. Its parts and sources are also provided in [20].

---

[5] A device attached to the camera lens that physically manipulates the focus ring and thus the position of the focal plane. It is often motor-driven and remote-controlled.

Surprisingly, we also found that the people we recorded behaved more *naturally* in front of the camera, which was also confirmed by the operator. Due to the remote control and the automatic bouncing mode, we could remain at a distance from the setup. We had never considered any effects on people in front of the camera before the shooting.

Overall, we see a strong indication that our prototyping platform generally meets the requirement of high quality *smooth camera motions* and of *system stability* for field use we had set out to test. Even though we are aware that it does not reach the level of sophistication of professional equipment, we believe it can still serve as a research platform for new user interfaces prototypes and field observation. During the recording, the slider was indeed controlled wirelessly. However, this was done by a second trained person using a command line interface on a laptop holding it with one hand and typing with the other. We focused on evaluating the collected hardware requirements and not yet the user interface requirements. The user interfaces for end-user control presented below were designed based on insights gained from this first field evaluation.

5   Controlled Experiment on the Effects of a Low Degree of Automation on Workload and Control

In order to meet the requirement of displaying the camera stream, we chose to implement the user interfaces on a tablet capable of this task. We implemented a *touch-based* UI that used the whole screen as an input area for direct control on the camera stream. This design led to less occlusion of the stream by visual interface components and can be extended by further image-based control techniques. We compared this design alternative to a status quo *software joystick* that served as a baseline condition for remote control. Both remote control interfaces were also compared to full *manual control*, a human control baseline without motorization. The human baseline condition allowed us to interpret the data collected beyond a relative comparison between both remote control conditions.

5.1   Measurements

The degree of automation (DOA) in a systems design can be located within a spectrum ranging from full human control to full system control. As presented by Miller and Parasuraman [28], design decisions on this scale are characterized by a trade-off between the reduction/increase of workload and the in-/decrease of the results' predictability (Fig. 3, left). With an increased degree of automation usually comes a decrease in predictability of the results, and with it a decreased sense of control. On this basis we chose a low degree of automation and determined its effects on *workload* and *sense* of control in this experiment. As work by Wen et al. [35] suggests, the quality of the results can itself be affected by the perceived level of control. We hence added a *quality* of control measurement. As no standardized tasks for measuring quality of control with cinematographic interfaces have emerged so far, we adapted a method used in the evaluation of automotive user interfaces established by Verster and Roth [33]. This method uses the standard deviation of lateral position (SDLP) to determine a driver's performance. Here, the deviation from the center of the lane is measured continuously while driving. In our study, we used the Rule of Thirds as a basis and continuously determined the deviation from the targeted third (Fig. 3, right).

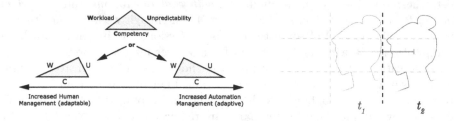

Fig. 3. *Left*: The trade-off between workload and unpredictability as described in [28], *right*: Adaption of the SDLP [33] measurement to the Rule of Thirds principle

5.2 Participants

For the study we recruited 18 participants (14 male). The average age was 24, with ages ranging from 21 to 31. Prior knowledge in tools for camera motion was reported by 4 participants.

5.3 Study Design

Each participant was asked to perform the task of following a person with the camera in movement direction while framing the person at the first third in the direction of the movement (Rule of Thirds technique). The three levels of the independent variable for *interaction technique* were full *manual control* (no motion control, human baseline), *software joystick* (motion control, remote control baseline) and *touch-based control* directly on the camera stream (motion control, touch-based remote control). For *manual control*, the slider carriage needed to be manipulated physically by the participants to move the camera and to frame the person. In the other conditions the slider carriage was driven by a motor and needed to be controlled via a remote control user interface offering continuous control options. In a within-subjects design each participant executed all conditions. The order was counter-balanced based on a Latin Square design.

5.4 Apparatus

An unmotorized slider, for the manual control condition, and a motorized slider, for the other conditions, were mounted on tripods at the same height and placed in front of each other. To provide the participants with the same delay that would appear in the video stream in the remote control conditions, the video stream was also displayed in this condition. A smartphone was therefore mounted on top of the manual slider carriage to display it. The stream was recorded by a DSLR camera (Canon EOS 60D) mounted on the carriage of the motorized slider. The camera was connected to a video encoder (Teradek Cube 255) via HDMI cable situated on top of the camera. The encoder provided an RTSP video stream of the camera image via WiFi and recorded the stream for post-hoc evaluation. The stream was also presented on the tablet used for the *software joystick* and *touch control* interfaces.

5.5   Procedure

First the participants were welcomed and informed about the study and how their recorded data was handled. They then were handed out a declaration of consent. After declaring consent, a demographic questionnaire was handed out and after its completion, the Rule of Thirds framing task was explained. An example video of the expected results was presented.

The order of the conditions was counterbalanced with a Latin-Square design to order to avoid learning effects. For each condition, the task was executed ten times. For each trial, the video material was recorded for the analysis of *quality of control*. After each condition the participants filled out an extended version of the NASA Task-Load-Index (TLX) [19] questionnaire to determine *workload* and *sense of control*. To determine the latter, the original TLX questionnaire was extended by one item. The question we added was *'How much did you feel in control during the task?'*. The wording of the question was taken from the sense of control scale developed by Dong et al. [15]. Here, the authors propose a 6-point rating scale as the response format. In order to minimize effort and confusion for the participants, we decided to stay consistent with the 20-point scale format used in the TLX. After carrying out all objectives, a semi-structured interview regarding the presented conditions was conducted.

5.6   Results

We conducted Shapiro-Wilk Tests for the data collected on *workload, sense of control* and *quality of control*. They showed significance for multiple conditions. In consequence, a normal distribution across all of the data cannot be assumed. We therefore only used non-parametric tests (Friedman's ANOVA and Wilcoxon Signed-Rank) to test for statistical significance. A Bonferroni correction with a value of $\alpha^* = .016$ was applied to account for pairwise comparisons. The post-hoc comparisons were only conducted after a significant main effect was found.

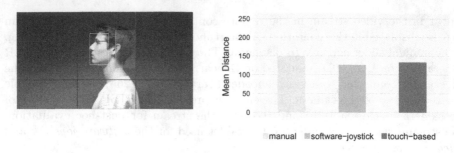

Fig. 4. *Left*: Determining the distance (blue) between the tracking target (yellow) and the first third in movement direction automatically, *right*: Mean distances to the target (Color figure online)

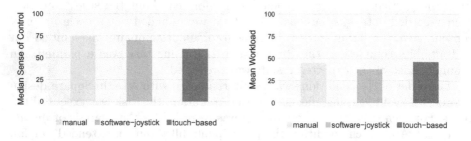

Fig. 5. *Left*: Results for *sense* of control, *right*: Results for the occurring *workload*

Quality of Control. The data determining *quality of control* was extracted from the recorded video material after the study. We developed an analysis tool to detect the face of the person walking by in each frame thus further determining the person's center (also available electronically [20]). The distance from the first third in movement direction to the person's center (blue area in Fig. 4, left) in pixels (px) was logged. The resulting data was analyzed with the Friedman test. No significant main effect could be identified ($\chi^2(2) \leq 3.44, p \leq .18$) with mean distance values of 149.94 px (SD ≤ 54.4) difference for *manual control*, 126.19 px (SD ≤ 23.19) for *software-joystick* and 133.03 px (SD ≤ 30.76) for *touch control* (Fig. 4, right).

Sense of Control. For analyzing the self-reported data regarding *sense of control*, we also used the non-parametric Friedman test as the use of parametric tests on self-reported data in rating-scale format is controversial as pointed out by Carifio and Perla [7]. Here also, no significant effect was found ($\chi^2(2) \leq 5.03$, $p \leq .081$), with median values of 75 for *manual*, 70 for *software-joystick* and 60 for *touch* (Fig. 5, left).

Workload. We determined the *workload* using the TLX for each user interface. Analyzing the overall workload for the different UIs with the Friedman test, we found no significant main effect ($\chi^2(2) \leq 7.00$, $p \leq .03$). With mean values of 45.09 (SD ≤ 15.18) for *manual* control, 37.78 (SD ≤ 13.47) for *software joystick* and 46.16 (SD ≤ 13.06) for *touch control* (Fig. 5, right).

5.7 Discussion

Based on the data we collected, we could not identify any significant negative effects on the *sense* or the *quality* of control due to the use of remote-controlled tools incorporating a low degree of automation. There was also no significant influence on *workload* when using remote-controlled tools. This seems to be in line with prior findings as presented by Miller et al. [28]. We further examined the data on workload more closely and found that in the dimension of *physical demand* there is a rather large difference in median values of 62.5 for *manual*, 15 for *software-joystick* and 30 for *touch-based*. When inspecting only this dimension, the Friedman test results in a significant difference ($\chi2(2) \leq 29.6$, $p \leq .001$) between the conditions. The pairwise comparisons revealed significant differences between all conditions (with $p \leq .003$ or less). So, when only concerned with physical demand, we observed that the remote-controlled tools could lead to a decrease in workload. However, the difference in this dimension was not strong enough to influence the participants' overall experienced workload significantly when measured with the TLX questionnaire.

6 Controlled Experiment on the Effects of a Medium Degree of Automation and the Review of Results

In the previous study, no negative effects on *sense* of control became apparent, which was surprising to us. Also, no effects on *quality* of control were observed that could have influenced perceived control indirectly. This could be attributed to multiple causes: the low degree of automation, a too coarse measurement tool or to the unawareness of the consequences on the quality of control by the participants. Regarding the precision of the evaluation tool, a single questionnaire item measured only after one trial might not be sensitive enough to show an effect in the analysis. Additionally, when examining the recorded material, we found that shaking and jerky motion was much more visible in the manual condition, however this had no effect on the sense of control reports. As there was no reviewing of the material, the participants potentially could not estimate the quality of control themselves properly. Providing the possibility to review the results - as usual in cinematographic practice - might influence their perception of control (similar to the findings of Wen et al. [35]) and provide a more externally valid result. To better understand the effects on perceived control, we conducted a second study addressing the issues mentioned above.

6.1 Conditions

Addressing the single degree of automation issue, we now used two designs with a low and medium degree of automation. For the low degree condition, we again used the software-joystick interface of the prior study. For the medium degree condition we prototyped a UI that used keyframe selection as an input technique. The user interface used a Through-The-Lens [23] approach. The participants could see the scene on the tablet and use it as a viewfinder. They could move the tablet freely and select certain positions as keyframes. The motion-controlled slider would then interpolate a motion path between all chosen keyframes. For the implementation of such a technique, known points of reference are necessary. These can be provided, e.g., via optical tracking or by synchronizing the tablet with a virtual model of the study room. These models consequently need to be updated when the tablet is moved, e.g., through the tracking of markers or the accelerometer data of the tablet. Such an implementation is technically complex as it needs to handle noisy data and requires low latencies. As we were mainly interested in the effects on the perception of our participants, we prototyped it in a wizard-of-oz style. To create the illusion of an automated system capable of this functionality, we asked the participants to select a pre-defined set of keyframes by showing sample images during the explanation of the study task. The motion control tool was accordingly pre-programmed so that the "selected" keyframes were matched by the resulting motion.

6.2   Measurements

To address the issue of a too coarse measurement tool, we now used a visual analog scale to ask for the preferred level of control. The captions on each side of the visual-analog scale read "I control the system and the results manually" and "The system controls the results". Additionally, we also increased the overall number of data points by taking multiple measurements during the study trials. As we used a wizard-of-oz approach with a pre-defined result, we did not collect data on the quality of control as in the prior study.

6.3   Participants

We recruited 12 participants (8 male) for the study. The average age was 25, with ages ranging from 21 to 32. No prior knowledge in tools for camera motion was reported by the participants.

6.4   Study Design and Procedure

We first welcomed the participants and introduced them to the study procedure. Then we handed out a declaration of consent to the participants. Having declared consent, they were given a detailed explanation of the study conditions. Each participant was then assigned to one of two groups. The groups were exposed to the conditions in counterbalanced orders. Before we started the first trial, we took a measurement on the preferred level of control to collect a baseline. Then the participants were exposed to both conditions. After finishing the trials we took a further measurement on the preferred level of control. Now the participants could determine their preference in reference to the varying degrees of automation. Then we gave the participants the possibility to review the results and again took a measurement. This time we determined the preferred level of control in reference to their perception of the quality of control in each condition. This addressed the missing review opportunity mentioned earlier. After all trials and measurements the participants were debriefed and thanked for their participation.

6.5 Results

We conducted a Shapiro-Wilk Test for the collected data. It showed no significance and therefore, a normal distribution of the data can be assumed. To stay consistent with our prior analysis, however, we again used Friedman's ANOVA to test for significance. The test indicated no significant differences between the 3 measurements ($\chi^2(2) \leq .359$, $p \leq .836$) with mean values of 40.28 (SD ≤ 18.26) for the baseline measurement, 36.58 (SD ≤ 25.38) for the measurement after exposing participants to the conditions and 39.33 (SD ≤ 23.21) after reviewing the results (Fig. 6).

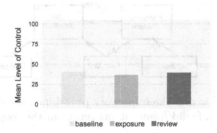

Fig. 6. Results on the measured preferred level of control

7   Reflecting on Our Mixed-Methods Design and Evaluation Approach and Its Results

The camera is generally moved synchronously by multiple operators following a defined workflow with little room for errors. A similar situation – collaborative work in established practices with little room for error – was found by Mackay and Fayard in [24]. Reflecting on their design process, they proposed a framework for HCI research. They recommend a triangulation between *theory*, the design of *artifacts* and *observation*. As HCI is an interdisciplinary field, the application of only certain methods threatens the generalizability or validity of the findings. In lab studies, conditions and variables can be controlled, however the situation is artificial and users might behave unnaturally. In contrast, users behave naturally in field studies, but it is hard to establish cause and effect relationships as influencing factors can interfere. We also used such a mixed-methods approach applying various techniques in our design and evaluation process (Fig. 7). To provide an overview of all of the applied methods, we provide a summary in Table 2.

For the human-automation interplay, user interface design and cinematography, *theory*, design guidelines as well as approaches can already be found in related work [21,28,29]. We therefore mainly focused on the development of a physical prototype, i.e., the design of an *artifact* with following *observations*. Addressing the challenges mentioned in Sect. 1 and the issues mentioned in Sect. 3, we built a motion-controlled camera slider with wireless remote control as a prototyping and research platform. Its use for prototyping is (a) *manageable* and *affordable*. Also (b) the occurring workload in control can be handled even by *non-experts* (non-exclusiveness). Through the wireless interface, it can easily (c) serve as a research platform as various user interfaces (e.g., mobile devices, gestural recognition devices etc.) or computer vision-based systems can be connected and evaluated. Additionally, it can (d) be *transported easily* and therefore is suited for lab as well as field evaluations.

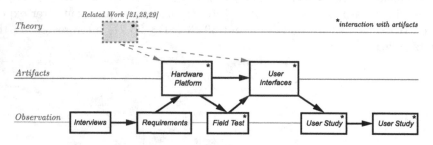

Fig. 7. Our work located within the framework of [24] incorporating control strategies as proposed by [21]. Black (solid frame) items represent the scope of this work.

As our physical implementation is mainly based on open source technology, we also provide it for reproduction and customization. Therefore the changing needs of researchers and practitioners can be met in varying contexts beyond the traditional scope of cinematography, as shown by the examples presented in Sect. 2. Identifying user roles, hardware and feature requirements with experts in a user-centered fashion helped us to minimize the risk of possible user rejection due to poor design or build quality in the implementation of our prototype. Experts in cinematography are often used to high-end equipment and thus bringing a prototype to the set has to be considered with caution. This was reflected by the fact that only after the first session and the screening of the results we were granted further access to the expert users and field environment and consequently were able to gather our insights.

Compared to virtual camera control, physical camera control faces different challenges due to in-situ constraints. Therefore it is hard to apply findings from virtual environments to the physical world. Our system is designed for application in the physical world and can be used in lab environments and in field studies alike. Sometimes, natural interaction processes and phenomena such as *unexpected use* emerge only in-the-wild. This is described by Marshall and colleagues [27]. These phenomena can give further insight into the users' actions, reasoning and experiences. In our case, one surprising and mentionable field insight was that untrained people tend to behave more naturally when filmed by an autonomously operating or remotely operated system. We also observed that the operators would ask to explore more variations of the same shot at different speeds, to have more options in choosing the fitting material for the rhythm of the cuts and the soundtrack in post-production.

We additionally examined two particular research questions in controlled studies. First we wanted to gain insights on how workload as well as sense and quality of control were affected by the introduction of a low degree of automation compared to a full human baseline. In conclusion, we could not find any negative effects regarding either sense or quality of control in our data. Although we could find a reduction in workload when only concerned with physical effort, this did not significantly decrease the overall workload score in our data set.

Table 2. The methods we used in our mixed-methods design and evaluation approach

Method	Results
Online survey (N = 3)	User roles from practitioners
Expert interview (N = 1)	Hardware and user interface requirements
Expert evaluation (N = 1)	Testing hardware implementation,
	Contextual inquiry with field insights,
	Iteration of user interface requirements
Controlled user study 1 (N = 18)	Data on the effects of introducing automation
Controlled user study 2 (N = 12)	Data on the effects of introducing a review phase

Given our experiences from the field evaluations, we were surprised *not* to find a difference. We had expected that a missing screening of the results might have affected the reports, in particular, on sense of control. In the full manual condition more and more noticeable jerky motions were observable in the recorded material. Participants however might have been unaware of it without a review phase. We hence conducted a second controlled user study examining the effects of adding a review phase to the evaluation process. Based on our collected data, we concluded that the introduction of a review phase had no significant effect on the participants' perception of control even when increasing the level of automation. To mimic the recording practice we observed on set and given that jerky motions might only be discovered after a recording, we would still recommend its integration in the evaluation process in field as well as laboratory environments.

Besides the general triangulation approach proposed by Mackay and Fayard, Shneiderman et al. [30] propose the use of a cascade of evaluation techniques in particular when evaluating creativity support tools (CST). We consider camera motion control tools to be a peculiar kind of CSTs and as such, their evaluation should not be conducted on performance measures alone. As pointed out in [30], performance measures might be part of the evaluation, but field observation and other quantitative measurement dimensions should also be considered as for example proposed by Cherry and Latulipe [11] in their Creativity-Support Index (CSI) questionnaire.

Expanding automation in the domain of creative expression seems paradoxical at first. Delegating camera motion to machines might result in a more robotic aesthetic than in manual operation as found in related work [10]. However, such tools can add to the vocabulary and expressiveness of the discipline as in time-lapse, high-speed or aerial shots, which can hardly be controlled manually. Additionally, smart, easy to use tools offering fast implementation of ideas that might lead to more exploration.

Evaluating and quantifying such aspects is a limitation of the presented work. With sense of control, we did consider an experience measurement beyond the performance measures of workload and quality of control. In our field observations, we also observed how the use of our tools influenced expressiveness and exploration of various speed settings in order to shape different versions for post-production. Expressiveness and exploration are, for example, dimensions measured by the CSI. We did not investigate these or any other dimensions covered by the CSI in detail.

Given the early development stage of our prototype and the controlled study design and goal-oriented study task (adapted SDLP), the environment was not particularly well suited for determining aspects such as "results worth effort" or "enjoyment". These are clearly important aspects that CSTs should support and that should be evaluated. However, we believe they also require an open-ended task and potentially an even more stable system.

8   Conclusion

For user interface design and prototyping in cinematographic motion control camera systems we identified a number of challenges. For example, we found that translating new ideas into working prototypes can be hard as expertise in multiple fields is required. Bringing together the expertise of camera operators, a mechanical engineer and computer scientists, we contribute a tool that can be used for prototype development. In expert interviews we identified hardware and user interface requirements. We integrated those in our implementation of a motion-controlled camera slider. It serves as a research platform, as through the wireless remote access that it provides, any type of user interface integrating Bluetooth, such as mobile devices, gesture recognition or wearable devices can be connected. In five on-assignment shootings with an expert we found strong indication that our system fulfills the collected requirement and thus is qualified for field use. We further reported two user studies (N = 18, N = 12) examining the effects of different degrees of automation on sense and quality of control of the participants. We could not determine any negative effects caused by the use and automated motion control tool, even when compared to a full manual control baseline. We also examined the effect of including the review of results in the evaluation process and found no indication that its integration led to significant differences in self-reports on the preferred level of control. Providing the system as open source, we encourage its reproduction, customization and extension by researchers and practitioners.

References

1. Freefly MIMIC for MöVI. http://freeflysystems.com/mimic
2. Soffer/Follow-Focus · GitHub. https://github.com/soffer/Follow-Focus
3. Star Wars Visual Effects, from AT-ATs to Tauntauns. https://www.youtube.com/watch?v=mIlYk7KQe-s
4. STYPE KIT - 3D Virtual Studio and Augmented Reality System Stype Grip. http://www.stypegrip.com/stype-kit
5. Bowman, D.A., Kruijff, E., LaViola Jr., J.J., Poupyrev, I.: 3D User Interfaces: Theory and Practice. Addison-Wesley, Westford (2004)
6. Byrne, K., Proto, J., Kruysman, B., Bitterman, M.: The power of engineering, the invention of artists. In: McGee, W., de Ponce Leon, M. (eds.) Robotic Fabrication in Architecture, Art and Design 2014, pp. 399–405. Springer, Cham (2014). doi:10.1007/978-3-319-04663-1_30
7. Carifio, J., Perla, R.J.: Ten common misunderstandings, misconceptions, persistent myths and urban legends about likert scales and likert response formats and their antidotes. J. Soc. Sci. **3**(3), 106–116 (2007)
8. Carr, P., Mistry, M., Matthews, I.: Hybrid robotic/virtual pan-tilt-zom cameras for autonomous event recording. In: Proceedings of the 21st ACM International Conference on Multimedia, MM 2013, pp. 193–202. ACM (2013)
9. Chen, J., Carr, P.: Autonomous camera systems: a survey. In: Workshops at the Twenty-Eighth AAAI Conference on Artificial Intelligence, Québec City, Québec, Canada, pp. 18–22 (2014)
10. Chen, J., Carr, P.: Mimicking human camera operators. In: IEEE Winter Conference on Applications of Computer Vision, WACV 2015, pp. 215–222. IEEE (2015)
11. Cherry, E., Latulipe, C.: Quantifying the creativity support of digital tools through the creativity support index. ACM Trans. Comput. Hum. Interact. (TOCHI) **21**(4), 21 (2014)
12. Christie, M., Hosobe, H.: Through-the-lens cinematography. In: Butz, A., Fisher, B., Krüger, A., Olivier, P. (eds.) SG 2006. LNCS, vol. 4073, pp. 147–159. Springer, Heidelberg (2006). doi:10.1007/11795018_14
13. Christie, M., Normand, J.M.: A semantic space partitioning approach to virtual camera composition. Comput. Graph. Forum **24**(3), 247–256 (2005)
14. Christie, M., Olivier, P., Normand, J.M.: Camera control in computer graphics. Comput. Graph. Forum **27**(8), 2197–2218 (2008). Blackwell Publishing Ltd
15. Dong, M.Y., Sandberg, K., Bibby, B.M., Pedersen, M.N., Overgaard, M.: The development of a sense of control scale. Front. Psychol. **6**, 1733 (2015)
16. Fitts, P.M.: Human Engineering for an Effective Air-Navigation and Traffic-Control System. National Research Council, Division of Anthropology and Psychology, Committee on Aviation Psychology (1951)
17. Gebhardt, C., Hepp, B., Nägeli, T., Stevsić, S., Hilliges, O.: Airways: optimization-based planning of quadrotor trajectories according to high-level user goals. In: Proceedings of the 2016 CHI Conference on Human Factors in Computing Systems, CHI 2016, pp. 2508–2519. ACM, Santa Clara (2016)

18. Gleicher, M., Witkin, A.: Through-the-lens camera control. In: Proceedings of the 19th Annual Conference on Computer Graphics and Interactive Techniques, SIG-GRAPH 1992, pp. 331–340. ACM, New York (1992)

19. Hart, S.G.: NASA-task load index (NASA-TLX); 20 years later. Proc. Hum. Factors Ergon. Soc. Ann. Meet. **50**, 904–908 (2006)

20. Hoesl, A.: CameraMotion · GitLab. https://gitlab.lrz.de/lmu08360/CameraMotion

21. Hoesl, A., Wagner, J., Butz, A.: Delegation impossible? Towards novel interfaces for camera motion. In: Proceedings of the 33rd Annual ACM Conference Extended Abstracts on Human Factors in Computing Systems, CHI EA 2015, pp. 1729–1734. ACM, April 2015

22. Hulens, D., Goedemé, T., Rumes, T.: Autonomous lecture recording with a PTZ camera while complying with cinematographic rules. In: Proceedings of the 2014 Canadian Conference on Computer and Robot Vision, CRV 2014, pp. 371–377. IEEE Computer Society, Washington, DC (2014)

23. Lino, C., Christie, M., Ranon, R., Bares, W.: The director's lens: an intelligent assistant for virtual cinematography. In: Proceedings of the 19th ACM International Conference on Multimedia, MM 2011, pp. 323–332. ACM, Scottsdale (2011)

24. Mackay, W.E., Fayard, A.L.: HCI, natural science and design: a framework for triangulation across disciplines. In: Proceedings of the 2nd Conference on Designing Interactive Systems: Processes, Practices, Methods, and Techniques, pp. 223–234. ACM (1997)

25. Marchal, D., Moerman, C., Casiez, G., Roussel, N.: Designing intuitive multi-touch 3D navigation techniques. In: Kotzé, P., Marsden, G., Lindgaard, G., Wesson, J., Winckler, M. (eds.) INTERACT 2013. LNCS, vol. 8117, pp. 19–36. Springer, Heidelberg (2013). doi:10.1007/978-3-642-40483-2_2

26. Marchand, E., Courty, N.: Image-based virtual camera motion strategies. In: Fels, S., Poulin, P. (eds.) Proceedings of the Graphics Interface 2000 Conference, GI 2000, pp. 69–76. Morgan Kaufmann Publishers, Montréal (2000)

27. Marshall, P., Morris, R., Rogers, Y., Kreitmayer, S., Davies, M.: Rethinking 'Multi-user': an in-the-wild study of how groups approach a walk-up-and-use tabletop interface. In: Proceedings of the SIGCHI Conference on Human Factors in Computing Systems, CHI 2011, pp. 3033–3042. ACM, New York (2011)

28. Miller, C.A., Parasuraman, R.: Designing for flexible interaction between humans and automation: delegation interfaces for supervisory control. Hum. Factors J. Hum. Factors Ergon. Soc. **49**(1), 57–75 (2007)

29. Nielsen, J.I.: Camera Movement in Narrative Cinema: Towards a Taxonomy of Functions. Århus Universitet, Institut for Informations- og Medievidenskab (2007)

30. Shneiderman, B., Fischer, G., Czerwinkski, M., Myers, B., Resnick, M.: NSF Workshop Report on Creativity Support Tools. Technical report, Washington, DC, USA (2005)

31. Stanciu, R., Oh, P.Y.: Designing visually servoed tracking to augment camera teleoperators. In: IEEE/RSJ International Conference on Intelligent Robots and Systems, IRDS 2002, vol. 1, pp. 342–347. IEEE (2002)

32. Tognazzini, B.: The "Starfire" video prototype project: a case history. In: Proceedings of the SIGCHI Conference on Human Factors in Computing Systems, CHI 1994, pp. 99–105. ACM (1994)

33. Verster, J.C., Roth, T.: Standard operation procedures for conducting the on-the-road driving test, and measurement of the standard deviation of lateral position (SDLP). Int. J. Gener. Med. **4**(4), 359–371 (2011)

34. Ware, C., Osborne, S.: Exploration and virtual camera control in virtual three dimensional environments. In: ACM SIGGRAPH Computer Graphics, vol. 24, pp. 175–183. ACM (1990)
35. Wen, W., Yamashita, A., Asama, H.: The sense of agency during continuous action: performance is more important than action-feedback association. PLoS One **10**(4), e0125226 (2015)
36. Zhang, Z., Liu, Z., Zhao, Q.: Semantic saliency driven camera control for personal remote collaboration. In: IEEE 10th Workshop on Multimedia Signal Processing, MMSP 2008, pp. 28–33. IEEE (2008)

Author Index